FREDERICK LAW OLMSTED

FREDERICK LAW OLMSTED

WRITINGS ON LANDSCAPE,
CULTURE, AND SOCIETY

Charles E. Beveridge, *editor*

THE LIBRARY OF AMERICA

Visit our website at www.loa.org.

All works reprinted by arrangement with
Johns Hopkins University Press. All rights reserved.

The illustrations in this volume were underwritten by grants
from the Gould Family Foundation
and
Furthermore: a program of the J. M. Kaplan Fund.

Endpapers: *Greensward Study No.5: View Southwest from
Vista Rock on Reverse Line of Sight from Study No.4.*
Courtesy of the NYC Municipal Archives.

This paper meets the requirements of
ANSI/NISO Z39.48–1992 (Permanence of Paper).

Distributed to the trade in the United States
by Penguin Random House Inc.
and in Canada by Penguin Random House Canada Ltd.

Library of Congress Control Number: 2015935690
ISBN 978–1–59853–452–8

———

First Printing
The Library of America—270

Frederick Law Olmsted:
Writings on Landscape, Culture, and Society
is published with support from

THE ARTHUR F. AND ALICE E. ADAMS
CHARITABLE FOUNDATION

FURTHERMORE:
A PROGRAM OF THE J. M. KAPLAN FUND

THE GOULD FAMILY FOUNDATION

THE LEON LEVY FOUNDATION

Contents

Illustrations

(following page 700)

FREDERICK LAW
OLMSTED

Autobiographical Fragment B

My father's father and two of my father's great uncles I remember in part by direct memory, for they lived, one at least, till I was nearly ten. But as a baby I was danced on the knee of each of them, and how much of what is in my mind about them I have by memory and how much by personal tradition I cannot be sure.

They had been seafaring men and in the revolutionary war martial men, both ashore and afloat, and their brother captured on a privateer died in the prison ship in the Wallabout. My grandfather himself regarded one of his living brothers as a hero and told me something of an action in which the British sloop of War Ostrich of 16 guns, Captain Peter Rainier had been compelled to lower her colors to a French letter of Marque of which my uncle (Captain Gid. he was called) though but a guest on board and serving in the action as a volunteer, was at the moment in command, the French master and every commissioned officer having been killed or sent below disablingly wounded.

Of his own adventures I do not seem to have ever been able to get any account from my grandfather and the impression he left with me was that though he had been to the most distant parts of the world his life had been quiet and devoid of interest.

Once I had heard an account read from a book of the winter's march through the wilds of Maine of the expedition sent to capture Quebec and I was told that my grandfather had been in it. I wanted to hear more particulars of the matter from him and plied him with questions more than I often dared. I remember only that when I asked if, when they were in a starving condition, he cut the leather off the tops of his boots and fried it, he laughed heartily and called my grandmother to tell her of it.

There was a single exception to his inability, for I do not think it was indisposition, to tell of what he had done and seen. One day I was lying with my head between the roots of a lofty elm, looking up at its swaying boughs and leafage, when he came out of the house and hobbled toward me. It must have been a Sunday or holiday, for he was dressed in his best. His

3

best, although he was in straitened circumstances, was finer than anything we see now. Ruffles on his bosom and wrists; small clothes, stockings and silver buckled shoes; a long silver headed Malacca cane as a walking stick in his hands (I have it now), his gray hair in a queue with a bow of broad black ribband at the end. There was an old cocked hat in the garret with a quadrant, charts, bunting, and small matters of cabin furniture, but I never saw it in his hand. He wore a hat of the then common fashion of real beaver fur.

I rose as he approached and he asked, looking up, did I not think it a fine tree? Then he told me that he himself had planted this tree when a boy. Others near by he had helped to plant, but this one was all his own, and he described to me how he had dug it in the swamp and had brought it on his shoulder and been allowed to plant it all by himself. It came to me after a time as he went on talking about it that there had been nothing in all his long life of which he was so frankly proud and in which he took such complete pleasure as the planting and the beautiful growth of this tree.

Shortly after this I heard a tree spoken of as a Honey-locust, and I got a pod from it and tried to eat the bitter meat I found in it, in order that I might better realize what hard fare that was that poor John the Baptist had to live upon in the wilderness. The seeds, which I could eat no more than the pods, I planted in my garden and a year afterwards I imagined that a sprig of leaves that I found among the weeds then growing had sprung from this seed and I set a stake by it and watched it and it really turned out to be a little honey locust tree and I was proud to show it and call it mine. When I was twelve years old I dug it up and replanted it in another place, a very suitable place in respect of soil and it flourished. Forty years afterwards I went to look at it and thought it the finest honey locust I ever saw. Lately I went again and it had been felled. After a moment's thought I was glad of it, for its individual beauty was out of key with the surrounding circumstances and its time had fully come.

I can see that my pleasure began to be affected by conditions of scenery at an early age; long before it could have been suspected by others from any thing that I said and before I began to mentally connect the cause and effect of enjoyment in it. It occurred too, while I was but a half grown lad that my parents thought well to let me wander as few parents are willing their children should.

Within thirty miles of where they lived there were a score of houses of their kindred and friends at which I was always welcome. They were mostly farm houses and had near them interesting rivers, brooks, meadows, rocks, woods or mountains. Those less rural had pleasant old gardens. Of the people, two only shall be referred to particularly. One a poor scholar who, after a deep affliction, lived in seclusion with no occupation but that of reading good old books to which he had formed an attachment in happier days. One of his favorite authors was Virgil, and he took pleasure in reading and translating him to me. He was quaintly mild, courteous, and ceremonious, of musing and contemplative habits, and in this and other respects so different from most men whom I knew that as he commanded my respect and affectionate regard, I recognize him to have had a notable influence in my education.

The other had inherited a moderate competence and been brought up to no regular calling. He lived in an unusually fine old village house with an old garden, was given to natural science, had a cabinet, a few works of art and a notable small library. He was shy and absorbed and I took little from him directly, but he was kind and not so careful of his treasures that I could not cautiously use them as playthings and picture books. He introduced me to Isaac Walton. He had no man servant—indeed no servants, his handmaids being of the order then called help, and he was on precisely the terms with them as it now seems to me that he might have been with helpful sisters, though they did not sit at table with him.

A man came from without the household for the heavier work of the place, giving but a small part of his time to it, and there was a boy to do the light chores who received no wages but worked for his board, books and schooling. One of the boys who thus became my play fellow afterwards made his way through college, studied law, and came to be a member of Congress and Governor of a state. For the rest my kinsmen and friends were plain, busy, thrifty people, mostly farmers and good citizens.

If in my rambling habits I did not come home at night it was supposed that I had strayed to some of these other homes where I would be well taken care of, and little concern was felt at my absence; but it several times occurred before I was twelve years old that I had been lost in the woods and finding my way out after sunset had passed the night with strangers and had been encouraged by my father rather than checked in the adventurousness that led me to do so.

It was my fortune also at this period to be taken on numerous journeys in company with people neither literary, scientific nor artistic, but more than ordinarily susceptible to beauty of scenery and who with little talking about it, and none for my instruction, plainly shaped their courses and their customs with reference to the enjoyment of it. As a small boy I made four such journeys, each of a thousand miles or more, two behind my father's horses and two mostly by stage coach and canal boat. Besides these, many shorter ones. When fourteen I was laid up by an extremely virulent sumach poisoning, making me for some time partially blind, after which, and possibly as a result, I was troubled for several years with a disorder of the eyes and the oculists advised that I should be kept from study.

It followed that at the time my schoolmates were entering college I was nominally the pupil of a topographical engineer but really for the most part given over to a decently restrained vagabond life, generally pursued under the guise of an angler, a fowler or a dabbler on the shallowest shores of the deep sea of the natural sciences.

A hardly conscious exercise of reason in choosing where I should rest and which way I should be going in these vagrancies, a little musing upon the question what made for or against my pleasure in them, led me along to a point at which when by good chance the books fell in my way I was sufficiently interested to get some understanding of what such men as Price, Gilpin, Shenstone and Marshall thought upon the subject.

Rural tastes at length led me to make myself a farmer. I had several years of training on widely separated farms, then bought a small farm for myself which I afterwards sold in order to buy a larger and upon this I lived ten years. I was a good farmer and a good neighbor, served on the school committee, improved the highways, was secretary of a local farmer's club and of the

County Agricultural Society, took prizes for the best crops of wheat and turnips and the best assortment of fruits; imported an English machine and in partnership with a friend established the first cylindrical drainage tile works in America.

But during this period also I managed to make several long and numerous short journeys, generally paying my expenses by writing on rural topics for newspapers. As it would have been an extravagance otherwise, however, I first crossed the Atlantic in the steerage of a sailing vessel and nearly always travelled frugally. In all these tours I took more interest than most travellers do in the arrangement and aspects of homesteads and generally in what may be called the scenic character of what came before me.

The word scenic flows from my pen unbidden and I venture to let it stand. Some writers of late are using scenic for the purpose it serves, but this is confusing, scenic having been so long used with regard exclusively to affairs of the drama.

All this time interest in certain modest practical applications of what I was learning of the principles of landscape architecture was growing with me. Applications I mean, for example, to the choice of a neighborhood, of the position and aspect of a homestead, the placing, grouping and relationships with the dwelling of barns, stables and minor outbuildings, the planning of a laundry yard and of conveniences for bringing in kitchen supplies and carrying away kitchen wastes, for I had found that even in frontier log cabins a good deal was lost or gained of pleasure according to the ingenuity and judgement used in such matters. Applications also to the seemly position of a kitchen garden, of a working garden, for flowers to be cut for the indoor enjoyment of them, to fixed outer flower and foliage decorations, to the determination of lines of out-look and of in-look and the removal or planting accordingly of trees, screens, bridges, windbreaks and so on, with some consideration for unity of foreground, middle ground and back ground, some consideration for scenic effect from without as well as from within the field of actual operations. I planted several thousand trees on my own land and thinned out and trimmed with my own hand with reference to future pleasing effects a small body of old woodland and another well-grown copse wood.

Never the slightest thought till I was more than thirty years old had entered my mind of practicing landscape gardening except as any fairly well-to-do, working farmer may, and in flower gardening or of any kind of decorative or simply ornamental gardening—any gardening other than such as I have indicated—I was far from being an adept.

But I gradually came to be known among my neighbors and friends as a man of some special knowledge, inventiveness and judgement in such affairs as I have mentioned and to be called on for advice about them. At length, growing out of such little repute, I was unexpectedly invited to take a modest public duty and from this by promotions and successive unpremeditated steps was later led to make Landscape Architecture my calling in life.

OFF HONG KONG: SEPTEMBER 1843

To John Olmsted & Mary Ann Bull

At anchor off Hong Kong,
September 5th, 1843

Dear Parents,

We arrived at this port day before yesterday, one hundred and thirty-two days from New York.

I wrote you at "Anjer" on the 9th of August, which place we left on the following evening having procured a supply of yams, sweet potatoes, plantains, bananas, cocoa-nuts, tamarinds, fowls, ducks & paddy (rice in the "hull") to feed them on, pumpkins and *fresh water*. Of these, the yams & water alone were intended for the benefit or use of the "people." To be sure, we would occasionally get a plantain or banana smuggled out of the maintop by a boy setting to'gallant studd'n sails in the night, and we were welcome to the cocoa-nuts' shells—rinds, I should say—after the Captain had drunk their contents. East Indians never think of eating them except with a spoon when in a pulpy state, as it were.

We bought "amongst us" two large green turtles—but when the first was killed, the best part of it was taken for the Captain's table & supplied it for some days, while we had but one meal. The other was launched overboard. They called it *sick*, but the way it struck out for Cochin China was a caution to doctors.

We had a most remarkable passage through the "straits." We had anticipated a very hard & dangerous time. There is a beautiful clipper built English vessel now lying by us which was over three weeks getting through; anchoring every night. I think we were but three *days*, and did not anchor once. The second night we were becalmed and all hands kept up some time expecting to anchor. The magazine was opened, guns loaded with grape, &c, for you know this sea ("Java Sea") is infested with Malay pirates, who *very* often attack vessels. But just as we were about to drop the kedge, a light breeze sprang up. It soon became strong & so favorable that we could lay our course. Sunday (twelfth, I think) P.M. land was made right ahead, and at dark we were almost enclosed by it. Before midnight we passed "Jasper" Island at the head of the ("Jaspar" or "Gaspar") Straits & were in the China Sea.

The next morning I made three sail from the royal masthead. Before night we were near enough to see that they were "Malay Proas." Our course was altered a little & next morning they were out of sight. We were now standing before the regular "monsoons"—which gave us plenty of work. Thus at daylight we are "right before it" carrying lower, topmast, topgallant & *royal* stud'n sails on both sides.

The wind shifts a little over our starboard quarter. "Brace the yards!" "Let go to stab'd." "Man the lee braces." "Fore brace!" "Hold on to starb'd!" "Well!" "Make Fast." "Topsail brace"—"well!"

"To'g'l't brace"—"well!"

"Royal brace a small pull—belay!" "Haul taut to stab'd!" "So!" "All Well."

"Main brace!" And so with all the main braces. (He takes another look.)

"Braces a little more!" "In lower stud'n sail!" (larboard).

It hauls still more. Braces again. We haul the stud'n s'l tacks as taut as possible, but they shake.

"In fore topmast stud'n s'l." "Clap on the downhaul." "Take in to'g'l't stud'n sail, Sir!" "In to'g'l't s'ls." "Up into the top, you boys. Haul in fore & main t'g'l't & royal stud'n sails. Make them up in the top."

By the time all this is done, the wind is coming back again. The first thing is to set the lee foretopmast stud'n sail. (The hardest sail in the ship to set.) Then royal & to'gallant stud'n s'ls or these first, lower stud'n sails. The wind continues hauling and the same operation goes on: bracing to starboard, slacking larboard stud'n sail tacks—tauting the starboard & soon taking them in one after another & perhaps setting spanker, gaff topsail, jib & flying jib. These two operations perhaps occupy us for an hour or two.

A dark cloud is seen rising on our larboard bow. Those that have a chance perhaps put on an oil jacket. The cloud rises small, or rather narrow, but long. Likely, we see a distant water spout (we *did* notice several). The wind is perhaps subsiding. All hands on deck busy washing down, feeding the fowls, &c. & paying no attention to the weather, till: "Stand by fore-royal halyards!" Then we all knock off work & soon one is standing by the main royal & to'gallant & fore royal & to'gallant halyards.

The squall strikes us. Everyone is wet through & those not "standing by" crowd under the lee of the rail. The old man comes on deck having noticed the barometer. "Clup fry'l" ("Clew up the fore royal.") "Haul down flying jib." "Clew up main-royal." "Lay aloft you b'ys & furl 'em."

One boy goes to each royal (in the first place, I should have got in all the studding sails & braced her sharp up—for the wind comes out ahead in the squalls & we are not "Full & bye.") By the time the boys are at work aloft: "Look out for yourselves on the to'g'l't yard!" They are hauled from below & the fore & main to'gallant sails are doused, but hardly ever furled.

In ten or fifteen minutes (from commencement) the squall breaks. "Hoist the main-to'g'l't sail!" then the fore. The royals are loosed, sheeted home & hoisted up, flying jib set & gaff topsail. Then we have a bracing spell—or rather a squaring—for as the squall passes, the wind is coming on her quarter again; & one after another, the studdingsails are set.

Oh! This is the weather to kill sailors. Any one of us had rather see a gale & reef topsails, than a light fair wind & the everlasting studding sails. We were often kept at work with scarce a minute's rest the whole night watch. But about two weeks before our arrival to our great astonishment we were becalmed & when we did get a wind it was ahead. And so it continued all day & night. The Captain was expecting it to change every hour, but to our delight we were still braced sharp up. No studding sails for forty-eight hours afforded us great relief. But such a thing in the "regular monsoons" had never been heard of before. It was at least a month too early. What could it mean? Deuce a bit did we care. So it did not mean to come back again.

We now had fine times—working at jobs in the daytime & in the night. "Come on deck to sleep & go below to rest." That is, when it was not squally, as it still often was. But often, if not generally, the watch below slept on deck. At eight bells, perhaps, throwing the blanket off & putting on a pea jacket. Then, if it was not one's lookout or wheel, coiling away on the studd'n sail again.

By day all hands were employed fitting the ship for port & for show. A flying skysail was made & royal stud'n sail soon after we left the straits, & the skin is yet to grow where I barked my shins on the to'gallant & royal shrouds & backstays, becketting & unbecketting that bothering little pocket-handkerchief flying kite. Now three or four hands were sewing on the poop & boat awnings. The guns and gun-carriages were scraped & painted & much of the iron work was scraped & oiled. The carpenter was employed on the gig which with the surf boat & pinnace were painted in the best manner. The best seamen were pointing & grafting gun gear, making fancy boat gripes &c, &c.

For my part, I had a job which I liked very well: it was making an enlarged (800%) chart of the entrance to Canton River, including Macao & Hong Kong. (By the way, that should be "*Hong* Kong," not "*Hong Kong*.") The Captain was much pleased with it, & I presume on that account, partly, has made me his clerk here.

On the 30th of August we made land (about noon) and next morning were in sight of the island or the islands of which Hong Kong is one. It was not till noon of the 2nd instant that we got up opposite the town—which will show you what kind of winds we have been among lately. (Twenty-seven miles.)

Hong Kong, September 7th, 1843

I was three days in the cabin copying invoices, writing (advertising) circulars, &c., during which time I eat at the second table with second mate, carpenter & sailmaker. I wrote the above in knock-off time and such "spells" as I could manage to get while there. I have had no time to go on with it.

Whampoa, Sept. 25th, 1843
P.S. I open to say that it is uncertain how soon the *Talbot* (not the *Panama*) is to sail: but as she has taken on board a chop boatload of sweetmeats, we judge it will be soon.

A TOUR OF WHAMPOA: NOVEMBER 1843

To Maria Olmsted

Bark *Ronaldson* at anchor, Whampoa,
Thanksgiving day, 1843

Dear Aunt Maria, dear coz. & my dearest sisters,

It's just about the right time of day, & I am imagining you just about well to work on the turkeys & cranberry. Though, in matter of fact, you are more likely preparing for Dr. Hawes' *great* yearly discourse. Miss Fan, the *Dido*, British man of war, has just struck four bells—afternoon watch. Can you calculate what time it is where you are? I wonder if you girls are at a side table this year. I suppose Mother has the "boiled & oyster," as usual, while Father performs on the roast & criticizes the dressing. So? as the Frenchman says.

As for me, being yet on the sick list, I luxuriate on broth; while the few well men yet on deck have an hour or two ago helped themselves out of two iron bound wooden tubs to rather dry, tough, but fresh buffalo and "*taro*" (which is a kind of yam—which is a tropical substitute for our excellent potato) eating it without salt, from their tin pans, cutting it with their sheath knives or jack knives (which they are now using with the tar bucket or slush pot in the rigging) & using the forks that nature provided—hardly as white (clean!) as your silver ones. Take care, Bertha. That's a big drum stick, but I guess you'll manage it with one hand.

I hope you *won't* think I've neglected answering your letters—the pleasure of receiving which, you can scarcely imagine—any longer than I could help.

I was obliged to give up my attempt to write you, as above, as I found I was not well enough. It is now about a week later and I am considerably better, but I have to write with caution. For if the mate should see me, he would be very likely to say I was well enough to "turn up," when in fact I am so debilitated that Dr. Green assures me I should be very likely to be laid up with a relapse, which would prove very dangerous. But the mate tells the men they must not mind what the Doctor says, but get to work as soon as they are able. This morning he has hustled a poor fellow out, to work at sennit, (under a bamboo shed, as it rains) who will most certainly have the "*shakes*" this afternoon, as usual. But the old hazer says—"work while you are able."

By the way, it is the same man, that a few weeks ago, was not expected to live fifteen minutes, who made his will (sailor), gave his *real* name, which no body in the ship knew before, his father's direction, &c., &c.—who turned to long before he was able, and in consequence has been laid up again on the sick list, with the fever & ague & other complaints.

A most agreeable circumstance occurred to me last evening. The mate was gone to Canton with a boat's crew, when Dr. Green came on board and invited me to take a sail with him in his sanpan—equivalent to "taking a ride or airing in his sulky." Nothing could give me more pleasure as I had not left the ship for more than a month. But I must not be particular. I'll spin the whole yarn to you one of these days, I hope. I laid down on a mat with a bamboo pillow, & we proceeded to Boston Jack's at Whampoa—this a noted Chinaman who visited Boston in his youth, & has since amassed a fortune as "Compradore" or "provider" of naval stores (to American ships mostly) from a mast, anchor or long boat, to a half dozen of eggs (duck's) or a roll of soft tuck (which I get of one of his clerks or assistants every other morning). On Dr. Green's expressing a wish to see him, he came out from his residence in the rear, into his office. Doctor told I had been sick, &c., &c. & he told me to come in. So I entered & rested myself on a cushioned chair. You must recollect I'm a sailor, swinging in tarry trousers, check shirt, with the lanyard of a jackknife in place of a cravat, monkey jacket, &c.

After resting myself some time I took a short walk with the Doctor & Chinese attendants, in the streets of Whampoa, occasionally entering the shops & stores, & seeing the Chinese in their every day life. Old *gentlemen* of fortune with rich dresses & robes reaching to their feet, their long tails richly interwove with silk cord, little black satin skull caps with bright turk's heads or topknots on the *unshaved* part of their crowns. These "old knobs" we often saluted, which they gravely returned, each repeating "*chin chin*," which like a great many of their phrases means many things of a similar character—as "Good evening," as in the present instance, "Good bye," "Thank you," &c. Their sons of every age,—little covies, not much bigger than Mister Albert—strutting about in precisely similar dresses, as gravely as Dr. Cox, or Parson Brace in the "marriage ceremony." However, speak to any of 'em big or little, & you find them full of fun enough, & they'll joke and laugh from Dan to Beersheba. Ay, & talk all the time as much nonsense as the main to'gallant studding-sail topping lift blocks, that we had stuck aloft without any thing rove through 'em all the way from New York here.

And you "women kind" will be glad to know I had an opportunity of seeing the fashions, for I met three *ladies*. That is as much of ladies I suppose as Whampoa can boast, for the *rale ginuine ladies*—of Hong merchants families, for instance—are never seen in public. But I was glad enough to have an opportunity of seeing 'em hobbling (exactly as if with wooden legs) on their tiny peg tops—what would you call 'em—not feet certainly—about three inches long. [🥿 The shoes they wear are shaped something like that. If I get well enough to go to Canton, I may possibly get a pair—but I very much fear I shall not be allowed to go up. And if so, I shall come home, with my chest as empty of anything Chinese, as when I left.

If I could afford it I'd get a tail; for they *can* be procured. Some of the crew of the *Congress* had two or three, which they whipped off the thieves they took, with their cutlasses. A sufficient punishment I hope the Mandarins thought it. For our sanpan boy, Jo, says, "Suppose you gi' me vive undret dollar no cut him off, suppose gi' me dis sip—suppose de whole fleet—not cutty him," &c.

But the ladies' head dresses, they would be as great curiosities to you I presume as the men's. They were all bare headed except I suppose a large quantity of what you call "false hair." Why, I saw a wash woman dressing her hair in a sanpan fastened to our quarter, & she had three or four *hanks* yet to be put *on*, & the Lord knows how many she had built on before. But these, had—mercy! as much again as I had ever seen before—say as much as Mr. Stearnes would care about lifting on the big pitch fork. Each of them had a parasol or umbrella—bamboo, I think they are. I mean to get one of them, too, if I can, and a Chinese gentleman's straw hat. The rest of their dress was plain enough: Nankeen I think—loose gown kind of jacket, *long*, & trousers— blue. But law! if I ran after the women in this style I shall get in a scrape & no mistake. Never get where I started for, at any rate.

But I must mention one thing more before I go back to Boston's. Now *gals*—I was looking into the doors to see a good interesting place to sit down at, for I wanted to rest every half minute. Passing a half open door, I thought the noise inside, which was low, sounded sort o' kind o' natural, as if it was familiar to me at sometime. A moment's thought & I had it. I feared to intrude (I fear a *native* would not believe *it*).

"Sam," to the attending Fuckee. "This China (*chiny*) school— make learn, Eh? Catchy read?" (That's the way Fanquis talk to the common people or generally to all.)

"Ya (yes). Suppose & want ya—can go." (If you wish you can enter.)

So opening the door, we entered. It was a long room, not very light. The pupils generally were standing up, though there were a few desks, with books on them. I suspect they study at home mostly, as I met some boys afterwards in different places with books, who I think were going to recite. The boys all stared & generally laughed as I came in, and some young rascals said in a low tone "Fanqui!" I suppose the master half rose & bowed to me, but coming in from the open street, I did not perceive him at first.

At any rate, the little fellow before him never once looked up or altered his tone as he followed the letters on his book (with his young nails some half inch long). He read with a kind of singsong—first high & then low—about two pages; closed his hornbook; about face, & was trotting off without taking the least notice of me, when I took the liberty of stopping him by catching hold of his tail (about eighteen inches long). He whipped round and laughed in my face! However, I gave him a bit of Mandarin cake (which I had bought for Jack on board) (composed, they say, of rice flour, sugar & dry lard—very delicate & nice they are, too) for saying his lesson so perfectly. He chin chin'd me & went about his business.

I looked at the "boss," who bowed & smiled. He was about forty years old, I think, & looked very sedate. Before I turned, though, there was another young Celestial singing away as before. On the desk, there was a earthen vase, with brushes (pens), &c. and a *large rattan* split a dozen times half down. I took it out. All the boys laughed and the old man, too, for that matter. He took & laid it over one of them—two or three coming up for him to show us what it was for—not hard, of course.

But enough of the school. Returning with the Doctor, I looked at some pickles in what appeared a mere huckster's shop, but which proved to be a very extensive preserve factory & storehouse, having a salesroom in Canton. I passed through half a dozen rooms, in which men were at work chopping all sorts of vegetables, &c, or which were filled with chests, cases and jars of sweetmeats, &c. & a yard as large as the "orchard" full of jars, the size of a half barrel, containing "soy," a fish & soup sauce; I presume, as the jars were uncovered, not yet completed. I tasted his ginger, (the doctor would not allow me to eat a plateful that was handed me,) as sample. It was far superior to anything of the kind I ever saw before: extremely delicate & rich, and a beautiful color. I should have taken a small 50 cent jar then, but he refused to take (copper) mace,—cash—which was all I could offer, wanting silver. A case of four jars, he asked three dollars for.

But at this rate I shall never get you back to "Misser Boston's" which the Doctor & I did about sunset. Outside were three young buffaloes, the number he has killed every night, to supply the ships next day. We found Jack at tea with his partners—two—on the platform by the waterside, in front of the store. On the table were various dishes of vegetables, or rather of "greens," two of lobsters, and crabs, shrimp, and the invariable large dish of rice, probably curried, stood near at hand. There was *soy*, too, which Boston said they had eaten with their soup.

Apparently they had been engaged some time, and were now enjoying their tea, wines, and liqueurs, of which there were several choice kinds on the board, such as sherry in a beautiful cut glass, short octagonal perfume bottle, Cherry brandy in a queer old fashioned Dutch concern, with a copper plate and a jaw-breaking name of the maker on one of the sides, three or four wines and French liqueurs—London porter, &c. while the old boy smuggled "Samshew" (a wretched fiery Chinese spirit, which has killed more English soldiers than any of their weapons) out of a tea pot, drinking from a cup the size of a large thimble.

Some of these, however, were unnecessarily brought on for our special benefit—I mean the Doctor's—though I was soon invited to a seat at the "board" where I had an opportunity of enjoying the best supper of cold ham, excellent eggs, bread, &c. and such capital tea, with loaf sugar, (such a contrast to our shushong with molasses). I was soon on intimate terms with our polite entertainers, and was induced by their gentlemanly and complaisant manner, imperceptibly to drop the fo'c'stle. All that I've been writing, dear Aunty, will have been but the shell to you. Now "stand by" for the "meat."

"Mr. Boston," says I, "do you happen to remember many years since, an American Captain by the name of 'Olmsted?'"

"Humstet?—no—I no. . . ."

"Ha!" interrupted one of his partners, an old man sitting next to me; "*Me sabé* (know—Portuguese) him. No come here, long time—twenty year, more. S'ip 'untress—I think—he come."

"Yes sir! Yes sir. That's him. I am very glad you recollect him."

"'hem! You *sabe* him?"

"I have the honour of being his nephew."

"Eh?"

"He my uncle—you sabe? My father's uncle."

"Me sabe! Me sabe!"

"I sabe him children you know."

"Ah! he no come long time. Suppose him catchee die."

"Yes—long time since—before I was born." And quite a conversation, very much as above, ensued. (I have endeavoured to follow as much as possible the words we used, to show you a specimen of the Anglo, Macao (Portuguese) Chinese always used here.)

I suppose, I rose very much in their opinion, when they found I was "connected," (as Boston expressed it) with a rich and honourable *captain*. The old man enquired about his family, &c., with apparently much interest, & you may be sure I was not backward in satisfying him. I told him they would be glad to hear from their father's old acquaintance, which appeared to please him very much. If I am not mistaken, he was his boat attendant or "sanpan." And it is customary if a captain once has a man, he is pleased with, for him to obtain his services for successive years, if he is not engaged.

About this time it threatened to rain. A large close awning was spread and lights brought on—Chinese candles about the size of your little finger of wax with stems, so they stood three or four inches above the candlesticks (after the Fanqui fashions). Before we left, the doctor called for a glass of water. An attendant, of which perhaps twenty stood near us, brought two. But our hosts would by no means allow me to drink it, as it would not do for my stomach, recommending me to drink cherry brandy or tea instead. They were undoubtedly right as this river water, unless it has been a long time "settling," produces violent dysentery &c.

I don't suppose I have drunk a half a pint for a month past. But *tea*, Lord bless you! morning & night. It's a caution to Dr. Alcott to say nothing of Dr. Taft (to whom my best respects). Gracious! but you ought to see these "China-men." When the ginseng merchants were aboard of us, they had some thirty or forty coolies employed along our decks, sifting it, sorting it, &c. Then there were two hands who did nothing else but bring up large waiters of tea from their boats & pass it around to them. I don't recollect whether it was another one or not that kept them supplied with little paper cheroots. But their masters on the poop had I think each one a pipe bearer, who also managed the tea cup performance. The gang of stevedores, too, in heaving out our bale goods, had a tub of tea standing at hand, and every few minutes would file off and bale it out, having one man whose business it was to keep it ready for them! There's one ship near us, that I am told allows the men to drink no water, but furnishes her men with tea—hot from the coppers—four or five times a day.

So the youngster eats more than John and I both, eh? Aunty—perhaps you'd think Fred would do better than all three, if you could have seen him sometimes last July putting down the salt—Oh! I have it—"*junk*" and hard tack. How many slices of *bread* (how my mouth waters, when I think of Mrs. Kelley's *soft* bread) would you think he'd be likely to eat in a bowl of milk, if you could see him devouring a couple of (mouldy) "ironbound sea cakes" soaked in a quart of tea dashed with 'lasses? And then "retiring" on the (so-called) "*beef*" kid, to get well ballasted, for a four hour's—I don't know what to call it;—sleep won't do—for "lubbers, along shore," pretend to sleep—say, four hour's—"below"—"bunked in"—that "over-hauls fair"—or a two hour's "bright lookout there for'a'd!" ("bright lookout it is, sir!") and a caulk under the lee of the long boat; unless interrupted by "Clew up fore & main r'yal!—lay aloft you b'ys & furl 'em"—or, "You, Frederick! Up there and unbecket the main skysail"—or—"Haul down that starb'd main-to'gallant stud'n sail.—Into the top & roll it up one of you boys. Send the gear down on deck, & rig in the boom!" or some such agreeable intelligence from the Mr. "Cock of the walk" on the weather side of the poop.

And you've nobody to "*taze* ye, have ye." Faith! Wait a day (or a month or two for that matter perhaps) and if that's what bothers ye (as appears by your letter), nevar belave me, if I don't aze yer mind of it.

(Postscript)-No. 3. To Miss Maria Olmsted & Co. 34 Ann St.

Remember me with respects to Coz Charles and Mr. Ayres. I regret he does not succeed better with his school. I am sure he must deserve to.

We have had some five or six days of severe storm. As our "Repealer" says, "Och! It don't rain then? Faith! It's for want of time to pour." The to'gallant forecastle deck not having the usual "wetting down" has leaked a good deal. In truth, the cook and one man have been *flooded* out of the berths. Fortunately, Chips had just the new "boys' house" finished, and two of them "moved in" that night. Next morning, Jake, one of them, was found sick; the house leaking considerably. I have since been much troubled by sundry aches and pains in head, back, ears, neck, chest, stomach, thighs, groin, legs, knees, ankles, arms, &c., resulting probably from two *trickles* of water, which would have been much more acceptable when we were at sea.

However, we were all enlivened yesterday (Sunday) the 17th by the arrival of a "chop" with some cassia which the Stephen Lurman could not take, and a letter informing the mate that the teas would be coming down immediately. And, as the Doctor says, we may sail, the latter part of the week. The Lurman hove up to drop below to the 2nd bar this morning—but a remarkably fair wind having since arisen, it is not improbable she may have sailed immediately to get down the river. In which case I shall send by the *Mary Ellen* bound for New York, to sail tomorrow. Other ships will probably be leaving all the week, by one of which John & perhaps Father may expect to hear from me. If we get away before New Year's day, you may expect to hear considerable louder from me, perhaps by May Day. That, after all, I may put off to first of June as you did last year.

It was pretty cold, certainly, for a week after we left, but I did not suffer much, having a powerful Homeopathic remedy. Except the first day, before I could get out thick clothes from the "Combin," which as happens Chips was employed all Sunday razeeing. He swears that the maker was either out of work or was in debt to "y'r old man," and wanted to make a "high" job of it; that he owned a share in a nail factory & was creditor to a hardware dealer. He has already recovered eighty screws, & expects some days more work on it: cutting it down one half— as the Captain advised him to "throw the lumber overboard."

My kind friend, Jim, became pretty well acquainted with you while I was seasick. He begs to be mentioned with his compliments to you—whose name, by the way, he says he always associates with ginger nuts. You'll hardly believe that I eat many of them 4th July—and a few left nearly a month after—though partly injured by salt water, which penetrated my chest at last, with some damage to sundry articles.

I don't think, girls, you could write with much pains, or be as successful as you were in what you wrote me, if your light came from a window 6 inches long and another the space of an auger hole; three men shaking their sides with laughter at a good yarn or joke. This with brandy, "to be well-shaken," being their only remedy for the shakes, with which each expects to be attacked during next 24 hours; as their shipmate in the lower bunk there is fairly making the bowsprit appear a divining rod. Then your ink must have the interesting property of coming out of the pen a beautiful white—& not tarnishing for some time. I meant to have said more & talked about the fruit, my "little cabin," the new horse—but apologizing for shortness of letter & sending, instead, therefore, *love*, I remain "Freddy."

CHINESE CIVILITIES: SEPTEMBER–DECEMBER 1843

The Real China

In early life I once lived for four months on a vessel lying at anchor near the mouth of the Great South river of China. The Opium War had just ended and British frigates which had brought desolation and more bitter poverty to many a poor household on its banks were moored near us. It was naturally to be supposed that the traditional antipathy of the people to foreigners had been greatly exasperated, and when we first began to go on shore we were cautioned that we could not be too careful to avoid offending the prejudices of those we might meet, not to go far from our boats and to keep together for common defence in case of necessity. It was said that some English merchant seamen had been roughly handled and that one who had strayed away and not reappeared was supposed to have been murdered.

From the first, however, such warnings were little regarded by most of my shipmates, some of whom were rough and reckless men such as sober quiet people anywhere in the world are shy of. Some too would at times be a little the worse for liquor, heedless, boisterous and quarrelsome.

Once a man in this condition lurched against a woman who was carrying a child in one arm and an earthen jar in the other, striking her with his elbow in that to save herself from falling she had to drop the jar. As I saw the jar fall I thought that he had knocked it out of her hand and it looked as if he might have struck her. There was a little outcry and something like a mob at once gathered about us, looking at us menacingly, but the woman apparently explained that she thought there had been no wrong intention, the rest of us expressed our regret, and in a few moments there was a general bowing and smiling and a way was opened for us to go on.

As a rule at all the villages and even at lone farm houses where the people had been accustomed to see foreigners we were allowed to wander freely and were treated with a degree of civility that in view of all the circumstances seems to me now quite wonderful.

If I had been a full blown admiral in a "brass coat" greater respect could hardly have been paid to me. I was in fact a very insignificant working man in my shirt sleeves. I am not sure that I was not barefooted and I much doubt if my hands were free from the slush and tar of the rigging in the repair of which I had just before been engaged.

On another occasion I boarded an armed Chinese vessel, said to be the floating quarters of a Mandarin or high officer, and met with even warmer hospitality, dishes of stewed meat, rice, fruit and a little cup of spirits being set before me as well as tea and tobacco.

Once, when on shore, hearing a hum like that of an infant school, I looked in at the window of the house from which it came and saw an elderly man with great spectacles teaching about twenty little boys. As soon as he observed me, he laid down his book, came forward and throwing open a door invited me to enter and then proceeded with great cleverness by gesture and example to show me how he taught the boys to read.

Once when we were fatigued and dry while one of these little mobs was hanging upon and jeering us we saw a boy who was carrying a pot of water. By motions we made him understand that we would pay for a drink from it. After a little while a bolder boy took the pot and bringing it near to us, set it upon the ground and with a laugh ran away. After we had satisfied ourselves we laid some "cash" by the side of it and drew back, whereupon the same boy, a ragged, half starved Chinese hoodlum, took the jar and kicked the money toward us, laughing again and shaking his head.

We had a man known as Sam attached to our ship while she lay in the river who ran errands with a small shore boat for the Captain, acted as an interpreter, and made himself useful in any way he could either in the cabin or on deck. He was a willing and skilful servant and the Captain tried to engage him to go to America with us. At last our steward falling ill, the Captain offered him very high wages, double as much as he had proposed to pay at first. Sam persistently declined and told me if the Captain doubled his offer again he would not go. I remonstrated with him for we would all have liked him as a shipmate, when he explained that he was the only son of an aged man and that it would therefore be infamous for him to go away from home.

If his father did not need his care he would have jumped at the Captain's offer.

I had made a friendly acquaintance with a merchant's clerk by giving him some lessons in the English alphabet. Shortly before we went to sea he came on board and remarked to me that when Chinamen ventured upon the ocean they set up Joss in their cabin before which from time to time they set cups of tea and burned joss sticks and paper prayers. He did not see any Joss in our cabin and he asked me if I would not be more comfortable when a great storm arose if such a recognition of our dependence upon the good will of a Superior Being has been observed? It was a simple friendly inquiry made in a perfectly well-bred way.

Following some other sailors at a little distance I once entered a building which, though no idols were to be seen, I took to be a place of worship of some sort. It was dark and overhead and in recesses on the right and left rafters, wainscot and tile were to be dimly made out through a thin veil of smoke. A table or altar stood opposite the door upon which joss sticks were burning. There were numerous inscriptions on the walls and on paper and silk lanthorns, banners and tags hung from them and from the ceiling. There were also several quaint bells and gongs. The sailors had made their way through a little crowd of Chinese who stood before the altar and some of them had gone behind it and were lifting the banners and shaking the lanthorns. Others were striking the bells and gongs with their fists and knives. As I stood peering in at the door and gradually making out what I have described, a sailor called out to me with an oath: "What are you keeping your hat off for in a heathen temple?"

Presently, as my eyes became accustomed to the gloom, I saw an old gentleman observing me from a side door. As our eyes met he bowed and directly came forward and beckoning me to follow him, led the way into a little room where there were piles of books and manuscripts. He laid open one of them which appeared very ancient, and showed me that it contained plans of the building and tried in a gentle, patient way to make me understand something of its origin and purposes. He could use a very few words of Pigion English, and, rightly or wrongly, I made out that the object of the structure was to keep the memory green & preserve the sayings of some good men who lived many generations ago. Afterwards the old gentleman took me through the main room calling my attention to the decorations of the bells and other things which he thought admirable and when I left he gave me several printed papers which I presumed to be religious tracts.

It was only when we pulled up some of the creeks or bayous to a distance from the fleet, where the people had had no direct dealing with foreigners and knew them only as rapacious enemies, that we met with anything but kindness and hospitality. These were holiday excursions. Leaving our boat in charge of a hand or two, we would be making our way along the dykes of the rice fields toward a pagoda, burial ground or village when we would hear a shrill cry, soon repeated by other voices, and presently see boys running together and shouting in concert a phrase which it was understood among us was equivalent to "Here come the heathen!" It seemed to be a make-believe rather than a real alarm. People nearby would look up as they heard the cry and regard us curiously. Idlers perhaps would smile, women would pick up their children and draw back out of our way, but nobody stopped work or looked at all threateningly except the vagabondish boys and they seemed more disposed to make fun of us than to injure or repel us. Sometimes as these gained boldness with numbers they would get behind us and menace us with brick-bats and pelt us a little with balls of mud. But though we heard that some other sailors had been driven into a miry place out of which they escaped with difficulty, I doubt if it had not been after some aggravated provocation.

We roved wherever inclination led us, hardly ever saying by your leave but taking that for granted, much as I have since seen a band of saucy Comanches do in a Mexican border village. Thus we made our way, often interrupting men and women at their work, into shops and factories, boat builders' yards and potteries, gardens, cemeteries and houses of worship; even into private houses; seldom receiving the rebuffs or rebukes which I am sure that we deserved, often invited and assisted to gratify our curiosity.

This good natured disposition was, as far as I can remember, universal. We met, to be sure, few but the poor and lowly. Yet we occasionally encountered some of the more fortunate classes. Once, for example, we had alongside of our ship an elegant yacht in which a wealthy merchant had come to deal for some part of our cargo. After quitting work in the afternoon I went to the gangway of this singular craft (which was very like those described by Marco Polo in the Thirteenth Century) and, by lifting my eyebrows to one of the crew, asked if I could come on board. The man stepped into the cabin and returned with a well dressed young fellow—perhaps the owner's son—who at once offered his hand to assist me in coming on board and then extended it as an invitation toward the cabin into which he followed me. The cabin was rich with carvings and contained some pretty furniture of black work inlaid with ivory and mother of pearl, and a number of musical instruments. All these were shown to me in a pleasant way. In a corner there were two gentlemen over a table, playing chess I think. When we came near them they bowed and smiled and, the servant at this moment bringing in the tea things which were placed upon another table, they rose and one of them handed me a cup of tea. Delicious tea it was. They each took a cup of it with me, then offered me cigarettes and finally waited upon me to the gangway and bowed me over the side with perfectly grave suavity.

I suppose that civilization is to be tested as much by civility as anything else. And I have recalled these incidents as illustrations of a personal experience which made a strong impression upon me, tending to a higher estimate of the social condition of the masses of the Chinese people than I think generally prevails.

ON A CONNECTICUT FARM: JUNE 1845

To John Hull Olmsted

Chateau L'eau roche Jeune 18th, 1845

Mon Cher Jean,

But—I think I'll write in English this time.

Your package of Tribunes by mail thankfully acknowledged.

Pleasant ride, very, I had, up, that day—but I survived with the assistance of an occasional pull at the pocket flask, its effects as usually known illustrated or held up in a Temperance lecture by the driver—who appears, by the way, a pretty clever honest fellow, fully competent to take charge of a small sack of oranges, cocoa nuts, &c., just received and landing from Brig So & So from St. Kitts, Barcelona, Barbados, I mean, or any such sort of thing.

I have been ploughing, since, breaking up old—old enough—old as the hills I'm sure, though they say it was ploughed thirty years ago—fallow—without no rocks nor roots nor nothin'. All as smooth as the lee side of the sand spit in a north*wea*ster or that favor'd bit of Connecticut, that the sailors told about, where they have to grind the sheeps' noses to a point 'fore they send 'em to pasture, so they can get 'em down between the stones. I haven't dislocated my hips nor my right wrist nor my neck yet—have, all the rest.

Received also last night a grand bundle of newspapers &c. from home—a summer jacket, for which I am obliged to you—a frock of same stuff as your plaid. I mean to send your jacket down but shall not have it wash'd here.

I sent a letter to Father yesterday in answer to one I received from him last week in which he gave me a lecture on Rash marriages, &c., saying that matrimony was a subject for me not to think of for years. I've no intention of marrying for three or four years. But I'd just as lief as not be engaged, if I came across a suitable person, before I took a farm on my own account, fearing that after that I should have no good opportunity of selection. I think I should like to cruise for about a year, then fall desperately in love & lay off and on till I could bring about an engagement. At any rate I should hope to be married before I am twenty eight. Don't you think I am reasonable? Well, under favorable circumstances I should do better than that, but I've "got a pretty large *caution*," Gibson says.

This fellow makes fun for me with his Phreno-lingo. "That 'ar' man," says he, speaking of an overgrown chap that drawls out his talk like a psalm tune in slow time on a hand organ, "That 'ar' man's got a pretty considerable development of the lymphatic narve." "He wouldn't be afraid o' nothin'. D'ye s'pose he would? D'ye obsarve his head? He 'ant got no caution. Not none 'tall." He gives me a pretty good character: large caution, large firmness, small destructiveness, large veneration, large philoprogenitiveness, small hands, large eyes, small mouth, large belly. What do you think of it?

Let me hear from you and the boat as often as possible.

I write this to have ready when opportunity occurs.

I have some great "settoos" with Gibson. How do you spell that? "Set-to?" I s'pose so. He's strong & has the advantage of me by long odds, but he does not. He isn't quite sure of it yet. He guards altogether too well & hits—very palpably.

18th. I've been all day hoeing potatoes & am gratified to find that I can keep up with Mr. Welton very well without much fatigue. I find by breakfasting on bread & milk I can do without drink between meals. I think I shall live on it, pretty much. They don't have anything else—proper good—but butter & cheese, which is very superior. They have a miserable mess of soured switchel which they think is "beer," and they pay dear for their infatuation. I'm too temperate for it—by a pailful.

We've had a horse—mare, filly. No! She wasn't a *dumb* baste at all, but a Yankee hoosier gal "to tea"—a character, rich! Regular Miss *Higgins*—Miss Squeesh. I've a good joke to tell you—fat! Awful! Enclosed for home, etc. as you'll see.

Your'n

agr—ic' (ula)
A Greek

"AN ORATOR FOR THE FOURTH": JULY 1845

To Charles Loring Brace

Waterbury, July 9th, 1845
July 10th

My dear Charly,

I received a letter from you some time last week. What a complete blunderer you are anyhow. But I had entirely forgotten that there were letters in that bundle except for Emma and you and John. I'd no intention of troubling you with them. They were of no consequence, but I'm obliged to you, all the same.

I have been in Hartford luxuriating on green peas and ripe cherries for some days, and now returned half sick to bread (half-baked rye dough by accident this week) and milk. By the way, I had the gratification of eating some of Emma's own bread at your house, and it was as good as could be, I assure you. I was at your house twice. Nobody there but your father and Emma, but I could not have had a much more agreeable time than I did.

I went up on the Fourth, and was fortunate enough to hear Mr. Case's performance, of which you have seen some notice. Oh! It was *rich*, though, I tell you. Decidedly a stupendous splurge. In the first place, I believe Mr. Case inquired of some friend if he knew any town that was desirous of obtaining the services of an orator for the Fourth. Certain public spirited individuals having learnt this, and it having come to their knowledge also that he had been engaged in the composition of an Independence address two years before, it was resolved that the result of so much distinguished labor should not be lost, but if possible secured for the edification of their own fellow citizens. Accordingly, a *self-constituted* Committee waited on the notable author and very readily obtained his acceptance of the appointment of "orator of the day."

So, on the morning, appeared on every lamppost and nuisance wall a handbill headed with a spread eagle with the flying motto of "Keep up the Spirit of '76" informing the public that *the* oration would be delivered at the foot of the State House yard by Seymour N. Case, Esq., after the reading of the Declaration of Independence, &c, "per order *Com. of Arrangements*." Agreeably to this call at four o'clock I found perhaps a thousand persons, or half of it, waiting there in lively anticipation.

Considerable apprehension of disappointment (is that a bull?) was evident, but it was said Mr. Case had been called on early in the afternoon and found rehearsing before a glass. However as he did not appear a committee went to look him up. He had locked himself into his room, and refused them admittance, telling them indignantly that he was not to be imposed upon. (Some friends had advised him that he was *sold*. It is supposed to have been Mr. Toucey.) Admission having been obtained however by a match key, his various personal acquaintance (who are they not?) severally assured him that there was no hoax, at least as far as they were aware. And each as friends privately advised him that if such had been the case, it would be much to his credit & renown to get the better of them, by carrying it through in a masterly manner, at the same time offering their countenance and protection.

Colonel Waterman (the Sheriff) came in hoping anxiously that he would delay no longer, as the people were getting excited and he feared it would be impossible to restrain them much longer. There were ten thousand men waiting impatiently and he did not know where it might end, &c. This evidently affected him and he inquired who was to be the *reader. Chas. T. Bull* was mentioned and several others, to each of which he objected (as guises I suppose). Mr. *Skinner* he thought would be just the man (quite complimentary to John wasn't it!) Mr. S. accepted and was agreed upon.

A procession was started immediately—thus: Marshall of the day (Colonel Waterman), Orator of the day carrying his roll, Reader of the Declaration of Independence with a big sheep covered book (arm in arm), Erastus Goodwin, Esq. (solus), assistant grand marshall, Committee of Arrangements, and the escorting committee with faculty and students of Trinity College, as an escort armed with canes; citizens (two deep) and strangers, three young ladies from the country in white dresses (accidentally), young gentlemen of the public schools, &c.

The crowd parted respectfully and permitted the "set" to enter the American Hotel, on the lower balcony of which they presently appeared. The adjoining windows and other balconies were crowded with beauty and white dresses. A table with chairs and a small awning were provided. And the meeting having been called to order by the Marshall, Mr. Skinner read the Declaration, after which the Orator was presented and received with every demonstration of delight. The cheers subsiding, Mr. Case unrolled a scroll of close written foolscap, which frightened some of the country folk who wanted to go home that night.

He commenced reading very loud and continued amidst general cries of "louder!" When it was evident he had reached the highest capacity of his voice, the Marshall requested the audience to keep order and silence was partially restored. The most rapturous applause, however, hailed every sentiment—generally in the middle of its delivery—and a running accompaniment of laughter, "good!" "louder!" "great!" "That's fine!" "Splendid!" "My!" &c., &c. was kept up.

Bouquets were thrown from the windows behind him, which he acknowledged with peculiar grace & benignancy. His modesty however would not allow him to wear a wreath, with which a young gentleman with the best intentions, acting as the representative of the ladies, endeavoured to adorn his brows.

When he had finished, Mr. Chapman, Major Ely, Lawyer Goodman, the Comptroller (Tyler), and others of our first public men were called upon, but severally excused themselves mostly on the plea that they dare not risk their reputation in extemporaneous speaking after such a well prepared and brilliant production as they had listened to. No lawyer could better the *case*, &c.

But the best of it was to see him try to look calm and composed sitting in the sunshine burning with blushes, his hair *wilted*, chin & nose dripping with sweat, & holding a bouquet as big as your hat, tied to a broom handle. He was escorted by the enthusiastic crowd to the City Hotel, where he held a levee where many distinguished strangers were presented to him, each retiring with a deep impression of his *peculiar* affability, &c.

It struck me as a peculiar feature of the affair that the whole crowd in which there must have been many strangers, appeared to understand the thing perfectly. Do you suppose that *he* did? Not a bit of it. John Skinner said he made a congratulatory call on him the next morning and he remarked "Ah! Mr. Skinner, yesterday was the happiest day of my life! The proudest moment of my existence!" &c. "Ah Sir! There is nothing—there is nothing, Sir, so cheering to the soul, as the murmurs of popular applause!" I hope the address will be published for your benefit.

I will try to recall one sentence: "The proud bird of liberty *clap'd* his wings, and scouring through the etherial element perched upon the topmost cloud of heaven's array, proclaimed to the sordid scions of royalty, *America is free!*"

John started with "liph," on Monday for New Hampshire, and perhaps Montreal. I rode up with them as far as "Alford's" where I left them in good spirits. Frank and his step brother were in company in a buggy. I do hope this journey will set John up again.

I should like to know when you expect to be in Litchfield. Our folks are to visit that way sometime in August, and I think *I* shall, if *you* do at that time.

Yours,

Fred

"FULL OF 'DOUBTS'": AUGUST 1846

To Frederick Kingsbury

Fairmount, August 22, 1846

I have not been very well for a few days—ate too many apples &c. and then took brandy to counteract them—and then not being better off, took apples to counteract the brandy. And so I have been going on, but it's confounded hard to make the proper average. This morning I felt stupid as an owl at noon day—and tried to balance accounts by eating half a dozen green pears and drinking a stiff dose of brandy, and going to bed. Now I have got up—but don't feel any better. Under such circumstances I should never think of answering a letter that came from anybody but you, unless a mere business inquiry as to how I'd have the money sent, or the like. I suppose that sounds like anything but a compliment, but 'tis one.

I am very sorry you cannot come; that's all I've got to say about it. I guess I shall be here in September, and I shall hope to see you then. I don't know where I shall be this coming winter. Perhaps I shall try to get onto Norton's farm in Farmington— perhaps with Townsend in East Haven—perhaps on *my own*. I shall try to be situated so as to be likely to study more than to work. Do you think I shall be contented on a farm—15 miles from New Haven, and three miles from neighbors? I mean civilized ones, gentlemen, doctors, lawyers and ministers.

By the way, I am beginning to have a horror of ministers. They are such a set of conceited, dogmatical, narrow minded, misanthropic, petty mind tyrants. I am most afraid to have such opinions but the fact is, I have acquired for good or evil a great many independent and agrarian and revolutionary ideas and ways of thinking which would frighten such kind folks as my good mother, or Mrs. Baldwin, not a little.

And now I am about it, it was just on this account that I wanted to see you. I don't know what to think about many things—and I wanted you to help me. Nobody can understand what I mean but you. I am full of speculation; and I respect one set of men so little above another, that now I have no very decided opinion on any subject that I have not examined for myself. I mean that I am not to be led by the nose any longer by any man or men—by any teacher, priest, party or church. I give no man leave to call me Whig or Presbyterian, and no man has the right to say I am not a Patriot and a Christian. I have not joined any church—I cannot believe it is best I should—nor am I likely to at present.

As for identifying myself with that set of men, the most bigoted, self complaisant, pharisaical, anti-advancing, anti-reforming, stiff necked old Jew Christians, agreeing on one thing, and that without a true meaning—to call themselves Presbyterians—if I am to have my feelings, dispositions, and opinions, I might almost say, known by my name I would prefer to be called Unitarian or Universalist. I suppose you would be very sorry to hear that I was one—so I tell you I am not by any means—but I should be neither frightened or horror struck to hear that you or John was. I suppose every reasoning creature must be full of "doubts" and in my opinion the more a man doubts, the more of a thinking animal he is. How intellectual I must be! I doubt everything pretty near—but understand such doubting does not affect (at least for worse) my happiness.

In fact my doubts are built on this—I will think and act right, I will find Truth and be governed by it, so far as I can, with the light God is pleased to give me. I will be accountable to no one but God for my opinions and actions. Trusting in Him for light I will not fear for nor care for what man thinks of, or does towards me. I am liable to mistake myself—but so far as I *do* judge myself, this is my paramount governing principle. I hope so anyway, and except from the consciousness of yielding to temptation, and thinking and acting contrary to my own more solemn, more rational and better intentions—as I often do most wickedly—what can I be sorry for? Whether it is because I am endowed with a sluggish, unfeeling heart, or I am a Philosopher or a Christian I do not know, but I certainly do not feel disappointments much or have gloomy anticipations.

I certainly have been declaring Independence this summer, and cutting myself loose from the common rafts of men. I shall hitch on again I suppose when I think there's occasion—but I shall attach myself not by proxy. I don't give my helm to Father, Mother, Schoolmaster, editor or minister, again.

I suppose it was because perhaps a little, I had this vagabond feeling that I fancied Sartor Resartus. Why, it took me three weeks to read through the first book, but when I got along about the "Everlasting No!" I was enchanted with it and some parts I have laid on my bed and read and thought over by hours—again and again. One of my temptations in the wilderness is coming off now, and the very consciousness of fighting the devil with a posse of Presbyterian priests and Methodist elders, and infidels and so forth at his back and fighting for Truth and God's glory is better than 'tis to be following your file leader like a machine.

But the mail won't stop for me to write nonsense. I am very glad Charley is not more broken down by the loss of his father. I had written a letter of sympathy and condolence to him but so unsatisfactorily expressed, and looking so much like a ceremony I would not send it.

We are all cursedly selfish—guess you are not worse than the rest except when you have got the dyspepsia blues. You are not romantic—imaginative enough to be in love. Otherwise you are reasonably in love as much as I am.

Ask John how to direct—or direct here so 'twill be forwarded. Love to the "46."

Yours truly,

Fred.

To Charles Loring Brace

South side March 25th 1848

Dear Charley,

I received a letter from you coming by way of "Guilford Sachem's Head" and Hartford, last week, in which like a good humored savage you raked me and particularly my amiable but unfortunate brother for transgressing your right angled laws of friendship. Well, as long as there are circumstances in the events of the world, or digestion in my body, or variations in the humours of my mind, I shall hold out an outlaw. So don't be *inclement*.

There is not much room for argument in regard to the *metaphysics* of your letter, as your positions are matters of opinion which reasoning has little to do with. Still the drift of some of it I must protest against. I think, Charley, I never knew the man that had graduated at a Theological Seminary that showed ordinary *charity* in his heart. I do believe it is harder for an editor and a clergyman to enter the kingdom than for a rich man. This was an observation independent and had no connection with your letter. So don't feel bad.

I believe it was suggested, however, or followed the groan I gave on noticing how much importance you do in your heart attach to matters of belief—questionable matters which can not be decided in this world and which I think it is right down wicked—absurd—filthy to look upon and act upon as absolutely decided. "Doing," and "settling" on questions of "*Belief*"— you write on the same line—as of equal importance—and the amount accomplished of each (acts and opinions) (doing good and *thinking* not good, but some way, decidedly, not *acting* decidedly) you speak of as companion labors in the work you have to do—as equally progressing you towards the object of your existence.

Now I thank God, Charley, you are not *settled* yet, not absolutely pinned down to any or but comparatively few Theological dogmas—(I hope *political* too.) May this unsatisfactory state that you weep and mourn about so much—in God's name—bother, fret, and spur you till you are perfected in the fullness of light. For just as soon as you reach the state I must infer from your letter you pray for, it will be perfectly impossible for you practically to have charity for those that differ from you. And I believe that one spark of charity is of more value than all the *results settlings*, of all the study, the light (or Grace of Belief), the candid beginning of Investigation (for candor can not progress with growing opinion) of Drs. Taylor, Edwards, Luther, Calvin (whose opinions have been a terrible curse), the Holy Fathers, or the Apostles to the Hebrews & Gentiles. Without the Charity and Love they preached and which made them preach, they would stand a poor chance to be saved. Without half their opinions, in my opinion, they would have borne more sweet fruit and less bitter, sickening, cursed high taxes on Goodness.

(Except the absurdities I have written—one or two back there.) Why the devils themselves (if there are any) believe and tremble, but what good does it do 'em? Why don't they accomplish more good? How much satisfaction it must be to Beelzebub to reflect "how much he has settled upon in belief." "Life is hurrying away and how much have I *done* or *settled upon* in Belief?" That's what you say.

Take all the Commandments God has given through the Scripture and through the natural impulses of your heart, as far as they agree with conscience or reason. Can not you perform them without being firmly settled on the damnation of infants—or the salvation of infants, if you believe God's mercy is consistent with both? And if you don't, is not the belief in God's mercy a vast deal the most important of the two—more important than settling on authenticity of the passages from which you might draw the arguments against it?

What in the world do you want? *Pure Religion*, don't you—to save you—and that is "to visit & relieve the widows and fatherless." It "*is before God.*" Now can you not do that without believing in—"what you do not understand," as your ridiculous conscience tells you you ought to, and makes you half miserable for not doing.

You ask—and I think it is the very damndest piece of unbelief even you ever started—whether, if you are "investigating *honestly,*" the Just and Merciful Father "will forgive" your "*mistakes?*" Why, what blasphemy! What would your earthly father do? And who was it said "Forgive them, for they know not what they do?" Is it not a good reason? And we believe that He shall come to be our Judge.

Now is your belief more culpable than that which led those men to the acts which seemed to need forgiveness? How any man can believe that Jesus Christ is one with the Father and yet be *settled* in his belief of eternal punishment to those who do—they know not what—does puzzle me as much as the Trinity itself. God has given me the Bible but I should never know it to be His word if he had not given me Reason to judge it by. And my Reason—it condemns a good deal of it. The Bible is not consistent with itself. Well, I *do not* believe the Bible to be the Word of God.

I have tried hard to believe the Bible, but I'll be hanged if I can. That is, I am not settled on it, and I never expect to be in this world. What earthly (or other) motive you can imagine yourself to have for being dishonest I can not imagine. Really, are you not splitting hairs?

You say you don't know as I can help not settling on points of belief. I can (practically) but not without, Pharoah-like, hardening my heart. You must conclude when you are settled, that every one who differs is wrong; and in consequence that their salvation is doubtful. Now, what rule have we to judge men by, but their fruits?

A Bishop of the Church of England lately preached a sermon on the death of a man that had never been baptized, never communed, and that differed in creed most essentially from the XXXIX Articles. (What a fence about truth XXXIX makes.) "Can we doubt" (said he) "that he was in danger whose whole life was an unwearied comment on evangelical Christianity? To give a moment's heed would be a libel on Christianity itself." His life was his preparation. In death he gave no sign. His life was the sign & seal. And can you not find scores of *Christians*—as Orthodox in belief as the Devil himself, for all you know—whose life is anything but a sign of their Heavenlymindedness? And can you find the man whose actions tell, speak, a heart of Love—who imitates Christ in mercy, who is eloquent against tyranny & vice, yet charitable to the vicious even, whom you can feel God will not be merciful to? I had for my part rather be in Horace Greeley's shoes, an Infidel as your schoolmen call him, than in Dr. Bacon's or Dr. Taylor's.

You ask if it is possible for a man to have true Repentance, without that knowledge of his sin which can only be obtained by a knowledge of the Infinite Sacrifice which was necessary to *wash his guilt* away. I do not believe that I ever had that knowledge (in your sense) and I do believe that I am a Christian. This can not be argued upon (this necessity). I believe that God did appear in the world as Christ: that as God, with His power and goodness, and as man with his weakness—his temptation to use the Power to punish those who injured him (or sinned) and man's capability of suffering, he came for the salvation (from temporal, perhaps eternal misery) of His children. Here He displayed His Infinite Goodness, which the natural man was incapable of trusting without, whilst He showed us the Height of excellence and triumph over Human failings we might strive to attain, in the forgiveness of His enemies. He led us to worship such goodness (and thus presented us with a true God to worship). To Love such Goodness and to Love Him—consequently to hate sin—to hate ourselves. Not to worship Happiness. To worship Goodness. Not to love our depraved selves. To love God and the God-like in ourselves.

So as a lamb that suffered for the sins of men, He poured out his blood freely and gladly that we might see and believe that no atonement was necessary to reach His Mercy: that we might have Faith in His Infinite Goodness, Mercy, and through this Faith we might be led to Love Him. Worship Him. Strive to be like Him. Strive for a new life. More! Knowing the frailty of our fallen nature and the temptations that beset us; pitying us as a Father pitieth His children and as a Father ready to give good gifts to them that ask him, He has promised that to them that have this Faith—if they heartily believe (for if so they will heartily desire it) that He is so good and so ready to help them—He will quicken and renew in their hearts His holy spirit, that as new creatures in Christ they may hereafter live to Him & Goodness, not to Sin and themselves.

"God judgeth the heart." It is not the past sin, but the present purpose which *is* a man's heart.

I skipped this page accidentally. It comes after the next leaf.

When I say I don't believe the Bible, of course I mean that I do not firmly, fixedly, *settled*-ly believe it: and I really rather think we can not depend on it, as a settling thing for all doctrine, for it does seem there is a good deal of man's handiwork in it.

I ought to fill this page out with the *French Revolution*. But—as everybody else says, wait till the next steamer arrives. I think that scene in the Deputies, with those bold presaging words—the voice of Divine decree as it were—that low, calm voice, to be for the next twelve-months the nightmare of all tyrants—*It is too late*. I think it will stand as about the most impressive scene in History.

I wish I were that man. Jeremiah will stand no higher. It is too late. Hear it, fools. Hear it, slaves, and have Faith. Hear it, Nicholas! Hear it, Metternich! Hear it Irish landlords! Hear it Scotch lairds and English hunters. Hear it Slaveholding sons of America and prepare to meet—or avert—your fate. (Whoop!)

I wish I was a German now. I wouldn't stay here long. I am going to join the European Revolutionary Vigilance Committee. Hurrah for a General War—only a short one. I only wish now Henry Clay was President or Daniel Webster or any statesman. Only there is not any other. Oh, if I was a Pole now wouldn't I! I'd open a recruiting office in five minutes. Give you the chaplaincy—Blackcoat.

I really revel in a *Righteous* War. As it is, I don't see as you and I can do much but pray & praise—and burn tar barrels and hurrah. I mean to do that thing next week. I keep a bright look to Sandy Hook for the "*Caledonia.*" Horrid ship wreck wasn't it? See you perhaps next week.

P.S. Just in time it comes! I congratulate you on the *Republic*! God bless Lamartine!

Stoned from under, House of Lords!

"FOREVER THE PEOPLE'S OWN": MAY 1851

The People's Park at Birkenhead, near Liverpool

Birkenhead is the most important suburb of Liverpool, having the same relation to it that Brooklyn has to New-York, or
Charlestown to Boston. When the first line of Liverpool packets
was established, there were not half a dozen houses here; it now
has a population of many thousands, and is increasing with a
rapidity hardly paralleled in the New World. This is much owing
to the very liberal and enterprizing management of the land-
owners, which affords an example worthy of consideration in
the vicinity of many of our own large towns. There are several
public squares, and the streets and places are broad, and well
paved and lighted. A considerable part of the town has been
built with uniformity, and a reference to general effect, from the
plans, and under the direction of a talented architect, Gillespie
Graham, Esq., of Edinburgh.

We received this information while crossing the Mersey in
a ferryboat, from a fellow passenger, who, though a stranger,
entered into conversation, and answered our inquiries, with
frankness and courtesy. Near the landing we found, by his direction, a square of eight or ten acres, enclosed by an iron fence,
and laid out with tasteful masses of shrubbery, (not trees,) and
gravel walks. The houses about were detached, and though of
the same general style, were sufficiently varied in details not to
appear monotonous. These were all of stone.

We had left this, and were walking up a long, broad street,
when the gentleman who had crossed the ferry with us, joined
us again, and said that as we were strangers, we might like to
look at the ruins of an abbey which were in the vicinity, and he
had come after us; that if we pleased he might conduct us to it.
What an odd way these Englishmen have of being "gruff and
reserved to strangers," thought I.

*   *   *   *   *

Did you ever hear of Birkenhead Abbey? I never had before.
It has no celebrity, but coming upon it so fresh from the land

of Youth as we did, so unexpecting of anything of the kind—
though I have since seen far older ruins, and more renowned,
I have never found anything so impressively aged.

*   *   *   *   *

At the Market place we went into a baker's shop, and while
eating some buns, learned that the poorest flour in the market
was American, and the best, French. French and English flour
is sold in sacks, American in barrels. The baker asked us if
American flour was *kiln dried*, and thought it must be greatly
injured, if it was not, on that account. When we left, he oblig-
ingly directed us to several objects of interest in the vicinity,
and showed us through the market. The building is very large,
convenient, and fine. The roof, which is mostly of glass, is high
and airy, and is supported by two rows of slender iron columns,
giving to the interior the appearance of three light and elegant
arcades. The contrivances to effect ventilation and cleanliness,
are very complete. It was built by the town, upon land given to
it for the purpose, and cost $175,000.

The baker had begged of us not to leave Birkenhead without seeing their new Park, and at his suggestion we left our
knapsacks with him, and proceeded to it. As we approached
the entrance, we were met by women and girls, who, holding
out a cup of milk, asked us—"Will you take a cup of milk, sirs!
Good, cool, sweet, cow's milk, gentlemen, or right warm from
the ass." And at the gate were a herd of donkeys, some with cans
of milk strapped to them, others saddled and bridled, to be let
for ladies and children to ride.

The gateway, which is about a mile and a half from the ferry,
and quite back of the town, is a great massive block of handsome Ionic architecture, standing alone, and unsupported by
anything else in the vicinity, and looking, as I think, heavy and
awkward. There is a sort of grandeur about it that the English
are fond of, but which, when it is entirely separate from all other
architectural constructions, always strikes me unpleasantly. It
seems intended as an impressive preface to a great display of art
within. But here, as well as at Eaton Park, and other places I have
since seen, it is not followed up with great things—the grounds
immediately within the grand entrance being very simple,
and apparently rather overlooked by the gardener. There is a

large archway for carriages, and two smaller ones for those on foot; on either side, and over these, are rooms, which probably serve as inconvenient lodges for the laborers. No porter appears, and the gates are freely open to the public.

Walking a short distance up an avenue, we passed through another light iron gate into a thick, luxuriant, and diversified garden. Five minutes of admiration, and a few more spent in studying the manner in which art had been employed to obtain from nature so much beauty, and I was ready to admit that in democratic America, there was nothing to be thought of as comparable with this People's Garden. Indeed, I was satisfied that gardening had here reached a perfection that I had never before dreamed of. I cannot attempt to describe the effect of so much taste and skill as had evidently been employed; I will only tell you, that we passed through winding paths, over acres and acres, with a constant varying surface, where on all sides were growing every variety of shrubs and flowers, with more than natural grace, all set in borders of greenest, closest turf, and all kept with most consummate neatness. At a distance of a quarter of a mile from the gate, we came to an open field of clean, bright, green-sward, closely mown, on which a large tent was pitched, and a party of boys in one part, and a party of gentlemen in another, were playing cricket. Beyond this was a large meadow with rich groups of trees, under which a flock of sheep were reposing, and girls and women with children, were playing. While watching the cricketers, we were threatened with a shower, and hastened back to look for shelter, which we found in a pagoda, on an island approached by a Chinese bridge. It was soon filled, as were the other ornamental buildings, by a crowd of those who, like ourselves, had been overtaken in the grounds by the rain; and I was glad to observe that the privileges of the garden were enjoyed about equally by all classes. There were some who even were attended by servants, and sent at once for their carriages, but a large proportion were of the common ranks, and a few women with children, or suffering from ill health, were evidently the wives of very humble laborers. There were a number of strangers, and some we observed with note-books, that seemed to have come from a distance to study from the garden. The summer-houses, lodges, bridges, &c., were all well constructed, and of undecaying materials. One of the bridges which we crossed was of our countryman, Remington's patent, an extremely light and graceful erection.

I obtained most of the following information from the head working gardener.

The site of the Park and Garden was ten years ago, a flat, sterile, clay farm. It was placed in the hands of Mr. Paxton in June, 1844, by whom it was laid out in its present form by June of the following year. Carriage roads, thirty-four feet wide, with borders of ten feet, and walks varying in width, were first drawn and made. The excavation for a pond was also made, and the earth obtained from these sources used for making mounds and to vary the surface, which has been done with much *naturalness* and taste. The whole ground was thoroughly under-drained, the minor drains of stone, the main, of tile. By these sufficient water is obtained to fully supply the pond, or lake, as they call it, which is from twenty to forty feet wide, and about three feet deep, and meanders for a long distance through the garden. It is stocked with aquatic plants, gold fish and swans.

The roads are McAdamised. On each side of the carriage way, and of all the walks, pipes for drainage are laid, which communicate with deep main drains that run under the edge of all the mounds or flower beds. The walks are laid first with six inches of fine broken stone, then three inches cinders, and the surface with six inches of fine rolled gravel. All the stones on the ground which were not used for these purposes, were laid in masses of rock-work, and mosses and rock-plants attached to them. The mounds were then planted with shrubs, and Heaths, and Ferns, and the beds with flowering plants. Between these, and the walks and drives, is everywhere a belt of turf, which, by the way, is kept close cut with short, broad scythes and shears, and swept with house-brooms, as we saw. Then the rural lodges, temple, pavilion, bridges, orchestra for a band of instrumental music, &c., were built. And so, in one year, the skeleton of this delightful garden was complete.

But this is but a small part. Besides the cricket and an archery ground, large valleys were made verdant, extensive drives arranged—plantations, clumps, and avenues of trees formed, and a large park laid out. And all this magnificent pleasure-ground is entirely, unreservedly, and forever the People's own. The poorest British peasant is as free to enjoy it in all its parts, as the British Queen. More than that, the Baker of Birkenhead had the pride of an Owner in it.

Is it not a grand good thing? But you are inquiring who *paid* for it. The honest owners—the most wise and worthy town's people of Birkenhead—in the same way that the New-Yorkers pay for the Tombs, and the Hospital, and the *cleaning*, (as they amusingly say,) of their streets.

Of the farm which was purchased, one hundred and twenty acres have been disposed of in the way I have described. The remaining sixty acres, encircling the Park and Garden, were reserved to be sold or rented, after being well graded, streeted and planted, for private building lots. Several fine mansions are already built on these, (having private entrances to the park,) and the rest now sell at $1.25 a square yard. The whole concern cost the town between five and six hundred thousand dollars. It gives employment at present, to ten gardeners and laborers in summer, and to five in winter.*

The generous spirit and fearless enterprise, that has accomplished this, has not been otherwise forgetful of the health and comfort of the poor.† Among other things, I remember, a public wash and bathing house for the town is provided. I should have mentioned also, in connection with the market, that in the outskirts of the town there is a range of stone slaughter-houses, with stables, yards, pens, supplies of hot and cold water, and other arrangements and conveniences, that enlightened regard for health and decency would suggest.

The consequence of all these sorts of things is, that all about, the town lands, which a few years ago were almost worthless wastes, have become of priceless value; where no sound was heard but the bleating of goats and braying of asses,

---

*"When the important advantages to the poorer classes, of such an extensive and delightful pleasure ground, are taken into consideration, no one will be inclined to say that such an expenditure does not merit the most unbounded success, and the deepest public gratitude. Here nature may be viewed in her loveliest garb, the most obdurate heart may be softened, and the mind gently led to pursuits which refine, purify, and alleviate the humblest of the toil-worn."
†"Few towns, in modern times, have been built with such regard to sanitary regulations, as Birkenhead, and in no instance has so much been done for the health, comfort and enjoyment, of a people, as by those energetic individuals with whose names the rise and progress of Birkenhead are so intimately connected." *Dr. J. H. Robertson.*

complaining of their pasturage, there is now the hasty click and clatter of many hundred busy trowels and hammers. You may drive through wide and thronged streets of stately edifices, where were only a few scattered huts, surrounded by quagmires. Docks of unequalled size and grandeur are building, and a forest of masts grows along the shore; and there is no doubt that this young town is to be not only remarkable as a most agreeable and healthy place of residence, but that it will soon be distinguished for extensive and profitable commerce. It seems to me to be the only town I ever saw that has been really built at all in accordance with the advanced science, taste, and enterprising spirit that are supposed to distinguish the nineteenth century. I do not doubt it might be found to have plenty of exceptions to its general character, but I did not inquire for these, nor did I happen to observe them. Certainly, in what I have noticed, it is a model town, and may be held up as an example, not only to philanthropists and men of taste, but to speculators and men of business.

After leaving the Park, we ascended a hill, from the top of which we had a fine view of Liverpool and Birkenhead. Its sides were covered with villas, with little gardens about them. The architecture was generally less fantastic, and the style and materials of building more substantial than is usually employed in the same class of residences with us. Yet there was a good deal of the same *stuck up*, and uneasy pretentious air about them, that the suburban houses of our own city people so commonly have. Possibly this is the effect of association in my mind, of steady, reliable worth and friendship with plain or old fashioned dwellings, for I often find it difficult to discover in the buildings themselves, the elements of such expression. I am inclined to think it is more generally owing to some disunity in the design—often perhaps to a want of keeping between the mansion and its grounds or its situation. The architect and the gardener do not understand each other, and commonly the owner or resident is totally at variance in his tastes and intentions from both; or the man whose ideas the plan is made to serve, or who pays for it, has no true independent taste, but had fancies to be accommodated, which only follow confusedly after custom or fashion. It is a pity that every man's house cannot be really his own, and that he cannot make all that is true, beautiful, and good, in his own character, tastes, pursuits and history, manifest in it.

But however fanciful and uncomfortable many of the villa houses about Liverpool and Birkenhead appear at first sight, the substantial and thorough manner in which most of them are built, will atone for many faults. The friendship of nature has been secured to them. Dampness, heat, cold, will be welcome to do their best. Every day they will improve. In fifty or a hundred years, fashions may change, and they will appear, perhaps, quaint, possibly grotesque—at any rate, picturesque—but still strong, homelike, and hospitable. They have no shingles to rot, no glued, and puttied, and painted gim-crackery, to warp and crack, and moulder, and can never look so shabby, and desolate, and dreary, as will nine-tenths of the buildings of the same denomination now erecting about New-York, almost as soon as they lose the raw, cheerless, impostor-like airs which seem almost inseparable from their newness.

AT THE NORTH AMERICAN PHALANX: JULY 1852

To Charles Loring Brace

Dear Charley,

Mr. & Mrs. Field, Rosa, Dr. Neidhard & myself were the party. Dr. Neidhard is an unusually sensible, reliable, good-hearted, stout, heavy, common-looking, democratic, socialistic, Christianic, German Homeopathic physician, standing high in this profession & having a profitable practice in Philadelphia. Had seen your letters in Bulletin—not your book. Was sorry not to see you & would be glad to do so when convenient to you.

The Navesink Highlands are a narrow range of hills extending down the shore but little further than we went with Benny. Then along their southern base comes the Shrewsbury or Neversink River, embouching into the *inlet* opposite the ocean house a few miles below our *peach-harbor*. Going up this 7 miles or so to Redbank—a very beautiful country. The south shore flattish & rather marshy. North, hilly with beautiful slopes to the shore—on which are woods, orchards & cultivated fields—very charmingly mingled. Finer than Staten Island.

From Redbank we start for the Phalanx by a *diligence*. Country very pretty—sandy & sterile but by marl & capital culture bearing fine crops. Hilly, well wooded & watered. Further you go less pretty—more half cleared land, less diversity of surface &c.

About ten miles—you come to the domain—no indication of approach—woody country—large old brown mill—water & steam power, saw & grist &c. Enter a farm gate & by a good road through pretty wild wood 50 to 100 rods to the phalanstery. No grounds—an old barrack attached to a little old Dutch cottage, & back of this a few rods, a rather fine neat large, brown colored, wood, hotel looking building.

We land on the piazza of it & enter a cold reception room. Plain, matted floor—engraving, head of Fourier & Swedenborg & plaster angel & a vase or two. Visitors' register on table. Nobody in sight for some time & we *waiting*.

I am looking out of window & see from the aforesaid barrack a human being approaching. It is Horace Greeley in a Bloomer. The same high expansive noble benevolent forehead & eye—rather withered in the sensual. The same floxy hair—& a devil may care air about looks & a take it easy carriage & expression. She is between 30 & 50 & looks healthy & good spite of the outrageous oddity.

She comes & salutes us mildly. Tells us most of Field's acquaintances are not here. (Spring for one, for your luck.) But others are brought, dinner ordered, & Mrs. Arnold, as good a specimen of the best sort of New England little oldish woman as I ever saw. Mild, loving, earnest, simple, thin, and monstrously over-worked. She is our hostess & we are made guests—dine, and Field & I, with a young pair of Arnolds, look over the crops, the marl pit &c.

There are about 100 members & 50 visitors, children, & probationers. No one can join until after a year's probation he or she is accepted by a majority vote. Visitors pay cost (same as members for dishes at table & $2 a week for profit & 37¢ for rent. So it costs as a mere boarding-house $3 to 5 a week.)

The attention of the community has thus far been evidently

given to merely financial success. They have evidently worked hard & constantly. And though from inexperience they made a good many errors at first and have had a great many peculiar difficulties, they have succeeded in *making it pay*. A great success. They have done little but in agriculture to make money by. And when you consider how hard it is to live by agriculture in general, you will acknowledge they have shown a great advantage in the co-operative principle as applied to it.

They have, as I intimated, neglected anything else almost in the endeavor to make money. There has been little thought of beauty or moral or mental advancement. Education of the young has been forgotten in a great measure. There is surprisingly little concern for appearances. They all talk and act *naturally*, simply and unaffectedly. Evidently care little, too little, about the *world* outside. Pay but little attention to visitors and greatly love one-another.

They generally are very strongly attached to the Phalanx, feel confident that it is the right way to live. Have enjoyed it & succeeded in their purposes in it much better than they had expected to. "I *wouldn't* leave for worlds." "Couldn't live any other way." "It is heaven compared with the life I had before," &c., we heard from different individuals.

It is considered a great privilege to be permitted to join them and they reject a great many. I can not tell what sort of people they were. Mostly New Englanders I should think—of various classes—the majority working people. Few or none independently wealthy. Whether any considerable number were actually mere laborers living from hand to mouth, uneducated and uncouth, I could not be satisfied. Some of the later ones were. Many of the old ones might have been and if so have been a good deal refined and civilized by the associative life.

If we compare their situation with that of an average of the agricultural class—laborers & all—even in the best of New England, it is a most *blessed* advance. They are better in nearly all respects. And I don't see why, if such associations were common, and our "lowest class" (I mean poorest & least comfortable and least in the way of improvement moral & mental) of laborers could be drawn of their own will into it, they should not be in the same way advanced in every way. Put a *commonplace* man (if a common-place man would choose to be so put) of our poorest Agricultural or Manufacturing laboring class into *such circumstances*, and it looks to me every way probable that he would be greatly elevated—be made a new man in a few years.

On the other hand, take the average of our people of all classes, including the wealthy and gay fashionable—including our merchants & shop-keepers & lawyers & ministers—and I think on the whole the influence of the system, if they would keep to it, would be favorable. They would live more sensibly, be happier & better.

If you take our most intelligent religious & cultivated sensible people, I think it would depend on individual character, on individual tastes. I half think (though my taste would say otherwise) it would be better for me. For you & J.H.O. & Field it would require a change, a good deal of a struggle, to come handsomely and profitably into it.

The long & short of it is I am *more of a Fourierist* than before I visited the Experiment. The conglomeration of families even works better than I was willing to believe. Nevertheless I am not a Fourierist for myself: but for many, a large part of even an American community (people) I am. It wouldn't suit me—certainly not Field or J.H.O. But I think it would the majority. An Associationist—a Socialist—I very decidedly more am than I was before I went to the Phalanx. The advantages of cooperation of labor are manifestly great. The saving of labor immense. The cheapening of food, rent, &c., very great. It would make starvation, abundance. The advantages by making knowledge, intellectual & moral culture, and esthetic culture more easy—popular—that is, the advantages by *democratizing* religion, refinement & information, I am inclined to think might be equally great among the *associated*. They are not at the N.A. Phalanx & yet are manifest among some.

Those who came there refined, religious, (moral at least) & highly intelligent may have suffered. I saw no evidence that I know that they had, but I should have thought they would. Because they have given themselves up to too narrow ranges of thought—have worked too hard to make the association succeed—or, if you please, too hard for the benefit of others.

It is not, by any means, yet a well-organized & arranged establishment. They are constantly improving—seeing errors and returning to do up matters which in the haste of a struggle to get started were overlooked. Yet they see an immense deal to be attended and better arranged when they get time. Nor are they *very* intelligent people or very refined and genteel and of high ideals—*any of them*. There are lots of conveniences they might have—that would be necessary to the comfort of some wealthy people, even for you & I prospectively; that they know nothing about &, of course, care nothing about. They are not any of them *first class* people, or if so they have forgotten some of their 5th Avenue notions. I mean *silver-forks* & such like—(napkins.)

One great thing they have succeeded in perfectly. In making *labor*, honorable. Mere *physical* labor they too much elevated, I think, but at any rate the "lowest" & most menial & disagreeable duties of civilized community are made really reputable & honorable. A man who spent a large part of his time in smoking & reading newspapers & talking and recreative employments only would feel ashamed of himself, would feel small & consider it a privilege to be allowed to black boots & sweep and milk for a part of the time.

It is in this way it would do me good to go there. No, not in making labor honorable, but in making idleness disagreeable & labor of all sorts (moderately) agreeable—in removing much that is disagreeable. Thus I should hoe corn very comfortably, if I had you in the next row to talk to about the Shuss cogsslocken del Espelntatzellin, and should black my own shoes & yours too if you paid me for it, if all that I needed to do was to toss them into a hopper and turn the stop-cock and let on the steam.

The whole of work of the community is apportioned to different *groups*. Rather, first to series; as the "Agricultural Series," the "Domestic Series," "Live Stock Series," &c, & the series into groups. Thus, the Agricultural into the market garden, orchard, experimental, marling, &c., groups. The Domestic Series into—Cooking, Washing, Ironing, Baking, Dairy, &c.

On joining the community I enter my name on the list of whatever group I please—thus on the dairy, the orchard and the market-garden. I work an hour, say, at the churn, six hours at picking apples for market, and three at sorting potatoes. I am credited by so much on each of the groups' books. Each group votes on what the time of each member is worth. The ordinary "day's work" is from 90 cents to a dollar.

The *chiefs* of all the groups of a Series hold conclaves with the "chief of a series" & arrange matters for the series. The series chiefs also meet under a head chief or *chief of the phalanx* & legislate on matters of more general character.

A man works at anything that he finds himself suitable for. Many are members of a good many groups. If a man does not work with any group with which he has registered his name during two months, he is considered to have left it, &c. If a man works only occasionally, irregularly, his time is valued at a lower figure.

The dining room is much like that of a first class hotel—spacious & neat & comfortable. Tables arranged as in an eating-house, but large enough for perhaps a dozen to each. The *carte* of each meal lies on the table (*carte du jour*) with the prices (cost) of the dishes, which as you know are very low. But every little item counts. Bread 1 cent, butter ½ cent or 1 cent, plate of ros' beef, 3 cents, &c. Ice cream "*a la français*"—a big saucer full, 2 cents. The cost varies with the season. During drought & short pasture, buttercakes are graduated in stamping a little smaller, &c.

The waiters are the prettiest & most refined and graceful young ladies of the community mainly—some of the "most respectable" young fellows, too. You are introduced to the waitress of your table.

Miss Mundy mine was, a very good-looking, lady-like young woman, intelligent accomplished & well informed—dressed with great taste. It was odd enough & not altogether agreeable to hold a conversation with her upon *social* topics in which she showed a philosophical mind and a cultivated and refined judgement, she bending over my shoulder. She takes part in the general conversation of the table, but comes & goes as there is occasion. Is a very good waiter indeed—clean, sweet, and good-natured.

Why do all the best of the young people choose to be waiters & so be deprived of the social enjoyment of the meals with their friends in a great measure? They all dine to-gether afterwards, and as they *are* the *best*, it is a privilege to dine with them—of course to wait with them. If it was not, they would be paid the best—(or should be.) So the most cultivated of the men are *attached* to the domestic groups (more or less—they generally also attach themselves to some of the out-door-exercising groups as well.) The chief of the series is a French physician. There are other foreigners, fine-looking gentlemen, also in it and among the waiters, head waiters, carvers, &c.

There is one I must speak of particularly. He was son of a wealthy, aristocratic family. Brought up in style; "got religion," became an Episcopal clergyman, was eloquent & much beloved & esteemed. Had a country church with a salary of $1,000. Didn't see that he was doing good. Worried & fretted & studied & prayed & fasted. Concluded the system was wrong & he was not sincere. Gave it up sick of life. Wandered & wasted. Accidentaly came hither. Stayed a week. And one night ran out & threw up his hat & declared the problem was solved. Here was a Christianity as was a Christianity & a church as was a church. Threw off his black coat & asked leave to work. Got tremendously tired, feverish &c. Found it wouldn't do. But was determined to work with his hands—"in labor is prayer."—& went into domestic series. And we were introduced to him, a fine, sad, quiet gentlemanly fellow—*peeling potatoes.*

N.B. Nobody blushes or boasts or seems to consider such employments at all to be kept in the dark or anything less of a regular thing than taking off their clothes for themselves when they go to bed. The fact is they have reconstructed a world for themselves & have forgotten the ways of the world *outside.*

I must tell you something of Mr. Arnold's history. He was a merchant in N.Y. greatly interested in Five Point philanthropies. Gave himself much up to them—so too his wife. Both Massachusetts saints. He was finally so much interested in his reforming labors that he gave his whole time to them & the Unitarians made him *minister at large* with a roving commission much such as you would like.

He then threw himself into it. Gave himself to the work—until he got perfectly sickened, disgusted, and overwhelmed. With large means & doing nothing else, he found it was stopping leaks in a rotten ship. The more you stopped the breech up the more it was *widened.* Had a conviction much like that of the Episcopal clergyman that the system was wrong, that the so-called Church of Christ was wrong. That it was not Christianity he was preaching—that Christians did not love-one-another, &c., &c., &c.

Went to the West and found the most solitary place he could & there lived hermit-like with his family for several years. His wife says, it was the greatest relief & happiness to her to feel that there they could do others but *little* harm & others could do them but *little*.

While so situated, Mr. Spring (his wife's brother) went to Europe with * Fuller—& while gone certain Fourierite periodicals that he had taken were sent to him (Arnold). He did not like them, but read them. So did his wife, until after a year both suddenly found each-other converted. They came to the Phalanx & are fully convinced that it must be by this way only that the kingdom shall come.

The arrangement of the dormitories is much like that of a hotel; a large number of small bed-rooms for single parties and suites of rooms for families. There are three or four tenements adjoining the main-house, built into it like a *block* with no communication with it or with each other except by a gallery in the rear to enable the inmates to go to the dining-hall or the work rooms (kitchen &c.) dry shod. There is also one entirely detached cottage.

These families could have their meals sent to them (by some additional payment) but in fact none do—all preferring the common refectory. Here families have their usual tables separate from others if they choose. Families separate, though, a good deal. Husband & wife & the younger children generally together, but the older children "follow their attractions." That is, being generally *engaged* as soon as they are big enough, they sit with their espoused.

In the evening from supper till 10 o'clock or later there was a good deal of recreation, walking parties, rowing parties, dancing & music. There are 6 pianos in the establishment & several guitars, &c. There was a music teacher & a French teacher. Also one of the French refugees teaches fencing & dancing, &c. But recreation of this sort was not *general*. The less cultivated however spent the evening much more elevatingly than most country people do—in conversation & discussions. There is very little reading done.

Most of the young ladies & some of the older men dressed *à la Bloomer*, generally not very tastefully. Some appeared to much greater advantage when so than in long skirts. A graceful *action* was much more graceful and gratifying where the movement of the leg could be seen. Some were very short skirted. Usually the kilt reached an inch or two below the knee, or enough to reach over it in sitting. Not always though. There was the most perfect natural propriety & good sense among them all. The Bloomer has been naturalized, and in an hour you are as accustomed to it as you would be in China. It is "all right." Many who wore Bloomer in A.M. were in "evening dresses" later. Some appeared better & some worse for the change.

As to creeds, the majority are Swedenborgians, but there is nothing peculiar to the community. I should think persons of all the great nominally Christian churches from Catholics to Unitarians, or rationalists.

The very shortest Bloomer had me by the button sitting under the trees for half the evening telling me of her Spiritual Supping experience. She had had, during two months, frequent intercourse with her father who died eight years ago while she was a child, & received most delightful words from, and practical advice and assistance. She believed it all as fully as she did or could anything not absolutely tangible. She recognized the influence of spirits constantly upon her as she did heat & light. It was a regular thing. Thought there was much humbug. Foxes & Fishes were imposters. Others fools—self deceived. Her yarn didn't amount to much. She was a person that would be easily imposed upon.

I have been, since last sheet, reading Tribune of Saturday (23rd.) If you haven't it's worth it—on Spiritual Manifestations & the *Shekinah* article on Judge Edmonds. And I add a little more.

She was convinced or held her faith entirely from the *moral* evidence—the general character of the communications she had received. First, though, she was startled by receiving answers to questions and suggestions in her own mind which she had not uttered or expressed in any way. As for material manifestations, she had certainly seen tables lifted and taken across a room. She had stood on a table and been moved gently and steadily across the room & back to the exact spots on the carpet that the legs occupied before—no person being near the table, at 4 o'clock P.M., open daylight. It was in Massachusetts last spring or winter. The table was moved at her request to give evidence of the ability of the spirits to exercise material agency. Was guided as she directed, &c. As I said, she was the sort of person that would be easily imposed on and be run away with by her own imagination. Nevertheless, her facts & her faith impressed me with a little more respect for the matter.

As to the people of the community in general, I have a strong respect for them as hard-working, earnest, unselfish livers in the faith of a higher life for man on earth as well as "above." There were fewer odd characters than I should have expected to find. Generally, there was much simplicity and self-containedness among them. I think they are living devoutly & more in accordance with the principles of Christ—*among themselves*—than any equal number of persons I ever saw living in the usual neighborhood intercourse together.

There is a certain class that they very much need to have associated with them. I could not help wishing Charles Elliott had joined them. Believing a good deal in their principles as I believe he does, he would have been exceedingly useful to them. They much need mechanics, but I think it is the fault of their theory that they do not have them. Their success without them is the more wonderful. I believe they have only one carpenter & a watch maker, or some such nearly useless thing to them. Having to pay high, of course, for all mechanics brought to do work for them from a distance.

What they need for improvement as a community of moral creatures is more attention to the intellectual. They want an *Educational Series* very much. They have no fit teacher—a Frenchman for want of a better acts as schoolmaster to the fry. But there is no proper nursery department & the children, & not the children alone, are growing without any proper discipline of mind. A rum set one would think they would make. But I must confess those who are breaking into manhood & especially into womanhood tell well for the system. They are young *ladies* & young *gentlemen*. Naturally and without effort or consciousness, so.

You had better go there next fall. I'll go with you. Mr. Arnold was sorry you didn't come with us. And others would be glad to see you. If you could give them a lecture on Hungary they would be gratified. Hadn't you better get one up—with some reference to present position of things? Remodel your old one a little. I told them you would come bye & bye.

If we can make a boating-party for several days it will be pleasant in peach season—*October* rather too late. Charles Elliott ought to go with us. Be valuable to him as a market gardener.

All the folks here. Nothing of importance. Beckwith not yet bought. In a fortnight I may leave home for a little while.

Yours Affectionately,

Fred.

P.S. I have condensed this for the Tribune. Told them if they didn't want to print it to direct to you & you would get it at the office.

"THIS BEGGARLY FARMING": MARCH 1853

The South

LETTERS ON THE PRODUCTIONS, INDUSTRY AND RESOURCES OF THE SOUTHERN STATES

NUMBER SEVEN

The Connection of Slavery with Agricultural Prosperity in Virginia—Discussion of the Comparative Value of Free and Slave Labor—The Amount Accomplished in a Day by a Slave and by a Free Laborer Compared—Labor and Wealth—The Humiliating Position of Virginia—Its Probable Cause.

To the Editor of the New-York Daily Times:

I did not intend when I commenced writing these letters to give much attention to the subject of Slavery; but the truth is, the character of the whole agriculture of the country depends upon it. In every department of industry I see its influence, vitally affecting the question of profit, and I must add that everywhere, and constantly, the conviction is forced upon me, to a degree entirely unanticipated, that its effect is universally ruinous. My first impression upon crossing the country was, that to account for the general superior prosperity asserted of the North, we need go no further than to examine the soil; the main source of wealth at the South being agriculture, no cheapness of labor could make profitable the culture of such poor soil as that which at first fell under my observation. It did, indeed, occur to me that only by the low value of slave labor, could such land have been so long retained in cultivation. Would you think it possible that a man could live by cultivating ground that only produced three bushels of wheat to the acre? The very slightest possible cultivation of the soil, and the mere seed and sowing of it without the slightest tillage, would cost a northern farmer as much as the value of the crop. Such crops are common in Virginia. I do not exaggerate in saying so. I have heard of repeated instances where the crop of a whole, large plantation was not over three bushels to the acre! Without asserting, as, however, I am much inclined to think, and as many Virginians confess to me they are themselves convinced, that the system of slavery is responsible, by its enervating effects upon the minds of the superior race, for this beggarly farming; there is not room for the shadow of a doubt across my mind, that slave labor makes the cost of cultivating such lands greater, and the profit (!) less, than it would be under free labor.

But the soils from which I derived the impression I have spoken of, are by no means to be taken as a criterion of the ordinary lands of this country; I have since seen large tracts of as fine wheat land, deep and rich upland of clayey loam; or alluvial meadows of the best description of soil for general cropping, that I ever saw in any country, and even on the same old piney land—or worn out tobacco fields—under a system of agriculture of moderate enterprise and skill, I have found that fair crops of all sorts can be made. And under free labor, and the direction of men exercising the ordinary intelligence and skill applied to Northern farms, I am wholly convinced that there is not in all the Northern States, or in all of Europe, a district of country where the business of farming would be so profitable, as in Eastern Virginia. I shall hereafter discuss the inducements offered under present circumstances to emigration. As to the capability of the soil, I heard this morning that a Northern man last year purchased a farm in Southern Virginia, but a few miles from a railroad, and but twenty from a seaport, for which he paid $5 an acre. It had not ordinarily produced wheat at the rate of five bushels the acre, and had never been plowed over four inches in depth; upon which, by plowing eight inches, turning up not only virgin soil, but clay to mix with the sand of the surface, and applying 150 barrels of guano, costing $3.75 to the acre, he obtained a crop averaging twenty bushels an acre, and from which he realized much more than sufficient money to pay for the cost of the land it grew upon, and the expense of growing it. I have seen land of a similar description, which has been sold, with its improvements, during the last year, for $2.25 an acre.

As I may hereafter wish sometimes to assume the superior cheapness or economy of free labor, I will in addition to the reasons I have before given for it, state here a few more.

I have compared notes with several farmers, planters and manufacturers, capitalists and contractors, and I arrive at the conclusion to which they have without one exception conceded, that the wages of laborers, measuring them merely by power of muscle, or brute force, without regard to energy or will, are at this time at least 25 per cent. higher in Eastern Virginia, than in the State of New-York.

In addition to this difference there is to be deducted from the profit of the slave the loss of time occasioned by his sickness (or absence from any cause); which loss does not fall upon the proprietor under the free labor system, and the temptation to counterfeit which is not offered to the laborer. The loss of this to the slave farmer is of various consequence, sometimes small, often excessively embarrassing, always a subject of anxiety and suspicion. A farmer told me for the purpose of showing me the weakness of the family tie and the promiscuous intercourse among slaves, that having allowed one of his men, a mechanic, to work some time in a shipyard at a city, soon after his return, and at a time when he was pressed for labor, he suddenly found twelve hands, male and female, and all of them married parties, laid up with a disgusting disease, and was obliged to procure, at a great expense, a physician to come from town twice a week to examine the whole force, to prevent its spread among them. After all, an old "nigger doctor," a slave in the neighborhood, was more successful in curing them with an empirical remedy, than the regular practitioner. I mention this as indicating that this complaint is not unfrequent among them. A decoction of pine leaves is one of the negro remedies.

As to sham-sickness or "playing 'possum" I heard much complaint of it, and it is said to be nearly as hard to treat negroes in sickness as it is children, because they use their imagination so much, greatly puzzle the doctors by lying as to their symptoms, and from their neglect or refusal to take the remedies left for them. They will generally conceal pills in their mouth, declare they have swallowed them, and it is only discovered that they have not by their failing to have any effect. This is a general custom, but probably arose from the fact that unless very disagreeably ill they are loth to recover from that which exempts them from labor.

Amusing incidents illustrating this difficulty I have heard, showing that the slave rather enjoys getting a severe wound that lays him up. He has his hand smashed by accident, and says: "Bless de Lord—de hand b'long to massa. I don't reckon I'se got no more corn to hoe dis year, for sartin."

On the other hand the suspicion that when a hand complains he is "playing 'possum" and the refusal to allow him to "knock off" often aggravates what might be otherwise a slight and temporary indisposition, into a long and serious illness. From this reason, the labor of women on a plantation, as a large planter assured me, "actually does not pay for their salt." After they get to the "breeding age" they do no more work of any account. "They are forever complaining of 'irregularities.' They don't come to the field, and you ask what's the matter, and the old nurse always nods her head and says, 'Oh, *she's not well*, sir; she's not fit to work, sir,'—and you have to take her word for it."

I believe that the slaves are generally very kindly and considerately treated in sickness, but the profit of slave labor is all the less from this, from the encouragement to the slave to make the most of sickness and so to withdraw his labor and be a mere "bill of expense" to his master.

Then the slaves sometimes *refuse* to labor, or "balk," from mere "rascality," which, as I have before shown, is sufficiently common and inexplicable as to be considered a disease. They are then inconceivably stubborn, and can barely be driven to work by the lash, and in no way restrained from recklessly or malevolently doing much injury to their master's property.

"How do *you* manage, then, when a man misbehaves, or is sick?" I have been asked at this point of the discussion.

"If he is sick, I simply charge against him every half day of the time he is off work, and deduct it from his wages. If he is careless, or refuses to do what in reason I demand of him, I discharge him, paying him wages to the time he leaves. With new men in whom I have not confidence, I make a written agreement, before witnesses, on engaging them, that will permit me to do this. As for 'rascality,' I never had but one case of anything approaching to what you call so. A man contradicted me in the field; I told him to leave his job and go to the house, took hold and finished it myself; then went to the house, made out a written statement of account, counted out the balance in money due him, gave him the statement and the money, and told him he must go, and had not another word with him. I've no doubt he was a good and respectful man to his next employer."

The slave master, in case he finds he has a "tartar" on his hands, has no remedy, if he has hired him, but to ask a deduction of what he has paid from his owner, on the same ground that you would if you had hired a vicious horse, and instead of helping you on your journey he had broken your leg; or, if he is an owner, to *sell* him "to go South."

That the slaves have to be "humored" a great deal, and often cannot be made to do their master's will, is very evident,—I do not think they will do from fear nearly as much as Northern laborers will simply from respect to their contract or regard to their duty. The gentleman I before spoke of as employing white laborers on a farm, had been especially struck with this. A dam had given way, and it was necessary to do a good deal of work very promptly in the water. He was greatly surprised to find how much more readily than negroes his white men would obey his orders, jumping into the water waist deep in the midst of winter without the slightest hesitation or grumbling. He had noticed the same on all emergencies, when it was desirable to work late at night, &c., or to do any very disagreeable job. A farmer in England told me that he had once, in a very bad harvest season, had laborers at work without a wink of sleep for sixty hours, himself heading them, and eating and drinking with them.

Finally, to come to the point of the amount of work which will be done under the Northern and the Southern system. I regret that I cannot get more exact data here. The only close observation of the work done in a day by slaves that can be fairly compared with that by free laborers, that I have been able to obtain, was made by Mr. T. R. Griscom, of Petersburg; a man remarkable for the accuracy and preciseness of his information on all subjects. I was recommended to call upon him, as a man possessing very intimate knowledge with regard to the agriculture of the district in which he lives, by as strong a pro-Slavery man as I have met. He formerly resided in New-Jersey, and has had the superintendence of very extensive and varied agricultural operations in Virginia.

He tells me he once very carefully observed how much labor was expended in securing a crop of very thin wheat, and found that it took four negroes one day to cradle, rake, and bind one acre. (That is, this was the rate at which the field was harvested.) In the wheat-growing districts of Western New-York, four men would be expected to do five acres of a similar crop.

Mr. Griscom further states, as his opinion, that four negroes do not, in the ordinary agricultural operations of this State, accomplish as much as one laborer in New-Jersey. Upon my expressing my astonishment, he repeated it, as his deliberately formed opinion.

I have since, again called on Mr. Griscom, and obtained permission to give his name with the above statement. He also wishes me to add, that the ordinary waste in harvesting, by the carelessness of the negroes, above that which occurs in the hands of Northern laborers, is large enough to equal what a Northern farmer would consider a satisfactory profit on the crop.

I do not think there is a man in Virginia whose information on this point would be more reliable or whose opinion would be formed with less prejudice to either side and is entitled to greater respect than Mr. Griscom's.

I have at second hand the result of the experience of another man who has superintended extended labors of a similar character, both at the North and in Virginia, which precisely agrees with Mr. Griscom's. I am not able now to see him and obtain the facts directly, but have been promised a statement of them by him in writing.

In a late article by H. M. Brackenridge, in the *National Intelligencer*, copied in the New-York Times of Dec. 29, reproving the spirit of *Uncle Tom's Cabin*, and containing many very sensible observations on Slavery, the result, the writer says, of ten years observation and much reflection, it is stated that "the day's labor of the slave is notoriously not more than half that of the white man; and if left to himself (it would be) not more than half that."

Another gentleman here, who formerly resided in Connecticut, told me that he believed that a Northern laborer would finish a negro's day's work by 11 o'clock in the forenoon.

I have stated that I had met no farmer that was not convinced of the superior economy of free-labor (if the slaves were not on their hands and in some way to be provided for), but few however are willing to concede or can believe the difference to be as great as the above opinions would indicate. On mentioning them to one, he remarked, that although the four men might not have done more than at the rate of an acre a day, it must have been because they were not well driven. He thought that if driven hard enough, threatened with punishment, and *punished* if necessary, they would do as much work as it was *possible* for any white man to do. The same man, however, has told me that slaves were very rarely punished—he thought not more than apprentices were at the North—that the driving was almost always left to overseers, who were the laziest and most inefficient dogs in the world—frequently not worth half so much as the slaves they pretended to manage—and that the wages of an overseer were often not more than half as much as one of the negroes put under his control could be hired out for.

A planter on the coast, whom I asked to examine these statements, and my conclusions with regard to this subject, that he might, if he could, refute them, or give me any facts of an opposite character, replied: "Why, I have no doubt you are right, Sir; in general, a slave does not do half the work he easily might, and which, by being harsh enough with him, he can be made to do. When I came into possession of my plantation, I found the overseer was good for nothing, and I soon told him I had no further occasion for his services, and I went to driving the negroes myself. In the morning, when I went out one of them came up to me saying, 'Well, massa, what'll you hab me go at dis mornin'?' 'Well, ole man,' said I, 'you may go to the swamps and cut wood.' 'Well, massa,' said he, 's'pose you wants me to do kordins we's been use to doin' here: ebery niggar cut a cord o' wood a day.' 'A cord! that's what you have been used to doing, is it?' said I. 'Yes, massa, dat's wot dey always makes a niggar do roun' heah—a cord a day, dat's allers de job.' 'Well, now, ole man,' said I, 'you go and cut me two cords to-day.' 'Oh, massa! two cords! Nobody couldn do dat. Oh! massa, dat's too hard! Nebber heard nobody's cuttin' more 'n a cord in a day roun' heah. No niggar couldn do it.' 'Well, ole man, you have two cords of wood cut to-night, or to-morrow morning you shall get two hundred lashes. Now, go off and be about it.' And he did it, and ever since no negro has ever cut less than two cords a day for me, though my neighbors never get but one cord. It was just so with a great many other things—mauling rails—I always have twice as many rails mauled in a day as it is the custom of the country to expect of a negro, and just twice as many as my negroes always had been made to do before I managed them myself."

Allowing that the opinions of the practical men who have had experience at the North and the South, that I have given, somewhat exaggerate the difference in the amount of work accomplished by a slave and a Northern free laborer (though I did not give them because they were extreme, but because they were the only exact statements that I could obtain)—allowing that I have been unfortunate in this way, and that a longer residence in the State would give me information that would much modify these estimates, there still remains, beyond a doubt, a very great loss in using the labor of the slave. These statements would make the loss between three and four hundred *per cent.* Now although they were the calculations and deliberate estimates of men who had enjoyed a liberal education, and who had unusual facilities for observing both at the North and South—men who employ slaves, and who sustain Southern opinions on the political questions arising from slavery—I am not disposed to insist upon full credit for them. *Cut them down one-half*, and we still have a loss of nearly *one hundred per cent.* Even if you will have them to be utterly mistaken, and calculate that the slaves accomplish equally as much—man for man—as Irishmen under wages contract, yet consider how large a sum would pay for clothes, time lost by sickness or otherwise—five or more additional holidays, which custom gives them, and for all that they pilfer or damage and destroy through carelessness, improvidence, recklessness and rascality!

Can there be a reasonable doubt that the State of Virginia loses fifty per cent. on the cost of labor, in employing slaves in preference to freemen!

Suppose that half the cost of a crop is expended in the human labor given to it, the profits of the farmers of Virginia would then be increased 25 per cent. per annum, if they could substitute the labor of freemen for that of slaves.

Labor is the creator of wealth. There can be no honest wealth, no true prosperity without it, and in exact proportion to the economy of labor is the cost of production and the accumulation of profit.

Remembering this, I cannot but ask the people of Virginia to read again the facts that follow, which I extract from the leading article of the Richmond *Enquirer* of this date (Dec. 29), and seriously and candidly reflect for themselves with regard to them.

> Virginia, anterior to the Revolution and up to the adoption of the Federal Constitution, contained more wealth and a larger population than other States of this Confederacy.

> ———

> Virginia, from being first in point of wealth and political power, has come down to the fifth in the former, and the fourth in the latter. New-York, Pennsylvania, Massachusetts and Ohio stand above her in wealth, and all, but Massachusetts, in population and political power. Three of these States are literally chequered over with Railroads and canals, and the fourth (Massachusetts) with Railroads alone.

> But when we find that the population of the single city of New-York and its environs exceeds the whole free population of Eastern Virginia, and the valley between the Blue Ridge and Alleghany, we have cause to feel deeply for our situation. Philadelphia herself contains a population far greater than the whole free population of Eastern Virginia.

> —The little State of Massachusetts has an aggregate wealth exceeding that of Virginia by more than one hundred and twenty-six millions of dollars—a State, too, which is incapable of subsisting its inhabitants from the production of its soil. And New-York, which was as much below Massachusetts, at the adoption of the Federal Constitution, in wealth and power, as the latter was below Virginia, now exceeds the wealth of both. While the aggregate

wealth of New-York, in 1850, amounted to $1,080,309,216, that of Virginia was $436,701,082—a difference in favor of the former of $643,608,134. The unwrought mineral wealth of Virginia exceeds that of New-York. The climate and soil are better; the back country, with equal improvements, would contribute as much.

All true, and facts and contrasts more striking and far more humiliating might have been shown you. Why be driven by fanaticism and bigotry to shut your eyes to the most simple and evident explanation of them?

I shall next show why it is not possible for any single farmer or manufacturer to relieve himself of his proportion of this tax to support slavery and increase his products and profits in a corresponding ratio, and make it evident that only by the general action of the people, their "commercial vassalage" can be remedied.

FREE LABOR AND SLAVE LABOR: MARCH 1853

The South

LETTERS ON THE PRODUCTIONS, INDUSTRY AND
RESOURCES OF THE SOUTHERN STATES

NUMBER EIGHT

Why Free Labor is Not More Profitable than Slave Labor, Now, in Virginia—The Difficult Question of Disposing of the Slaves—Their Condition—The Condition of the Free Blacks at the South.

To the Editor of the New-York Daily Times:

In my last, it was made to appear that the cost of employing Slave labor in Virginia over free labor in New-York, was equal to an addition of one dollar to every dollar now expended for labor. This loss, be it remembered, is not a loss merely to the employer, but is a loss to the whole body politic—an abstraction from the general wealth of Virginia, of the United States, and of the world.

And it by no means follows, that, by disposing of his slaves, as things are at present, and hiring free laborers, any farmer in

Virginia can make a saving of 100 per cent. The principle of demand and supply here comes in. The laborer that, in New-York,
gives a certain amount of exertion for a certain price, soon finds
that for that price here a less amount of work is customarily
expected. He adopts slave habits of labor—he suits his wares to
the market. He sees that the capitalists of Virginia give a high
price for a poor article—he furnishes the poor article. But there
are also other laws, besides this of demand and supply, that affect
this matter.

"Man is a social being." The large amount of labor performed
in Virginia is and long has been done by negroes. The negroes
are a degraded people; degraded not merely by position, but
actually immoral, low-lived; without healthy ambition, but little
influenced by high moral considerations, and in regard to labor
not at all affected by regard for duty. This is always recognized,
and debasing fear, not cheering hope, is in general allowed to be
the only stimulant to exertion. A capitalist was having a building
erected in Petersburg, and his slaves were employed in carrying up the brick and mortar for the masons on their heads; a
Northern man standing near remarked to him that they moved
so indolently it seemed as if they were trying to see how long
they could be in mounting the ladder without actually stopping.
The builder started to reprove them, but after moving a step
turned back and said, "It would only make them move more
slowly still when I am not looking at them, if I should hurry
them now—and what motive have they to do better? It's no
concern of theirs how long the masons wait. I am sure if I was
in their place I shouldn't move as fast as they do."

Now let the white laborer come here from the North or
from Europe; his nature demands a social life; shall he associate
with the poor, slavish, degraded, low-lived, despised, unambitious negro, with whom labor and punishment are almost
synonymous, or shall he be the friend and companion of the
white man in whose mind labor is associated with no ideas of
duty, responsibility, comfort, luxury, cultivation or elevation
and expansion either of mind or estate—as it is, where the ordinary laborer is a free man, free to use his labor as a means of
obtaining all these and all else that is to be respected, honored
or envied in the world?

Associating with either or both is it possible that he will not be demoralized, hate labor, give as little of it for his hire as he can, become base, cowardly, faithless—"worse than a nigger."

I ask *you, Virginians,* if this is not so—if you do not know it to be so? Is not this a simple, reasonable, satisfactory explanation of those failures in the substitution of free laborers for slaves to which you are in the habit of referring as settling this question?

See you not that it is Slavery still, that, like the ship-worm, is noiselessly and imperceptibly ever opening the leaks by which your state, the greatest of all, the vanguard of the fleet, rolls helplessly water-logged far astern of all?

Nine out of ten of the thinking men of Virginia are so convinced, and whisper among themselves, what is to be done? And the rest of the crew double-shot the starboard battery, and loudly threaten what they *will do* if we of the North don't mind our business, and quit advising and pitying them, and send back the rats that swim away from them.

Well, it's all very true that we can't help them, and that our attempts to do so only embarrass them, and that we have among us plenty of bad and more weak and foolish people that would do better to mind their own business and leave them to their fate; that we have beams enough in our own eyes; that the condition of *some* of our laborers is bad, as bad as theirs, worse than theirs; that this shows a rottenness in the planks of our system which we would do well to probe and study to mend. I am convinced of it all—the more so, the more sadly and earnestly so, for what I see here. There is wrong in both systems. Too much competition and self-seeking in our labor as there is too little in theirs. They prove it to me; I thank them for it; they cannot object if I, with no unkind or invidious purpose, frankly describe the nature of the evils they themselves have to deal with.

And they must understand that we have an interest and a certain responsibility in whatever of evil belongs to them, as we have in all that concerns the human family. That with a fair understanding of the nature of this evil, and of all its relations, we shall find that we have little or nothing to do about it ourselves, but to quietly wait and pray, for them in wisdom to move, is not improbable; and I hope and believe, that what I shall have occasion to write in regard to it, will favor such an understanding.

A proper appreciation of the difficulties that embarrass the people of the South in connection with the subject of Slavery, that lie in the way of any action favorable to even the amelioration of the condition of the slave by the action of law, would do more to restore friendly feeling and confidence between the two great sections of our country, than all the compromise measures that could be contrived, however strictly and conscientiously carried out. Only let it be known at the North in addition to a slight appreciation of these difficulties, that there was a general disposition to boldly, manfully, look them in the face, and to deal with them in a broad, Statesmanlike and Christianlike spirit, and the fanaticism of Abolition is dead and buried.

Only let the North show a disposition in future to regard the subject of Slavery as one *over which she has no control*, let indignation be quieted and turned to the injustice, and barbarism in her midst, let fierce denunciation and exciting appeals and even senselessly unpractical counsels be silenced, and I rejoice to state my conviction that in Virginia at least, hosts of great, good, and talented men, are all ready and earnestly purposed to give themselves with all their energies to the mighty task.

Even the men who have no concern above dollars and cents are well convinced this day, and it is commonly calculated among them, that if the Slaves could be quietly removed from their limits, the State would fill up so rapidly with free-men, and its sources of wealth would be so much more speedily and economically developed, that in five years' time the increase in the value of all real estate would more than pay for the value that the Slaves are now reckoned by their masters to be worth.

I am ready to give it as my present opinion, after what I have seen already of Slavery, that the African race whether it has been elevated or degraded by subjection to the whites of the South, is in many respects, and shows itself in the majority of instances to be, happier, intellectually, morally and physically, in Slavery than in what passes at the South under the name of Freedom, and that almost is the only freedom that it is practicable at present to be permitted to it.

Slavery in Virginia, up to the present time, however it has improved the general character and circumstances of the race of miserable black barbarians that several generations since were introduced here, has done nothing to prepare it, and is yet doing nothing to prepare it, for the free and enlightened exercise of individual independence and responsibility. THEREFORE, is Slavery the greatest sin and shame upon any nation or people on God's earth. The slaveholders say that we and others, by our impracticable interference, are responsible for this sin and shame. Let God judge, and let us keep silence.

I wish now to give you some idea of the condition of the freed blacks at the South; in Virginia. I shall incidentally refer to the condition of those at the North.

In one county of Virginia, a few years ago, an inventory and estimate of the value of the property of all the free blacks was made by order of the magistracy. With one exception the highest value placed upon the property of an individual was two dollars and a half ($2.50.) The person excepted owned one hundred and fifty acres of land, a cabin upon it, a mule and some implements. He had a family, including only his wife and children, of nine. Of provisions for their support, there were in the house, at the time of the visit of the appraisers, a peck and a half of Indian meal and part of a herring. The man was then absent to purchase some more meal, but had no money, and was to give his promise to pay in wood, which he was to cut from his farm. And this was in Winter.

This shows their general poverty. That this poverty is not the result of want of facilities or security for accumulating property, is proved by the exceptional instances of considerable wealth existing among them. An account of the death of a free colored man who devised by will property to the amount of thirty thousand dollars, has been lately in the newspapers. I have ascertained the general accuracy of the narration though one somewhat important circumstance was omitted. It was stated that the man preferred that his children should continue in the condition of slaves, and gave his property to a man who was to be their master. He gave as a reason for this that he had personally examined the condition of the free blacks in Philadelphia and Boston, as well as in Virginia, and he preferred that his children should remain slaves, knowing that their master would take better care of them than they were capable of exercising for themselves. This was substantially correct, and I have conversed with a gentleman who tried to persuade him to act otherwise, to whom he gave these reasons. He had been, however, for a long time before his death, in a low state of health, and I know not how sound, or uninfluenced by others, his mind might have been. The circumstance omitted was, that these were illegitimate children, by a slave woman, although he had a wife that was a free woman, and had had a child by her—which, however, died young. It is a general custom of white people here to leave their illegitimate children, by slaves (and they are *very* common) in slavery. The man was himself a mulatto. I know of a very respectable and very wealthy man who sold his own half-brother to the traders to go South, because he attempted to run away.

I have heard of another case of a free negro in Virginia, supposed to be worth at least $5,000.

At the present rate of wages, any free colored man can accumulate property more rapidly in Virginia than almost any man, depending solely on his labor, can at the North. In the tobacco factories in Richmond and Petersburg slaves are at this time in great demand, and are paid one hundred and fifty to two hundred dollars, and all expenses, for a year. These slaves are expected to work only to a certain extent for their employers; it having been found that they could not be "driven" to do a fair day's work so easily as they could be stimulated to it by the offer of a bonus for all they would manufacture above a certain number of pounds. This quantity is so easily exceeded that the slaves earn for themselves from five to twenty dollars a month. *Freemen* are paid for all they do at rates which make their labor equally profitable, and *can* earn, if they give but moderate attention and diligence to the labor, very large sums. The barber under the Bollingbroke Hotel has a younger brother, who works in a tobacco factory, whose wages last year amounted to over nine hundred dollars. Of this he has laid up not one cent, and such is the case with nearly all the hands so employed in the town; they spend their wages as do the slaves their "over money," almost as rapidly as they receive it, and as foolishly and as much to their own injury as do sailors, or the manufacturing workmen in England. Of the truth of this, I have assurances from every quarter, and from men of all opinions.

Formerly, I am told, the slaves were accustomed to recreate themselves in the evening and on holidays a great deal in dancing, and that they took great enjoyment in this exercise. It was at length, however, preached against, and the "professors" so generally induced to use their influence against it as an immoral practice, that it has greatly gone "out of fashion," and in place of it the young ones have got into the habit of gambling, and worse occupations, for the pastime of their holidays and leisure hours. I have not seen any dancing during these holidays, nor any amusement engaged in by the blacks that was not essentially gross, dissipating or wasteful, unless I except firing of crackers.

Improvidence is generally considered here a natural trait of African character; and by none is it more so than by the negroes themselves. I think it is a mistake. Negroes, as far as I have observed at the North, although suffering from the contamination of habits acquired by themselves or their fathers in Slavery, unless they are intemperate, are more provident than whites of equal educational advantages. Much more so than the newly-arrived Irish, though the Irish are soon infected with the desire of accumulating wealth and acquiring permanent means of comfort. This opinion is confirmed by the experience of the City Missionaries—one of whom has informed me that where the very poorest classes of New-York reside, black and white in the same house, the rooms occupied by the blacks are generally much less bare of furniture and the means of subsistence than those of the whites.

I observed that the negroes themselves follow the notion of the whites here, and look upon the people of their race as naturally unfitted to provide for themselves far ahead. Accustomed like children to have all their necessary wants provided for, their whole energies and powers of mind are habitually given to obtaining the means of temporary ease and enjoyment. Their masters and the poor or "mean" whites acquire somewhat of the same habits from early association with them, calculate on it in them, do not wish to cure it, and by constant practices encourage it. The negroes depend much for the means of enjoying themselves on presents. Their good-natured masters (and their masters are very good-natured, though capricious and quick-tempered) like to gratify them, and are ashamed to disappoint them—to be thought mean. So it follows that with the free negroes, habit is upon them; the habits of their associates, slaves, make the custom of society—that strongest of agents upon weak minds. The whites think improvidence a natural defect of character with them, expect it of them as they grow old, or as they lose easy means of gaining a livelihood, charitably furnish it to them; expect them to pilfer; do not look upon it as a crime; if they do, at least, consider them but slightly to blame, as, indeed, they are; and so every influence of association is unfavorable to providence, forethought, economy. I shall continue this subject in my next.

SLAVERY IN VIRGINIA: APRIL 1853

The South

LETTERS ON THE PRODUCTIONS, INDUSTRY AND RESOURCES OF THE SLAVE STATES

NUMBER NINE

Condition of Free Blacks at the South—Free Blacks at the North —Evils of Enfranchisement—Aversion to Colonization— Dependence of Negroes on the Whites—General Sentiment on Slavery in Virginia.

To the Editor of the New-York Daily Times:

With such influences upon them, with such a character, with such education, with such associations, as I described in my last letter, it is not surprising that Southerners say that the condition of the slave who is subject to some wholesome restraint, and notwithstanding his improvidence is *systematically* provided for, is preferable to that of the free black. The free black does not in general feel himself superior to the slave, and the slaves of the wealthy and aristocratic families consider themselves in a much better and more honorable position than the free blacks. I have heard their view of the matter expressed thus "_____ *dirty free niggers!—got no body to take care of 'em.*"

It is for this reason that slaves of gentlemen of high character, who are treated with judicious indulgence, and who can rely with confidence on the permanence of their position, knowing that they will be kindly cared for as they grow old, and feeling their own incapacity to take care of themselves, do often voluntarily remain in slavery when freedom is offered them, whether it be at the South, or North, or in Africa. A great many slaves that have been freed and sent to the North, after remaining there for a time, have of their own accord, returned to Virginia, and their report of the manner in which negroes are treated there, the difficulty of earning enough to provide themselves with the luxuries to which they have been accustomed, the unkindness of the white people to them, and the want of that thoughtless liberality in payments to them which they expect here from their superiors, has not been such as to lead others to pine for the life of an outcast at the North. Among those so returning, have been many of Mr. Randolph's slaves, I understand.

And here let me say, as I am most happy to do, that I am convinced that the real kindness of heart and generosity of the people of Virginia, makes practically of no effect their unjust, cruel and cowardly laws with regard to free negroes—unjust, because they interfere with a man's quiet possession of the rewards of his own labor—cruel, because they separate friends, break up families, and make men homeless outcasts among strangers—cowardly, because they attempt to throw upon others a danger and evil which is the natural result of the peculiar constitution of their own society.

The spread of intelligence of all kinds among the slaves is remarkable. A planter told me that he had frequently known of his slaves going twenty miles from home and back during the night, without their being missed at all from work, or known at the time to be off the plantation. Another told me that he had been frequently informed by his slaves of occurrences in a town forty miles distant, where he spent part of the year with his family, in advance of the mail, or any means of communication that he could command the use of. Also, when in town, his servants would sometimes give him important news from the plantation, several hours before a messenger dispatched by his overseer arrived.

I do not wish to be understood as intimating that the slaves generally would not like to be freed and sent to the North, or that they are ever really contented or satisfied with slavery; only that as having been deprived of the use of their limbs from infancy, as it were, they are not such fools as to wish now suddenly to be set upon their feet, and left to shift for themselves.

They prefer, if they have sufficient worldly wisdom, to secure at least plain food and clothing, and comfortable lodging, at their owner's expense, while they will return as little for it as they can, and have only the luxuries of life to work for on their own account. It is not easy to deprive them of the means of securing a good share of these.

These luxuries to be sure, may be of very degrading character, and such as, according to our ideas, they would be better without. But their tastes and habits are formed to enjoy them, and they are not likely to be content without them.

But, to live either on their own means, or the charitable assistance of others, at the North, they must dispense with many of them. It is as much as most of them—more than some of them, with us—can do, by their labor, to obtain the means of subsistence, such as they have been used to being provided with, without a thought of their own, at the South. And if they are known to indulge in practices that are habitual with them, they will not only lose the charity, but even the custom, of most of their philanthropical friends; and then they must turn to pilfering again, or meet that most pitiful of all extremities— poverty from want of work. Again: Suppose them to wish to indulge in their old habits of sensual pleasure, they can only do so by forsaking the better class of even their own color, or by drawing them down to their own level. In this way, Slavery, even now, day by day, is greatly responsible for the degraded and immoral condition of the free blacks of our cities, and especially of Philadelphia. It is, perhaps, necessary that I should explain that licentiousness and almost indiscriminate sexual connection among the young is very general, and is a necessity of the system of Slavery. A Northern family that employs slave domestics, and insists upon a life of physical chastity in its female servants, is always greatly detested; and they frequently come to their owners and beg to be taken away, or not hired again, though acknowledging themselves to be kindly treated in all other respects. A slave owner told me this of his own girls hired to Northern people.

That the character and condition of some is improved by coming to the North, it is impossible to deny. From a miserable half barbarous, half brutal state they have been brought to the highest civilization. From slaves they have sometimes come to be intelligent, cultivated, free-thinking, independent-minded, and good and even great men. Frederick Douglass is a *great* man, if poetry, eloquence and vigorous original thought make greatness. He is but little less great that the vindictive energy with which he pursues the enemy that prevents his being recognized as so, that even *taboos* him from the society of the cultivated and refined, sometimes carries him beyond the bounds of calm reason and good taste.

It is minds of such character originally that slavery is most galling to, and in which the intelligence and energy necessary to obtain freedom is most likely to reside. For this reason the condition and character of the fugitive slaves does not give a fair indication of that of the mass, and yet it surely is not such, take them all in all, as to make it appear that if the great body of slaves should be sent to free States they would be better off than they are now. I doubt if we have reason to think their children would. In my opinion, this is the greatest reproach to slavery, but the fact remains against *hasty* measures to destroy it.

As to slaves set free by the masters, without any previous education for it and sent to the free States, I have no doubt they often come to great suffering; and if it should be a frequent or general practice, the result would be anything but desirable. I know of one case in which seven were thus permitted to go to Philadelphia, of which five died in three years, two returned to Virginia, and only one remains—of whose condition I am uninformed, but have no reason to think, and do not believe it at all better in any way than when he was a slave.

As to Liberia, it is certainly true that the negroes, either slave or free, are not generally disposed to go there. It is a distant country, of which they can have but very little reliable information, they do not like the idea any more than other people do of emigrating from their native country. But I really think that the best reason for their not being more anxious to go there is that they are sincerely attached in a certain way to the *white race*. At all events they do not incline to live in communities entirely separate from the whites and do not long for entire independence from them. They have been so long accustomed to trusting the government of all weighty matters to the whites, that they would not feel at home where they did not have them to "take care of them." As I pointed out before, they do not feel inclined to take great responsibilities on themselves, and have no confidence in the talent of their race for self-government. A gentleman told me that he owned a very intelligent negro who had acquired some property, and that he had more than once offered him his freedom, but he would always reply that he did not feel able to fall entirely upon his own resources, and preferred to have a master. He once offered him his freedom to go to Liberia, and urged him to go there. His reply was to the effect that he would have no objections if the Government was in the hands of white folks, but that he had no confidence in the ability of black people to undertake the control of public affairs.

To conclude this letter, I will tell you what I think the continued existence of Slavery in Virginia depends upon. First—

Upon the very low and degraded condition of the mass of the people. The proportion of those who cannot read and write in the State is *more than thirty times as great as in Connecticut.* From their want of intelligence they are duped, frightened, excited, prejudiced and made to betray their most direct and evident interests by the more cultivated and talented, spendthrift and unprincipled of the wealthy class. These, who, without the slightest prudence or care for the future of the Commonwealth, live dependent for the means of their selfish extravagance on the slave labor of today, form "public opinion" by their reckless energy.

Meanwhile the truly wise and good men of the State suffer themselves to be left in the background, suffer themselves to appear in a false position, even aid by their apparent countenance of the wicked and foolish, the general expression of attachment to Slavery, because the question, What can be done, is too great for them, and because they really think the only remedy that is proposed would be productive of greater evil than the disease.

No one speaks a word aloud of it, but not a sober, thinking man of the State is there that does not know that Slavery is a Curse upon him and his, and that if it were possible to remove the effect of causes that are not alone in the future or the present, Virginia would be a hundred times richer, a thousand times happier, if Slavery were not.

P. S.—Since I wrote this letter I have been convinced that the sentiment I have described in the last paragraph is even deeper and more general with the mass of the people than I then imagined. I must mention an incident indicative of it. I was standing on the platform of a railroad car at a station where a gang of slaves had been waiting to take our train to proceed South, but the "servant's car" being full they were left behind. Two men, one of whom I afterwards learned to be a bar-keeper, the other an overseer, stood with me on the platform. As we moved off one said to the other:

"That's a good lot of niggers."

"Good! I only wish they belonged to me, I wouldn't ask for anything else."

They continued in conversation, *starting* with this, for some time, though I heard but little of what they said. They were talking of their different occupations, and grumbling that they succeeded no better. One, I heard say, that the highest wages he had ever had was two hundred dollars a year, and that year he did not lay up a cent. Soon after, one of them spoke with much vehemence and bitterness of tone, so I do not doubt their whole previous conversation had had reference to the point.

"I wish to God, old Virginny was free of all the niggers!"

"It would be a d____d good thing if she was."

"Yes, and I tell you, it would be a—d____d *good thing for us poor fellows.*"

"Well, I reckon it would, myself."

But, mind you, these same "poor fellows" understand the impracticability of instantly abolishing Slavery and having on their hands a vast population of freed slaves—more degraded and impressible with exciting prejudices than even themselves—as well as any body, and would be the very first to tar and feather an "Abolitionist" if he came to advise them to it.

"THE LAWS OF THE SOUTH": JULY 1853

The South

LETTERS ON THE PRODUCTIONS, INDUSTRY AND
RESOURCES OF THE SOUTHERN STATES

NUMBER TWENTY-EIGHT

Slaves Owning Horses, Guns, and Dogs—The New Code of Alabama—Illicit Trade with Negroes—Pilfering—The Socialistic Aspect of Slavery—The Paternal Aspect of Slavery.

In returning from the "Cracker meeting" to the plantation, we passed a man on horseback, who had the appearance of one of the civilized native East Indian gentlemen; his complexion dark olive, with good features, and a thick moustache. He was well-dressed, and raised his hat in bowing to us with a courteous and well-bred air. I asked who it was.

"He is one of our people—Robert—a very valuable servant. He is the watchman, and has charge of the engine and all the stores."

We met a wagon with a pleasant family party of common fieldhand negroes. They also belonged to Mr. A. I inquired if they usually let them have horses to go to Church.

"Oh, no; that horse belongs to the old man."

"Belongs to him! Why, do they own horses?"

"Oh, yes; William (the House servant) owns two, and Robert, I believe, has three now; that was one of them he was riding."

"How do they get them?"

"Oh, they buy them."

"But can they have money enough to buy horses?"

"Oh, yes; William makes a good deal of money; so does Robert. You see he is such a valuable fellow, father makes him a good many presents. He gave him a hundred dollars only a little while ago. The old man was getting infirm, and could not get about very well, so father gave him a horse."

I afterwards met the man, Robert, at the mill, where he lived as "watchman," or steward, in a cabin by himself, at a distance from the quarters of the other negroes. His language and manner was confident, frank, and manly; contrasting as much as possible with that of the negroes or mulattoes of ordinary circumstances. He wore a belt, on which were hung a large number of keys, and he walked about with his owner and me, to open the doors of the mill, barns, storehouses, and stables, conversing freely, and explaining a variety of matters with much intelligence.

I learned that he was employed while a boy as a house-servant, until, at his own request, he was put in the plantation black-smith's shop; after acquiring this craft, he learned to make cotton-gins, and then, as he wanted to become a machinist, his master took him to Savannah, where he remained living at his own pleasure for several years. At length his owner, finding that he was acquiring dissipated habits and wasting all his earnings, brought him back to his plantation, and by giving him duties flattering to his self-respect, and allowing him peculiar privileges, made him content to remain there. He had made all the alterations and repairs necessary in running a steam-engine and extensive machinery during seven years, and his work was admirable, both in contrivance and execution.

Elsewhere I saw another negro engineer of remarkable intelligence; the gentleman in whose employment he had been for many years, esteemed him very highly, and desired to make him free. His owner, a large capitalist, a gentleman moving in our best society, and a church-member, resides at the North. He does not think it a good plan to emancipate slaves, and refuses to sell him at even a great price for that purpose. He (the owner) receives two hundred dollars a year as the wages for his services.

Though in reality a slave, being himself the property of another, cannot possess property, yet in the same way that our children and minors have things "*for* their own," they acquire many articles which few masters would be mean enough to take from them, except they were of a character to hurt them—such as ardent spirits—or such as they might be afraid of their using to the injury or annoyance of others.

The new code of Alabama, which, in one or two particulars, is less inhumane than the laws of any other Southern State, except Louisiana, in its provisions with regard to the negroes, has

one article forbidding slaves to own dogs. As it seemed to me
by the incessant yelping at night that every negro in the State
must keep half a dozen curs, I asked a legal friend what was the
object of the law. He could not tell me, but assured me that it
would never be enforced. I presume it was intended to abate the
great destruction of sheep by negroes' dogs (or rather the destruction which the negroes attribute to dogs, to shield a theft
of one of themselves), an evil which is everywhere complained
of at the South, and which operates to prevent more extensive
wool-growing there. It will probably not be enforced except on
extraordinary occasions.

Other provisions of this code, enumerated by a writer in the
Times a few days since, as examples of the humane amelioration of the laws of the South in favor of the negroes, seem to
me of value only as expressing the views of the enactors on
certain minor moralities of Slavery, such as that forbidding the
separation from their mothers (*mothers* only) of children, before they are ten years old, in sheriff's sales, unless their owner
deems that his interests require it (for this is all it amounts to),
and to prevent the separation of relatives in mortgagee's sales,
where they can just as well be sold together in family lots. The
gratification which "Walpole" finds in such provisions for the
more humane use of negroes, in a State which he considers to
be "rapidly advancing in all that constitutes true civilization,"
and as "leading the way" by such measures in a glorious work
of reformation, well shows with how much smaller a progress
than most Northern men would have been apt to suppose safe
and practicable, even the most intelligent, liberal, humane, and
hopeful Southerners would be content—bearing out the views
I have before expressed upon this point.

I fear many of your readers will have been surprised to find
such a man touching upon it as a great thing—a reformation to
be pointed to as an honor to the civilization of the good people
of Alabama—that the law does not violently separate, for the
fault or indiscretion of another person (their owner, as it deems
him), a child under five years of age from its mother, under any
circumstances, nor remove a child under ten years old from its
mother, unless the said owner will make and deliver to an officer
in charge an affidavit that his (the said owner's) interests will
be materially prejudiced by the sale of them together. The law

does not even propose to hinder, by so much as requiring an affidavit to be made that he will make money by it, the owner of a mother and child who pays his debts, from selling one to go to Texas, and retaining the other. This would be thought exceeding the appropriate duties of legislation—too great an interference with the natural laws of commerce.

I have often suggested the propriety of such laws as "Walpole" refers to, to prevent the internal slave trade, and have been answered that it was impossible to make such laws efficient. In Georgia, I was told, there is a law forbidding the introduction of slaves from abroad to be sold within the State; but it is constantly evaded. The law does not forbid persons without the State selling to those within, nor the transfer of slave property between resident citizens. The slave trader, therefore, has merely to have a partner, or confederate resident, execute bills of sale of his Virginia importation to him, and the latter may then resell without let or hindrance. I entirely agree with "Walpole" in his views of the principles on which Southern Statesmanship should be guided on this subject, and if I had the least ability to influence the South, I would not wish to use it in any other direction than that in which his enthusiasm flows.

If I err in my statement of facts, or if I have misapprehended public sentiment at the South, on this or any other subject, I shall consider it a favor to be corrected by those whose residence at the South gives them means of more reliable information and better judgment, than I can hope to have enjoyed. But I ask you, Southern readers, to remember, that a stranger to their habits and proceedings in connection with Slavery, must reflect from so different and distant a standpoint from that in which familiarity places them, that it will not be strange if what appears light to them, sometimes remains dark to him, and that a movement which to them is great and important, is to him almost imperceptible.

The watchman, Robert, besides owning three horses, had in his possession *three guns*—one of them a valuable fowling piece of a noted London make. Upon further inquiry, I found that several of the field hands also owned guns, which they kept in their cabins. Nothing could show better than this how small is the fear of insurrection where the negroes are managed discreetly, and treated with a moderate degree of confidence and kindness. I have not examined the laws of the State upon the subject, but it was probably illegal, as I know it would be in Alabama and Louisiana for them to be possessed of these weapons. The negroes had purchased them or, in some cases, received them as presents from their owner.

On inquiring of him what were their privileges in buying and selling, he informed me that during a large part of the year all the industrious hands finish the regular tasks required of them by one or two o'clock in the afternoon, and during the remainder of the day are at liberty, if they choose, to labor for themselves. Each family has a half-acre of land allotted to it, for a garden, besides which there is a large vegetable garden, cultivated by a gardener for the plantation, from which they are supplied, to a greater or lesser extent. They are at liberty to sell whatever they choose from the products of their own garden, and to make what they can by keeping swine and fowls. His family had no other supply of poultry and eggs, except what was obtained by purchase from his own negroes; they frequently, also purchase game from them.

The only restriction upon their traffic was a "liquor law." They were not allowed to buy or sell ardent spirits. This prohibition, like liquor laws elsewhere, unfortunately could not be enforced, and of late years, Irishmen moving into the country and opening small shops, buying stolen goods from the negroes, and selling them poisonous washes under the name of grog, had become a very great evil; and the planters, although it was illegal, were not able to prevent it. They had combined to do so, and had brought several offenders to trial; but as it was a penitentiary offence, the culprit would spare no pains or expense to save himself from it, and it was almost impossible, in a community constituted as theirs was, to find a jury that would convict.

A remarkable illustration of this evil had just occurred. A planter, discovering that a considerable quantity of cotton had been stolen from him, and suspecting one of his negroes to have taken it, from finding him drunk and very sick from the effects of liquor soon after, informed the patrol of the neighboring planters of it. A lot of cotton was prepared by mixing hair with it, and put in a tempting place. The negro was seen to take it, and was followed to a grog-shop, several miles distant, where he sold it, its real value being nearly ten dollars, for ten cents, taking his pay in liquor. The man was arrested, and the theft being made to appear, by the hair, before a justice, obtained bail in $2,000 to answer at the higher Court.

In a community where the greater number of families live miles apart, and have but rare intercourse with one another, where occasion for Law and Government is almost unknown, where one part of the people, poor, untrained, illiterate, recklessly and improvidently live almost from day to day on the bounty of Nature, making rude log huts, every man for himself; of restless disposition, and frequently, from mere caprice, leaving them and moving away to make new homes; habitually a law to themselves, while they are accustomed, from childhood, to the use of the most certain deadly weapon; and where, in the other part of the people, a barbarous, patriarchal system of government exists, within another Government—as far as possible, with this circumstance, of the most republican and enlightened form—it is really wonderful that Law has so much power, and its deliberate movements and provisions for justice to accused parties are so much respected, as, spite of calumny and occasional exceptions, is usually the case in our Slave States. Why are not these villainous scamps scourged out of the district, and their dens burned, where the Law is so slow and uncertain with them?

This evil of the grog shops, and other illicit and criminal business with negroes, is a great and increasing one at the South. Everywhere that I have been, I have found the planters provoked and angry about it. A great swarm of Jews, within the last ten years, has settled in nearly every Southern town, many of them men of no character, opening cheap clothing and trinket shops, ruining or driving out of business many of the old retailers, and engaging in a clandestine trade with the simple negroes, which is found very profitable. The law which prevents the reception of the evidence of a negro in Courts, here strikes back with a most annoying force upon the dominant power itself. In the mischief thus arising, we see a striking illustration of the danger which stands before the South, whenever its prosperity shall invite extensive immigration, and lead what would otherwise be a healthy competition to flow through its channels of industry.

Mr. A. remarked that his arrangements allowed his servants

no excuse for dealing with these fellows. He made it a rule to purchase everything they had to sell, and to give them a high price for it himself. Eggs constituted a circulating medium on the plantation; their par value was considered to be twelve for a dime, at which they would be exchanged for cash or taken on deposit at his kitchen.

Whatever he took of them that he could not use in his own family, or had not occasion to give to others of his servants, was sent to town to be resold. The negroes would not commonly take money for the articles he had of them, but would have the value of them put to their credit, and a regular account was kept with them. He had a store, well supplied with articles that they most wanted, which were purchased in large quantities and sold to them at wholesale prices; thus giving them a great advantage in dealing with him rather than with the grog shops. His slaves were sometimes his creditors to large amounts; at the present time he owed them about five hundred dollars. A woman had charge of the store, and when there was anything called for that she could not supply, it was usually ordered by the next conveyance of his factors in town.

Here you see an illustration of what, I believe, I have before suggested: Slavery is a grand, practical, working system of *Socialism*. It brings up, too, another aspect of Slavery—its happiest and best.

The negroes came to us from barbarism as from a cradle, with a confused, half-developed mind, with strong and simple appetites and impulses, but whimsical and unreliable; forming attachments quickly, and cleaving closely to their protectors and superiors; but, if removed from one, forming the same relations quickly, and with equal strength, with another; subject to violent and uncontrollable passions, and altogether undisciplined, uneducated, unchristianized.

Here I see their master, dealing with them as a father might with such children; guarding them sedulously against dangerous temptations, forbidding them to indulge in bad practices, rewarding the diligent and obedient, and chastising the perverse and indolent; anticipating and providing for their wants; encouraging them in the provident use of their little means of amusement, and comfort, and luxury; all the time furnishing them the necessary support of life; caring diligently for them in sickness; and only when they are of good age and strength, so long as he is their guardian, demanding of them a certain amount of their labor and assistance, to increase his own comforts, provide for his age.

Were but all Slavery this, and were but this all of Slavery!

"A THOROUGH ARISTOCRAT": DECEMBER 1853

To Charles Loring Brace

Cumberland River, December 1st, 1853

Dear Charley

At Louisville we called on Prentice with a letter from C. M. Clay—an elderly, bright, keen, sorrowed looking man. He said he had written to Greeley and to Raymond to know if they could recommend any talented young man to him to assist in editorship of the Journal. He much wanted to find one. Probably would pay well. Raymond had not replied to him at all.

We also called on Dr. Short, a wealthy old hunker at a beautiful place 5 miles out of town—introduced to him by Dr. Gray.

From Louisville, rather than start two nights' coaching, we came to Nashville by the river down Ohio & Cumberland. Were laid up *every* night by fogs and were aground two days, so were a week getting to Nashville. Very tedious & disappointing.

At Nashville we met a classmate of John's, *Allison*. A good specimen of the first class gentleman of the South. We spent nearly all our time in Nashville, two days, in conversation with him, and he gave us a dinner at the hotel. He is wealthy, a bachelor, connected with the largest slaveholding in Tennessee: chivalric and believes in pistols and bowie knives. His argument being similar to Cooper's.

We confess to each other that he silenced us and showed us that our own position was by no means consistent and satisfactory. He has lately been running for Congress and though running very honorably ahead of his ticket, was beaten by Zollicoffer, a Whig and veteran politician who last year shot a man across the street at his office door. He gave us an amusing account of the canvass.

He and Z. went in company to all parts of the district, each speaking twice at a place in opposition to each other (such places as "T. Golb's Grocery," "the second gate on the Tobroke 'pike") &c., the crowd varying from 50 to 2000 in number— men, women, children & niggers, all excited and betting. His own body servant came to him after the election and asked him to lend him $10, as he had lost his watch on the election & he could get it back for that.

He carried a pair of pistols loaded in his pocket for a few days as Zollicoffer had the reputation of a fighting man. But he found them such a bore to carry that he put them in his saddle-bags and he got through without any "difficulty."

In the cars in Kentucky a modest young man was walking through with the handle of a Colt out of his pocket-skirt behind. It made some laugh & a gentleman with us called out, "You'll lose your Colt, Sir." The man turned and after a moment joined the laugh and pushed the handle into the pocket.

John said, "There might be danger in laughing at him." "Oh no," replied our companion, evidently supposing him serious, "he would not mind a laugh." "It's the best place to carry your pistol, after all," said he. "It's less in your way than anywhere else. And as good a place for your knife as anywhere else is down your back, so you can draw over your shoulder."

"Are pistols and knives generally carried here?"

"Yes, very generally."

Allison said *commonly*, but he thought not generally.

Allison declared himself a Democrat very strongly, but we confused him by proving to him that he was not; that he be- lieved in two distinct and widely separated classes of society. He afterwards defined his Democracy to consist in holding to a strict construction of the Constitution (nevertheless he favored the building of Pacific R.R. by the government) and following the views of Jefferson rather than the Federalists. He admitted that practically there was no difference between the parties at the present time.

He and other gentlemen in Nashville hated Seward as "a devil incarnate." He thought he ought to be hung as a traitor. He was guilty of treason in the Senate—the gravest of all crimes. He thought it a deep misfortune to the country that he could be reelected to the Senate. D. S. Dickinson he thought a true Statesman and the only prominent man at the North who had been true at all times to the country—consistent, reliable, patriotic and unselfish, free from demagogism. He remarked at another time regarding the next President that he had been in correspondence with leading Southern Democrats upon the subject and that there was a general disposition to look to Dickinson as the Democratic candidate for next President. At any rate there was no other northern man the Southern Democrats would support.

Allison and other gentlemen I have seen in Nashville & Kentucky have changed the views I had with regard to the feelings of the South about extension of territory. Allison said they *must* have more slave territory. It was a necessity upon the South which every one saw. He thought California would be a Slave State. He also looked to the Amazon as a promising field for Slave labor. There was no disposition to hasten the matter.

There was a general dislike on the part of the South to a general war in Europe such as was now imminent because it would injure the value of cotton & of course of negroes & everything else. But on some accounts they would like it. In case of a general war which would involve France & England & perhaps Spain, advantage would be taken of it to get possession of Cuba and perhaps of Mexico, as England & France could not then interfere. He hated England & liked France & thought the South did generally. It seems to me probable that the Government at Washington is acting on similar views. He evidently supposed so. He wouldn't go to fighting without some honorable excuse.

His whole idea of honor is of this sort. Mere deference to time honored rules and conventionalisms it seems to me, though he thinks them spontaneous honorable impulses. Oddly enough, with all his hodge podge of honor & morality, he was reading secretly (as he confessed to us) Strauss' life of Christ and some of Parker's books.

Most moral people at the South were Church members. Not that they believed much in particular, but thought that was on the whole the best way. Every man could not expect to have his individual opinions accommodated in systems, & systems were necessary. He was not a church member himself. He thought there was a happy gentlemanly medium in which a man would be sufficiently religious (that is, sufficiently to satisfy his poetical nature, I suppose) and yet not deny himself sensual and social pleasures—"spree moderately," I think he expressed it.

He did not believe there was a gentleman in the whole Northwest (the western free states), especially including Cincinnati. And he evidently thought there were very few, and they but poorly developed, anywhere at the North. There was not a man in Yale College who had anything of the appearance or manners of a gentleman, from the North, except a few sons of professional and commercial people who had been brought up in the large towns. There were no gentlemen at the North out of the large towns. He had once met some of the old Dutch aristocracy of New York (your Schuylers, &c.) and he did think them thoroughly well bred people.

There is a great deal of truth in his view. I tried to show him that there were compensations in the *general* elevation of all classes at the North, but he did not seem to care for it. He is, in fact, a thorough Aristocrat. And altogether, the conversation making me acknowledge the rowdyism, ruffianism, want of high honorable sentiment & chivalry of the common farming & laboring people of the North, as I was obliged to, made me very melancholy. With such low, material, and selfish aims in statesmanship as the best men of the South have and with such a low, prejudiced, party enslaved and material people at the North, what does the success of our Democratic nationality amount to—and what is to become of us. Of course, I have told you but little of the whole conversation that so impressed me.

I must be either an Aristocrat or more of a Democrat than I have been—a Socialist Democrat. We need institutions that shall more directly *assist* the poor and degraded to elevate themselves. Our educational principle must be enlarged and made to include more than these miserable common schools. The poor & wicked need more than to be let alone.

It seemed to me that what had made these Southern gentlemen Democrats was the perception that mere Democracy as they understand it (no checks or laws upon the country more than can be helped) was the best system for their class. It gave capital every advantage in the pursuit of wealth—and money gave wisdom & power. They could do what they liked. It was only necessary for them, the gentlemen, to settle what they wanted. Or if they disagreed, the best *commander* of the people carried his way. The people doing nothing but choose between them. He had no conception of higher than material interests entering into politics. All that these sort of free traders want is protection to capital. Agrarianism would suit them better if they could protect that and use what they consider their rights.

But I do very much feel inclined to believe that Government should have in view the encouragement of a democratic condition of society as well as of government—that the two need to go together as they do at the North in much greater degree than at the South or I suppose anywhere else. But I don't think our state of society is sufficiently Democratic at the North or likely to be by mere *laisser aller*. The poor need an education to refinement and taste and the mental & moral capital of gentlemen.

I have been blundering over this and have not, I think, expressed at all what I wanted to. In a steamboat cabin—dark, shaking, and gamesters and others talking about the table—I can't collect my ideas. But to put some shape to it. Hurrah for Peter Cooper and Hurrah for the Reds.

The great difference I feel between such fellows as these gentlemanly, well informed, true and brave Southern gentlemen, whom I admire in spite of my Democratic determination, whom I respect in spite of my general loathing of humbugging dignity; the great difference between them & those I like and wish to live among & wish to be is the deficiency in one & the sense in the other of what I must call Religion (the intrinsic religious sense) as a distinct thing from Belief, Obedience, Reverence, and Love to Personal Deity. The quality which God must have himself. They do not seem to have a fundamental sense of right. Their moving power and the only motives which they can comprehend are materialistic or Heavenalistic—regard for good (to themselves or others or to God) in this world or in another.

I have something which distinguishes me from them, whether the above explains it or not. So have you. So has Field, Elliott, all our earnest fellows. Allison couldn't approach to it and therefore he is a Conservative and a Democrat of the American School.

I am a Democrat of the European School—of the school of my brave porter of Bingen. And these so-called Democrats are not. They are of another sort; material, temporary, temporizing, conservative. I wish I had Victor Hugo's speech now to read you.

The Southern sort are perhaps larger—more generous and braver minds than ours—and they act up to their capabilities better. But ours are more expansive and have need to be more humble as being less true to their principles and feelings.

Allison & his friends evidently had no power of comprehending a hatred of Slavery in itself—no I can't think that. Put themselves in the place of the slave and they would cut their own throats, if there was no other way out, without hesitation. But they didn't & I believe couldn't imagine that the North would be governed by any purpose beyond a regard for self interest (including the gratification of pride, envy, spiritual pride, &c.) with regard to slavery. They could not see how the North could be so *foolish* as to determinedly prevent the extension of Slavery. Its own interest would suffer so much—commerce be injured, market for manufactures not enlarged, &c. Individuals might profit, but the whole would so certainly be injured by this injury for commerce, and beyond this they could not be got. So completely had they swallowed the whole hog of Free Trade. Admitting commerce & trade on the whole to be benefitted, it was a corollary that the measure would be for the highest good. What on the whole injured capital, consols, niggers, State credit, was wicked. What benefitted it, was Godlike. This was the end of their track.

Well, the moral of this damnedly drawn out letter is, I believe, go ahead with the Children's Aid and get up parks, gardens, music, dancing schools, reunions which will be so attractive as to force into contact the good & bad, the gentlemanly and the rowdy.

And the state ought to assist these sort of things *as* it does Schools and Agricultural Societies—on the same plan, with the same precaution that the State of New York now does. I believe that it can do so safely. I *don't* believe the friction compensates for the increased power of the machinery.

And we ought to have that Commentator as an organ of a higher Democracy and a higher religion than the popular. And it ought to be great—sure of success—well founded. Bound to succeed by its merit, by its talent. A cross between the Westmin-ster Review & the Tribune, is my idea. Weekly, I think, to give it variety & scope enough for this great country & this cursedly little people. Keep it before you.

Yours affectionately,

Fred.

SLAVES & NON-SLAVEHOLDING WHITES: JANUARY 1854

The South

LETTERS ON THE PRODUCTIONS, INDUSTRY AND RESOURCES OF THE SOUTHERN STATES

NUMBER FORTY-SEVEN

General Conclusions—The Condition of the Slaves—The Condition of the Non-Slaveholding Whites.

Southerners often represent the condition of their slaves to be so happy and desirable that we might wonder that they do not sometimes take measures to be made slaves themselves, or at least occasionally offer their children for sale to the highest bidder. Yet there are many among us who always assume these accounts to be the only reliable information that we have upon the subject. On the other hand, there are many who always picture the slave as a martyr, with his hands folded in supplica-tion, naked, faint with hunger, dragging a chain, and constantly driven to extremity of human exertion by a monster flourishing a cart-whip.

A Scotchman, who had been employed at home as foreman of a large stock farm, came, a year or two since, to America, to better his condition. He spent some months in Canada and afterwards in New-England, looking in vain for a situation suited to his capabilities and habits. His little capital being nearly expended, he used what remained in paying his passage to Richmond, Va., learning that the proprietors of farms in the Slave States generally employed overseers, as in Scotland. On arriving at Richmond he immediately walked into the country, and at nightfall came to the plantation of the gentleman who related his story to me. He informed the proprietor of his circumstances and solicited employment, presenting, at the same time, a recommendation from his last employer in Scotland, and a testimonial of his piety, good character and education from the pastor of the church he had belonged to in the old country. Before, however, the gentleman had read these, he said to him, "By the way, Sir, there are a number of your niggers loose in the lane."

"What?"

"As I was coming up the lane to the house, Sir, I met a number of niggers just going off loose, without anybody to look after them."

"Yes, I suppose they have got through their work, and are going to their quarters."

"But they were *loose*, Sir; just straying off, nobody looking after them. If you wish, Sir, I'll run down and catch them."

The Scotchman had always been informed, as he afterwards told the gentleman, that the slaves were treated exactly like cattle, and probably would not have been much surprised if he had been ordered to put half a dozen of them into stalls to be fattened for the butcher.

I think that any one who has read the accounts I have given of the negroes upon the different plantations I have visited, and the chance-observations I have made on others, will have obtained a correct and reliable idea of the *customary* manner in which the slaves are treated by the whites. It may be desired of me, however, to give the conclusions at which I have arrived upon certain points which have been most fruitful of unprofitable controversy.

Are the slaves hard-worked, poorly fed, miserably lodged and clothed, and subject to frequent brutal punishment?

Any sensible man, at all familiar with the Black-laws of the Southern States, can anticipate the true answer to these questions from his general knowledge of human nature. There is all the difference in the treatment of slaves by different masters that there is of horses by their riders, or of children by their parents. The laws have very little power to restrain cruelty or to enforce care and provide adequate sustenance for the negroes. They have less effect than the laws to secure humane treatment of animals at the North, because the violations of the laws at the South would be much more seldom witnessed by persons anxious to secure their enforcement, and because Southerners respect the individuality of each other more than Northerners, and are more loth to meddle in matters that do not *especially* concern themselves. Public Opinion is favorable to humanity and care—in some districts very strongly and effectually so. In general its influence is not very valuable to the negro, for the same reasons that the laws are not. What power has Public Opinion on the treatment of domestics and farm laborers at the North? Except in extreme cases, none. Competition is the balance wheel of cupidity.

But as I have said, in describing the character of the people of the South, they are as kind to their slaves as any people could be imagined to be—much more kind than one whose whole experience of human nature had been obtained at the Northern States would be likely to imagine them to be.

If the labor of the slaves were voluntary—if he were exhilarated with the spirit of the ambitious free laborer, with a loved wife and children to enjoy the fruits of his toil in proportion to its amount, his work would in nearly every case, as far as I could judge, be light. As it is, on the far Southern large plantations especially, it seemed to me that the negro was *driven* at his work more tediously and fatiguingly than agricultural laborers often are in any other part of the world that I have visited.

The negroes, I should think, were *generally abundantly* provided with coarse food—more so than the agricultural laborers of any part of Europe.

They are sufficiently clothed, *in general*, to enable them, if they are at all pains-taking, which they seldom are in this particular, to appear decently, and to protect them from any degree of cold weather to which in the mild climate of the South they are subject. Their habitations are *generally* very deficient in comfort, and are much too small for the number of occupants that are crowded into them. Rapid improvement in this respect, however, is now making; neat (exteriorly) quarters for the negroes having become a fashionable part of every gentleman's plantation. The negroes seldom or never want for fuel.

There are but few plantations in which the negroes are not frequently punished by being whipped, and that not seldom with what I should think would be generally considered at the North, severity. In this respect I think the condition of the negroes is just about what that of the seamen has formerly been in our Navy, and still is in the English service, varying on different plantations as in different ships. Cases of disgusting cruelty are not very rare. I never asked a middle aged Southerner the question (and I put it perhaps twenty times) who was not able to tell me a case within his own knowledge, and occurring, probably, in the near vicinity of his residence, of a slave killed by severe punishment from its master. I do not believe slaves are killed by their masters one tenth as often as sailors are by the cruelty or carelessness of their masters. I believe very few overseers punish their slaves entrusted to them so wantonly, brutally, passionately and cruelly as I have seen a clergyman in New-England punish boys entrusted to him for education. On some few plantations punishment of adult and well-broken negroes is very rare. But it requires a man of peculiar temperament and governing abilities, to efficiently control and direct a large body of persons, dependent on him and subject to his uncontrolled authority, whether they are negroes or sailors, or peasants or children, without the use of the lash or other humiliating punishments.

Are the slaves "happy?"

Any one who thinks that a drunkard can be made happy by supplying him to his full content with the only thing in the world that he craves, might answer this question as it generally is answered by Southern writers and their Northern disciples. And, in this sense, I believe it is true that the negro in Southern slavery is sufficiently degraded to be as happy on an average, as most men are in the world; as happy (in this sense) as the majority of the negroes who enjoy the freedom to live, if they can, in contempt and obloquy at the North.

Are the slaves often separated against their will from their families?

It is astonishing that any one can be so careless as to deny it. In every State of the South, except Florida, Missouri, Delaware, and in Texas, which I have not yet visited, I have known of slaves separated from their families without the slightest indication that it was not a frequent and almost an everyday occurrence. I can show evidence that would satisfy any court that it is a common practice in every Slave State. If any one says that they have never known such a case in their own neighborhood, as our Southern friends often do, and, no doubt, believing that they speak truly, the chances are that if you ask them to let you look at the newspaper published nearest their residence, you will find an advertisement in it of slaves, in which some half dozen will be noted as the children of another, all to be sold singly and with no more restriction as to their future fate than if they were cattle, and at public auction. In a paper now before me there are nine mentioned as of one family, to be sold separately, but the suckling infants of two of them, and the child aged 3 years, and infant aged two months, of a girl aged 19, are to be sold with their mothers. Public opinion is opposed to the sale of old family servants, yet they not unfrequently are sold. I have several friends at the South who have each purchased more than one such, from mere humanity, to save them from being "sold away"—that is, from being separated from their wives and children. It is not a very common thing to sell a slave except "for fault," unless the owner has especial need of money. But this reason for selling a servant will be held over him as a threat, at every trifling occasion for blaming him. It is not common in most communities to sell a single slave, particularly if he is married, without mentioning the intention to do so, to him some time previously, and giving him leave to look about to find some person that he will like for a master, to purchase him. A price is often mentioned at which he is warned to sell himself, or after a certain time he will be sold to the traders. At almost every slave auction, however, the anxiety of the negroes to be purchased by some person living near their old master and their families, and their grief, if they are disappointed, is painfully evident.

The trade of a slave-dealer is about as reputable at the South as that of a horse jockey is at the North. They are generally considered knaves, and I think *therefore* are not admitted into the society of honorable gentlemen. To say that they are not so, merely because they buy and sell human flesh, is thoughtless, because there are very few of the honorable gentlemen of the South that have not themselves either bought or sold servants.

I have heard respectable planters speak of their friends as having borrowed money to speculate in negroes. "Negroes are the *consols* of the South," is a proverbial expression with

Southerners—certainly indicating the frequent and general transfer of this species of stock. Virginians who visit the North, often angrily deny that any one in that State makes a business of breeding negroes for market. Perhaps not, but I have heard men in Virginia speak publicly of purchasing women with reference to their breeding qualities, and of taking the most suitable care of them for this end. Men speak in railroad cars of "turning off" so many negroes every year, precisely as a Connecticut farmer speaks of "turning off" so many head of neat stock to the drovers every Spring.

A gentleman whom I visited in Mississippi, to show me that the condition of the negroes in that State was much more desirable than that of those in the Atlantic Slave States—after enumerating certain luxuries and privileges that were generally allowed them there, such as an allowance of molasses and better variety of food generally, a perquisite of money in proportion to the cotton sold, and permission to cultivate cotton, for sale themselves, on Saturday afternoons and holidays—added that the negroes were very much less frequently sold off the plantation and separated from their friends.

"A cotton planter here," he said, "buys all the negroes his credit is good for, and keeps all he can get. Why, in Virginia, if a youngster wants to get a fine horse, or a young lady wants a piano, they teaze their father to sell one of the young negroes to get the money for it; a negro is reckoned just the same as cash." It is undeniable that the human life, sold and exported every year from Virginia, far exceeds in value that of the total of all other of its productions. It is always gratifying to find Virginians ashamed of this, as the cultivated gentlemen and the religious people generally are. The sale and purchase of men, women and children, regarding them so distinctly as property, and property entirely, is such an insult to the human race, that nothing else that disgraces the name of man more demands the shame and the indignant protest of all men who claim to be gentlemen of honor and chivalry.

Are the negroes in Slavery improving and being christianized and becoming fitted gradually for freedom, as was anticipated and expected by the founders of the Republic, both of the North and South, at the time of the Revolution?

Beyond a doubt, the men who signed the Declaration of

Independence, and who formed the Constitution of the United States (to judge from the expressions which the most prominent among them are recorded to have made), would be exceedingly disappointed with the present state of things. Not less so would be the men who composed various provincial Conventions in Virginia and North Carolina. Most disappointed would be Jefferson, who even at that early day pronounced in the gravest and most formal manner, in his history of Virginia, that Slavery was a great and dreadful curse upon his native State, the speedy end of which was to be demanded by every consideration of Justice, Humanity and Expediency.

The condition of the slaves is doubtless improving, and has greatly improved since the Revolution, in all the long settled parts of the country, in respect to the kindness with which they are treated. I mean that they are better fed, clothed and lodged, and are less subject to brutal punishment. The present tendency in the Cotton States to the enlargement of plantations, and to gathering negroes in larger bodies, I deem exceedingly unfavorable to their happiness.

The negroes are necessarily acquiring more of the outward forms and habits of civilization and Christianity every day, and many of those engaged in the domestic service of white households, and those living in towns, and the denser and more commercial communities, are growing intelligent, religious and moral. I must doubt if this is the case with the mass. I think they lose as much that is desirable of their original savage virtue from the influence of Slavery, as they gain in character from the influence of Christianity. Manliness, reliability, natural sense of and respect for that which is noble, self-respect and responsibility to conscience, and the natural affections, are all dissipated under the influence of Slavery, and are poorly compensated for by the mixture of formalism and irrational, idolatrous mysticisms, which generally passes with them for Christianity. I am aware that the opinion of most of the religious people of the South does not agree with that which I have been led to form. That of the majority of slaveholders and of all classes, however, so far as I could judge, does so.

There are very, very few Southerners who are not determinedly opposed to the indefinite improvement and elevation of the negroes. If this is doubted, ask any Southerner what is his private opinion with regard to the destiny in the future of the Gulf States, and ten to one, if his answer is made freely and candidly, he will be obliged to admit that his view is incompatible with any great degree of intelligence on the part of the negroes. It is the general belief that in the great cotton, sugar and rice districts, Slavery will, and should, be indefinitely perpetuated. Ignorance and indolence of mind, and want of ambition, energy and intellectual capacity to struggle for freedom, are rightly considered necessary to Slavery.

With regard to the instruction of Slaves, it is well known that in the majority of the States it is forbidden by law to teach them to read and write. Nevertheless, with women and children, higher law notions seem to prevail, and it is not uncommon to find that some of the domestic servants of a family have been taught to read by their mistresses or white playfellows. To express my information as definitely as possible, I should roughly guess that one in five of all the household servants, and that one in one hundred of the field-hands on the plantations of the South, might be able to read haltingly. Half of this number might be able to write intelligibly to themselves. In certain Districts the proportion is much larger.

In this series of letters (which will be concluded with the next number) it has been a minor object with me to show the peculiarities of character and the habits of the Southerners, by describing what appeared to me remarkable in their manner of life and conversation. This class of my observations has been confined, in a great degree, to the less intelligent and cultivated people. It remains for me only to give my conclusions with regard to their condition in general.

It is estimated by a Southern writer, that five-sevenths of the whole white population of the South are non-slaveholders. Of course, this body has the political power to entirely control the destiny of the Slave States. Less information has, nevertheless, been usually given by travelers with regard to them, than the wealthy and hospitable proprietary—and their condition and character is nearly always entirely ignored by Southerners themselves in arguing the advantages of their slave system.

So far as they can be treated of as a class, the non-slaveholders are unambitious, indolent, degraded and illiterate—are a dead peasantry so far as they affect the industrial position of the

South. That they are illiterate, will not only have been evident to the readers of the Times, from observations I have given, but may be proved from official statistics. Notwithstanding the constant and immense influx of an uneducated pauper class from Europe into the Northern States, the proportion of those who cannot sign their names to marriage contracts and other legal papers, is much greater in every Slave State than in any Northern State—so far as the facts have been made known. I am writing in a steamboat, fast aground in the Cumberland River, and cannot refer to the authorities—but they are to be found in all good libraries, and are essentially accurate and reliable.

With regard to their moral condition, I have several times made inquiries of physicians—who almost alone of the educated class, have any valuable knowledge of them—and have invariably been informed that the number of illegitimate children among them was very great; and that many of those living together as man and wife, are never ceremonially married.

That they are non-producers, except of the necessaries of their own existence, is evident from their miserable habitations and other indications of hopeless poverty. I have just been in conversation with a gentleman of Georgia (much the most enterprising of the Southern States) who is returning home after spending the Summer at the North. He observes with regard to the white laboring class: "Poor people in our country seem to care for nothing more than to just get a living. We cannot get them to work steady, even if we give them high wages. As soon as they have earned any money, they quit, and will not go to work again until they have spent it." Of course, as he says, there are some exceptions, but what is the exception at the South is the rule where labor in general is voluntary and not forced.

I have heretofore explained the reason of this—the degradation of all labor which is affected by Slavery. It was very concisely explained to me by a white working mechanic to-day—a foreigner, who had worked at the North, and lately moved to the South to obtain higher wages, but who was returning to the North again, dissatisfied. "Why, you see, Sir, no man will work along side of a nigger, if he can help it. It's too much like as if he was a slave himself."

The mode of life of the greater part of the non-slaveholders— the poor white people in the country—at the South, seems to be much the same. Some of them are mere *squatters*, living by sufferance on the land of others; many own a small body of unproductive land, and in the Eastern Slave States especially, a large part of them occupy a few acres of forest land, which is let to them by the owner for a term of years, on condition that they clear it and perhaps otherwise improve it. They build a small cabin or shanty, of logs, upon the ground, in which to live, with the simplest housekeeping utensils. They raise swine in the forest, and generally own a horse or a pair of cattle, and perhaps a cow—all of the meanest description. They raise on their clearing a meagre crop of corn and a few potatoes, and this, with the game they shoot, furnishes them with food. The women spin and weave, and make most of their clothing. When the land reverts to the owner, they may continue to occupy it by paying him a share (usually one-third) of the corn they raise. They are very seldom observed at work, but are often seen, like young Rip Van Winkle, lounging at the door of a grocery, or sauntering, with a gun and a dog, in the woods.

I speak not less from what I have almost everywhere seen, than from accounts given me by planters of the non-slaveholding class of their own neighborhood, in almost every district I have visited. I may be wrong in supposing such to be the condition of the larger part of the class, when the farmers of the mountain regions and some frontier districts, where few slaves are owned, are included among them; but setting these aside, the condition of the majority of the remainder cannot be much, if any superior, to that indicated in my description.

I think I have had as good means of knowing, and of painfully appreciating the evils which arise from excessive competition, to the laborers of the North, as any man, and I cannot hesitate in affirming that there is no class in the Free States, with the exception of recent immigrants and victims of intemperance, whose condition is not far better than that of the non-slaveholding population of the South. I do not forget the occasional distress of factory hands and mechanics, crowded in large towns. I have been informed of similar distress reaching to an equally painful point in manufacturing towns of the South. The real difference seems to be that the Southern work-people, hoping for less, are less demonstrative of their suffering. The only apology that I can find for the assumption constantly made by almost all Southern gentlemen and by Mrs. Tyler, that evils similar to those arising from over-competition are never found in Slave countries, is the fact of the very slight acquaintance they usually have with the vagabonds that surround them. I have hardly visited a single planter, however, who did not complain of the annoyance which the vagrant and dishonest habits of some of his poor neighbors gave him.

The unfortunate condition and character of these people, so far as they differ from those of the laboring class of the North, is mainly the direct effect of Slavery, and their material, moral and intellectual elevation will be commensurate with that of the negroes. Their ignorance and the vulgar prejudice and jealousy of low minds at present generally prevent their perception of this fact. They may, however, at some future time become a "dangerous class," as they now are a useful one to Southern legislators. Railroads, Manufactures and other enterprises, necessary to be encouraged for the prosperity of the South, will be of more value to them than would be even the gift of common schools. There is no life without intelligence—no intelligence without ambition.

GERMAN IMMIGRANTS IN TEXAS: MARCH 1854

A Tour in the Southwest

NUMBER EIGHT

THE REFUGEES FROM EUROPEAN DESPOTISM IN TEXAS

San Antonio de Bexar, March, 1854
Previous to 1848, the European emigration to Texas was largely composed of the least intelligent and poorest class of the German and Germanic-French population. Many were paupers, and some were petty criminals, whom lenient magistrates handed over unpunished to the Emigration Company, satisfied to rid their country of them. There were among them, however, many bold and enterprising young men, some of whom were induced, by special offers, to strengthen and encourage the emigration.

There were also a few who accepted the offers of the company merely from love of liberty and discontent with the political and social evils of their native land.

In 1847 the Emigration Company failed. In 1848 the German people burst from the grasp of their masters, but, caught with fair words and perjury, were again held to the ground.

Since then the emigration to Texas has included a remarkable number of high-minded, intellectual and cultivated people. I should judge a considerably larger portion of these than the emigration to the North. A few of them are voluntary emigrants; many have fled to save their lives, having been condemned to death as traitors; many more have been driven to seek a new country from the destruction of their property, or from having all means of obtaining an honest and honorable livelihood obstructed, on account of their acknowledged political opinions, by the management of the police.

Few of this class have been able to bring with them any considerable amount of property, and it is wonderful how they are generally able to sustain their intellectual life and retain their refined taste, and more than all—with their antecedents—to be seemingly content and happy, while the necessity of supporting life in the most frugal manner by hard manual labor is imposed upon them.

One evening, at a log house, after the most difficult and beautiful music of the noblest of German operas, and the dearest and most patriotic hymns of the fatherland had been sung, there were gentlemen, some of whom had had the rank of noblemen, waltzing to gay music with two ladies, each of distinguished beauty, grace and accomplishments. One of the company observed to me, "I think if some of our German tyrants could look upon us now, they would be a good deal chagrined to see how we are enjoying ourselves, for there is hardly a gentleman in this company whom they have not condemned to death or to imprisonment for life."

I have visited one gentleman, the taxes on whose estate, previous to 1848, were not less than $10,000. He had enjoyed unusual advantages of education, even for a wealthy German, and had resided several years in England, in France and in Italy. He had been led to adopt and to publicly express Democratic political views, and, on the breaking out of the Revolution he was called upon by the people to head the first movement in that part of Germany in which he lived. He obeyed the call, tearing himself from his weeping wife on the very day of a deep family bereavement, separating himself from nearly all his relations and former friends, vainly striving to lose a private grief in the enthusiasm of a momentous public struggle. Three months' fighting, and a popular constitution was yielded by their Duke. But soon came Prussian bayonet and reaction, and he was forced to flee. With the moiety of his fortune which he was able to take with him, he purchased a farm in Texas. He has now a comfortable house, a small library, and an excellent musical instrument, and his wife and children are all with him.

He employs no hired laborers on his farm. His two sons work with him till 11 o'clock in the forenoon in Summer, and till 12 in Winter. In the afternoon they are engaged in study. During the last year they have cultivated sixty acres of land, raising 2,500 bushels of corn, besides some wheat, tobacco and cotton. His sons are as fine pictures of youthful yeomen as can be imagined, tall, erect, well-knit, with intelligent countenances, spirited, ingenuous and gentlemanly. In speaking of his circumstances, he simply regretted that he could not give them all the advantages of education that he had himself had, but he added that he would much rather educate them to be independent and self-reliant, able and willing to live by their own labor, than to have them ever feel themselves dependent on the favor of others. If he could secure them here, minds free from prejudice, which would entirely disregard the conclusions of others in their own study of right and truth, and spirits which would sustain their individual conclusions without a thought of consequences, he should be only thankful to the circumstances which exiled him.

One morning in the mountains, we met two herdsmen, riding in on fiery mustangs, at a dangerous gallop among the rocks, searching for cattle. We halted, and were presented to them. One was a doctor of Philosophy from Berlin, the other a baron of ancient and honored name. The latter invited us to call at his "castle," which was appropriately placed on a prominent rocky elevation in the vicinity. We were there received with the most cheerful hospitality and refined courtesy by his lady, who served us lunch, consisting of jerked beef, corn-bread and tin goblets of hot *bouillon*. The baronial residence was made of logs, and had been built entirely by the hands of its owner. The larger part of it he was obliged yet to use as a barn, and the "family apartments" were separated from this by a partition composed partly of deer-skins and partly of calico. The logs were plastered with mud however, the outside door fitted tightly, and, though all the furniture and upholstery was of household manufacture and of the most rude and rustic description, the only essential comfort wanting was—room. This was now the more noticeable from the presence of a late addition to the family, a fine healthy baby, which the Baroness assured us weighed nearly twice as much as children at its age usually did in Germany. There was not the slightest indication of a repining spirit.

It is a strange thing, the like of which, I think will occur to one hardly anywhere else than in Texas, to hear teamsters with their cattle staked around them on the prairie, humming airs from "Don Giovanni," or repeating passages from Dante and Schiller as they lay on the ground looking up into the infinite heaven of night, or to engage in discussions of the deepest and most metaphysical subjects of human thought, with men who quote with equal familiarity, Hegel, Schleiermacher, Paul and Aristotle, and who live in holes in the rock, in ledges of the Guadalupe, and earn their daily bread by splitting shingles.

A gentleman, much beloved by the people of his native district for his benevolence and generosity, who has been President of an important institution for the elevation of the working classes, for several years a member of the Chamber of Deputies, and in 1848, of the National Assembly of Prussia, arrived here a short time ago. I saw him to-day with a spade working on the road-side, a common laborer, earning a dollar a day. This occupation will be but temporary, nor is he under the absolute necessity of engaging in it. He simply prefers it to idly waiting for more satisfactory duties to be offered him.

Another gentleman I have seen to-day, highly accomplished as a scholar, able to converse in six languages, an author; in 1848 the President of one of the Provincial Assemblies of Germany; since then, two years in prison, and finally escaping in the night and coming safely to Texas, where he supports by his labor a large family. I never saw a man more cheerful, strong in faith, and full of boundless hopes and aspirations for the elevation of all mankind, (including Africans.) I have had the no small blessing of being in his company most of the time for several days; not the slightest evidence of disappointment, dejection, or anything of bitterness have I seen in him.

I have never before so highly appreciated the value of a well-educated mind, as in observing how these men were lifted above the mere accident of life. Laboring like slaves (I have seen them working side by side, in adjoining fields), their wealth gone; deprived of the enjoyment of art, and in a great degree of literature; removed from their friends, and their great hopeful designs so sadly prostrated, "their mind to them a kingdom is," in which they find exhaustless resources of enjoyment. I have been assured, I doubt not with sincerity, by several of them, that never in Europe had they had so much satisfaction—so much intellectual enjoyment of life as here. With the opportunity permitted them, and the ability to use it, of living independently by their own labor—with that social and political freedom for themselves which they wished to gain for all their countrymen, they have within themselves means of happiness that wealth and princely power alone can never purchase or command.

But how much of their cheerfulness, I have thought, may arise from having gained during this otherwise losing struggle to themselves, the certain consciousness of being courageously loyal to their intellectual determinations—their private convictions of right, justice, and truth.

Truly, it has seemed to me, there may be a higher virtue than mere resignation, and our times may breed men as worthy of reverence as the martyrs of past ages.

What have not these men lost—voluntarily resigned—that mean and depraved and wicked souls are most devout to gain. And for what? For the good of their fellow men—they had nothing else to gain by it. For their convictions of truth and justice. Under orders of their conscience. In faithfulness to their intellect. And they have failed in every earthly purpose, but are not cast down—are not unhappy. What shall we think of those from whom life was also taken—who as cheerfully and bravely gave their life also?

I was looking at some portraits of gentlemen and ladies—the gentlemen decorated—in a room here, the other day. "Those are some of my relatives that remain in Germany." "And who are these?" I asked, pointing to a collection on the opposite wall, of lithograph and crayon-sketched heads. "These are some of my friends. That one—and that one—and that one—have been shot; that one—and that one—are in prison for life; that one—poor fellow—is in Siberia, and that one—he has been made to suffer more than all the others, I am afraid."

I once, when in Germany, met an American clergyman, who, I have since seen it said in the papers, has been sent to Asia, to teach the Hindoos Christianity; and he was good enough to inform me that all the German Republicans were mischievous, cut-throat infidels; who well deserved to be shot, hung, and imprisoned for life; and that I very much wronged those who were doing this for them, in my feelings about it. He had dined, only the day before, with several of the higher classes, with a number of Prussian and Austrian officers, and he never met with more gentlemanly and kind-hearted men. When I mentioned the fact that one of these officers had, a few days before, knocked down upon the pavements, with a blow of his fist, an aged laboring man, for coming, guiltlessly, into the street with red stockings on, he presumed that he had thought it his duty to do so; harsh measures had to be used to support the laws when the people were so exceedingly depraved. I believe he did not alter my feelings about it, very much; but I confess that these refugees in Texas have taught me something.

"Hate?"—said one of them—"hate? we do not hate. It was with injustice, imposture, oppression, degradation and falsehood, we struggled. We did and do not hate our enemies; they are the growth and the natural fruit of the system which they sustain, and we are only sorry for them. We have no personal enemies. It is an insane enmity that B_____ has, because the police killed his wife, and he has never recovered from it; so he still talks of revenge. A healthy mind can have no hatreds. We fought with men because they stood for ideas; but it was the ideas we fought against, not the men."

YEOMAN

POLITICS AND THE PARK: 1848–1858

Passages in the Life of an Unpractical Man

The agitation for a public park in New York began with an article published by Mr. Downing in 1848 in which he eloquently urged his strong conviction that properly planned and managed public recreation grounds would have a most civilizing and refining influence on the people of our great cities. This was followed from time to time by other papers having the same object until his lamentable death four years afterwards.

Mr. Downing's writings on the subject were much copied and favorably noticed by the leading newspapers and shortly before he died the Common Council of New York, at the instigation of Mayor A. C. Kingsland, took action which led to an act of the state legislature providing for a park on a tract of 150 acres of land situated on the East River. The following year a small politician, jealous of the advantages which another might gain by the success of this scheme, undertook to "head it off" by an alternate project. The idea striking him that a plausible argument could be made for a larger park more centrally situated, in a moment he adopted for his purpose the site afterwards accepted as that of the Central Park, neither knowing nor caring whether the ground was at all suitable in other respects than its geographical centrality.

The land was not fully acquired until 1856 and, the legislature having as yet made no provision for its government, in the latter part of that year Fernando Wood, the Mayor, near the end of his second term, obtained an act of the Common Council under which he with his Street Commissioner Joseph S. Taylor took charge of it. They appointed a chief Engineer and a large corps of assistants, and expenditures were made and liabilities incurred on account of the park, as was alleged by their opponents, to the amount of $60,000, as the result of which all that could afterwards be found of value to the city was an inaccurate topographical map of the ground.

There is a power which ordinarily lies ineffective back of all the political vices of our cities. At times it is stirred with shame, disgust and indignation; organizes itself and makes a loud demand for reform. The politicians out of office take advantage of the opportunity not only to secure the removal of those who have been in office but to make them as they go forth serve the purpose of scape goats. A few changes of form and method are made and the citizens are reconciled to a system under which the old vices are cherished only more warmly than before.

One of these storms of reform was rising at the period of which I have spoken and Fernando Wood was to be the chief scape goat by whose outgoing the indignation and wrath of the people was to be appeased.

Wood being a Democrat, the Republicans, who held the majority of the state legislature, took advantage of the momentary popular disgust with him and his associates to take the regulation of certain parts of the city business from the elected government of the city and to give it to a series of professedly non partisan Commissions. One of these, composed of nine members, part Republicans, part Wood Democrats, part "reform" Democrats, part non-descript, was appointed to supersede Wood and Taylor in the special government of the Central Park. It had to go to the Common Council of the city for its supplies, and a majority of the members of the Common Council siding with the Mayor were disposed not to honor its requisitions. Eventually they would be obliged to do so unless indeed a decision of the court could be obtained, as they professed to expect, declaring the Act of the legislature unconstitutional. But supplies could be delayed, and when yielded given in driblets, and various difficulties and obstructions could be put in the way of the Commission.

Two considerable influences were working in favor of the Commission: first, a desire with many that some progress should be made in turning to use the property in the land appropriated to the park which had cost the city five million dollars; second, the desire of the laboring population to obtain the employment which the construction of the Park was expected to give. This latter influence was strongest in those parts of the city where Wood and his supporters in the Common Council had hitherto obtained the most votes and on their popularity in which they depended for reelection.

To counteract it, the act of the Legislature was denounced as a tyrannical usurpation of power by which the Black Republicans and Abolitionists were to put themselves in office and plunder the city against the will of the local majority.

But these denunciations had to be uttered in the face of the fact that the Commissioners were to receive no pay; that they had elected a Democrat as their President, another Democrat as the Treasurer, and had reappointed Wood's whole Engineer corps. They had gone so far in this respect that a clamor was beginning to rise from the Republican side that the Commission was wholly given over to the Democrats.

At this period in its history one of the Commissioners came to spend a Sunday at a sea side inn near New Haven where I had been finishing the manuscript of my Journey in the Back Country. Sitting next to him at the tea table, he told me what I have just recited of the history of the Commission and added that they were now taking on a force of laborers. Having no money as yet at their command, each of the men employed was required to sign an agreement releasing the Commissioners from personal liability on account of the wages he might earn, and in lieu of wages, due bills against the city were to be issued which would be payable when the Common Council should make the appropriation, in favor of which an additional element of popular interest would thus be established. He added that at their next meeting they intended to elect a Superintendent and it was thought necessary that he should be a Republican. There were several candidates, but no Republican had offered with whom he was much pleased, and he asked if I knew of a suitable man. I inquired what would be the duties of the Superintendent?

He would be the Executive Officer of the Chief Engineer with respect to the labor force and would have charge of the police and see that proper regulations were enforced in regard to public use of the Park.

Must he be a politician?

No, a Republican but not a politician; much better he should not have been a practical politician. The Republicans could do little without the cooperation of the reform Democrats and were ready to compromise, on the understanding that the park shall be managed independently of politics.

"I am delighted to hear it," I said; "There's no limit to the good influence a park rightly managed would have in New York and that seems to be the first necessity of good management."

"I wish we had you on the Commission, but as we have not, why not take the Superintendency yourself? Come now."

Till he asked the question, the possibility of my doing so had never occurred to me, though he probably suspected I was thinking of it. I at once answered, however, smiling:

"I take it? I'm not sure that I would not if it were offered me. Nothing interested me in London like the parks and yet I thought a great deal more might be made of them."

"Well, it will not be offered you; that's not the way we do business. But if you'll go to work I believe you may get it. I wish that you would!"

"You are serious?"

"Yes; but there's no time to lose."

"What is to be done?"

"Go to New York and file an application; see the Commissioners and get your friends to back you."

"I'll take the boat tonight and think it out as I go. If no serious objection occurs to me before morning, I'll do it."

Accordingly, the next day I was looking for my friends in New York. At that season they were much scattered, but one I found who took up the matter warmly and my application was in a few days fortified by a number of weighty signatures. I shall presently refer to the fact that there among them was that of Washington Irving.

The President of the Commission being out of town on my arrival in New York, I first called on the Vice President, bearing a letter to him from my friend in New Haven.

The Vice President, who was a Republican, repeated that it was desirable that the Superintendent should not be a Democrat, yet that he should be as little objectionable as possible to the Democrats. He seemed to think that my prospects in this respect were good. He offered to introduce me to one of the Democratic Commissioners who was a very practical man, and also to the Engineer who again he described as a very practical man; if their judgment should be favorable, I might count on his support.

The practical Democratic Commissioner having ascertained that I had had no experience in practical politics, even no personal acquaintance with the Republican leaders in the city, that my backing would be from unpractical men, and that I responded warmly to virtuous sentiments with regard to corruption in both parties, after a long conversation gave me to understand that I might hope that if the Republicans brought me forward he should be less inclined to oppose me than a possible Republican who had been deep in the mire of city politics and who disapproved of the practice of virtue in politics.

The Engineer I found at a house on the Park about which was a crowd of laboring men, each bearing a letter addressed to him. On the ground that my letter was from a Commissioner, I was allowed to precede those who had stood waiting outside the door before me. The room in which the Engineer sat at a desk was crowded with applicants for employment whose letters were collected in batches by men wearing a golden star on the breast of a very dirty and seedy jacket and handed to the Engineer. These letters were chiefly from members of the Common Council. As each was opened and its writer's name recognized, the bearer was either abruptly told that there was no work for him at present or his name was taken and looked for on a list furnished by the writer of his letter in which it appeared that a limited number had been named whom he wished to have preferred among all those to whom he gave letters. If found there, the applicant was without further examination given a ticket and told to call again on a given day.

At the first opportunity I presented my letter and card. Reading a few lines, the Engineer glanced at me, dropped the letter and went on with his canvass of the laborers. I stood among them half an hour and then pointing to my card asked if I might hope to find him less engaged later in the day. As he seemed to assent, I walked out a little way looking at the ground for the park. I returned and withdrew again three times before I found the enlisting business ended. As I came in the last time, the engineer was about leaving. I walked with him & took a seat by his side in the street car running to the city.

I then had an opportunity to state on what grounds I had ventured to think that he would find me useful as an assistant in his work. He replied that he would rather have a practical man. I did not learn why I could not be regarded as a possibly practical man, but it was only too evident that the gate of hope was closed to me in that direction.

Calling by appointment on the Vice President the next day, I was not surprised to find that doubts had been growing over night in his mind, as to whether the office of Superintendent should not be filled by a practical man.

Some time after my election, which occurred at the first subsequent meeting of the Park Board, another of the Commissioners told me that this objection would have defeated me had it not been for the autograph of Washington Irving on my papers. That turned the balance.

But one member in a full board of nine stood out in the final vote; it was Mr. Thomas C. Fields, the best partisan I ever knew, and he never forgave me for it.

It is hardly necessary to say that even after my election I did not quite feel myself out of the woods. Had it been concluded that it was after all just as well not to have a practical man? Or had they been convinced that after all I was a practical man?

These gentlemen, most of whom had themselves made large fortunes in business, would hardly defer to Washington Irving on such a point. No, I owed my election to something else than their estimate of my value as a practical man—and to what I did not understand.

When I next came to the office on the park, my first experience was repeated until I said to the Engineer; "I was instructed to report to you for orders, Sir;" Upon this he called to one of the starred men: "Tell Hawkin to come here." Then to me: "I have given my orders to Mr. Hawkin. He is what I call a practical man and I will tell him to show you what you have to do."

Mr. Hawkin, a cautious, close-mouthed, sensible looking gentleman, wearing no coat and with trousers tucked in the legs of a heavy and dirty pair of boots, here opened the door and said, "Want me?"

"Yes; this is Mr. Olmsted, the new Superintendent. Take him round the park and show him what work is going on and tell the foremen they will take their orders from him after this."

"Now?"

The Engineer looked at me.

"I am quite ready, Sir."

"Yes, now."

In truth, as I had intended this to be rather a call of ceremony or preliminary report to my superior officer, I was not quite as well prepared as I could have wished to be for what followed.

Striking across the hill into what is now the Ramble, we came first upon a number of men with bill hooks and forks collecting and burning brush wood. Under a tree near by a man sat smoking. He rose as we approached:

"Smith, this is Mr. Olmsted, your new Superintendent. You'll take your orders from him after this."

All the men within hearing dropped their tools and looked at me. Smith said, "Oh! that's the man is it? Expect we shall be pushed up, now." He laughed and the men grinned.

"What is Mr. Smith doing?" I asked.

"He's grubbing round here and burning up what he can get together," and Mr. Hawkin moved on.

"See you again, I suppose," said Smith still laughing.

"Yes Sir; good day for the present."

And this process was repeated with little variation as we passed from gang to gang to the number of perhaps fifteen, there being at this time about 500 men at work. As they were nearly all Democrats and all appointed by a Democrat, and a Democrat who had himself been appointed first by Wood, and as they were mostly introduced to him by Democratic members of the Common Council, the presumption that the Commission was to be managed exclusively in the interests of the Republicans and as a means of defeating Wood was considerably weakened.

As I stood in the office, I had not been able to observe that the slightest consideration was given to the apparent strength or activity of the laborers. Each man undoubtedly supposed that he owed the fact of his preference over others, often much abler than himself to do a good day's work, to the fact that a member of the Common Council had asked his appointment. He also knew that the request of his patron was made not because of his supposed special fitness to serve the city or the park, but because of service that he was expected to render at primary meetings and otherwise with a view to the approaching municipal election. He knew too that he was for an indefinite period to receive no pay for his work, but only a promise to pay which he must turn to account by selling it at a discount.

Under all the circumstances it was plain enough that when Foreman Smith pleasantly remarked that he supposed that they would be pushed up now and the men laughed with him at the suggestion, it was because the idea that I might expect a day's work from them for each day's due-bill was thought a good joke.

Neither Foreman Smith nor any other that day said anything aloud to me about my not being a practical man, but I saw it in their eyes and their smile and I felt it deeply. In fact, for other reasons, I could have wished long before our round was finished that I had worn a pair of high legged boots and left my coat behind me, for it was a sultry afternoon in the height of the dog days and my conductor exhibited his practical ability by leading me through the midst of a number of vile sloughs in the black and unctuous slime of which I sometimes sank nearly half leg deep.

He said but one word to me during the afternoon beyond what his commission strictly required. As I stopped for an instant to kick the mire off my legs against a stump as we came out of the last bog, he turned and remarked:

"Suppose you are used to this sort of business."

I believe that he was some years my junior and it is probable that I had been through fifty miles of swamp for his one. There was not an operation in progress on the park in which I had not considerable personal experience, and he spoke with apparent gravity. Nevertheless, I felt very deeply that he was laughing in his sleeve, and that I was still a very young man. So I avoided a direct reply by saying that I had not been aware that the park was such a very nasty place. In fact the low grounds were steeped in the overflow and mush of pig sties, slaughter houses and bone boiling works, and the stench was sickening.

For several days there continued to be something that stimulated good humor in my appearance and in the inquiries and suggestions which I made as I walked from gang to gang feeling my way to an intelligent command of the business. It was as if we were all engaged in playing a practical joke. The most striking illustration of this good fellowship that I remember occurred, I think on the third day, when a foreman who was reading a newspaper as I came suddenly upon him, exclaimed "Hallo Fred—get round pretty often, don't you?"

Having no power to discharge or secure the discharge of a man, I found it was better to give every offender the benefit of the largest possible assumption of ignorance, forgetfulness and accident and urge him to give more attention to his duties and use more care.

THE GREENSWARD PLAN: APRIL 1858

Description of a Plan for the Improvement of the Central Park

"Greensward"

REPORT

TOPOGRAPHICAL SUGGESTIONS

A general survey of the ground allotted to the park, taken with a view to arrive at the leading characteristics which present themselves, as all-important to be considered in adapting the actual situation to its purpose, shows us, in the first place, that it is very distinctly divided into two tolerably equal portions, which, for convenience sake, may be called the upper and lower parks.

THE UPPER PARK

The horizon lines of the upper park are bold and sweeping and the slopes have great breadth in almost every aspect in which they may be contemplated. As this character is the highest ideal that can be aimed at for a park under any circumstances, and as it is in most decided contrast to the confined and formal lines of the city, it is desirable to interfere with it, by cross-roads and other constructions, as little as possible. Formal planting and architectural effects, unless on a very grand scale, must be avoided; and as nearly all the ground between the Reservoir and 106th Street (west of the Boston road) is seen in connection, from any point within itself, a unity of character should be studiously preserved in all the gardening details.

THE LOWER PARK

The lower park is far more heterogeneous in its character, and will require a much more varied treatment. The most important feature in its landscape, is the long rocky and wooded hillside lying immediately south of the Reservoir. Inasmuch as beyond this point there do not appear to be any leading natural characteristics of similar consequence in the scenery, it will be important to draw as much attention as possible to this hill-side, to afford facilities for rest and leisurely contemplation upon the rising ground opposite, and to render the lateral boundaries of the park in its vicinity as inconspicuous as possible. The central and western portion of the lower park is an irregular table-land; the eastern is composed of a series of graceful undulations, suggesting lawn or gardenesque treatment. In the extreme south we find some flat alluvial meadow; but the general character of the ground is rugged and there are several bold, rocky bluffs, that help to give individuality to this part of the composition.

Such being the general suggestions that our survey has afforded, it becomes necessary to consider how the requirements of the Commissioners, as given in their instructions, may be met with the least sacrifice of the characteristic excellencies of the ground.

PRELIMINARY CONSIDERATIONS

Up to this time, in planning public works for the city of New York, in no instance has adequate allowance been made for its increasing population and business; not even in the case of the Croton Aqueduct, otherwise so well considered. The City-Hall, the best architectural work in the State, and built to last for centuries, does not at this time afford facilities for one-third the business for which it was intended. The present Post-Office, expensively fitted up some ten years ago, no longer answers its purpose, and a new one of twice its capacity is imperatively demanded. The Custom-House expressly designed for permanence and constructed to that end at enormous expense less than twenty years ago, is not half large enough to accommodate the present commerce of the city.

The explanation of this apparently bad calculation is mainly given with the fact, that at every census since that of 1800, the city's rate of increase has been found to be overrunning the rate previously established.

A wise forecast of the future gave the proposed park the name of Central. Our present chief magistrate, who can himself remember market-gardens below Canal street, and a post-and-rail fence on the north side of City-Hall park, warned his coadjutors, in his inaugural message, to expect a great and rapid movement of population toward the parts of the island adjoining the

Central Park. A year hence, five city railroads will bring passengers as far up as the park, if not beyond it. Recent movements to transfer the steamboat-landings and railroad stations, although as yet unsuccessful, indicate changes we are soon to expect.

The 17,000 lots withdrawn from use for building purposes in the park itself, will greatly accelerate the occupation of the adjoining land. Only twenty years ago Union Square was "out of town;" twenty years hence, the town will have enclosed the Central Park. Let us consider, therefore, what will at that time be satisfactory, for it is then that the design will have to be really judged. No longer an open suburb, our ground will have around it a continuous high wall of brick, stone, and marble. The adjoining shores will be lined with commercial docks and warehouses; steamboat and ferry landings, railroad stations, hotels, theatres, factories, will be on all sides of it and above it: all of which our park must be made to fit.

The demolition of Columbia College, and the removal of the cloistral elms which so long enshadowed it; the pertinacious demand for a division of Trinity churchyard; the numerous instances in which our old graveyards have actually been broken up; the indirect concession of the most important space in the City-Hall park for the purposes of a thoroughfare and the further contraction it is now likely to suffer; together with the constant enormous expenditure of the city, and sacrifices of the citizens, in the straightening and widening of streets, are all familiar facts, that teach us a lesson of the most pressing importance in our present duty. To its application we give the first place in our planning.

THE TRANSVERSE ROADS

Our instructions call for four transverse roads. *Each* of these will be the single line of communication between one side of the town and the other, for a distance equal to that between Chambers street and Canal street. If we suppose but one crossing of Broadway to be possible in this interval, we shall realize what these transverse roads are destined to become. Inevitably they will be crowded thoroughfares, having nothing in common with the park proper, but every thing at variance with those agreeable sentiments which we should wish the park to inspire. It will not be possible to enforce the ordinary police regulations of public parks upon them. They must be constantly open to all the legitimate traffic of the city, to coal carts and butchers' carts, dust carts and dung carts; engine companies will use them, those on one side of the park rushing their machines across it, with frantic zeal at every alarm from the other; ladies and invalids will need special police escort for crossing them, as they do in lower Broadway. Eight times in a single circuit of the park will they oblige a pleasure drive or stroll to encounter a turbid stream of coarse traffic, constantly moving at right angles to the line of the park itself.

The transverse roads will also have to be kept open, while the park proper will be useless for any good purpose after dusk; for experience has shown that even in London, with its admirable police arrangements, the public cannot be secured safe transit through large open spaces of ground after nightfall.

FOREIGN EXAMPLES

These public thoroughfares will then require to be well lighted at the sides, and, to restrain marauders pursued by the police from escaping into the obscurity of the park, strong fences or walls, six or eight feet high, will be necessary. One such street passes through the Regent's Park of London, at the Zoological Gardens. It has the objection that the fence, with its necessary gates at every crossing of the park drives, roads or paths, is not only a great inconvenience, but a disagreeable object in the landscape.

To avoid a similar disfigurement, an important street; crossing across the garden of the Tuileries, is closed by gates at night, forcing all who would otherwise use it, to go a long distance to the right or left.

The form and position of the Central Park are peculiar in respect to this difficulty, and such that precedent in dealing with it is rather to be sought in the long and narrow Boulevards of some of the old Continental cities of Europe, than in the broad parks with which, from its area in acres, we are most naturally led to compare it. The Boulevards referred to are, however, generally used only as promenades, not as drives or places of ceremony. In frequent instances, in order not to interrupt the alleys, the streets crossing them are made in the form of causeways, and carried over on high arches. This, of course, prevents all landscape gardening, since it puts an abrupt limit to the view. Some expedient is needed for the Central Park, by which the convenience of the arrangement may be retained, while the objection is as far as possible avoided.

THE PRESENT DESIGN

In the plan herewith offered to the Commission, each of the transverse roads is intended to be sunk so far below the general surface, that the park drives may, at every necessary point of intersection, be carried entirely over it, without any obvious elevation or divergence from their most attractive routes. The banks on each side will be walled up to the height of about seven feet, thus forming the protective barrier required by police considerations; and a little judicious planting on the tops or slopes of the banks above these walls will in most cases entirely conceal both the roads and the vehicles moving in them, from the view of those walking or driving in the park.

If the position which has just been taken with regard to the necessity for permanently open transverse thoroughfares is found to be correct, it follows necessarily that the 700 acres allowed to the new park must, in the first instance, be subdivided definitely, although it is to be hoped to some extent invisibly, into five separate and distinct sections, only connected here and there by roads crossing them; and if the plan of making these thoroughfares by sunken roads is approved, they will, as it appears to us from the nature of the ground, have to be laid down somewhat on the lines indicated on the plan. If so, the problem to be solved is narrowed in its dimensions, and the efforts of the landscape gardener can be no longer directed to arranging a design that shall agreeably use up the space of 700 acres allotted, but instead to making some plan that shall have unity of effect as a whole, and yet avoid all collision in its detailed features with the intersecting lines thus suggested. It is on this basis that the present plan has, in the first instance, been founded. If the sunken transverse roads were omitted, the design would not be less complete in character; but it is, on the other hand, so laid out that the transverse thoroughfares do not interfere materially with its general or detailed effect.

SURFACE TRANSVERSE ROADS

After having planned the park drives agreeably to these views, we observed that three additional, moderately direct, transverse roads had occurred. These will afford facilities for crossing the park to all vehicles of classes which it will be proper to admit upon them, such as hackney coaches and all private carriages; and thus seven transverse roads will be really provided to be used during daylight. Four roads will probably be amply adequate for the night traffic needing to cross the park; but it might be questionable if this number would be sufficient during the day.

THE EXTERIOR

As it is not proposed that the park proper shall be lighted at night, it is well worth while to consider if the advantages which it offers as an interesting promenade, may not yet in some way be obtained at night.

FIFTH AVENUE

The ordinance that regulates the width of Fifth avenue, allows a space of fifteen feet on each side, exclusive of the sidewalks and the roadway; consequently, a space thirty feet in width, for promenade, is already on this side of the park for its whole length.

EIGHTH AVENUE RAILROAD

On the Eighth avenue, a similar arrangement may probably be effected, and as there would be no occasion to back up carts against the park side of the avenue, it is feasible to carry the railway tracks close to the edge of the promenade, thus leaving a clear space for carriages on the building side, and making the access to the park side more clean and convenient.

FIFTY-NINTH AND ONE HUNDRED AND SIXTH STREETS

On the southern boundary it is not desirable to reduce the already moderate width of the carriage way. It is, on the other hand, a question whether, as the streets and the park both, in reality, are the property of one owner—the City—this street should not be treated in a similar manner. It will, from its position, be in time rather crowded with traffic, and will, therefore, have some claim to be widened on this ground alone. As a question of beauty of arrangement for the park itself, however, it is conceived that if by this management a more stately character than could otherwise be obtained will be secured to the outer boundaries of the park, it will be cheaply purchased at the sacrifice of a few feet, at the south end, off its present length of two and a half miles. In riding along any of the avenues, the eye cannot fail to be struck with the great difference in dignity of effect, between such streets as Fourteenth and Twenty-Third, and those intermediate; and it would be a matter of regret, that the source of effect so easily obtained, should be lost in connection with the grand approaches to the park because it does not happen that its boundaries at present coincide with the wide streets laid out on the working plan upon which the city is being constructed. If, moreover, the advantage of the evening promenade is allowed to be of importance, we should be sorry to dispense with this section of it, which would be the only portion having a direct communication from the Sixth and Seventh avenues.

TREATMENT OF BOUNDARY LINES

For the purpose of concealing the houses on the opposite side of the street from the park, and to insure an umbrageous horizon line, it is proposed, as will be seen in the plan, to plant a line of trees all around the outer edge of the park, between the sidewalk and the roadway. On approaching the Fifth and Eighth avenue entrances, this line of trees along Fifty-Ninth street will come prominently into view, and have a handsome effect if the street is widened; but if Fifty-Ninth street is allowed to remain as a narrow street, it is feared that it will be difficult to prevent this boundary line of the park from having a contracted and somewhat mean appearance. Hence, we have thought it proper in our plan to assume the advantage and practicability of this arrangement to be conceded; but, if this should not be the case, it will be readily perceived that it forms no essential part of our design.

On the space originally provided for a sidewalk on the park side of the streets and avenues, there will, in any case, be room for such a line of trees as we have proposed. The continuous exterior mall should by no means be given up, even though it cannot be made in all parts as wide as we have proposed. At many points, and frequently for quite long distances, it will form an elevated terrace, commanding extensive views over the park, of the most interesting character; and a mere parapet-wall three or four feet high will, in such cases, be all-sufficient for the safety of promenaders and the protection of the park from interlopers.

FIFTH AVENUE ENTRANCE

The handsomest approach from the city is certain to be along the Fifth avenue, and it has been thought necessary to view with special care the angle of the park first reached from this direction, because it will be generally felt that immediate entrance should be had at this point.

The grade of the avenue has been established so high, that considerable filling-in would be required to avoid a rapid descent; but directly this single difficulty is overcome, the ground beyond has great advantages for the purpose of a dignified entrance to the park. A massive rock that will be found in connection with this requisite made-ground offers a sufficiently large natural feature to occupy the attention, and will at once reduce the artificial feature to a position of minor importance. If, next, we stand upon that portion of the rock which (a little north of the large cherry-tree) is at grade-height, we find that there is another rocky hillock within a short distance, in the direction a visitor to the park would most naturally pursue—that is to say, towards the centre of the park. This can be easily reached by slightly raising the intermediate ground; by then sweeping to the right, the natural conformation of the surface offers an easy ascent (by the existing cart-way over Sixty-Third street) to a plateau (two rods west of the powder-house), directly connected with the extensive table-land which occupies the centre of the lower half of the park.

From this plateau (now occupied mainly by the nursery) a view is had of nearly all the park up to the Reservoir, in a northerly direction; and on looking to the south and west, we perceive that there are natural approaches from these directions, which suggest that we have arrived at a suitable point of concentration for all approaches which may be made from the lower part of the city to the interior of the park.

THE AVENUE

Vista Rock, the most prominent point in the landscape of the lower park, here first comes distinctly into view, and fortunately in a direction diagonal to the boundary lines, from which it is desirable to withdraw attention in every possible way. We therefore accept this line of view as affording an all-sufficient motive to our further procedure. Although averse on general principles to a symmetrical arrangement of trees, we consider it an essential feature of a metropolitan park, that it should contain a grand promenade, level, spacious, and thoroughly shaded. This result can in no other way be so completely arrived at, as by an avenue; which in itself, even exclusive of its adaptability for this purpose, contains so many elements of grandeur and magnificence, that it should be recognized as an essential feature in the arrangement of any large park. The objection to which it is liable is that it divides the landscape into two parts, and it is therefore desirable to decide at what point this necessity can be submitted to with the least sacrifice to the general effect. The whole topographical character of the park is so varied, so suggestive of natural treatment, so picturesque, so individual in its characteristics, that it would be contrary to common sense to make the avenue its leading feature, or to occupy any great extent of ground for this special purpose. It must be subservient to the general design, if that general design is to be in accordance with the present configuration of the ground, and we have therefore thought that it should, so far as possible, be complete in itself, and not become a portion of any of the leading drives. There is no dignity of effect to be produced by driving through an avenue a quarter of a mile long, unless it leads to, and becomes an accessory of, some grand architectural structure, which itself, and not the avenue, is the ultimatum of interest. An avenue for driving in should be two or three miles long, or it will be petite and disappointing. We have therefore thought it most desirable to identify the idea of the avenue with the promenade, for which purpose a quarter of a mile is not insufficient, and we can find no better place for such a grand mall, or open air hall of reception, as we desire to have, than the ground before us.

THE PROMENADE

In giving it this prominent position, we look at it in the light of an artificial structure on a scale of magnitude commensurate with the size of the park, and intend in our design that it should occupy the same position of relative importance in the general arrangement of the plan, that a mansion should occupy in a park prepared for private occupation. The importance that is justly connected with the idea of the residence of the owner in even the most extensive private grounds, finds no parallel in a public park, however small, and we feel that the interest of the visitor, who in the best sense is the true owner in the latter case, should concentrate on features of natural, in preference to artificial, beauty. Many elegant buildings may be appropriately erected for desirable purposes in a public park; but we conceive that all such architectural structures should be confessedly subservient to the main idea, and that nothing artificial should be obtruded on the view as an ultimatum of interest. The idea of the park itself should always be uppermost in the mind of the beholder. Holding this general principle to be of considerable importance, we have preferred to place the avenue where it can be terminated appropriately at one end with a landscape attraction of considerable extent, and to relieve the south entrance with only so much architectural treatment as may give the idea that due regard has been paid to the adornment of this principal promenade, without interfering with its real character.

This avenue may be considered the central feature in our plan for laying out the lower park, and the other details of arrangement are more or less designed in connection with it.

PARADE GROUND

To the west is the parade ground, containing about 25 acres, that may, at a moderate expense, be levelled and made suitable for its purpose; and also some eight or ten acres of broken ground, that will be more or less available for military exercises. Such a broad open plane of well-kept grass would be a refreshing and agreeable feature in the general design, and would bear

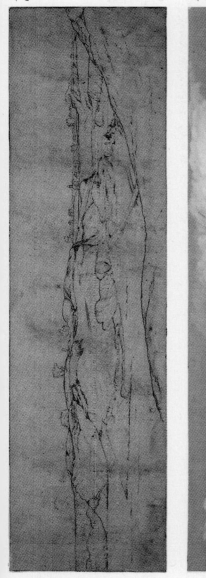

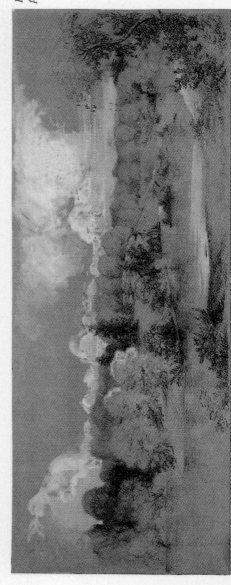

1. Frederick Law Olmsted & Calvert Vaux, *Greensward Study No. 1: View North across Pond from near Entrance at 59th Street and Fifth Avenue*, 1858.

2. *Greensward Study No. 2: View South across Playground in Southwest Section of Park.*

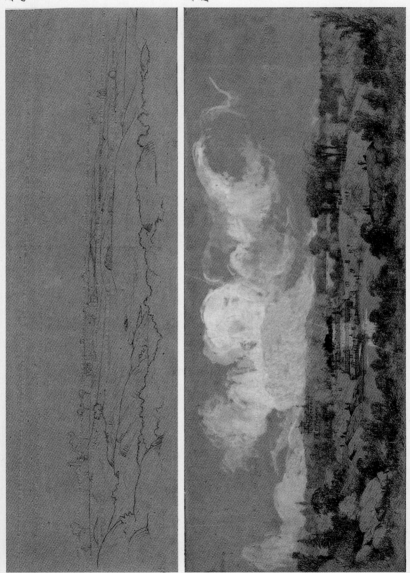

3. *Greensward Study No. 3: View South toward Terrace from Ramble.*

4. *Greensward Study No. 4: View Northeast toward Vista Rock.*

Present outlines

Effect proposed

5. *Greensward Study No. 5: View Southwest from Vista Rock on Reverse Line of Sight from Study No. 4.*

6. *Greensward Study No. 6: View from Ramble on Same Line of Sight as Study No. 5.*

7. *Greensward Study No. 7: View South across Playground in Upper Park from Bogardus Hill near 103rd Street and Eighth Avenue.*

Present outlines

Effect proposed

8. *Greensward Study No. 8: View East from Same Point as Study No. 7.*

9. *Greensward Study No. 9: View West from Edge of Proposed Arboretum
on Reverse Line of Sight of Study No. 8.*

10. *Greensward Study No. 10.*

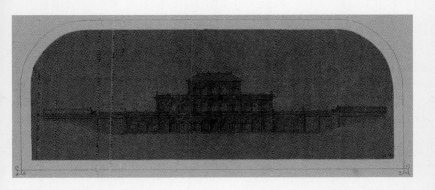

11. *Greensward Study No. 11: Plan for Flower Garden at Fifth Avenue and 74th Street.*
Top: Garden Arcade Building. *Bottom:* Flower Garden.

12. Andrew Green, George Waring Jr., Calvert Vaux, Ignaz Pilat, Jacob Wrey Mould, and Frederick Law Olmsted (*l. to r.*) on Willowdale Arch, Central Park, New York, September 23, 1862.

13. Bethesda Terrace under construction, 1862.

ON THE RAMBLE,
NEAR THE LAKE.

THE RUSTIC BRIDGE.

MOONLIGHT ON THE LAKE.

THE MARBLE BRIDGE.

14. Four views from Louis Prang's *Central Park Album*, 1864.

15. *Central-Park, Winter: The Skating Pond.*
Lithographed by Lyman W. Atwater, after a painting by Charles Parsons,
published and printed by Currier & Ives, 1862.

16. Frederick Law Olmsted, c. 1860.

17. Calvert Vaux, c. 1860.

to be of much greater extent than is here shown, if the lot were of a different shape; but under the circumstances, 25 acres seems as much as can well be spared for the purpose. A military entrance from Eighth avenue is proposed to be made at Sixty-Ninth street, which has been already, at considerable expense, cut through the rock at this point, and offers a suggestion for a picturesque approach, with a portcullis gate, and with the main park drive carried over it at a higher level.

PLAYGROUND

The natural southern boundary of the table-land occupied by the parade ground is a rapid slope that occurs about in the line of Sixty-Sixth street; in this slope it is proposed to sink one of the transverse roads; and on a level plane below it, stretching to the south, a playground, about 10 acres in extent, is located, as indicated on the plan. We have thought it very desirable to have a cricket ground of this size near the southern boundary of the park, and not far from the Sixth and Eighth avenue railroads, which offer the most rapid means of access from the lower part of the city.

In this playground, sites are suggested for two buildings of moderate dimensions: one for visitors to view the games, which would be appropriately located on a large rock that overlooks the ground; and the other for the players, at the entrance from the transverse road, by which an exit could be obtained from the playground after the other gates were closed. Only one mass of rock of any considerable magnitude would require to be blasted out for the purpose of adapting this ground to its intended purpose; its position is indicated on the plan by a red cross, and the object of its removal will be seen on examination. This part of the design is illustrated in study number 2. The ground at the south-west corner of the park it is proposed to fill in sufficiently to make, on the plan indicated, an agreeable Eighth avenue entrance.

THE LOWER LAKE

To the south-east of the promenade, and between the Fifth and Sixth avenue entrances, it is proposed to form a lake of irregular shape, and with an area of 8 or 9 acres. This arrangement has been suggested by the present nature of the ground, which is low, and somewhat swampy. It is conceived that, by introducing such an ornamental sheet of water into the composition at this point, the picturesque effect of the bold bluffs that will run down to its edge and overhang it must be much increased; and that by means of such a natural boundary this rocky section of the park will be rendered more retired and attractive as a pleasant walk or lounge. The proposed effect of this part of the design, as it will appear from the Fifth avenue entrance, is indicated on study number 1.

THE ARSENAL

To the south-east of the promenade will be found that portion of the park in which the present Arsenal is situated. This ground is undulating and agreeable in its character, and will offer pleasant opportunities for shady walks. The arsenal itself, although at present a very unattractive structure, and only tolerably built, contains a great deal of room in a form that adapts it very well to the purposes of a museum. It is proposed, therefore, to improve its external appearance, so far as may be necessary, without changing its shape or usefulness, or going to any great expense; and as it occurs rather near the Fifth avenue entrance, and is, therefore, likely to occupy too considerable a share of attention if left exposed to view from the south, it is intended, as early as possible, to plant in its vicinity forest-trees calculated to become handsome specimens of large size, and that will, after a few years, prevent the museum from attracting an undue share of attention in the general landscape.

MUSIC-HALL

To the east of the promenade, there will be a half-mile stretch of lawn and trees extending from the vicinity of Fifty-Ninth street to Seventy-Second street, and this will be the dress ground of the park; and in a prominent position on this ground, and immediately connected with the grand mall, the site for a music-hall, called for in our instructions, has been set apart; and we have suggested that a palm-house and large conservatory should be added to this music-hall whenever it is built.

This site is recommended because it is conspicuous, without being obtrusive, and is easy of access from the promenade and from one of the leading avenue entrances; while, to the north, it commands from its terraces and verandas the finest views that are to be obtained in the lower part of the park. It also overlooks the site which we have selected as most appropriate for the flower-garden, called for in our instructions; and this we consider a decided advantage, as the most attractive view of a flower-garden is from some point above it that will enable the visitor to take in at a glance a general idea of the effect aimed at.

THE FLOWER GARDEN

The garden is located in low ground to the north-east of the promenade, and is designed close to Fifth avenue, the grade of which at the centre line of the garden is about twenty feet above the present level of the ground; this, for the reasons above stated, we consider a desideratum, and have suggested that over the arcade or veranda that we propose should be built against the east wall of the park in connection with the garden, a structure should be erected, with an entrance on a level with the avenue, so as to give an opportunity for a view of the garden, both from this level and from another story above it. This idea is not, of course, necessary to the design, and the sketch submitted is merely a suggestion, to show what may be done at some future time.

The plan of the flower-garden itself is geometrical; and it is surrounded by an irregular and less formal plantation of shrubs that will serve to connect it with the park proper. In the centre it is proposed to construct a large basin for a fountain, with a high jet; other smaller jets are prepared for, as indicated; and, in connection with the north wall, which will be somewhat below the surface of the ground below, it is proposed to arrange some such wall foundation as the celebrated one of Trevi. The water for this fountain will, in the present case, be supplied from the overflow from the skating pond, and also from the Reservoir, and will fall into a semi-circular marble basin, with a paved floor. Such a fountain is out of place unless it can be furnished with an ample supply of water; but, in the position assigned to it on our plan, there will be no difficulty in procuring all the water that can be required for the purpose; and it seems desirable, therefore, to take advantage of the opportunity offered, for the effect of a sculptured fountain of this sort is quite distinct from that produced by a jet d'eau.

A colored plan of this part of the design is illustrated to an enlarged scale on study number II.

To the north-west of the promenade is a slope, offering an appropriate site for a summer-house that in such a situation should have some architectural pretension; and further to the west, near Eighth avenue, is a stretch of table-land, terminated by an abrupt rocky descent, that suggests itself as well suited for a Casino or refreshment house.

From the upper end of the promenade the rocky hill-side to the north, surmounted by Vista Rock at its highest point, comes into full view; and on this rock it will be generally conceded a tower should be erected—but by no means a large one, or the whole scale of the view will be destroyed. To the north and north-west of the promenade, a tract of low ground is proposed to be converted into the skating pond called for in our instructions; and the picturesque scenery between Vista Rock and the promenade will thus be heightened in effect, when seen from the south side of this lake, of about 14 acres. A terrace approach, as shown on the plan and on study number 3, is proposed, from the avenue to the water. This feature, although by no means absolutely necessary, would add much to the general effect, and could be introduced at any future time, if it is preferred at present to treat the ground occupied by it in a less artificial style.

Immediately in the vicinity of Vista Rock is the south wall of the present reservoir. This wall occupies the whole of the middle of the park, and is a blank, uninteresting object that can in no way be made particularly attractive. We have, therefore, thought it necessary to bear this in mind in arranging the general plan, and have given a direction to the lines of drive leading this way from the lower part of the park that will enable them to avoid the wall of the reservoir altogether. The necessity for doing this has induced us to commence diverting the lines of drive at the south end of the grand promenade, which seems to offer a sufficient reason for so doing, and to lead them afterwards on their northerly course in such a way that they may pass naturally to the east and west of the reservoir. If any drive proceeded in the direction of the line of avenue, and at once crossed the ground proposed to be occupied by the lake, the reservoir would inevitably become the terminal feature of the lower part of the park, and this would be disagreeable. The skating pond will offer a sufficiently natural barrier to this direct mode of proceeding, and will furnish a reason for locating the promenade in its proposed position, and also for terminating it where suggested; and by carrying a road along the edge of the water, an opportunity will be given to lengthen out the drive commanding the principal views in this vicinity; the lake will also help to give a retired and agreeable character to the hill-side beyond, which is well adapted for pic-nic parties and pleasant strolls. Even if the reservoir did not occur in its present position, the conformation of the ground is such that the roads would naturally take, to a considerable extent, the direction indicated, leaving the centre of the park undivided by a drive.

The management of the ground between the skating pond and Vista Rock appears to be indicated by its form and the character of its present growth. It is well sheltered, and large masses of rock occur at intervals. The soil is moist, and altogether remarkably well adapted to what is called in Europe an American garden—that is, a ground for the special cultivation of hardy plants of the natural order Ericaceae, consisting of rhododendrons, andromedas, azaleas, kalmias, rhodoras, &c. The present growth, consisting of sweet-gum, spice-bush, tulip-tree, sassafras, red-maple, black-oak, azalea, andromeda, &c., is exceedingly intricate and interesting. The ground is at present too much encumbered with stone, and with various indifferent plants. By clearing these away, and carefully leaving what is valuable—by making suitable paths, planting abundantly, as above suggested, and introducing fastigiate shrubs and evergreens occasionally, to prevent a monotony of bushes—the place may be made very charming. Where the hill-side approaches the lake, sufficient openings are proposed to be left for occasional glimpses, or more open views, of the water; and glades of fine turf are intended to occur at favorable intervals, so as to offer pleasant spots for rest and recreation.

PLAYGROUND

To the east and south-east of the present reservoir, the general conformation of the surface continues to be of the same easy, undulating character as that to the east of the promenade, and can be treated in a similar manner. The whole space is intended to be occupied with stretches of well-kept turf, with fine groups and single trees, so planted that they may appear to advantage, and not crowd each other. That portion which is immediately east of the reservoir is set apart for one of the playgrounds; and in the strip of land between the main drive and the reservoir wall, a reserved garden is provided for, with gardener's house attached; this will be needed in connection with the flower-garden already described. On the west side of the reservoir, the ground is of an irregular character, which continues past the old and new reservoirs to the upper end of the site. The spaces remaining for park use will, however, be so much contracted by the reservoir walls and embankments, that extended landscape effects are out of the question.

WINTER DRIVE

It is intended, therefore, as the soil and situation are adapted to the purpose, to arrange in this locality a winter drive about a mile and a half in length, and to plant somewhat thickly with evergreens, introducing deciduous trees and shrubs occasion-ally, to relieve the monotony of effect that otherwise might occur. Large open glades of grass are introduced among these plantations of evergreens, as the effect aimed at is not so much that of a drive through a thick forest, crowded with tall spin-dling trees, as through a richly wooded country, in which the single trees and copses have had plenty of space for developing their distinctive characteristics to advantage.

BERCEAU WALKS

Immediately south and west of the present reservoir, terraces have been already formed, and these can readily be converted into continuous arbors, or berceau walks. Access will thus be provided to all the gates of the reservoir, and the wall will itself be planted out. The effect of these closely shaded walks will also, it is conceived, offer an agreeable contrast to the views obtainable from Vista Rock, in the immediate vicinity.

POLICE STATION

In the northern section of this locality, and in connection with one of the transverse roads, will be found the house of the Su-perintendent, the office of the Commission, the police station, and other necessary buildings, such as stables, &c. The site is not far from the one at present occupied by the police, and is thought to be well suited for its purpose. By making a private entrance along the wall of the reservoir, the whole establishment can be immediately connected, by means of the transverse road, with the city streets, and at the same time be central and elevated without being unpleasantly prominent. It is proposed, as will be seen on the plan, to make short connections from the park roads to the transverse thoroughfare north of the present reservoir, so as to admit of visitors shortening the drive in this way if preferred.

RESERVOIR RIDE

The new reservoir, with its high banks, will take up a great deal of room in the park, and although it will offer a large sheet of water to the view, it will be at too high a level to become a landscape attraction from the ordinary drives and walks. It is suggested, therefore, that all round it a ride shall be constructed, and carefully prepared for this purpose only; and although this feature may be somewhat costly in the first instance, it is conceived that the result would be worth the outlay, for the sake of its advantages as a ride over a mile and a half in length, commanding the view of the reservoir, and uninterfered with by the regular drives, although in connection with them at different points.

On the east of the new reservoir, the park is diminished to a mere passage-way for connection, and it will be difficult to obtain an agreeable effect in this part of the design, unless some architectural character is given to it. It is not recommended, however, to attempt any such effect immediately, or out of the funds of the Commission, but to accept the high bank of the reservoir as a barrier to the west, for a few years; because it is thought that as soon as this part of the city is built up to any considerable extent, it will not be difficult to obtain an enriched architectural effect, appropriate to the purpose, without expense to the Commission. An arcade, 100 feet deep, could be substantially built, and the drive could be carried above this arcade, on a level with the reservoir and overlooking Fifth avenue, the remainder of the ground being filled in; and it is thought that as this arcade may be lighted from the rear, and will face a fashionable thoroughfare, it will offer, at not distant period, very valuable lots for stores, or other purposes; and as it is a third of a mile in extent, it may be a source of revenue, in rent, to the park fund, instead of a burden on it.

TOWER ON BOGARDUS HILL

The north-westerly portion of the park, above the new reservoir, is planned very simply, in accordance with what we conceive to be the suggestion of the ground. The evergreen drive is continued nearly to the foot of Bogardus Hill, and then, somewhat changing its character, turns to the east. At this point a branch road crosses a brook that is made to expand into a pool a little below the bridge; and this road then winds gradually to the top of the hill, which offers an available site for some monument of public importance, that may also be used as an observatory tower. If, as is not improbable, the transatlantic telegraph is brought to a favorable issue while the park is in an early stage of construction, many reasons could, we think, be urged for commemorating the event by some such monument as the one suggested on the plan, and in study number 9. The picturesque effect of a spring of clear water, that already exists in this vicinity, may be heightened, as suggested in study number 10.

The central portion of the upper section of the park is left as open as possible, and can be levelled so far as may be required for the purposes of the playgrounds indicated on the plan, and on study number 7. At present, it is hardly thought that it would be necessary to make the Sixth avenue entrance to the north; but its position is indicated.

THE ARBORETUM

The north-east section of the upper park is shown as an arboretum of American trees, so that every one who wishes to do so may become acquainted with the trees and shrubs that will flourish in the open air in the northern and middle sections of our country.

This arboretum is not intended to be formally arranged, but to be so planned that it may present all the most beautiful features of lawn and wood-land landscape, and at the same time preserve the natural order of families, so far as may be practicable. The botanical student will thus be able to find any tree or shrub without difficulty. We have selected this tract, of about 40 acres, in the upper angle of the site, so as to interfere with the more special requirements of the park as little as possible. The spot chosen is in some measure separated from the rest of the grounds, by a ridge of land between Fifth and Sixth avenues, and includes the buildings on Mount St. Vincent. The wooden structures would be removed, and the brick chapel converted into a museum and library of botany, similar to that at Kew, but with more specific regard to landscape and decorative gardening. In the park itself there will be numerous specimens of all the trees, native or foreign, that are likely to thrive; but it is proposed to limit this particular collection to American trees, because the space necessary for a complete arboretum would occupy several hundred acres, and also because it will afford an opportunity to show the great advantage that America possesses in this respect. No other extra-tropical country could furnish one-quarter the material for such a collection. In the whole of Great Britain, for example, there are less than twenty trees, native to the island, that grow to be over 30 feet in height; while in America we have from five to six times that number. There are, indeed, already over forty species of the largest native trees standing in the park, which is nearly equivalent to the number to be found in all Europe.

It is proposed to plant from one to three examples of each species of tree on open lawn, and with sufficient space about each to allow it to attain its fullest size with unrestricted expanse of branches; the effect of each tree is also to be exhibited in masses, so as to illustrate its qualities for grouping. Space is provided to admit of at least three specimens of every native tree which is known to flourish in the United States north of North Carolina; also for several specimens of every shrub; these latter, however, except in particular instances, are not expected to be planted singly, but in thickets, and as underwood to the coppice masses—as may best accord with their natural habits and be most agreeable to the eye. Further details of this part of the design will be found in the explanatory guide to the arboretum, submitted with the plan, in which the proposed arrangement of all the trees is set forth in order.

The leading features of the plan have now, it is thought,

been referred to. It has not been considered necessary to especially particularize the different trees proposed to be used in
the various parts of the park. For the purposes of the avenue,
the American elm naturally suggests itself at once as the tree to
be used; and it is to be hoped that the fine effect this produces,
when planted in regular lines, may in a few years be realized in
the Central Park.

There is no other part of the plan in which the planting calls
for particular mention, except to the south of the skating pond;
an opportunity is there offered for an exhibition of semi-tropical
trees, and it is intended to treat that portion of the park in the
manner suggested in study number 5. A list of the trees to be
used is appended to the explanation of the arboretum.

The plan does not show any brooks, except a small one in
connection with the pool at the foot of Bogardus Hill, which
can always be kept full by the waste of water from the New Reservoir. Mere rivulets are uninteresting, and we have preferred
to collect the ornamental water in large sheets, and to carry
off through underground drains the water that at present runs
through the park in shallow brooks.

As a general rule, we propose to run footpaths close to the
carriage roads, which are intended to be 60 feet wide, allowing
a space of four feet of turf as a barrier between the drive and
the path. Other more private footpaths are introduced, but it
is hardly thought that any plan would be popular in New York
that did not allow of a continuous promenade along the line of
the drives, so that pedestrians may have ample opportunity to
look at the equipages and their inmates.

It will be perceived that no long straight drive has been provided on the plan; this feature has been studiously avoided,
because it would offer opportunities for trotting matches. The
popular idea of the park is a beautiful open green space, in
which quiet drives, rides, and strolls may be had. This cannot be
preserved if a race-course, or a road that can readily be used as
a race-course, is made one of its leading attractions.

A PARK FOR WASHINGTON HEIGHTS: AUGUST 1860

To Henry H. Elliott

August 27, 1860

My Dear Sir:

The Herald of today publishes statements, in one of its peculiar playful slang-whang articles, which doubtless misrepresents the intention as well as the action of the Commission, but which contains some good suggestions, as these articles generally do, and also presents certain ideas which you gave me to understand in our conversation a few days ago were favorably considered by a majority of the Commissioners. For convenience's sake, having no clearer statement than the Herald's, I want to take that as a text for some observations upon them.

The Herald's first notion, though not directly expressed, evidently is that the high and picturesque grounds of the territory to be laid out should be made to take a peculiar character, different from the adjoining flat land and from the rest of the island. It proposes that each should constitute a department by itself, or, there being three great hills, that there should be three departments, each with a departmental road.

This road, to refer now to your suggestions to me, as the Herald is less particular in certain respects, is to be comparatively narrow, so it may be cheaply built by taking advantage of natural terraces or the flatter parts of the ground along the steep sides of the hills.

The remaining ground of each department will, says the Herald, constitute a park; a park, only the ground will be studded with private demesnes and handsome villas, and all owned by private individuals in parcels of various forms and sizes (precisely as at present).

This sounds pleasantly, and possibly, if carried out, the name of Fort Washington Park would, under the idea that it must mean something pleasant, attract some attention from those who wished to suit themselves with a site for a villa near the city.

Imagine yourself a dozen years hence, a stranger to the district, and that I am a real estate broker to whom you have applied to assist you in your search for a fine villa site. As agent

for the Fort Washington Park land-sellers in general, I drive
you out over the new 40, 50, or 60 ft. road. We enter the park
somewhere near the Deaf & Dumb establishment and have got
up into the vicinity of what is now the Fort Washington road.

"When shall we come to the park," you ask.

"Oh," I reply, "We are in the park, have been in it these ten
minutes past."

"Indeed! I did not observe any gateway."

"No, there is none."

"No gateway? Then there can be no special regulations enforced by which any nuisance can be excluded."

"Well no, not upon the road. You see, it was necessary that
there should be a road in this part of the island, open for all
purposes of an ordinary public road."

"Then in fact this road is not really a part of the park?"

"No, it only runs through it, but, you see, as the park lies on
both sides of it, it gives you a pleasant drive to your residence,
if you should have one out here."

"That certainly is an advantage, but what security is there
that the property on each side here will remain in its present
condition?"

"It is so steep that it is absolutely worthless for any purpose
except to maintain a distance between the residences on the
flatter ground above and those on the flatter ground below
and the road."

"What is the market value of this steep ground?"

"It cannot be sold except in connection with some of the
flatter ground; hence it might just as well be public property,
for all the benefit its owners derive from it."

"But here the slope is less; what is this horrible bare spot we
are coming to?"

"This was a piece of twelve acres that was sold to Mr. Abbot,
who when it began to be a rage to build in the park, intended
to establish a ladies' university on it. He got up a company for
the purpose, and they went so far as to cut off the trees, and to
lay off the steep slope in terraces and grade the upper ground,
but Mr. Abbot died, and the subscribers did not pay up and
the hard times came on, and so the work stopped. Then in the
spring there came a storm just as the frost was breaking up, and
the terraces not having been sodded, there was a land-slide. It

tore up the road and quite destroyed a gentleman's place on the lower side. When they repaired the road they had to build a regular retaining wall 40 feet high on the river side, as you see."

"Yes, it's rather an improvement to have the trees removed on that side, it opens up such a fine river view. But what is it smells so like a pig-sty?"

"I believe there are some large pig-sties down there under the wall."

"How is that—in the park?"

"The fact is there is an Irish settlement just down below there, but it's only temporary; they expect to have them cleared out."

"How did they get their shantees stuck in here?"

"Oh, they are only squatters, I believe."

"But how is it there are squatters in the Park?"

"Well, they got in here when they were rebuilding the road, some of them. Then there were a lot of Dutch people that got in afterwards when they built the great cellar of the Tiger brewery. This is it on the right. This is the outer wall of the cellar. It is eight feet thick and fifty feet high, and there is another wall inside of it. Then there are great vaults which come under the road, and subterranean passages to the buildings below on the wharf. It is the greatest Lager brewery in the world. There is a garden up above and on Sunday they sometimes have 15,000 people there. There is an observatory on the highest ground 300 feet high & it's a great place for target shooting & balloon ascensions. They have an artillery target and two of the new rifled ninety-eight pounders for practice. Gerrin pays a thousand dollars a year for this wall to stencil advertisements upon."

"This part of the park won't suit me. I should think the brewery & garden would destroy the value of land for residencies in the neighborhood."

"Indeed it does. Land is wanted here for nothing but Dutch boarding houses and groggeries, and but little for those. It's all held on speculation & will hardly sell now at any price."

"Why did they allow such a monstrous nuisance to get into the park?"

"The gentleman, a rich Cuban by the name of Torres, who bought this ground, had agreed with Mr. Abbot that they should have a private road running so as to accommodate both places. They had to buy a right of way of a man who held some land in the rear in order to get a road to suit them, because the difficulty of this brewery place was that it was not conveniently accessible from the departmental road. They paid a great price for the right of way, and Mr. Abbot was going to remove a ridge of rock that stood in the way of the private road to get material for his terraces. After his work stopped, Torres got disgusted with the delay and sold the place to the Gemeau Company. Several persons who had bought about here with the intention of building gave it up when it came out what was going to be done with the place. In fact several law suits grew out of it, and that, I suppose, is the reason that that pig-sty settlement has been allowed to grow up down below there."

"There are some very common houses."

"Yes; after they built the brewery and those stores near it, it got to be unfashionable just here, and as the land would not sell for villas, the owners got tired of holding it as dead property, and put up cheap tenement houses on it."

"There is a fine old house; it is sadly out of repair though, & the grounds are gone to waste."

"It's too good yet to be pulled down, you see, yet too near town, at least too near the brewery, to be fashionable, so it remains as it is, and is used for a boarding-house."

"Here is another dreary spot on the hill-side."

"Yes, this is a minor's estate, and there is some dispute about the title, and it has been neglected; and there's another nest of Irish folks down there at the foot of the hill who keep their goats on it and get in at night & steal the timber."

"What is that drumming?"

"I suppose it is a target company going out to Conrad's."

"What's Conrad's?"

"That's Bennett's old place, you know; my horse is a little restive, I don't know as I can drive him by them."

"It is no matter; I do not care about going any further. The fact is, although it is called a park, I don't see that there is any difference between this region and any other suburb of the city. I remember very well when Bloomingdale road below Manhattanville and Jones' Wood was in this way. All the old villas had not been given up. Mayor Wood, and the Clendennings & Chestermans and Doctor Williams and a few other people held on to their old places—but most of the good houses had got to be taverns (One was called the Claremont, another Elm Park, another Burnham's, but all had been fine old country places), and the road was lined with shantees and mean little temporary houses."

Are such glimpses, my dear Mr. Elliott, of the possible future of Fort Washington at all more improbable, than a view of the present state of things in the central part of the island would have seemed to you, when you first visited friends on the Hellgate, Old Boston or Bloomingdale roads? How can it be prevented? By narrow or crooked or steep roads? What is to prevent a future legislature from forming a Commission to straighten, widen and re-grade roads, to open streets through your villa grounds to accommodate the brewers & grocers and coal merchants on each side of them? There is nothing to attract commerce to the heights, you say. What attracts commerce to Jones' Wood? The river shores cannot be docked, and they are yet grading streets far south of it thirty or forty feet deep through solid rock. A very few years ago it contained the choicest residencies on the island, with circuitous private roads laid out as the Herald proposes they should be on Washington Heights, according to the needs & tastes & whims of the individual proprietors of the Wood. There is not a factory, nor a store or grocery, on it to this day so far as I know, but do gentlemen of fortune who desire a luxurious country residence within convenient reach of the Exchange and the Opera House, go to Jones' Wood to look for it? If Jones' Wood had been named Jones' Park, it would have been all the same, would it not? If you wish further assurance of this danger, go to Staten Island. Certainly Washington Heights can claim no advantage over the heights of Clifton and New Brighton in respect of inaccessibility from the city. Yet where five years ago there was nothing but elegance & fashion, you now see unmistakeable signs of the advance guard of squalor, an anxiety to sell out on the part of the owners of the finest villas, no sales except for public houses, and an absolute deterioration in value of property. Look again at the Brooklyn suburbs. Jersey City. See the process repeated at Philadelphia & Boston.

You ask me if there are not cases abroad where roads have been laid out in the suburbs of a town, as a landscape gardener would lay them out if the adjoining ground were a park, at St. George's Park in Liverpool for instance, and where the ground has on this account become rapidly occupied by villas and gained a value for villa residencies too great to leave any danger that it will be encroached upon by shops, etc.?

St. George's Park is a picturesque road, with gates at each end, with a real park, or space of common pleasure ground beautifully laid out & kept on one side, while the ground on the other side is held in parcels of considerable breadth and depth, each built upon & occupied by an individual proprietor. The park, however, is permanently common to all, is controlled no more than the road by any individual, and lies between all of the villas and the nearest public road or street. There are other similar instances. It is frequently to be seen that a comparatively small bit of planted ground—or an attractive promenade in any form, which secures an appearance of elegant seclusion to the vicinity—has served to permanently establish a neighborhood or quarter of handsome private residencies.

The expedient most commonly used abroad to secure seclusion for residencies in or near a town, is that of building in what are called crescents. A crescent is a series of villas, or a range or block of buildings, the front or fronts of which form a curved line, concave towards the public road. In front of them is a bow-shaped piece of ground, and the wood of the bow will represent a private road by which each front door is approached; the bow-string, the public road or street; and the space between the bow and string, a piece of planted ground which screens the houses from the street. A large proportion of the recently erected houses in the most fashionable part of London are thus planned. Another method used in London is to build houses pointing upon a cul-de-sac, or a street entered from a great thoroughfare, but closed at the other end and with no other opening.

The essential point aimed at by the Herald, and probably by the Commissioners, is to establish an elegant rural character for the three districts or departments, and to offer some assurance to those who wish to build villas that these districts shall not be bye and bye invaded by the desolation which thus far has invariably advanced before the progress of the town. Is this possible? Not by the Herald's plan of adding the word park to the name of a locality, running a rural road through or around it, and leaving all difficulties to convenient subdivision and closer occupancy to be solved by necessity. Nothing would be more certain than such a lazy and temporizing plan to accomplish the contrary purpose, namely to make sure that ways of meeting numerous local necessities should arise, which would after a time be compromised and combined upon new plans which would introduce new elements into the district, entirely at discord with those upon which its occupants had previously built.

Is it possible to have it otherwise?

Only by making all the ground, in the first place, of more value for villa residencies than for anything else, and in the second place, by securing such solid special advantages for this purpose that a class of residencies shall be planted on it, too good ever to be given up to any other possible use, and too good to be superseded even by fashion.

How can this be done?

This we can answer by considering what goes to make ground essentially valuable for villa purposes, and whether our heights possess or can in any feasible way be given this primarily essential value; and second, whether special substantial advantages can be given to these heights which can not be had elsewhere, so that for villa residencies they will permanently stand absolutely beyond competition.

To begin with, the heights offer the essential rural requirements for villa residences. But there are other things a rich and cultivated family want near their residence. They want the advantages of society, of compact society, of the use of that professional talent in teachers, and artists and physicians and mechanics, which can only be adequately paid for and maintained in the midst of a compact society. They want to be served in a regular, exact, punctual and timely manner with superior comestibles and whatever else it is desirable to have supplied to a family, freshly, frequently or quickly on demand.

The Northern heights of the island possess these advantages perhaps more than any other ground which can be put in competition with them at present—yet by no means in as great a degree as is desirable and as may be secured.

What else is essential in a villa residence? The grand advantage of the villa over the town mansion is that the villa possesses tranquility and seclusion—freedom from the turmoil of the streets—and means and opportunities for amusement and exercise which can not be had in a town mansion, certainly not without the liability of observation from neighbors or the public in the streets.

It is when this tranquility and seclusion can no longer be had in a villa residence that it becomes irksome to its owner & unattractive to anyone else, when it can no longer be had in what has been a fashionable villa road or district that the character of this road or district changes to that at present possessed by the Bloomingdale road or the Jones' Wood district and which Clifton Avenue, Staten Island, is just beginning to unmistakably take on. Nobody will think now of buying land on either for a villa because they no longer possess an aspect of tranquility or seclusion. Yet there are many essential advantages for the residence of cultivated & luxurious families on the Bloomingdale road which were wanting when it was a fashionable villa quarter. Every advantage of compact society is far more accessible than formerly. Churches, operas, balls, may be enjoyed, for instance, with far greater frequency & far greater convenience, by reason of closer vicinity and of paved & gas lighted roads; butchers & bakers will call more frequently & regularly & serve better; doctors and teachers, piano tuners and stove pipe setters, are nearer at hand when wanted. Water is better & more abundant. All these are undoubted advantages. Yet its old inhabitants flee from it, and those who demand luxury in their residence shun it.

Why? Not because of these metropolitan advantages surely, but because the road on which these villas face, by which they must be approached, and which passes close beside their walks and lawns, has become a common business thoroughfare; and inasmuch as butchers and bakers and tinkers and dramsellers and the followers of other bustling callings need to expose their wares and advertise themselves by signs and place themselves so they may be conveniently called upon without requiring their customers to go out of the way, the ground not actually occupied by villas fronting upon this thoroughfare has been extensively built upon for these purposes, and this has given employment to numerous mechanics & laborers and so occasioned a demand for cheap tenement & boarding houses along the road; and so gradually from a quiet & secluded neighborhood, it is growing to be a noisy, dusty, smoking, shouting, rattling and stinking one.

What helps a road or street, and what hinders it from becoming such a thoroughfare? Steep grades do not, as anyone knows who has been in Boston, Liverpool or Edinburgh. Neither does narrowness of roadway; it only impedes the passage of vehicles which would otherwise pass through the road, so as to make it more crowded, more noisy, more destructive of quiet and privacy to the neighborhood. Moreover, steep grades are bad for the carriage as well as for the cart, and if purposely established, detract from the essential advantages of the neighborhood of the road for villas as well as for anything else.

In proportion as the following rules apply to a road on the outskirts of a town, I think you will perceive that it is sure to become a business thoroughfare: First, it shall lead directly toward the business part of the town. Second, many streets or roads not themselves business thoroughfares shall open upon it. Third, these tributary roads shall approach it upon an angle leading toward the town. (If any of these tributary roads have other and more distant roads opening upon them, the effect will be greater.) Fourth, there shall be no roads, or few roads, running toward town from the same quarter.

To prevent a road from becoming a thoroughfare, these rules must be reversed: First, it shall not lead with special directness toward the town. Second, it shall have few, if any, public streets or roads opening into it, and such as do lead into it shall be short. Third, tributary roads shall not approach it from a direction opposite the town. Fourth, there shall be at no greater distance from it a road or roads running approximately parallel to it, but more directly toward the town.

If the 11th Avenue is extended as far north as practicable and the 10th Avenue is extended through the island in a straight or nearly straight line, and if cross roads can be arranged to enter these avenues at frequent intervals, especially if they can be arranged to lead from all other parts of the territory toward these, and with an inclination toward the town, these avenues will answer all the requirements of the first series of rules. If then a road is laid out on either of the heights on courses at all adapted to the contours of the natural surface—that is to say,

circuitously or indirectly between any two distant points—and
if the public roads opening upon it instead of being tributaries
to it shall be rather outlets from it leading toward the straight
avenues—that is to say, toward the town—then such a road will
answer all the requirements of the last series of rules, for long
roads cannot lead into it from the side opposite the Avenues on
account of the nearness of the rivers.

Thus it will not be difficult at the outset to give a peculiar
character to the heights, favorable to their occupation by villas,
and giving a certain degree of assurance that this occupation
may be permanent. That is to say, business will be perfectly
accommodated without using the heights' roads for any other
purpose than to supply the wants of the residents. Even for this
purpose the principal road would be very little used, for supposing a tradesman's cart were going to a house some distance
from the south end of the heights road, it would be quicker &
easier to drive up 11th Avenue until the diagonal tributary road
were reached, the other end of which, upon the heights road,
was nearest to the house. If, however, the tradesman and others
whose business led them or their wagons often to the heights
should long remain in considerable numbers at a considerable
distance townward, there would be danger that more direct
access would be demanded for them, and that the property
holders of the South part of the district would be tempted, by
the prospect of selling small lots at high prices for stores, to
move for an extension of the 12th Avenue, or that other projects
would get afoot for more direct roads leading into the district
for business purposes.

It is also certain that the road, if laid out as I have supposed,
especially if lined with well kept grounds, would soon be much
resorted to for pleasure driving. This is not to be objected to—
for pleasure driving, so long as its road is not crowded, is not
open to the same objections with the ordinary business street
traffic, and nothing is more likely to enhance the value of the
property for residencies and thus withhold it from other occupation than its being voluntarily visited by great numbers of
people of leisure or possessing the necessary means for pleasure
driving, and its becoming associated in the minds of these with
their pleasure & with the frequent recognition of friends of
their own class.

This very circumstance of its becoming resorted to for plea-sure driving would undoubtedly bring many persons to it who would not be desirable, and would suggest to many the estab-lishment of taverns and shops and stores upon the road, and at any rate the quality of seclusion would diminish. As the land grew more valuable it would be divided into smaller lots for sale, and if you consider the character of the ground, you will see that even if sold in pieces of not less than five acres and a front-age of five hundred feet upon the road, it would in many cases be quite impossible to have a private carriage entrance from the public road, as it would be necessary, in order to get easily up or down the declivity to a comfortable distance for the house to be situated from the road, to turn the approach road so frequently as to entirely destroy any landscape beauty of the grounds. This would only be avoided by the clubbing of neighbors, that is to say by the terrace-arrangement on a large scale. In this case the ground outside of the terrace-road would be virtually common ground, and if fenced off from the terrace road, might for all practical purposes just as well be public-ground.

PARKS: AN ENCYCLOPEDIC VIEW: 1861

Park

PARK: originally in England a portion of a forest enclosed for keeping deer, trapped or otherwise caught in the open forest, and their increase. Grants for this purpose were made by the sovereigns to the nobles. Rich land of an open pastoral charac-ter, with trees sparingly distributed and having broad stretches of greensward pasturage, would naturally be chosen for this purpose; and this character would be intentionally increased by felling a portion of the trees and unintentionally by the effects of the browsing of the confined deer. Hence the word is used to describe this sort of scenery. Parks of this character at length became very numerous. In the reign of Henry VII. there were in Kent and Essex alone 100, each of several miles in circumfer-ence. The earl of Northumberland possessed 21 in three of the northern counties, containing 5,771 head of deer, besides others in the south. At that time, tenants sufficient to cultivate the land being difficult to obtain, parks were enclosed from motives of profit. As the country became more densely occupied and the landlords more numerous, sites for residences were generally taken within the parks for their proprietors. Thus the mansion was originally fitted to the park, not the park to the mansion. Parks at length came to be considered luxurious appendages to the dwellings of the rich, and to be formed and planted for this purpose.

There yet remain a large number of private parks of considerable size in England. There are more than 50 in the single county of Warwick, each from one to 5 miles in diameter. Most of these are open to the public, with some reasonable restrictions, and in many cases the whole people of the neighboring farms and villages have rights of way in footpaths through them. Not unfrequently parish churches are situated in the midst of old private parks. Most of the parks formed and held for the king's use came gradually to be considered in a measure as public grounds. Even earlier than the reign of George II., the use of the park of St. James in the suburbs of London had been so long enjoyed and was so highly valued by the people, that when the queen asked what it would cost to transform it to a garden, suitable to be attached to the palace which fronts upon it, closing it to the public, Horace Walpole says that his father replied: "Only three crowns," meaning a revolution. As England has advanced from feudalism, and the power of the people has increased, the royal parks have more and more been adapted to the wants of the citizens.

Almost every large town in the civilized world now has public pleasure grounds in some form. Those of London are the following: Kensington gardens (262 acres), Hyde park (389), Green park (55), St. James's park (59), Regent's park and Primrose hill (473), Victoria park (248), Greenwich park (185), Battersea park (175), and Kennington park (35). The first four are in a chain (though not at all connected in plan), being partly separated by streets. There are also a great number of small pleasure grounds, termed squares, comprising about 1,200 acres. Besides these there are several large royal parks and grounds in the vicinity of London, much resorted to by its inhabitants; for instance, Windsor (3,800 acres), Hampton Court and Bushy (1,842), Richmond (2,468), and Kew (684). These can all be reached in less than an hour from the central parts of London, as can Epping forest, and several large commons, which are equally pleasure grounds for all the people. Thus, there are of free public pleasure grounds, within the town, above 3,000 acres, and suburban at least 10,000. In addition there are several noblemen's parks which are in a measure open to the public, and the grounds of societies, as the horticultural and the crystal palace, to which the public are admitted on payment of a gate fee. The crystal palace company's grounds comprise 200 acres, laid out by Sir J. Paxton, and 50,000 visitors have been in them at one time. The number ordinarily using the public parks of London has not been accurately ascertained, but on certain Sundays when music has been performed more than 100,000 persons have been counted at the gates of Victoria park in a day. The largest number counted was 130,000 in a day, in the Ring road in Hyde park; it is about 3 m. in length, and varies from 27 to 60 feet wide. The fashionable riding course of London is in the same park, and is popularly called Rotten Row, a corruption of *la route du roi*, or the king's road, its official name; it is 90 feet wide, and a mile in length. Kensington gardens, Green park and St. James's are only skirted by carriage roads and there is but little carriage road in either of the other metropolitan parks. That of Victoria park is but 22 feet wide, and seldom crowded.

Phoenix park at Dublin (1,752 acres) is a fine upland meadow fringed and dotted with trees. In its natural character it is the best public park in the world, but it is badly laid out and badly kept, being much larger than the town requires or than government can afford to maintain for it. Birkenhead park is a piece of ground of 185 acres in a suburb of Liverpool, and is surrounded by villas, the grounds of which connect with it. Though small, it is by its admirable plan the most complete, and for its age the most agreeable park in Europe. It was designed and its construction superintended by Sir Joseph Paxton and Mr. Kemp. Birmingham, Manchester, Bradford, and other manufacturing towns of England have each recently acquired parks by subscriptions of citizens or by joint stock companies formed under the limited liabilities act. To that at Birmingham a charge of a penny is made for entrance, and this affords a fund by which, after the payment for improvements and maintenance, the cost of the land is being rapidly defrayed; as soon as paid for, the admission will be free. At Halifax an admirable park has been formed and given outright to the town by a benevolent citizen. Derby is provided in the same way with an arboretum. Most of the small towns of England have some place of general promenade, as for instance the old city walls and the river bank above the town at Chester, the common and the old castle grounds at Hereford, the river banks at Lincoln, and the cathedral green at Salisbury and Winchester. These consist in each case either of a long, broad, walk, pleasantly bordered and leading to fine views, or a few acres of smooth turf well shaded, where, after church on Sunday or on a fine summer evening, considerable numbers of the largest classes of the people may always be seen in their best presentation of themselves. Most villages in England have a private park near them which the people are allowed to use; when this is not the case, it is rare that even a hamlet is found that has not at least a bit of cricket ground or common, where, on benches under a patriarchal oak or elm, the old people meet to gossip and watch the sports of the vigorous youth.

The old towns of the continent have generally provided themselves with pleasure grounds by outgrowing their ancient borders of wall and moat and glacis, partly razing the wall, filling part of the moat, and so, with more or less skilful arrangement of the materials, making the groundwork of a garden in the natural style. This is done admirably at Frankfort, Leipsic, and Vienna. Elsewhere, simple broad roads bordered with trees have been laid out upon the levelled ramparts, as is the case with the circuitous portion of the boulevards of Paris. The boulevards of Brussels are simply straight streets about 125 feet wide, and with in some cases different classes of communications running through their length, each divided from the other by a row of trees; one, for instance, has on the outside a gravelled walk 21 feet wide, next a macadamized carriage road 36 feet wide, next a soft gravelled horseback road 21 feet wide, next a paved business road 30 feet wide, and then another walk, which is perhaps flagged for rainy weather. Town houses of a good class front upon this boulevard, removed from the too close observation of promenaders by the interposition of small private gardens or forecourts. Brussels also has an old park and two botanical and zoological gardens.

The newly formed Avenue de l'Impératrice at Paris is a

straight promenade, between Paris and the Bois de Boulogne.
It consists of a carriage way 60 feet wide, there being a pad for
saddle horses on one side and a gravelled walk on the other,
each 40 feet wide, and separated from the carriage road by
a simple wooden hand rail; on the outside of all is a slope of
turf planted in the rear with groups of trees and shrubs in the
natural style; back of this, on both sides, a narrow road adapted
to heavy traffic is carried, which also gives access to a line of
detached villas, the grounds of which, being outside of all, form
the background of the view from the promenade.

The Bois de Boulogne is an ancient royal forest of some
2,000 acres, in the suburbs of Paris. The soil is naturally sandy
and poor, and the scenery flat and uninteresting. The trees are
generally thickly grown, stunted, and weak. Several departmental roads—broad, straight, paved wagon ways—pass through it.
Except for its vicinity to Paris, and the refreshing wildness of a
large and entirely untrimmed forest, it offered as late as 1855 but
little to attract a visitor. It was, however, already a favorite resort
of the Parisians, and Napoleon III. saw, in the very neglect to
which it had been abandoned, the opportunity of making one
of those sensations to the frequent succession of which he owes
so much of his popularity with his subjects. The coarse silicious
soil, although unfavorable to fine old trees, is much less costly
to handle than better earth, and its form may be remodelled
with ease and rapidity. Good roads are cheaply graded in it, and
the materials of a sufficiently firm superstructure for so porous
a base may be had on the spot by simply screening its pebbles;
for the same reason, scarcely any artificial drainage, so important in heavy soils, is necessary. There were some large open
meadows in the vicinity reaching to the banks of the Seine. All
these circumstances were skilfully taken advantage of, and the
various opportunities they afforded for the purpose in view were
adroitly combined. Possession was obtained of the meadows,
and roads were cut through the old wood in such a way as to lay
open all that was most agreeable in it, at the same time bringing its close scenery before the visitor in rapid alternation with
the open expanses of the meadows. Long and narrow lakes,
the largest having two long and narrow islands in the midst of
it, were excavated, and the excavated material was thrown into
hillocks along the shores. Thus, with but a very short removal

of the light material, a very rapid change of scenery, and this in views of no inconsiderable distance, was effected.

Rocks of soft stone were then selected at Fontainebleau, split into fragments convenient for transportation, floated down the Seine till opposite their intended site, and then moved to the banks and hillocks of the lakes and put together again in their original form. This, with an addition of artificial rock, made chiefly of water cement, and an admirable planting of evergreens, furnished bits of really picturesque scenery. Each of these pieces of rock-work, however, is only excellent in itself; they are rather studies of rock pinned against the landscape of the wood than naturally incorporated with it. The principal rock-work is much more like an operatic fairy scene than any thing in nature; and as its great size prevents it from being regarded as puerile or grotesque, like Chinese garden scenes, it may be considered to have been conceived in an original style to which the term romantic may be rightly applied. In its way it is admirably done. It contains 58,015 cubic feet of rock, and, with the reservoir of water behind it, cost upward of $30,000. It furnishes a grotto through which during promenade hours a subterranean stream passes, forming at the mouth a cascade 32 feet in breadth and 27 in depth of fall, and using 176 gallons of water each second when in full flow. The water for this cascade, for the lakes, and for the sprinkling of the ground, is chiefly diverted from aqueducts constructed for the general supply of Paris. Some is obtained from the Seine by a steam pump, and an Artesian well is under construction especially for the supply of the wood.

All the above works, commenced in 1855, together with a race course and a great number of rustic architectural structures, the planting of 420,080 trees and shrubs, of which 1,550 were too large to be lifted by hand, and a general improvement of the surface throughout the wood and meadow, had cost, at the end of the year 1858, $1,414,000; and no money ever better effected the object of its expenditure, nothing else done under the auspices of the present emperor being regarded by all classes of the people of Paris with such universal admiration and satisfaction. The Bois de Boulogne contains, with the meadow, 2,155 acres, thus divided: wood, 107 acres; open turf, 675; water, 74; roads, 265, nurseries and flower beds, 71. The length of carriage road

is 86 miles, varying from 24 feet 6 inches to 32 feet 8 inches
in width; of bridle road 7 miles, generally 16 feet in width; of
walks 16 miles, generally from 8 to 10 feet in width. Much of
the wood is still in an unimproved state.

The Bois de Vincennes is a close natural forest on the opposite side of Paris from the Bois de Boulogne, the improvement
of which, in a manner similar to that of the latter, was commenced some years ago, but has been discontinued. It encloses
a vast plain used for heavy gun and shell practice, drilling in field
fortification, and manoeuvres on a large scale.

The garden of the Tuileries with the Champs Élysées forms
the most magnificent urban or interior town promenade in the
world. Its central feature is an avenue of horse chestnuts, which
leads straight from the clock tower of the palace, through the
Place de la Concorde, the Champs Élysées, and the triumphal
arch, to the bridge of Neuilly, a distance of 3 miles. In its centre,
on the Place de la Concorde, stands the obelisk of Luxor, with
fountains near it, and there are at different points other fountains which give brilliancy to its vista. On either side in the
gardens are groves, shrubberies, and parterres of flowers; and
in the Champs Élysées, gay coffee houses, concert halls, and
booths for the exhibition and sale of playthings. The garden of
the Luxembourg is another interior promenade of Paris. It is
also in the formal style, with a central avenue, groves, and flower
beds, music and coffee houses, but is especially notable for its
rose garden; it is about a mile in circumference. Both gardens
are open to the public, and in fine weather an immense crowd
of all classes of the people daily make use of the privilege. At
certain hours thousands of children, attended generally by their
nurses, may be found in them at play.

The interior pleasure grounds at Vienna have been already
mentioned. Its principal rural promenade is the Prater, the chief
feature of which is a straight carriage road, over a mile in length,
with a walk on one side and an equestrian pad on the other.
It contains near the town a great number of coffee houses and
play houses; but being 5 miles in length, considerable portions
are thoroughly secluded and rural. Before the recent improvements of the Bois de Boulogne it was the most frequented
park in the world, all classes of the Viennese, from the emperor
to his most humble subject, resorting to it at certain seasons

almost as if it supplied a necessity of life. The English garden at Munich was laid out under the inspiration of Count Rumford, by the Freiherr von Skell, and its scenery, in the English style, is more agreeable than that of any other large public park on the continent. It is about 4 miles long and half a mile wide. The Thiergarten at Berlin contains over 200 acres of perfectly flat land, chiefly a close wood, laid out in straight roads, walks, and riding paths. Its scenery is uninteresting. The Prussian royal gardens of Sans Souci, Charlottenburg, and Heiligensee are all extensive grounds, the two former in mixed, the last in natural style. The public gardens of Dresden, Stuttgart, Hanover, Brunswick, Baden, Cassel, Darmstadt, Gotha, Weispar, Worlitz, Schwetzingen, Töplitz, Prague, and Hamburg, are all worthy of mention. Coffee houses are important adjuncts of all the German public gardens. The refreshments furnished are generally rather coarse, but of a wholesome sort, and the prices very moderate. Many families habitually resort to them for their evening meal, especially when, as is frequently the case, there is the additional attraction of excellent music furnished by the government. The gardens of Antwerp, the Hague, and Warsaw are also remarkable.

The famous summer gardens of St. Petersburg are not extensive, being but half a mile in length by a quarter in breadth, and formal in style. They contain very fine trees, are rich in statuary (boxed up in winter), and are the most carefully kept public gardens in the world, so that it is said a policeman watches every leaf to catch it, if it falls, before it reaches the ground. In the exceeding luxuriance, freshness, and vigor of the plants and flowers, and in the deep greenness of the turf, this care finds its reward. During the evenings of the short summer the garden is crowded with loungers, and it is here that the ancient annual wife fair is held—marriageable girls, tricked out with every evidence of wealth in trinkets which their parents can manage to obtain, standing for hours together, for the express and avowed purpose of affording an opportunity to those wanting wives to make their selection. The more fashionable promenade of St. Petersburg is in the gardens of Catharinehoff, where on the 1st of May "all St. Petersburg" turns out, and there is an endless procession of carriages headed by that of the emperor. The gardens are full of bowling alleys and restaurants. Many of the islands of the Neva contain pleasant gardens, both public and private, their chief distinguishing characteristic being the abundance of glass and the success with which exotics are cultivated. One of the most remarkable gardens in the world is that of Tzarskoe Selo, in which is the residence of the imperial family, about two hours' ride from St. Petersburg. It consists of about 350 acres of diversified scenery, wooded and open, and contains, besides the palace, temples, banqueting houses, and theatres, a complete village in the Chinese style, a pyramid and obelisks in the Egyptian style, a Turkish mosque, a hermitage, and numerous monuments of military and other achievements. Notwithstanding this great and incongruous variety of artificial objects, beautiful and secluded rural scenery is not wanting. The keeping of the grounds employs 600 men, and costs $80,000 per annum.

Stockholm has a great variety of delightful waterside rural walks, and the chief object of pride with its people is the Djurgard, or deer park, which is a large trace of undulating ground about 3 miles in circumference, containing grand masses of rock and fine old trees. It is beautifully kept. The Haga park, also at Stockholm, is very picturesque in character, and has the peculiarity of natural water communications between its different parts and the city, so that it is much visited in boats. The environs of Copenhagen contain many grounds of public resort, but the notable promenade of the city is the royal deer park (Dyrhave), a noble forest. In the midst is a large green where a great annual fair is held.

In all the Italian cities, the chief public rural resorts are gardens attached to the villas of ancient noble families. The *cascine* of Florence are pastures of the ducal dairy, on the banks of the Arno, passing through which are broad straight carriage drives. These contain little that is attractive within themselves, but command delicious views. At a space where the different roads concentrate, a band of music usually performs at intervals during the promenade hours; and it is the custom for carriages to assemble just previous to the commencement of each piece of music, and rapidly disperse at its end, taking a short drive and returning. The fashionable carriage drive of Rome is on the Pincian hill, which has little natural attraction except in its magnificent distant views. At Naples the fashionable world turns out in carriages upon a broad street called the Riviera di Chiaja, near the bay, but separated from it by the public garden of the Villa Reale, the length of which is about 5,000 feet, breadth 200. The garden is partly in the Italian and partly in the natural style; but with the bay of Naples to look out at, the visitor finds little in its scenery to hold his attention.

Most Spanish and Portuguese towns, and towns founded anywhere in the world by the Spanish and Portuguese, are provided with a place of promenade under formal avenues, to which at certain hours custom brings the ladies in open carriages and gentlemen on foot or horseback.

In the United States there is, as yet, scarcely a finished park or promenade ground deserving mention. In the few small fields of rank hay grasses and spindle-trunked trees, to which the name is sometimes applied, the custom of the promenade has never been established. Yet there is scarcely a town or thriving village in which there is not found some sort of inconvenient and questionable social exchange of this nature. Sometimes it is a graveyard, sometimes a beach or wharf, sometimes a certain part of a certain street; sometimes interest in a literary or a charitable, a military, or even a mercantile, enterprise is the ostensible object which brings people together. But in its European signification the promenade exists only in the limited grounds attached to the capitol and to the "white house" at Washington, and in the yet half-made park of New York. It is a remarkable fact that in the second year after any portion of the roads of the latter are open, and while they are still incomplete and encumbered with the carts of the workmen, and there is but the faintest suggestion of park scenery, the promenade seems to have been fully established as an institution of the city. There are indeed few gayer or better attended promenades in Europe, it having been not at all unusual during the last year (1860) for 2,000 carriages and 10,000 persons on foot to enter the gates of a fine autumn afternoon, while, although 5 miles distant from the city hall, 100,000 have been drawn to it on special occasions.

The central park of New York is being formed on two pieces of ground a little less than a mile apart, one of 331 acres, the other of 166, connected by two narrow strips containing together 137 acres, between which stand two great artificial reservoirs of water for the supply of the city, which occupy 142 acres. The park enclosure will therefore contain 776 acres, to which an addition of 68 is contemplated. The site of the central park, having been chosen on account of the impracticability of extending the ordinary street arrangements of the city over it, presents great obstacles to satisfactory park arrangements. In overcoming these, many peculiarities, by which it will be distinguished from all other parks, must result. The plan, which is still incomplete in details, contains about 9 miles of carriage road, 5 of bridle road, and nearly 20 of walks. A lake, which, with many deep bays, occupies 20 acres, is furnished with pleasure boats in summer; and in winter, its depth being reduced to 4 feet, at which elevation its banks are terraced, forms a skating field to which sometimes as many as 50,000 persons have resorted in a day, furnishing a scene of gayety and intricate motion almost without parallel. Fifty acres in different parts of the park are prepared especially for the recreation of ball playing. A district called the ramble, which can only be entered on foot, consists of a series of walks carried, in constantly changing grades and directions, through 80 acres of ground of very diversified character, the aspect of natural arrangement being everywhere maintained, while the richness of cultivation is added. The profusion of rocky surface, without the barrenness of vegetation which usually accompanies it, renders this very interesting and attractive; and, in the incomplete condition of the rest of the park, it is often inconveniently crowded. At a point where the best interior view of the park is to be had, exterior scenes being obscured, and where the various communications are so arranged that visitors must pass near it, a series of terraces, staircases, and arcades offer temptations and facilities for a large number of people to tarry and so dispose of themselves while resting or lounging as not to be in each other's way. This is effected by a peculiar architectural arrangement, the details of which themselves invite observers to leisurely contemplation.

Mr. F. L. Olmsted and Mr. C. Vaux are the designers of the plan, which was obtained by a remarkable competition, the commissioners appointed to lay out the park having offered premiums amounting to $4,000 for the best, which induced 35 studies to be presented to them, some coming from Europe. It is chiefly remarkable as an effort to reconcile the necessities of a park which is to be the centre of a crowded metropolis with scenery, the predominating quality of which shall be rural and in some parts even rudely picturesque. Its purely constructive features are for this purpose kept below the general plane of sight, and to some extent are completely subterranean. Its artistic intentions are described in a recent report of a legislative committee to be, "in the first place, to obtain large unbroken surfaces of smooth meadow-like ground wherever the natural obstacles to this mode of treatment are to be overcome, even by heavy expenditure. The immediate borders of these spaces are planted in a manner to hide or disguise any incongruous quality in the grounds beyond. The rocky and broken surface which originally characterized the whole site, however, admits of the application of this evident preference of the designers to but a small portion of the grounds thus far finished; and elsewhere its capabilities for picturesque effects have been revealed. The different classes of communications are so arranged that, by a peculiar system of arched passages, it never becomes necessary for a person on foot to cross the surface of the carriage roads, or the horseman's track, or the horseman to cross the carriage roads, though he may ride upon them if he prefer."

Philadelphia, Baltimore, Brooklyn, Hartford, and Detroit have each recently taken steps to obtain a park. In Philadelphia some fine old villa grounds, beautifully situated on the Schuylkill near the Fairmount water works, have been purchased. These contain 128 acres, upon which operations adapting them to public purposes have been commenced, and it is intended to add to them 80 acres on the opposite bank of the river, the two sections to be connected by bridges. The alterations to be made are designed and superintended by Messrs. Sidney and Adams. There are fine trees already on the grounds, and they possess many very valuable advantages in position, character of soil, and beauty of natural surface. At Hartford a competition of plans was held, but the committee having the matter in charge were dissatisfied with all that were offered, and undertook to form one for themselves which should avoid all the objections they found to each of them. The result was an ill-digested design, badly fitted to a rather difficult piece of ground. At Baltimore, Mr. Daniels, who had previously laid out a number of rural cemeteries, has been employed to adapt a very beautiful old private park to public purposes. The Brooklyn park commission is acting under the advice of Lieut. E. L. Viele, formerly of the U.S. army, but has not yet adopted a plan. Mr. Olmsted has been consulted with reference to the Detroit park, but nothing is yet determined in regard to it. Near St. Louis private munificence has formed and opened to the public a botanic garden. The common of Boston is a piece of undulating ground of 48 acres, in most of which trees have been planted without method, and a great many walks laid out with no other purpose than to offer short cuts through it from every entrance in all directions. It has a few fine trees, and the Beacon street mall, a broad avenue walk by the side of one of its boundaries, has a unique though perfectly simple character. The old public grounds of Cambridge, New Haven, and other towns often exhibit the beauty and value which trees acquire with age, when planted with ever so little art. These grounds are matters of town pride, and are assumed to have great value to the communities which possess them; but they are inconveniently arranged, badly kept, and bear a similar relation to a well designed and well kept park that a wigwam does to a well appointed mansion. Savannah has a great number of small public squares, some few of them laid out and planted with taste, but most of them mere untidy spaces, too small for a walk or any purpose of recreation, except playing a game of marbles, and which apparently serve no purpose but to increase the distances between the houses of the town and enlarge its geographical size. At the Bonaventura cemetery, near Savannah, a natural assemblage of old live oaks, hung with moss, forms one of the finest scenes of druidic beauty in the world.

Landscape gardening in the United States has hitherto been chiefly directed to the improvement of naturally wooded scenery, and that on a small scale, yet in many instances, of which the best are on the banks of the Hudson, with admirable results. Publicly the art has been chiefly directed, also, to the improvement of naturally wooded, picturesque scenery in the formation of rural cemeteries. The motive of economizing space for graves, the association of funeral solemnity with shade, gloom, and seclusion, and the custom of yielding the planting of each allotment of ground for a family to the caprice or confined local purpose of its purchaser, have in these cases rendered the application of true art scarcely possible. Yet, though our rural cemeteries invariably contain much that is hideous, particularly in iron and marble, and are entirely without breadth or repose of scenery, many of them are very beautiful; and the older ones especially, although yet in their youth of the best tree life, exhibit the wealth of the country in elements for landscape art. The rural cemetery, which should, above all things, be a place of rest, silence, seclusion, and peace, is too often now made a place not only of the grossest ostentation of the living but a constant resort of mere pleasure seekers, travellers, promenaders, and loungers; and this indicates, as much as any thing else, the need that exists in every town and village for a proper pleasure ground.

The most notable pleasure grounds of remote antiquity of which we have any clear account, were those formed by Nebuchadnezzar, at Babylon, to satisfy the longing for picturesque scenery of his home-sick Median bride. If we credit the accounts of Diodorus and Strabo, nothing has been attempted in modern times to compare in magnificence with what was there achieved. The ancient Persian gardens seem to have been designed with the same motives which rule in those of modern Turkey. The intention in these is to secure a luxurious repose, which is to be accomplished by establishing a sense of security and privacy; hence "the wall about" is an important feature, and is not hidden from view. Trees are planted in rows, in order that the wind may draw currents between them. Small fountains of water or streams of running water, to increase the sensation and association of coolness, are required. Flowers are cultivated for perfume and beauty. Inducements to exercise are not desired. Distant views, which would be calculated to distract the mind from the present enjoyments, are not sought for. The proprietor commonly proceeds, on entering his garden, immediately to a seat near its centre, where he remains until he is ready to leave. Enclosures were sometimes made by the Persians for keeping wild beasts, and aviaries were common. Terebinthinate evergreens were esteemed a luxury.

The Greeks derived their ideal of gardens from the Persians, and seldom attempted any essential improvements upon it; which leads Lord Bacon to remark that "men came to build stately sooner than garden finely, as if gardening were the greater perfection." Athens had its public park, however, called *Academia*, which in the height of its civilization seems to have wanted nothing that we should deem essential for the purpose, considering the climate and the different customs of the people. Originally a rugged piece of ground, it was laid out by Cimon, who formed pleasant walks, introduced a stream of water, and planted groves. Facilities were designedly offered for robust exercises as well as for contemplative recreation. At the entrance the first altar, dedicated to Love, was placed. Scattered through the grounds were statues and monuments to the most worthy citizens. The best evidences of Athenian civilization are connected with this park.

When Rome was in her glory, her citizens were proud of their country houses and pleasure grounds. The sites for these were chosen with the greatest care, and shaped elaborately in stately terraces about the mansion. The grounds were profusely furnished. Pliny's Tusculan villa was provided with a court for chariot exercise, and another for horseback riding; with terrace walks suitable for the general assemblage of his guests, and retired paths for those disposed for solitude. In the grounds were an enclosure for wild animals, an apiary, a snailery, and a dormice house. There was also a flower garden, with fountains flowing from marble vases. Adjoining the house proper, the park was strictly formal and symmetrical with the architecture; the walks were lined with box and plane trees sheared to the shape of walls, and in some parts trained in fantastic figures. These have been generally considered as mere puerile conceits, but no one who has thoroughly felt the peculiar charm of Italian landscapes can fail to comprehend how they may have been used to add to the enchantment of the view of which they furnished the foreground; and it is to be remarked that Pliny describes at length how his seats and windows, even his bath and place of rest, were arranged with express reference to the best distant views over the Campagna. It is then probable that the shearing of his trees was intended to make them subordinate to the highest beauty of the natural scenery beyond his own possessions. This must be assumed, or we are left to suppose that a style of landscape improvement which was the foundation of all essays in rural art in Europe till the earlier part of the last century, and which had its origin in the golden age of Roman architecture and in the closest connection with it, was itself without any basis of art.

We have no need to trace its lapses and revivals, its advances and degradations. As practised in England, at least, it had long lost the slightest element of the artistic feeling, which still in Italy it cannot be denied to possess. This is shown in the opinion of Sir William Temple that the best example of gardening at home or abroad was that at Moor Park, a garden which, according to Walpole, would have lost none of its beauty if designed by one "who had never stirred out of Holborn"—in other words, if utterly dissevered from all sentiment of nature. The real artistic qualities of the ancient style were thus entirely overlooked, and its mere excrescences and frivolities had come to be considered its essential features. In Addison's ridicule of these ("Spectator," No. 414), and in his praise of a shrubbery which Bridgman, the court gardener, had formed out of some old gravel pits in the palace grounds at Kensington, the first evidence of the practical revival of art in gardening is found. It is supposed that the earliest innovations upon the fashionable style were suggested by travellers' descriptions of the somewhat grotesque imitations of nature which for centuries had been the delight of the Chinese in their gardens. They were made very cautiously, usually as a mere incident of nature within a formal garden. Years after Addison's paper in the "Spectator" appeared, it was considered a bold eccentricity which carried the Serpentine through a corner of Kensington gardens with shores aligning with nothing in their vicinity. The first garden in which formality was attempted to be laid aside, and the intricacy of nature aimed at, is believed to have been that of Pope at Twickenham. Addison's garden, laid out also in defiance of the fashion by himself, and still existing near Rugby, is informal without being picturesque.

The first man to attempt to form really a landscape in England was Kent, who had been a student of art in Italy, and who on his return was recommended by Lord Burlington to paint the ceilings at Stowe, and afterward as an architect, in which capacity he first gave his attention, as all architects should, to the connection of his buildings with the landscapes of their vicinity. Naturally enough, seizing in his design upon that which was most important, he swept away the rubbish which now represented the ancient style, and undertook the creation of scenery upon the ground at his command on the same principles that he would select a subject in nature for his canvas. The new style soon became the fashion, but like all fashions it was too generally adopted with little appreciation of the real basis it had in art. To avoid "three trees in a line," to form meaningless slopes, tame rivers, and monotonous groves, was not a difficult task even to the old gardeners, whose box Venuses and hornbeam hedgehogs had become dead stock. A host of servile followers after Kent supplied the demand for change which rapidly extended to almost every country seat of importance in the kingdom; and in their haste to demonstrate the landscape capabilities of the ground which they were called to improve, too often the destruction of noble avenues and terraces was involved, the value of which when rightly placed had probably been disregarded by Kent merely out of disgust with their general misplacement.

In the latter part of the 18th century, landscape gardening, in the hands of most of its professors, had thus well nigh again become a mechanical business, instead of the liberal art which Kent had made it. The ground was made to suit a plan the features of which were constantly repeated, instead of a plan being made to meet the suggestions of the ground. "Most of our large gardens," says a writer of the day, "are laid out by some general undertaker [contractor], who introduces the same objects at the same distances in all." Thus, except where proprietors became artists themselves, talent was not demanded nor sustained, and the monotonous repetitions, the dulness, and the common marks of the respectability of fashion characterized nearly all the gardening of the time, until poetic and artistic genius again combined to criticize and create, as in the time of Pope, Addison, and Kent. In the various "Picturesque Tours" of Gilpin, and the voluminous "Essays on the Picturesque" by Sir Uvedale Price, the true principles of art applicable to the creation of scenery were laboriously studied and carefully defined. Shenstone, Mason, and Knight, by their poems, materially aided the revivification of the art. In more recent times the good service of Repton, Loudon, Paxton, Kemp, our own Downing, and other artists and writers on the subject during the present century, merits warm acknowledgment. Downing's works especially should be in every village school library.

The natural style had soon after its adoption in England

become fashionable on the continent, and writers there treating of it had even exercised some influence on the improvement of taste in England. An artistic sense is more generally perceptible in the detail of grounds on the continent than in those of England itself. In all close scenery, as well as in vistas, peeps, and what a landscape painter would consider "good bits" for sketches, the continental gardeners are often faultless; but the formation of entirely artificial complete landscapes, or the improvement of broad scenes throughout their whole scope and to remote distances, all in imitation of nature, is to this day the peculiar art of England.

AFTER BULL RUN: JULY 1861

To Mary Perkins Olmsted

Sanitary Commission, Washington, D.C.
Treasury Building, July 29, 1861

Beloved!

We are in a frightful condition here, ten times as bad as anyone dare say publickly. I think we are getting better, but are also growing nearer a crisis—an attack. Why Beauregard does not attack I can not imagine unless he be—no general. I have not been to bed since I have been here without a strong apprehension that I should be waked by cannonading. The demoralization of a large part of our troops is something more awful than I ever met with.

There is but one Sanitary measure to be thought of now & that is discipline. We want numbers of fresh men for the moral effect on ourselves and on the enemy; but practically, for action, numbers will only increase confusion, until they are a thousandfold better disciplined than the most of those now here or than those who were spoiled for soldiers at Bull Run.

I will have a Report on the subject soon.

Write to me and make the best of our affairs. I could not flinch from this now if it starved us all to stay.

Yours.

Tell all our friends to stiffen themselves for harder times than we have yet thought of. Unless McLellan is a genius as well as a general & unless he becomes a military dictator & rules over our imbecile government, we should & must have a revolution before we can do anything with the South.

You will see from this that I am overwhelmed. I have suffered intense humiliation. Our Commission can do something and I from my position in it can do something to set public opinion in the right direction & to overcome in some details the prevailing inefficiency & misery. You would not have me do less than I can.

I remain pretty well, having got off my cold. I need not confess that I am working harder & longer than is good for me & have been in want of sleep. I am doing well under the circumstances. Many regiments are not a mob; they are parts of a disintegrated herd of sick monomaniacs. They start and turn pale at the breaking of a stick or the crack of a percussion cap— at the same time they are brutal savages. That is the meaning of "demoralization." It is a terrific disease. They are fast recovering. Most may now be called recoverd of those that remain. Thank God, McEntee escaped the disgrace of Bull's Run. What it was will never be told publickly. Human nature has seldom showed itself so degraded.

ANATOMY OF A ROUT: SEPTEMBER 1861

FROM *Report on the Demoralization
of the Volunteers*

GENERAL SUMMARY

From these investigations, combined with information derived from official reports of the generals commanding; from published statements in rebel as well as loyal journals; from previous investigations of the inspectors of the Sanitary Commission as to the condition of the troops, and from other sources, it is manifest that our army, previous to and at the time of the engagement, was suffering from want of sufficient, regularly-provided, and suitable food, from thirst, from want (in certain cases) of refreshing sleep, and from the exhausting effects of a long, hot, and rapid march, the more exhausting because of the diminution of vital force of the troops due to the causes above enumerated. They entered the field of battle with no pretence of any but the most elementary and imperfect military organization, and, in respect of discipline, little better than a mob, which does not know its leaders. The majority of the officers had, three months before, known nothing more of their duties than the privates whom they should have been able to lead, instruct, and protect. Nor had they, in many cases, in the meantime, been gaining materially, for they had been generally permitted, and many had been disposed, to spend much time away from their men, in indolence or frivolous amusement, or dissipation.

It appears that many were much exhausted on reaching the field of battle, but that, supported by the excitement of the occasion, they rallied fairly, and gradually drove the opposing forces from Sudley Spring to the lower ford, and from the lower ford to beyond the Stone bridge and the Warrenton road; that, at this time, (half-past three,) when congratulated by superior officers, and congratulating themselves on having achieved a victory, and when having repulsed reinforcements sent from the extreme right of the enemy to support their retreating columns, they were just relaxing their severely-tried energies, there appeared in the distance "the residue" of the forces of General Johnston, (see McDowell's report, Dr. Nott's letter to a Mobile paper, and correspondence of Charleston Mercury,) a single brigade (Elzey's) coming up from the Manassas Gap Junction railroad, marching at double-quick to engage our troops at the right who had been hotly fighting unrelieved by reserves during the day. This brigade, joined with the two regiments of Kershaw and Cash, "turned the tide of battle." (See in Richmond Dispatch, July 29, statement "of a distinguished officer who bore a conspicuous part on the field of battle on the 21st of July.")

Our troops, ignorant of the fact that they had been contending against and repulsing the combined forces of Beauregard and Johnston; and believing that this inconsiderable remnant of Johnston's forces, which they now saw approaching, to be his entire column; and feeling their inability, without rest or refreshment, to engage an additional force of fresh troops nearly equal in number to those with whom they had been contending during the day,—commenced a retreat, not very orderly, but quite as much so, at first, as had been the advance in which they had driven back the forces of the enemy. Their (nominal) leaders, who too often had followed them in battle, were, in many cases, not behind them on retreat.

As they retired, however, a sense of disintegration began to pervade their ranks; each ceased to rely on his comrade for support, and this tendency was augmented by the upturned wagons blocking the road, which served to completely break the imperfect columns.*

The reports of the inspectors give no evidence that the panic infected the extreme left, or the reserves, to any sensible degree. It was uncontrollable only with the troops on the extreme right, among whom it originated. Many at the centre and the left were surprised when the order came to retreat, and for a time considered it as merely an order to change position in view of a still further general advance. Some officers state that they "warmly remonstrated"—"too warmly, perhaps"—when they received the order to retire.

The returns of the inspectors are not conclusive on this point; but from the result of subsequent specific inquiries by Mr. Elliott and the Secretary, it can be stated with confidence that indications of terror or great fear were seen in but a comparatively very small part of the retreating force. Most trudged along, blindly following (as men do in any mob) those before them, but with reluctance, and earnest and constant expressions of dissatisfaction and indignation, while no inconsiderable number retained, through all the length of the privation and discomfort of their dreary return to Washington, astonishing cheerfulness and good humor, and were often heard joking at their own

---

* From a consideration of all the evidence, Mr. Elliott states that he has himself formed the following opinion:

"The *retreat* was immediately due mainly to *delusion*, on the part of the troops of the Union, respecting the force of the enemy, especially of the reserves advancing from the railroad to engage our forces, combined with extreme physical exhaustion; that the *rout* was due, in part at least, to the too near approach of the wagons of the volunteers to the field of battle, thereby dividing their columns on retreat; and that the sense of disintegration, and consequent *panic*, (so far as it existed,) was due to want of discipline, to physical exhaustion, and to want of all provision for securing an orderly retreat, combined."

misfortunes, and ridiculing the inefficiency of their officers. The Germans of the reserve were frequently singing. None of the reserves were in the slightest degree affected by the panic, and their general expression with reference to the retreat was one of wonder and curiosity.

The reserve, nevertheless, suffered much from fatigue, and subsequently exhibited most decided demoralization.

The Commission met in Washington on the 26th of July, and most of its members suffered the pain of witnessing something of the general condition of the army at that time. As there are no means of recording it with exactness, it is important to the purpose of this report that the impression then received should be in a measure recalled, analyzed, and traced to its foundations.

A victorious enemy was known to be within ten miles of the capital, and was presumed to be cautiously advancing. Never could the occasion for military vigor, energy, promptitude, and thoroughness of action seem to be greater. It was the belief that the utmost and best directed efforts of every one who had to do directly or indirectly with the army should be concentrated at Washington; that, without previous concert, brought the majority of the Commission thither. Arriving, as they did, soon after daybreak, and passing from the railroad station toward the President's House, the aspect of the streets was in the strongest possible contrast to that which would be imagined of a city placed by a stern necessity under the severe control of an effective military discipline. Groups of men wearing parts of military uniforms, and some of them with muskets, were indeed to be seen; but, upon second sight, they did not appear to be soldiers. Rather they were a most wo-begone rabble, which had, perhaps, clothed itself with the garments of dead soldiers left in a hard-fought battle-field. No two were dressed completely alike; some were without caps, others without coats, others without shoes. All were alike excessively dirty, unshaven, unkempt, and dank with dew. The groups were formed around fires made in the streets, and burning boards wrenched from citizens' fences. Some were still asleep, at full length in the gutters and on doorsteps, or sitting on the curbstone, resting their heads against the lamp-posts. Others were evidently begging for food at house-doors. Some appeared ferocious, others only sick and dejected; all excessively weak, hungry, and selfish. They were mainly silent, and when they spoke, it humiliated a man to hear them. No pack of whining, snarling, ill-fed, vagabond street dogs in an oriental city ever more strongly produced the impression of forlorn, outcast, helpless, hopeless misery. There was no apparent organization; no officers were seen among them, seldom even a non-commissioned officer. At Willards' hotel, however, officers swarmed.

They, too, were dirty and in ill-condition; but appeared indifferent, reckless, and shameless, rather than dejected or morose. They were talking of the battle, laughing at the incidents of the retreat, and there was an evident inclination among them to exaggerate everything that was disgraceful. Since they had not a victory to boast of, they made the defeat as dramatic and notable as possible. They seemed to be quite unconscious of personal responsibility for the results of the battle.

"Where is your regiment?" one was asked.

"Completely demoralized, sir; completely demoralized."

"Where is it now?"

"All disorganized—all disorganized."

"But where are the men?"

"I'm told that there are two or three hundred of them together somewhere near the Capitol, but I have not seen them yet since the battle."

A captain sat with his feet on the window grating, smoking; a man outside said to him, "Captain, there are two hundred of our men just beyond the Long Bridge, and they have not had anything to eat to-day."

"Where's the Quartermaster?"

"I don't know: there isn't any officer there."

"They don't want me, do they?"

"They have not had anything to eat to-day, and there's no officer to get it for them."

"Well, it's too bad;" and the Captain continued smoking, and ten minutes afterward had not put his feet to the floor. It was not till a Provost Guard of regulars drove these officers out of the town, almost at the point of the bayonet, that they seemed capable of entertaining any purpose of duty. As to the men, it was nothing but starvation, in many cases, that brought them back to theirs. In how many ways the humiliating confession of cowardice was heard; how piteously the desire was expressed to go home; how distrustful the officers were of the men; how universally those who did not acknowledge cowardice and homesickness were disinclined to resume duty, or to continue under the same officers as before, cannot be statistically told. It was enough to establish the conviction that the army was, for the time being, quite broken up and useless. For a time it seemed as if there was no government, civil or military, at the seat of government. The newspapers re-echoed the words of the Secretary of War, "the Capital is safe;" because, as every one understood, the Capital could be defended with no spirit, confidence, or resolution, even by the large body of soldiers in it who had not directly participated in the battle. To re-establish in them some degree of confidence was the first necessity. With this the Capital would be safe. But this was wanting. All power of exercising confidence, all respect, every social sentiment seemed to have been for the time lost to them. This but feebly indicates the nature of that condition of the government forces which was generally denominated their "demoralization," and which was considered the direct result of the battle of Bull Run.

It did not seem sufficiently accounted for by the simple facts of the battle as generally related; that is to say, by an advance against the enemy, which was everywhere successful, until a check to the right wing caused with some a panic, and led to a general discontinuance of the aggressive movement, both armies resuming the position held previously, the enemy having suffered much the most, as was then generally believed, and, so far as yet appears, truly.

Considering that it was desirable that its real causes should be more clearly ascertained and defined, the investigation was set on foot, the results of which, to the present time, have now been laid before the Commission. Regarded as an attempt to find in the minor circumstances attending the battle adequate causes for the condition of the army which succeeded it, the investigation has not succeeded. Should it warrant the conviction, however, that no sufficient cause of the demoralization was to be found in the circumstances immediately attending the battle, it may be that a further investigation would be induced, which would yield results even more important than were originally anticipated.

The Secretary has executed the duty which he had proposed

to himself, in the analysis of the facts of the battle directly bearing on the question. The duty of a complete exploration of the causes of the demoralization of the army in July he trusts will be assumed by a committee of the Commission.

That there is a broad field for such an exploration yet remaining to be entered, and that it will involve the consideration of many questions, a satisfactory decision of which will have a direct and important bearing upon the welfare of the country, the Secretary is prepared to give his reasons for believing. In doing so, he will not attempt to reserve an expression of his own judgment upon the questions which naturally arise, because it will be found that some of these involve questions of his official duty, and in regard to which it is proper that the Commission should be informed how he is impelled to act; for which reason also he desires, as a constituent member of the Commission, to be allowed to present views to which he has no assurance that the Commission is prepared to assent.

"TO SEVER THESE SINEWS": NOVEMBER 1861

To the Editor of the New-York Times

THE REBELLION

How to Reason with the South—
How to Deal with the Slavery Question

Washington, Thursday, November 29, 1861
Those who say that the people of the South can never be made to submit to the Government are either repeating a cant phrase without meaning anything more than that their personal sympathies are with the rebels, or they forget what a different thing is the submission of a people struggling against a cruel despotism, from the submission of a people merely unwilling, as a matter of feeling, to return to an old habit of self-government, under a few general laws, in the making of which they themselves were consulted, and had a fair and honest part, and under which they have for many years enjoyed great freedom and light taxation. The case of the Irish, the Hindoos, the Poles,

and the Hungarians, was very different from this, and if, after long years of desperate resistance, their submission to a foreign force seems to have been somewhat reluctant and imperfect, it forms not the slightest ground for assuming that our own misguided citizens will never accept peace under their old and honored flag, as soon as certain delusions by which they are still influenced have been dispelled.

The rebellion is justified at the South under the name of revolution. Thousands of men are fighting for it now, who, a year ago, denounced the movements which initiated it, as criminal. What justifies a revolution, and what makes rebellion criminal? Success, or the prospect of success. It was confidence in the military force of the Slave States, as compared with the Free, then, that turned the scale, and alone made rebellion formidable. "Revolution" sinks to "rebellion" again when this confidence is destroyed, and thousands now fighting for it will then again denounce persistence in it as criminal.

One of the delusions which has led to the false estimate of the comparative power of the rebels and of the Government, which prevails at the South, is that of the anarchical condition of the Free States, and the military feebleness of the Government so far as it is dependent on them. The habit of using arbitrary authority reduces the capacity of sympathy, and our power of understanding men's motives and characters is proportionate to our ability to sympathize with them. The state of society in the Free States is very different from that in the South, and there is nothing to which men adapt their habits of thought with more difficulty than social conditions to which they are unaccustomed. Of this, the English writers, in their comments on our affairs, give no infrequent evidence in their habitual assumption that there necessarily must be something in this country corresponding, though in a diluted form, to their gentry and peasantry, with an intermediate stratum, poor relation to the one, and jealous, contemptuous, timorous neighbor to the other. They cannot get the notion out of their minds, that, in some way, class interests are acting one against another, or, one in combination with another, in all our politics. Much less easily can the Southerners be freed from the idea that where there is so much industry there must be a master class and a servile class, the one more or less wisely caring for government as the safeguard of property, the other regarding government inimically, as a social power by means of which they are kept under control, and which it is consequently their interest to weaken as much as possible. The intelligent slaveholder appreciates even less than the Englishman, therefore, that deep-seated, unconscious and instinctive conservatism, formed in the habits of a people where the status of a man is never felt to be fixed, which in moments of peril places a sudden feminine strength at the disposal of the agents of Government, such as no mere ruler over a land ever possessed, and which is the natural compensation of that very dependence of the government upon the will of the governed, that renders it powerless for many purposes readily assumed by rulers of weaker nations, more pompously powerful and ostentatiously dignified.

The thick habit, however, under which the slaveholders have been led to doubt and defy the strength of the gathering tempest of our Northern loyalty, is already worn with a conscious awkwardness under their recent experiences. This is plainly shown in the disgraceful falsehoods to which Davis, Beauregard, and others who labor to control public opinion at the South, are driven; in their efforts to maintain the impression that the Union army has been mainly formed of hireling foreigners, and that it is incited only by lust and greed. This new delusion, if it prevails at all, is far less formidable than that which it is intended to fortify, namely: that diffusion of power is absence of power; diffusion of patriotism, want of patriotism; and that weakness of the agents of Government is equivalent to weakness of Government itself.

The cupidity and baseness of England is another delusion which is being slowly relinquished at the South. England has ever talked little and done much. Now she talks much because, though the necessarily slow process of our war costs her some, she has the heart to do nothing to establish a nation on a basis which, above all other things, she hates. The blockade is no longer laughed at in the South.

A minor delusion has been that ships could do little against shore batteries. Hatteras and Port Royal have effectually dispelled that, as the evacuation of Tybee satisfactorily informs us.

The grandest delusion of all, industriously fostered by many public teachers of the South, and discountenanced during the last twenty years by few, until, absurd as it may seem to us, a generation has almost grown in its habit, is, that slaves are a source of military strength to those who possess them. Till now, the war has been mainly carried on by Government as if it had been for our interest, as perhaps it has been, to strengthen this delusion. While thousands of negroes have been employed to resist the enforcement of the laws, all use of them in sustaining their supremacy has been as much as possible avoided.

In the conduct of the slaves at Port Royal, if our information can be trusted, the South is presented with the first tangible evidence of the *essential weakness of this main prop of the rebellion*. Government had offered no inducement for the slaves to desert, had offered them no protection. There is in all the South no other district in which the slaves were less likely to be intelligently informed, or where they could as easily have been deceived as to the motives of the attacking force. The fact, therefore, that when the forts were taken, the slaves refused to withdraw from the vicinity with their masters, and that numbers of them were shot down in the vain attempt to prevent their falling into our hands, is of more value in demonstrating to the people of the South the futility of the struggle into which they have been inveigled than all else that has been as yet accomplished by our arms.

Negroes in the rebel States are property, and, as property, are the very sinews of the rebellion. The occurrences at Port Royal indicate that, at least whenever our forces penetrate the rebel States, it is in our power to sever these sinews, and by so much destroy the strength of the rebellion. For the sake of our friends in Kentucky and Maryland, we may spend a few hundred millions before we systematically use this power, but we cannot avoid estimating its value and availability. Nor can the rebels flatter themselves that we shall yield them independence before we have made use of it.

The use of slaves as property depends on the degree in which their services are controllable. This control is never perfect; if it was, there would have been no need of the whip, no need of the Fugitive Slave law, no need of discountenancing the instruction of slaves in the common arts of writing and reading. There is always more or less of what the overseers call "ugliness," or resistance to control, to be overcome and to be guarded against. On a large plantation some of "the people" are almost always "out," or "in the swamp;" that is to say, they have, through insubordination, carelessness, or sheer indolence, or disinclination to work, incurred the prospect of punishment and have hid themselves away to avoid it. In doing this they have no hope before them of attaining permanent freedom, but only a respite from Slavery. They reason, as has often been explained to me, that whenever they are caught or choose to return, the punishment they will receive for running away cannot be much heavier than that they would have received for the previous offence, without injuring their value as property. They would use the proverb, "It is as well to be *paddled* for a sheep as for a lamb." If even a remote chance of escaping punishment altogether is seen by the slave, he often seizes it with a spirit, which, in a slave, is wonderful and admirable. It not unfrequently appears in the advertisements of Mississippi, that a runaway is supposed to be "making for the Free States," hundreds of miles distant; and I have seen a fugitive in Mexico who had felt his weary way thither, at what enormous risks I need not say, clear from Louisiana. If Government should take possession of certain districts of the South, or even mere fortified points at convenient distances around the planting region, as at Wilmington, Hilton Head, Fernandina, Pensacola, Bayou Calcasieu, Galveston, San Antonio, Fort Smith and the mountain passes of Kentucky and Tennessee, and should offer at all of these a safe harbor for all negroes, there can be no doubt that slave property throughout the South would become rapidly less controllable than it is at present and as rapidly less valuable.

That a knowledge of these asylums would soon reach every plantation is quite certain. I have often been told by planters in the interior that information of important National events had reached them through the negroes long before it came by mail.

It is not to be supposed, however, that all the slaves would at once run to obtain the protection of these sanctuaries of freedom, but while thousands would do so, all would have such a resort in view and be affected by it in their daily conduct, and thus sensibly deteriorate in value. Not only would they fail in their accustomed tasks in the fields; they would, while still remaining on the plantations, pilfer and waste and carelessly and mischievously damage much other property besides that of their own labor. A hostile force would thus invade the enemy in his very stronghold. With every negro who ran away and escaped immediate pursuit, the tendency to disregard control among those remaining would increase in strength.

The need to call back from the army every active, strong, and resolute man would be less imperative for the pursuit of the actual fugitive than for the overseeing of those of feebler enterprise who remained behind.

Organized insurrections and St. Domingo massacres are not, in my judgment, to be apprehended under any circumstances. The slaves are neither as savage, nor as civilized as those who entertain this fear suppose. But, whatever danger of this kind there may be, there will be less, if a prospect is offered those more discontented, of escaping from their masters by flight, and the measure that will present such a prospect to them will set on foot a quiet and inactive method of exhausting the effective resources of the rebellion, which will increase and become more and more irresistible, the longer all other methods of attack are incompletely successful.

It is unquestionably in the power of our Government to do all that I have suggested; and probably at a tenth of the cost of our present operations, such posts could be constantly held, and the fugitives reaching them be safely and humanely cared for. Suppose we are unsuccessful in our advances into the interior of the South, while this depleting and demoralizing process continued, and only otherwise successful in resisting invasion of the Free States and in maintaining the blockade, with what confidence of success would the rebellion continue? Where would be the military strength founded in Slavery?

But the instigators of the rebellion say, that they can make their slaves fight for them, and several negro regiments are reported to be now enrolling. In the construction of their earthworks, military roads, &c., it is known that the rebels employ many slaves. The African nature inclines to the pomp and circumstance of war, and yields more readily and completely to discipline than any other in this country. By taking advantage of the disposition of the negro to imitate, and where practicable, to emulate, the whites, and by working upon his vanity and love of approbation he can doubtless be rapidly brought to a high condition of drill and discipline. But he would be a far better soldier on our side than on theirs. On theirs it is impossible that he should not be affected by the constant assertion of the Southern camps, that the Lincolnites are fighting for the negro. On ours it is equally impossible that he should not be affected by the knowledge that to surrender would be to him death, or hopeless Slavery. Placing him under martial discipline, is not offering encouragement to the horrors of a servile war, but exactly the contrary. It is preventing a servile, by substituting a civilized war. There are many military duties to be undertaken in which negroes, properly trained and officered, would be far better than white soldiers. Even if the rebels had not set us the example of them, the provision against which they hypocritically cry out in advance, for forming regiments of their black deserters to be turned back threateningly upon them, is not merely a justifiable act of war, but is in all respects a humane and honorable one.

The best reason for it, however, is the effect it would have in aiding the removal of the delusion out of which the war has partly grown, namely: that the peculiar property which the South holds gives the right of revolution to a wicked rebellion, by supplying peculiar means of offence and defence. Whatever will prove to the Southerners that the advantages they suppose themselves to hold are common to all who enter their territory in arms, will not merely tend to make the war shorter and cheaper, but will also tend to enforce the necessity for a policy in peace upon them, the neglect of which hitherto has been the foundation of all their political troubles.

YEOMAN

"FOR THE ARMY OF A COMMON COUNTRY":
FEBRUARY 1862

To George Frederic Magoun

6 February 1862

To the Rev. Geo. Magoun:
Secy Iowa Army Sanitary Commission
Sir:

I yesterday received your favor of January 28th, in which you suggest that a connection should be formed between your Association and the Sanitary Commission. You do not state the object to be gained by the connection, nor indicate any advantage which would arise from it. As there will be sufficient time for letters to be exchanged between us before the next meeting of the Commission, at which it will give me pleasure to propose any plan of connection which you may think desirable, I should be glad to hear further from you on this point.

You will excuse me for reminding you of a few circumstances which must influence the Commission in whatever action it may conclude to take.

Our loyal fellow countrymen in Tennessee are suffering persecution, their crops and cattle have been taken for the support of the rebel hordes, their houses burned, their stores plundered. Sick and weary, thousands hide in the mountains biding their time. How they support life, God knows. They certainly have nothing to spare, and though many of them have broken through the defensive lines of the enemy, if they had to spare, it would not be possible to send their goods where they are more wanted than they are at this moment in Tennessee. But of those who have escaped, the strong and healthy men to the number of two or three thousand, are fighting our battles in Kentucky side by side with your Iowan heroes. Those who are not strong and well fill the homes of our noble and hard tried brethren of "the dark and bloody ground," and these have enough to do to provide for their necessities.

Virginia, in like manner ravaged by War, furnishes seven thousand men to fight the battles of our common country.

This Commission received the other day seventeen thousand

dollars in hard cash, collected in one of the states of New England. It has received within two months in hospital stores, from the same state, sufficient supplies for ten times as many men as that state has sent to the field. The troops of Iowa and Virginia and of Tennessee have received within two months at least as great advantages from these contributions as those of that state.

Do you wish Iowa troops to be dependent on the contributions of New England? On the other hand, do you wish to spurn for Iowan volunteers the patriotic offerings of New England? Would you at such a time as this say to New England: "Mind your own business," would you say to Virginia and Tennessee, "Take care of your own sick folks and we will take care of ours"?

Suppose that in the next battle in Kentucky the brunt should be borne by Iowans and some thousand of them should be thrown on the Surgeons' hands—do you wish that the Surgeons should refuse all assistance for them until it can be sent from Iowa? Would you be unwilling that they should be dependent for a time on the provision for such an emergency to which the women of New England have contributed so liberally? Whether you would or not; they will be so dependent: they have been so dependent; and at this moment some of your Iowan sick, I do not doubt, rest on beds sent from New England, and their strength is sustained by wine sent from New-York.

This being so, are you willing that when in the next battle in Virginia the husbands and fathers and sons and brothers of the women of New England are brought low, Iowa shall have contributed nothing (except in the form of a tax) by which their lives also can be cherished?

Of course I do not ask these questions reproachfully; upon their answer seems to me to depend the answer which should be made to your proposal. In the work of this Commission no State is known; all contributions to it are to a common stock, for the Army of a common country. It has received, as it happens, by far the most from those states for whose men it has done least. Whether aided by Iowa or not, it will be as ready to aid Iowa, as to aid New York, New England, Ohio, or Tennessee.

You may ask how far it has done so? I do not know because I have never thought of asking how far it has aided one or another. I know that its agents, under their orders, can never regard one and disregard another.

To be more explicit, however, I will give the outlines of the arrangements of the Commission for collecting and supplying hospital stores.

Dépôts for hospital supplies are established at different points, with reference to accessibility for different columns of the Army. Four of these are at the four largest seaports; one at Washington, for the Army of the Potomac; one at Wheeling for Western Virginia and Kentucky; one at Louisville; one at Cairo, and one at St. Louis for the columns operating in the Mississippi valley and Missouri. Another will probably be established soon further West. There is also one at Port Royal; one at the Tortugas, and one at Ship Island. At each of these dépôts it is intended to keep a stock of hospital goods in reserve. A further reserve is also usually maintained at Cleveland intermediate between those of the East and West, and which is intended to be drawn upon both from the East and West upon occasion.

There are three associate secretaries of the Commission, one of whom is responsible that the goods given in charge to the Commission are distributed as far as possible to those most in need of them on the Atlantic. The second is in like manner responsible for the necessary distribution to the Armies between the Alleghanies and the Mississippi, the third for those west of the Mississippi. The duty of the latter is however complicated and embarrassed somewhat by the existence of a Commission organized by General Fremont, which has undertaken to do the same work in the same field, believing that it can do so harmoniously without being in subordination to the same rules. The national Commission has thought best, while it regards the arrangement as a bad one, to yield to the wishes of the excellent men at St Louis, who under official sanction, have established a local institution which they are perhaps, naturally indisposed to make merely auxiliary to the national system. This local institution however, while it has an independent dépôt and makes independent collections therefor, and exercises duties other than those undertaken by the Commission, is perfectly national and catholic in its purpose. Although its members all live in St Louis it takes thought as much for the sick Illinoisian or Ohioan, as for the sick St. Louisian or Missourian. It can therefore work harmoniously with the Commission. The Commission is, however, obliged in order to carry out its plan completely, to maintain an independent dépôt at St Louis free of any provincial control, and always ready like those in New York, Cleveland, and Washington, to serve any demands of the sick and wounded of the Army or Navy anywhere they may arise. At any of these dépôts contributions are received from the various societies of patriotic women throughout the land counting by hundreds in every state east of Iowa and north of Kentucky, and including some in Kentucky as well. It is not known, and it never will be known, how much the women of one state have given, and how little those of another. All who contribute, contribute freely according to their means, to a common stock.

The advantage of this common stock thus divided is almost daily illustrated. For instance:

A considerable force has been recently massed and placed in movement in the mountain region of Virginia, west of the field previously occupied by the Army of the Potomac and east of that occupied by the Army of Western Virginia. Owing to the difficulty of transportation, this force was without tents, and being obliged to bivouac in bad weather at mid-winter in a highland region, a large sick list was rapidly formed. An inspector of the Commission had been sent a week ago to look after it, but it was not till the day before yesterday that information of its wants was received by the Associate Secretary of the Commission for the army of the Potomac to which the column was subordinate. To send goods to the position in question from Washington, or any of the Eastern dépôts, it would have been necessary to move them several days' journey by waggon, and with considerable hazard. A supply of hospital stores for a thousand patients was consequently ordered by telegraph from Wheeling whence, although needed for the Army of the Potomac, it was sent by Railroad at least sixty miles nearer to the point of demand, than it could have been by any Railroad from the East. At the same time, the agent at Wheeling was advised by telegraph that if his supply ran short it would immediately be replenished from Cleveland and those in charge of the dépôt at Cleveland were advised that although the dépôts at New York and Philadelphia had been drawn low to supply Naval Expeditions, a considerable reserve existed at Boston, upon which, if they were not amply provided for all probable demands from Kentucky and Missouri, they should immediately make requisition. This, however, was found to be unnecessary, the industry of the women of Michigan, Western New York, and Ohio, having at this time supplied a very large accumulation at Cleveland.

There has been no time to my knowledge during the last six months when any demand made upon any one of the dépôts of the Commission has failed to be met, and yet the Commission has been during all that time giving out to hospitals nearly two thousand articles of clothing every day, and no Surgeon has allowed a want of hospital clothing in his regiment to become known to the Commission or to any of its twenty Camp Inspectors, or other agents, that a supply has not been immediately placed at his disposal. Since our dépôts were fairly established at Cleveland, Wheeling, Cairo, and St Louis, I am not aware that any demand upon any one of them has failed to be met at once. Nevertheless, urgent appeals have been frequently made by ignorant persons to New England, New York, New Jersey, and Pennsylvania for goods immediately needed for a regimental hospital within fifty or a hundred miles of those dépôts and many tons of freight have been conveyed unnecessarily and at great cost from the Atlantic to the Mississippi in answer to such appeals.

The Commission cannot engage that its dépôts always will be fully supplied, it cannot engage that all proper demands upon it shall be met. This will depend upon what is supplied to it. It can engage, having better means of information than any organization of a local character, or any not in immediate communication with the War department can have, that what it receives shall as far as possible be so distributed as to be of the greatest good to the greatest number of soldiers of the Union, come whence they may, go where they may.

At each dépôt where goods are received to a considerable amount by direct contribution, there are local organizations auxiliary to the Commission, composed of its Associate Members and other men, with a body of women, and young people, who undertake the onerous labor and expense of opening, assorting, packing and accounting for goods, and of the necessary correspondence. These auxiliary organizations also frequently purchase articles needed by the sick, which they fail to receive as contributions in kind, in sufficient quantity. They pay the local rents, &c. A large working staff is constantly required and is maintained for these purposes. An expenditure of many thousand dollars in each case has thus been saved the Treasury of the Commission.

There are many hundred sub dépôts maintained in the same manner, again auxiliary to these, no one of which however is expected to be constantly ready to meet a sudden demand as is the case with the regular directly auxiliary dépôts of the Commission among which besides those already named, there is a very important one at Chicago, for the State of Illinois: another at Cincinnati for Southern Ohio, &c.

If the good people of Iowa believe that they can best serve the common cause by directing their energies exclusively to the supply of their own neighbors and relatives gone to the War, it is no part of my duty, nor am I disposed to argue against that conviction. At the same time, I cannot conceal that my own judgment is led to a different conclusion, and it is within my duty to fully explain and justify the plan of the organization I represent, which plan would certainly fail if none should take a different view of their duty, from that which I find indicated in your letters and publications. There seems to me to be a stain of the very soil, out of which the monster Secession has grown, when such a complete machinery as you have formed in Iowa is confined in its operations by State lines.

But if you contribute to the common stock, it may be asked what assurance will you have that Iowans will not be neglected? I might ask in reply what assurance has Massachusetts, New York, or Ohio? But a better answer is found in the fact, that no Surgeon from Iowa or anywhere else, has for months past asked for a single article which it was not in his power to get, as a right directly from a Government source, that it has not been supplied to the full extent of the entire resources of the Commission, and as soon as possible.

That the Iowan hospitals have nevertheless wanted much is to be accounted for

1st   By the constant movements and frequent changes in the plan of the campaign in Missouri which for a time rendered all attempts at systematic supply abortive.

2nd   The failure of the arrangements instituted under

General Fremont to relieve the national Commission of duty in Missouri, it having been understood that these would render unnecessary if not impertinent any undertaking on its part to provide systematically for the wants of the forces within the field of the St Louis organization.

3rd The neglect of the Surgeons to call upon the Commission,—excusable when it is considered what a variety of sources they are invited to resort to for the same articles, as for instance, first the government stores, second, the Sanitary Commission, third, the St Louis Sanitary Commission, fourth, the Iowa Army Sanitary Commission, fifth, various village Sanitary Commissions, which, as I observe by your report, supply directly as well as through your state organization, sixth, Eastern Local Societies, seventh, Church Societies &c. in St Louis, eighth, individual benevolence.

I am advised that an impression prevails with you that our organization has chiefly confined its operations to the East. On the contrary, the very first action of the Commission after its complete organization, before it looked at the Army in Maryland was to send its president along with a special resident Western Secretary to look after the Troops then beginning to concentrate in Illinois and Missouri. The first Iowa Volunteers were visited by the President of the Commission and Dr Newberry in June last and before the Commission had met in Washington except in part for the purpose of organizing.

You observe in your own report of a visit to the hospitals at Mound City, on the Mississippi, the largest Military hospital in the United States: "The Surgeons assured us that they could not possibly carry it out, but for the Sanitary Commission. Said one, 'You will find a hundred articles here from the Sanitary Commission where you will find one from the Government.'" By reference to our report of operations in the West for the three months ending 30th November, you will see that these supplies were from our dépôts at New York and Cleveland, and that at that time upwards of 90,000 articles had been sent from the Cleveland depot alone, to Western hospitals. In the first report of the Chicago branch of the Commission p. 4, you will find reference to "repeated visits of the members of the U.S. Sanitary Commission to the camps and hospitals at Cairo."

The meetings of the Commission are held at Washington, because Washington is the headquarters of the Army, and the seat of Government, with whom it is a part of the duty of the Commission to constantly advise. A majority of the members of its central board reside in the East, because it is necessary that they should be frequently and quickly assembled. For the same reason its Central Office is established at Washington.

If the army of the Potomac has been better supplied than that of Missouri, it is because the former has been closely concentrated and at rest. Systematic provision for it has therefore been more practicable. But precisely the same machinery of supply has been extended throughout the West. And as soon as it became apparent that the Commission should reassume the duty of providing for the forces in Missouri, one of its Secretaries, familiar with all the details of its operations in Maryland, was sent to reside in Missouri, and all the resources of the Commission placed at his command. Obviously however, if other organizations undertake the supply of the hospitals in Missouri, obtaining their supplies from the neighboring sources, our Secretary for Missouri must either enter into a competition with them for these supplies, or obtain supplies at greater and unnecessary cost from other sources, which he can have no certainty will be required.

The explanation I have thus given of the existing arrangements of the Commission will, I trust enable you the more readily and definitely to determine in what manner your very efficient State organization can be honorably and advantageously brought into connection with it.

The Commission will probably meet at Washington about the 20th inst.

Reciprocating your assurance of sympathy in the cause and the work

I am most respectfully yours

(Signed) Fred. Law Olmsted
General Secretary

A PLAN FOR THE SLAVES AT PORT ROYAL:
FEBRUARY 1862

To James Reed Spalding

Private.

U.S. Sanitary Commission, Washington, D.C.
15th February 1862

My Dear Sir,

The advantage which I happen to possess for dealing with the Port Royal problem, from having some years ago, made a careful study of the rural economy of that district, to which you allude in a manner so complimentary to me in the World of today, authorizes me to call your especial attention to the Senate Bill of Mr Foster, in the preparation of which I had the honor to be consulted, and which I believe to be altogether the best bill which would have any chance to be acted upon favorably at present.

The urgent importance of the earliest possible action, and of adopting some thoroughly comprehensive, and at the same time *elastic*, scheme can not be too strongly stated.

We have on our hands, from fifty to a hundred of the most valuable plantations on the continent, with on an average, the full complement of working hands for their cultivation. The Treasury agents estimate that they will be able to gather and send from these plantations the value of a million and a half of cotton. During the months of January and February the operation of *listing* the cotton fields, in preparation for planting is performed. In March and April cotton is planted. Not the first stroke of work has yet been done in the cotton-fields. If there should be another month's delay, nothing can be done this year, and we have on our hands 12,000 paupers to be supported in the main at public expense.

Mean-time, I am already informed that our soldiers are suffering for want of a due supply of vegetable food, and Commodore Dupont has sent home one of his best ships to recruit the crew, in which the fearful scourge of scurvy had begun to rage. As the weather grows warmer the want of a proper diet will become a more serious evil.

But a decent regard for the national honor, a decent respect to the science of social economy, a decent reverence to the demands of Christianity, should forbid our dealing any longer with these people in a desultory, stingy, temporizing, penny-wise, pound foolish, way. The Bill is drawn with especial care to avoid all issues of a radical character. Neither slave-holder nor abolitionist would be compromised in voting for it—and, as it will not stand in the way of more thorough measures, one way or the other, when the policy of the country with regard to slavery, is determined; it may be hoped to unite all who do not wish to establish at Port Royal, another evidence of the folly of ever hoping to see negroes usefully employed in any other condition than that of abject slavery.

The opportunity of proving to the South, the economic mistake of Slavery, which is offered us at Port Royal, is indeed invaluable. It has for months engaged my profoundest attention, and I am heartsick at the listlessness, indifference and utter childish cowardice with which it is regarded by controlling minds at Washington.

Hoping that you will agree with me as to the urgency of the case, and excuse me for intruding so long upon your valuable time.

I am, dear Sir, yours most Respectfully,

Fred. Law Olmsted

Mr. Spalding.

"THE DUTY OF GOVERNMENT TO THESE NEGROES":
MARCH 1862

To Abraham Lincoln

U.S. Sanitary Commission
Adams House, 244 F. St.
Washington, DC   March 8th 1862

Dear Sir

At the request of several gentlemen—I mention Dr Howe, Prof^r Bache, Dr Bellows and G W Curtis—I shall offer you my thoughts about the management of the negroes at Port Royal. That I can suppose it worthy of a moment of your time is to be accounted for simply by the fact that it chances to be more mature than most men's thoughts on this subject can be, the occasion which has arisen having been practically anticipated by me several years ago.

Aside from military considerations, the duty and function of government with regard to the negroes is included in and limited by these two propositions:

1. To save the lives of the negroes, except possibly as death may be a natural punishment of neglect of duty.

2. To *train* or *educate* them in a few simple, essential and fundamental social duties of free men in civilized life: as, first, to obtain each for himself the necessities of life, independently of charity; second, to regard family obligations; third, to substitute for subordination to the will of their former owners, submission to Laws—or rules of social comity with the understanding that these are designed to correspond to the natural laws of their happiness; 4th, to discriminate between just authority under the Laws as above, and despotic authority—between the duty of obedience to administrators of law and obedience to masters by might.

I do not know that there are any more than these: if there are, they should be clearly defined before they are sought to be inculcated by the use of the money or agents of government.

Whoever is entrusted with the administration of the duty of government to these negroes should be under no necessity or temptation to engage in purely philanthropic, benevolent or charitable duties toward them.

If the two classes of duties (governmental and charitable) are not absolutely inconsistent one with another, the exercise of the latter by the same person with the former will do much to maintain a confusion of ideas which exists in the minds of the negroes and from which it is a large part of the duty of government as an economic operation to free them. It should be laid down as an absolute rule that government will do nothing merely for charity. The negroes are not to be in the least fed & clothed for charity but because either they are expected to be valuable to the state, and for that purpose their lives must be conserved, or because it is tacitly agreed upon between every civilized man and the community to which he attaches himself that in dire extremity of misfortune he shall not want protection against the coup de grace of cold & hunger. To accomplish these points, the agent of gov^t should have the means within his control beyond all peradventure:

1   To place within the reach—upon proper conditions—of each negro, what is barely necessary for the support of his life. The limit of expenditure for this purpose should be strictly defined and the agent should be rigidly and accurately held within it, but within it there should be nothing left doubtful.

2   To offer employment and wages to each negro which will enable those who are diligent to provide something more than what is barely necessary for the support of life; which will, for instance, at least enable parents to provide for their children's necessity.

A very moderate sum to be attainable by each laborer daily will suffice for this; but the sum however large in the aggregate should be provided beyond any possibility of failure; otherwise the second proposition will fail and the unsuccessful attempts to realize it will accomplish results precisely the opposite to those required.

It would be better for the state, and more merciful to the negroes to guillotine them at once, than to educate them by any means in beggary, distrust of themselves and cowardly hatred of the first duties of freedom.

sgd. Fred. Law Olmsted

Argument Addressed to the Secretary of the Treasury and Afterwards to the Secretary of War, After the Former Had Asked Me to Take Charge of the Negro Population of the Sea Islands

In the stubborn refusal of the people of the slave states to entertain any proposition favorable to the abolition of slavery, there doubtless is much of selfishness, much of cowardice, and much of willfully blind and deaf prejudice and passion, but it can hardly be that there is not also some element of common sense to which it is the part of wise statesmanship to accommodate itself. Such an element as well as the relation to it which the dealings of government at this time with the negroes of the Sea islands must have, it is my purpose to demonstrate.

The man whose twenty first birth-day comes on the fourteenth of November will be allowed to cast his vote at an election on that day when he will not be allowed to do so on the thirteenth. Why is it his right tomorrow and not today? Nature knows no such line. It is an artificial boundary arbitrarily fixed by law. And on this ground I have heard a proposition to abolish it gravely made and argued, it being forgotten that human government can proceed not a single step without classifying men, and dealing with them differently, each after his class. Is not this truth too much lost sight of in the advice commonly given the people of the slave states?

There are some men under twenty one years of age of much more mature intellect than others who are above that age. Yet common sense acquiesces in the law which receives the vote of the latter class and rejects that of the former. There are negroes in slavery who have attained to a higher civilization, and a purer morality than some white men, who are, nevertheless, neither confined in the madhouse, nor the penitentiary. The distinction of classes established by law, has, in all such cases, a certain basis in nature. There is equally a basis in nature for a *distinction* between the negro class of the South and all other classes of its society. It is true that if we examine the most obvious grounds of this distinction—those of form and color—we find them in reality of no importance *except* as of marks of historical peculiarities. But do not these historical peculiarities necessarily involve mental and moral peculiarities? Unquestionably. We know that whoever possesses them must have inherited whatever congenital idiosyncrasy would naturally result from the circumstance that his stock during some five or six generations had one after another been condemned for life to hard, unrequited labor upon a crude, monotonous diet. He is also very sure to be in direct descent, and but a few generations removed from a completely savage and heathen people.

Being thus distinguished from all other classes in the republic, and the distinction being thus marked and defined, there can be nothing essentially unreasonable or unrepublican in the idea that special enactments of law *may* be required with reference to this class.*

If we concede this, we must also concede that a majority of the citizens of any state may rightly *demand the enactment* of such provisions.

Concede this, and we may, at any moment, be brought face to face with the question: To *what* peculiar liabilities or disabilities, temporary or otherwise, in their requirements, shall Africans residing in the state be *made* subject?

To this question, what to the citizen of a slave state will always be, while it remains a slave state, the simplest and readiest answer? Obviously this: "Those already on our statute books."

"I know these Africans," says the citizen of the South, "and in my judgement they demand different supervision and requirements of law from those which are necessary for the rest of our community; a supervision which it would be expensive, and, in the main, useless to maintain with the races of Europe; police requirements which it would be irksome and equally useless to have forced upon me and my family. There is an existing system which meets this demand. You propose to abolish

---

* The Hon. Charles Sumner, in an address to the people of New York at the Metropolitan Theatre, 8th of May, 1855, says: "While discountenancing all prejudice of color and every establishment of caste, the Antislavery Enterprise—at least so far as I may speak for it—does not undertake to change human nature, or to force any individual into relations of life for which he is not morally, intellectually and socially adapted; nor does it necessarily assume that a race, degraded for long generations under the iron heel of bondage, can be lifted at once into all the political privileges of an American citizen."

it. What substitute do you offer? Will it raise cotton? Will it
prevent vagabondism? Is it compatible with my dignity and
interests? Is it likely to be satisfactory in my household? Where
can I see it at work? Where is all you assert of it, demonstrated?
Nowhere,—no demonstration? A mere theory that something
might be done? I'll hear no more of this idle talk. The evils of
Slavery I know and can bear with; the evils of an untried system
of dealing with these savages, who are but just now well broken
in to a useful part in our social economy, I will not think of
venturing upon."

Mr. Secretary, I shall be excused for observing before proceeding to what must be necessarily a matter of opinion, that
my opinions upon this subject are not closet opinions, and they
have not been hastily formed. I some years since spent considerably more than one whole year in daily personal intercourse
with the citizens of the slave states for the express purpose,
constantly in view, and I believe, constantly with a sincere and
honest endeavour, to gain a trustworthy knowledge, and to
form trustworthy opinions, upon it. And I have long entertained the opinion, that, for the security and permanence of our
government, nothing was so much needed, as an opportunity
of demonstrating to the citizens of the South upon their own
soil that there was another alternative to the Slavery of this class
of their population besides that of merging it in the existing
classes, which might be adopted with reasonable certainty of
satisfactory results. We now have such an opportunity, and with
it we have an administration which was elected by the people
with a distinct understanding that, within just, reasonable and
constitutional limits, it would favor freedom. It has gone so far
as to declare its disposition to offer a compensation to the owners of Slaves, as an inducement to them in favor of freedom. It
has not declared, but, it is about to demonstrate, what it thinks
should be done by the states with and for this class in its first
step of freedom.

There are three courses, one of which this administration
must and will take, concerning the opportunity to which I refer:

1st   It may neglect it altogether.
2nd   It may use it in such a way as to give grounds for the
assertion that it has found the African inhabitants of the Sea

Islands freed from the liabilities of slavery; that it acknowledges its duty as a government toward them; that it has taken out of their reach the products of their last year's labor, that it has allowed its highest military and financial representatives on this ground to solicit charitable donations for them, that it has encouraged and co-operated with a system of eleemosynary supply for their wants, and that it has thus presented to the citizens of the Slave States

ORGANIZED BEGGARY

as the only alternative to slavery which it is able to adopt when it undertakes the duty of dealing directly with the Africans upon the soil, and in the climate of the South. Assertions of this character are already publickly made. Can it be said that they are entirely without foundation?

3d   It may use it in a way to make as complete and consistent a trial as is practicable of the abolition of slavery in the South, with twelve thousand plantation negroes, for the most part upon their plantations; securing to them for this purpose every reasonable legal advantage and requiring of them all just and proper service. It may thus not only demonstrate the good faith with which it has professed to regard slavery as an evil, but at the same time demonstrate that there may be a just alternative to slavery, to the willing adoption of which there can thereafter be no obstacle except ignorance and passion, which the declaration already made at the suggestion of the administration will not go far to remove.

Of these three courses the first, that is to say, an entire neglect of these negroes by government, would have simply the objection that it might cause much privation and suffering to an innocent people. This however is but a common and unavoidable contingency of war, and might be much more merciful than the second which in aiding to fix a demoralizing and wasteful policy upon the country would be entirely inhumane, unwise and disasterous. Doubtless there will be found occasion for cavilling in any case but I speak now with regard to men who mean to be honest and reasonable, and who yet sustain slavery. These men in my judgement will not fail to be told that what shall have been done with and for these twelve thousand plantation negroes was what this administration, what Lincoln and the northerners, would have done if they could, with all the Slaves upon all the plantations of the South. And I think that there will be some reason for them to believe it. Therefore I think that the larger the amount of assistance which these negroes have forced upon them of a merely charitable character, or of what may seem to be of a fortuitous character, without order, system or responsible return of the results, such as the army may incidentally throw to them, as a hunter throws the offal of his game to his dogs—the larger the amount of all such assistance they get, the stronger will be the hold of that old prejudice, against which the plan initiated by this administration, and against which every plan for relieving the country of this terrible Old Man of the Sea of Slavery, will have to contend in the forum of popular discussion.

But there remains the third course; namely, to establish a policy of dealing with the negroes on the Sea Island plantations in which the primary duty of government toward such a class of its population shall appear to have been recognized; which shall be in substantial accordance with the principles of law which this administration would be willing to see the governments of the Slave States adopt, and to so carry out that policy as to present a real vindication of those principles and demonstrate to the honest common-sense of the citizens of the South when this excitement shall be overpast, the sufficiency of such a policy for all the purposes of just dealing, with all the negro class in their midst.

Precedents involving the principle applicable in the case, do not seem to be entirely wanting. Sir, what do the peculiarities—the idiosyncracies of the class in question amount to? The negro has, it is said, but an imperfect intelligence; he is childish; he is improvident; he is sensual and exciteable, and his temper is to be distrusted. Have we no precedents for special legislation as to men possessing such peculiarities? What then is the matter with the inmates of your District workhouse, and of your five and twenty institutions, State and National, for the treatment of lunatics and weak minded persons? And are there not special enactments of law for the supervision and provision of minors?

Suppose that a Governor or Superintendent or Guardian

should be appointed for these negroes, who like the insane of the Army and Navy can properly be regarded as under no state government, and who consequently have at this time got to be looked after, if they are adequately looked after at all, by the National Government, what in accordance with these precedents of our laws, will be his first duty? Unquestionably it will be to see that his wards are provided with the means of supporting life. Let it be assumed that for this purpose the use of the abandoned plantations on which they are found living is entrusted to him, and that until these are available for their entire support, government will make the necessary advances afterwards to be returned out of the proceeds of the sale of their surplus productions, or in fresh provisions to be supplied to the Army. Then his second duty will be to guard against their peculiar vices or frailties, so far at least as they would otherwise cause inconvenience or expense to the community, that is, to the nation. For this purpose it is essential that he possess all necessary legal authority, and power to enforce legal authority, to prevent them from becoming an unnecessary burden upon others, or upon the Treasury. This authority will be of the same character as that of a Tradesman with an idle apprentice, or as that of the master of a Merchant Ship with a truculent seaman.

And his third and most important duty will be to make the Negroes comprehend that this authority is not the same as that by which a master compels a slave to work for his own purposes, namely that of ownership; and again, that it is not merely the natural authority of a superior intellect over an inferior, or of a good man over a bad man. But that it is *the sacred authority of Government* to enforce a natural duty of each man to all other men; an authority before which all white men are expected and required to bow equally with black, an authority to which their Governor or Guardian is himself subject equally with them. In other words he must be to them the representative and the instrument of that Common law to which they in common with white men are hereafter to hold themselves subject and their loyalty to which, especially in this particular of industry, it is to be hoped will demonstrate that their slavery or subjection to the merely private interests of another man has been heretofore unnecessary.

It may seem to be too nice a distinction to be comprehended

by such people—this between subjection to the authority of an owner backed by statute law, and subjection to the authority of a guardian backed by Common Law—but if the guardian is armed with the authority of government to be to them not merely its instrument to compel them to their duty, but equally and at the same time its instrument to protect them in the rational exercise of their just and proper rights, to secure to them the natural reward of their labor, and to guard them against the lazy rapacity of other men, there need be no fear that they will long remain without a wholesome and happy respect for the corresponding exercise of authority by which he protects the nation against their inclination to indolence and other vices. It will then be essential to success that he possess means of controlling all the dealings which others may need to have with the negroes so far at least as to prevent violence and frauds upon them. For this purpose he must either be clothed with the authority of a magistrate himself, or he must have a ready and efficient appeal to someone else who is clothed with this authority. Thus only will he be able to command the confidence of the negroes as their true governor, guardian, superintendent or legally appointed protector and friend.

To properly execute his trust, therefore, he must be possessed beyond all question of the following endowments from government

1st Means of securing to the Negroes temporarily, at least, protection against hunger, cold, &c. (conditionally it may be upon their good order and industry)

2nd Means of offering them some sort of wages for work;

3rd Means of entailing upon them a sure punishment for indolence and other vice;

4th Means of securing them against unlawful violence and the impositions and tyranny of others.

All this is nothing less than it is the simple duty of the administration to offer and secure to them, and unless this much can be attempted, I can not but gravely doubt if it would not be better for me and for all good citizens, in view of the great interests of our race which are involved, to refrain from aiding or taking part with the administration in carrying out a plan which will necessarily cause so large a body of our brethren hereafter to offend, and that upon a point so vital to our national existence. They will die then, says the Secy of the Treasy. Let them die. What are ten thousand lives longer or shorter in a question of this magnitude? Four millions of Negroes here today to be eight millions tomorrow. What shall we do with them?

In its relations to that question, the importance of the business of Government with this insignificant ten or twelve thousand unfortunate men, women and children, wrecked by process of War, on the Sea Islands, is very far from being limited by the measure of its mere duty to them.

Yet as regards these Negroes alone, what is the duty of government?

You have taken their corn; you have taken their mules and horses and wagons; you have prevented them from preparing the soil for their only staple crop; you have through the criminal negligence or more criminally contracted judgement of duty of your Medical Bureau introduced small pox and have propagated other diseases among them. Can you say that what is being now done, is all the duty that government owes them?

I know, Sir, that the Secy of the Treasury is doing what he can in his own department and that he is willing to stretch his authority to the utmost to meet the more important demands of humanity, but with how little confidence, Sir, can it be possible for his agent to proceed in the attempt to realize a consistent policy of executing the duty of government, I ask you to judge after hearing the statement of the Secretary himself addressed to that agent & which thus defines and limits his authority in the case:

"The whole authority of the Department over the objects of your report is derived from the 5th Sec. of the act *to provide for the collection of duties*, approved July 13, 1861, by which the President is authorized to permit *Commercial intercourse*, with any part of the country declared to be in a state of insurrection, under such rules and regulations, as may be prescribed by the Secy of the Treasury."

"As incidental to this authority alone have I any power to sanction any measures for the culture of the abandoned estates in the Port Royal or other districts."

Under the administration of your predecessor, Sir, I endeavored to induce your Department to adopt a comprehensive plan of dealing with these plantations and with this people, which had come under its control and were held and used under its control as an incident of War. It had not occurred to me, Sir, nor did it occur to the gentleman long connected with government, with whom I then consulted about it, that the necessity which existed for government to take action in the premises, *was* a necessity incident to the collection of duties.

Such, however, was, I think, Sir, owing only to its preoccupation of mind by more imperative duties, preventing deliberation, the conclusion adopted by the administration, and accordingly I was then unable to obtain the attention of the Department. Without knowing the reason therefor, I cheerfully submitted to its wisdom.

Learning however, from the Inspector of the Sanitary Commission that no measures were being taken at all adequate to the demands of the case; sometime subsequently I called upon the Secy of the Treasury, in company with two other gentlemen who had a benevolent interest in the matter, to represent the importance of such measures.

The Secretary informed us that he had employed a person whom he believed to be fully competent to superintend the business and that he possessed all requisite authority of action.

Though I did not feel authorized to occupy his time in argument, from my own knowledge of the circumstances I could not with all respect for his judgment agree with him, and I felt obliged in my conscience to act in another channel.

I consequently drew up the Bill, sometime afterwards presented by the Honble Mr Foster to the Senate. I have been informed that the Secy of the Treasy did not wish that Bill to pass, it did however at length pass the Senate by a vote of 24 to 14. And I have reason to believe that it would have passed the House, some of the ablest and most conservative minds of the House having assured me that it would receive their active support in debate.

At this time however the Secy of the Treasy sent for me and let me know that he did not wish the Bill to pass; at the same time, he proposed that I should myself take entire charge of the negroes and the superintendence of the government duty to them.

Never doubting that the authority of such an agent would be

adequate for the duties which I deemed it necessary governmt should undertake, I requested the gentlemen who had most interested themselves in the Bill in the House to let it sleep while I took the proposition of the Secy into consideration.

It is only within a few days that I have fully understood the state of the case—having learned from the Secy of the Treasury that he had never read the Bill in question, that he entirely misapprehended its scope and purpose, and that he regards himself as having no power to confer any authority upon an agent which would have the slightest practical value.

In fact, Sir, I understand that really the only authority which is pretended to be exercised, as a legal authority, over this population, *is* a military authority and so far as this is exercised with any regard to any of the objects—whether of state or of charity, to which I have had the honor to be allowed to ask your attention—it is by reason of a letter borne by the Agent of the Treasury Department addressed by *you*, Sir, to the *Military* authorities, recommending him to their countenance and such assistance as—incidental to the operations of *War*—they may find it convenient to give him.

I respectfully submit, Sir, that this is a complicated arrangment—that it has the inherent fault of all unnecessarily complicated arrangments of government, the creation of undefined responsibilities and imperfect duties.

I do not feel willing Sir, to accept a responsibility which is morally so great, and legally so questionable in its scope.

It may seem to you, Sir, immodest in me to tender my services to your department in a manner which implies that I consider that tender as an inducement to you to undertake the duty of government in the premises. You will believe my assurance, however, Sir, that I do so simply because I trust that you regard it as important that some man possessing certain qualifications which I suppose myself to possess, and who is thoroughly imbued with a sense of the responsibility resting on the administration in the premises, should be appointed for this purpose, and it is because I wish to testify to the administration in the most emphatic manner the fact, that it is very doubtful if a man so imbued will assume that responsibility with only such means of executing it satisfactorily to his conscience, as the Secy of the

Treasury can offer, while he will readily do so, if you desire it and will give him the support morally and materially which I suppose it to be in your power to do.

Mr Secy, I have endeav^d to show you that the administration has a duty to those negroes, which is incident to the operations of war. This duty, Sir, will meet every imperative requirement of the case which can properly be made upon government. There is another Class of duties, Sir, which it is important should not be confused with those of gov^t. If gov^t will attend to the economical demand of the case, I am authorized to pledge the faith of the leading citizens of Boston, New York & Phil^a that the religious and educational demand which it presents, shall be also generously met—generously and in an orderly, quiet, respectable and systematic way. I refer, Sir, to the gentlemen composing the associations organized at the instance of the Secy of the Treasy, committees from each of whom are now here. They are willing to undertake this—are not willing to be responsible for the duty which the Secy of the Treasy has been disposed to leave to them.

But, Sir, if I have not succeeded in impressing you with the conviction which I possess that it is the proper duty of your department of this administration, as a consequence of the incident of war, which deprived these innocent people of their usual means of subsistence, to provide for their government in the only proper way they can be governed, then I wish to put it on another ground which I deem conclusive as to the question of your authority.

As Secy of the Sanitary Commission, Sir, I have received much evidence that the army on the Southern Coast is already suffering from a lack of sufficient provision of fresh vegetable food. In that climate a larger quantity of vegetable food than is provided for in your rations is an absolute necessity of health. I do not exaggerate the case when I state that your army can not live without it.

This necessary provision can in no way be obtained with any regard to economy except by the cultivation of those plantations, and those plantations can in no way be cultivated for this purpose so efficiently, so economically, as under the direct superintendence of your department.

I only ask, Sir, that you give me the authority to employ

precisely those agencies which would be most economical for this purpose, and I will engage to accomplish all the duty of government so far as that is practicable by any means from this time henceforth, until the final adjudication of this whole great question of the government of the rebellious districts.

HOSPITAL TRANSPORTS: MAY 1862

Labors of the Sanitary Commission

Its Attentions to the Wounded and Sick Soldiers in Eastern Virginia—

REPORT OF MR. OLMSTED, THE SECRETARY, TO DR. BELLOWS, THE PRESIDENT, OF THE COMMISSION

Steamboat Wilson Small,
Off Yorktown, Thursday, May 15, 1862

My Dear Sir:

The Commission is throwing itself into so many gaps that I not only cannot find time to make full reports to you, but it is impossible to recollect much detail, of more or less importance, determined and acted upon at the instant of necessities, even of only day before yesterday. I think you are fairly well informed of the outline of our work till then. We had on our tender, the *Small*, twenty-five severely wounded men, two dying and one or two dead; we had the night before sent two portions of our company, with such stores as could be at a moment's notice sent with them, to two vessels conveying wounded from the battle of Williamsburgh to Fortress Monroe; another portion was with the wounded of West Point, on the *Star*.

These drafts had left us no more on the *Small* than was necessary for the care of those on board of her. Yet the boat was crowded, and for a week, most of the men have slept, when they could, out on deck, the cabins being occupied by the wounded. Early in the morning the *Webster* arrived. We ran alongside and took from her some much-needed stores. We breakfasted on board, and were delighted with her arrangements and the good order which prevailed on her, contrasting so favorably with the impromptu ill-considered arrangements and disorder of everything else of which we have had recent observation. I immediately reported her ready to receive two hundred patients to the surgeon in charge of the Yorktown hospitals, and having received your telegram announcing the definite withdrawal of the *Ocean Queen*, I went on board the *S. R. Spaulding*, and finding her, though lamentably inferior to the *Queen* for our purposes, the best, in fact, the only available vessel for outside service, I obtained an assignment of her to the Commission from the Quartermaster's Department, and took measures to have her at once given coal and water.

Arranged also for the coaling of the *Knickerbocker*, and put a company on board, to fit her for a surgical hospital. Got a wharf-berth for the *Webster*, near the hospitals; but, finding that she could not get in, on account of spiles broken off near it, got an order to take any small steamboat for lighterage, and secured a tug, and running this alternately with the *Small*, until near eleven o'clock at night, took off, and put safely and comfortably to bed on her, 240 sick and wounded men. After this, rearranged her hospital service, so as to transfer from her all who could by any means be spared, and to put on her such of our company as it was necessary to part with. Had an estimate of stores necessary for her return trip made, and at daylight sent what she could spare, on the *Small* during the night.

I found everything working beautifully on the *Webster*, every man knowing his place, and not trying to do the duty of others. I cannot speak too highly of the service of Dr. Grymes. He is just the man for the duty. At 9 A.M. the *Webster* weighed anchor, and we turned our attention to the other vessels which were being fitted. We had a company at work on the *Elm City*, another on the *Knickerbocker*, and were supplying stores to the *State of Maine*. We found them getting on as well as possible with the limited force we could spare on the *City*, but the *Knickerbocker*, after twice running through the fleet in search of her, we had to conclude was missing. Going to the Quartermaster's, we learned that, at 11 the night before, a requisition had been made upon him for the *Knickerbocker* to go to our advanced position on the Pamunkey, and forgetting that she had been assigned to the commission, he had given a written order to the Captain to take her there. Four of our company, including two ladies, were on board of her. The only relief to our anxiety for them was the assurance that she would undoubtedly return at once.

After considerable other business at the Quartermaster's office, we got from the Military Governor a detail of carpenters and other privates, and an order to destroy a platform erected by the rebels, which would furnish lumber for the fitting up of the *Spaulding*.

We left the *Small* to take this on board, and went to the shore hospital, where after considerable debate with D^r W, Surgeon in Charge, we agreed to have the *Elm City* ready by 2 o'clock to take on the sick, and see the *State of Maine* immediately fully supplied to follow the *Elm City* without delay. Returning to the *Small*, were met by a note from the Quartermaster, enclosing a telegram from the Medical Director, at Williamsburg, demanding a boat provided with straw and water to take on two hundred sick within two hours at Queen's Creek. "This is of the utmost urgency—see Mr. Olmsted," concluded the dispatch. The only boat in the fleet that had a fair supply of water on board, and which could be otherwise made anywhere near ready in less time than a half a day, was the *Elm City*, and she had no provision of food.

We had a day's supply on the *Small*, and I at once wrote to Dr. Greenleaf, that to meet an order of the Medical Director I had to withdraw the *Elm City* but we would send supplies to the *State of Maine* at once, so that she could take her place. We then ran near the *Elm City*, hailed her to fire up and be ready to go up the river in half an hour; ran alongside the *Spaulding*, threw the lumber and carpenters on board of her, arranged plan of berths and set them to work; then steamed off to the *Alida*, and sent her with the supplies for *State of Maine* and others; returned past the *Elm City* and ordered her to follow us; ran up to the mouth of Queen's Creek and anchored by the side of the *Kennebec*, which was being loaded with wounded secession prisoners, brought out of the creek by the lighter steamers. Went up the creek in our yawl to Bigelow's Landing, and saw the process of embarkation, which was rude, shiftless and painful, the poor wretches being made to climb a plank set at an angle of forty-five degrees, which they could only do by the aid of a rope thrown to them from the deck.

There was a small guard to carry up those who had suffered amputation or other severe injury. You can imagine, perhaps, what a cruel process it was by which they accomplished this. There being no officer to whom we could report, and nothing apparently for us to do at this place, we went (Knapp, Ware, Wheelock and myself) in a couple of returning ambulances to Williamsburgh, to report to the Medical Director. We had in this drive a sufficient experience of the abomination of two-wheeled ambulances. Our road, for a mile or more, lay through the midst of the field of battle, of which we saw many marks. On inquiring for the hospital at Williamsburgh, the reply was, "Every house on the main street is a hospital." We found the Medical Director surprised at our promptness. Not having supposed such a literal compliance with his orders possible, he was unable to take advantage of it, but promised to send us two hundred sick and wounded in the morning. We returned late in the evening, and at five the next morning all hands were again up to complete as far as possible the preparations of the *Elm City*, for we were very short-handed, and an imperfect make-shift organization and arrangement was alone possible.

At the first step I was met by a brigade surgeon from the *Kennebec*, who said: "No, this shall be so and so; I shall take charge here." As he persisted, after I showed my authority, and refused to compromise, I said that I should allow no sick to come on board. He then said he should go to the Medical Director. "The very thing I wanted, and I will go with you. Meanwhile the sick, if any arrive, shall come on and Dr. Ware will see that they are cared for temporarily."

We then went to the landing and saw the lighter loaded with sick in the same manner as yesterday. When the lighter was full, the surgeon told me that he should return and see the sick properly disposed of on the *Elm City*.

"But I thought we were to appeal to Dr. Tripler."

"I have concluded not to go to him, and have *written* to inform him that my authority is questioned." I deemed it best, upon this, to make sure of a written order from Dr. Tripler, and after a tedious delay got passage on a forage wagon, loaded with oats.

This was a hard ride—a continuous atmosphere of thick yellow dust, and the jar of the heavy wagons over execrable roads. I found Dr. Tripler—got a copy of an order which the Brigade-Surgeon should have received but had not, and the failure of which justified officially his assertion of authority over any transport for the sick at that anchorage. Returned to Bigelow's Landing, and, the lighters having grounded, waited there on the banks of the creek, along with a hundred sick men, being devoured by mosquitoes and sand flies. On returning, at length, to the *Elm City*, found that, owing to the conflict of authority, and the insufficient number of attendants, the sick were, with difficulty and slowness, taken care of.

After the hundred brought off with me had been taken on, the count was over four hundred, or twice as many as the Medical Director had estimated, or I had calculated on, in considering the supply of water, medicine and stores.

After sunset, I went again up the creek, and found eight men on the beach, left there sick—some very sick—without a single attendant or friend within four miles, while only the night before two of our teamsters had been murdered in the woods near by. After they were on board, I asked who was in charge of the party, wishing to make sure that no stragglers were left. A man was pointed out, who, because he was stronger and more helpful than the rest, seemed to have been regarded by them as their leader, though he had no appointment. He was able to answer my inquiries satisfactorily, and then told me his own story. His name was Corcoran. After the battle of Williamsburgh he was sick for three days. Then there was an order to march. His Captain said, "Good God! Corcoran, you are not fit to march; go into the town and get into a hospital." He walked three miles, carrying his knapsack, and when he came to a hospital, the surgeon told him he must bring a note from his Captain, and refused to receive him. He went out, and as he was very sick he crawled into something like a milk-wagon and fell asleep.

He was awakened by a man who pulled him out by his feet, and he fell on the ground and was hurt. He begged the man—a Secessionist, he supposed—for some water, and he brought him some, and said he would not have done it, only he wanted his wagon. He tried to walk away, but pretty soon fell down and fell asleep. By-and-bye a negro man woke him up and asked him if he shouldn't help him to a hospital. The negro man was very kind, but when he came to a hospital (it was in a church) the doctor said he couldn't take him because he hadn't a bit of a note. Then he said, "For God's sake, give me room to lie down here somewhere; it's not much room I'll take any how, and I can't keep up any longer." It was then three days since he had tasted food. Then the doctor told him he could lie down, and he had not been up since till to-day. I have told the whole of this story, simply because the man, as I just now chanced to learn, died a few hours afterwards, kindly attended, in his last moments, by our sisters of mercy. He has been buried to-day at Yorktown. A letter to his mother was found in his pocket, and one of the ladies has written to her.

The weather being unfavorable, we laid at anchor off Queen's Creek during the night, and by midnight had got all our affairs in pretty good trim. Knapp had been to and returned from Yorktown in the *Small*, with stores for the *Elm City*, and reported the arrival of the *Knickerbocker*, and that the *State of Maine* was loading with sick.

This morning we returned to Yorktown, and took on thirty more sick from a steamboat which had brought them from Cumberland on the Pamunkey. At 10, the *Elm City* left for Washington. Knapp went ashore to carry telegrams, and get some more lumber, and I went to bed. After noon I went ashore; called on the surgeon in charge and the Military Governor; made our arrangements for a trip up the river to collect sick from the advance, and to tow our *Wilson Small* up to West Point for repairs; for she has become completely disabled. Were met by an officer with a telegram, begging that a boat should be immediately dispatched to Bigelow's Landing, where an ambulance train master had reported that a hundred sick had been left on the ground in the rain without attendance or food, "to die." Bigelow's Landing is up a narrow, shoal, crooked creek, and we ran about the harbor looking in vain for a boat that could be expected to get there. At length we determined to take our whole fleet there, and leaving the *Knickerbocker* and

Alida outside, to try to get up with the storeboat *Elizabeth*, she being the shortest.

We ran to the *Knickerbocker*, but before we could get her under way, a steamboat came alongside, and a letter was handed me begging that I would take care of one hundred and fifty sick men on it, who had been taken on at West Point early in the morning, and who had had no nourishment during the day. It was at sunset, and stormy-cold. I at first refused, on the ground of the greater need of those at Bigelow's Landing, but the surgeon in charge induced me to take a look in the cabin, and I changed my mind. The little room was as full as it could be packed of sick soldiers sitting—not lying—on the floor; there was not room for that. Only two or three were at full length; one of these was dying—was dead the next time I looked in.

We immediately began taking them on the *Knickerbocker*. It is now midnight. Knapp started with Dr. Miller and a part of our company, and the two supply-boats, five hours ago for Queen's Creek, with the intention of getting to the sick at Bigelow's Landing if possible; if not, to go up in the yawl and canoe with supplies and firewood, and do whatever should be found possible for their relief. Two of the ladies are with him.

The rest are giving beef-tea and brandy and water to the sick on the *Knickerbocker*. These have all been put into clean beds, and are about as comfortable as it is possible to make them. But, to take decent care of 150 sick fellows at such short notice, on a steamboat, is not so easily accomplished as you might imagine. Dr. Ware and Dr. Swann are in attendance, aided most efficiently by Wheelock and Haight. Mr. Collins is the executive officer of the *Knickerbocker*, and Mr. Woolsey, clerk, taking charge of the effects of the soldiers. I am quite at a loss to know what I shall do to-morrow. Unless reinforcements arrive, we certainly cannot meet another emergency.

It will not be surprising if you find this report somewhat incoherent for I have several times fallen asleep while writing it. We have a cold northeast storm and thick weather, and I conclude that Knapp's expedition is unable to get down to-night. I have just been through the *Knickerbocker*, and find nearly all the patients sleeping quietly, and (a few typhoid murmurers excepted) with every indication of comfort.

May 16.—I was so soundly asleep fifteen minutes after I finished writing you last night, that it had to be several times repeated to me before I could comprehend what it meant, that the supply boats were coming alongside with over a hundred more sick. Anchoring the *Alida* outside, Knapp had attempted to get up the creek with the *Elizabeth*, but as I had feared would be the case, she went aground. Going on with the yawl, he found one of the steam lighters at anchor, with over a hundred sick lying on the deck, who were not only soaked with rain, but who had been obliged to wade out to her in knee-deep water. We learned that, further up the creek, a few men too sick to stand, and who, of course, were unable to wade off to the boat, had been left behind. No persuasion could induce the Captain to return for them, but a distinct assertion of authority in the case by Knapp, which he had from Gen. Van Vliet, and a threat to report him to headquarters, at length forced him to fire up and go back for them. There were eight of them, some in a nearly dying condition. These having been brought on board, and stimulants furnished them, the whole party was brought down and transferred to the supply-boats, the freight-rooms of which had, in the meantime, been as well as possible prepared for them. The ladies were ready with hot tea; there were plenty of blankets, and before the boats got down to us the larger part of the company were sound asleep. Those who were awake when I visited them were very ready to say that they wanted for nothing, and that they had not been as comfortable since they left Washington. We concluded to let them remain where they were for the night. They had been on the creek shore from ten to fourteen hours without a physician or a single attendant, a particle of food or a drop of drink. A cold, foggy day, with rain and mist after nightfall. With half a dozen exceptions, they appear marvelously well this morning and profoundly grateful for the kindness, which I need not say the ladies are extending to them. I am yet unable to make up my mind what to do with them. There is a hard northeasterly storm, with heavy rain, to-day.

Yours respectfully,

Fred'k Law Olmsted,
Gen. Sec.

H. W. Bellows, D.D., President San. Com.

"THE SICK ARE COMING IN VERY RAPIDLY": MAY 1862

To John Foster Jenkins

Sanitary Commission,
White House, Va   Floating Hospital,
May 21st 1862

My Dear Doctor,

I think that the enclosed sheet, in pencil, may have been omitted from the ms copy sent you yesterday. It should be inserted, if I recollect rightly, after the Hours of Meals.

I wrote you yesterday that things looked more promising ashore, except for the want of hands. Drs Ware, Draper and Armstrong, spent the greater part of the day, with some of the young men, in the hospitals, and their report at night was far far from favorable. The sick are coming in very rapidly, much more rapidly than the accommodations for them can be increased. The record is said to show a total of 1600. I suspect this includes the 256 taken on the Webster and all who have been discharged, as there certainly is not tent room for that number. There are five surgeons and assistants, one steward, no apothecary, and *no detail*. No nurses except those selected from the patients themselves. Two wells have been dug but the water of neither has been as yet fit to use for drinking. Water is brought from the White House well—nearly quarter of a mile distant—and until yesterday, the whole supply was brought by hand. It is now waggoned in casks. We sent up three casks of ice from the Webster's stock, which was found of great value. The greater part of the men are not very ill; with nice nourishment, comfortable rest, and good nursing, would be got ready to join their regiments in a week or two—but this is just what they are not likely to have. They have but two soup-kettles to cook for the whole number and the surgeon in charge, Baxter, seemed to think this enough—and, apparently, that they were doing well enough for soldiers altogether. He was nevertheless eager to throw them on board our boats.

I am in a quandary as to the best policy to be pursued. The weather is growing excessively hot and we are pushing forward in a malarious country in the face of the enemy. We have taken on one or two wounded men from the skirmishes yesterday. There is obviously great danger that they will be altogether overwhelmed with sick and wounded in a few days. If the recommendation of my telegram of Sunday is adopted—a complete hospital for 6000 sent here from Washington—there will be reasonable provision for the contingency. But I believe that the Surgeon General is wrong when he says that Tripler can accomplish this himself. He is dependent on the Quartermaster's department of the army, I suppose, and I have no idea that the Quartermaster's Department will listen to anything at present but getting forward rations and forage for the fighting Divisions. If I am wrong as to the means at his disposal I still do not believe that he can have faith enough in his power to be ready to exercise it. He does not, and can not be made to, believe it possible that when the Army is advancing, anything but very moderate and modest propositions will be listened to from the Medical Staff. There is no doubt that we can take care of three or four hundred or more on our boats—probably save the lives of some among them who will otherwise die from the inadequacy of the accommodations ashore—but considering what a week, or, for that matter, a day, may bring forth, I feel it right to throw them, still, on their resources—force them to enlarge their shore accommodations, believing that they are not doing half what they might, nor quarter what they ought to be able to do, in this respect. I have therefore patiently submitted to the delay of the Quarter Master's Department, in getting a wharf ready for the Elm city. Nor shall I be disposed to hasten the disposal of the sick on her. I shall endeavor to prevent any but serious cases from coming on. Then, as to the removal of the sick North, it is plain that the facilities so far offered in this respect have been greatly abused, and that serious evils have come of it. Those responsible for the care of the sick here,—I mean the military administrative as well as medical officers—have been encouraged to neglect all proper local provision for them, and to depend entirely on hurrying them on board vessels with the idea that they thus relieve themselves of responsibility about them. I saw this at our first freight, and have, (I wish the Surgeon General and our friends to be sure of this), constantly done all that I could to counteract it—not only by verbal protest—but by a habit of action, which I know that Knapp and other friends here, who have not had the duty to look at the matter so largely as I, have not been able always to regard as justifiable. But there is a greater evil than this. There is a great deal of home-sickness in the army, and among a hundred thousand men, there must always be a great many shirks. This is really the first experience of nearly all of our officers in active campaigning. They are learning to take care of their men as a matter of self-interest. The men themselves need to learn to make themselves content—of contented habit—to be away from home, to understand that this is in the bargain. It is obvious from the remarks we hear that the rumor that sick men are to be sent home has a demoralizing effect, encouraging neglect of precaution and provision against sickness with the officers and the surgeons; distracting the minds of the men from their business—their duty—by leading them to think of the chances of their getting home on sick leave. I find this appreciated by Gen'ls Williams, Van Vliet and Franklin, with whom I have conversed. It was one of many reasons for my sending the Webster to Boston, that, as no selection of New England men had been made for her, it would be seen that we did not study to send men near their homes. (It was suspected too that there might have been some management to get New York men on her, who wanted to go home, without regard to their necessity).

The Knickerbocker has arrived while I have been writing, thus I have all the elements of my plan approved by Tripler, on Monday.

The quandary is this: If they have several hundred more patients on shore than they have tents for, or beds, and among them all several hundred seriously ill—such as would properly be sent North—shall I break up my reserve and have no provision for the avalanche of suffering which a great battle before Richmond would send down upon us? I have more than fifty idle hands here—and the boats I hold, cost government three to four thousand dollars a day. I am afraid that I stand alone in my resistance to the demands of the present, and I may be induced to modify my plan.

I have just bought what is left of a cargo of ice—probably sixty tons—at $12., having been authorized by my own suggestion to do so, on acct of gov^t by Tripler. We are now very well supplied at all points I think; thanks to your good judgment and energy. There are doctors enough here, for the present, and if necessary, we could even man the D. Webster No. 2., which is clean, and which we shall have ready as a reserve sick transport, inside. Keep us informed of the accommodations at Washington, Annapolis and Baltimore. I am determined not to send sick people in any of these outguard boats outside. The only vessels we have, that I shall ever send out, of my own will, are the Webster No 1. & Spaulding.

As Dr. Bellows knows Warriner; suppose you refer the matter of Mrs Harlan to him, assuring Mr Harlan, that justice will be done. It is quite incomprehensible. Of course Mrs Harlan is in some way mistaken. I entirely approve the course you have taken. The immediate difficulty will be to satisfy Mr Harlan that there is no unnecessary delay in dealing with the matter.

night—We began taking sick on the Elm city the P.M. I am sorry to say that Dr Fisher proves good for nothing. He is excessively fussy, slow and without any authority or efficiency. I telegraphed you about the crowded state of the hospitals and about our feeding sixty men who had been turned away from them. I wrote to the surgn in charge about it & Knapp called on him with my note. He merely denied that there could have been as many as sixty turned away. He had a detail of ten men who were four hours getting their dinner, while sick men were being almost drowned in a very heavy rain. The water stood several inches deep in some tents of the hospital and the men brought on the Elm city had evidently been lying in a puddle which nearly came over them. These were selected by Ware as the sickest men, and their clothing was soaking wet. Ware helped to put up tents to protect men before the storm, and said that he saw half a dozen tents yet remaining not put up at night-fall, though men were constantly arriving and were left in their ambulances. If an engagement occurs this side of Richmond, my opinion is that we shall have all the horrors of Pittsburg landing in an aggravated form. I have tried in vain to awaken some of the Head Quarters officers to a sense of the danger, but while they admit all I say, they regard it as a part of war, and say "there *never* was a war in which the sick were so well taken care of"; "England does no better by her wounded,"—"true they will suffer a good deal for a time, but that is inevitable in war," &c.

The only comforting circumstance in our present situation is the fact that the prevalent sickness is not of a very serious character. Of the men we relieved today not more than six of the sixty, seemed to require anything more than rest and good diet for a few days, and half of them, after having had a little brandy and water, bread and tea, were inclined to walk about and amuse themselves. It was nearly twenty four hours since they had had anything to eat, except a few ginger nuts bought of a sutler.

The sutler nuisance, by the way, is dreadful here. I met a dozen boys peddling pies within a hundred yards of the Elm city today.

Yours Very Truly

Fred. Law Olmsted

"MORE APPALLING THINGS THAN WERE EVER
IMAGINED": JUNE 1862

To Henry Whitney Bellows

White House on the Pamunkey,
June 3d 1862

My Dear Sir,

Sick men arriving Friday (30th May) night by the Railroad, could not be provided for in the crowded field hospital ashore, which still remains but one fifth the capacity, in tent room, which I urged it should be made three weeks ago. To make more room, on Saturday morning (31st ulto.) we were ordered to take four hundred upon the Elm city. They were sent to her by smaller steamboats and the last load, which brought the number up to four hundred and fifty, arrived so late that she could not leave 'till Sunday morning. The orders were to deliver them at Yorktown and return immediately.

We had previously sent out two parties to look for straggling sick and visit the hospitals in the rear of the left wing. One of these returned at noon at Friday, having been by Cumberland to New Kent Court House. From Dr Allen who was in charge of the other I received a dispatch about sunset, stating that his party were assisting the surgeons in a field hospital to which wounded were crowding from a battle then in progress. Soon after midnight the party arrived on board, having come from the front with a train of wounded, and we then had our first authentic information of the fierce battle in which our whole left wing had been engaged, and which still continued, our forces losing ground, when the party left the field. We were left in painful anxiety as to the result.

Early in the morning an order came for the Knickerbocker to come immediately to the Rail Road landing. Before she could get steam up, she was twice again visited by a tug to repeat the order and hasten compliance with it. These orders came from the Surgeon General of Pennsylvania, only one of them was written; it was upon a sheet headed "Surgeon General of Pennsylvania"; was addressed "to the Surgeon in Charge of U.S. transport boat Knickerbocker," and was signed "by order of the Medical Director," with the signature of Dr Smith. The Knickerbocker had, with the written approval of Dr Tripler, been arrang^d for a *receiving* surgical hospital, and by permission of the Quarter Master, she had been especially exempted from the requirement made of others to keep her fires going. I did not feel at liberty to disregard the order, however, and all possible speed was made in firing up, but before she could move, a small steamboat came alongside with a hundred and fifty wounded men. As these came on board, they were duly registered, cleaned and dressed and each man's personal effects so disposed of that when taken from the boat they would go with him. I preceded the Knickerbocker to the landing, and finding Dr Smith in the tent of the Quarter Master & Provost Marshal, Captn Sawtelle, I reported to him the condition of the Knickerbocker and of our other boats. I then stated what our original orders had been from the Surgeon General and what had been agreed upon between myself and the Medical Director as to the use of the boats, and proposed in accordance therewith to assort the patients which should be placed on the Knickerbocker sending such as could be properly removed by sea to the Webster No. 1, which had been waiting two days for a load, and holding the rest for the Elm city to be conveyed to any point not outside the capes, all being dressed, and operations, so far as immediately necessary, being performed on the Knickerbocker. He said that each boat would be filled up as rapidly as possible and then anchored off to await orders, these being his instructions from the Medical Director. Having said this, he left the tent and I asked Captn Sawtelle, if Dr Smith had been given charge of all the boats to be used for hospital purposes on the river. He had not till now been aware he said that Dr Smith had any authority over them, but he had assumed it and seemed to be justified in doing so by a telegraph dispatch, which he had just exhibited, from the Medical Director. Captn Sawtelle seemed perplexed and said that he should call for distinct information on the subject. In the meantime, it was obvious that nothing could be done with our boats except in compliance with the orders of Dr Smith. I give you these details in order that you may understand why we have been diverted from our original plan of operations and somewhat embarrassed in our disposition to meet the emergency most effectually.

Passing over other incidents of the day—about five o'clock a train arrived with five hundred wounded. At the landing, next to the cars was a scow; next the Pennsylvania hospital boat Whillden the Hd. Q. of Dr Smith; outside of her the Commodore; outside the Commodore, the Knickerbocker. Doctor Smith had also ordered up the Webster No 2 and the State of Maine, on neither of which was there any hospital company or proper arrangments for the care of wounded or their sustenance. I again proposed to Dr Smith to so classify the patients that proper use could be made of the Webster and the graver cases be placed on our well-provided boats for Stillwater transportation. He answered that Richmond was being evacuated, that there would be more patients than all the boats could hold, and that there was no time to pick them out. He should put as many as possible on the Knickerbocker as fast as he could, as ordered by the Med. Direc. The K. is a very old boat, low between decks in the hull, with no means of ventilation under the main deck and consequently of scarcely more than half the capacity of other boats of not much greater length and with which she would by a careless observer be classed. The Surgeon of the Commodore told me that if necessary he could stow 700. I knew that half that number would soon breed a pestilence on the Knickerbocker, and I asked leave again, after filling her, to transfer as many from her, as the surgeon in charge of her might think best, to the Webster. He said that he should need the Webster to be filled up at once to her utmost capacity, in the same manner as the Knickerbocker. I replied that the Elm city would arrive the next morning & the Spaulding probably before the next night and between them they would take seven to eight hundred. At this moment Knapp reported to me that the Elm city was coming up. Five minutes afterwards she was made fast outside the Knickerbocker. She had been to York-town, landed her 450 patients and returned within the day. Dr Smith, however, declined any other arrangment than that al-ready ordered, and the wounded were presently brought across the scow, the Whillden and the Commodore to the Knicker-bocker; up and down, a hard road. Knapp suggested and urged some improvement but was answered: Our arrangments are already made and can not be changed. We began registering them as usual, but this caused delay and by Dr Smith's orders it was discontinued and those who could walk were turned in like sheep, no record being taken and no attention to the personal effects of the men. I had the captain prepared to move the boat with rapidity and directed the surgeon in charge to report to me when she should seem to have received as many as could possibly be taken *with safety*, allowing that one hundred should be removed within twelve hours. As soon as he did so, Dr Smith not being present to direct in the matter, I took the responsibil-ity of taking in the gang-planks and pushing the boat out. I ran her a mile down the river and anchored near the Webster No 1, (to which next morning—as no orders to sail were received—I had the hundred removed). She had—by estimate—three hun-dred & fifty on board; the night being fine, many were disposed of on the outer decks, and before I left at eleven at night, nearly all had been washed, dressed and put to bed decently and as comfortably as possible. All had received needed nourishment and such surgical and medical aid as was immediately required.

I came up in a small boat to the landing again where I found the Elm city with nearly five hundred wounded on board. Dr Smith had not been seen since they commenced taking them on. I ordered her to run down and anchor near the Knickerbocker.

There had been a special order in her case from the Medical Director to run to Washington; I judge that this was given under the misapprehension that she had failed to go to York-town and had her sick still on board. She was unable to go at once, for want of coal, which could not be furnished her till the evening of the next day, (Monday). The State of Maine was filled up with wounded in great haste immediately after the Elm City. The ladies on the Elm city sent some supplies on board of articles of immediate necessity and some of our men from the Webster were aiding in distributing them. We also put on board bedding and various stores of which there was evident need, from our supply boat without waiting to be asked, and without finding anyone to receive them, the surgeons being no doubt fully engrossed with pressing surgical duties. The battle had been renewed in the morning of this day (Sunday) and we had sent a party with supplies of stimulants, lint &c. to the battlefield hospitals. This party returnd about midnight with another train of wounded. All our force that could possibly be withdrawn from duty on the boats was employed in supplying drink to the wounded on the cars and in carrying them from the railroad to the boats.

The next morning, Monday, when I first went on shore, I found that a train had just arrived, and the wounded men were walking in a throng across the scow to the Webster No 2. I knew that she was not properly prepared, and I tried to stop them, and sent for Dr Smith. Dr Smith could not be found. I asked for the medical officer in charge of the Webster. The captain said there was none, and that he had had no orders but to come to the landing to take wounded. I sent for the surgeon in charge of the train and the answer was that there was no surgeon—there was no one in charge of the wounded. Mean-time, they were being taken out of the cars and assisted toward the landing by volunteer by-standers until the gangways of the boat, the scow and the landing were crowded. I finally con-cluded that Dr Smith must have ordered them to go on board, although I could find no one in the crowd who professed to have received his orders. At all events as I had no authority to stop them and as many of them seemed fainting in the sun, I advised the Captain to let them on board. He did so and they hobbled in till the boat was crowded in all parts. The Small was outside the Webster No 2, and our ladies administered as far as was possible to their relief. Going on shore, I found still a great number, including the worst cases, lying on litters, gasping in the fervid sun. I do not describe such a scene. Then and frequently since I saw more appalling things than were ever imagined in the wildest mania of delirium tremens. There were many volunteers busily doing what little could be done without any order or system or materials of relief, to mitigate the suffering of individuals. As is always the case under such circumstances, the greater number were giving orders and advice and grumbling because they were not regarded. Two or three men were working effectively and being accepted as leaders, Knapp & Ware among them. There were a few soldiers, engaged in carrying those on litters. I soon saw that these got their orders chiefly from and were working effectively under the orders of an active man, breezing about in his shirt sleeves, but with a stripe on his panteloons. As I was leading and ordering too, we soon, of course, ran foul. "May I ask who you are, Sir, & what is your authority?"

"I am Surgeon Ellis, lately post surgeon at New York, and am ordered by the Sgn Genl to take charge of wounded at White House."

"Thank God, but what has become of Dr Smith?"

"Dr Smith? I saw a man here last night who told me that he was Dr Smith; he was looking for Pennsylvania officers. He has not been about here today."

We had receivd several telegrams from the Medical Director, which indicated a great misapprehension on his part of the state of things. He could not understand my replies or would not believe my statements. For instance, one of his orders was to fill up the Knickerbocker, which I had already reported to be full; one of his messages ran in this way. "I was informed on Sunday that the Elm city had four hundred and fifty sick upon her, and that the Knickerbocker was empty. I have depended upon these statements. If the Elm city had four hundred and fifty sick on Sunday, how can she now Monday have four hundred and seventy wounded? The Elm city must discharge her sick and the Knickerbocker take on wounded." The climax was a message from the Medical Director to the Quarter Master saying that the boats held by the Sanitary Commission must be turned to use for the conveyance of the wounded. Before this I had dispatched a messenger with a letter explaining the actual condition of things, showing that every order has been followed to the letter, and that as far as possible we had pursued his intentions. Assuring him that, however incredible it might appear to him the Elm city had been here on Sunday morning with four hundred and fifty sick upon her, had proceeded to Yorktown, discharged them, returned and taken on four hundred and seventy wounded before eleven o'clock the same night. That the Knickerbocker had been empty the same morning and loaded the same night, and that as, at the time of writing, one was halfway to Washington and the other halfway to Newport News, according to the latest previous orders, it was not possible to comply with the last order of all, which was to immediately fill them (specifying these two boats) with wounded at White House. I telegraphed more briefly to the same purport and begged that Dr Ellis or Dr Watson, at the camp hospital, might be clothed with some discretionary power as to the transportation of the wounded at this landing, using the means which from hour to hour, might be most available. Dr Ellis telegraphed his orders from the Sgn Gnl at the same time and made a similar request. The reply was that 'till Dr Ellis reported to the Medical Director in person, he could not be recognized; this to Dr Ellis—to my suggestion of Dr Watson, no reply. It has got to be Thursday since I commenced writing and I have just now received another order from the Medical Director to fill up either the Knickerbocker or the Vanderbilt and send them to Portsmouth. Neither boat has been here during the last two days, and the Vanderbilt has never been under my orders. The telegraph has broken down since this order was transmitted and I can not reply or ask other instructions. Dr Tripler now explains to me (June 6th) that my telegraphic reports have not reached him, not until in some cases several days after they were sent and in irregular sequence.

At the time of which I am now writing, Monday afternoon, wounded were arriving by every train, entirely unattended or with at most a detail of two soldiers to a train of two or three hundred of them. They were packed as closely as they could be stowed in the common freight cars, without beds, without straw, at most with a wisp of hay under their heads. They arrived, dead and alive together, in the same close box, many with awful wounds festering and alive with maggots. The stench was such as to produce vomiting with some of our strong men, habituated to the duty of attending the sick & wounded of the army. How close they were packed you may infer from the fact which one of our company who was present at the loading of a car reported. A surgeon was told that it was not possible to get another man upon the floor of the car. "Then," said he, "these three men must be laid in across the others for they have got to be cleared out from here by this train." This outrage was avoided, however.

Shall I tell you that our noble women—true nobility, no empire was ever blessed with nobler—were always ready and eager, and almost always the first, to press into these places of Horror, going to them in torrents of rain, groping their way by dim, lanthorn light, at all hours of night, carrying spirits, ice and water, calling back to life those who were in the despair of utter exhaustion, or catching for mother or wife the priceless, last faint whispers of the dying. Dr Ellis was the only man who, at this time, claimed to act as a medical officer, he was without instructions and without recognized authority. Dr Ware was, for a time the only other physician on the ground. Before night however, the Spaulding opportunely arrived—not in a condition to be made directly useful being laden unfortunately with government stores, which could not be removed for twenty four hours. The physicians and students could never have been more welcome. I put one half her whole company on duty for the night on the Webster no 2. Captain Sawtelle, at my request, pitched a hospital tent for our ladies on the river Bank by the rail-road, behind which a common camp-kitchen was established. To this tent quantities of stores were conveyed, and soup and tea, prepared in camp-kettles, kept hot. Before this arrangment was complete, and until other stores could be landed, bread and molasses and iced molasses, vinegar and water were dealt out to all who needed. Many of the slightly wounded seemed almost famished, and the assertion that they had eaten nothing for three days was frequent. Before Tuesday night,

Captn Sawtelle had got up for us a dozen Sibley tents—since then a much larger number—into which, after the boats at the wharf had been crowded, the wounded were conveyed, not before, however, several score of them had been exposed to the rain for some time. The vicinity of the landing was a very inconvenient and every way bad place, for all this. Dr Ware took the main, medical charge ashore, besides doing much else. Dr Ellis and the two surgeons of the Spaulding, with their company, took the boats. I can not disentangle, now, the events of the two days, nor have I a very exact idea of the numbers we took care of. We put two hundred and fifty on the Webster No. 1, on Monday; among them were General Devin and Col. Briggs of Massachusetts, and fearing that all intermediate hospitals were full, in the absence of orders, I sent her to Boston. The same day the Vanderbilt was filled and sent. After her the Kennebeck. Today the Spaulding has been filled and sent and the State of Maine is filling a second time. The number of wounded thus far brought here this week is between two and three thousand. At least 9/10ths of these have been cared for exclusively while here, by the Sanitary Commission, with the constant aid of Dr Ellis and for some time that of the surgeons of the gun boat Sebago, Mr Odell, a member of Congress, the Revd Mr May, of Syracuse, and one or two others, who chanced to be here. We have sent away on our boats since Sunday morning seventeen hundred and seventy (1770) patients. These, after having been got upon our beds, have been all methodically and tenderly cared for. The difficulties which have had to be overcome in accomplishing this were enormous, and perhaps the greatest of them were of a nature which it would be ungrateful to describe. We have in these four days also distributed a large amount of hospital stores to the government hospitals and boats.

To Mary Perkins Olmsted

Sanitary Commission,
Floating Hospital
White House, June 11th 1862

Dear Wife,

We have got through with a terrible week's work, and now that we have an opportunity to catch breath again, my dear good friend Knapp, having worked a greater deal harder than anybody else, and accomplished more, proves to have made the worst expenditure for himself; and the doctors have ordered him to be turned out to pasture for a week at least. He promises to find and bring me word of you. It is more than a month since I have heard of or from you, and, knowing that you must have moved from Mt St Vincent, and that much must have happened, I need not say that my anxiety has become painful almost beyond endurance. I have written you six or eight times to the usual address. It is useless to speculate on the cause of my not getting letters from you. I find one or two others suffering in a similar way and as unaccountably. I should have been driven to go to you, if Bellows had not given me reason to believe that you and Marion were well and you in your usual condition—as you would not have been if anything very bad had happened to us, and if it would not have been the meanest sort of desertion of my post. I felt as if it were a post of some importance before the battle; since then—let Knapp tell you what it has been. It is worth while to have seen such awful suffering to have also the recollection of such relief and such gratitude. If we had not been just where we were and just so well prepared as we were, I can not tell you what a horrible disgrace there would have been here to our country. It will not be known in history but I want you to share the satisfaction of my consciousness that I am not playing an unworthy part—spite of my crippled body—in the great tragedy, consequently that you, left forlorner, if not as lonely, are doing your share, carrying your share, of the great weight under which the nation is staggering. It can not be equally distributed as you would know, had you seen the noble men, as I have seen them, in these last days, smiling in their last cruel struggle with death, or had you part in the crowd of those who are now coming here, eager to know how fell this or that son, brother or father, reported among the dead or missing. Thank God this comes not to us. Pray God it come not again in our time or with our children. The horror of war can never be known but on the field. It is beyond, far beyond all imagination. One of our most efficient men, who worked through all with untiring nonchalance, today, being the first day of rest, broke out in hysterics, and for hours afterwards, was in a swooning state. We send him home with an attendant tomorrow, if he is well enough. It is wonderful how the women not only retain their senses but their strength and spirit. I do hope you will think it right to come to me with Knapp. Do we not both need it? It will go far to break me down, if I can not at least be sure of hearing of you often hereafter.

Your husband

A WARTIME SKETCH: JULY 1862

To Mary Perkins Olmsted

Harrison's landing, James' River
July 3d 1862

Dear Wife,

I write in my stateroom on the Wilson Small, which lies two hundred feet East of the long pier of what we call, with some doubt if it is not another, Harrison's landing. The shore is like that of Staten Island at Redbank—or along near there. Immediately in front, it rises with a rapid slope for a distance of 1000 feet, and beyond is a table land or gentle slope northward. There are slight undulations right and left, about as on the Leveridge farm and from half a mile to a mile distant are open country in each direction, then irregular skirts of woods. At the highest point of the swell in front is a fine old brick mansion (the central hospital). The beach below the broken bank is filled with soldiers, some bathing, some washing clothes, many reading newspapers which have just arrivd from New York; some and I hope most are wounded—I can see arms in splints.

About the head of the pier there is a dense crowd of wounded, being led and carried one by one down to the hospital-boats at the end. From the edge of the bank, on the right for a short distance, there are rows of waggons, drawn up as "in line of battle"—that is, not in column—teamsters in their saddles, row after row, at right angles to the river; more are forming in the rear, and still further to the right, columns of them are moving this way. More to the left and along the crest of the hill, artillery is forming and moving off on a walk, till out of sight; over the next swell to the right, a body of cavalry is moving off—to the right. Further to the left, through the low trees & bushes on the bank there, is a city of tents to be seen. Out of them, we catch glimpses of infantry columns in movement toward the front and right. Head Quarters are a little to the left on swampy ground, and this is not far from the military centre of our position. There is a large fleet of transports in our rear and up and down the river, and at the extreme right and left are the gun-boats, with their heavy guns. The boat has swung since I commenced writing and I see down the river the turret of the Monitor—a puff and cloud of white smoke rises and is blowing away a large white gusty cloud, a heavy, shaking report and hoarse screech of shell (the sound is nearest like that of a violent steam escape, a rush, a buzz and a metallic ring combined, but with a varying, wavering intensity); then a duller one from another gun-boat, and another; something oftener than once a minute these, the heaviest reports; up the river a little further off, another set; from the front the reports, sharper but not as loud, come irregularly from one to twenty seconds apart (field artillery). Now we hear loud cheering, long and multitudinous and excited, caught up from one to another body, and then again by others more distant and then louder by those nearer again. The Hero comes up with six hundred, not more than six hundred, fresh troops, who cheer as they pass us, and we wave back their salutation with feeling, for though but a drop, we hope it is the drop of a coming shower, and we know how every drop brings its special relief to the parched and haggard heroes who have fought five battles in five successive days and each night after repulsing the attacks of double their number, made a forced march to gain a new position, who have had but two days' rations of uncooked food during these five days, who had their first night's rest last night, sleeping on their arms, without tents, blankets or fire, the rain falling in torrents, and who are now again advancing in line of battle, and who have tonight again to find strong picket guards.

Col. Howland's servant (Col. Howland is wounded, and on board) has just come off, and says their division has just been moved off; they were told it was for a special and important duty and they were expected to do their very best. Whereupon they cheered. The excitement keeps them up wonderfully, but I don't believe that braver, pluckier men were ever gathered in as large a number before on the same space of ground, as now within a radius of a mile and a half of this boat.

Letterman the new Medical Director has been on board and I am to go with the Small as quickly as possible to Washington to tell the Surgn General more fully than he can write what the condition & the medical needs of the Army are, and to bring back direct what it most urgently wants.

Wounded are arriving from the battle of today; which is now ended or suspended, though our line of battle is maintained. By climbing a mast, we can see it.

Our grand army is very nearly destroyed. I wonder whether they will let you know it. It is striving bravely and cheerfully—heroically to the last, but there is an end to human endurance, and if the enemy with his double force, keeps pushing upon it, it can not hold out much longer, unless reinforcements of considerable strength arrive.

Letterman estimates our loss in the last week at 30,000; our present force—effective—at 60,000; the enemy's at 150,000 to 200,000. The majority of our men have lost tents, knapsack and blanket, have saved only musket and cartridge box. Many in the line of battle are bareheaded and barefooted. Think what their condition will be in this shadeless plain when the July sun comes out tomorrow. I am going to get if possible, first, tents, or something that will cast a shade for the wounded.

Chesapeake bay, 4th July

We were all night feeling our way without a pilot down James river. We have met no reinforcements.

Your affectionate husband,

A CALL FOR REINFORCEMENTS: JULY 1862

To Henry Whitney Bellows

On board Steamboat "Wilson Small,"
Chesapeake bay. July 4th 1862

My Dear Doctor,

I left our anchorage off Head Quarters of the Army of the Potomac—where I wrote you last—about 4 o'clk yesterday afternoon, and am running for Washington, by request of the Medical Director, to advise the Surgeon General of the sanitary condition of the army and secure the immediate supply, as far as possible of its most urgent surgical and medical wants. As the rebels have put out the lights and we could get no pilot, we were all night feeling our way down the river, and shall not be able, with all we can do, to get to Washington till late tonight. I hope to get what is most necessary and leave on our return before night to-morrow. I telegraphed from Old Point to have everything advanced.

There is one want of the army, which on Sanitary grounds as well as every other, is so extremely urgent, that all other wants become insignificant, and I can think and care for nothing else, while it seems possible for me to use the smallest influence favorable to its supply. Why, in the name of God, if our public servants at Washington know the condition of the Army of the Potomac, do we, on this fourth of July, meet not a solitary boat load of re-inforcements going to it? Surely, they do not know it—the people do not know it—how anxiously those exhausted heroes, facing the enemy, who as they believe, presses still upon them with double their numbers, look over their shoulders, as they advance, to see if the help they have fought so hard to secure the chance of receiving, will not arrive in time to give them rest, before they faint with fatigue. No men ever deserved better of their country. They know it. They exult in it. They die exultant. But it is because they believe that by the sacrifice of their lives they have secured an opportunity to their country, of which it will now be eager and quick to take advantage.

Whatever is the truth, the Army of the Potomac believes this and lives in this belief: That its General has comprehended better than anyone else, the military opportunity, the military resources and the military cunning of the enemies of the country; also that better than anyone else he has seen how these could be successfully overcome in one blow; that the government had hitherto not seen the opportunity of the rebellion; had underestimated the value, in this opportunity, of its resources, and had failed to comprehend the motive of its moves. It has consequently refused to believe that the Army of the Potomac could not advance without reinforcements, it has not suspected that it could be threatened by overpowering numbers of the enemy upon whom it was called upon to advance, and it has attributed to an excessive caution, allied to cowardice, or to a weak ambition which it would be dangerous to gratify, the continued entreaty of its General to be supplied with the additional force, which he had from the first asserted to be essential to the sure success of his undertaking. This is suddenly ended by the enemy, who all at once throws upon three sides of this Army, with a vehemence and recklessness and prodigality of life which was calculated to overcome it as by a deluge, forces, which they believe to have been more than double their own in number. They are on low ground, untenable for prolonged defence; and they are hopelessly cut off from their base, and the enemy, again and again repulsed, reforms on the hills his broken lines and brings over fresh troops, and day after day renews with unabated confidence the purpose of overwhelming them. Every day they stand up in resistance, and every night they toil through the swamp roads, till at length on the sixth day, they have established a new base, and hold for the country the opportunity of remedying its mistake, and of yet ending the life of the rebellion at a blow. They believe the country appreciates this now and will throw everything else aside to avail themselves of it. They can not hold it long in their exhausted condition, and they believe that every hour will bring the beginning of the stream which is to flow in to stay, and, in its turn, to set back and finally to overwhelm the foe who still desperately renews the effort on which his all is staked.

Whatever measure of misapprehension of facts there may be in this, I am sure that not far differently from this believes nine tenths of the Army of the Potomac; and in this belief—this faith—that the country will regard them as having, by unparalleled exertion, endurance and heroism, saved it from a blow which would have established the confederacy, and as now holding, with even greater endurance and heroism, the forlorn hope of the battle against the Confederacy, and that the country will press forward to their rescue and the rescue of the opportunity of which they hold the key—in this faith it sustains the contest, looking every hour for large reinforcements to arrive.

I have seen and conversed freely with many staff officers and been among the men, wounded and well—if any can be called well where all are feverish with six days and nights of frightful fatigue and exhaustion and starvation and excitement. One, a Major General said, "I have not been asleep nor have I tasted food in five days—I have only sustained myself with coffee and segars." As to the men, the common and average statement is; "My regiment has had for the last five days before arriving here, two days' rations: what has been eaten of this has been eaten uncooked; during that time it has made five forced marches, and fought five battles; one third of it has fallen in killed or wounded and not one man has been shot in the back. One third of what remains is now on picket duty in the woods, which the enemy is shelling; the other lies yonder in the mud, sleeping on its arms." This was during the rain, which fell in torrents day before yesterday. Yesterday the enemy was attacking again, and when we left, the whole army was in line of battle, cheering the general, wherever he presented himself. The common saying was: "He knows now, that he can depend upon us for anything he wants, and we know that he can save us, if any man can." But still, there was a constant looking down the river for reinforcements from Washington, and looking across the river for Burnside.

The exultant confidence of the army in itself is beyond all verbal expression. It has grown out of the experience of the ability of its Generals to resist and foil and terribly punish with it, desperate assaults made upon it with forces greatly superior in numbers. It says, proudly and joyfully: "All that men can do, we can do," but there is also, the consciousness of a terrible strain upon their energies, of an unnatural strength, and the reflection is frequent that there must be a limit to every man's endurance.

Rest and recuperation, how are they to be had? The first, only by the relief of reinforcements; the second by good diet and favorable hygienic circumstances. Eastern Virginia is all malarious; the banks of James river notoriously so; the army is chiefly upon a moderately elevated, slightly undulating table-land; the river on the south side, swampy land at no great distance on the other sides. It is open, airy, dry, a healthful point, on the whole, as any that could be selected East of Richmond. But the sun will be exceedingly fierce upon it, and it is supposed the army has lost two thirds of its tents. Probably a majority of the men have lost also their knapsacks and blankets. Many were without caps or shoes. The area held is small and will be crowded. If the enemy is active as it would appear to be his policy, the officers will be too much occupied with the immediate military necessities of the position to give much attention to police duties. And if they should be disposed to guard against the great dangers which will arise if they are neglected, the excessively fatigued and exhausted condition of the men and the necessity of reserving their strength, from day to day, for the struggle with the enemy, will forbid the constant labor which would be necessary to prevent a terrible accumulation of nuisances, until at least reinforcements shall arrive so large that no more than the ordinary quotas will be required for guard and picket duty.

After such tension and trial, a rapid reduction of force must also occur from sickness, and those not on the sick list will suffer from the lassitude of reaction from excitement. Under these circumstances, all our experience shows that it will be hardly possible to enforce requirements, the observance of which must be essential to a healthy camp.

Unless large reinforcements speedily arrive, then, not only must the army feel that its heroism is unappreciated, and the object, for which it struggled, is to be lost by the neglect of others, and thus become dejected, dispirited and morally resistless to the dangers of disease, but it will be physically impossible to establish such guards against these dangers as are most obviously and directly called for.

(Private) Letterman thinks our loss may be 30,000, our present force 60,000—our net loss of artillery is probably about 50 pieces—mostly small field pieces; one battery(?) of 20 pounders.

There is a general large degree of confidence that with the aid of the gun-boats which are throwing shell on the flanks at frequent intervals, we can hold the position, till sufficient reinforcements come to place it beyond question, but, no one speaks with entire confidence, and the nearer to the head, the graver seems to be the apprehension—though with all, there is that strange exultation—ready to break out in laughter like a crazy man's. There are some few—Casey's old officers chiefly—who are utterly despondent and fault-finding. One in an important position for his rank, predicted openly that McClellan would surrender today. But there is less of this than ever before, and fewer stragglers and obvious cowards. Nothing like what was seen by Douglas, he says, after Pittsburg landing. Of what we saw after Bull Run there is not the slightest symptom. In short we have then a real grand army, tried, enduring, heroic: worth all we can give to save it.

Yours Respectfully,

Fred. Law Olmsted
General Secretary

H. W. Bellows. D.D. Pres't. San Com.

"OUR MOST URGENT WANT": AUGUST 1862

To Charles Loring Brace

Washington, Aug. 25th 1862

My Dear Charley,

I came back to Washington last week; I have been ill, and still am far from well, being very deeply jaundiced, but avoiding acute illness by every dodge to which with the best medical advice, I can from hour to hour, resort.

In looking over my trunk full of postponed letters, I find yours of July 9th in which you ask me for the grounds of my strong judgment of Stanton. They are chiefly personal. I mean that my personal intercourse with him leaves me with a strong "instinctive" conviction that he is a bad man, a coward, a bully and a swindler. My judgment of the facts of his dealing with McClellan, agree with those of the enclosed paper from "the World" which I only just now met with.

Upon the question you put—"Is not the great fault of the campaign—the making the peninsula the base—his? (McClellan's)" I answer, no. I am convinced it is Stanton's. That is, if McC.'s plan of landing all of McDowell's corps at Urbanna, marching it across to West Point & then cutting off the enemies' peninsula army from its base, had been carried out, it would not have been a mistake. I have lost my respect for Lincoln since he assumes the responsibility of the order which prevented that. Whoever is responsible for that ought to be hanged, it seems to me.

McClellan is not a Napoleon and he has the great merit of not thinking himself a Napoleon. He has got to be successful, if at all, by wise and considerate action, not by audacity or strokes of genius. If you like to have very common intellects undertake to fight in the method of very great military geniuses, I commend you to Pope. But Pope is said to have always been a notorious liar, as well as profligate ass. He and Fremont bear the worst reputations of all men who have been in the army and escaped being kicked out with official infamy by a court-martial, and there is no doubt in the mind of any regular officer I know, that Fremont would have been if Benton had not intrigued to save him. I believe them both to be great scoundrels, intriguers, just fit to plan with Stanton.

We have not any genius. We may hope, but we have no right to expect to succeed by genius. What we want is conscientious, *industrious, studious* men, who will do their duty, carefully, thoroughly. We want them in all ranks and this is our great want, our most urgent want. The inefficiency, the want of men who can be depended upon to be energetic and thorough in the execution of any trust committed to them, is the appalling circumstance of our case. It is equally apparent in all departments. I see it most directly in surgeons & chaplains, but I also see it in sergeants & captains & colonels and Generals. Men with great responsibilities are careless about them, will not take the trouble—apparently can not—to study carefully & thoroughly how they can be best executed, but *get along somehow & guess it will do.* Damn them. *Guess it will do* when the life of the nation & much more may depend on it. I have seen hundreds of lives lost which would have been saved by half as much expenditure of brainpower as would be needed to comprehend the simplest problem of Euclid. What is our Educational System worth, if this is the result? But the worst of all are these lazy loafers trained in your Theological seminaries. They could not step out of their ruts to save their own lives. Our strength & merit is cheerful or sullen endurance. In stupid British, blind lumbering momentum we beat the British themselves. By the way, why do you not come as a chaplain? It seems exactly what you have always wanted & you could be immensely useful.

Let me hear from you.

My love to Letitia.

Yours affectionately

Fred. Law Olmsted

"OUR MANY SIDED WORK": SEPTEMBER 1862

To Mary Perkins Olmsted

U.S. Sanitary Commission,
Adams' House, 244 F Street,
Washington, D.C.   Sept. 21st 1862
Sunday

Dear Wife,

You know I wanted a month to arrange a report so the Commission when it met could take a comprehensive view of things & not go off half-cocked on seeing some one or two sides of our many sided work. Vaux's illness kept me, so I finally got here (after a fatiguing *twenty* hours passage in poor stinking day cars from New York, missing connections all the way & bothered with military trains) after the third meeting of the session was well in progress and everything going at sixes & sevens just as I apprehended. I rushed to the rescue with all my might & for two days was busy eno' heading off all sorts of mistaken impressions, theories & projects. I couldn't help getting the Governor quite red in the face sometimes, in resisting the strong set of his will. He had for instance three times up a peremptory order for immediately undertaking the weekly publication of a Hospital Directory & if I couldn't do it, getting some Antioch professor put in charge of it. I "cuss'd and swore," so about it, that they yielded to my will until I got half an hour to deliberate upon it, when I demonstrated that instead of a small newspaper it would be equal in letterpress to two large quarto volumes of 240 pages each & would require several hundred clerks and the largest steam-printing establishment in the U.S. This was a sockdolager. After three days, I got up my papers & went in for a "field-day." I had Knapp to help me, and beginning at 10 A.M. gave them a sort of familiar history of our more important work of the summer & how things stood. They were (really) intensely interested & didn't want to break up until I got quite through about 4 P.M. I carried their convictions & sympathies & regained their entire confidence. Dr Bellows immediately afterwards retracted all his doubts, apologized for them & expressed his strong conviction of the wisdom with which everything had been managed during the summer. And I think I stand better with the whole Commission than I ever did before—I mean that they are more disposed to trust my judgment and leave the business to me untrammelled with specific instructions.

In the midst of all this, were the exciting telegrams of the great battles finally culminating in that of Antietam, and we were rushing to the rescue. I sent agents & $3500 into Pennsyl^a to purchase & push thro' stimulants from the North; got on six "quarter masters" (old hospital transport men) from New York; sent all we could by rail, but fearing the trains would choke the road, bought, hired & borrowed waggons & horses and sent them through by the turnpike, ("National road"). The Rail Road did get choked, and all the government medical stores as well as ours were held back somewhere in twenty miles of cars, behind ammunition & subsistence, so that our waggon trains passed them & were twenty four hours ahead of anything else on the battle fields. Agnew is there with half a dozen of our best inspectors and a score of distributory assistants. We have sent 20 or 30 tons of soup, wine &c. & are constantly yet pushing it.

Of course I have been working my brain like fury & my blood boils.

Jenkins, ordered off by the doctors to save his life, goes home today with three weeks' leave of absence with pay & a present of $250.

All the world comes to our office now, to enquire about hospitals, wounded men &c.

I have your collection of letters from Aug 4 to Septr 14th &

have enjoyed them very much as a cool breeze in the battle. By the way have you read the Tribune correspondent's report of the battle of Antietam? If not, do so, it's reprinted in most of the papers & is the most extraordinary literary production as well as the best possible large loose sketch of this great battle that you will see in the next ten years.

I wrote "Mrs Vaux is alone" they put for alone, alive. This gives you the key to all I said & did. It was for you to judge how much she needed you & how well you could come considering the children's health & your own. You know he has gone to Dr Brown's. I am greatly perplexed and perhaps not in a position or state of mind to consider healthily & with confidence, what I ought to do. I wish you would advise—I don't mean tax your energies but give me your impressions from your superficial general view. The park & Vaux's interests pull me toward New York; I am intensely held here. It don't seem as if I could do justice to both. Which shall be paramount? Self interest says the park I think. Benevolence, duty (?) & gratitude say San. Com. The San Com. are gentlemen, liberal, generous, magnanimous.

I have rather favorable intelligence regarding Vaux, but shall be surprised if he gets out for work this fall. Poor fellow, how it will annoy & depress and perplex him that he has been liable to go crazy & may be again.

I enclose check for $100. I had to borrow $300 of father, to pay Vaux's office rent &c. & make sure they did not suffer for money.

Write a word daily if you can.

Fred

Didn't you get a letter from me when in New York about Vaux & about Masons?

My impression is we can best live, especially if Vaux is going to be in poor trim, in one of the houses of Cook's block in 78th St, rent probably $400, he says they are comfortable small houses & the situation is as nearly right for me as possible.

THE UNION LEAGUE CLUB: NOVEMBER 1862

To Oliver Wolcott Gibbs

New York, Nov 5th 1862

My Dear Gibbs,

Your request can not be passed by, this direful day, but I can only give it stolen time.

The method must be built up from the motive.

Of your motive I judge from our short conversation and the name you gave your suggestion—"Loyalists' Club."

We regard ourselves as distinguished from some others by our loyalty to something, to which they, whatever they profess, whatever they may, even, believe of themselves, are not, in our estimation, loyal. We desire to recognize this distinction as a ground of a certain alliance, by which we may express our greater pleasure in the society of those who agree with us, and something more.

To what are we loyal and they not?

We agreed that Belmont and Stebbins must be of the other sort. To what are they not loyal? Both will swear allegiance to the Constitution. Stebbins within a year has declared to me that slavery must & should be abolished and the rebels exterminated. Supposing him sincere I still could not suppose him to be sympathizing with what loyalty includes with me. I feel that Liberty and Union is not all. Neither Belmont nor Stebbins could with sincerity say, I believe, that they would not, if they could, have a priviledged class in our society, a legal aristocracy. Both, I believe, hold, in their hearts *European* views on this subject. Both regard our society as "a failure" because of the want of a legally priviledged class. Both feel something of contempt for a man—at least they feel themselves to be the natural superiors of a man who does not feel himself to belong to a class, which he thinks ought to be priviledged. I, on the other hand, feel a certain contempt or a sense of superiority to a man, who wants any such legal setting up. They sympathize with what has always been the prevailing sentiment of the aristocratic and cultivated class abroad, and avowedly of only a very vulgar, presuming and peculiarly snobbish class here.

We sympathize with what has been a prevailing sentiment with the highest quality of men peculiarly in our own country, the men, too, who formed our country and gave it to our keeping. To their sentiment in this respect and to this quality given by them to our nationality, we are loyalists—they are renegades. We are the hereditary, natural aristocracy—they are parvenus; we are rich, they are vulgar. Your club then would be a club of true American aristocracy, the legitimate descendants and arms-bearers of the old Dukes of our land, of our law-givers: Loyalists. Difference of opinion within this should be tolerated; we would only require that in this, our disposition, and sense of personal dignity, should not be braved or erased. We wish also to establish the fact that there is an "aristocratic class" in New-York, which in this respect, is not European—which shall not be felt by an English gentleman to be the mere ape and parrot of a European gentry.

To this end the foundation should be very securely and cautiously laid.

Let us begin with a club, clubbing to canvass for a club. The Ante-Club. Agnew, Van Buren & yourself say, the tripod of it. Calvinistic, Catholic and cautious, (Man with his savage energy and directness; man fraternated and deliberatized; man philosphized and re-led to nature). Now close the doors and let in no man who has not blue blood to your certain knowledge; no man who does not burn with the sacred fire. Get in 15 to 30 of this elite of the elite, all of whom must, in the nature of the case, be too much personally interested, not to be willing and able to help with serious deliberate exercise of judgment. Select them, one by one, with great caution. Then classify them, not by set numbers, but according to their peculiar geniuses, knowledge and habits of judgment, into committees, to consider different questions of organization. One of these upon the shibboleth or test question for loyalty; another upon other conditions desireable to be required of membership; another upon Constitution & Byelaws with a sub committee—or a subsequent—upon plans of operation; rooms etc.

Of the first point, I have indicated the direction my views take at first opening ground. Of the second: three classes should be regarded: *first*, men of substance and established high position socially. I mentioned Minturn & Brown as first occurring to me, last night. Men of good stock or of notably high character, of legal reputation, would be desireable: Strong and Jay. So men of established repute in letters or science. And especially those of old colonial names, well brought down, as old Col. Hamilton. A larger proportion of this sort I should consider absolutely essential to success in the purpose I see. They must be in the centre. *Second*, clever men, especially of letters, wits and artists who have made their mark. *Third*, promising young men—quite *young* men, who should be sought for and drawn in and nursed and nourished with care, but especially those innocent rich young men of whom I see many now, who don't understand what their place can be in American society, gentlemen, in the European sense, in a society which has no place for "men of leisure"; they are greatly tempted to go over to the devil, (boss devil). The older and abler established men ought to fraternize with them, to welcome and hold every true man of them in fraternity—so soon they may govern us if they will.

The question is: what can be offered each of these classes, and what shall be asked of them?

As to the first class, everything must be asked; can anything be offered but the satisfaction of a patriotic and Christian purpose? This with some, if it can be well presented, will go a great way. Can anything be added?

Of the second; it is only necessary to ask little. This is essential. Let me mention names: Kapp, who knows more & talks better upon the vital cords of American history than any man I know. Cap Curtis, Col. Waring, Capt[n] Worden; Col. Elliott—all men who must live on their pay & all who must live carefully & feel every dollar. If these repeat the password, they ought to come in easily, for, once in, they will be the best working members. The fee should not be high then.

For the third class, good rooms with something to do, is alone essential (what else is needed, follows). Billiards & Reading and smoking at least. I should question if all that is necessary could not be got by arrangment with some Hotel or Restaurant of the better sort. A club suite of rooms opening out of, or by a side door into, the Maison Doree for instance; at least to its kitchen and some of its service.

I have not considered the question, whether the club should be actively engaged in propagating the faith? From within the club the faith should be actively propagated outwardly, I think, and by reason of the club, but not by the club as a club, a sufficient objection being, that certain members would be forced to quit by the expense if it were to be; (there are others).

For this reason & for others it should be understood that those who join the club do so from other motives than those which usually influence gentlemen to join clubs, and that they will aid its purposes otherwise than by their fees and annual dues. A committee of correspondence and publication should be provided with a special fund by contributions of members, not assessment, for instance. (All propagative correspondence & publication to be in the name of members, not of the Club).

The club should be, *as a club*, quiet and as little as practicable known by people not its members. So far as known, it should be purely in its *social* quality: Absolute secrecy as to its inner purpose is perhaps not to be required, but I should think it might be best that no member should propose or suggest to anyone else that he should join the club until, after having in private obtained assurance of his "loyalty," he had been proposed in the club, considered, and his election provisionally assured. Such assurance by the by could be best obtained negatively: by the question, "Don't you *hate* such & so?" rather than: "don't you love such and so?" It is easier to profess true hate than true love.

These matters & much else having been well discussed and determined in your Ante-Club, I should then set all to work to cautiously and adroitly canvass for members, not admitting them to the Ante Club & not organizing the Club of the Club till a sufficiently large list of men unanimously regarded as desireable had been made tolerably sure of, as ripe enough in loyal spirit to join it heart & soul when asked. Then organize the Club proper, the members of the Ante Club being its first members and first officers; bring in the marked men in squads rapidly, but so that those of each may fully understand it & their part in it, and have their say about those proposed still to be added before the latter are addressed on the subject.

Yours very Cordially,

Fred. Law Olmsted

Wolcott Gibbs Esqr

THE WOMEN'S COUNCIL: NOVEMBER 1862

To Henry Whitney Bellows

November 24, 1862

My dear Doctor,

The number of women in attendance upon the Council is sixteen. It has necessarily occupied my attention almost exclusively since the Commission adjourned. The objects in view have all been most successfully accomplished. After full discussions the judgment has been unanimous upon the various points upon which I wished advice. There were three delegates from the West, one from Louisville and two from Chicago. The difference between our Western operations and our Eastern has been fully brought out, and the Westerners seem to be fully convinced that ours is a better and nobler way. I detained Dr Newberry to take part in the discussions, perceiving that it would have great advantages. The Chicago ladies say that Judge Skinner told them that the California money ought all to be used by the Central Society and if it was determind to divide it among the branches, he should not be disposed to take any for Chicago, believing that it would do more harm than good. After you left the other day I had a very frank conversation with the Cincinnati men. They tacitly acknowledged that we were right, but as often as they were brought to this, they retracted and gave me to understand that right or wrong the people of Cincinnati had determined to have their share with St Louis of the bounty of California, and there was little use in reasoning about it. St. Louis was their rival, and they were merchants & there was not much use in convincing them of what was right in the matter. The people thought they were going to have $50,000 or more and they would be disappointed and angry if they didn't get it. Finally, that was all there was about it. However they gave me to understand and I thought intended to do so, that they would resist the popular clamor, as far as they could without sacrifice of their personal popularity, and do their best to prevent rash action. They left with profuse and hearty expressions of gratitude and good feeling. You can judge what they are worth. I think *they* are well disposed and rather ashamed of their position as attorneys of the O.B.D.

They were commissioned to bully us, were rather surprised at their ill-success, and ashamed of the attempt and not unwilling (if they saw how they could) to apologize for it and give it up.

After full consideration Newberry declined to take any of the Eastern inspectors. The West is better supplied with Inspectors than the East and he has two new ones to come in. I gave him the best of our Relief Agents and offered him any of the others, but he declined taking any more. Various arrangments are concocted between us, the final determination of them to be upon reports which he is to make as soon as he gets to Louisville and has conferred with Judge Skinner & others. I have given him some suggestions which, if he is able to act upon them, will, I think, give Cincinnati the opportunity of coming into line, gracefully.

Let me refer to the statement which you and others so often made that the greater part of our expenditures had been at the East. Goods & money coming to us come to a common stock. From that common stock, the wants of soldiers are to be everywhere supplied justly, equitably. No one says their wants at the West have been less attended to or not as well supplied as at the East. No one who knows anything about it: No one says it with truth. At the West certain advantages are secured from government more freely than at the East. Certain classes of stores fill our dépôts more readily and fully than at the East. The Cincinnati Branch & others at the West have foolishly chosen, instead of sending money to our treasury, to expend the money for themselves, *giving* us certain stores, which at the East *we* have purchased. This & this only is the foundation of the impression you have. And in the form in which it was frequently stated during the session, it is mistaken and unjust. It is utterly and completely false, first & last from beginning to end, that the Commission by accident or design favors the East or gives the East any advantage over the West, and I cannot allow the Commission to show the slightest appearance of entertaining that idea without protesting against it. I beg that nothing shall be done or said which shall seem in the slightest degree to intimate an admission that we entertain the charge or are affected by it. To do so will only confirm & establish the ignorant in their mistake, and the rascals in the belief that we can be bullied out of our well considered, just and honest arrangments.

My attention is at this moment called to a Resolution passed in my absence Saturday night, requiring me to submit to the Exec. Com. all augmentation of salaries. I don't think such a resolution should have been considered in my absence. I think it was unnecessary, will be very inconvenient and can do only harm. I have always referred my intentions in this respect in cases of any importance to you or the Exec. Com. if not to the Board. A request from you that I should do so would certainly have been all sufficient to correct any want of consideration in this respect. If I have ever refrained from it, it has been because I did not think you wished to be troubled in the case, that it was too unimportant—or because there were special causes for immediate decision. I think it impracticable to comply with this order without loss of efficiency, & request you to ask the Exec. Committee in my behalf, to direct its suspension.

————————

(The ladies are making arrangments to call on the President of the U.S.)!

————————

Speaking of salaries, what was the action of the Exec. Committee upon my suggestions? There was some action. Mr Strong requested me to give formal shape to it for record. I did so, with an addition which was in harmony with the views expressed, by members, though not upon motion, but all the rest (in effect) was on motion. Was this adopted or rescinded, and just how does it stand now?

Will you please direct that copies of proceedings of the Ex. Com. shall be transmitted to me daily?

I beg the Surgical Committee to find me some good general inspectors.

Yours Respectfully,

Fred. Law Olmsted

Revd Dr H. W. Bellows
President

THE EMANCIPATION PROCLAMATION: FEBRUARY 1863

To Charles Janeway Stillé

Altoona, Feb'y 25th 1863

My Dear Mr Stillé,

I have read "Northern Interests and Southern Independence" with the greatest interest and pleasure. I regard it as being of the highest value to the nation and have a renewed sense and enlarged sense of the great indebtedness in which we are all placed to you. I disagree with you in opinion as to the proclamation and regret, deeply regret, that you were compelled to express the views given in the pamphlet. I do not even agree with you as to the disastrous results which it has produced. It has served to unmask the traitors in our midst, I do not believe it has made one. I do not believe that the administration or the war has one intelligent opponent which it had not before, though both have many more active and open enemies. Of its effects on the army it is yet too early to judge. The public reports from Louisiana are unfavorable, but I have received today a letter from my brother who is camped side by side with a negro regiment at Baton Rouge, and all he says about it is in the highest degree commendatory and encouraging. My brother is not an abolitionist, or was not. The proclamation has been made the excuse or cover for a great deal that is exasperating and its results seem to be bad among ourselves, but recollect that Seymour of Connecticut and every other man of real prominence opposed the war, opposed the administration quite as decidedly (and with greater real courage) a year ago, as now. But whatever evil it has done at home is in my judgment far more than compensated by the advantage it has given us abroad. Neither the French nor the English government will as willingly as before, face the consequences of directly aiding to establish a slave-holding nation; of making a legally free people slaves. The danger of recognition, or of the encouragement of recognition, in England has been completely removed. England is today on our side; her influence is on our side. It was not before the Proclamation. The favor of Germany is ten times as strong as it was before emancipation, and France must proceed with more hesitation than she otherwise would to work against us. This is all known and felt & must be acted upon at the South. Davis's hope of creating a cry of indignation is all gone. The world is with us, is against him, and he and they know it.

And I for one, would rather the war never stopped, would rather suffer the deep humiliation of a peace with the certainty that it was but a mockery and would be but a short and ill-kept truce, I would rather go through the farce of acknowledging Southern independence, than have the Union ever again as it was. Slavery and republican liberty can not exist together. I do not wish to call Alabama my country when the law will neither protect my life there nor attempt to punish my assassinators. I wish that my children may be free to travel safely throughout my country and yet I wish them to be free to form the opinion that slavery is not right, or expedient. I have never said that it was not right, I have never said that emancipation was expedient before the proclamation, but having written calmly of what I have seen, my books have been burned, my property injured, my reputation vilified, I have been libelled and slandered, and my life threatened publickly. I don't want my children to be subject to this without redress in their own country. I don't mean they shall be. I opposed the proclamation until it was issued. I shall stand by it now as long as I live, and I shall try to bring up my children to make it good. I shall be for continual war, or for Southern independence rather than go back one step from it. There is but one way in which I believe prolonged peace to be practicable—it is called extermination.

I seldom express these opinions; I have never expressed them so strongly before. Perhaps I have never held them so clearly. This is the result of my reflections upon your argument—that portion of it addressed to those who think with me. I feel that when I tell you how greatly I value your pamphlet as a whole, I should not be honest to hold this difference back.

I trust it may be as largely circulated as the previous one has been and do as much good. I hope especially that it may be sent to any democrat who can read, in Connecticut, and to every member of the next Congress (who can read).

I am, dear Sir, gratefully yours

Fred. Law Olmsted

C. J. Stillé Esqr

A VISIT WITH GENERAL ROSENCRANS: MARCH 1863

Journey in the West

Spring 1863

NASHVILLE TO MURFREESBORO
WITH ROSECRANS

(Murfreesboro') March 7th 1863
At midnight, we went to the office of the hotel to arrange for
leaving in the morning: the clerk informed us that the train left
at 7 o'clk, we should be called at 5¼.; bkfast at 6 and leave by
an omnibus at 6:15 for the R.R. Station.

"There's no need of calling us so early—call us at 5:45."

"Can't do that."

"Why not?"

"Our rule is 5:15."

"I don't care for your rule. We wish to be called at 5:45."

"Can't do it."

"Certainly you can send a servant to rap at our door at any
hour, can't you? We take the risk of being late, if that is what
you mean."

"Well, 'twouldn't be safe. It might be forgotten; I couldn't
undertake to remember it."

"But put it on your memorandum."

"Reckon, I might forget to look at it if I did."

And all persuasion, expostulation and argument was in vain.
It is the custom of the country for the public to accommodate
itself to the convenience of the great hotel keepers, to the Rail
Road and steamboat men, and individual non-conformists will
not be tolerated. So we were visited at 5:15; had fried beef steak
and coffee without milk, and slapjacks, in the dining room before
the fires were lighted, at 6, and ten minutes after we took our
seats were told that the omnibus was ready. We packed into it,
and were furiously driven, as if the time were short, to the station,
where we waited again nearly three quarters of an hour. The
omnibus following us, driven as if the occasion for speed were
still more desperate, capsized upon one of the rocks in the road

and a lady and gentlemen badly bruised were lifted out and led to the station.

Again the ladies' car was sternly guarded, and we were driven into a steerage, close and filthy. The atmosphere high, stove-heated, dense, rank, pipe-tobacco-smoke, the cushions of the seats damp, the floor everywhere sole-deep with a shine of tobacco spittle, clay tracked in, pipe ashes, bread, cake and apples, left by yesterday's passengers. These things make some people sick but not the large mass of the travelling public, when women and men who travel with them and Major Generals, (for I observe that Major Genl Mitchell, Commander of the Post of Nashville, goes in with the women) are withdrawn. It is not agreeable to us and we would keep the window open, but K. has a cold, and it rains and is raw and gusty. On the whole, the majority of those in the car probably like it rather better for not having been cleaned. There is not a shadow of choice where any man shall spit or empty his pipe or drop his apple cores and parings, and at least nineteen in twenty of the passengers are smoking pipes, or chewing tobacco or apples. Don't suppose, however, that conversation is suspended. I think our English friends give a rather exaggerated idea of our taciturnity. As we leave the town and K. asks: "What are those earthworks?" an answer comes from before and behind, and this leads to conversation and frank relations of personal experience with the army & the people hereabouts. And this is our universal experience—the people one meets by chance are directly approachable, obliging, communicative and accommodating: much more so than in England, according to my experience. There they are obliging in a different way, with formality and consciousness. Here, no one thinks of saying thank you for being accommodated with roadside information. A man asks: "What place is this? How far is it from Murfreesboro'?" of the company at large within hearing. He does not acknowledge an answer as a courtesy by so much as a look. He feels ill-used, if nobody answers, and so, someone says: "Must be about fifteen miles. I never was here before, looks like they had had a scrimmage here. There's two bullet-holes through the target of that switch-handle. There was a little dépôt building that they burnt there."

The rail-road had been very thoroughly demolished by the

enemy; for many miles there was a continuous series of the remains of fires made from the wooden ties and sleepers, with the iron rails laid on them and when thus heated, bent so as to be useless. As on the road from Louisville to Nashville, every bridge had been destroyed. But our army had completely rebuilt everything except the station-houses and the new bridges were always protected by guards, having stockades and rifle-pits, and sometimes more complete earth-works of defence. Burnt farm-houses were frequently seen and near those which remained the absence was notable of all domestic animals except horses mounted by soldiers or attached to army waggons. The devastation was worse than on the other side of Nashville. We were glad to be assured that the rebels had left not much of this sad work to be done by our men. Not a few planters' houses remained uninjured: yet the track of war could generally be traced in broken fences, campfire-brands in their door-yards or recent waggon roads run through them. Very few of the inhabitants, white or black, were to be seen.

The Rail Road runs through nearly the centre of the field of the battle of _____ before Murfreesboro' (battle of Stones River) and the ground was at once recognizable by the clusters of fresh graves, generally a few dozen together, once or twice several hundred, rarely one isolated. Scores of dead horses lay still unburied.

Having arrived at Murfreesboro', we were guided by a fellow passenger with a major's shoulder-straps, along deeply mired roads crowded with army waggons and soldiers, horse and foot, to the square of the village, at a corner of which was a relief station of the Sanitary Commission, after visiting which and looking into a few of the village stores, long, narrow rooms, occupied as hospitals for the wounded, who seem to be doing well and were neatly cared for, we proceeded to call on General Rosecrans. He occupied the most comfortable house of the town, a short distance from the square. There were lounging sentries—that is to say, "American citizens," wearing army clothing and holding muskets on their shoulders or resting upon them, but completely free from any uniformity of appearance one with another or from any resemblance to the European idea of a soldier in carriage, manner, or style of wearing their dress. They looked at us as we passed them and entered the front-door of the Head Quarters house but said nothing. Officers, orderlys and citizens were standing in conversation or moving through the hall. As it seemed to be the function of no one present to advise or direct strangers, we opened a door into a side room, where we found a number of young officers, all busy writing at desks. Evidently the aids, young fellows, at once seen to be of a superior class—selected men, refined, intelligent and giving promise of promptness and courtesy. One immediately stepped from his desk to receive us. "Is Col _____ here?"

"He is out at this moment."

"We have letters to Gen'l Rosecrans to whom we wish to pay our respects when it will be convenient for him to receive us."

"The General is just now at breakfast; if you will come with me, I will take you to General Garfield, his Chief of Staff."

Going into another room, we found Gen'l Garfield, who, knowing nothing of us except from our statement that we were of the Sanitary Commission, made us at home in the midst of his business, in the simplest and heartiest and most good humored way possible, talking and writing, soon making familiar friends of us, on the ground of our knowing one and another of his old friends. Presently we found an old acquaintance in one of the staff who came in with papers, and then while we were talking, a man walked in rapidly, saying: "Did you see that statement of the Chicago Times, Garfield? That must be stopped. Write a peremptory contradiction of it."

"Will you show about what you want it to be on paper. Here it is. Take my chair. These gentlemen have letters to you from Bache of the Coast Survey and Dr Bell of Louisville. Mr Olmsted, Mr. Knapp. General Rosecrans."

"I'm glad to see you Sir. I am glad to see you Sir. Keep your seats"; and he gives us his hand, fixing his eye, searchingly but with a pleasant twinkle, upon us for a moment, and then turning to the desk, where he writes carefully, with pauses, paying no attention to those who come in until he has written three or four lines. "There, something in that way, Garfield. When have you seen Prof^r Bache, Mr Olmsted? What a nice little hand he always writes," and then he opens the letters. While he is reading them, a telegraphic dispatch is brought in, Genl Garfield reads it and says: "_____ telegraphs that he hears heavy guns to the Southward."

Genl Rosecrans lifts his head, holding Prof' Bache's letter still: "That must be Sheridan. Telegraph _____ & _____ to see if they have heard firing today?"

"I have already done so," said Captain Bond.

"Anything from Davis?"

"Nothing; he no doubt moved two brigades to Salem this morning."

"He should have three days' rations."

"He has."

"Let's look at the map," and he rose and walked with Garfield & Bond into the next room. Presently coming back, he was saying: "Let them all have three days' cooked rations."

"They are all about ready. Could move in half an hour."

"That's right," and he took his seat by the desk and read the letters through; then rose, and said: "Come into my room, gentlemen," and we walked into a room with a large four post bed; a silk ensign hanging over it. "Take seats, take seats. Have a cigar? Mr. Knapp: have a cigar? Your association has done a heap of good here. There is a great deal of benevolence in our people, but benevolence is very often misdirected and wasted so that it does more harm than good. You have done just what was wanted to be done in giving system and order to it. It was a capital good thing for us."

"I am glad you so regard it. Let me thank you for your assistance to the purpose of the Commission. Your letter was not only very gratifying to the Commission, but it has been of great value in getting the popular attention directed to the mistake of schemes for aiding the army which have state or local limits. I must say, General, that I think the Sanitary Commission has more claims upon the gratitude of the country for what it has done in a quiet, unaggressive way to lead the people out of their old narrow state and local bounds of interest and sympathy and to foster a purely national exercise of patriotic sentiment, than for the assistance which it has been able to bring to the Medical department in relieving the sick and wounded. Your letter helps greatly to establish precisely that conviction which the Commission has been constantly endeavoring to carry to every fireside in the loyal states, since the war commenced."

"I am glad if it will help at all in that. It's hard when people are bent on doing something for the relief of soldiers from their own district, to check them, and tell them it is not their soldiers but the soldiers of the country they are to help. It looks almost unkind, but it is the only real Kindness and certainly the only real patriotism. It would have been better that some of the sick and wounded should have suffered and died from want, than that anything should have been allowed which would encourage that very spirit at the North which we are fighting against at the South. We have got to conquer it and trample it out, or it will destroy us. They are so set upon being little nigger aristocrats that they will sacrifice everything else to it. What is their spirit of chivalry? It's the same spirit which loves to bully niggers. And it grows out of that. It's contemptible meanness. They boast of their honor. Their honor! What does it amount to? They reverence it just so long as it keeps ahead of their self interest and passions, but as soon as their passions or selfish interest come in play, honor falls behind. They are honorable just so far as it jumps with their convenience and pleasure to be honorable. Beyond that they are the meanest men in the world, full of miserable pride, violent and uncontrollable in their selfishness. That's my experience with them, here and everywhere. We've a great work before us here. Please God, we'll do it. My only hope is" (here he paused, turned in his chair, took his cigar from his mouth and threw his head forward looking at us, first one and then the other, keenly in the eyes and after a pause nodding two or three times, I nodded in response. He nodded again, significantly, and his eyes gleamed.) "My only hope is—that God is just." (pausing again) "We were not a war-like people. I wish that we had been a virtuous people. But we have a wonderful patriotism standing opposed to the selfish pride of those little nigger-tyrants. I have studied history with some care but I don't believe, I do not believe that as much pure patriotism—pure patriotism, without mixture of self interest—was ever found in the common run of any people on the earth before. Men, common men in the ranks deliberately make offering of their lives for the sake of the nation. Selfishness has not as deep a root as usual in men who really do that, really, without any humbug. I saw a man the other day: He was mortally wounded and he knew that he could not live more than a few hours. 'It's all right,' said he, 'all right,' as cheerfully as I can say it now. 'I made up my mind when I listed,' said he, 'that I would give up my life for the country, and now it's all right. I have nothing to say against it. It's all right, General.'"

We referred to Garesche, whom we had known and loved in Washington. "Garesche," said the General, "gave his life to save this nation as fully, as truly and as simply as ever any man gave his life to any cause. He expected to be killed in that battle. He fully prepared himself for it. He asked my leave to retire for a short time half an hour before he was killed. I know what he retired for. He was all ready to meet death. I never saw anything finer in my life than his face when he drew his sword. You would have thought it the happiest moment of his life. He knew where he was going."

This is a poor report of the opening of our conversation. I perceive that I have failed to catch the style of General Rosecrans's language, which was in the highest degree direct, forcible and plain, boldly idiomatic and with frequent unhesitating reference to fundamental religious principles, but I have followed my memory of his very words as precisely as possible. We remained in the bed-room two hours and a half, the General twice insisting upon our remaining when we rose to go. He discoursed to us during more than half of this time and always in much the same tone; manifesting the strongest devotion to our nationality; the strongest aversion to everything of a disintegrating tendency. He hated the policy of politicians. Justice must save us—nothing less. Justice is our policy. What is the most truly and permanently just, that is best. The just policy is the wisest policy, and in the end it will take with the people. Politicians make the greatest mistake about that. They would hit the favor of the people a great deal easier, oftener and better, if they would go right straight ahead as they thought absolutely just, and not ask what the people want. In the end the people will find out and hold fast by a just man. He referred to the evils growing out of the interests of Governors and other elective officers controlling appointments and promotions as one of the grandest difficulties which the army had to struggle with but readily and emphatically assented when I said evils of this kind were not peculiar to American armies.

Further advices by telegraph coming in, a consultation of Generals was held, in the midst of which a parcel which had come by our train was opened, and found to contain maps, sent from the Coast Survey office, one being of Eastern Tennessee. This and others were studied, and various surmises canvassed of the intention of the enemy in the movements of which symptoms were reported. (Three regiments of ours had been taken prisoners by Van Dorn's cavalry the day before.) Among the Generals present was Jeff. C. Davis, who invited us to visit him in his camp. He did not remain long, and left with orders to have everything in readiness to move instantly upon an order, the intention being to move his division, seventeen miles to the right that night, upon a certain anticipated contingency.

Before leaving, we expressed a wish to look at the army in its camps, and were advised to visit a part of Davis's division which was only two miles out, and which might be in movement by the time we reached them. "I should like to have you see them on the march," said the General. A verbal order was given to provide us with two horses and an orderly. As an indication of the character, not of General Rosecrans, but of our army and people, I cannot omit to mention that my horse appeared never to have known a curry comb and to have lain the last night and for many nights in mud; the bridle had been plainly stomped under foot in clay, it was knotted at the end, where the buckle had been torn loose, and clods of fresh clay were still attached to it; the saddle, the regulation dragoons' saddle—a McClellan frame strapped upon a ragged blanket—was equally rude and dirty. I had some difficulty in mounting and the orderly did not offer me the slightest assistance, obliging me to step out in the deep mud of the street while he kept his seat. Once mounted, the horse proved an excellent one; active, spirited, plucky, untiring, and perfectly well-trained as a saddle-horse, and the orderly proved a remarkably intelligent, patriotic and obliging man, a very pleasant leader and companion, for our excursion.

We galloped out upon a road dangerously crowded with army waggons, the empty ones driven recklessly, the six mules to each waggon not unfrequently disobeying orders when at full speed and by some eccentric action, when attempting to turn out, suddenly throwing the waggon into the ditch, giving occasion for a frightful expenditure of oaths and lashes, from the rude fellows who drove postilion fashion, with a single line to the leaders.

Genl Davis's quarters were pointed out to us at a small

dilapidated house, without furniture, in heavily wooded low ground; mud and water fetlock deep to the door, before which there was a rude rack at which horses were hitched. There were a few scattered tents before it, and among them, a camp forge, with the blacksmiths shoeing horses. There were sentries and officers about the door, but they paid no attention to us, and we walked in and found Gen'l Davis alone writing at a rude table, the room containing two chests, a case of maps, a camp-bed and some personal equipments.

SOUTHERN ILLINOISANS: MARCH 1863

Journey in the West

Spring 1863

LOUISVILLE TOWARD CAIRO

Cairo, supra Mississippi,
March 13th 1863

By a fracture of the promises of the Ohio and Mississippi Rail Road Company, we were yesterday thrown upon our resources for twelve hours, at a small way station, in the midst of the great prairie region of Illinois, just as Mr Trollope was at Centralia. There were a score of men besides ourselves and some women left in the lurch with us. I walked the length of the railway platform several times during the day, to see if I could find the American, as seen in numbers, and described by Mr Trollope at Centralia under similar circumstances. There were individuals "walking the deck" and smoking solitarily and silently, but never did I find twice the same man thus engaged, nor of the score was there more than one who was not during the greater part of the day joined to one of the several groups which I invariably found engaged in conversation or playing euchre. The one solitary man who answered to Mr Trollope's description of the American with twelve hours on his hands at a rail-road station in the far West, was an American Indian, who did exhibit precisely that taciturn, self-wrapped and stolidly self-sufficient aspect in which Mr Trollope saw so many of his fellow-detained white men. I thought when I read Mr Trollope's book that this description was very clever and true, though it was mysterious to me, how it could be so and I have often since. I spoke of it to gentlemen at Cincinnati and Louisville and they were decidedly of the opinion that it was a mere accident of the occasion from which Mr Trollope had generalized carelessly. They, who had travelled much in the West and a little in Europe, were quite sure that men were more ready to converse, more likely to be quickly on familiar terms with each other in America—in the West especially—than in Europe, than in England particularly.

This accords with my experience yet I recognized something familiar in Mr Trollope's picture. It reproduced sensations of my Southern experience. I think this is true: that the American is more content to be solitary and silent upon occasion, than the European; that though this Indian habit is not constant with him, it sits more naturally upon him when he lacks satisfactory opportunity for social life, than, under similar circumstances, it does upon the European. Mr Trollope is an exception to his countrymen, if, under the circumstances described, he was not unusually morose, not to say crabbed and quarrelsome, while forced by the mismanagement of the railway company to wait twelve hours on a miserable railway junction platform, with not the smallest object of interest to him in the neighborhood and no better dinner to be had than was to have been expected at a prairie hamlet in Illinois. I thought yesterday, supposing twenty Englishmen averaging first, second and third class railway travellers had been set down here in this way without even a decent ale-house or skittle yard to resort to, or a fine bit of scenery or of architecture to regale their eyes upon—only this dreary prairie to the monotonous horizon—how would they have talked? The whole day would have been consumed in selecting associates to grumble with and in grumbling. I think that of our twenty Yankees, ten gave vent to their disappointment at the moment they discovered how we were situated, in one or two sound oaths and imprecations upon the Ohio and Mississippi Rail Road Company. The remainder acted precisely as if they had expected it and bargained for it, and after one minute of swearing, I did not hear a word on the subject during the day. It is a misfortune and a fault of our national character that we bear evils too patiently and carelessly. If every American traveller was made crabbed for a day by every rail-road company's or inn-keeper's mismanagement that he suffered from, if some one of every twenty would write for the Times, or even, as I do, once in ten thousand cases, complain, in a book, of these things, our progress in civilization would be more sure.

Nothing was more unsatisfactory to me in Mr Russell's book than his picture of the American on the prairies of Illinois. I knew that it must be incomplete and untrue in its incompleteness from the mere statistics of Illinois, but I thought that there must have been more that was disagreeable and unpromising in the condition of our prairie population than I had before supposed and less that would be agreeable to see than I had imagined, or that so keen, careful and generally good humored an observer as Mr Russell would not have failed to see it. Yesterday was my first day on the prairies of the free states. I am glad to be obliged to think that either Mr Russell was very unfortunate, or that I was very fortunate in my experience. And yet I saw some of the most disagreeable people and one of the most tiresome landscapes that I ever met with. I saw all that Mr Russell describes so graphically and most of it was as hateful to me as it was to him. But I saw a good deal that he did not see and which would have made his first day on the Illinois Central Rail Road much pleasanter if he had seen it.

I will describe some things that I saw.

First; two small, low, very rude, log-cabins, connected by a roof so as to make a third apartment open to the weather and the road on one side; by the side of it a log corn-crib, both standing in the midst of a small (for the prairies) corn-field, in which stood a number of very poor horses and cattle. A man and woman and a number of children were sitting, lounging or moving listlessly in the roofed space or before it. They were ill-dressed, perhaps ragged; dirty and forlorn looking. The picture was very familiar to me and I have described it before. I could swear that man moved to "The Illineyes" from the slave states many years ago; that he has got corn and hogs more than enough, sells enough to buy tobacco, molasses and store-goods, and to warrant not a few visits to one of the dram-shops of which so many were seen by Mr Russell; that he thinks it's getting too close settled round here, but don't want to go north, and don't want to go back to "a nigger state" and don't find any place in Southern Illinois that is not getting too close settled up to suit him to begin on, so he can't be induced to sell out to his neighbors who would gladly unite to pay him twice the market value of his property to get him to move away from them. I could swear that he has never written a letter in his life; that he takes no newspaper, that he thinks the Vice President is a mulatto, that the President is a despot, that he means to resist the execution of the Conscription Act and to refuse to pay any war taxes; that he thinks Northern and Southern Illinois ought to be two states, and that he hates a Yankee "worse than a nigger"; that he is in short a poor white of the South out of place. There are many such in Southern Indiana and Illinois. He has his good qualities. He helped to drive the Indians away from here, as well as the panthers and wolves. And much as I pity him and his children, if I was obliged to live here on the prairie, I would rather live under his roof than in a wigwam, I would rather be him than to be the savage that I have seen. He has done some work by which others have benefitted as well as himself. He has not the smallest particle of servility; I should not be surprised if he were a member of some church and meant to do God's will, according to his light; and on the whole, I must say that I think that the average English agricultural laborer leads even a less enviable life than this poor man on the prairies. He never had any fear that he could not get food for his children or that he might have to come on the parish.

"A VISIT TO THE ARMY": APRIL 1863

To John Olmsted

Sanitary Store Boat, "Dunleith,"
on the Mississippi, above Memphis;
April 1st 1863

Dear Father,

We are returning from a visit to the army before Vicksburg, which we reached on the 22d. General Grant's command consists of four army corps: one under Gen'l Hurlbut is in Tennessee; there being detachments at Columbus; Is^d No 10; New Madrid, Jackson, Helena, and considerable bodies at Corinth and Memphis. A second corps is amphibious between Helena and New Providence, under Gen'l McPherson; a third, having been recently drowned out of camp at Young's Point, near the canal across the neck, is now at Milliken's bend, ten miles above; Sherman's corps alone remains in direct observation of Vicksburg. It is camped on a series of plantations, from one to two miles above the canal. Head quarters is on the steamboat Magnolia, which lies, nose up, on the only ground which I saw, above water, outside the levee below Milliken's bend. There were a dozen large steamboats at the same place, two being quarters of Col. Bissell's Western Engineer Regiment; two ordnance boats, (loaded with ammunition) one medical store-boat; one hospital boat, several transports and forage boats, and one immense floating ware-house containing Commissary stores; also a score or two of flatboats loaded with coal. The space of ground out of water is about 1000 feet in length. At the other end of Sherman's encampment, there are half a dozen more Commissary boats. There are near here also three or four iron-clads and rams, and in the mouth of the Yazoo, which is just opposite Hd. Q., the flag boat of Admiral Porter, half a dozen mortar boats, another iron-clad, and some more rams and a naval hospital boat. Most of the Squadron, and considerable force from each army-corps were absent on the Sunflower and Blackwater expeditions, from which they were getting back as we left; the sternwheel transports, wonderfully knocked to pieces; their smoke-stacks all down, so that the black coal-smoke was thrown directly upon the hurricane decks, which were necessarily crowded with men, who must have been nearly suffocated by it.

The day after our arrival Gen'l Grant sent an aid on board our boat to take us as near to Vicksburg as it would be safe to go. It was near enough to set our watches by the town-clock and to see negroes shovelling earth upon the breast-works. Bissell was building a case-mate battery for two 30 lb^r Parrotts, concealed from the enemy by the levee, at the point nearest the town; from which it was intended to open fire upon their R.R. station and Commissary storehouse, the morning after we left. The next day we went with Medical Director Hewit, to look at the camps, riding on the levee, and across one plantation on a corduroy road. The ground inside the levee even, is elsewhere impassible, the ground being all soaked, where it is not flooded, with the "seepage-water" straining through and under the levees. The camps are near the levee; the tents being furnished with bedsteads made of saplings, lifting the men a few inches off the ground; the men of one battery, having been flooded out elsewhere, had pitched their tents on terraces cut in the slope of the levee; forming a very picturesque camp; the levee is here about 14 ft. high. A part of McPherson's men whom we visited opposite Yazoo pass were camped on a strip of the forest left above water, not more than fifty feet wide; the water so nearly over it, that the swell caused by our boat rolled into one of the tents. The water had risen an inch and a half during the night, and you would say it was about the most dismal place and the most dismal prospect upon which an army could be put. So here of Sherman's corps: the ground all asoak and water backing up on them in every direction except where the levee restrained it. The levee itself was lined with graves; there being no other place where the dead could be buried, on account of the water, which at once fills every cavity. These graves, which must be seen by everyone, there being no other road to travel near the camps, have helped, I suppose, to give the impression that Grant's army was in a terribly diseased state. I suppose country people would get the impression that a fearful epidemic was prevailing if they should see the burials daily occurring in any town of 40,000 inhabitants, or if they should see all the graves made within a month placed in two lines, head to foot, as they are for this army, on the levee.

In fact the health of the army, tho' not quite as good as that of the army in general, is amazingly good. You can not conceive how well and happy the men in general looked. They are mostly now well broken in, and know how to take care of themselves. Considering that they were living athletically and robustly, with plentiful air; I don't know anything that they wanted. I have enough of the Bedouin nature in my composition to envy them. I never saw men looking healthier or happier. The food is abundant, varied and most excellent in quality. I don't believe that one in fifty ever lived as well before. They were well-clothed and well-shod. If I were young and sound, I would like nothing so well as to be one of them.

We dined at Sherman's Head Quarters, which are in a

planter's house in a little grove of willow oaks and Pride of China, just greened out, but dinner was served in a tent. Here I met Captain Janney, Sherman's staff-engineer, with whom I rode a couple of hours in the afternoon and whose talk I enjoyed greatly. He has had a half artist education in Paris and was warm on parks, pictures, architects, engineers and artists. Reminiscences of Cranch and Fontainbleau; of student-life at the Politechnique and Centrale, discussions of the decoration of the Louvre, had a peculiar zest in the midst of raw upper Louisiana plantation, where nature's usual work is but half-done; looking across the River into tree-tops hung with the weird Spanish-moss, vultures floating above; shouts and turmoil of a gang of contrabands tearing down the gin-house of the plantation—Captain Janney wants the material for bridges—the drums beating and bugles sounding for evening parade behind and the distant boom of Farragut's big guns on the Hartford, pitching shells at intervals into my quondam host's, Dick Taylor's, rebel batteries at Warrenton. Another excellent fellow here was Sherman's Medical Director, McMillan, whom I have known before; indeed have met often since the war began. He was Stoneman's Medical Director on the Peninsula. He was grossly abused by the Herald's correspondent, for "entire neglect to make any provision for the wounded" at the battle of Chickasaw bluffs, whereas his arrangments were really the most complete that have ever been formed before a battle, with perhaps a single exception, and he is one of the most humane, industrious, enlightened and efficient surgeons in the Army. It is oftener than otherwise that the really good surgeons are maligned and held up to public execration, and the surgeons who always fail in an emergency pass for the best.

McMillan & Janney rode with us to call on Gen'l Steele, living in a large room of a planter's house, which had been half finished years ago, and since inhabited in its unfinished state. There were school-classics left behind on the mantel-piece. From Gen'l Steele's we rode to Gen'l Blair's also quartered in a planter's house. (The boat shakes so, it is scarcely possible to write legibly—but a pencil can be better managed).

Janney, by the way, who has charge of the Young's Point Canal and employs several hundred contrabands, and who also employed a large number while Sherman's corps was at

Memphis, speaks well of the negroes as industrious, disciplinable, grateful and docile. They have less vigor and endurance than whites, can not do as much hard work and seem generally to be of weak constitution. A remarkable proportion of them are deformed or mutilated, apparently from injuries in childhood. Nearly all bear the marks of injuries which they are unable to explain. You know that I have contended that the negro race in slavery was constantly growing in the mass less and less qualified for self dependence; the instinct of self-preservation being more and more worked out, and the habit of letting "master take care of his nigger" bred in to the race. Janney believes that slave children while more precocious than white, suffer more from accidents than the children of the poor with us. The most valuable negroes, who are also, as a rule, the cleverest, have generally been taken away from the plantations by their owners, the least enterprising and those who would be most bewildered in trying to look out for themselves, and who are worth least for army purposes, being left as they are always told to "look after things" on the plantations. Wonderfully little it is they have to look after, however. A good many who are taken away, however, contrive to escape and return to the plantation or to their relatives and friends who follow the Union army. They often show strong attachments in this way, not to their owners but to localities and to their families. Among the company which was working under him at Memphis, Captain Janney said that there was one very active, sharp, industrious and faithful fellow, who had left a plantation about twenty miles off. Soon after his good qualities had attracted Janney's attention, his owner—a rank rebel, came as they often do, with complete assurance, to ask that he should be given up to him. Janney assured him that the country needed his services and it could not be thought of at present. Some weeks after this the same negro came one morning to Janney's tent and said: "Here's a right good fowling-piece, Captain, and I want to gib it to you."

"Where did you get it?"

"Got him ob my old massa, Sah."

"How is that? What did he give you his fowling piece for?"

"Did'n gib'm me, Sah; I took 'em."

"When?"

"Last night."

"Has your master been here again?"

"No Sah, I been down dar, to de old place, myself lass night, and I see de gun, dah, and I tort he was a rebel and he ortn't to be let hab a gun, and I ort to take 'em away, tort dat wus right, Captain, wusn't it? He ain't no business wid a gun, has he? Only to shoot our teamsters wid it."

"What sent you out there?"

"Well, I went dah, Sah, for to get my wife and chile dat was dah. I tried to get 'em nodder way but I was cheated, and I had to go myself."

"What other way did you try?"

"I'll tell ou, Sah; I want my wife and chile: dey was down dah on de ole plantation. Last Sunday when we'd got our pay, I seen a white man dat libs ober dah, and he tell me if I gib him my money he get my wife for me. I had thirty dollars Sah, and I gib it to him, but my wife did'n come. So I went myself. My wife, house servant, Sah, and I creep up to de house and look into de windah: de windah was open and I heah de ole man and de ole woman dere snorin in de corner, and I put my head in and dah I see de gun standing by de fi' place. I jumped right in and cotch up de gun, and turn roun' and hold em so. Says I, 'Master, I want my wife.' 'You can take her,' says he, and he didn say another word, nor move a bit, nor Missis eider. My wife she heerd me, and she come down wid de chile and we just walk out ob de door; but I tort, I'd take de gun. He ain't no Union man and he ortn't to hab a gun, Captain. You'll take it, Sah, won't you?"

"Yes, I'll turn it in for you."

Returning to the Magnolia, we took tea with Gen'l Grant. He told me of the return of Admiral Porter and the failure of the "Sunflower" expedition. He said there seemed to be no way open to attack Vicksburg but by direct assault in front and an attempt to take it in this way would involve a frightful loss of life. He was obviously full of grave thought and concern and I avoided keeping his attention at all. He lives in the ladies' cabin of the boat, there is a sentry, or an apology for one, at the boat's gangway, but he stops no one from going on board, and there is free range in the cabin for anyone to and beyond the table, which the General, with others, writes upon, near the stern. He is more approachable and liable to interruptions than a merchant or lawyer generally allows himself to be in his office, and in my observation, citizens who had been allowed to come to the army to remove bodies of the dead for their friends; or on other pretexts, several times came in and introduced themselves to him; one man saying, "I hain't got no business with you, General, but I just wanted to have a little talk with you because folks will ask me if I did." The General had just received a number of Vicksburg papers by a deserter, which he invited me to look over. He was reading these and writing during most of the evening, while I was conversing with the gentlemen of the staff; when I rose to go, he got up and said: "I wish you would be in as much as convenient while you stay, I am not always as much occupied, as I am tonight, and whenever you see that I am not, understand that I shall be glad to talk with you." The next night I went in and had an hour's conversation with him. He is one of the most engaging men I ever saw. Small, quiet, gentle, modest—extremely, even uncomfortably, modest—frank, confiding and of an exceedingly kind disposition. He gives you the impression of a man of strong will, however, and of capacity, underlying these feminine traits. As a general, I should think his quality was that of quick commonsense judgments, unobstructed by prejudices, and deep abiding quiet resolution. He confided to me in a comic, plaintive, half humorous, half indignant way, the annoyances, obstructions, embarrassments and hindrances to which the Governors of the various Western states constantly subjected him, and keenly reviewed their various methods. The Governors of Iowa and Wisconsin were moderate in their inflictions and seemed to have some appreciation of his situation. He must do them the credit to say that they were forbearing and thoroughly patriotic. The Governor of Illinois was an amiable and weak man. He seemed to think it his business to help any citizen of Illinois to anything he wanted. "He must be in the habit of signing papers without reading them, and the quantities of letters he writes me urging me to grant favors to people who come here with them, is appalling. Favors too, which he ought to know that I have no right to grant—no more than you would have. It's very hard, especially when he sends women here, to get favors for their sons. It's a pastime to face a battery compared with facing a woman begging for her son, you know. These letters from the Governor of Illinois being all open letters, are written in the most earnest tone of personal and official anxiety. "He could not be more in earnest if he were pleading for his own son. And yet there are so many of them, they can't mean anything. I've been expecting a letter from him to tell me that he did not want me to pay any attention to them. It's different with the Governor of Indiana. He is perfectly cold-hearted. He seems to think, because I have some Indiana regiments, that he has a right to demand my assistance in any way he chooses, to carry out his state political arrangments. By the way, doctor, there's a lady from _____ on the _____ which arrived this afternoon, who has a great many favors to ask. I've seen her; I can't see her again. You must answer her. It's easier for you to say no to a woman than 'tis for me. Some things she wants, can be granted; some can't; you'll see how it is, when you talk with her. But don't leave it necessary for me to see her again."

I had some suggestions to make to the General; he heard me patiently, met me quickly, almost eagerly, adopted and advanced upon my views, allowed me to prepare a draft for an order in accordance with them, which next day he adopted adding one clinching sentence, and handed over to his adjutant General, who at once gave it the form of an order, signed, copied, printed and issued it. The openness of mind, directness, simplicity and rapidity of reasoning and clearness, with consequent confidence, of conclusion, of Genl Grant is very delightful. Those about him become deeply attached to him. Towards Sherman there is more than attachment, something of veneration, universally expressed, most by those who know him most intimately, from which I suspect that he has more genius than Grant.

We spent one day chiefly among the iron-clads and gunboats. Admiral Porter is a gentlemanly, straight forward and resolute sort of man. Breese his flag-captain a smiling, cheerful and most obliging and agreeable man. He assumes friendship from the start, but, with all this, one gets an impression of strong will & great certainty that when the time comes for boarding or cutting out, he will bear his part with the same ingenuous ease and grace. Some of the new men of the navy whom we saw did not strike us so favorably. Scurvy was threatening the squadron and we put on 200 barrels of potatoes and onions on the flag-boat.

April 3d   Cairo

We have just arrived here, all quite well.
Expect to go to St. Louis this evening.
Your affectionate Son,

Fred. Law Olmsted

John Olmsted, Esqr
Hartford, C^t
(Please send this to Washington.)

"EXTERMINATION OF THE REBELS": APRIL 1863

To Charles Eliot Norton

Washington, April 30th 1863

My Dear Sir,

I am truly obliged to you for your favor of the 22d in reply to my note to Mr Forbes.

The slip enterprise is certainly a most effective measure for good, and if I should be able, at any time, to contribute to it, I shall gladly avail myself of your invitation.

To establish our nationality on a firm and permanently firm basis, it will be necessary that we have no dealings with slave-holders and rebels or disaffected people at the South, except as with criminals who have no civil rights, who have—as such—no property; as with men to whom nothing can be conceded, who can have nothing to give us but submission, and with whom consequently all idea of compromise is out of the question. As Mr Seward said the other day, whenever the people have made up their minds to a long war, the war is at an end. That is to say, as soon as it is known that we will never give up, that we want no peace and will have no peace with traitors, no one can doubt—no one at the South can doubt, what the result will be. It is simply a question of whose resources will hold out longest.

Everyone at the South must see that as the nation's will. Every man then who would not prefer death to submission, will be under a constant temptation to ask: "If I have got to submit, might I not as well submit now?" This would not at once or soon bring resistance to an end but would only make that end sure—the result sure. To reach it the leaders and desperate men, and those whom they could control, would keep together as armies as long as they could, afterwards as bands in the mountains and swamps, and a large part of the population would continue, while nominally submissive, to give them all the aid, and the civil officers of the nation, all the embarrassment possible. Probably for many years, in parts, no considerable part of the population will take part in elections or hold civil office, and those who do take office will be in danger of assassination and all manner of underhanded annoyance and obstruction. War will then continue for years as civil war, having the more common characteristics of civil war. Practically, therefore, what we need of the people is that they should say no more, ever, of peace with the South. Peace is to be come at by a gradual process, not by a treaty of peace, not by any act of Congress, least of all by any compromise, but by the gradual wearing out, dying off and killing off—extermination of the rebels.

Now I think the great work of those who are in a position to lead the people, is that of familiarizing them with this idea, of rooting out of their minds the idea that the war is to be ended by an event—the Tribune idea, the sensational idea. I think an appetite for sensations is clearly not as strong as it was and yet I fear that the promise of a peace, jubilee-holiday with fire-works and a grand inflation of business, would reconcile a good many of us to the prospect of having Southern gentlemen back again in Washington society. It is this danger we need to fortify the people's mind against now.

At the West, especially in the Southern part of the Western states and in the large towns, not only is Copperheadism and hatred of New England and a hankering after the nobility of the South very strong, but with loyal men to a great extent, the passion of money-making, especially by land speculation, constantly struggles with patriotism. Patriotism will lose a great advantage in this struggle when the Mississippi shall be opened. There will from that time be a strong and constantly increasing disposition throughout the West, but especially in the Western large towns, to make some arrangment with the rebels—no matter what, so the Mississippi trade can be resumed.

Hence I hope that you will do all you can to propagate the resolution that peace shall be gained in Alabama only as it has been, partially, in Maryland and Western Virginia and Kentucky and Missouri. That the rebels are to be exterminated, and the process of extermination is likely to continue for years.

That is the spirit of the unconditional Union men of the border states. Let us insist upon it that that is the spirit of loyal men everywhere.

I really think, however, if we can manage to keep the war along only one year more, get a hundred thousand negroes habituated to working only for wages, and have a few regiments of them stand up well, side by side, with the white ones, in some great battles, the disintegration of Southern Society—of the Slave Social System—will be permanently established.

Thank God, we live so close upon it. It is more than I had expected a hundred years would bring the world to.

I do not know enough of Genl Banks' arrangment to judge fairly of it. But if he can get a quarter part of the slaves who were in Louisiana to work for money-wages, I think he will have struck the heaviest blow at Slavery that it has yet received. My impression is that you overestimate the danger to be apprehended from any intermediate state between Slavery and Freedom. Men who have been accustomed to manage negroes as slaves, will not be able to do anything with them in any condition which closely resembles but is not slavery. It will be easier for them to deal with them as free-men than as apprentices. The contradictions of Slavery itself are an intolerable embarrassment. The self control which would be required by an apprenticeship would be impossible. They could never help taking the aims of an owner and getting themselves into trouble thereby.

A year more of war and slave-holders will be mere lingering survivors of a nearly extinct class of mankind. They are out of place in the world.

With sincere respect, I am cordially Yours

Fred. Law Olmsted

Chas. Eliot Norton Esqr

FOUNDING "THE NATION": JUNE 1863

Prospectus for a Weekly Journal

This Pamphlet is printed for private circulation only,
and it is requested that it may be returned to the Trustees.

It is proposed to establish a weekly journal, the main object of which would be to secure a more careful, accurate and elaborate discussion of political, economical and commercial topics, than is possible in the columns of the daily press, and a more candid and honest discussion of them than the constitution of the daily press admits of. The way in which the latter treats the questions of the day, is necessarily imperfect, slip-shod and inaccurate, if for no other reason, for the mere want of time of its writers to do better. Each topic has to be handled on the very day on which it comes up, and, let the writer who takes hold of it be ever so conscientious or pains-taking, he is compelled to dispose of it by the aid of such knowledge as he happens to command at the moment, and in most cases with the aid of scarcely any reflection. The result is, in appearance, an essay, but in reality an extemporaneous speech, containing simply a first impression, delivered as hastily as the pen can be made to move over the paper. It would, consequently, possess little value, even if there was a positive certainty that the article was the product of sincere and unbiased conviction. But this is not likely to be the case, owing to the fact that nearly all the daily newspapers of influence and importance, are either the organs of men who seek political prominence, and who make them subservient to the advancement of their personal fortunes, or else are compelled, owing to the smallness of their price as compared with the weight of their expenses, to follow that course which will secure the largest circulation. A sufficiently large circulation can only be secured by bending to the demand of a portion of the public not the most intelligent, by reflecting its prejudices, and by endeavoring to solve every problem in legislation or political economy in the manner which will be agreeable to it. The result is that every event of the day is colored so as to make it serve either the purposes of the editor, or of the party to which he belongs, or in a manner to commend itself to minds which are not given to a consideration of fundamental principles.

Before the present convulsion in our affairs, these defects of the press, though by no means unnoticed, were not seriously felt. It did not much matter to many educated men, how things were publicly discussed, about which their own minds were not deeply occupied. Since the commencement of the rebellion there has been a wide change in this respect. Questions of the most momentous importance come up daily, and exact grave consideration from all. The experience of most persons will confirm the assertion that the manner in which the daily newspapers deal with these questions is most defective and unsatisfactory. Their false prophecies, their abandonment of all attempt to sift evidence—often unavoidable, it is true—their constant sacrifice of the truth to the demand for startling effects, the factious, flippant and reckless way in which many of them deal with the most serious topics, constantly remind their more intelligent readers that they are prepared to suit the requirements of the greatest number, but not by any means the best qualified, of those whose judgment goes to make up that force in human affairs called public opinion.

A weekly journal, of the kind contemplated, would not be open to these objections. There would be time for the deliberate preparation of its articles. The public would look to it for careful rather than early comments on subjects of interest. The editor could, therefore, exact from his contributors all the accuracy, completeness and finish which his space would admit of, and the readers would find in it the matured views of competent authorities, instead of the first impression of writers not always possessing special qualifications for their task. It would be its place to lead public opinion rather than to follow it.

If this purpose should, at first thought, be considered quixotic, it must be remembered that while, four years ago, intelligent men could avoid giving much consideration to questions of government and legislation, this is no longer the case; henceforward they *must* give consideration to these questions or prepare themselves to accept the destruction of their country. There is nothing clearer than that the time in which anybody was competent to administer our affairs is forever gone by. Whatever may happen, we have before us a future of standing armies, of large navies, and of complicated foreign relations, and we shall have to add to these, the grave task of reducing a disaffected population of four millions into order and submission, and of raising the same number of degraded slaves into the ranks of industrious citizens. A government which has problems of such magnitude to work out must be aided and supported by men more thoughtful, more far-seeing, more attentive to remote consequences than those whose demand establishes the character of our present daily press. It is a necessity of the country that studious men should take hold of public affairs, and be felt as a power; it is important that they should come closer and more constantly together—should be organized and possess means which they have not hitherto had of making themselves heard and their influence felt. It should be remembered, however, that even if it were practicable to obtain such articles daily as ought properly to appear in a paper which would answer this purpose, people would not pay for such a mass of erudition and ability every day, and, if they did, could not, in a society like ours, read and digest it. Even such a paper as the London *Times* can not be read as our daily newspapers are mostly read—as, for instance, in the street cars. But at some time in the course of every week many men can find an opportunity, and will have the inclination, to deliberately read three or four articles in which real thought and study are brought to bear upon matters of public interest.

The strongest objection that is raised against the establishment of such a paper is the difficulty which, it is alleged, would be experienced in finding writers. There is, however, very little doubt that this would be mainly a question of money, though partly a question of the amount of influence which would be exercised by the paper. In all the professions, as well as outside of them, there are men of high attainments, to be found, who would be willing to write upon their special subjects, if paid well enough, and if the place in which their articles were to appear would command for them consideration and influence. And a weekly paper would be exempt from the disadvantage, under which the daily papers labor, of being compelled to seek its contributors in the place of publication. The editor of the latter is forced to depend, for the most part, on men attached to his office. Even on political topics, the editor of a weekly paper might collect his articles over an area of five hundred miles, and as regards the purely economical, commercial, literary, and social articles, they might be written in any part of the Union. This is, of course, an uncommon advantage, as it gives the whole country for a field of selection, and there are undoubtedly a large number of skilled writers, who, writing poorly every day, would write once a week very well, and still a larger number who, utterly unable to write every day, would produce once a fortnight, or once a month, contributions of great value. That many of this latter class would be brought to light by the existence of a periodical anxious to get their articles, and willing to pay well for them, there is no doubt.

It is obvious, however, that a publication of this kind could not, under the most favorable circumstances, rely upon a circulation so large as to make it possible to keep the price very low. The most careful writing on any subject is not, even in a periodical form, either read or appreciated by very large numbers, and those who are interested in seeing thought and study applied to politics, necessarily form in every community a comparatively small minority. The same thing may be said of those who really desire and appreciate careful and conscientious criticism in science, art and literature; so that it is not anticipated that such a paper as is proposed could be sold at much less than ten dollars a year.

This raises, what is, without doubt, the most serious question of all: whether at this price, such a periodical would find purchasers in sufficient numbers to make it successful. Are there, in short, in the loyal States several thousand persons of sufficient taste and education to make them desire to have on their tables, every week, a periodical, professedly critical, and not merely popular or partizan? The answer to this must, of course, be mainly conjectural, but the following are some reasons for giving it in the affirmative:

That there is such a class, that it already is not small, and that it is increasing, is proved by the sale of many high class works of all kinds, native and foreign. There is no country, except England perhaps, in which books which require a good deal of previous culture for the enjoyment of them, are so widely diffused as in America at this moment. An illustration of this may be found in the fact, that more than two thousand copies of such a book as Mill "On Liberty," which is very abstract in its subject and style, and not by any means popular in its opinions, have actually been sold here within a few months. Moreover, the number of authors in all departments whose claims to places in the front rank is everywhere acknowledged, is increasing every year. This could not happen unless the class which has the wealth, taste and culture to enable them to appreciate their works were also increasing, for, from this, writers as well as readers must come. Readers are the soil from which writers spring. It is also proved by the increasing interest in, and love of art, as shown by the large and growing production of pictures of a high order, and which find ready sales at high prices. There is hardly a doubt that those who are interested in books and pictures, are also interested in having competent, careful, and impartial critiques upon them, and these are things which, at present, are not to be found in the newspaper press, and which it would be one of the main objects of the proposed journal to supply. So it may be said, that there is some basis to start upon, and a fair prospect of a circulation which would increase in the direct ratio of the progress of the country in every direction.

It must not be forgotten, too, that such a paper would have no rival. There is nothing in the field which, in the least, resembles what is now proposed. It would at once gather to itself all the materials for success which actually exist, and would have the best chance of appropriating those still to be created. It would, however, have to depend mainly for success on the power and accuracy of its writing rather than on advertizing. It could not be puffed into circulation. So that at least one year, and perhaps two, might be expected to elapse before it would be established on a firm commercial basis. Consequently it would not be prudent to attempt to start it with less capital than would be sufficient to cover its entire expenses for a year.

No one should be asked to subscribe to its stock merely for the ordinary purposes of commercial speculation, but it is thought that in the present condition of public affairs, motives may be found which will appeal no less powerfully to many than purely commercial ones. The federal system is at this moment in greater peril than it has ever been in since the Union was formed. The rebellion has shaken the popular faith in its strength if not in its value, and on this faith, its durability must be greatly dependent. A convulsion has occurred which even the authors of the *Federalist* pronounced all but impossible, and, rousing the people suddenly from dreams of peace and security, it has thrown them into a state of doubt, of which malcontents and demagogues are eagerly availing themselves. The very same doctrines, uttered in almost the same language, which formed the main impediments to the formation of the government, are now used to aid in its overthrow. The people are urged to leave it to its fate, by the same arguments by which their fathers, eighty years ago, were urged not to establish it. The dangers of concentrated power, and of standing armies, are painted in frightful colors,—the overwhelming importance of local interests is energetically and insidiously preached. One of our most powerful demagogues has even gone so far as to propose the separation of the town from the State, for the advantage of the local politicians,—a point far beyond the wildest theorizing of the earlier enemies of the Union. A Union resting on the mere inclination of the members of it, is declared to be the only Union possible; although this is the very kind of Union which was tried under the old confederacy, and found worthless. The necessary inconveniences of the Union as it is, are made to wear the appearance of wrongs or calamities, while the possible advantages of separation are constantly hinted at. The State is held up as our real mother and protector, as something entitled to the devotion and affection of all its citizens, while the Federation is represented as a mere machine, to be maintained as long as it runs well, but not worth very great sacrifices for its preservation. All these devices were encountered by the founders of the government, but they are more formidable now than they were then, because the independence of the State organization was, at that day, associated in the popular mind with dissension, repudiation and stagnation at home, and with weakness and contempt abroad. The people had tried it and found it wanting. Now, however, it is the Union which is presented in association with evil and misfortune. It is for the perpetuation of the federal system, and the propagation of the federal idea, that the country is passing through its present throes, and it is consequently a comparatively easy task for the enemies of both to cheat the ignorant, the unreflecting or the timid into the belief that the remedy for what we are now suffering, lies in the relaxation of the federal bond, and the exaltation above all else of the individual States. War and heavy taxation have come in the Union, and it is, therefore, easy to persuade many that peace and security might be found outside of it. The worst and greatest dangers that can befall us, threaten us, they are told, from such an alleged augmentation of its strength as is necessary to carry on a war with its enemies in arms, while our dearest blessings might survive its overthrow, were it destroyed tomorrow.

There is amongst us, also, a large body of sympathizers with Southern theories of government, who, under the pretence of sustaining the States' rights doctrine, are intentionally laboring for the maintenance of Slavery and the overthrow of popular government. They zealously ascribe our troubles to the very nature of our popular institutions, and lose no opportunity of drawing unfavorable contrasts between the administration of our affairs, and that of monarchical or aristocratic societies. They have, it cannot be denied, already achieved a good deal of success among the men of property of our eastern cities. It only remains for them to win over the education and cultivation of the nation to insure the triumph of their ideas. With property and intelligence lost to popular government, it is easy to see that it might become so intolerable for all, that we should take refuge in the only refuge which would be left us, sheer absolutism. For nothing can be more certain than that for a society such as ours, based on an equality of conditions, there is no resting place between broad democracy and pure despotism. We have neither the men nor the manners for a mixed system, and if we acknowledge that the people cannot manage their own affairs, we have no resource but to surrender them into the hands of one able and energetic ruler.

It is, for all these reasons, more necessary than it has been at any period of our history, that there should be some publication, largely devoted to the task of holding up to the eyes of those who should be the leaders of public sentiment, the now forgotten perils and inconveniences of petty sovereignties, the innumerable dangers to our prosperity, and even to our civilization itself, of such a state of things as we should certainly drift into, if the so-called rights of States became the paramount consideration in our politics. From whatever point of view we look at it, there is nothing so essential to the future peace and happiness of our country, as a general and clear perception of the relations which exist between events of constant occurrence and the fundamental principles of our national as distinguished from our State and commercial existence. But to keep the attention of the people fixed upon the remote consequences of apparently insignificant occurrences, the daily press is too superficial, while the monthly and quarterly magazines necessarily lag behind the period of popular interest in the various events of which they treat.

For these reasons, it is believed, that there is no way in which capital can be so well invested, regard being had to the overruling interests of all, as in the promotion through the instrumentality of such a publication as is proposed, of careful, candid and conscientious study of the deeper nature and remoter bearings of the leading events of each passing week.

The proposed paper would somewhat resemble the London *Spectator*, in appearance, and arrangement, as well as in character, though less heavy and less elaborate, both in the selection of subjects and in the treatment of them. It would be made up—

1. Of three pages of short comments on the principal occurrences of note, legal, social, commercial and political—of the preceding week.

2. Of three or four carefully prepared articles on the leading topics of the day.

3. Of about the same number on questions of social, economical, literary or scientific importance—including under the term "scientific," jurisprudence, political economy, agriculture and manufactures.

4. Thoroughly careful and impartial critiques on the books, pictures, and theatrical and musical performances of all the leading cities.

5. Correspondence from Paris and London giving a popular summary of all that is most interesting in the literary, social, and political world in England and on the Continent: amongst other things, a condensed account of the most noteworthy discoveries and inventions made in Europe and elsewhere.

It is intended that all those articles shall be marked by such an amount of research and accuracy as shall give the publication a value in this respect, peculiar to itself.

For the fund to be contributed to establish the paper above proposed, the undersigned have consented to act as Trustees, and subscriptions to the said fund may be made to them.

Howard Potter,
George T. Strong,
William J. Hoppin

AFTER GETTYSBURG: JULY 1863

To Edwin Lawrence Godkin

Sanitary Commission,
Frederick, July 15th 1863

My Dear Godkin,

I spent two days and nights at Head Quarters on Beaver Creek near Williamsport. I saw Genl Meade a few hours after the escape of Lee was established. He is tall, thin, stooping, but has a most soldierly and veteran-like appearance; a grave, stern countenance—somewhat Oriental in its dignified expression, yet American in its race-horse gauntness. He is simple, direct, deliberate and thoughtful in manner of speech and general address. On the whole he impressed me very favorably. He is a gentleman and an old soldier. He expressed disappointment at the escape of Lee, but said: "With the information that I had yesterday, I could not on the whole have been justified in— [hesitating]—saying that if we attacked yesterday there were sufficient grounds for a conviction that we should not get the worst of it."

"I had ordered an attack this morning. I was myself rather disposed to try it yesterday, but all my corps commanders except one were decidedly against it, and my own conviction was not strong enough to warrant me in acting against theirs."

"We are not as strong as we are supposed to be. I dare not say how weak we are." Reinforcements were constantly arriving; it was raining hard, the Potomac was rising. I suppose that we were by reinforcements and improvement of position ten thousand stronger on Tuesday than on Monday morning. I think Meade somewhat hoped that Lee would be tempted to attack on Monday. I went out on Monday P.M. Our line had been advanced during the day nearly a mile, and was advanced quarter of a mile while I was with it; the men & batteries all in line of battle and with slight entrenchments, which they seemed to construct almost of their own accord or as a matter of course. In the woods or behind woods as soon as the line was formed, they began felling timber, so that it would answer the purpose

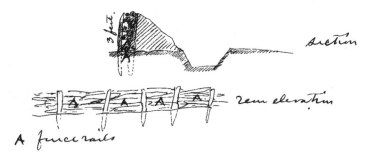

of abatis. I went through the line and advanced to the outermost skirmishers who were driving the rebel skirmishers slowly back from tree to tree in the woods. I crept up with General Crawford amongst them to a point where with a glass we could see through the wood and caught a glimpse of an earthwork before us and could see the dirt thrown (throwing) up from the ditch upon it.

I believe that in my estimate sent you a week or more ago of the forces at Gettysburg, I overstated ours. I had a hint that nobody was allowed to know how small it was, & I could see that those who knew best were not willing that I should believe some parts of the Army to be as weak as I know they are. All who were likely to be well informed, unquestionably believe that Lee outnumbered us. They say we could not possibly have held out fifteen minutes longer and for half an hour the chances were felt to be evenly balanced. We could not spare a man, and it seemed as if the slightest additional force on the part of the enemy would have broke us.

The old army of the Potomac is in fine condition, marches twenty or thirty miles a day & accepts what comes to it without hesitation—its chief discouragement arises from the smallness of the regiments, many being as low as 200 men. Many who were brigade commanders at Antietam and are now division commanders have fewer men under them now than then. The statement made by Wilson Senator, before the riots, that the draft was to be immediately enforced & the drafted men used to fill up the old regiments, was received with prolonged cheering. It is what all want—want more than anything else.

I enclose a note about the position from one of our inspectors, written on *Monday*. ("The hermaphrodite Medico," means "Miss Walker M.D.", "Doctoress Walker," "Walker M.D. on the war-path," as one of ours describes her).

I bruited the matter of the Weekly to the Surgeon General, who received it in the warmest manner possible. He said that he would do everything he could for it. I asked if he could recommend any writers in the Army. "I will write for it, I will write on Sanitary and Social Science all you want." He told me who was the best man in the army on projectiles, & said that he thought he could be got & he would introduce me to him in Washington. We discussed others.

I have heard nothing from New York—of the subscriptions. Nothing had been done when I left. Bellows & Agnew have been absent. Our operations have been on a much larger scale than ever before. I will send you some notes in a few days showing their magnitude. The immediate movement of the Army after the battle, taking its administrative offices, left the necessity for our aid, peculiarly at Gettysburg. The Army trains are astounding. The daily consumption of forage by the Army (before the recent reinforcements) was 1000,000 lbs of oats (at 3½ cents) 300,000 lbs. of hay (at 1½ c.) 150,000 lbs of corn, (at 2 cents).

I don't think the riots will harm our enterprise. How I wish it was started & we could pitch in! I think you should take the ground that the most dangerous foes of the republic are in New York City, that the government has now the right and duty to put them down; that from this moment to the end of the war, government should deal with New York and other insurrectionary towns & districts, as it does with Baltimore & Nashville and New Orleans. Let Barlow & Bennett & Brooks and Belmont & Barnard & the Woods & Andrews and Clancy be hung if that be possible. Stir the govt up to it. I didn't mean to omit Seymour.

Our inspector who has arrived this moment from Berlin says there is no intention of crossing for *three days*. I can't understand it. He says he thinks there was an apprehension that the enemy would resist the crossing. We have two pontoon bridges laid below Harper's ferry—and hold both sides at Harper's ferry—though not in force on the Virg^a side.

When Meade telegraphed that the enemy had gone, Halleck replied that he must acquit himself for allowing him to escape by his energy in pursuit of him &c. the tone being regarded by Meade as insolent. Genl Ingalls came into the tent as he was reading it & Meade said: "Ingalls don't you want to take command of this army?"

"No, I thank you. It's too big an elephant for me."

"Well, it's too big for me, too, read that," and then he immediately wrote in reply that his resignation was at the service of the Department. Two hours afterwards he received for answer to his reply that neither the President nor the General in Chief wished to be understood as blaming General Meade for the escape of the rebel army. This I know to be true, but as I can't mention my authority, it should not be made public except in general terms. I was at Hd Q at the time.

Yours Very Truly

Fred. Law Olmsted

TROPICAL LANDSCAPES: SEPTEMBER–OCTOBER 1863

To Ignaz Anton Pilat

Panama, September 26, 1863

My dear Mr. Pilat:

I have never had a more complete satisfaction and delight of my love of nature than I had yesterday in crossing the isthmus. You will remember that I always had a reaching out for tropical effect, but I found the reality far beyond my imagination, resting as it did upon very inadequate specimens, hastily and imperfectly observed. I constantly wished that you and Mr. Fischer were with me, and much more I wished that we could have seen five years ago what I saw yesterday, and received then the same distinct lesson which I did yesterday, and of which I certainly had some sort of prophetic feeling, and desire to avail myself in some of our study of the park planting. The groundwork was not extraordinary to us, the topographical characteristics not differing essentially from those of the park; yet the scenery excited a wholly different emotion from that produced by any of our temperate-zone scenery, or rather it excited an emotion of a kind which our scenery sometimes produces as a quiet suggestion to reflection, excited it instantly, instinctively and directly. If my retrospective analysis of this emotion is correct, it rests upon a sense of the superabundant creative power, infinite resource, and liberality of Nature—the childish playfulness and profuse careless utterance of Nature.

This is what I felt most strongly, and, after my excitement was somewhat tempered, I naturally fell to questioning how it was produced, and whether, with materials that we can command in the temperate regions, we could to any marked degree reproduce it. I think that I was rather blindly and instinctively feeling for it, in my desire to give "tropical character" to the planting of the island, and luxuriant jungled variety and density and intricate abundance to the planting generally of the lake border and the Ramble and the River Road. Of course, it is the very reverse of the emotion sought to be produced in the Mall and playgrounds region—rest, tranquillity, deliberation and maturity. As to how it is caused—I mean how the intensity of it which I yesterday experienced is occasioned by any details which I can select in tropical scenery—it is unnecessary to ask, if we can assume that these details do naturally contribute to it. Taking it for granted that they do, what is there here that we have not something similar to, or that by management we can bring something that we have to resemble?

First, we have nothing that will resemble cocoanut or date palms (none of our established materials) or bamboo. These are the most striking things we see. But does this esthetic effect of the tropical scenery depend greatly upon them? In the center of the isthmus we passed considerable intervals where palms were absent from the foreground. The tropical picture was much less complete as merely a picture of the tropics, but the sense of the luxuriance of nature produced was not less complete. Indeed, I think the association of the palm with the open, flat monotonous desert, and with many scenes of barrenness, as on the rocky, parched and sterile coast of Cuba, makes it not absolutely essential, but only favorable to this impression. The banana or plantain is a great help and is of the greatest possible value, but it appears only occasionally, and is also not indispensable, though more desirable than any other of the family. On the high grounds, especially, there was often nothing of which we have not a typical representative in our scenery; the great difference being that we have no scenery in which there are not qualities which are altogether absent here, and we have no scenery in which those qualities which are common to both are seen in anything like the same profusion and combination. I frequently thought, looking at any ten or twenty square feet of which I saw before me, and omitting the palms, it would only be necessary to assemble various bits of scenes to have a complete scene resembling and producing in considerable degree the moral effect of a scene before me. Palms or palm-like trees were never out of sight, though sometimes, as I said, absent from the foreground. Well, it was then a great satisfaction to find that the trees most markedly different from our common temperate-zone trees, at a little distance, could not be distinguished from what we were trying to get and what we know it to be possible to get on the island. It is true, nature uncontrolled, except by a most rare accident possibly, never quite gives us the palm, or palm-like tree in our distances,—but she sometimes comes near it. By selection and special treatment, we can then produce trees, which, seen at a distance of a couple of hundred feet, shall lead a man to say, "I have seen such trees before only in the tropics."

This is what we are aiming for on the island. Wherein are we wrong? As far as the palm-like effect is concerned, only in not pushing our plan far enough. The length of stem and smallness of head is more than I had supposed, often more marked than I had supposed, I mean at a distance, the trunk frequently is imperceptible, and you see the head apparently floating unsupported. The trees growing in this way are not palms or not all palms, but in their foliage so nearly like the Ailanthus that at no great distance (as a landscape painter would depict them) you would not know them apart, at least an average observer would not. Another of our prominent trees on the island, the Aralia, is, if I mistake not, itself in several varieties, actually present and frequent and not unimportant in the minor scenery of the isthmus. I saw these two trees (something resembling the Ailanthus

and the Aralia) on the shore of lagoons and rivers and on islands
in these, not a few hundred yards away, not differing at all from
those on our island, except as they stretched themselves higher
toward heaven and had smaller bunches of plumes at the top.
I saw also great lengths of shore, where the immediate border
of the water consisted wholly of shrubs and grass or herbage,
which would in the middle distance of a picture be perfectly
represented by a copy of a bank, very densely grown (horizontally over the water) of our Holly-leaved Barberry and beds
of Sweet Flag and Tiger Lily with vines running through and
over them. These vines are thinly leaved with leaves like Kalmia,
but longer, and a blossom like a white Convolvulus. The only
noticeably frequent blossom or flower at all conspicuous was
not to be distinguished a few rods off from the Convolvulus,
sometimes white and sometimes purple. A speck of scarlet was
sometimes seen in the herbage, but I could not catch the form.
There were also great broad leaves of the color of the Skunk
Cabbage and others which I could not distinguish from the
Paulownia. A small tree was sometimes seen also having exactly
the effect of the Paulownia four to five years old in rich soil.
These then are all details which (seen across water) we can very
well produce.

Other plants, of the general density, form, size and best color
of the *Berberis aquifolia*, including some of broader leaf and
greater pliancy, are mixed with that. The Forsythia and the
Oriental Magnolias represent closely other shrubs which I saw
distinctly by the roadside. I saw also, as it seemed to me, our
Wild Raspberry, the fragrant variety, or a purple dark leaf of
the same form (a single shrub of Purple Barberry would meet
the effect in a bank). I saw also our common rushes and the
Cat-tail Flag, but without seed-stems. Of many scenes, there
was no other marked detail. Of trees which I could distinguish
in the general body of foliage, there were besides those spoken
of, what I suppose to be Tamarinds, not essentially differing in
landscape effect from our Honey-locust, and one resembling
in its structure our Sycamore, with a thinly scattered foliage of
leaves like the *Magnolia grandiflora*; I almost think it is that,
grown very large and straggling under tropical heat. There were
glaucous-leaved small trees which the *Magnolia glauca* would
tolerably replace and all the varieties of Magnolia, generally

growing in clusters and not large, much the most marked of these not differing from our great-leaved Magnolia when young and in rich soil. Young shoots of this growing as it would if from a stool with the different stems cut down one or two every year, and none growing over five years, would give what was of most value of the great-leafed trees not palms and not of the Paulownia character. I saw no great-leafed trees more than twenty feet high, always excepting palms. As a general rule, in the landscape, these and whatever trees there were, were lost completely (as individuals) in the intricacy of whatever went to make up the mass of luxuriance, but especially under the all-clothing garment of vines and creepers.

You know how we see a single tree—most frequently a *Juniperus Virginiana*—lost completely under the Cat-briar. Frequently—generally—the whole forest is lost in the same way here. You often see nothing but the foliage of the vines, and this is generally so small and delicate in detail that you distinguish nothing individual except in the immediate forground. Palms and everything are lost under it. As far as I could make out, the largest and highest trees were completely covered with a most delicate vine with a close narrow long leaf, gray-green in color, or more likely with a small white or gray blossom, which gave that effect. When growing over shrubs or small trees, a hundred feet distant, it was not essentially different in landscape effect from the Clematis as we often see it showered over a Sumach.

If you could have large spreading trees like the Chestnut or Sycamore growing on a steep hillside, and completely cover them with Clematis as the Sumach is covered, only here and there little branches and twigs of the other trees I have mentioned pushing up through, you would have the effect of the tropical forest much as I saw it yesterday across the Chagres River. There are all sorts of other vines. I saw, as I suppose, the yellow jessamine (of Georgia) and the Trumpet Creeper, but the Virginia Creeper would at a little distance answer better the purpose of what was more common. But also there were many more delicate in structure and smaller leaf, but larger and more cord-like in trunk. Very often it seemed as if hundreds of cords (½ inch) were stretched from every part of the great spreading tops of trees, fifty to a hundred feet to the ground. All large trees seem to have strained themselves to the utmost to get their foliage away from the smothering density of the ground-growth, the smaller trees and shrubs, but not to have been able to get away from the vines and creepers. Thus there is often, as it were, an upper and a lower growth, of which the cocoanut palm growing out of a jungle, but itself overgrown by the creepers, is the extreme type, thus:

There are parts of the Ramble where you will have this result, in a considerable degree, after a few years—the lower stratum being a few shrubs that will endure the shade and the upper, low spreading-topped or artificially dwarfed trees, assisted by vines. I don't doubt that in the interior of these forests you would find spots where the ground-growth was killed by density of shade and the trunks only supported a canopy or extended parasol rendered complete and impervious by the vines and by the absence of shade above. The theory of adaptation of varieties thus accounts for the palm-like growth of so many tropical trees and shrubs or sub-trees. Our Sassafras as it grows in the sassafras grove in the Ramble is a perfectly tropical tree in character. But for tropical or tropic-like scenery you must get the utmost possible intricacy and variety and can have no breadth or mass of color or simple continuity of outline, for instance:

This is a correct sketch of the profile of a hillside, a span of the Andes, as I now see it two miles away, against the sky. Many of the trees must be of the largest size.

The country is rocky but, except where there are cliffs or precipices (where stone is being quarried, generally by the Rail Road Company), *all the rock is covered with verdure*. The most beautiful thing in itself is the young (or a small variety of) banana—or what I suppose to be that. Is there nothing which would give something of that exquisite, transparent, glaucous green, which, by strawing and all manner of practicable winter protection, you could get on the lake shore? You get no conception of its beauty when it is grown as an object by itself in a tub under glass. It wants a little play of light, derived from its own motion and that of other foliage reflected on it. I assume, as I said at starting, that as a general rule, these things which I have mentioned as the most obvious parts (except those clearly out of our power to produce) which combine to constitute tropical scenery all help to that emotion, the root of which seems to be a profound sense of the Creator's bountifulness. I don't know how, without considering the probable reason (in the tropics) for this upper growth of certain and many trees, we can be led to this emotion by witnessing it, but I am inclined to think that it plays its part without this reflection being induced, as well as everything else. Therefore, in trying to make the best of our materials to the same purpose, I should not neglect to use it—to train up by continual selection of a leader and pruning off anything below its junction with the trunk, until a very unusual height was attained and so on by knife and training and manure. I think we could get objects to represent all the prominent details. Then general richness of soil and the removal or covering up and making intricate with vines and creepers of everything else, would under favorable natural circumstances, I believe, produce an effect having at least an interesting association with or, so to speak, flavor of tropical scenery and I should hope some little feeling of the emotion it is fitted to produce. For this purpose, however, we must make much of trees of the smallest size and large shrubs, and consequently must subject all large trees to peculiar treatment, so as not to destroy the minor scale of the landscape, and also not to crowd out and destroy the important small trees by shade.

If I were, after this experience, in your place on the park, I should aim to have something of this character all around the lake, but especially on the east shore of the main lake. We always, or at least originally, intended to get water-plants in there. The mass of foliage on the shore opposite and to the north of the island is, I think, more monotonous than was originally intended—very much. Is it too late to break into it and reducing the surface in some places to water-level, get flags and coarse water-grasses and lilies, etc., to grow? On the island, I would cut away all the deciduous growth which inclines to run more than four feet high, except the Aralias and Ailanthus and push these as high as possible (except also the vines, of course). I question whether I would keep the cedars, but if I did, I would confine them in a network of vines to the narrowest limits consistent with the life of the lower foliage. I would remove from the island the Deciduous Cypresses. The adjoining bank, I would, if it were possible, treat in the same way for a short distance, and then make sure of great intricacy above and a water edge (where Flags would not grow) of overhanging glossy (with spots of glaucous) foliage. I would have every rock (and evergreen) in this immediate vicinity shrouded under Cat-briar or Clematis, completely so. Of course I would get in the Indian Corn here and there if I could. I think the Sorghum would have a canelike effect, would it not? And of course I would have some show of the Ailanthus and the cut-down Paulownia along the edges, as well as Callas, etc. By callas I mean plants having the general appearance of callas. I was delighted the last time I was in the park, with the appearance of the Cypresses on the west shore and thought I would be glad to have the masses of them enlarged. Would it not be well to move those on the island for that purpose? I did not like the Weeping Willow at the bridge, but don't mind their being tried. Cut them away when you feel like it. I would have the Catalpa and the Paper Mulberry once or twice more repeated along the lake-shore. I thought the knife was badly wanted to bring out the dark on the point opposite the terrace and at a few other points. I meant to have said all this to you and more, but had no time.

I hope you will continue to pay particular attention to the enrichment of the soil on the intermediate border of the lake, especially where the rocky parts are. Up to this time there has been no part of the work which has disappointed me more than these rocky and stony parts of the lake-shore, particularly the bay opposite the terrace and the east side of the point, the north bay and the west side of the passage to the crypt, where the blasting drill-hole is still seen and where the richest luxuriance of foliage was wanted, there is rawness, bareness, and sharpness of form, and poverty. Couldn't you have some large pocket-holes blasted or quarried near the water's edge in those rocks in the north bay, the crypt-cove and the terrace bay and fill them with rich soil so as to get vines growing over them from beneath? By some means or other the bareness of these rocks should be overcome whatever its cost, for it detracts greatly from the value of all that has been done about them.

Off Cape Corrientes, October 6th
Since the above writing, we have landed at Acapulco and Mansanillo bay in Mexico, and I have strolled a little among the trees. I find the true palms seldom except in groves and clusters by themselves, generally in low alluvial ground, and what I have said above is confirmed, except as the distinctive character of tropical foliage is less on the Mexican coast than at the isthmus. We have coasted for days within short distance of the shore. What I chiefly feel that I have above disregarded or neglected to refer to, is the peculiar beauty in tropical landscape which is due to the frequent cavernous depths of shade, to the constant recurrence of these on the forest slopes. You can easily see how these result from the circumstances I have mentioned; the umbrella-like trees, overhanging dense undergrowth and the vines making a drapery, all natural ravines and cliffs of rock and caverns of rock, which form the characteristic topography of this coast as of parts of the Italian and English coasts, being thus clothed with foliage. The play of light and shade even at noonday is most refreshing. One can often hardly believe that the forms of foliage are not artificial, so like are they when seen at a distance in effect of light and shade to the old clipped arbors and boweries and hedge figures. You have all this in some degree about the crypt and the rustic arch and with care to push the vines and coax the branches over, so as to get, not merely caverns and depths of shade, but caverns of foliage, dark and yet reflecting light at every leaf-point, and depths of shade in green, such as elsewhere in our climate we see only in gray and brown, you will get it perfectly. When you do, to the utmost extent that is possible with the materials which the climate allows you to use in those situations, I believe it will be a revelation of beauty to the people, and even to gardeners and artists, for although in some, indeed in many particulars, they have the advantage of us in England, in their materials, especially dark and glossy foliage, they cannot approach us in materials for canopy and drapery effects of foliage, and there are few situations where soil, exposure and rocky skeletons can be so happily combined for the production of this class of effects as in the Ramble and

along the lake-border. I have seen my ideal of the treatment of several points, done by the unaided hand of Nature (with the tropical sun) a number of times this morning and as I never saw before.

Please tell Mr. Green that I fully intended to have spent a day with him on the park before I left, and regret that I was so pressed as to be unable to.

With regards to Mr. Fischer and Mr. Rolland,

Very truly yours,

Frederick Law Olmsted

FIRST IMPRESSIONS AT MARIPOSA: OCTOBER 1863

To Mary Perkins Olmsted

Bear Valley, 15th Octr 1863

Dear Wife,

Pieper & family arrived just now, (7 A.M.) after a fearful journey from Stockton by the stage. He says the driver was frequently obliged to stop his horses to let the dust blow off, not being able to see anything of them or of the road. But they are very well, with a great appetite, and that is the case with us all. I really think that I am already experiencing the health-giving quality of the air. I don't think I could have stood the fatigue of the last two days and feel so perfectly fresh as I do now—on the Atlantic.

It needs health, at least, to compensate for this terrible dryness. It is a desolate country. Of all those streams shown on the map of the estate, I don't think there are three in existence & these three are mere threads, used over & over & over again, so valuable that a man's eyes will sparkle when he points them out to you. They are coaxed to the mills and made to wash gold again & again by ingenious contrivances and what finally gets away is seized upon by China-men and made the most of by their painstaking industry.

Well—I visited Princeton, Mt Ophir & Green Gulch yesterday. The mills were in excellent order, the mining very bad; the men in charge very good, the whole aspect of the country detestable.

I rather think that if I had known what the place was I should not have asked you to come here.

You must be prepared for a very hard life; I can hardly face it yet and see what you are going to do. But it's too late to retreat; so the sooner we trim sail to the wind the better. You will have to live in the mountains. A region possessing less of fertility—less of living nature—you scarce ever saw. The style is Cyclopian, but the vegetation Lilliputian. The population—roving adventurers, China-men and Diggers—living for the most part in camp—that is, under temporary shelters of boards, or booths. The houses of the villages proper, the residencies of the quartz miners of the estate, the mechanics, clerks &c. are all of a temporary character, with rough & ready moveables—dirty of course—the dust is everywhere. No waggon passes on the road that I don't need to have Charles come and dust off the table.

It must be very hot here in summer. At the hottest, mercury above 110°, the breeze if there is one gives no comfort. It seems to come out of an oven. The plains to the Westward are still hotter. This intense heat extends through all California (which means *furnace-hot*) only that the strong sea-gales temper it on the Coast. They say this place is cooler than the mining regions to the Northward, and much cooler in general than the plains & valleys below (to the Northward as well as Westward). But it is very hot on the hills as well as in the valley. Mrs Fremont used to say—they repeat—that it was *ten degrees* cooler on the top of Mt. Bullion than in the valley, but nobody else has experienced it. The place of their camp seems to be off the estate, on a table land over the top of the ridge of Mt Bullion—on the highest land in the vicinity, chosen because of a small spring there—the only place above the valley where so far as is known water can be had. It is several miles away by a mountain trail, inaccessible by waggons.

I should think it most likely we should have to choose some rocky spur of the mountain to which water could be forced by the mill engines, and build a chalet, with any contrivance you can think of, for shielding off the sun. For in all ordinarily hot weather (90° to 100°), the breeze is the grand desideratum. Fremont's mansion is a poor shantee—quite intolerable, as hot as it can be, by position—otherwise the position is agreeable—regarding distant landscape &c.

17th *Sunday*

If I had been writing you last evening, without reference to what I have previously written, I might have said: "I never enjoyed a pleasanter drive or passed through a more lovely landscape than in coming from Mt. Ophir to Bear Valley this evening." The explanation is that I came during twilight, when the ground appeared all the same as turf, and the vegetable productions, as trees. If you can look to a distance the views are fine—as in Italy.

But—aside from the general fact thus indicated—I regard the situation much more favorably than when I wrote the former part of this letter. Friday—after writing—I drove to the North end of estate. It is not far from here to the divide, when you look out of the valley to the Northward, and the scenery there changes completely. It is far more barren and rude but becomes grand—not picturesque but sublime in no contemptible degree. You see nothing but steep mountains, the lower Sierra Nevada, almost completely bare of trees, but many of them covered closely with low shrubs, that which is most abundant and which gives color and character to the general surface, being in landscape effect, like the gorse, furze or whins of England. They are quite like the heathery peaks of Scotland. The descent to the Merced is very steep and the ravine is very deep, the river is a muddy rill—of no account in landscape at this season, (it appears nearly dry). We rode on, keeping to the right of the openings of Josephine mine, to a spur from which there was a view up the valley of the Merced which was still finer— El Capitan—the white cliff of Yo Semite being seen in the distance—a grey precipice, the upper portion only, for it is 4000 feet deep, 4000 feet perpendicular, (think of it 13 times as high as Trinity spire).

We went down the hill by the serpentine Railway, a slightly built tram-road in bad order, but perfectly safe and very—hot. The mills were fine—admirable—the mines extensive, heterogeneous, dirty—as it struck me—under slovenly management. We rode back by the "English Trail," a road for pack-mules finely engineered through the ravine called Hell's Hollow. It is as fine a mountain bridle road as you ever saw—perhaps two miles long and we galloped the whole distance. So here—take the Yo Semite view and all is a very delightful ride for you of about six miles—from Bear Valley. Take it in a couple of hours before dark and you will much enjoy it. There are some small distances for which mules would be more in character than horses.

Yesterday we had a drive of thirty six miles in the Southern part of the estate. The soil is less sterile, the trees less miserable and occasionally they are quite respectable. In many places there is a young growth of white pines 15 or 20 ft high, which promise well and are agreeably dense & fresh in color. I really believe that this part of the estate must be very charming in summer. The Surface is beautifully undulating: high rounded hills and deep dells, with oak trees scattered park-like everywhere. A *few* of these oaks are beautiful trees—some variety which retains freshness even at this season—and there are a *few* respectable in size and form—their delapidation being picturesque. In general, however, they are individually poor (stunted & infirm). There are some hills covered with the gorse-like shrub, and one dell dense with it and a number of other shrubs, growing closely, which was very beautiful in color.

The valleys are all ploughed—sometimes ten feet deep, for gold, and wherever there is a rivulet—no matter how small— wherever there is a puddle, no matter how thick—water springing to the surface but not making a stream from the rapidity of evaporation and absorption—there are Chinamen hard at work, digging and washing. Even where there is no water, they are found throwing up heaps of gravel and constructing ditches and little dams and reservoirs in preparation for the rainy season. They are all more or less in Chinese Costume, half of them in full rig. They work steadily and rapidly. I saw scenes exactly such as I have seen in China. This for instance—a treadmill used here

to raise water for Long Tom—goldwashers; in China for paddy fields. We passed through one village, chiefly Chinese—a few Germans on the outskirts—probably forty houses built closely on a narrow street with Chinese signs—one quite gay two story restaurant. There were women & children and dandies on the porches of the houses & shops.

In the Southeastern part there are abundant granite boulders and the surface, but for want of foliage, is quite like that of the Ramble. Shivered boulders and ravines, with knobby hills & hillocks. The Mariposa river, the most important stream running through the estate, is, at the best, six inches deep and ten feet wide: the diggings on it are enormous and, in the landscape, horrible. It is used, however, also for irrigation of gardens and there are a number of these most refreshing to see. Fruit trees as well as culinary vegetables of all kinds flourish wonderfully. We were freely supplied with as handsome large, fair thin-skinned apples as I ever saw—of good quality, crisp and juicy. The peaches were fair but not fine. Grapes pretty good. Pears enormous not well ripened. Figs & almonds are said to thrive and bear abundantly but we saw none. They all have to be watered, by turning on a stream for one night, once a week, otherwise they shed their fruit prematurely.

Mariposa, here considered "a large and flourishing town, county-seat of Mariposa County," is "regularly laid out"—the main street at the North end turning up an impassible hill—and contains a hundred shantees, one pretty good German inn—in the Rossville style, several brick, one story, stores, and half a dozen comfortable little houses. There are three physicians, two newspapers and a general assortment. A lawyer, employed by the estate, who called on us at the Inn, where we dined, appeared a gentleman with whose family we should associate pleasantly. I was told that there were others, and it looked as if there might be.

Mariposa is 8 or 9 miles from Bear Valley. Ten miles beyond there, on the mountains, you come to Pine Woods said to be fine trees. There are two or three very tall fine pines near Mariposa and the young growth there is very pretty and promising.

What the estate wants & must have if a million or two of dollars would get it—is water. I am germinating great plans of washing all the gold out of the surface of the valley and then, making a garden of the debris. I think it possible. The hills, below here, will make the finest sheep range imaginable—say 20,000 acres, and I have a plan budding for that.

I have omitted the mines proper. I have "examined" twenty veins, half of which have been more or less worked, and know— as much as I did before. If I was to believe what is believed by someone with regard to each of them, there is gold enough on the estate to bridge the Atlantic with. On the whole, my belief is that there is an enormous amount of gold, as favorably situated for mining, so far as natural circumstances are concerned, as any in the world, but for all that, it will be an enormous work to "realize" upon it. The difficulty is—will be—to persuade the company to lay out as much capital as is required at each or any spot. If there were twenty companies, each with a floating capital of a million, I guess that, in twenty years, they would on an average have done exceedingly well; but some would have failed.

I went yesterday to the bottom of a mine, and there knocked out pieces of quartz, in which with a candle, I could see the particles of gold. The vein was a clean seam through a hill like that above (varying some in width, generally 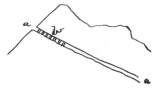 three feet), and the mine completely removed it so the hill was sliced in two—or had a thin slice taken out. The top part is prevented from falling down by wooden supports (b)—logs 12 to 20 inches thick set a few feet apart (3 to 10). These logs cost the estate last year $12000 and the plank used with them, (so), as much more. Going through any of these mines is very hard work climbing wet crags with a candle in your hand, but you will not be able to resist their fascination, I presume, any more than the rest of us.

Bring or send a plan for the house. It should secure coolness and ventilation to the last degree. It should have deep piazzas or galleries with low shades. It should have a bold, rough-hewn character in outline as well as detail (of which Knapp's cottage at Walpole, is the best example I know.) The walls may be of small pieces of slaty stone (2 inches thick x), the corners and string courses of lime stone—or if very much desired, of granite but granite would be very expensive, lime stone is scarce. Slate, for a rough wall, cheap. There is a steam saw mill and pine in abundance twelve miles away (not a planing mill), and lumber is the common & cheapest building material. This store is of the fragmentary slate, laid up with galore of poor mortar, and hardly weather-proof in consequence. To save it from falling down they are now covering it with cement-stucco. Kitchen should be detached probably, (that is customary) and chimneys outside. All the chimneys are stove-pipes in this town, but there is plenty of brick clay (some adobe huts,) and bricks are made at Mariposa Town. They might be cheaper for walls than stone. I should have preferred boards, as probably cheaper, but stone would be cooler. It is impossible to make too much allowance for shrinkage of all wood-work. Billiard balls, boiled in oil, sent here from San Francisco will crack. Doors made in New

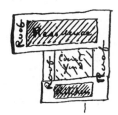

York & refitted at San Francisco, shrink to pieces here. Nice work you cannot have, therefore try for thick, substantial work, rude in surface, admirable in lights and shadows. The pine has a good reddish yellow color. Let everything be calculated for rude mechanics. Steam power (for sawing detail) will be

cheap to us. Iron & glass, dear. Freight on everything you bring or order will be 2 cts a pound from San Francisco—perhaps more if in winter—but only in special cases. Time, ten days. I should like nothing better than your favorite chalet curtained gable to the valley the roof over hanging everything. Being on a hill-top, there should be a cellar front. It must have shade around it and be shaded, independently of trees, & look shady; and as if knocked up by some mountaineer with a genius, and an axe & steam saw mill.

You can try to get Garretty to come out & build it. I enclose a memorandum.

The weather is delightful, just the finest autumnal weather you ever saw, the sun somewhat scorching toward noon, but quite as cool as you want it in the shade, and the mornings & evenings delicious. All agree as to healthfulness of the valley & hills—no fever & ague—nothing in particular. If men die, they die with their boots on. The natural death of the country is cold lead in the brain. There are no churches in Bear Valley but we had a horse race in the main street, at which a great deal of money changed hands, at noon today. The only other sign of Sunday is a Chinese woman very smart in tarry hair and sky blue pantaloons. The Italians are gambling in the Roman way—loudly. Mills & mines are stopped. We have a lot of Italians in the village.

Beef, mutton & vegetables good & cheap. Fowls & eggs scarce and dear. Fish "perch" from the Merced. They are like a coarse bass a pretty good fresh-water fish. In the spring they get salmon. Quails very abundant, good size, less gamey than ours, rather dry—very cheap, being shot by Indians. Rabbits & hares plenty & cheap.

There are a good many birds—doves, a large blue-bird, jackdaws, sparrows, larks. There are said to be plenty of rattle-snakes—though not nearly as many as formerly as the Chinese eat them—horned toads are known. Bears—grizzlies & black are occasionally seen on the mountains. Deer only in winter, but they are not far off. Vegetables are all excellent and cheap. Fruit also.

There are no servant girls in town. China men do scullery work, and there are French cooks. There is an excellent French bakery, and—a Bath House!

I have not heard a word from any of you since I left New York.

Affectionately

Fred. Law Olmsted

P.S. Mrs Pieper is "delighted" with the country and astounded and sickened by the want of female servants and the cost of washing.

P.P.S. Evening services consist of a dog-fight—a deep interest is felt by the whole population.

—A walk at sunset was very pleasant—to the top of a large knoll, or sugar-loaf hill, in the middle of the valley, a few Ilexes upon it, and some clumpy chaparral (with very little leaf) and young pines; the view down the valley, with a perfect Indian summer haze, with the heathery hill of Mt. Ophir closing up the vista, birds singing softly, in minor key, with a very rich deep color (violet grey, Martin says) which (so far) always follows sunset here for a few minutes—all made up a most soothing Sunday evening. Twilight is considerably shorter here than at Washington—darkness always overtakes us unexpectedly, but there is no sudden chill. The night air is cool but agreeable; you don't feel inclined to have a fire, but to put on a coat, and close the window perhaps. In fact, as to the climate at this season, it is the finest imaginable: it is in fact, as I said, much like our very finest autumnal weather, though somewhat warmer in the middle of the day.

A CALIFORNIA CEMETERY: MAY 1865

FROM *Preface to the Plan for Mountain View Cemetery, Oakland, California*

TO MAJOR R. W. KIRKHAM, U.S.A.,
President of the Board of Trustees:

SIR:

Having made a study for laying out a burial ground upon a site selected by your Board, I desire in the present paper to review some of the leading considerations by which I have been influenced.

Under the authority of the State, you have assumed the duty of meeting the demand of a large community for a place of burial of the dead. The ground has been selected with care; you propose to have it laid out with care; you propose to make a large expenditure upon it; it will be consecrated with solemn ceremonies; you are forbidden to make sales within it a matter of pecuniary profit to yourselves, or those who provide for the expenditures to be made upon it; and in all your doings, you will act under special privileges of the law, and be held to peculiar responsibilities before the law.

Plainly, something more is contemplated in this than providing a place where spaces of ground are to be held ready for sale to those who may have bodies of the dead in their houses, which they wish to put away; something more, also, than a place where monuments may be erected by individuals or families, over the remains of their dead. A heathen and savage people might want all this. What more does the character of a religious, civilized and republican people require a place of burial to be? The answer is: "A place of our common grief, our common hopes and our common faith; a place wherein we may see and feel our sympathy one with another." Hence, no place of burial is satisfactory to us, which does not exhibit, besides evidences of respect paid by individuals and families to the memory of their own dead, evidences also of respect paid by the community of the living to the community of the dead.

Your central purpose, then, is to prepare a place in which those feelings, sentiments and aspirations which religion and civilization make common to all in presence of the dead, may be expressed and excited independently of the promptings of individual affliction and individual memories.

Your ground will be well or ill laid out, accordingly as this purpose is fittingly accomplished.

The success of those who have undertaken a similar duty for communities in our Atlantic States, where solemn groves and sheltered glades abound, and where turf forms naturally over all the soil which is not shaded by foliage, is mainly due to a judicious selection of ground at the outset.

Ground similarly suitable for the purpose does not exist in the vicinity of San Francisco. Here, there is no Cypress Hill, or Laurel Hill, or Greenwood, or Spring Grove, to be appropriated.

You must then look to an entirely different way of accomplishing the end in view, and to entirely different measures from those made use of in the East; or you must undertake, as a preliminary duty, the formation, by art, of a groundwork similar to that which Nature offers ready-made, to those who look for it at the East.

I believe that you will find it best not to undertake the latter course, and for the following reasons:

With graves and monuments studding the ground, and paths approaching them at frequent intervals, an absolutely natural landscape in a burial-ground is of course out of the question; but as far as it is possible to harmonize the general purpose with a naturally picturesque landscape, this has usually been attempted to be done in the Eastern Cemeteries. In laying them out, a picturesque, natural style is had in view; and if the roads and walks in them do not follow what are called natural lines, and the trees and shrubs and plants in them do not stand and group in a natural, picturesque manner, it is because of a necessity, which is regretted, or through want of skill to accomplish what is intended.

This style of gardening originated in England, and has been carried to much higher perfection in that country than anywhere else in the world. The reason of this is that certain conditions, favorable for the peculiar beauty sought for, are found in the British Islands in a degree exceeding that of any other part of the world. These consist, in part, of a steadily moist atmosphere, and of soils to which a remarkably large variety of plants is indigenous, and which are, at the same time, extremely hospitable to exotics. In France, Germany, or the Northern Atlantic States, with the same ideals in view, the soil must be deepened and the roots of trees and grasses induced to extend themselves vertically, to avoid the effects of the dry atmosphere and the parching of the surface of the ground. Even these expedients are often insufficient, and arrangements have to be made for artificially watering the surface, before even an approach to the beauty of the English lawns, formed in this style, can be secured. It is safe to say, that a certain degree of beauty and convenience in New York, will cost the gardener, following this style, four times as much labor as it would in England, while, as before asserted, its highest perfection is absolutely out of the question there.

The difference between the circumstances with which you have to deal, and those of the Eastern States, is even greater than between those of the East and of Great Britain. Scarcely anywhere in the world, except in actual deserts, is the indigenous vegetation so limited in variety as in the country about

San Francisco. It is subject to long-continued rains and to flowing torrents of surface water, at one season; it becomes dry and
powdery, withering vegetation, at another. To what extent it
will prove kind to exotic trees, cannot yet be ascertained, as the
trial of none has passed an adolescent period.

Prima facie—what is peculiarly fit and becoming for your
purpose in England, and what is a little less fit and becoming
for the same purpose on the Atlantic coast, is likely to be quite
unfit and unbecoming for the same purpose here.

By a very abundant use of artificial means of watering the
ground, it might be possible for you to follow after the same
ideal that has been had in view by those who laid out the best
Eastern Cemeteries. But the capital, the skill, and the constant
expense for labor which would be required to secure even an approach to the beauty, convenience and fitness of these grounds
for their purpose, would be incalculably larger in your case, and
the result, after all, would be satisfactory as a triumph of art
over difficulties, rather than for its intrinsic beauty and fitness.

A part of your ground is a plain surface, mainly level. It is as
far as possible, therefore, from being suggestive of picturesque
treatment. You will observe, that in the portion of the plan
which I offer you covering this part of the ground, each road
is carried from one end to the other in a straight line, and bordered by rows of trees forming an avenue. This is, under the
circumstances, the simplest and most natural course; whereas,
on the hill-sides, to secure ease of ascent and descent, and to
avoid rocks and sharp declivities, it is more natural and easy
to proceed by curved and sinuous courses. The Cemeteries
to which we are accustomed in the East, are laid out entirely
in curved lines, and in proposing to you to depart from their
fashion in this respect, I have not disregarded, without reason,
certain considerations which are commonly supposed to demand an adherence to it.

Curved lines are said to be natural lines, straight lines to be
artificial, that is, unnatural; and it being common to regard
what is called nature, as if it were more directly the offspring of
the great Creator, and therefore purer and better, more full of
truth and beauty than any work of man can be, it is argued that
in a Cemetery the gardener's art should only appear as if used
in an humble waiting on Nature. But, even if we were willing

to carry out this principle, choosing only natural forms for our granite and marble and bronze, which we are not, we should be but following out a fallacy; for the brain and hand, the taste and judgment, and skill and genius of man, are also agents of the Creator—are as much agents of the Creator as the wind and rain, as blight and drought and heat, as the instinct of the birds or the coral insect. If man's purpose be pure and good, his handiwork will manifest the love and beauty and truth of the Almighty, at least as truly as that of any of His soulless agents; and however much the beauty of trees, the seeds of which have been sown by birds and winds and floods of waters may manifest the love of God, this so-called natural beauty can be no more pure and beautiful, no more fitting and becoming to our purpose, than if the trees had been planted by the hand of man, and with a single purpose to manifest Christian tenderness and care in the presence of the dead.

It is for this purpose that marble is to be quarried, and carved and set up; for this purpose trees are to be planted and nursed and watered and trained. Why desire to conceal the fact of art with them, any more than with the marble? Why not make the trees obviously and avowedly subordinate and auxiliary to this purpose—the solemn purpose of waiting on the dead?

But, it may be said, grounds in the picturesque, natural style—aside from all questions of fitness—are intrinsically more beautiful. It is true, they are so, under favorable circumstances. But, even where circumstances of climate and soil are favorable, the requirements of a place of burial constitute circumstances which are never favorable to the beauty aimed at in that style; for example, the charm of grounds laid out in the natural style, depends in a great degree upon the breadth of shadow which can be secured in connection with a graceful modulation of surface, and a free sweep of outlines. But a cemetery necessarily contains a large number of very small divisions of the surface, each of which must, of necessity, be within a short distance of a roadway. The ground must therefore be much cut up, the groups of trees must be small; and if individual taste or caprice is at all indulged in the family lots, it must be at a sacrifice of all breadth of effect. No plat of ground, of a hundred square feet, can be made a landscape by itself; no number of plats of ground, each planted by itself, and with a view limited by its boundaries, as family burial lots usually are, and each containing its monument of stone, can be made to constitute a landscape, or can be given a high degree of the beauty which the picturesque style of gardening seeks to produce. Even, where a piece of ground of great natural beauty is in the first place selected, this necessity of a cemetery makes it certain that its purely landscape beauty will be marred, rather than advanced, as the general result of what shall be done.

There may seem to be an exception to this rule, in cases where a large extent of ground having been appropriated, a portion of it having the greatest landscape beauty, is carefully preserved from the operation of the rule—only that which is less attractive being given up to graves. It will be obvious, that in these cases, the real burial-ground is treated as the stables and outhouses of a mansion usually are by an architect—as if honor to the dead were an entirely secondary or subordinate purpose. The result is a park or pleasure-ground, with a burial-place attached to it. The care of the dead is not expressed in the beauty of the park, however great the skill in gardening, or the truthfulness to nature may be, which is there displayed.

If, then, you desire to manifest respect for the remains of the dead, you will be likely to accomplish your purpose better, if you start with that purpose directly in view, and not with the purpose of first making a beautiful landscape, and then finding a place where your dead may be buried without great injury to its beauty. Not only marble, but trees and earth and everything else should be treated in such a manner as (consistently with the nature of these materials) will best serve your purpose.

There are certain social circumstances which affect the question of what that manner should be, and which I propose next to consider.

In the community for which you are to provide, as in all young and rapidly enlarging communities, yet in a degree exceeding any other of equal numbers, there will be an extraordinary proportion of single men, of travelers and temporary sojourners. Under these circumstances, associations of various kinds are sure to be numerous. Many of these associations will desire portions of ground distinctly set apart for their purpose, in each of which the names of all members, or of all who are buried by the association possessing it, may be inscribed on a common monument. Your ground should be so laid out that such divisions and monuments may be made to contribute to the general effect desired, showing forethought, order, and decorous regard by all these associations, to the common purpose of honoring the memory of all the dead, as well as the particular purpose of each. Large provision should be made for single graves and for small family lots. Some of the former should be situated favorably for the commemoration, by prominent monuments, of citizens or travelers in whom the public may have especial interest. While these are so placed that they may be readily distinguished, and the monuments over them be conspicuous, it is not desirable that they should be very greatly isolated, nor that the monuments should not seem to group and associate in architectural harmony with all that surrounds them. A lonely grave suggests a dreary life and the absence of cordial affection, even when it is marked with stately honors.

The social peculiarities of the community last referred to enforce another reflection, which is perhaps the most important of all, to be kept in mind in constructing your plan.

In old communities, society has gradually become organized in such a way that there are always a large number of persons who have had the opportunity of educating their tastes in constructive activity, and who have had sufficient relief from the demands of ordinary commerce to acquire contemplative habits of mind. Many public interests fall to the care of this class, and they come, sometimes unconsciously to themselves, and without distinct recognition by others, to be the leaders of public opinion in all fields of common interest wherein the esthetic exercise of the judgment is of great importance. By their example, and by quiet persuasion in ordinary social intercourse, they direct the action of many men of greater energy and practical ability, but of less mature taste than themselves. In your community, this class of men will not only be small, but society will for a long time be very loosely organized, and the functions they perform in older communities will therefore be exercised but imperfectly. The consequence will be seen in the neglect of public opinion to act in such a way as to cause the exercise of a refined common sense in those parts of what is common property and common duty, which are matters of taste. The members of the community will be too much engrossed with their individual occupations to give much attention to these—at least, to actively interfere against what they feel to be bad—and their occupations will have unfitted them to originate and carry through, and maintain in operation, the proper remedies.

It follows, that in the organization of a public enterprise like yours, the probability of this general neglect and of individual eccentricity, working unchecked by public opinion, should be regarded and provided against. Questions of taste should, as far as possible, be deliberately and thoroughly considered by express determination at the outset. What is right and best should be resolved upon, and fixed and tied up in bylaws and otherwise, so that it cannot be afterward set aside through carelessness, forgetfulness, or individual bad taste. And your plan should be made complete, so as to leave little to the future; and in such a form that no considerable deviation from it, or interference with it, by individuals, will be easily overlooked or tolerated.

The peculiarities of your climate enforce the same duty. Nowhere else is the danger of dilapidation from the alternation of Summer drought and Winter torrents, of stormy winds, and of vermin, so great; nowhere is dilapidation so inappropriate and offensive, and therefore so much to be guarded against, as in a cemetery.

The principle of mutual assurance, of coöperative labor, of joint stock association, is at the basis of your enterprise. Every man who buys a lot in your ground becomes a stockholder, a participant in the assurance you offer against dilapidation, neglect and irreverence. The greater and more obvious you make this assurance, the larger the common advantages you offer; the more perfectly and completely you provide what the public really needs to have, the more surely will you succeed, and the higher will what you have to offer be valued.

Having due regard to the peculiar social and climatic circumstances which have been thus considered; and looking ten years ahead, thinking what San Francisco is to be, what its wealth is to be, how great will then be the difficulties of rapidly providing other suitable grounds, it must clearly be your true policy to make much more generous, substantial and in every way well-guarded arrangements in yours, than are customary. At the same time, a character of simplicity and of unity, and an orderly co-relation of parts, is essential to the solemnity and dignity which it should be your first object to secure and preserve.

"THE GREATEST GLORY OF NATURE": AUGUST 1865

Preliminary Report upon the Yosemite and Big Tree Grove

It is a fact of much significance with reference to the temper and spirit which ruled the loyal people of the United States during the war of the great rebellion, that a livelier susceptibility to the influence of art was apparent, and greater progress in the manifestations of artistic talent was made, than in any similar period before in the history of the country. The great dome of the Capitol was wholly constructed during the war, and the forces of the insurgents watched it rounding upward to completion for nearly a year before they were forced from their entrenchments on the opposite bank of the Potomac; Crawford's great statue of Liberty was poised upon its summit in the year that President Lincoln proclaimed the emancipation of the slaves. Leutze's frescoe of the peopling of the Pacific States, the finest work of the painter's art in the Capitol; the noble front of the Treasury building with its long colonnade of massive monoliths; the exquisite hall of the Academy of Arts; the great park of New York, and many other works of which the nation may be proud, were brought to completion during the same period. Others were carried steadily on, among them our own Capitol; many more were begun, and it will be hereafter remembered that the first organization formed solely for the cultivation of the fine arts on the Pacific side of the Globe, was established in California while the people of the State were not only meeting the demands of the Government for sustaining its armies in the field but were voluntarily making liberal contributions for binding up the wounds and cheering the spirits of those who were stricken in the battles of liberty.

It was during one of the darkest hours, before Sherman had

begun the march upon Atlanta or Grant his terrible movement through the Wilderness, when the paintings of Bierstadt and the photographs of Watkins, both productions of the War time, had given to the people on the Atlantic some idea of the sublimity of the Yo Semite, and of the stateliness of the neighboring Sequoia grove, that consideration was first given to the danger that such scenes might become private property and through the false taste, the caprice or the requirements of some industrial speculation of their holders; their value to posterity be injured. To secure them against this danger Congress passed an act providing that the premises should be segregated from the general domain of the public lands, and devoted forever to popular resort and recreation, under the administration of a Board of Commissioners, to serve without pecuniary compensation, to be appointed by the Executive of the State of California.

His Excellency the Governor in behalf of the State accepted the trust proposed and appointed the required Commissioners; the territory has been surveyed and the Commissioners have in several visits to it, and with much deliberation, endeavored to qualify themselves to present to the Legislature a sufficient description of the property, and well considered advice as to its future management.

The Commissioners have deemed it best to confine their attention during the year which has elapsed since their appointment to this simple duty of preparing themselves to suggest the legislative action proper to be taken, and having completed it, propose to present their resignation, in order to render as easy as possible the pursuance of any policy of management, the adoption of which may be determined by the wisdom of the Legislature. The present report therefore is intended to embody as much as is practicable, the results of the labors of the Commission, which it also terminates.

As few members of the Legislature can have yet visited the ground, a short account of the leading qualities of its scenery may be pardoned.

The main feature of the Yo Semite is best indicated in one word as a chasm. It is a chasm nearly a mile in average width, however, and more than ten miles in length. The central and broader part of this chasm is occupied at the bottom by a series of groves of magnificent trees, and meadows of the most varied, luxuriant and exquisite herbage, through which meanders a broad stream of the clearest water, rippling over a pebbly bottom, and eddying among banks of ferns and rushes; sometimes narrowed into sparkling rapids and sometimes expanding into placid pools which reflect the wondrous heights on either side. The walls of the chasm are generally half a mile, sometimes nearly a mile in height above these meadows, and where most lofty are nearly perpendicular, sometimes over jutting. At frequent intervals, however, they are cleft, broken, terraced and sloped, and in these places, as well as everywhere upon the summit, they are overgrown by thick clusters of trees.

There is nothing strange or exotic in the character of the vegetation; most of the trees and plants, especially those of the meadow and waterside, are closely allied to and are not readily distinguished from those most common in the landscapes of the Eastern States or the midland counties of England. The stream is such a one as Shakespeare delighted in, and brings pleasing reminiscences to the traveller of the Avon or the Upper Thames.

Banks of heartsease and beds of cowslips and daisies are frequent, and thickets of alder, dogwood and willow often fringe the shores. At several points streams of water flow into the chasm, descending at one leap from five hundred to fourteen hundred feet. One small stream falls, in three closely consecutive pitches, a distance of two thousand six hundred feet, which is more than fifteen times the height of the falls of Niagara. In the spray of these falls superb rainbows are seen.

At certain points the walls of rock are ploughed in polished horizontal furrows, at others moraines of boulders and pebbles are found; both evincing the terrific force with which in past ages of the earth's history a glacier has moved down the chasm from among the adjoining peaks of the Sierras. Beyond the lofty walls still loftier mountains rise, some crowned by forests, others in simple rounded cones of light, gray granite. The climate of the region is never dry like that of the lower parts of the state of California; even when, for several months, not a drop of rain has fallen twenty miles to the westward, and the country there is parched, and all vegetation withered, the Yo Semite continues to receive frequent soft showers, and to be dressed throughout in living green.

After midsummer a light, transparent haze generally pervades the atmosphere, giving an indescribable softness and exquisite dreamy charm to the scenery, like that produced by the Indian summer of the East. Clouds gathering at this season upon the snowy peaks which rise within forty miles on each side of the chasm to a height of over twelve thousand feet, sometimes roll down over the cliffs in the afternoon, and, under the influence of the rays of the setting sun, form the most gorgeous and magnificent thunder heads. The average elevation of the ground is greater than that of the highest peak of the White Mountains, or the Alleghenies, and the air is rare and bracing; yet, its temperature is never uncomfortably cool in summer, nor severe in winter.

Flowering shrubs of sweet fragrance and balmy herbs abound in the meadows, and there is everywhere a delicate odor of the prevailing foliage in the pines and cedars. The water of the streams is soft and limpid, as clear as crystal, abounds with trout and, except near its sources, is, during the heat of summer, of an agreeable temperature for bathing. In the lower part of the valley there are copious mineral springs, the water of one of which is regarded by the aboriginal inhabitants as having remarkable curative properties. A basin still exists to which weak and sickly persons were brought for bathing. The water has not been analyzed, but that it possesses highly tonic as well as other medical qualities can be readily seen. In the neighboring mountains there are also springs strongly charged with carbonic acid gas, and said to resemble in taste the Empire Springs of Saratoga.

The other district, associated with this by the act of Congress, consists of four sections of land, about thirty miles distant from it, on which stand in the midst of a forest composed of the usual trees and shrubs of the western slope of the Sierra Nevada, about six hundred mature trees of the giant Sequoia. Among them is one known through numerous paintings and photographs as the Grizzly Giant, which probably is the noblest tree in the world. Besides this, there are hundreds of such beauty and stateliness that, to one who moves among them in the reverent mood to which they so strongly incite the mind, it will not seem strange that intelligent travellers have declared that they would rather have passed by Niagara itself than have missed visiting this grove.

In the region intermediate between the two districts the scenery generally is of grand character, consisting of granite mountains and a forest composed mainly of coniferous trees of great size, yet often more perfect, vigorous and luxuriant than trees of half the size are ever found on the Atlantic side of the continent. It is not, however, in its grandeur or in its forest beauty that the attraction of this intermediate region consists, so much as in the more secluded charms of some of its glens, formed by mountain torrents fed from the snow banks of the higher Sierras.

These have worn deep and picturesque channels in the granite rocks, and in the moist shadows of their recesses grow tender plants of rare and peculiar loveliness. The broad parachute-like leaves of the peltate saxifrage, delicate ferns, soft mosses, and the most brilliant lichens abound, and in following up the ravines, cabinet pictures open at every turn, which, while composed of materials mainly new to the artist, constantly recall the most valued sketches of Calame in the Alps and Apennines.

The difference in the elevation of different parts of the district amounts to considerably more than a mile. Owing to this difference and the great variety of exposure and other circumstances, there is a larger number of species of plants within the district than probably can be found within a similar space anywhere else on the continent. Professor Torrey, who has given the received botanical names to several hundred plants of California, states that on the space of a few acres of meadow land he found about three hundred species, and that within sight of the trail usually followed by visitors, at least six hundred may be observed, most of them being small and delicate flowering plants.

By no statement of the elements of the scenery can any idea of that scenery be given, any more than a true impression can be conveyed of a human face by a measured account of its features. It is conceivable that any one or all of the cliffs of the Yosemite might be changed in form and color, without lessening the enjoyment which is now obtained from the scenery. Nor is this enjoyment any more essentially derived from its meadows, its trees, streams, least of all can it be attributed to the cascades. These, indeed, are scarcely to be named among the elements of the scenery. They are mere incidents, of far less consequence any day of the summer than the imperceptible humidity of the atmosphere and the soil. The chasm remains when they are dry, and the scenery may be, and often is, more effective, by reason of some temporary condition of the air, of clouds, of moonlight, or of sunlight through mist or smoke, in the season when the cascades attract the least attention, than when their volume of water is largest and their roar like constant thunder.

There are falls of water elsewhere finer, there are more stupendous rocks, more beetling cliffs, there are deeper and more awful chasms, there may be as beautiful streams, as lovely meadows, there are larger trees. It is in no scene or scenes the charm consists, but in the miles of scenery where cliffs of awful height and rocks of vast magnitude and of varied and exquisite coloring, are banked and fringed and draped and shadowed by the tender foliage of noble and lovely trees and bushes, reflected from the most placid pools, and associated with the most tranquil meadows, the most playful streams, and every variety of soft and peaceful pastoral beauty.

This union of the deepest sublimity with the deepest beauty of nature, not in one feature or another, not in one part or one scene or another, not any landscape that can be framed by itself, but all around and wherever the visitor goes, constitutes the Yo Semite the greatest glory of nature.

No photograph or series of photographs, no paintings ever prepare a visitor so that he is not taken by surprise, for could the scenes be faithfully represented the visitor is affected not only by that upon which his eye is at any moment fixed, but by all that with which on every side it is associated, and of which it is seen only as an inherent part. For the same reason no description, no measurements, no comparisons are of much value. Indeed the attention called by these to points in some definite way remarkable, by fixing the mind on mere matters of wonder or curiosity prevent the true and far more extraordinary character of the scenery from being appreciated.

It is the will of the Nation as embodied in the act of Congress that this scenery shall never be private property, but that like certain defensive points upon our coast it shall be held solely for public purposes.

Two classes of considerations may be assumed to have influenced the action of Congress. The first and less important is the direct and obvious pecuniary advantage which comes to a commonwealth from the fact that it possesses objects which cannot be taken out of its domain that are attractive to travellers and the enjoyment of which is open to all. To illustrate this it is simply necessary to refer to certain cantons of the Republic of Switzerland, a commonwealth of the most industrious and frugal people in Europe. The results of all the ingenuity and labor of this people applied to the resources of wealth which they hold in common with the people of other lands has become of insignificant value compared with that which they derive from the price which travellers gladly pay for being allowed to share with them the enjoyment of the natural scenery of their mountains. These travellers alone have caused hundreds of the best inns in the world to be established and maintained among them, have given the farmers their best and almost the only market they have for their surplus products, have spread a network of rail roads and superb carriage roads, steamboat routes and telegraphic lines over the country, have contributed directly and indirectly for many years the larger part of the state revenues, and all this without the exportation or abstraction from the country of anything of the slightest value to the people.

The Government of the adjoining Kingdom of Bavaria undertook years ago to secure some measure of a similar source of wealth by procuring with large expenditure, artificial objects of attraction to travellers. The most beautiful garden in the natural style on the Continent of Europe was first formed for this purpose, magnificent buildings were erected, renowned artists were drawn by liberal rewards from other countries, and millions of dollars were spent in the purchase of ancient and modern works of art. The attempt thus made to secure by a vast investment of capital the advantages which Switzerland possessed by nature in its natural scenery has been so far successful that a large part if not the greater part of the profits of the Rail Roads, of the agriculture and of the commerce of the kingdom is now derived from the foreigners who have been thus attracted to Munich its capital.

That when it shall have become more accessible the Yosemite will prove an attraction of a similar character and a similar source of wealth to the whole community, not only of California but of the United States, there can be no doubt. It is a significant fact that visitors have already come from Europe expressly to see it, and that a member of the Alpine Club of London having seen it in summer was not content with a single visit but returned again and spent several months in it during the inclement season of the year for the express purpose of enjoying its Winter aspect. Other foreigners and visitors from the Atlantic States have done the same, while as yet no Californian has shown a similar interest in it.

The first class of considerations referred to then as likely to have influenced the action of Congress is that of the direct pecuniary advantage to the commonwealth which under proper administration will grow out of the possession of the Yosemite, advantages which, as will hereafter be shown, might easily be lost or greatly restricted without such action.

A more important class of considerations, however, remain to be stated. These are considerations of a political duty of grave importance to which seldom if ever before has proper respect been paid by any Government in the world but the grounds of which rest on the same eternal base, of equity and benevolence with all other duties of a republican government. It is the main duty of government, if it is not the sole duty of government, to provide means of protection for all its citizens in the pursuit of happiness against the obstacles, otherwise insurmountable, which the selfishness of individuals or combinations of individuals is liable to interpose to that pursuit.

It is a scientific fact that the occasional contemplation of natural scenes of an impressive character, particularly if this contemplation occurs in connection with relief from ordinary cares, change of air and change of habits, is favorable to the health and vigor of men and especially to the health and vigor of their intellect beyond any other conditions which can be offered them, that it not only gives pleasure for the time being but increases the subsequent capacity for happiness and the means of securing happiness. The want of such occasional recreation where men and women are habitually pressed by their business or household cares often results in a class of disorders the characteristic quality of which is mental disability, sometimes taking the severe forms of softening of the brain, paralysis, palsey, monomania, or insanity, but more frequently of mental and nervous excitability, moroseness, melancholy, or irascibility, incapacitating the subject for the proper exercise of the intellectual and moral forces.

It is well established that where circumstances favor the use of such means of recreation as have been indicated, the reverse of this is true. For instance, it is a universal custom with the heads of the important departments of the British Government to spend a certain period of every year on their parks and shooting grounds, or in travelling among the Alps or other mountain regions. This custom is followed by the leading lawyers, bankers, merchants and the wealthy classes generally of the Empire, among whom the average period of active business life is much greater than with the most nearly corresponding classes in our own or any other country where the same practice is not equally well established. For instance, Lord Brougham, still an active legislator, is eighty eight years old. Lord Palmerston the Prime Minister is eighty two, Earl Russell, Secretary of Foreign affairs, is 74, and there is a corresponding prolongation of vigor among the men of business of the largest and most trying responsibility in England, as compared with those of our own country, which physicians unite in asserting is due in a very essential part to the advantage they have possessed for obtaining occasional relief from their habitual cares, and for enjoying reinvigorating recreation.

But in this country at least it is not those who have the most important responsibilities in state affairs or in commerce, who suffer most from lack of recreation; women suffer more than men, and the agricultural class is more largely represented in our insane asylums than the professional, and for this, and other reasons, it is these classes to which the opportunity for such recreation is the greatest blessing.

If we analyze the operation of scenes of beauty upon the mind, and consider the intimate relation of the mind upon the nervous system and the whole physical economy, the action and reaction which constantly occurs between bodily and mental conditions, the reinvigoration which results from such scenes is readily comprehended. Few persons can see such scenery as that of the Yosemite and not be impressed by it in some slight degree. All not alike, all not perhaps consciously, and amongst all who are consciously impressed by it, few can give the least expression to that of which they are conscious. But there can be no doubt that all have this susceptibility, though with some it is much more dull and confused than with others.

The power of scenery to affect men is, in a large way, proportionate to the degree of their civilization and to the degree in which their taste has been cultivated. Among a thousand savages there will be a much smaller number who will show the least sign of being so affected than among a thousand persons taken from a civilized community. This is only one of the many channels in which a similar distinction between civilized and savage men is to be generally observed. The whole body of the susceptibilities of civilized men and with their susceptibilities their powers, are on the whole enlarged. But as with the bodily powers, if one group of muscles is developed by exercise exclusively, and all others neglected, the result is general feebleness, so it is with the mental faculties. And men who exercise those faculties or susceptibilities of the mind which are called in play by beautiful scenery so little that they seem to be inert with them, are either in a diseased condition from excessive devotion of the mind to a limited range of interests, or their whole minds are in a savage state; that is, a state of low development. The latter class need to be drawn out generally; the former need relief from their habitual matters of interest and to be drawn out in those parts of their mental nature which have been habitually left idle and inert.

But there is a special reason why the reinvigoration of those parts which are stirred into conscious activity by natural scenery is more effective upon the general development and health than that of any other, which is this: The severe and excessive exercise of the mind which leads to the greatest fatigue and is the most wearing upon the whole constitution is almost entirely caused by application to the removal of something to be apprehended in the future, or to interests beyond those of the moment, or of the individual; to the laying up of wealth, to the preparation of something, to accomplishing something in the mind of another, and especially to small and petty details which are uninteresting in themselves and which engage the attention at all only because of the bearing they have on some general end of more importance which is seen ahead.

In the interest which natural scenery inspires there is the

strongest contrast to this. It is for itself and at the moment it is enjoyed. The attention is aroused and the mind occupied without purpose, without a continuation of the common process of relating the present action, thought or perception to some future end. There is little else that has this quality so purely. There are few enjoyments with which regard for something outside and beyond the enjoyment of the moment can ordinarily be so little mixed. The pleasures of the table are irresistably associated with the care of hunger and the repair of the bodily waste. In all social pleasures and all pleasures which are usually enjoyed in association with the social pleasure, the care for the opinion of others, or the good of others largely mingles. In the pleasures of literature, the laying up of ideas and self-improvement are purposes which cannot be kept out of view. This, however, is in very slight degree, if at all, the case with the enjoyment of the emotions caused by natural scenery. It therefore results that the enjoyment of scenery employs the mind without fatigue and yet exercises it, tranquilizes it and yet enlivens it; and thus, through the influence of the mind over the body, gives the effect of refreshing rest and reinvigoration to the whole system.

Men who are rich enough and who are sufficiently free from anxiety with regard to their wealth can and do provide places of this needed recreation for themselves. They have done so from the earliest periods known in the history of the world, for the great men of the Babylonians, the Persians and the Hebrews, had their rural retreats, as large and as luxurious as those of the aristocracy of Europe at present. There are in the islands of Great Britain and Ireland more than one thousand private parks and notable grounds devoted to luxury and recreation. The value of these grounds amounts to many millions of dollars and the cost of their annual maintenance is greater than that of the national schools; their only advantage to the commonwealth is obtained through the recreation they afford to their owners (except as these extend hospitality to others) and these owners with their families number less than one in six thousand of the whole population.

The enjoyment of the choicest natural scenes in the country and the means of recreation connected with them is thus a monopoly, in a very peculiar manner, of a very few, very rich people. The great mass of society, including those to whom it would be of the greatest benefit, is excluded from it. In the nature of the case private parks can never be used by the mass of the people in any country nor by any considerable number even of the rich, except by the favor of a few, and in dependence on them.

Thus without means are taken by government to withhold them from the grasp of individuals, all places favorable in scenery to the recreation of the mind and body will be closed against the great body of the people. For the same reason that the water of rivers should be guarded against private appropriation and the use of it for the purpose of navigation and otherwise protected against obstructions, portions of natural scenery may therefore properly be guarded and cared for by government. To simply reserve them from monopoly by individuals, however, it will be obvious, is not all that is necessary. It is necessary that they should be laid open to the use of the body of the people.

The establishment by government of great public grounds for the free enjoyment of the people under certain circumstances, is thus justified and enforced as a political duty.

Such a provision, however, having regard to the whole people of a State, has never before been made and the reason it has not is evident.

It has always been the conviction of the governing classes of the old world that it is necessary that the large mass of all human communities should spend their lives in almost constant labor and that the power of enjoying beauty either of nature or of art in any high degree, requires a cultivation of certain faculties, which is impossible to these humble toilers. Hence it is thought better, so far as the recreations of the masses of a nation receive attention from their rulers, to provide artificial pleasures for them, such as theatres, parades, and promenades where they will be amused by the equipages of the rich and the animation of crowds.

It is unquestionably true that excessive and persistent devotion to sordid interests cramp and distort the power of appreciating natural beauty and destroy the love of it which the Almighty has implanted in every human being, and which is so intimately and mysteriously associated with the moral perceptions and intuitions, but it is not true that exemption from toil, much leisure, much study, much wealth are necessary to the exercise of the esthetic and contemplative faculties. It is the folly of laws which have permitted and favored the monopoly by priveleged classes of many of the means supplied in nature for the gratification, exercise and education of the esthetic faculties that has caused the appearance of dullness and weakness and disease of these faculties in the mass of the subjects of kings. And it is against a limitation of the means of such education to the rich that the wise legislation of free governments must be directed. By such legislation the anticipation of the revered Downing may be realized.

> The dread of the ignorant exclusive, who has no faith in the refinement of a republic, will stand abashed in the next century, before a whole people whose system of voluntary education embraces (combined with perfect individual freedom), not only common schools of rudimentary knowledge, but common enjoyments for all classes in the higher realms of art, letters, science, social recreations and enjoyments. Were our legislators but wise enough to understand, today, the destinies of the New World, the gentility of Sir Philip Sidney, made universal, would be not half so much a miracle fifty years hence in America, as the idea of a whole nation of laboring men reading and writing, was, in his day, in England.

It was in accordance with these views of the destiny of the New World and the duty of a Republican Government that Congress enacted that the Yosemite should be held, guarded and managed for the free use of the whole body of the people forever, and that the care of it, and the hospitality of admitting strangers from all parts of the world to visit it and enjoy it freely, should be a duty of dignity and be committed only to a sovereign State.

The trust having been accepted, it will be the duty of the legislature, to define the responsibilities, the rights and the powers of the Commissioners, whom by the Act of Congress, it will be the duty of the Executive of the State to appoint. These must be determined by a consideration of the purposes to which the ground is to be devoted and must be simply commensurate with those purposes.

The main duty with which the Commissioners should be charged should be to give every advantage practicable to the mass of the people to benefit by that which is peculiar to this ground and which has caused Congress to treat it differently from other parts of the public domain. This peculiarity consists wholly in its natural scenery.

The first point to be kept in mind then is the preservation and maintenance as exactly as is possible of the natural scenery; the restriction, that is to say, within the narrowest limits consistent with the necessary accommodation of visitors, of all artificial constructions and the prevention of all constructions markedly inharmonious with the scenery or which would unnecessarily obscure, distort or detract from the dignity of the scenery.

In addition to the more immediate and obvious arrangements by which this duty is enforced, there are two considerations which should not escape attention.

First; the value of the district in its present condition as a museum of natural science and the danger—indeed the certainty—that without care many of the species of plants now flourishing upon it will be lost and many interesting objects be defaced or obscured if not destroyed. To illustrate these dangers, it may be stated that numbers of the native plants of large districts of the Atlantic States have almost wholly disappeared and that most of the common weeds of the farms are of foreign origin, having choked out the native vegetation. Many of the finer specimens of the most important tree in the scenery of the Yosemite have been already destroyed and the proclamation of the Governor, issued after the passage of the Act of Congress, forbidding the destruction of trees in the district, alone prevented the establishment of a saw mill within it. Notwithstanding the proclamation many fine trees have been felled and others girdled within the year. Indians and others have set fire to the forests and herbage and numbers of trees have been killed by these fires; the giant tree before referred to as probably the noblest tree now standing on the earth has been burned completely through the bark near the ground for a distance of more than one hundred feet of its circumference; not only have trees been cut, hacked, barked and fired in prominent positions, but rocks in the midst of the most picturesque natural scenery have been broken, painted and discolored, by fires built against them. In travelling to the Yosemite and within a few miles of the nearest point at which it can be approached by a wheeled vehicle, the Commissioners saw other picturesque rocks stencilled over with advertisements of patent medicines and found the walls of the Bower Cave, one of the most beautiful natural objects in the State, already so much broken and scratched by thoughtless visitors that it is evident that unless the practice should be prevented not many years will pass before its natural charm will be quite destroyed.

Second; it is important that it should be remembered that in permitting the sacrifice of anything that would be of the slightest value to future visitors to the convenience, bad taste, playfulness, carelessness, or wanton destructiveness of present visitors, we probably yield in each case the interest of uncounted millions to the selfishness of a few individuals. It is an important fact that as civilization advances, the interest of men in natural scenes of sublimity and beauty increases. Where a century ago one traveller came to enjoy the scenery of the Alps, thousands come now and where even forty years ago one small inn accommodated the visitors to the White Hills of New Hampshire, half a dozen grand hotels, each accommodating hundreds are now overcrowded every Summer. In the early part of the present century the summer visitors to the Highlands of Scotland did not give business enough to support a single inn, a single stage coach or a single guide. They now give business to several Rail Road trains, scores of steamboats and thousands of men and horses every day. It is but sixteen years since the Yosemite was first seen by a white man, several visitors have since made a journey of several thousand miles at large cost to see it, and notwithstanding the difficulties which now interpose, hundreds resort to it annually. Before many years, if proper facilities are offered, these hundreds will become thousands and in a century the whole number of visitors will be counted by millions. An injury to the scenery so slight that it may be unheeded by any visitor now, will be one of deplorable magnitude when its effect upon each visitor's enjoyment is multiplied by these millions. But again, the slight harm which the few hundred visitors of this year might do, if no care were taken to prevent it, would not be slight, if it should be repeated by millions. At some time, therefore, laws to prevent an unjust use by individuals of that which is not individual but public property, must be made and rigidly enforced. The principle of justice involved is the same now that it will be then; such laws as this principle demands will be more easily enforced, and there will be less hardship in their action, if the abuses they are designed to prevent are never allowed to become customary but are checked while they are yet of unimportant consequence. It should, then, be made the duty of the Commission to prevent a wanton or careless disregard on the part of anyone entering the Yosemite or the Grove, of the rights of posterity as well as of cotemporary visitors, and the Commission should be clothed with proper authority and given the necessary means for this purpose.

This duty of preservation is the first which falls upon the State under the Act of Congress, because the millions who are hereafter to benefit by the Act have the largest interest in it, and the largest interest should be first and most strenuously guarded.

Next to this, and for a similar reason preceding all other duties of the State in regard to this trust, is that of aiding to make this appropriation of Congress available as soon and as generally as may be economically practicable to those whom it is designed to benefit. Had Congress not thought best to depart from the usual method of dealing with the public lands in this case, it would have been practicable for one man to have bought the whole, to have appropriated it wholly to his individual pleasure or to have refused admittance to any who were unable to pay a certain price as admission fee, or as a charge for the entertainment which he would have had a monopoly of supplying. The result would have been a rich man's park, and for the present, so far as the great body of the people are concerned, it is not, and as long as the present arrangements continue, it will remain, practically, the property only of the rich.

A man travelling from Stockton to the Yosemite or the Mariposa Grove is commonly three or four days on the road at an expense of from thirty to forty dollars, and arrives in the majority of cases quite overcome with the fatigue and unaccustomed hardships of the journey. Few persons, especially few women, are able to enjoy or profit by the scenery and air for days afterwards. Meantime they remain at an expense of from $3 to $12. per day for themselves, their guide and horses, and many leave before they have recovered from their first exhaustion and return home jaded and ill. The distance is not over one hundred miles, and with such roads and public conveyances as are found elsewhere in the State the trip might be made easily and comfortably in one day and at a cost of ten or twelve dollars. With similar facilities of transportation, the provisions and all the necessities of camping could also be supplied at moderate rates. To realize the advantages which are offered the people of the State in this gift of the Nation, therefor, the first necessity is a road from the termination of the present roads leading towards the district. At present there is no communication with it except by means of a very poor trail for a distance of nearly forty miles from the Yo Semite and twenty from the Mariposa Grove.

Besides the advantages which such a road would have in reducing the expense, time and fatigue of a visit to the tract to the whole public at once, it would also serve the important purpose of making it practicable to convey timber and other articles necessary for the accommodation of visitors into the Yo Semite from without, and thus the necessity, or the temptation, to cut down its groves and to prepare its surface for tillage would be avoided. Until a road is made it must be very difficult to prevent this. The Commissioners propose also in laying out a road to the Mariposa Grove that it shall be carried completely around it, so as to offer a barrier of bare ground to the approach of fires, which nearly every year sweep upon it from the adjoining country, and which during the last year alone have caused injuries, exemption from which it will be thought before many years would have been cheaply obtained at ten times the cost of the road.

Within the Yosemite the Commissioners propose to cause to be constructed a double trail, which, on the completion of our approach road, may be easily made suitable for the passage of a single vehicle, and which shall enable visitors to make a complete circuit of all the broader parts of the valley and to cross the meadows at certain points, reaching all the finer points of view to which it can be carried without great expense. When carriages are introduced it is proposed that they shall be driven for the most part up one side and down the other of the valley, suitable resting places and turnouts for passing being provided at frequent intervals. The object of this arrangement is to reduce the necessity for artificial construction within the narrowest practicable limits, destroying as it must the natural conditions of the ground and presenting an unpleasant object to the eye in the midst of the scenery. The trail or narrow road could also be kept more in the shade, could take a more picturesque course, would be less dusty, and could be much more cheaply kept in repair. From this trail a few paths would also need to be formed, leading to points of view which would only be accessible to persons on foot. Several small bridges would also be required.

The Commission also propose the construction of five cabins at points in the valley conveniently near to those most frequented by visitors, especially near the foot of the cascades, but at the same time near to convenient camping places. These cabins would be let to tenants with the condition that they should have constantly open one comfortable room as a free resting place for visitors, with the proper private accommodations for women, and that they should keep constantly on hand in another room a supply of certain simple necessities for camping parties, including tents, cooking utensils and provisions; the tents and utensils to be let, and the provisions to be sold at rates to be limited by the terms of the contract.

The Commissioners ask and recommend that sums be appropriated for these and other purposes named below as follows:

For the expense already incurred in the survey and transfer of the Yosemite and Mariposa Big Tree Grove from the United States to the State of California	$2,000
For the construction of 30 miles more or less of double trail & foot paths	3,000
For the construction of Bridges	1,600
For the construction and finishing five cabins, closets, stairways, railings &c	2,000
Salary of Superintendent (2 years)	2400
For surveys, advertising, & incidentals	1000
For aid in the construction of a road	25,000
	$37,000

The Commissioners trust that after this amount shall have been expended the further necessary expenses for the management of the domain will be defrayed by the proceeds of rents and licenses which will be collected upon it.

The Yosemite yet remains to be considered as a field of study for science and art. Already students of science and artists have been attracted to it from the Atlantic States and a number of artists have at heavy expense spent the Summer in sketching the scenery. That legislation should, when practicable within certain limits, give encouragement to the pursuit of science and art has been fully recognized as a duty by this State. The pursuit of science and of art, while it tends more than any other human pursuit to the benefit of the commonwealth and the advancement of civilization, does not correspondingly put money into the hands of the pursuers. Their means are generally extremely limited. They are likely by the nature of their studies to be the best counsellors which can be had in respect to certain of the duties which will fall upon the proposed Commission, and it is right that they should if possible be honorably represented in the constitution of the Commission.

Congress has provided that the Executive shall appoint eight Commissioners, and that they shall give their services gratuitously. It is but just that the State should defray the travelling expenses necessarily incurred in the discharge of their duty. It is proposed that the allowance for this purpose shall be limited in amount to four hundred dollars per annum, for each Commissioner, or so much thereof as shall have been actually expended in travelling to and from the ground and while upon it. It is also proposed that of the eight Commissioners to be appointed by the Executive, four shall be appointed annually and that these four shall be students of Natural Science or Landscape Artists. It is advised also that in order that it may be in the power of the Governor when he sees fit to offer the slight consideration presented in the sum of $400 proposed to be allowed each Commissioner for travelling expenses as an inducement to men of scientific note and zealous artists to visit the State, that he shall not necessarily be restricted in these appointments to citizens of the State. The Yosemite being a trust from the whole nation, it seems eminently proper that so much liberality in its management should be authorized.

A PARK FOR SAN FRANCISCO: MARCH 1866

FROM *Preliminary Report in Regard to a Plan of Public Pleasure Grounds for the City of San Francisco*

V.

LIMITATIONS UPON THE SCOPE OF
THE PLAN, FIXED BY PHYSICAL CONDITIONS
OF THE LOCALITY

The special conditions fixed by natural circumstances, to which the plan must be adapted, are so obvious that I need not recapitulate them here. Determining for the reasons already given, that a pleasure ground is needed which shall compare favorably with any in existence, it must, I believe, be acknowledged, that, neither in beauty of greensward, nor in great umbrageous trees, do these special conditions of the topography, soil, and climate of San Francisco allow us to hope that any pleasure ground it can acquire, will ever compare in the most distant degree, with those of New York or London.

There is not a full grown tree of beautiful proportions near San Francisco, nor have I seen any young trees that promised fairly, except, perhaps, of certain compact clumpy forms of evergreens, wholly wanting in grace and cheerfulness. It would not be wise nor safe to undertake to form a park upon any plan which assumed as a certainty that trees which would delight the eye can be made to grow near San Francisco by any advantages whatever which it might be proposed to offer them. It is perhaps true that the certainty of failure remains to be proved, that success is not entirely out of the question, and it may be urged that experiments on a small scale should be set on foot at once to determine the question for the benefit of future generations; but, however this may be, it is unquestionably certain that the success of such experiments cannot safely be taken for granted in any general scheme that may, at this time, be offered for the improvement of the city.

The question then is whether it be possible for San Francisco to form a pleasure ground peculiar to itself, with a beauty as much superior to that of other such grounds, *in any way*, as theirs must be superior to what it can aspire to in spreading trees and great expanses of turf.

I think that it can.

VI.

SPECIAL ADVANTAGES POSSESSED BY
SAN FRANCISCO FOR FORMING AN ATTRACTIVE
PLEASURE-GROUND

Strangers, on their arrival in San Francisco, are usually much attracted by the beauty of certain small gardens, house courts and porches, and, if they have any knowledge of horticulture, they perceive that this beauty is of a novel character. It is dependent on elements which require to be seen somewhat closely, and which would be lost or out of place in such expanded landscapes as form the chief attraction of parks and gardens in the East. It is found in the highest degree in some of the smallest gardens in the more closely built and densely populated parts of the town, in situations where park trees would dwindle for want of light and air.

These results of private and unorganized experiments sufficiently indicate the limits within which we can proceed with entire confidence in planning a public pleasure ground, and, omitting a discussion here of the less difficult questions to which my attention has been given, I will now proceed to give the general conclusions of my preliminary enquiry as to the special requirements which the plan of a public pleasure ground for San Francisco should be adapted to meet.

VII.

GENERAL CONCLUSIONS OF DISCUSSION
AS TO THE CONDITIONS TO BE OBSERVED
IN A PLAN

In any pleasure ground for San Francisco the ornamental parts should be compact; should be guarded from the direct action of the northwest wind, should be conveniently entered, should be rich in detail, close to the eye, and should be fitted to an extensive system of walks, rides, drives and resting places. These latter should also be sheltered as much as possible from the northwest wind; should be of such a plan that their public use can be efficiently regulated without cumbrous, unusual, or very expensive police arrangements, and should be easily kept clean and free from dust. No ground should be selected for this improvement which is already of very great value, yet the neighborhood should be of a character which will ultimately invite the erection of the best class of private mansions and public edifices. Entrance to it should be practicable at no great distance from that part of the town already built up; it should extend in the direction in which the city is likely to advance, or should be so arranged that an agreeable extension can be readily made in that direction hereafter. At the same time it should have such a form that when the city shall be much enlarged it may so divide it that, without subjecting the trees and shrubs it contains to destruction during great conflagrations, it shall be a barrier of protection to large districts which would otherwise be imperilled. It is further desirable that it should not make any great change in the present plans of sewerage, lighting and water supply necessary, should not present any insurmountable obstructions to the ordinary ways of passage or business transportation between different parts of the city, should not block the city railroads or other public works and should not greatly disturb buildings already erected, streets already graded, sewered and paved, or otherwise cause heavy losses or depreciation of value to the existing property of the city, or that of corporations or private citizens.

If there is any scheme by which all these seemingly conflicting requirements can be met, no arrangement which can be proposed, that falls short of it, will long be considered satisfactory. Changes of detail, revisions, repairs, temporary expedients to meet special difficulties, will constantly be suggested, discussed, and from time to time adopted; and thus in the end any less comprehensive plan will prove excessively inconvenient and expensive. It will be much more economical to adopt a plan which comprehends everything that is likely to be wanted at the outset. The whole scheme of improvements should, as far as possible, therefore, be definitely established at the outset, and the plan of the city in all respects adjusted to suit it.

VIII.
EXPEDIENT PROPOSED FOR OVERCOMING
THE CHIEF SPECIAL DIFFICULTIES

The expedient by which I would propose to overcome the chief difficulties imposed by the conditions of the case, will be most readily understood, if it be imagined that there had originally been a creek crossing the site of the city, not far back of that part of it which is at present occupied by buildings of an expensive character; that streets had been formed on the banks with houses facing towards the creek, and that cross streets had, at such intervals as would be required by convenience, been carried over it on bridges. (This may be seen in reality at Stockton, but it will be better to imagine the creek passing through a hilly country, instead of a flat one, and the houses facing toward it to be stately mansions instead of shops and warehouses.) Let it then further be imagined that the course of the stream which formed the creek had been divided, so as to leave its bed dry; that a road had been formed with broad walks in the middle of the old bed; that the banks had been dressed in agreeable shapes, the lower parts turfed and the slopes planted with shrubs and trees, with a thicket of hardy evergreens all along the top, and that hydrants had been set at proper intervals on the edge of the streets above and the road below, so that, (with hose and punctured pipes, such as are used for watering the lawns and roads of the Bois de Boulogne), the dust could be kept down, and the turf and plantations readily sprinkled as often as necessary. If all this had been done, provided the course of the creek had been originally from southwest to northeast—that is to say, across the sea-wind—it will be seen that a sheltered promenade or boulevard would have been possible within the city limits, which would meet all the prescribed requirements.

As nature has not provided such a creek-bed as has been imagined, what I propose to do is, first, to secure a similar condition by an artificial excavation, and then proceed to obtain a similar result, but of a much higher character.

The citizens of San Francisco would in this way be provided with an extended walk, ride and drive, which would be open at all times to those seeking health, recreation, and social intercourse in the open air; but within which the dust, din, and encounters with vehicles, moving in various directions, to which they are subject in all the present public places, streets and roads in and about the town, would be entirely avoided.

IX.
MILITARY AND PLAY-GROUND; SEQUESTERED GARDEN; MARINE-PARADE AND SALUTING GROUND; PLACES FOR MUSIC, FIRE-WORKS, AND PUBLIC CEREMONIES

But a mere promenade is not all or nearly all that should be provided in a metropolitan scheme of public grounds. Places are needed where military and athletic exercises can be carried on without conflicting with the pursuit of business and the safety or the quiet of those not interested in them. Civic ceremonies, music and fireworks should also be provided for, and a more secluded, quiet, and purely rural district should be added, in which invalids, and women and children may ramble, or rest in the open air, free from the disturbance of carriages and horsemen. There should also, if practicable, be a landing-place, with suitable surroundings, at which guests of the city could be welcomed, salutes fired and processions formed without interference with the public use of the streets or the commercial wharves.

San Francisco is so situated that it requires arrangements of this kind even more than other great cities, and no system of public grounds will be complete until they are added, even if it should be impracticable to plan them in such a way that they would be attractive and useful in every condition of wind and weather. Obviously, however, they should, as much as possible, be protected from the wind, and as near the present built part of the town as practicable.

To provide a parade ground in such a situation, large enough for the manœuvering of a brigade or division, would cost too much, and it would be otherwise objectionable. For such a purpose the city should secure a large tract of ground some miles distant from the present centre of the town; but for each of the other purposes a smaller area will answer, and suitable positions should, therefore, be found without going far out.

For a municipal landing place and marine parade, suitable to the commercial position of the city and to the duties which it will be proper for it to assume as holding the portal of the republic on the Pacific, where foreign dignitaries and our own national representatives will land and embark, and a port of refuge to which men-of-war of all nations may at any moment be obliged to resort, there seems to be a suitable place on the east side of the ridge of Point San José, between the fort and the Pioneer Woolen Mills. It enjoys considerable protection from the sea wind, as is shown by the growth of shrubs, and there is a good depth of water immediately off shore, with good anchorage. Here there should be a suitable landing quay and a plaza, with a close and thick plantation of evergreens on the west side, faced with banks of shrubs and flowers. The plaza or parade should be open and large enough to be used for a drill ground by a battery of artillery or a regiment of infantry, with some standing room and seats for spectators. It should also contain an elegant pavilion for the accommodation of committees of reception and their guests and a band of music, and should be decorated with flagstaffs, marine trophies, and eventually with monuments to naval heroes, discoverers and explorers. It should not, however, be very large or fitted for extended ceremonies, being considered rather as the sea-gate of the city than the place of entertainment for its guests.

The best place for a rural ground, to be retired from the general promenade, that I have been able to find near the city, is in a valley sheltered on the north, west and southwest sides by hills lying north and west of what is designated the "hospital lot" on the city map, and not far from the Orphan Asylum. This valley is not only unusually protected from wind, but the soil is moist, and I have observed that in the driest season the shrubs and herbaceous plants, of which there is very abundant natural growth within it, retain their freshness and health better than anywhere else.

There is a considerable extent of low level ground in the same vicinity, suitable for a parade and play ground of moderate size, which being close on Market Street, near the Mission, will be readily accessible from the present town. It is also very centrally situated with reference to all the suburbs of the city, and is just within the lines to which the streets of the city are laid out by the map of 1865. As beyond this point to the westward the rectangular system of streets will probably have to be abandoned, owing to the steepness and ruggedness of the hills, it offers also a convenient point of division between a scheme of grounds intended for the use of citizens during the next ten or twenty years, and a scheme for future improvements.

For these reasons I would propose to place here, as far as practicable, all those parts of the general system of pleasure grounds which require considerable lateral expansion. In European town parks, the more strictly rural portions are generally associated with the parts intended to be used as a promenade, in which but little lateral space is really needed. As by the arrangement already sketched out the social public promenade is provided for elsewhere, and as only a moderate area will be needed for military use here, the parade ground proper being located further out in the country, it will be desirable to bring this area in juxtaposition with the tract to be set apart for the more secluded garden ground, in order to gain a greater general impression of spaciousness than either alone would give. As, however, the purpose of each is quite distinct from that of the other, they should, in the detailed arrangement of the design, be very completely separated. I propose, therefore, to place between them a grand terrace or tribune, readily accessible from each, as well as from the general promenade, and from the common streets of the town. This structure might be formed in two levels, one set apart for persons in carriages, the other for those on foot. On two sides of it might be rich parterres or formal flower gardens with fountains, and the whole might be given a highly architectural character with rich parapets of stone; or it might be cheaply finished with turf banks, bastions and bays, and plain iron or wooden handrails. In connection with this grand central concourse there should be suitable stands for music, for fireworks, and for public speaking. These should face toward the parade ground, in which a crowd of many thousand persons might be assembled without danger of injury to plants or objects of art, and where a regiment might be manœuvred, or a division reviewed in marching column. Additional accommodation for spectators on foot and in carriages should be arranged all around its margin. It should be placed at as low a level as practicable, with higher ground and thick plantations on the windward side.

On the other side of the terrace or tribune, in a still more thoroughly protected position, I would have a small garden formed in a nook of the hills, facing to the southeast, with a grove of trees in the upper part and in that part nearest the tribune, the remainder being thrown into a surface of pictur-esque form, with rocks and terraces, and planted closely and intricately with shrubs and vines, with walks running among them, and frequent seats, arbors, and small sheltered and sunny areas of turf and flowers. In the lowest part there should be a flatter space, in which there should be laid out and kept up at any expense for maintenance that might be found necessary, a small clear lawn of turf sloping down to the shore of a pool of still water, on the other side of which there should be the finest display of foliage in natural forms which art could command. From within this garden, no carriage road or buildings, except those of a rural character, inviting rest, should be seen, and no pains should be spared to make it a spot of pure and tranquil sylvan loveliness. If it is a question whether anything of this kind could be maintained in a large city without being misused, and rendered practically valueless for those who would most enjoy it through the misbehaviour of lawless men and boys, the Ramble in the Central Park, parts of which in a great degree realize what I should attempt, gives a sufficient answer.

For some years to come such a series of grounds and structures as I have suggested near the Orphan Asylum, with a Marine Parade at Point San José, and a spacious promenade between them, would probably suffice.

A line between these two points would be nearly parallel to a line equally subdividing the present population of the city, being within ten minutes' drive of the City Hall and the Lincoln School-house respectively; and the best course for a promenade to be laid out between them, having regard merely to the beauty and fitness of the promenade itself, would be a moderately direct one, carried in a succession of easy curves, generally in the depression of the hills.

If, however, the value of the land which would need to be purchased, and the disarrangement of the present lines of streets and properties which would be required to carry out this plan, should be thought a very great objection to it, it would be practicable to make use of Van Ness Avenue, from the water line to Eddy Street, and I think it best to presume that this would be deemed advisable.

X.
THE GENERAL PROMENADE

Taking Van Ness Avenue, I should add to it one tier of building lots on each side, which gives a space of 390 feet wide. Fifty-five feet of this space on each side might be appropriated to streets, into which the cross streets now falling into Van Ness Avenue would lead, without there being necessarily any change in the present plans for their grading, paving, sewering or piping. The present middle tier of lots of the blocks on each side of Van Ness Avenue would then be front lots on these two streets, which would be in all respects formed in the usual manner, except that it might be considered best not to lay any walk on the sides opposite the houses. There would remain a space to be given up to the promenade and ornamental ground 280 feet wide. With this an excavation would be made, varying in depth a little, according to the shape of the surface, but everywhere at least twenty feet deep. The sides of the excavation should slope so as to leave a nearly level space at the bottom 152 feet wide. In the centre of this might be formed a mall 24 feet wide, flanked on each side by a border, to be used as will hereafter be described. Between the borders and the foot of the slopes might be two roadways, each 54 feet wide, 15 feet being made of loose sifted gravel, as a pad for saddle horses, and the remaining 39 feet finished with hard rolled gravel for carriages. Immediately outside the roadways, the surface should usually rise very gently and be occupied by beds of turf or flowers, which should be carried up irregularly until lost under plantations of shrubs and trees. The upper part of the slopes adjoining the streets should be everywhere planted with coniferous trees set closely and trimmed so as to form a lofty hedge or thick screen sufficient to break off the wind from the less sturdy plants within.

At such intervals as might from time to time be deemed advisable, bridges, to carry streets across the promenade grounds, would have to be constructed, and at each of these bridges entrances should be arranged by which persons on foot could reach the mall. Access to the roads may be obtained by carriage approaches descending the slopes in lines diagonal to the general course, starting midway between the bridges.

After crossing Eddy Street, the promenade might fork into

two branches, that to the left going straight to the south-west corner of the present Yerba Buena Park, where the Pioneer monument is to be placed, which would form the vista-point of the mall. Here it would terminate with an entrance on Market Street, six blocks out from Montgomery Street. The fork to the right would be at right angles to the first, and run parallel to Market Street until it reached the vicinity of the low ground near the Orphan Asylum, where it would connect with the terrace before described. Here it would be divided, one branch of the roadway being carried around the garden, following the hills; the other making the circuit of the parade ground; the mall being arranged to branch out into the garden walks, and also to lead around the parade.

The system of roads and walks after leaving this point, would resume more or less of the original restricted form, and would be carried on as far as might be thought advisable, as an extension of the general promenade. Between the Pioneer Monument and the old Spring Valley Reservoir near the Orphan Asylum, little having been done toward the carrying out of the existing plan of the city streets on the west side of Market Street, I think it would be best to revise the city map, both to secure greater convenience for business purposes, and to increase the dignity of the approaches and surroundings of the parade and garden. The small pieces of ground now reserved in this vicinity for public squares, may as well be thrown into streets and lots, and the streets at present laid out to divide the property between Market Street and the proposed promenade, be given up, and a more simple and symmetrical plan adopted.

The accompanying map, marked A, shows the position and relation to the *present* street system of the city, of the ground which would require to be taken for these improvements, so far as I am able to define it without a special survey. In the plan marked B, a suitable arrangement of the side entrances to the general promenade is shown, and the plan and section marked C, illustrates a method of bridging the promenade for the common streets of the city, and of giving access from them to the mall. The plan marked D, shows all the pleasure grounds, as well as the changes above proposed to be made, between Eddy

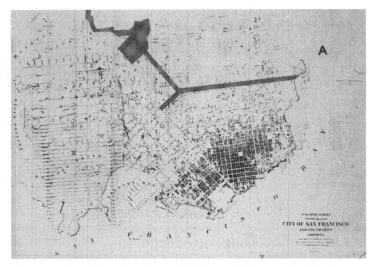

Plan A: Map of San Francisco with Olmsted's Plan for Public Pleasure Grounds Superimposed

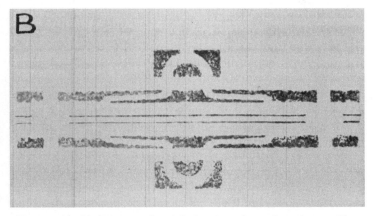

Plan B: Sketch of Promenade, with Carriage Access from Streets Above

Plan C: Method of Bridging Promenade, Shown in Elevation and Bird's-Eye View

Street and Market Street, and between the Yerba Buena Park and the city line.

If such a plan should be adopted as I have suggested, each section of the general promenade formed by the bridges, should receive a somewhat different treatment, especially in the border between the mall and the roadway. In some sections, the border may be treated in a natural style, in others, in a formal style. The latter would be especially applicable where the level of the natural surface and the adjoining streets is highest, and the cuttings deepest, as in these situations, it may be best to employ retaining walls, and throw the ground into terraces on the exterior slopes; then, at some points, the border may be decorated with vases elevated on pedestals, baskets of flowers, yuccas, aloes, orange trees, or other exotic plants in tubs, which would admit of their being placed under shelter. Another section of the mall should be planted with fastigiate trees and shrubs, another with cactuses, another with standard roses, another with a particular class of flowering shrubs, another with creeping plants pegged down, another with a vegetable embroidery upon fine turf, another with beds of tulips, of violets, or of callas, etc.

At some points, the walks should be carried out to the edge of the roadway, (as shown in the vicinity of the bridges, upon the sketch C), so that people can step upon it from their

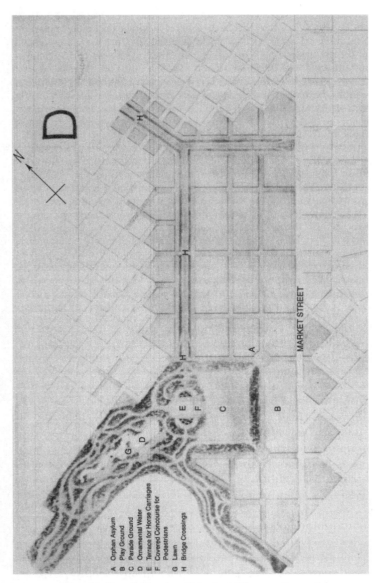

Plan D: Detail Showing Principal Pleasure Grounds

carriages, or converse with those upon it without getting out. Some of these openings should be covered by pavilions of rustic or lattice work, overgrown with vines and creepers, and furnished with seats; at other points the walk may be thrown out to the road on each side, and the centre occupied by smaller pavilions, or by fountains, statues, cages of birds, dove cotes, rabbit hutches, small paddocks of gazelles or antelopes, tanks of aquatic plants, globes of fish, or such suitable objects of art or curiosity, as may from time to time be acquired by the city, either as gifts or by purchase. By slight modifications of the general plan, the details could be modified to an indefinite extent, and every desirable object might be placed in the position most suitable to exhibit it to advantage, either from the carriage road or the walk, or from both. Portions of the mall, for instance, might be made lower than the adjoining road, and divided, so as to run within narrow rocky ravines, in the ledges and crevices of which would be the most delicate plants, or the rocks might be covered with ivy.

Thus, in minor points, the design could be everywhere varied, always taking care, however, that the slopes should be of a somewhat larger style than the one adopted for the borders of the central mall. At the same time, if considerations of economy should be required to control the design in this respect, a plain turf finish might be given to the borders, and the slopes might be planted with masses of common shrubs and small trees, such as the lilacs, mock-orange, calycanthus, acacia, flowering currant, elder, laburnum, buckeye, manzanita, photinia, ceanothus, magnolias, laurels, azaleas, œdenostema, eriodictyon, golden-leafed chestnut, holly-leafed berberry, and many others which may be obtained in large quantities from the cañons of the coast range. Some sections might be devoted to an illustration of the shrubs of California, others to those of Australia, China, Japan, or Siberia, in so far as they would suit the situation.

As, however, the winter of San Francisco is peculiarly adapted, whenever it is fair weather, to the enjoyment of the promenade, I should prefer to plant much the larger part almost wholly with evergreens, especially with the smooth-leaved evergreen shrubs and vines, like the laurel, myrtle, rhododendrons, Chinese magnolias, and ivy. With a smaller expenditure than several individuals in Europe and the Eastern States have made for the purpose, the citizens of San Francisco might, I believe, provide themselves in a few years, with a "Winter Garden" more beautiful than any now to be found in the world.

Beyond the central parade and garden I should be disposed to make the protected ground somewhat wider, and perhaps of varying width, and to plant it in a more rural and decidedly picturesque manner, introducing the approaches more circuitously, as indicated in the southwest branch leading out of the garden in the drawing D. The bridges may be formed mainly of timber, as shown in the section C. The principal timbers should, however, be massive, and the details artistically designed. A large part of the bridges may be covered with vines on wire trellises. Whenever desired in the future, bridges of masonry or wrought iron can, of course, be substituted for timber structures. There should be balconies on the bridges overlooking the promenades, thrown out from the line of the sidewalks as indicated in the drawing C.

Much less water would be required to keep the plants on the slopes in flourishing condition than would be needed if they were on the open ground, and the water would be distributed with much greater rapidity and economy. The water may be obtained by special contract with the water company, or by a system of wells from which the water would be raised to small reservoirs at the higher points on the banks by windmills or engines.

The principal advantage of placing the mall, as proposed, between the two roads, besides that of doubling the carriage and bridle ways without a corresponding expense of construction, is that it completely protects persons on foot from all danger, or feeling of apprehension, of being run over at any point within the pleasure ground; a matter of great consequence, not only to the infirm and to timid women and children, but to all who are disposed to enjoy the ground in a tranquil way, and especially to those in carriages or on horseback, who would otherwise need to be constantly on the alert, to avoid collisions, as now in the common streets.

Another advantage would be found on occasions when it would be desirable to use one of the roads for a procession.

The width of each road is sufficient to admit of the march of a military column by company front, and the whole mall, as well as the balconies of the bridges, might be occupied by spectators, without at all interrupting the ordinary pleasure-driving upon the other road, the width of which would allow four carriages to be driven freely abreast without crowding upon the bridle road.

The total length of carriage road would be over nine miles; of bridle road, the same; and of the mall, between three and four miles. There would be four or five miles more of walking ground in the walks of the central garden and about the marine parade.

This, I presume, is as much as would be required, or as it would be best for the city to undertake to finish and maintain for several years to come. It will be obvious, however, that a system of drives, bridle roads, and walks within quite narrow lateral boundaries, such as I have suggested, is one that is well suited for indefinite extension, and that the cost of the ground required for the purpose, provided the purchase of it should not be too long delayed, would be light.

The sketches which are now presented provide for extensions in two directions; one of these might be carried to the flat land lying southeast of the hill shown on the large map in the City Surveyor's Office, with the name upon it of Cady & Gardiner, which is the most suitable ground that I have seen between the present city and the ocean, for an extensive parade ground; the other around the leeward slope of the hill west of the hospital lot, and by easy grades to the lowest point in the saddle of the hills near where the old toll-gate house upon the Ocean House road stands. Thence the latter might be carried either through the valley to the southward, and terminate upon the shore at Point Avisadero or Point San Quentin, or it might be carried (as much as possible near the bottom of the valleys), to the Laguna Mercedes and the ocean beach, or again it might be extended indefinitely into the country, toward San Bruno. It might be forked, and take any two or more of these routes. But it will not be practicable to determine upon any definite plan of extension for the promenade, or to secure the required amount of ground without an understanding of the general plan yet to be adopted for the extension of the common street system of the city. As already observed, it will hardly be practicable to attempt to push the present rectangular arrangement much further, and this consideration leads me to offer in conclusion a few observations relative to the general plan of the city.

To the present time the street plan of San Francisco has been contrived with scarcely any effort to adapt it to the peculiar topography of the situation. On a level plain, like the site of the city of Philadelphia, a series of streets at right-angles to each other is perfectly feasible, and the design is as simple in execution as it appears on paper; but even where the circumstances of site are favorable for this formal and repetitive arrangement, it presents a dull and inartistic appearance, and in such a hilly position as that of San Francisco, it is very inappropriate. If the present site, as it was in 1850, had now to be laid out for a large city, it would be desirable to adopt a different arrangement in many respects.

If hills of considerable elevation occur within the boundary of a site marked out for a city, this salient difficulty should be met at the outset, and a series of main lines of road should be arranged that will ascend these hills *diagonally*, in such a way as to secure sufficiently easy grades. The skeleton lines being thus determined on, a series of transverse and connecting streets should next be provided that will divide the whole into sections of moderate size, and each of these intermediate districts should then be planned separately, and with as much regularity as the circumstances of the case admit.

The city of San Francisco is unquestionably in a very different degree of advancement from what it was in 1850; but even now it is evident that by far the larger portion of the city remains to be built up. Although, therefore, very much has been done that it would be impossible to think of changing, and the interests involved in the portions that are not improved, are, doubtless, so numerous as to make a change anywhere difficult and troublesome; still the future advantage to the city of a judicious reconsideration of the whole subject at this time can hardly be over estimated, especially with reference to that portion of the city that remains entirely unoccupied by buildings of a permanent character.

The first cost of constructing the streets upon such a plan

as has been suggested, would probably be less than upon the present; and the advantage in the saving of wear and tear to horses and vehicles, to say nothing of fatigue to persons on foot, would be incalculable.

There are many side questions in connection with the general scheme I have presented, to which I have given the consideration necessary to satisfy myself that any difficulty likely to arise in carrying it out might be satisfactorily overcome; but the whole matter has already been laid before you in a more detailed form than properly belongs to a preliminary report, and I now leave it in your hands, sincerely hoping that you will be as strongly impressed as I am with the commercial, social, and moral importance to your State of an early attempt to develop on a liberal scale some such plan of metropolitan improvement as I have here sketched out.

Respectfully,

FRED. LAW OLMSTED
Olmsted, Vaux, &. Co,
Landscape Architects

SITUATING A COLLEGE: JUNE 1866

FROM *Report upon a Projected Improvement
of the Estate of the College of California,
at Berkeley, near Oakland*

When I first visited the ground at your request, it was proposed that the buildings to be erected for the Institution should be placed upon a site which looked down upon the surrounding country on every side except that which would be to their rear, and that the remainder of the property should be formed into a *Park*, for which it was desired that I should furnish a plan.

After some preliminary study, I advised you that whatever advantages such an arrangement might have in a different climate and soil, it would in my judgment be inappropriate to your site and inconvenient to your purposes, while it would permanently entail burdensome expenses upon your institution.

My objections to the original project having been deemed conclusive, I was requested to review the whole question of the placing of the College buildings and the disposition to be made of the tract within which it had been determined that a situation for them should be selected. The general conclusions to which I was brought by this review having been verbally presented to your Committee, I was instructed to draft a plan in accordance with them. This I have done, and in the present report I have to show how this plan is adapted to serve the main purposes of your corporation, as well as some others of public interest.

The question as to the local circumstances that would be most favorable to the attainment of the objects of a College, is mainly a question of adjustment between a suitable degree of seclusion and a suitable degree of association with the active life of that part of the world not given to the pursuits of scholars. The organic error in this respect of the institutions of the middle ages and the barrenness of monastic study in the present day, is too apparent to be disregarded. Scholars should be prepared to lead, not to follow reluctantly after, the advancing line of civilization. To be qualified as leaders they must have an intelligent appreciation of and sympathy with the real life of civilization, and this can only be acquired through a familiarity with the higher and more characteristic forms in which it is developed. For this reason it is desirable that scholars, at least during the period of life in which character is most easily moulded, should be surrounded by manifestations of refined domestic life, these being unquestionably the ripest and best fruits of civilization. It is also desirable that they should be free to use at frequent intervals those opportunities of enjoying treasures of art which are generally found in large towns and seldom elsewhere.

Such is the argument against a completely rural situation for a College.

On the other hand, the heated, noisy life of a large town is obviously not favorable to the formation of habits of methodical scholarship.

The locality which you have selected is presumed to be judiciously chosen in respect to its proximity to San Francisco. Although it has the advantage of being close by a large town, however, the vicinity is nevertheless as yet not merely in a rural but a completely rustic and almost uninhabited condition, two small families of farmers only having an established home within half a mile of it. This is its chief defect, and the first requirement of a plan for its improvement is that it should present sufficient inducements to the formation of a neighborhood of refined and elegant homes in the immediate vicinity of the principal College buildings.

The second requirement of a plan, is that, while presenting advantages for scholarly and domestic life, it shall not be calculated to draw noisy and disturbing commerce to the neighborhood, or anything else which would destroy its general tranquillity.

The third requirement of a plan is, that it shall admit of the erection of all the buildings, the need of which for college duties can be distinctly foreseen, in convenient and dignified positions, and leave free a sufficient space of ground for such additional buildings as experience may hereafter suggest, as well as for exercise grounds, gardens, &c.

I proceed to a consideration of the means of meeting the first of these requirements.

San Francisco is so situated with regard to the commercial demands of various bodies of the human race, that it may be adopted as one of the elements of the problem to be solved, that many men will gain wealth there, that the number of such men will be constantly increasing for a long time to come, and that a large number of residences will be needed for these suited to a family life in accordance with a high scale of civilized requirements. If these requirements can be more completely satisfied in the neighborhood of the college than elsewhere, it may be reasonably anticipated that it will eventually be occupied by such a class as is desired.

We have to consider then, what these requirements are, and whether, by any arrangements you can make or initiate, they may be provided for in an especially complete way, on the property which you have to dispose of.

We shall gain but little light in this matter, by studying the practice of those who have had it in their power to choose the circumstances of their residence, the difference in this respect being very great, and leading to no clear, general conclusions.

Some, for instance, as soon as they are able to withdraw from the active and regular pursuit of their business in towns, seem to have cared for nothing but to go far away from their friends, and to rid themselves of the refinements of life and the various civilized comforts to which they have been previously accustomed. Others can only make a choice among lofty structures, the windows of which look out on busy streets, so that the roar of toiling, pushing crowds, is never escaped from, while for any enjoyment of natural beauty, the occupants might as well be confined in a prison.

In England, the prevailing fashion of wealthy men for several centuries, has been to build great stacks of buildings, more nearly represented by some of our hotels, than anything else we have, and to place these in the most isolated positions possible, in the midst of large domains, with every sign of human surroundings not in a condition of servility or of friendly obligation to themselves, carefully obliterated or planted out.

This fashion, growing as it doubtless has, out of a conservative disposition in regard to feudal social forms, has also been frequently followed in a cheap and shabby way by many in America, especially in the Southern States, yet no argument can be needed to show its utter inadaptation, even with profuse expenditure, to the commonest domestic requirements of our period of civilization.

The incompleteness of all these arrangements is easily traced to the ordinary inclination of mankind to over-estimate the value of that which happens to have been difficult to obtain or to have seemed to be so, and to overlook the importance of things which are within comparatively easy reach.

It is only by reference to some general rule that will satisfy the common sense, that the comparative value of one or the other of the possible conditions of a residence can be safely estimated, so that those things which are essentially important, may not be sacrificed to matters which are of value only as they gratify a temporary personal fancy or caprice of taste.

Such a general rule may, I think, be stated as follows:

The relative importance of the different provisions for human comfort that go to make up a residence is proportionate to the degree in which, ultimately, the health of the inmates is likely to be favorably influenced by each, whether through the facility it offers to the cheerful occupation of time and a healthful exercise of the faculties, or through any more direct and constant action.

Every civilized home centres in an artificial shelter from the elements; a contrivance to shut out rain, and wind and cold. But little judgment is required to make a shelter sufficiently large and effective. To accomplish this in a way that will be compatible with a due provision of sunlight and fresh air, however, is more difficult. In fact, perfect shelter at all times and as free a supply of fresh air and sunlight as is desirable to be used by every human being at intervals, is impossible. Yet, as their use seems to be always free to the poorest and least intelligent of men, it seldom occurs to such as are intent on making good provision in other respects for the comfort of their families, to take great care to make the use of sunlight and air easy and agreeable. The consequence is that their houses are really no better in this respect than those of careless and indolent men; often not as good, the advantages of the latter in this one particular being sacrificed by the more prudent to more complete arrangements for accomplishing the primary purpose of shelter.

More unhappiness probably arises from this cause, in houses which are in most respects luxuriously appointed, than from any other which can be clearly defined and guarded against.

Attractive open-air apartments, so formed that they can be often occupied for hours at a time, with convenience and ease in every respect, without the interruption of ordinary occupations or difficulty of conversation, are indeed indispensable in the present state of society to the preservation of health and cheerfulness in families otherwise living in luxury. The inmates of houses which are well built and furnished in other respects, but in which such apartments are lacking, are almost certain, before many years, to be much troubled with languor, dullness of perceptions, nervous debility or distinct nervous diseases. The effort to resist or overcome these tendencies, except by very inconvenient expedients, such as traveling abroad, or others of which it is impossible to make habitual use without a sacrifice of the most valuable domestic influences, leads to a disposition to indulge in unhealthy excitements, to depraved imaginations and appetites, and frequently to habits of dissipation.

It may be thought that this is a defect which, in most houses with private grounds about them, might be so easily remedied that it is hardly credible that I do not exaggerate the degree in which it mars the happiness of families who are so fortunate as to live out of the midst of towns. But it is a great mistake to suppose that it is a simple matter to make it convenient and agreeable, to delicate women especially, to spend much time healthfully in the open air. Lord Bacon, three hundred years ago, sagaciously observed:

"God Almighty *first* planted a garden, and, indeed, it is the purest of human pleasures; it is the greatest of refreshment to the spirits of man, without which buildings and palaces are but gross handiworks: *and a man shall ever see that when ages grow to civility and elegance, men come to build stately sooner than to garden finely—as if gardening were the greater perfection.*"

In the formation of country residences of the smallest pretensions far greater study and a far larger proportionate expenditure is generally made in England, and in most countries where civilization has been long established, upon matters of out of door domestic convenience than in America. Yet the difficulties to be overcome and the need to overcome them, are incomparably greater in America, and especially in California, than in England. The truth is they are so great that they are commonly regarded as insurmountable, and a deliberate effort to make sure that the out of door part of a residence shall be conveniently habitable and enjoyable is not thought of. The "garden" and "grounds" are regarded merely as ornamental appendages of a house, marks of the social ambitions of the owner, like the plate and carpets within, rather than as essentials of health and comfort, like the beds and baths. Yet the frequent action of free sun-lighted air upon the lungs for a considerable space of time is unquestionably more important than the frequent washing of the skin with water or the perfection of nightly repose.

Another class of civilized requirements frequently forgotten by men who have earned, by their skill and industry in providing for the wants of others, the right to live luxuriously, consists of those which can only be met by the services of numerous persons who are not members of the family requiring them, such as purveyors of various articles of food and bodily refreshment;

artisans, musicians, nurses, seamstresses, and various occasional servants. (Physicians, teachers and clergymen might be added, but the absence of these from a neighborhood is less frequently overlooked.) Townspeople who have been accustomed to find those able to render such services always within ready call are particularly apt to neglect to consider how much of their comfort is dependent on this circumstance, and often discover it only after they have, by a large expenditure, made a home for themselves in which they are obliged to live in a state which, by comparison with their town life, seems one of almost savage privation.

The first of the two classes of requirements to which I have referred, it is obvious, can never be satisfactorily provided for in a town house, as towns are usually laid out. Hence, as statistics testify, families living in such towns, except where habitual resort is had to parks or gardens, or to annual journeys in the country, constantly tend to increasing feebleness of constitution, and generally become extinct from this cause in a few generations. The second class cannot be provided for in an isolated country house. Hence, in a great measure the frequency with which wealthy men who have spent enormous sums to provide themselves country houses abounding in luxury, are willing, after the experience of a few years, to dispose of them at great pecuniary sacrifice.

It is true, that by great expenditure, many of the usual inconveniences and deprivations of a residence in the country may be made of small account. But often it is found that with double the current expenditure in a country house of the most luxurious equipment, the same variety of civilized enjoyments cannot be obtained as are to be had in town houses of a much more modest description. There are certain very desirable commodities, indeed, that very poor families can enjoy when living in or near large towns, that even the very rich commonly dispense with when they live in the country. These constitute a large part of the attractions which such towns have for poor and rich alike.

There can be no question, that, as a general rule, people of easy circumstances, especially those who have the habits of townspeople, if they want to make the most of life, should not undertake to live where they will be necessarily dependent in any degree much greater than is usual in towns for the supply of their every day material requirements upon labor performed within their own walls, nor where they can be deprived at any time of year, much more than they would be in towns, of good roads and walks, and other advantages for exercise, and easy, cheerful use of whatever advantages there may be near them for social intercourse. Yet it is equally certain that if they fail to secure fresh air in abundance, pleasant natural scenery, trees, flowers, birds, and, in short, all the essential advantages of a rural residence, they will possess but a meagre share of the reward which Providence offers in this world to the exercise of prudence, economy, and wise forecast. But if we are thus compelled to seek the site for a residence "out of town," and to take care that all effort to secure comfort in it is not exhausted in the plan of the mere house, or shelter from the elements, we must also remember that to keep extensive private grounds in good repair, and perfectly fresh and clean, requires more skill and labor, as well as administrative ability, than all the rest of the ordinary housekeeping affairs of a moderate family. And as, unless they are so kept, extensive private grounds are not simply useless, but absolutely irksome, when associated with a family residence, and as it is hardly possible in America to maintain for any lengthened period a large body of efficient domestic servants, however extravagantly disposed a man may be in this particular, the folly of attempting to imitate the aristocratic English custom which has been referred to is evident.

It may be laid down, then, as a rule, to which there will be but few exceptions, and these only in the case of families not only of very unusual wealth, but of quite exceptional tastes, that for the daily use of a family, no matter how rich, if the site be well chosen, and the *surrounding circumstances are favorable*, a space of private ground of many acres in extent, is entirely undesirable.

If the surrounding circumstances are *not* favorable—if there are dirty roads, ugly buildings, noisy taverns, or the haunts of drunken or disorderly people near by, ground which it would otherwise be undesirable to hold may be wanted in which to plant them out of sight and hearing; if the country in the neighborhood is not agreeable to walk, ride, or drive through, a large space may be wanted in which to form extended private walks, rides, and drives, which shall be artificially agreeable; if one's neighbors are of surly, hot-blooded, undisciplined, quarrelsome character, he will want to buy them out of their land in order to have them at a greater distance, and to be free from the danger of their return. If he is himself of an ostentatious, romantic, and dramatic disposition, he may require, more than any other luxury, to have a large body of servile dependents about him, and may want to disguise the fact of his actual insignificance among his neighbors by establishing his house at a distance from anything that he cannot think of as belonging to himself or subordinate to his will. But the great majority of men who have the ability to gain or hold wealth in America come under neither of these heads, and in the choice of a place of residence will find it best, at the outset, to avoid, if they have the opportunity to do so, all such conditions as have been enumerated.

A respectable college could not be established in any locality without bringing to it a certain amount of neighborhood advantages, while if it is not positively repellant to, it at least can have no direct attraction for, the more common constituents of a bad neighborhood, that is, for those things which every man must wish to keep at a great distance from his house. If, then, you can make your neighborhood positively attractive in other respects, especially if you can make it in important particulars more attractive than any other suburb of San Francisco, you can offer your land for sale, for villa residences, in lots of moderate size, with entire confidence that you will thus cause to grow up about it such a neighborhood as is most desirable, with reference to your first purpose.

What, then, are the requisites (exterior to private ground) of an attractive neighborhood, besides good neighbors, and such institutions as are tolerably sure to be established among good neighbors? The most important, I believe, will be found in all cases to be that of good *out-goings* from the private grounds, whether with reference to social visiting, or merely to the pleasure and healthfulness of occasional changes of scene, and more extended free movement than it is convenient to maintain the means of exercising within private grounds.

For this purpose the common roads and walks of the imme-

diate neighborhood, at all times of the year, must be neither
muddy nor dusty, nor rough, nor steep, nor excessively exposed
to the heat of the sun or the fierceness of the wind. Just so far
as they fail in any of these respects, whatever is beautiful in
the neighborhood, whatever is useful—churches, schools, and
neighbors included—becomes in a certain degree disagreeable,
and a source of discomfort and privation. No matter what a
neighborhood may be in all other respects, therefore, if it fails
in these it must be condemned as unfit for a civilized residence.
It is folly to suppose that compensation for the ill-health and
the vexations that will daily arise from a poor provision in this
respect will be found in such other circumstances as a beautiful
prospect from a house, or a rich soil, or springs of water or fine
trees about it, or any other mere private or local possession,
for the lack of these can generally be remedied in large degree
by individual wisdom and expenditure, while the lack of good
out-goings cannot.

The desideratum of a residence next in importance will be
points in the neighborhood at which there are scenes, either
local or distant, either natural or artificial, calculated to draw
women out of their houses and private grounds, or which will
at least form apparent objects before them when they go out. It
will be all the better if many are likely to resort to these points,
and they thus become social rendezvous of the neighborhood.

Next to points at some distance from a house commanding
beautiful views, it is desirable to be able to look out from the
house itself upon an interesting distant scene. This is generally
not too little but too much thought of, the location of many
houses being determined by regard for this circumstance alone,
and things of far greater importance being sacrificed to it. It
will be found that when this is the case—when, for instance, a
house is placed in a lonely, bleak position, on the top of a hill
difficult to ascend—the most charming prospect soon loses its
attractiveness, and from association with privation and fatigue
becomes absolutely repulsive.

Nor is it desirable that a fine distant view should be seen from
all parts of the house, or of the grounds about it. This, indeed,
is impossible, if the house and grounds are in themselves completely agreeable. The first and most essential condition of a
home, is domestic seclusion. It is this which makes it home,

the special belonging of a family. If it is not attractive within itself, and chiefly and generally within itself, and made so by, or for the sake of, the family, it is no home, but merely a camp; an expedient of barbarism made use of to serve a temporary purpose of a civilized family. Yet it is a good thing to be able at times, without going far, within or without the house, to take a seat from which, while in the midst of the comfort and freedom from anxiety of a home, a beautiful or interesting distant scene can be commanded. It is not desirable to have such a scene constantly before one. If within control, it should be held only where it can be enjoyed under circumstances favorable to sympathetic contemplation.

The class of views most desirable thus to be had within easy reach, is probably that which will include all well balanced and complete landscapes. The general quality of the distant scene should be natural and tranquil, but in the details there should be something of human interest. No matter what the character of the distant outlook, however, it is always desirable that the line or space of division between that which is interior and essential to the home itself and that without which is looked upon from it, should be distinct and unmistakable. That is to say, whenever there is an open or distant view from a residence, the grounds, constructions and plantations about the house should form a fitting foreground to that view, well defined, suitably proportioned, salient, elegant and finished.

It may be observed that such an arrangement is not compatible with what some writers on landscape gardening have said of "appropriation of ground;" but it need hardly be argued that a man is going wrongly to work to make a home for himself when he begins by studying how he can make that appear to be a part of his home which is not so.

Even if this appropriated ground were public ground, to look at it from a private house without seeing a well defined line of separation between it and the family property, or without a marked distinction of character between the two, in the details of the scenery, would be to have the family property made public rather than the public property made private.

If it is desirable that the distinction between the character of the ground which forms a part of the home and of that which forms a part of the neighborhood beyond the home, should be thus emphasized, it is also desirable, and for a like reason, that there should be a somewhat similar gradation between that which constitutes the neighborhood and that which is more distant. In other words, a neighborhood being desirable, the existence of a neighborhood should be obvious, and for this reason the scenery which marks the neighborhood should be readily distinguishable. The view from the window or balcony should, in short, be artistically divisible into the three parts of; first, the home view or immediate foreground; second, the neighborhood view or middle distance, and third, the far outlook or background. Each one of these points should be so related to each other one as to enhance its distinctive beauty, and it will be fortunate if the whole should form a symmetrical, harmonious and complete landscape composition.

Of these three desiderata, the first only can be supplied by private effort. A site for a residence, therefore, should be selected, if possible, where the other two are found ready to hand.

For the purpose of ascertaining what was necessary to be supplied upon your ground to give it the advantages which have been described, and others, generally recognized to be essential to a neighborhood of the best form of civilized homes; I visited it under a variety of circumstances, in summer and winter, by night and by day, and I now propose to state what are its natural conditions; what are the artificial conditions required, and how these may be best secured.

First.—In respect of soil, exposure, natural foliage and water supply, your ground is, to say the least, unsurpassed in the vicinity of San Francisco.

Second.—There are few if any suburbs which command as fine a distant prospect. The undulations of the ground and the difference of elevation between the upper and the lower parts give the advantage of this prospect in its main features to a large number of points of view, so situated that the erection of buildings and the growth of trees at other points will be no interruption to it.

Third.—With respect to climate and adaptation to out of door occupation, persons who had resided upon the ground or who had frequent occasion to cross it, having stated that the sea-winds which nearly everywhere else near San Francisco are in summer extremely harsh, chilling and disagreeable to all, and often very trying to delicate persons, were felt at this point very little, I gave this alleged advantage particular consideration.

During the month of August I spent ten days on the ground, usually coming from San Francisco in the morning and returning at night. The climate of San Francisco was at this time extremely disagreeable, while that of the College property was as fine as possible. One morning, when I left San Francisco at nine o'clock, though the air was clear, a light but chilling north-west wind was blowing. The same wind, somewhat modified, prevailed at Oakland. At Berkeley the air was perfectly calm. Ascending the mountain side a few hundred feet, I again encountered the wind. Descending, it was lost, and the air remained calm until I left at five in the afternoon; the temperature being at the same time agreeably mild. During all the day I observed that San Francisco was enveloped in fog and that fog and smoke drifted rapidly from it over the bay and over Oakland. At five o'clock, in returning to San Francisco, after driving two miles toward Oakland, I had need to put on my overcoat. In the cabin of the ferry-boat, with doors closed, I saw women and children shivering, and heard the suggestion that the boat should be warmed in such weather. At San Francisco I found a blustering, damp wind and my friends sitting about a fire. The following day there was in the morning a pleasant, soft breeze at Berkeley, but late in the afternoon it fell to a complete calm. I determined to remain on the ground for the purpose of ascertaining whether this would continue or whether it preceded a change of temperature and a visit of the sea-wind after night-fall. At sunset the fog-clouds were rolling over the mountain tops back of San Francisco, gorgeous in rosy and golden light; the city itself was obscured by a drifting scud. At Berkeley the air remained perfectly serene, and, except for the fog-banks in the southwest, which soon became silvery and very beautiful in the moonlight, I never saw a clearer or brighter sky. It remained the same, the air being still of a delightful temperature, till morning, when the sun, rising over the mountains in the rear, gave a new glory to the constant clouds overhanging the heights on each side of the "Golden Gate." Going back in the afternoon to San Francisco, I again found the temperature, in contrast to that of Berkeley, disagreeably chilling, though the day was considered there an uncommonly fine one and the wind was less severe than usual.

I have visited the other suburbs of San Francisco and studied them with some care, and, without being able to express a definite estimate of the degree of difference between their climate and that of Berkeley, and without being able to assert from my limited observation, that the immunity of the latter from the chilling sea-wind is absolutely complete and constant, I think that I am warranted in endorsing the opinion that the climate of Berkeley is distinguished for a peculiar serenity, cheerfulness and healthfulness.

I know of no entirely satisfactory explanation of the fact. But it may be observed that it lies to the northward of the course of the north-west wind which draws through the Golden Gate and which sweeps the peninsula to the southward of the city and the Contra Costa country south of Oakland, and that there are to the northward and northwestward of it several spurs of the Monte Diabolo range, the form of which is calculated to deflect currents of air setting down the bay from the northward. The form of the trees on the top of the nearest of these hills indicates an upward deflection of the northerly wind.

FRONTIER SOCIETY: 1866

FROM *The Pioneer Condition and the Drift of Civilization in America*

SECTION I
A PIONEER COMMUNITY OF THE PRESENT DAY

This part of the country has been known to white men about fifteen years. The Indians who before lived here were of the weak yielding kind which is common west of the Cordilleras, too feeble of intellect to make any largely organized resistance and indisposed through indolence and pusillanimity to individually oppose any purpose of the newcomers. Nevertheless it happened, as they were pushed about and then pilfering and assassinating Indian habits caused a spice of vindictiveness to be added to the feeling of contempt with which they were chiefly regarded by the whites, a state of absolute war came to exist and continued, though generally pursued in a very desultory way, for several years. On certain occasions the whites formed volunteer military organizations and fought in short campaigns with some degree of system. These active periods were always ended by a sweeping massacre of Indians with comparatively small loss to the whites and a treaty of peace, the conditions of which practically amounted to this, that the whites in all that part of the country which they chose to occupy or travel through could do as they pleased if they would cease to make an organized business of killing Indians. Even after the last of these "fighting sprees," as I have heard them called, the surviving Indians within a distance of fifty miles of our village must, I think, have outnumbered the whites. A few hundred yet remain, and there is a fixed camp in which something more than a score of them live during the greater part of the year within a few minutes' walk of our house. At certain seasons, however, they leave the neighborhood altogether and at these times there are I presume tribal gatherings.

Within twenty miles to the East of us there are numerous miners' camps and graziers' cabins scattered through the valleys. Beyond that the mountains are so elevated that even their valleys are rendered impassible during the greater part of the year by the accumulation of snow. At the distance of an easy day's ride, therefore, in this direction, there is an uninhabited wilderness. Beyond this, at the distance of a hundred miles, in a flat desert region at the Eastern foot of the Sierras there is another line of miners' camps, beyond which again the red savage holds his own for several hundred miles. Also within a hundred miles to the Southward, there is a considerable body of Indians, living in valleys and high meadows of the Sierras, who do their poor best to keep away from white men. When, however, white men and these Indians meet each tries to kill the other. They are regarded and dealt with as beasts of prey. Some of our friends have lately exchanged shots with them, but they are so far off, and there are other settlements so much nearer them than ours that we have no concern with them. With regard to the Indians, therefore, we are not upon the advanced line, but rather upon a secondary line of settlement.

Nevertheless we are occasionally reminded of our close vicinity to the wilderness. Two grizzly bears have passed, unharmed, though one was shot at, and a wildcat has been killed, within a few hundred yards of our house, since we have been here. The Indians, in their primitive costumes, with bows and arrows and papooses strapped to the backs of the women, and with their primitive filth and vermin, and primitive stolidity of expression, often find their way into our doors and sometimes before they are discovered fall asleep in our entrance hall. On such occasions, if any notice is taken of them at all, the habit of most people here, of the several Irish, German, French and Chinese servants we have tried, for instance, is to address them in the same tone, and deal with them in the same manner, precisely, as a mangy street cur is spoken to & dealt with under similar circumstances.

We are some thirty miles within the outer line. This advanced line is formed by a very irregular series of cabins occupied mostly by graziers pasturing their stock in the mountains, with occasionally a camp of miners or prospectors. The graziers may be regarded as fixed settlers. Nearly all of them are emigrants from the Slave States, and have Indian "wives"—concubines.

There are men also who live for the most part along this line who cannot be classified either graziers or miners; men who have no particular occupation but most of whom live chiefly upon wild meat and who pay for their powder and lead, clothing, coffee, tobacco and whiskey mostly with bear and deer skins. Some of them have cabins of their own; most make one of the graziers' cabins a base of operations; sometimes spending several weeks at it and then assisting the grazier in looking after his stock. At times too they will join a party of miners or of prospectors or explorers or even lend a hand for a few days or possibly a few weeks at an occupation which requires some regular labor, such as harvesting a crop, building a cabin or a saw mill, a mill-dam or a sluice way for placer mining, or they will join a surveying or exploring party, taking the duty of supplying it with meat (game) or that of guide, or of cook and camp-guard, or of all three. Occasionally they come within the more populous districts in which case most of them "go on a spree." For the most part, however, as far as I have observed, they are not drunkards, though always ready to take a drink when it is offered them and generally carrying a little whiskey about with them which they use when by themselves sparingly.

If they become drunkards, like the Indians, they give up the wilderness and live wholly within the settlements, commonly dying very soon of delirium tremens in the County hospital or jail.

There is a much larger number of men whose habits are somewhat similar, and who are little if any more incorporate with the community than these last, the chief difference being that they spend the greater part of their time in prospecting, searching for gold and other treasures, getting their living mainly by placer-mining (washing particles of gold dust from sand). These also, however, occasionally engage for a day or a few days at a time in fishing, or helping farmers, millers or packmen, for thousands of people within a hundred miles of us live at a distance from waggon roads and receive their supplies either by pack trains sent out by the tradesmen with whom they deal or from pedlars who move their stock on the backs of mules or donkeys. Among the latter class (the solitary prospectors) I have found men of a good deal of intelligence and who have been fairly educated. Most of them have been trained or partially trained in some regular occupation in Eastern or European cities. Invariably, however, they are men of ill-balanced minds, many of them quite as much so, as some who are classed in our Eastern hospitals among the incurable cases of (mild) lunacy.

To return to the outer line of settlers and pioneers. These men are for the most part essentially as foreign to civilization, so far as I can see, as the Indians themselves—in fact more so, for among the Indians the primary crystallization of civilization is generally quite strongly shown in relationships of family and tribe, though here it stops. Among the white pioneers there is generally less of this. Their way of dealing with their women is less civilized than that of the male Indian. It does not follow, the reader should remember, that it is necessarily more cruel but that it is less based on sympathy and sense of unity of interest. Nevertheless these men appear to me to be & to have always been, as a class, more nearly akin, in the constitution of their minds to the Indians than to truly civilized white-men. If it were not for differences of language and the antipathetic prejudice originally given them by early education in a white community towards Indians as a body, they would prefer, I think, to live with a tribe of Indians rather than with a civilized community. I have heard some of them avow that they preferred Indian, negro, Mexican or Chinese women to white. One reason of this I judge to be that any white woman who would adopt their habits and be willing to associate with them on peaceable terms would necessarily be a very wretched and hateful specimen of the white race.

I do not wish to be thought to report altogether animadvertingly of these men. I have a kind and respectful and even admiring feeling toward some of them, but so it is true I have toward some savages. All I mean to express is that I have a strong impression of their essential incompatibility with civilized men and women.

Most of the outer settlers have Indian women living with them. It is the custom of the country to speak of these women as "Indian wives." They are not wives of course and quite the contrary, being thrown off with no more ceremony than they are taken on, whenever dissatisfaction is felt with the relation. Frequently no paternal obligation is recognized toward their children but this of course varies as does the degree of the constancy of hospitality toward the women, in each case, according to the varying strength of the natural force of amative attachment and of philoprogenitiveness.

The original family of the Indian wife often visits her and indeed frequently lives a considerable part of every year near by her master's cabin. The men, (her father, brothers—possibly her old husband), occasionally earn a little tobacco, whiskey, or cast off clothes or blankets by catching game, making baskets, hunting cattle that are far-strayed &c. The Indians who habitually have any peaceable association with the whites hereabouts, however, are mostly feeble, dispirited creatures, however, and rarely make themselves in any way in the slightest degree useful to the whites. A few only have courage to steal, even under favorable circumstances, so great is their terror of the white man's vengeance but when one of the outer settlers misses anything and chances to see an Indian, near at hand, he is very apt to assume that he is a thief, and that it is his duty to vindicate civilization, which he does on the spot either by shooting or if convenient by hanging him, the latter being deemed more "high toned." Our newspapers state that several Indians have been observed suspended from trees in this and the next county lately, one of them adds this comment: "supposed to have been thieves." Nothing more.

Still nearer where I write there are many mining camps, several ranches (cattle farms), villages, and within a half circle frontier ward of ten miles' radius, a population of several thousand, of whom a small minority are native Americans of the United States. The rest are Indians & Half breeds, Mexicans, Chinese and native Europeans in not very greatly unequal parts.

Most of them live in rude cabins, shantees, or booths, partly covered with canvas, some in "ratholes," shallow burrows made in clay banks; a few in tents; and there are several clusters of habitations having somewhat more pretence to comfort & permanence, being covered with clapboards and shingles and painted white, but divided through the interior by canvas screens. Houses of this sort are properly called pavilions by the French, being set up in a wooded country after saw mills have been put at work, almost as easily as a tent and burned down quite as easily. Collections of them here are commonly called "camps" unless there is a land speculation on foot in connection with them, when they may be made to take the title of city.

Our own place of residence in the ancient times (of Buchanan) bore the name of Bear Camp, and though the Postmaster General has given it another, that remains its proper name. It has a population of from two to three hundred and contains three general stores, two "hotels," five other establishments for supplying liquors & cigars, two supplied with Billiard tables and one with a piano, a Livery Stable, Bakery, Foundry, Machine Shop, Smithy and Cobbler's shop, two or three lodge-rooms and a public hall for dancing and other entertainments. It has a Mexican suburb, an Indian suburb and a Chinese suburb, the latter containing at this time about forty inhabitants. There are three good gardens near the camp, each well irrigated and admirably cultivated, one managed by an Italian, one by a Frenchman and one worked by a company of Chinese, who pay a small rent to citizens for the land but work on their own account, with admirable skill and painful thoroughness and industry.

I have been much puzzled to guess why there is this collection of people always here, and how it is supported. Plainly a considerable number cannot live by anything they earn here and now but besides these the number who seem to be making their living, and a pretty good living too, is more than a stranger can at once account for. The shopkeepers and tradesmen sell goods to miners living in smaller camps around us or to other shopkeepers and peddlars who supply these outer camps. The gardeners have the same market. But I have found it difficult to believe that its demand is so large or so varied as the supply that continues to be provided would seem to indicate. The fact undoubtedly is that the amount consumed or made way with per head of population, both of necessaries and of luxuries of certain kinds and these latter not a few, would very greatly outrun that of any community in Europe or the Atlantic States.

I was not prepared to find in a region so remote from the great centres of civilization so little of rural or backwoods sim-plicity. The English speaking people are no more unsophisti-cated here than in Piccadilly or St. Giles'. Even the farmers have more commonly the carriage, style and manners of unfortunate horse jockeys and dissipated market men than of solid, steady and frugal countrymen. Go where you will on the mountains, the hills or the plains, wherever the slightest trail has been formed or the smallest sign of industry—mining, mechanical or agricultural—is to be found, you may also find empty sardine boxes, meat, oyster and fruit cans, wine, ale, olive and sauce bottles, with playing cards and torn leaves of novels, magazines and newspapers, more commonly New York newspapers, but sometimes French, German or English.

Our camp is at the outside of a cluster of five stations of supply of similar character and among them within twelve miles to the Southward there are five public bakeries. We are supplied at our own door with fresh rolls as well as with milk every morning before breakfast. Our bread is of better quality than any I ever tasted made in New England. There are two public breweries, and no better beer is made in the United States than is supplied by one of them. There are three tolerable restaurants and several establishments which must be styled cafes and caba-rets rather than bar-rooms or dram shops; being provided with small tables, and two of them with vine covered arbors, where men sometimes rest and refresh themselves in a quiet and tem-perate way. When away from home I gladly resort to them as an escape from the parlors, dining rooms and bar-rooms of the hotels. Of these there are five of the ordinary dreary Western American kind, of which four on an average make each a new landlord bankrupt every six months. There are eight or ten public billiard tables; there are two hot bath establishments. There are eight or nine livery stables. There is a newsman, who keeps a reading room and also acts as carrier for the European and Eastern magazines and illustrated papers. The stock of clothing materials & of articles for the table to be found in the two dozen stores is much larger & more varied than would be found in most Eastern towns of several fold larger population & of several fold greater average wealth. There are established brokers, nurses, midwives, horolagers, barbers, sign-painters, metal-roofers. And this list of our sources of supply and distribution indicates another condition which I was not prepared to find in this remote wild region, in the variety of trades and handicrafts represented in the population. When it has happened that the services of a slater, thatcher, glazier, cooper, sadler, painter, confectioner, pastry cook, florist, piano tuner were wanted, someone previously unknown in the required capacity has come forth in good time from among our neighbors more or less fairly prepared for the occasion.

Few men, however, long hold fast by any single occupation. Our baker not only makes and distributes bread but sells cakes, beer, confectionary, tobacco and segars. At the same time & place he does business as a gold broker, as an express agent, as the Treasurer of two or three mining companies, and as Justice of the Peace. To customers who sit under his little awning to enjoy their cakes, beer or cigars, he gratuitously supplies the latest newspapers & magazines and cards or dominoes. German by birth of course, he is a well-disciplined, exact, honest, frugal, thrifty, sober and much esteemed citizen. Again there is a gentleman whom I personally know as a surgeon and a naturalist of large and varied observation, educated at the University of Paris. By his advertisements in the newspapers and otherwise I know that he is also proprietor of a white-smithing shop, an apothecary's shop, and manager of a mine; he has recently been admitted to the bar and offers his services as an attorney, counsellor and notary. He announces that he is prepared to draw up legal papers in French, Spanish and English. He is canvassing for capital for projected smelting works and is a candidate for the office of Coroner and Superintendent of the County hospital.

The two facts which I have indicated, that of an extraordinary average demand for certain material results of civilization and that of a general readiness and disposition to turn one's hand rapidly & frequently from one thing to another and to hold to nothing ploddingly or with long forecast, these two form the most striking distinctions of general application between the people here and any other I have observed.

Both may perhaps be reduced to one. In all old countries, public opinion acting in infinite forms is constantly operating with immense force on every man to prevent him from behaving not only illegally but improperly, that is inappropriately to his station, his station being the position in which he is expected to serve others & be served by others. For convenience sake, stations are classified into classes, and within certain limits the habits appropriate to each class and to many subdivisions of each class are so well established that everyone knows the indications of them which are given in forms, color, dress and carriage and is governed accordingly.

If an Englishman should be walking in the country at dusk of evening and an object should cross the road a little way off with regard to which, without having his attention particularly called to it at the time, he should be afterwards examined and cross examined, it would commonly appear that if he was able to state confidently that the object had been a man rather than a cow, he would also be able to express some idea about the social class of the man. Thus he would say, "I think he must have been a man of the lower class rather than a gentleman." Again if pressed he would find an impression which would lead him to regard it as more probable that the man was a factory workman than an agricultural laborer, that he was a small tradesman rather than a gentleman's servant and so on. If he had been sitting in a railway carriage with a man and had heard him speak a few sentences if only in answer to a traveller's enquiry about the road, he would make similar distinctions, similar reference to a class with much more precision and confidence.

More or less of this habit all civilized men must have. But the degree of it, the distinctness and tangibility of the classification and of the laws of duty and of requirement vary. Here by distinction not merely with England but with any community of the Atlantic or the Mississippi region, there is comparative abolition of class and consequent social anarchy. Our blacksmith is called upon to shoe two horses and make some repairs on a peddlar's waggon, in a hurry; he works hard, completes the job, is paid three dollars and being heated and dry, he goes where—to the pump; no, to the "hotel," and calls for, beer? gin? no; champagne or Burgundy, undoubtedly more refreshing & better for him.

There is a poor widow in the village whom my wife employs to do occasional chores, (a charwoman). She lately heard that a birth had occurred in the house of a friend ten miles away and at once ordered from the livery stable a handsome carriage with a pair of horses and a driver to take her to make a call of congratulation. Such incidents do not now impress me on account of the want of frugality which they illustrate as much as on account of the evidence they offer of the weakness here—the practical extinction of one of the great conservative forces of society. The precept and sense of propriety, which directs that a man should carry himself as becomes his station in life, assumes a continuity of occupation. The station of today must at least be built upon the station of yesterday. But here, when a newcomer is found among us it is impossible for us to judge him by reference to the standards of any station he has previously occupied. And we are all newcomers. The consequence is that the habit of dealing with others or of expecting to be dealt with by others with reference to such a standard is impracticable & is rapidly eradicated. There is a rapid increase of freedom of thought, freedom of suggestion and consequently a rapid multiplication of each man's wants, of each man's demands upon his fellow men or upon commerce, and a rapid weakening of each man's habit & disposition to follow any course which society seems to have laid out for him in a plodding, tedious, persistent or consistent way.

If a man who has shown ability in any direction, driving a stage coach or building a mill-dam, chooses to give advice in a question of law or medicine or theology or political economy to which he has never given an hour's study, it is not unlikely to be taken with as much respect & confidence as that of men who have labored hard through a course of years to fit themselves to give such advice.

Nearly all the advantages of civilization which depend on special and priviledged conditions of a part of the community, natural as well as artificial, are thus wanting here. The advantages, for instance, for serving the community which would be generally possessed by the son or daughter of parents who have always been in easy circumstances, who have long maintained a high reputation for thrift, honesty, and patriotism, & who have had a strong will as well as ability to educate their children carefully, are made of no account. They start on the same footing with the vagabond children of vagabond parents who have always been both reckless and helpless as to the training of their children. And the condition which I thus refer to is not due solely to the habits which a constant experience of dealing with persons of unknown antecedents must establish, but also partly to a prevailing disposition to distrust the reality of such advantages and a habit of confusing naturally established advantages of social position, standing, reputation or character, with those which in older communities are artificially imposed. I don't know but this over reaching rebellion is as strong with New Englanders as with Irish and Germans. The New Englanders here are many of them resolute Protestants against all the standards of respectability which are commonly held up in New England.

One man who has been very successful in gaining the confidence & respect of the community said to me of an applicant for employment as a clerk—"He told me he had a minister's certificate of his character—when a young man tells me that I always set him down for a sly one. No minister & no church can ever manufacture a character for me. I don't want a tub that can't stand on its own bottom."

"Life" here is remarkably open, a man's habits, qualities, tendencies are more generally displayed on an average than anywhere else in the world. And life is nowhere else I think so "many-sided." We turn from one thing to another, from one mental condition to another with frequency & with the facility and grace which comes of much practice. It is the soldierly habit, surging, joking, going in a drove careless to what like sheep;

then face to face with grimmest death, passionate, intense, sublime in self forgetfulness in love of cause or country, then again given to petty trickery, deceitful and ready to gain an indulgence of appetites either by the meanest petty larceny or the most awful piracy and murder. This many sidedness causes for a time a perplexity. Everyone recognizes, proclaims, and most insist emphatically and jubilantly in the fact that there is a grand difference between the public opinion, in what is approved, expected, required, demanded of a man here and elsewhere in the world wherein newspapers are printed and champagne or lager bier is within the reach of everyone. Is it greater love of justice, greater humanity, greater sympathy, greater honesty and frankness, greater willingness that others as well as oneself should be free? Each will be said on occasion but the next occasion will contradict it. There is an intenser love and intenser hate moving men here in one direction or another constantly than is often manifested in communities at the East or in Europe, and yet the means of developing & manifesting community of sentiment are exceedingly feeble. And it is not intenser love or hatred of freedom, truth, justice or of one another. No man having the question clearly before him and comparing event with event for many months will hold to any such theory. The condition about which all that there is here of peculiar conservatism and all that there is here of peculiar recklessness centres is I finally conclude that of Slipshod.

Men love so dearly to be slipshod that they will even for a time be systematic and intense and far-reaching in their efforts to quench whatever tends to put to shame, establish penalties or otherwise antagonize their continued following of slipshod ways.

I am confident that this is the one grand characteristic quality of the frontier, and without asserting that there are no exceptional instances I believe that if one carefully studies any striking example of energy of a kind which is at all characteristic of this rather than of any other Christian country, it will not be difficult to follow its stem down to a root of slipshod impulse.

Lynch Law itself, with all its outward show of thorough deliberation and system, is nothing but an intense form of the common effort to get along without real and prolonged deliberation and system. It is a darning together and inking over of the faded rags which the beggar would not if he could exchange for clean whole cloth. Just enough law or show of law to maintain the greatest degree of lawlessness under which men can have any use of neighbors.

There is then something more than a general forgetfulness or neglect of the constraints of old social order. There is a positive and wilful withdrawal from them, a contempt for and hatred of them as impositions, such as men feel toward discarded idols or superstitions which have lost their hold on them. There seems to be a commonly prevailing suspicion, at least, that whatever leads men to adopt habits of frugality, steadiness and plodding industry also fosters a disposition to override or outreach or oppress those of more open and careless habits.

I have been in the practice of going about the country within fifty miles, sometimes taking a pack mule and camping conveniences. Three times absent & sleeping always on the ground, several weeks—travelling each time on an average 250 miles entirely beyond fixed settlements, much of the way beyond any settlements even temporary. In these latter cases I have generally had some of my family with me and a guide or servant. I was leaving the tent the morning after I had first camped here in this way with my wife, intending to return to it for dinner, which was to be ready for us at a certain hour, when my wife said to the guide—"I hope you will not go out of sight of the tent, as there are some things in it which I should be very sorry to have stolen." The man swore that he would not leave it and, by way of further assuring my wife, said that I might hang him right up to the tree over the tent if I caught him away from it whenever we came back. "But," he added, "there ain't no need of watching it. There would not no man dare go nigh it that knows anything about California ways."

"Why not?" I asked. "What do you mean?"

"Why, Sir, suppose a man was to see the tent here and should want to go to it, how does he know that you ain't somewher around here; and, suppose you should see him, what would you do? Why he hain't no business there has he? Of course not and if you see him of course you'd shoot him, wouldn't you? Of course you would, if you see him going to your tent, cause you know he couldn't want to go there for no good. He knows you know that. Everybody knows you knows that. You bet there wouldn't nobody go to it. They'd go out o' their road to keep shut of it. You bet they would."

When we came back the man was not present, and no preparation had been made for dinner, and on going to the nearest watering place, which was not in sight of the tent, I found him lying on the ground asleep but for certain private reasons I did not hang him.

The village in which we live compares favorably in its general appearance with other villages that I have seen in a similar position in regard to the frontier. I am constantly told that seeing it now, I can hardly imagine what a different place it was a few years ago. Then a night seldom passed in which there was not a quarrel in which pistols were used by numbers of persons and a gentleman assures me that several times in the course of a few months that he lived here, on going out of his door in the morning, he saw the dead bodies of men who had been taken off in these entertainments, & who was killed last night was almost always asked at the breakfast table. The morning after I arrived here, I rode out with an old resident and presently passed about thirty unenclosed heaps of earth, some of them having stakes or small rude crosses stuck in them. "Graves—" said my companion as he observed me looking at them. "Yes—we used to always put 'em in here, fellows that died natural deaths—In their boots." I found afterwards that not all had been shot, but a majority. These are not the only uncared for graves. My little girl one day while playing near the house picked up something which like little Peterkin she brought in wondering what it was. A woman's skull, with a bullet hole through it. The body had been buried somewhere in the vicinity and probably so near the surface that beasts had torn it to pieces. And upon numbers of heaps of earth unmarked by stake or stone, I have come at different times, which I have generally found upon enquiry recalled to the older residents some "shooting scrape" of what they call "the old times."

Making all due allowance for the proneness to exaggeration which is very evident of those from whom I receive my accounts, it does not admit of doubt that a few years ago, not only in this but in all of the adjoining settlements which I have visited, deadly weapons were used with frequency, "every day," say my informants, speaking of various camps or villages, the population of which did not exceed three hundred on an average, men & women. The machinery of law was in existence; there were justices and sheriffs or sheriffs' deputies in these communities and lockups or jails in one or two of them but the officers of the law and the most sober and well educated men carried revolvers and knives and not unfrequently used them without law.

The many comments and explanations which I have heard made by men who were participants in the excitements and dangers of the earlier period all indicate that the condition from which the common insecurity of life most obviously & immediately resulted was not solely that of the diverse sources from which so many men came together and the consequent ignorance and want of confidence with which each man regarded most of those about him, but that it grew out of the fact that an unusual proportion of those thus brought together had already before they came here been established in habits of distrustfulness, of holding themselves in readiness to resist the disposition of others to cheat, oppress, and impose upon them—and that this habit was simply developed into a fiercer form by their sense of special ignorance of the character of the great mass of those with whom they were here thrown in contact. This ignorance was greatest toward those whose previous education and associations had been most different from his own. Towards these therefore suspicions, jealousies, prejudices, and ill-defined fears were readily roused and easily exasperated to a degree which especially under excitement of drink or anger, or mortal danger, almost made one a maniac and for the time being, quite made him a savage.

Every propensity in human nature, favorable to the production of deadly feuds, seems to have been indulged by every man to an unnatural degree—a degree which would have been unnatural to him in more maturely organized communities. Composed of such heterogeneous materials, there being in each settlement representatives of many nations and tribes, and those of the same nation born and bred often at the greatest distance apart actually and socially, whenever a stranger arrived he was as it were instinctively led to seek out his natural allies; almost every man had one or more "chums" or "partners," and each set of chums had alliances with other sets; alliances not made formally, but as came naturally from the readiness with which a good understanding could be arrived at. Such alliances were offensive and defensive and nothing was so evidently the requirement of prudence, as to look well to your friends. Of course it followed that the more careful each man was to take care of his friends the more careless he was in thought for the life or the rights in any way of those who were not his friends.

A large proportion of those who lost their lives appear to have been Mexicans or Negroes (Indians never count). Southerners come next, Irishmen next, I do not remember the grave of a single murdered New Englander, though there were not a few here and they carried arms and used them. In the large majority of cases these deaths resulted from some unfair dealing or suspicion of unfair dealing, cheating at cards, imposition in trade, robbery, attempt to carry a point, (perhaps a vain desire to appear well in conversation or debate), by false statements, brow-beating or unwarranted assumption. Whatever it was, the men with whom it originated seem seldom to have been the victims, but the moment either of them drew his weapon, others would draw and either side quarrels or a general "shooting scrape" result and death come to someone with no interest in the original quarrel. Of course all present on such occasions become more or less excited but many seem to become possessed of a blinding fever of destruction. Drawing and cocking their revolver they look for somebody to shoot at. The choice is made instantly and by instinct rather than judgment, and instinct discriminates in favor of those most akin. At least this is in part, I think, the explanation of the greater number of Mexicans and other colored men who fell, though it is also true that the Mexicans were more given to certain forms of imposition, more suspicious, more ready to resort to the knife, and not as well equipped with good firearms, on an average, as the men who came here from a greater distance.

As ignorance is the parent of credulity and passion is contagious, a ready credence was commonly found for any man's charges; complaints or suspicions against strange neighbors among all his more natural allies, and proposals to punish or enforce remedies for alledged wrongs or to guard against anticipated dangers by bold attacks were taken up with enthusiasm and executed with dash. Men not merely stood blindly by those to whom they would expect to turn for self-protection but against common enemies, no matter what made them enemies, practiced without compunction all the strategy ordinarily immoral which defensive war is ever supposed to justify.

Nothing seems to have been deemed mean or cowardly or unworthy of a man, by which a very distant or foreign neighbor, when for the time being considered an enemy, could be outwitted and overcome. One of my neighbors, an amiable & estimable man, told me that he had seen and had part in a distribution of presents to Indians, ostensibly as a peace-offering, in which were handkerchiefs intended to convey the poison of Small-pox. Another, that he had seen some Indian prisoners tortured by white captors in the indian manner, some mutilated and set free as a warning, and many white men wearing Indian scalps and even more barbarous trophies. Those most prone to these extreme degradations seem to have been European born. And though these may be considered occurrences of real war, it would appear that much the same feelings were always easily excited toward Mexicans, negroes and half-breeds, in which case they fared little better than Indians. And so generally the more distinct the line of seperation from one's natural friends or allies was felt to be, the less chance had any man the other side of it to be respected in any way. It was not to be supposed for instance in any fracas or difficulty involving numbers that an unknown man was possessed of honor, or honesty or rights of any kind, or that honor or honesty or a fair field was to be observed in dealing with him.

This is the general impression of the common tone of opinion & impulse which I derive from the many narratives given me by persons who in my experience of them are honest, honorable, brave and sober.

In such a state of society men appear to expose very rapidly qualities of character which they had not before been suspected even by themselves to possess. "It was a terrible school;" said one, "in three months after I landed in California, I did not know myself, my character was so changed."

Traces of it, or I should rather say, broad tracks which surely will not be effaced in more than one lifetime yet remain. The community, if there can be said to be a community at all, is so strangely unintegrate. Each man yet has his friends and allies, vaguely bonded with him perhaps, and his enemies to whom he is but vaguely antagonistic perhaps but beyond a limit more or less contracted, hardly anyone realizes and acts habitually upon the presumption which is the backbone of civilized society, that others have common interests with him or that he has common interests with others.

Of course there are alliances within alliances. A Mexican is nearer than an Indian I think to most of us whites; so is a Chinaman, though oweing to the fear of their competition hatred of them is more active & more frequently expressed. And there are alliances which are not the result merely of spontaneous, unexpressed understandings. Nowhere else have I known such organizations as Free Masons, Odd Fellows, Sons of Temperance and Knights Templars to be so important, as they are here. Political clubs also, both secret and acknowledged in their organization & proceedings, exist in every settlement & few voters of any class are not enlisted in them. Among the young men of my acquaintance I find that there are members of six different secret societies, each of which occasionally has meetings in the village. Two of them have established each a separate enclosure for a graveyard. I have no doubt the ends they have in view are good, and the time of the members is comparatively well spent at their meetings but it can hardly be that such organizations do not stand in the way of what is most needed here, an all-embracing relationship based on the confidence, respect and interest of each citizen in all and all in each.

Whatever degree of pure good fellowship there may be in the motive which causes men to form these formally organized & administered alliances, the broader & simpler ones to which I have referred clearly rest largely on an essentially selfish base. At the bottom is the thought, "You stand by me & I will stand by you." The want of regard for life, & much more for any right or possession less sacred than that of life, which is often manifested under conditions where an understanding of this kind is most difficult to be assumed, is even yet very shocking.

The formal organization of Law is necessarily of little value as a protection against wrong among such people as we have here. About an eighth of all are Indians, Mexicans, negroes and Spaniards, or men whose blood is a mixture of some of these &

that of some of the races of Northern Europe. Not one in fifty of them has the faintest comprehension of a civilized system of law and government. The exercise of the right of property is to them simply the exercise of the power of the stronger man, and they cannot yet see that assassination offers a means of enforcing this power less desireable than the baton of the constable, or the sabre of the dragoon except as it is less safe to him who makes use of it.

There is no definite line of separation between those who are more & those who are less barbarous in this respect. People of various education are singularly mingled. The house next mine for instance is occupied by an Irishman, the next by a Mexican, the next by a New Yorker, the next again by a Mexican, the next by a Chinese, the next by an Italian, the next again by a Chinese; on the other side, an African, a German, a German Jew, an Italian, a Virginian, an Irishman, a German, a South Carolinian, an Italian, follow one another. At this moment I see a group in the street composed of an Irishman, an Italian, and a Digger Indian woman with a white baby which she carries not in the Indian or the Italian but the English manner. She is dressed in printed calico, & wears shoes and white stockings, while the Irishman wears a blanket, as a Serape's, in the Mexican fashion. While I was writing the last sentence, they all went together into a bar-room which is kept by an Irishman; the mistress of this Irishman is a Mexican half-breed.

Precisely the same understandings of property rights or the same control of personal inclinations, passions & idiosyncracies in subordination to common interests as prevails in Kent or Lancashire, cannot be assumed by anyone to rule under these circumstances. With at least half the community the Law as law is never distinctly recognized. Our officer of the law is not known to them as an officer of the law. When the life of one of these persons is threatened, he does not think of the Law, that is of the community, as his protector, or if his property is stolen or taken from him by force, he does not know to whom or where to go for official assistance to recover it. He must depend on himself and the voluntary assistance of others, just as he must if he proposes to recover a horse that had broken his trail rope and strayed, or as he must if a bear had hugged him and broken his ribs, so he cannot provide himself with food in his customary way. Ultimately through friendly action the law may help him, the Sheriff may hear of the case, correspond about it with the Sheriff of the next county South—reaching a hundred miles from here, and possibly thus put agencies in operation by which the property will be recovered. But the injured man, even in that case, will very vaguely if at all comprehend that the Sheriff has been acting in any other than his individual capacity. He will respect him for his action, not as the representative of the community but as one man of great cunning and power in accomplishing what he undertakes, and with whom it will be well to be on friendly terms.

The practical result is I suppose as great a degree of safety both for the life & property of the civilized & well disposed part of the community as has yet been attained in many parts of Italy and Spain, or in Tipperary or even many streets of London.

In a conversation a few days since with our most worthy local magistrate, he remarked that of course very little could be learned from the records of our Courts of the amount of crime. He thought, for instance, that since he had lived here, (ten years?) at least four thousand horses had been stolen in the county and run off. Less than five hundred certainly had ever been recovered and even in these latter cases very rarely indeed had the thieves been brought to court. Indeed it was rarely that any attempt was made to apprehend them, though they were often shot, had been shot by their pursuers. Formerly the horse thieves were nearly all Mexicans, but lately a good many Southerners had been in the business.

The robbery of Chinese is of daily occurrence—literally so. "I do not think," said the Judge, "that in the last year and a half any twenty four hours has passed without a robbery of the Chinese in this County." It is so common that the Chinese scarcely ever complain of it—taking it as one of the misfortunes of business which all must expect to encounter occasionally. "Except in two or three cases where the Chinese have been so fortunate as to shoot them, I do not think any of the robbers in these cases have been punished. Sometimes the sufferers complain, but when they do nothing comes of it. Not long since a Chinaman here in front of my house raised a great cry, 'That man robby me! that man robby me!' closely following a wellknown robber, who being much hated by the people here was presently arrested and taken before a Justice. The Chinaman did not go into the Justice's office, but running about outside again & again told his story. The Justice must have heard him but did not ask him to come in. However, as the Chinaman's bag of gold dust was found on the robber and there was some other circumstantial evidence against him, and the Grand Jury was in session, the Justice sent him to Jail and a day or two afterwards he was brought before the Grand Jury who discharged him, for want of evidence, the Chinaman not being called before them."

"I heard," continued the Judge, "a dozen of our young men talking of this occurrence, and from what was said, I made up my mind that if the man had confessed the robbery, or if it had been proven against him beyond all question, a majority would have voted to discharge him." The views they expressed were that the Chinamen were a nuisance anyway, their competition with white men tended to reduce wages, and whoever helped to discourage them from coming here was a public benefactor, no matter what his character might be in other respects.

Very rarely indeed was any resistance made to these robbers of the Chinese, unless white men were present who were likely to suffer. Last week, a man lost a revolver here in the village. He learned that a Chinaman had found it, who had gone to some diggings on the Chowchilla Creek. A Chinese offered to guide him to the place and he accordingly went there, taking a friend with him. Arriving at the Chinese camp after dusk, they concluded to spend the night. During the night the camp was attacked by three white men. The visitors being angry at having their rest disturbed, got up and fired at the robbers, killing one, breaking the arm of another. The third escaped. It was ascertained that they belonged to a company of eight who were proceeding regularly through the district. The following week one of our County newspapers gave a playful account of their operations, (which, by the way, were not at all interrupted by this "accident,") as follows:

> Barring accidents, such as happened to them last week, they are likely to succeed in their undertakings, as they have shown great caution in their movements so far. To guard against any alarm being raised in their rear, as soon as they robbed one China camp they would march all the Celestials ahead of them to the next,

where they would increase their booty and number of hostages. They kept this up until their Celestial army began to languish for forage (the line of march being through an inhospitable region), when it was disbanded.

The other county paper contains nothing on the subject, and it is but very rarely that the incidents of this constant war are noticed at all, in the newspapers, almost never unless they are thought amusing.

In illustration of the more common proceeding, the Judge said,

A few days ago, on a creek which flows within half a mile of the Court House, two Chinamen were scratching away upon a poor claim they had recently acquired when a couple of white men riding by stopped and one getting off his horse clapped his hand on a Chinaman's shoulder, saying, "Well Johnny, how you get on?"

The Chinaman thinking it a friendly salutation, replied, smiling "Welly well."

"And how much gold you getty, eh?"

"Welly little—no good."

"How much?"

"Only dollar arf."

"Oh that won't go down, Johnny. We shall have to see what we can find."

Accordingly the two white men proceeded to search the two Chinamen, and to pull their cabin to pieces, but as they could find only about the value of a dollar and a half in dust, one asked:

"That a good knife?"

"Yes."

"Well, let's have it, and here's your dollar and a half, you want it more 'n we do, I reckon. We'll wait till we find one of you who'se been more lucky."

Three Chinamen were found hanged upon trees a few miles from here last week, and not a week passes that some Chinaman, Mexican or Indian is not killed.

The (late) District Attorney of the County confirmed the Judge's statements, but added that very rarely indeed did any white man who had not the reputation of being himself a robber and ruffian suffer, except from petty pilfering and horse-stealing.

"I have lived here eight years and have travelled about constantly, but no one ever attempted to rob me but once."

"Do you generally go armed?"

"Always. I never go from my office to my house—(a distance of a thousand yards in the middle of the shire town) at night, without carrying my pistol in my hand. Do you not go armed?"

"Never," said I, "unless when I am carrying bullion."

"By the way," said he, "here's a letter which Judge _____ asked me to give you, I had forgotten it till now." The letter informed me that the writer, a Judge of the adjoining County, had reason to believe that there was a plan to rob our "treasure" while it was being carried from the mills to my office, and he thought best to put me on my guard. (Three times besides this within a year and a half I had warnings of this kind, from Sheriffs or other officers of the law, but the attempt was never made.)

The County Sheriff informed me that since he had held his office, two men had been legally executed for murder.

"What proportion do these executions bear to the homicides in the County in that period?" I asked.

"Not one to thirty."

"Including Chinamen and Indians, do you mean?"

"No.—Oh! altogether? Not one in fifty, no, not one in fifty, certainly."

He made similar statements to those above reported of the Judge with regard to the Chinese and said that these crimes were increasing. As men learn that they can rob the Chinese with impunity, they resort to this method of filling their pockets more readily.

Yesterday Judge _____ asked me: "Did I not see J.B. in your office?"

"Yes."

"Are you doing much business with him, now?"

"He has some considerable contracts for transportation."

"I think I may as well tell you something that came to my knowledge about him this week. A few nights since, a negro man who lives on _____ (forty miles away in another county) came to my house and wanted to see me in private. He had something to say which he seemed to be afraid to disclose but after some encouragement it came out. He said that a few nights ago, while he was asleep in his cabin, the door was suddenly burst open and three men instantly sprang upon him, jerked him out of his bed, threw him on the ground and put a revolver to his head. They then lighted a candle and produced a paper and pen and ink. The paper was a bill of sale to J.B. of all his cattle, these being about all his earthly property, and they demanded that he should sign it, which in fear of his life, he did. The signature was witnessed, and then a bible was brought out; he was required to get on his knees and take an oath that he would never state what had occurred or deny that he had freely and for a satisfactory money consideration sold his cattle to J.B. He was then ordered to go to bed again, and one of the men stood guard over him till near daylight while the others drove away the cattle."

This man, J.B. ordinarily appears a rather amiable, frank, moderate and considerate but unpretending and not very intelligent man. Among his friends he bears the character of "a good fellow." There is nothing of the ruffian or the bravo about him, as I have seen him, and he has been in my office hundreds of times. I feel confident that under favorable circumstances, he would have grown up a very quiet and inoffensive member of civilized society. Yet if in civilized society, well organized, he indulged in his present habits of discussion, he would be seldom a week out of jail. Twice since I have known him, that is within two years, he has been shot once—at a ball, and once at a political meeting of his own party when a discussion became warm. He carries I believe two or three bullets in his body previously received, and I never saw him without a revolver at his waist. He was born in one of the Eastern Slave States but has been on the frontier for ten years or more. Although a violent secessionist, having often cheered for Jeff Davis, he was once bought by a candidate during the period of the war, for four hundred dollars in gold paid down, and a larger sum paid pro rata for all Union votes above a certain number cast at the precinct nearest his residence. It would be hardly just, perhaps, to say that he is a fair specimen of the Southerners here, but, if I had not been informed of his night-business, I should certainly have thought that he was at least not an unfavorable specimen of them. There are men living near here who are known to have been guilty of far greater crimes, and there are very few Southerners among the settlers hereabouts, whose sudden anger I should feel it

any safer to provoke by the expression for instance of my opinions about the rights of negroes, or the question of the true
economy of states in dealing with people of inferior civilization
when they had no pecuniary interest in my life.

Is there not a quite sufficient reason for this? Think what the
effect must have been upon European emigrants to be brought
into the relation of master of the enslaved and debilitated African savages of the South. Here there is another frontier, not a
tangible geographical frontier, but a frontier between civilization and barbarism quite as truly as that gradually moving line,
on which white men and red men have been contending so
long. A process of education has been going on upon that line
and here I see its immediate results. That "the black man has no
rights which the white man is bound to respect" is a conviction
fastened in the minds of my Southern neighbors so deeply that I
should no more expect to remove it by argument in most cases
than to restore the virtue of an abandoned woman by sermons,
or to induce the Indians yonder to adopt habits or regular labor
by the offer of high wages. Nor are they any more able to
practically believe that a coloured woman can be chaste or that
her chastity is a matter of consequence and should be guarded
by the community. They have been thoroughly educated in
a different conviction. That a considerable proportion of the
recent European emigrants who are here their fellow citizens
and tavern associates are very ready to adopt similar views of
the rights of colored people, I need not say. Nor can it be difficult for anyone to see what follows where Mexican, Indian,
Chinese and negro are all found together. The foundation of
civilized society is not a community of mutual requirement and
service, in the protection of the fruits of labor, of the condition
of chastity and other matters, which is bounded by *arbitrary*
lines, or by lines which may be stretched or contracted by individuals according to their personal opinions & prejudices.
These corruptions with regard to the Indian, the negro & the
Chinese cannot exist without making other corruptions. The
whole framework of Society is necessarily lax in these sparsely
settled communities, and the man who has learned to think
that negroes, Indians, Mexicans, Chinese, half-breeds, may
properly enough be treated as a sort of outlaws, or on different
principles of right and duty from other men, does not require

the inducement of a very strong demand from his passions, his prejudices, his lusts, his covetousness or his pride to be exerted to make him forget law, and civilized customs in dealing with any other men. Yet an alliance such as the more degraded whites are obliged to connect themselves with, extending & ever so feebly connecting them in interest with the great republic of the nation, is educative, so far as they realize it & are true to it.

I take from the newspapers of the day of this writing three short paragraphs, which will serve to illustrate not only the characteristic forms and methods of pioneer advance but the characteristic line of thought in regard to the murder of certain classes of men and women which prevails among the less ignorant and uncultivated members of pioneer bodies of the European race at the present day. Taken in succession the three reports will also furnish an indication of the usual stages of progress by which Indians disappear from and European communities occupy the wilderness. The first, from the Marysville Express is part of a correspondent's letter from a region which may be considered to be just fairly reached by the skirmishing parties of the advancing whites, which is described as follows:

> a barren sage plain, with no vegetation, and save a few lizards, horned toads, snakes, jackals, rabbits, grasshoppers and sage hens, not a living thing can be found. There are but few small alkali flats on the Snake, and where it has been tried, nothing will grow on these plains.

It might be supposed that the Indians who had fallen back upon such a region as this would be left to the peaceable misery which it offered them; the whites, however, are bound to go through it, and as usual an interchange of bullets and arrows has occurred. Reporting some of the incidents the correspondent goes on to speak of the Indians as follows:

> by long experience, I find they are civil and good only when dead. Then the tomahawk and scalping knife are at rest, and peace rests in the forest shades. Then wolves howl their requiems over the sad relics of their departed lords. Then life is safe, and there are no shuddering thoughts of the many innocent emigrants, endeavoring to blaze the trail and *break the sod of civilization* in the far West, who were inhumanly butchered by these ruthless savages. Yet the cry is, "Lo! the poor Indian."

A specimen of the second stage is found in the Owen's River Valley, a district of fixed agricultural settlements, where some cattle have recently been stolen from the settlers not, as is supposed, by the Indians of the vicinity, but by some marauders from a distance. It was enough to suspect that the thieves were Indians however and the correspondent of the "Sacramento Union" narrates what action the whites thought proper to take in the premises, as follows:

> the whites are killing off the Indians on all sides. At Big Lake thirty-five "went under," and two more eight miles below Bishop creek. One succeeded either in escaping or in drowning himself, it is uncertain which, at Bend City, in rather a remarkable manner. He had been confined in a house, his hands tied behind him, and was closely guarded. Under some pretense he was allowed to leave the house for the bank of the river, and though he was accompanied by two armed whites, as soon as he approached near enough to the stream, he dove, head foremost, into it, and that was the last seen of Lo! the poor Indian. This killing of the Indians may look barbarous to many, but so long as the Government neglects to protect the settlers, they must protect themselves.

There follows in the same paper from a correspondent at Fort Boise in an account of a third stage, in which the habits of the men, trained by such necessary warfare with the Indians, are more fully exhibited.

> Ferd. Patterson and his crew govern Idaho. On the principal thoroughfares eastward gangs of men collect to rob, steal and murder with impunity, there being no civil law to interfere with them. I think I am safe in saying that not a day passes in this part of the Territory without one or more men meeting a violent death. No one ever hears of a conviction for crime or punishment for an offense. It is a "weeping, wailing and gnashing of teeth." If Milton had lived now-a-days he would have banished Satan into Idaho in preference to the infernal regions. *Extract from a Letter to a Portland Merchant. Sacramento Union.*

The following is an official report of the Governor of Idaho, made in 1866.

> The following letter from Hon. Caleb Lyon, Governor of Idaho, dated Bois City, Indian Territory, March 13, 1866, has been received at the Indian Office:

Hon. D. N. Cooley, Commissioner of Indian Affairs:
Sir:

I regret to inform you of the massacre of some sixteen friendly Indians, on the 11th of this month, fifteen miles above this city, near the mouth of Moore's Creek, on the Boise River, by a party of citizens of Ada County, encouraged and incited to do this cowardly deed by the editor of the Idaho *Statesman* Jas. S. Reynolds, than whom a greater scoundrel never lived.

I make the following extract from his paper just after it: "Sixteen Los have bit the dust. We long to see this vile race exterminated. Every man who kills an Indian is a public benefactor. Who will not emulate this good example, and rid us of these nuisances? These are the wretches the Government pamper, and Gen. Lyon's sickly sentiment in favor of preserving them is all bosh. We say kill them off—the faster the better, without distinction—nits make lice."

There were but two grown males; the rest were women and children. The immediate settlers (miners) reported against the murder, and their statement I shall send you in a few days, showing that the Indians were defenceless and peaceable. If anything will serve to bring on a general Indian war, it is such acts as these. I have gathered the rest of the tribe and placed them under the protection of the military of this post. The excitement runs high, and I have all I can do to carry out my instructions against the depraved moral sentiment evinced toward the poor savages.

Things look stormy just now, but when the road to the Indian country becomes passable, I shall quiet the troubled waters. In no case that I have examined have I found the "Red Man" the aggressor, but invariably the trouble springs from some fiendish outrage of bad white men.

I have already stated that my reports of personal experience & observation, refer to what I am constantly assured is a state of society exhibiting a great improvement in civilization over that which existed here immediately after the Indians had been finally & effectually dispossessed. It is a state greatly better than that which is found in the more advanced pioneer settlements of the present moment, as the above writer indicates and as I have been often told by those who have been recently dwelling "over the mountains." It is greatly better than that which appears to exist in a region a day's ride to the South of us, wherein occurred the incidents referred to in the following newspaper matter.

[4th of July murders outlaws]

One of the reputed associates & friends of this outlaw spoken of has been lately residing among us, following the profession of a gambler. He once came into my office displaying two revolvers and a dirk-knife—and is an active man in our elections.

I have been more struck with the education in injustice, disloyalty (non fealty to law) and all the vices of barbarism which is constantly going on upon the frontier in the case of my friend ____, an amiable, law abiding, industrious New Englander, than anyone else. The remains of a man having been found some ten miles from his house, who it was suspected had been murdered, he proposed to me that an Indian known to be near at hand but against whom there was not the slightest evidence that would be listened to for a moment by a civilized Court, should be shot, quite as a matter of course. When I reasoned with him against such an atrocity, he answered, "Well I see I was wrong—but it's the way of the country and it never occurred to me before that it was not right."

Six months afterwards, an indian woman whom my wife had employed in washing while we were living in camp, told her that she was going to a mourning and could not be back for some weeks. My wife asked who of her kindred had died and found it was the indian who had been suspected of this supposed murder. The circumstances of his death were these. He had obtained some liquor at a camp where several indian women are kept by white men, and when drunk had made some disturbance. Having been turned out of a house, he staggered off some distance and being unarmed and quite drunk, began throwing stones toward the house. One of the stones broke a window, whereupon a white man walked out of the house, and shot him. The indian being well known, his death, which occurred some fifteen miles from the court house, was generally spoken of, but no coroner's inquest was held and I never heard the assassination alluded to in any terms other than such as would have been appropriate to the shooting of a bear.

Mr H. P. Arnold in his Recollections of Thomas Noon Talfourd, contributed to the Boston Post, says of him:

He was very eloquent, and could carry a jury with him to almost any point he chose. I heard him on one occasion make a superb argument in a case where his client was suing a man who had injured his horse by hard driving and cruel treatment. He obtained ample damages, but I don't think he spoke ten minutes about the horse. By some strange deviation he soon wandered from the subject, and, for over an hour, devoted himself to the horrors of African slavery. It was the most stirring, energetic and masterly speech on that matter which I ever heard.

If there is such a thing as eloquence for modern minds, it should not require much of it to make any intelligent man realize that want of respect for a brute, want of respect for a nigger and want of respect for the clearest individual rights of those nearest and dearest to him, all rest on one common criminal defect of judgment and will, and that he cannot protect the virtue of his wife, prevent his children from being brutally overridden, or enforce the smallest benefit from his own industry with any degree of manly energy unless he makes "common cause" with *all* who are inconsiderately abused.

The want of comprehensive, far extending prudence in the minds of the pioneers in this respect is just as obvious in their disposition to regard a criminal trial as a game between the accused person & a powerful association, foreign to themselves, called the Law, in which the accused is the weaker party, and stands most in need of aid and encouragement from mere spectators, as in their general disregard of fair play and readiness to sacrifice not merely the liberty, the happiness and means of living, but the lives, of others, in their frequent quarrels and tumults.

There were but few men among the pioneers who were not aware that in a community ruled according to law, they would have been made to feel themselves degraded and disgraced by the courses of life into which they had cast themselves and in which they were disposed to continue. So long as it was a fair race in carelessness and recklessness, a mere dash in the dark; so long as a man felt that he could hold his own, in a contest of short-wittedness, so long he would be perfectly willing to do without any law at all, but as this could not be the case for a single month with all, the wiser minds were at any early stage prepared to welcome the forms of a legal organization because they would perceive that they could have its strength on their side. No one would demand any more law, however, or any more strength in the hands of the representatives of the law than he judged would be perfectly convenient to himself. The friends of law would want strength enough in the law to help them protect themselves from the more reckless and dashing, but any more than this they would feel to be oppressive. Accordingly a considerable part of the community regarded the law as so much added to the strength of those who were not likely to be on their side in any contest and the remainder sustained the law just so far as, with the very feeble degree of power in looking far ahead or through a complicated process which they were accustomed to exercise in judging of their own interests, they felt inclined to do so.

To illustrate how far this was likely to be, I can imagine a man presenting himself to my friend M. and saying, "Stranger, I got into a scrimmage in the saloon over yonder and shot a man and the Sheriff's after me. Can you lend me a hole to hide in?" M. has himself been in a scrimmage twenty times and has drawn his revolver and if he has not shot men has come so near to it that so far from shrinking from his visitor on that account, he is, always supposing him to be a white man & to speak English, rather drawn to him by sympathy. For the moment he thinks of the Sheriff only as another white man; the Sheriff for all that he knows might just as well be "after" him. He would, as in fact I suppose he did, more than once, without hesitation give the murderer all the advantage for outwitting the Sheriff that he conveniently could. If this was the case with the American pioneers, far more so was it with the very large number of the more sober class of foreign born, who had been brought up to regard officers of the law as their masters or as the instruments of their masters, not in the least as their own agents.

(The disposition of juries to move in the same way.)

The progress of improvement is said to have been astonishingly rapid, but it has not advanced so far that the influence of the same habits of thought is not yet perceptible, although on ordinary occasions, a good deal complicated and obscured by more mature and wiser counsels.

At a late election chiefly for County officers the canvass has been very hot. There were some extremely bad men nominated by the Democratic party, a majority of the members of which

are Secessionists. As this party was successful at the previous
Presidential election, I was apprehensive these men would be
elected, especially as the candidate for the more lucrative office,
was a bold gambler, and was known to have disposed of considerable property, that he might be well supplied with cash. He
made a very strong fight, getting in at my own poll the votes
of a lunatic, a born idiot, and of a number of half-breeds who
could not speak English & who had never been seen in the vicinity before. Some of these as they approached carried a vote
in one hand and money in the other. They were all challenged,
and all "swore in" their votes; committing perjury, as I have
very little doubt. At the polls where he was personally present,
this candidate ran far ahead of his ticket and of the vote of his
party at the preceding election. Nevertheless, he and the worst
candidates on the ticket with him were defeated in the County.
I understand that he has stated that he would have been successful if some upon whom he depended at the polls which he
could not personally overlook, had not played him false.

I had subscribed to the election fund against him, and was by
special circumstances very intimate with & in the confidence of
some of the leading men of both parties, and I have taken some
pains to learn the secret history of the election. I believe that
the defeated candidate had paid out with reference to the election about eight thousand dollars. A part of this however, was
merely the payment of debts of long standing, and which probably never would have been paid under other circumstances.
He probably paid five thousand in direct bribes to secure the
services of certain persons, chiefly keepers of taverns or groggeries, who were also owners or part owners of mines, mills or
shops, or who in some other way employed or influenced the
employment of a number of laborers. To one such man whom
I know very well he paid one thousand dollars; to another, a
drover and butcher, five hundred dollars. I asked one of the
managers of the successful ticket how it had been possible to
defeat him. He replied in substance as follows:

> His party is composed largely of Arkansas men (frontier men)
> and foreigners. Most of the foreigners can always be bought, all
> the Arkansas men can. The only difficulty about it is that when
> we buy them, we can't depend on them. They take money from
> both sides & promise & swear to each alike. The only way to

hold them is to pay them something down at the last moment &
promise them something more & show them the money to be
paid contingent upon the vote at the precincts where you expect
them to operate. We kept a close watch on X and got pretty accurate information of how much money he could command, and
we took care at the close to be prepared to "go better." He had
bought _____ for $1000. On the night before election I saw
_____ and gave him $500 and told him I would give him $600
more after the election if we were ahead in his precinct. I assumed
of course in talking with him that he was on our side, always had
been, that he was deeply interested, and that he would need all
of this, for election expenses; treating, printing and all that. I
suppose he did use some of it so. He kept a free bar on election
day, and I guess he promised to forgive a number of men small
debts on condition that they should show him their tickets at the
polls. Of course it was known how he was going to vote by all his
crew, early in the morning.

  We carried the precinct by twenty majority (last year it was carried against us by the same vote). So it was elsewhere. We were
generally able to make the last bid, and on election morning we
had the longest purse to show. We raked and scraped every dollar
that could be found to do it.

(This was so much the case that there was a notable scarcity
of coin in the usual channels for a short time after the election.)
I took considerable pains to ascertain who the men were who
had received the benefit of this expenditure, and could hear of
but one native American of the free states who was included
among them. Several foreigners and Southerners who had been
previously regarded as Secessionists and who voted for McClellan at the previous election, were bribed successfully by the
Unionists, to my knowledge. I think that the whole amount of
money expended by both parties, with reference to the election, was equal to the amount of one dollar for each vote cast.
Nine tenths of this money was contributed by the candidates
and about one half of it was expended with the knowledge and
intention of the candidates that it should be the direct pecuniary consideration of votes.

I am told that this election has been an exhibition of purity
and respectability compared with those which were common
here at the earlier elections. And I have heard narratives from
men who had a hand in that of which they tell which almost

justify the assertion. The hero of one of the worst of these stories and bearing a most disgraceful and disgusting part in it, is now a Senator of the United States. We have a great deal of statesmanship in Washington which has been acquired in the same school and there are men who are proud of the circumstance.

The only ecclesiastical organization which seems to be administered with any thorough system, constancy and steadiness is that of the Roman Catholic Church. The official representative of the hierarchy of Rome is a French priest of the ____ order. He is well-bred, and learned; probably more so than any other man who has any direct personal relations with the people here. He is withal a modest, zealous, heroic man. I have known him to ride forty miles by mountain trails on a stormy night, swimming torrents by the way and encountering other great perils to visit a Mexican woman whose friends had sent for him, believing her to be near death. Nearly all his time seems to be taken up with duties to individuals, visiting the sick and wounded, baptizing children and attending funerals. His parish extends some hundred miles to the North and South of us and is limited to the Eastward only by the presence of hostile savages. I have met him but once, when he called on me in a matter of business and was induced to spend an hour or two with my family, who found him one of the most urbane, entertaining and instructive visitors that had ever come under our roof. But after all, I think it would be hard to find a man who appeared to be more unsympathetic and outside of the whole ordinary life of the people, even those of his own creed, a man more incapable of entering into their minds and of influencing them, except as an authority and a dealer who—as it might be—had certain articles of clothing which they might need to sometimes wear & which they could get only of him and which he would supply as a duty delegated to him, which his honor required him to fulfil to the uttermost and at whatever peril or actual suffering to himself. Twelve miles from us on one side and forty on the other there are small wooden churches, at one of which mass is ordinarily celebrated every Sunday.

Except by the clergymen of the Roman Catholic Church and such others as are bound to abide by ritualistic forms and as are responsible to authorities resident in better organized communities, public religious worship is very rarely conducted in a manner which is solemn, dignified or in any way attractive to the mass of settlers. I should use stronger language to express personal experience of it. Of my five thousand nearest neighbors I doubt if ten per cent have taken part in a religious exercise in the last ten years. This is chiefly oweing to the repulsions and jealousies which exist between the sects and schools within sects by reason of which any simple whole souled purpose of preaching Christianity and especially any general efficient cooperation for that purpose is impossible. The people here have been educated under several scores of so called churches.

Chief difficulty that the main object of religious services is ordinarily to glorify a particular organization of Christians, to progagate the tenets which it has adopted and denounce as unscriptural, unchristian and of infidel tendency those of which are held by other organizations, of some of which other the parents and dearest friends of nine tenths of the constituents of every community are likely to have been representatives. As under this barbaric, disintegrating management of the pastoral duty the pastor can have the hearty good will of but a few among any body of settlers, the members of his flock are generally widely scattered, incapable of effective cooperation, and the organization miserably weak, unreliable, disunited, stingy and poor. He is consequently driven to employ dramatic & sensational expedients to secure a sufficient basis for his own support. These expedients in the end do not favor a general improvement of the moral condition of the people but in the minds of many they do favor a habit of disdain for and a feeling of superiority to what is deemed the humbug and pretentious assumptions of those who set themselves up as the only authorized representatives of true Christianity. I must confess that those things which here stand as representative of the Church of Christ do not seem to be as well calculated to educate the people in habits of neighborly, catholic, large & generous sympathy which is the essence of Christianity, as in narrowing tribal self conceits and repulsions. Except of the Roman Catholic, I should judge that the number of sincere, interested disciples of the strongest of them does not exceed four per cent and of each on an average less than one per cent of the whole population.

There are nevertheless two or three buildings in the county which have been erected by the efforts of members of as many different churches or sects of Protestants, besides the places of worship of the Chinese, which are more numerous than those of the Christians. The former have all been built under the pressure of some special effort and excitement, which has long since passed off. They now without exception have a neglected, forsaken, delapidated and shabby appearance which is truly typical of the condition of their respective proprietorships. The only one of them in which services are held with constant regularity is avowedly attended by a considerable part of the small congregation which goes through the forms of worship therein not from religious motives, but because it has become the representative of a political faction and many of its supporters lead notoriously villainous lives.

There are several residents in the county who are called ministers, but I believe only one of them is under an engagement with any organization to act as its pastor with an obligation on the part of the organization to provide his means of living. The one who is so seems not to have been educated for the profession, to judge from his misuse of language. For instance, I have twice known him to speak of himself publicly as the Prelate of his congregation, apparently imagining that word to have the same meaning with preacher. On one of these occasions, however, mendicant would have been the more appropriate word. There are few things hereabouts that have seemed to me more abominable than the organization for servility, cowardice and general degradation of the representative of the civilized system of religious worship of which this man is the victim. An unskilled laborer here, a man who cannot read and who cannot count twenty, may get the wages of seven hundred dollars a year. This is for eight or ten hours' labor per diem, after doing which he may earn something more if he is disposed to do more work. This minister's regular wages under his contract with his church do not exceed half that amount. Whatever else he receives for his own support and that of his family he receives literally as a starving beggar receives it and with expressions of dependence and gratitude which would be proper to a starving beggar. He has a wife and several children. I doubt if there is as large a white family within a thousand miles of us whose provision if purchased at the ordinary tradesman's prices would not cost much more than the amount of this minister's salary. His daughters growing into womanhood are not dressed as well as most paupers in England. I am informed by one of his neighbors that they are sometimes kept indoors from regard to decency and that there have been at least two occasions within the last two years when the family lived for several days on meal and water, and when there was not a cent of money or more than a pan full of meal left in the house. Finding at these times that their servant was likely to die on their hands if nothing was done, some of his employers, women mainly if not altogether, have then set to work to organize begging expeditions and with contributions thus obtained they have replenished his stock and clothed his children. Most of the money has been obtained by school girls or young women who in a thoroughly civilized state of society would have been school girls, who have gone about in small companies calling at every white man's house, shop, office or digging within the beat which they took upon themselves to canvass and soliciting or demanding contributions of all without being particular as to their special personal religious opinions and obligations, their condition or their character. Of me they *demanded* a contribution most impudently and immodestly. They visited a gambling saloon and bar-room and interrupted the men before the bar and those who were playing at the time and got from each of them the price of a drink or a cigar. My informant who was present said that notwithstanding their own impoliteness they were treated with respect and deference and that each man made a contribution quickly with the desire to hasten them from a place in which not so much the impertinence as the impropriety of their visit was found to be painful to its ordinary visitors. Heathen Chinamen have been called upon and have contributed to these Christian foraging parties. But the sum total of all the poor beggar's income is not probably more than that which the public provides for its poorest mixer of fancy drinks, mule-driver or coal burner. It pays its Sheriff at least ten times as much, and the difference in valuation of the services of each thus represented is not as great by any means, I think, as the difference in the power to influence the character

of the community which is respectively exercised by the minister
of religion & the minister of law.

As I have said, there are several other men who preach occasionally but none with nearly the same appearance of influence
or standing in the community as this settled pastor. There are
some Mormons here, all Englishmen I believe, and a considerable number of families who belong to a religious organization which originated in the Slave States, and who are all of
the class of poor whites, exceedingly ignorant and exceedingly
hateing and despising all who have book-learning, it being one
of their tenets that religion is the peculiar property of the poor
and ignorant and that all others are the Devil's own. It was at
a protracted meeting of this sect, at which Elder Brown and
Elder Bounce alternately led the services that the following
dialogue occurred:

Elder Brown in the midst of a discourse setting forth the
claims of his organization as the true church. "We's the uns that
enters in dar—ain't we Brother Bounce?"

Brother Bounce from his seat in the midst of the congregation. "You bet we is, Brother Brown."

A camp-meeting is held every year in the county, in connection with which there are horse-races, gambling booths and
other facilities for amusement. The camp meeting indeed seems
to be the principal holiday of a considerable class of the population and that by no means a religious class. I have not attended
any of these meetings but have met troops of drunken fellows,
all well armed, riding home from them. They do not differ in
character or in incident materially from those which have been
often described by travellers in the Slave States.

Some readers will infer from what I have said that there are
no representatives of the Christian ministry here who stand in
any relationship to the people which is compatible with self
respect or extended personal influence favorable to nobility of
character or even to common morality. Many exceptions must
be allowed for, if all frontier populations, or all sparsely settled
wilderness populations, are to be judged by this one in this respect, but that the rule may with this caution be safely inferred
from these statements all I have seen of the back settlements of
the South and West, leads me to believe.

At points which I have visited, nearer the Pacific where the progress of the settlement of which was earlier and the progress of which has been less fluctuating, I have found a very great improvement in the habits of the people, greater efficiency of the law and all healthy social institutions in a much more flourishing condition on an average than they are here. And in settlements of a corresponding class formed fifty years ago in States East of the Mississippi a still higher advance in most of the more important characteristics of a civilized community is obvious.

SECTION 2

DEFINING CIVILIZATION

A few days after my arrival in California I fell in with a man who had been one of the first to emigrate after the discoveries of gold were made known. Having failed in business fifteen years before, he had left a wife and children in the East and come hither to make a fortune. Of his own accord he narrated much of his subsequent life. After listening for some time, I asked:

"How many times have you taken up a new business and failed in it since you came to California?"

"I have been dead broke six times."

"And how many times have you changed your business?"

"I'm sure I can't tell; I always change when I see a better chance."

A few weeks afterwards he made another change and leaving the part of the country where I was, I lost sight of him. Yet experience afterwards led me to regard this man as one much more likely to be successful in the long run, than most of those with whom I became acquainted, who had yielded to the California fever of 1849.

Some time afterwards a company of twenty four working men proposed to me to give them a lease of certain property in consideration of some desireable improvements which they proposed to make upon it. In drawing up a form of agreement for the purpose I assumed that each one of these men would do his part of the work, during the whole period required for the service, which was estimated at three months. But this was objected to on the ground that though they all now intended to continue at the work for that period, some would be sure to get tired of it and wish to quit and it would be necessary to provide for supplying their places.

"Do you not think," then said I, "that you could all depend on each other to go through with it?"

"No sir," replied their spokesman, who was the master workman, "I don't believe you could find twenty four men in California who could be depended on to stick together at any job for three months. There will always be some who will take a sudden start and when they do there's no reasoning with them. When they once get their heads set on it they are bound to go, no matter what they lose by it. I have known many men strike off and leave five or six hundred dollars that would have been coming to them soon if they had kept on where they were." To this there was a unanimous expression of assent from all present, of whom nine-tenths were European born and fully one half Englishmen.

What are called in California, Forty-niners, that is, early emigrants, frequently apply to me for employment, representing themselves to be of most industrious disposition but the victims of singular misfortune which has hitherto followed them wherever they have turned. They want to be tried in humble capacities, only asking that they may have before them a chance of working up to something better by hard labor and the exercise of the severest virtue. Generally, however, if successful in their application, they soon find some occasion for resigning the opportunity, often frankly avowing that they find it impossible to hold themselves steadily to any drudgery. Upon enquiry I find that this is a common experience and that the "forty niners" are good for nothing in any undertaking which requires long, plodding, steadfast application is generally understood. But it has occurred to me to question and the more I have thought of it, the more reason I have found to question whether the earliest emigrants are defective in this respect in a degree more marked when compared with the great body of emigrants who now occupy California than this body is itself defective in the same respect, compared with the population as a whole of New England, or of any part of Europe. The region about me has been "settled," as they say, more than fifteen years. For more than ten years its whole population has been covered by the forms of systematic civilized government, has had its actual courts of law, elections, taxes, sheriffs, post-offices with mails from San Francisco three times a week. It has its schools and churches, its dozen of lawyers' offices, its jail, its free hospital;

temperance societies, Odd-Fellows and Masonic lodges, two newspapers and a brass band. Much more than a million dollars in gold has been invested here in buildings, bridges, mill dams, fences and other substantial means of providing for civilized requirements. Nevertheless the people are very strikingly more shifting and consequently shiftless than those of any part of the Eastern states or of Europe. Since I have been here (two years) the District Attorney's office has been twice vacated by resignation and is now filled by the third incumbent. The two leading lawyers in the county have left it; four other lawyers have changed their residence. Three citizens previously engaged in other occupations have entered upon the practice of law. The principal capitalist, the largest merchant and three other leading merchants have left the county; at least a dozen other storekeepers have sold out and as many more come in. Ten men of my acquaintance who were running mills of various kinds (saw, grain and stamp), when I came here, have left them. In one case a mill has changed hands three times, in several others twice; I know of not one which has not changed hands. The Justice of the peace; the seven successive school-committeemen; three out of four of the physicians; the five butchers; the five innkeepers, eight out of twelve of the tradesmen and their assistants; the blacksmith; the two iron-founders; the two barbers; the daguerrotypist; the bathing-house keeper; the seven livery-stable-keepers; the three principal farmers; the three school-teachers and about seventy out of a hundred of the miners and laboring men who have lived nearest me or who have been most readily accessible and observable to me, have moved from one house, office or shop to another, or have left the county within two years. I count in this village forty-seven separate places of residence and of business which have been occupied by eighty-seven persons, not including housewives or children. Of these eighty-seven, eighty-five have changed their residences or place of business within two years. This has not been on account of a destructive fire or any extraordinary occurrence; population on the whole has not decreased, and so far as I can ascertain the changes have not been markedly greater than at previous periods of the early history of the district.*

---

* Within a year after this was written, great disasters occurred oweing to Wall Street swindling, and the shifting process went on at an accelerated pace.

In 1850 the population of San Francisco was thirty thousand (30,000). Twelve years afterwards it had advanced to 90,000. Distant from the mines, possessing the only good harbor in a coastline of fifteen hundred miles and being the centre of finance and wholesale commerce for nearly a third part of the United States and much of Mexico, this population was one of more steadfast character than any other on the Pacific coast, yet of five thousand five hundred of the more important merchants, tradesmen and manufacturers who were registered in the San Francisco Directory of 1861 only three thousand four hundred remained in 1862, and of the smaller dealers it is estimated by the compiler of the Directory that at least forty per cent had "declined business" during the same year. This was during a period of general prosperity and when the total number of business firms greatly increased.

An agricultural population is almost necessarily a more abiding one in its habits than any other, but the same characteristic unsteadiness is observable among the farmers of California, comparing them with farmers elsewhere. Of the agriculturists among my neighbors, seven out of twelve have moved within two years and those who have not are men who were originally bred for different callings & have late in life taken to farming. Going out of the county on the only road which I have had occasion to travel over enough to gain an acquaintance with the farmers on it, I have noticed that seven out of twelve properties have changed hands within two years, one of them twice.

The general fact thus illustrated is to be partly attributed to the experimental character of all industrial undertakings in new settlements and especially in California, owing to the variableness of its seasons and to the capricious distribution of its primary source of wealth in deposits of gold. But careful study has satisfied me that this is not the main cause of the more shifting character of its population compared with that of established civilized communities. The main cause is independent of all local and temporary conditions: it lies in the natal character of the population and in those qualities of character which govern the circumstances under which members of civilized communities most readily yield to the temptations to break loose from the opportunities and the duties in which they have become established.

I trust I have made it obvious to the reader that the organization of society here, however advanced from what it has
been at an earlier period, is yet very crude and that the reason
why it is so is that the people are generally unprepared to take
part in a higher organization. There is nothing which has been
more strongly impressed upon me than the absence of a desire
for a more coherent community on the part of the more intelligent, and the feeling, which is more than one of indifference,
of the greater number in regard to what should be the common
concerns of all. The explanation is a simple one, more personal
concern in common affairs would be equivalent to a loss of the
enjoyment of personal independence. Men do not constrain
others or influence others because to do so would be to invite
constraints upon their own caprice or judgment.

Most men who leave the old communities of the East for the
pioneer settlements do so with the hope of returning when they
shall have acquired a certain amount of wealth. This hope they
retain for many years more or less distinctly. It is nevertheless
notorious that most of those who succeed in returning are not
satisfied to remain long. They say that it appears to them that
the character of the old community has changed. It is not what
they had remembered it to be and there is something very oppressive to them in it. No doubt old communities do change;
old friends pass away or new interests and habits are taken on,
but in most of these cases the greatest change is that which has
occurred in the emigrant himself. In a frontier or immature
state of society, each individual becomes connected by ties of
interest or otherwise with a certain number of others who are
of distinct importance to him and to whom he is of distinct
importance. He knows what he has to do with everyone about
him and what everyone about him has to do with him. When
he comes into the midst of an older or more fully organized
community, he finds individuals *comparatively* unimportant and
a large part of every man's interest in others so indirect, at-
tenuated, ramified and subtle that it appears to him that there
is no genuine friendship, trust or truth, any more than there
is thorough-going hatred, enmity or manly courage in regard
to injuries. The fact is that friendship, the obligation of truth
and trust or dependence on others is exercised in a much more
extended and elaborate way, the heart and mind are both more

liberal than he is able to appreciate, and in truth it is he who has been growing contracted, concentrated and direct in the exercise of his natural qualifications for helping and being helped by his fellow-men otherwise.

Notwithstanding the constant changes which I have described, the immediate community about me is so small, and my business responsibility has been of such a character, that I have taken an interest more or less active in the condition, the habits and tendencies of nearly every individual sojourner near me. I have been anxious for the introduction of conditions favorable to progress toward a thriftier state of things, toward a community of larger and steadier commercial demands, larger and steadier productive power. On this account, it has naturally become a habit with me to weigh the value of individuals, with reference to the general end which I should like to feel that I am aiding my neighbors to approach, and I find that whenever my attention is called to a man I at once rank him according to an intuitive estimate of the part he is likely to bear, if any, in this respect. I find that for convenience of thinking I habitually classify my neighbors according to my estimate of their measurement by some scale which exists in my mind. I have never to this moment attempted to define clearly to myself what this scale is, but looking out the window as I write, I see two men and I know that both stand near the bottom notch and that the scale is too rude to show any difference between them. It interests me to find that this is the case because there are striking differences between them.

One stands idle but erect, and though of feeble form, with the pose of a noble statue; his face is streaked with vermilion; a quiver of undressed fox skin, full of arrows, hangs over one naked shoulder, a ragged blanket over the other and there is a bow in his hand. I saw him standing within six feet of where he now is an hour ago and with no difference of position except that his vacant eyes were directed toward the other end of the village. He is a dull, silent, stupid savage. He was born near here and when he was born his mother had never seen a white man.

The other reclines near the tavern-door. He has a cigar in his mouth, a Colt's revolver in one pocket, a Geneva watch in another and scores of machines and many hundreds of hands have been employed in preparing his apparel. When freshly and mildly stimulated, he has a very active mind and a ready utterance. It is not unlikely that tomorrow morning, after he has taken a warm bath, his cognac and soda water, coffee and one or two after breakfast drams, I shall again hear him discoursing, as I did this morning, with indignant eloquence on "the mockery of justice, the debasement of the ermine, the ignorance of law, the degrading demagogueism, the abominable infidelity by _____!" of a recent decision of a Court with regard to the rights of colored people in public conveyances, reported in a San Francisco newspaper. In twenty minutes he will have made use of words primarily prepared for him by Saxon, Roman, Greek, Sanscrit and I know not what other brains. Then again he will pass under my window humming a hymn of Handel, or I shall find him at the Post Office sitting in an arm chair, made for him in New Hampshire, and reading a novel first written in France, translated in England and printed for him in Boston. He will have been served before the day is over by your work and by mine and by that of thousands of other men, and yet will think of nothing so often or so intensely as the "cursed luck" by which he is served no better. And what will he do for us? Play a game of billiards with you or take a hand at cards if you want amusement, and if he wins money in this or any other way of speculating he will use it "generously." Within a year by pledging his word to drink no more he induced a poor hard worked widow to become his wife, having been previously the father of several children of different colors for whose maintenance or education he has never worked an hour or concerned himself a moment. He is a tall and large framed white man of English stock, born in a state of society which he speaks of as "the highest reach of civilization."

While I see no other men but these, I am reminded of two others by hearing the strokes of an axe and the dull rap of a hammer. The first comes from a Chinese servant preparing wood for the baker's oven over the way, the other from a crippled German shoemaker. These two men again I at once range together and very far above the Indian and the Fruit of civilization—not, perhaps more than half way to the higher notches—yet, not a majority of my neighbors stand higher than these two steady, plodding, short-sighted, frugal workers. But it is not industry, nor well-balanced demand and supply, nor sobriety and inoffensiveness only that I lay to the scale. There is some general quality which these lie back of and support perhaps, but which I look most for and find feeble in the stolid German and weazen Chinaman.

Trying one man and another and reflecting upon what it is in each that sets him high or low in my scale, I come to the conclusion that the highest point on my scale can only be met by the man who possesses a combination of qualities which fit him to serve others and to be served by others in the most intimate, complete and extended degree imaginable. Shall we call it communitiveness? Then I find not merely less of a community but less possibility of community, of communitiveness, here among my neighbors of all kinds than in any other equal body of men, I ever saw. And the white men, the Englishmen, the Germans, and other civilized men do not possess it often in as high degree as the Mexicans, Chinese and negroes—nor do the good men always possess as much of it as the rogues, the wild-fellows.

Of the thousand millions of human beings that are said to constitute the population of the entire globe, says Mr Mayhew in London Labor & London Poor, there are but two distinct and broadly marked races, namely, the wanderers and the settlers— the vagabond and the citizen, the nomadic and the civilized tribes.

I believe this in the main to be a true statement and that a similar division may be made of every so called civilized community. Every now and then we find in an Eastern society an Indian who lives peaceably and industriously, who has adopted the usual fashions and manners of the community very closely and who respects and obeys the laws as a good citizen. Yet those who know this man thoroughly are generally aware that the Indian propensities and habits remain and are really stronger than usual with him because of the prolonged suppression to which they have been subject. Occasionally in a furtive solitary way he gives rein to them. After a time, in many cases, he will suddenly, at what appears to be a great sacrifice, abandon whatever he has gained as a citizen, part from his friends, make his way to the frontier or to some other opportunity for escaping from the restraints of organized society and for the indulgence of his independent, vagabond, deep seated proclivities. White men brought up in mature communities are to be found with much the same proclivities. Under favorable circumstances they may be controlled and obtain little attention; under other circumstances they make men gamesters, filibusters and, whatever their ostensible profession or calling, speculators. If they are industrious it is in some irregular, unmethodic way, involving so much risk, guess work and shifts that on the whole it causes more embarrassment than it contributes assistance to the methods by which the community altogether advances in prosperity.

Such men are not solitary in their habits, they are by no means incapable of love, of generosity, of magnanimity; of staunch fidelity to friends or to the trusts which they assume. They enjoy the fruits of civilization, and are often extraordinarily covetous of them. But they seem to be incapable of catholic relationships or of faith in the existence of a unity of interests between themselves and any others to whom they are not bound by some special tie or assurance of sympathy. They are not disinclined to have a few chums; they can extend their chumming for special purposes so as to include a band. They are most thorough-going partisans. They are capable of strong family attachments and they can extend the chumming relation and the family relation and the partisan relation so as to include their tribe, clan or race, so far as the interests of tribe, clan or race may appear to be in conflict with those of others with whom they have no similar relationships. But aside from these ties which are all commonly very strong with the lowest savages, their instincts or intuitions toward other men seem to be those of beasts toward other beasts, as if their only interest in them could be as towards objects of prey or of preying.

I have been most struck by evidences of this characteristic in men who were most attractive from their boldness, tender heartedness and general natural nobleness.

This quality is the result of education and being transmitted like other educated intuitions from parent to child constantly gains ground in communities which are advancing in civilization. In communities falling back in civilization it diminishes.

It is very strongly impressed upon me that the representatives of all the older communities whom I find living together and constituting whatever there is that can be properly called a new community here were much behind the general state of advancement of those older communities when they came out from them, in respect to this quality, and that the most advanced are here falling back very rapidly.

A PLAN FOR GALLAUDET: JULY 1866

To Edward Miner Gallaudet

No. 110 Broadway, New York,
July 14, 1866

Dear Sir:

In accordance with your instructions we forward herewith a study for the general arrangement of your buildings and grounds.

As the school is of scarcely less importance than the college, we have thought it desirable to plan the entrance in such a way that each department of the institution may be easily approached from the principal gateway.

The chapel (which has a direct access for the public from the main entrance) and the dining halls of both school and college are located in the intermediate space between the college and the school buildings, with which they are proposed to be connected by an arcade. An artistic grouping may thus, it is hoped, be secured, and the chapel will seem to belong to neither department exclusively.

The principal college building is proposed to have a westerly frontage, chiefly because this arrangement allows of a comparatively large space being set apart as a lawn and ornamental ground, entirely distinct from the section devoted to the use of the school.

South of the chapel a terraced garden is proposed, of moderate dimensions, as indicated on the plan; this is suggested by the present formation of the ground, and its semi-architectural character is depended on to assist in bringing the different elements of the composition into one harmonious whole.

The arrangement proposed for the offices and subordinate buildings will be clearly seen on reference to the design.

It is very desirable that, in the general scheme to be adopted by your institution, provision should be made for the residences of the faculty and of the president.

It will, we think, be impossible to provide for these necessary features of a liberally conceived general design, within the exact dimension of your present lot; but if two hundred feet of ground to the west can be procured, a sufficient although by no means over-spacious arrangement can be made that will include sites for six residences.

It is evident that in the development of an institution for the deaf and dumb which is to be national in its character & sphere of operations, considerable expenditures must be involved in the erection of the appropriate structures; and as it would be very poor economy to spare expense for necessary ground while undertaking considerable outlays for necessary buildings, we

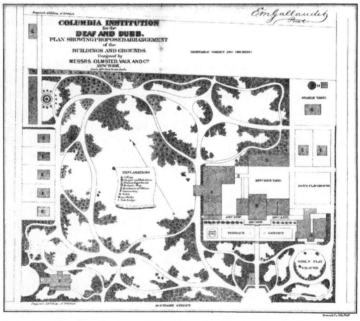

Plan for Campus of the Columbia Institution for the Deaf and Dumb, 1866

have no hesitation in pressing on your attention the serious importance of adding to your site, at this time, at least the two hundred feet indicated in our design.

There seems, moreover, beyond the mere question of convenience, another reason why, in your institution, a liberal appropriation of space should be set apart for ornamental ground in the vicinity of the college buildings; the inmates of your establishment being unable to hear or speak, any agreeable sensation or delicate perception must depend on the development of other faculties.

In a well-regulated garden the senses of sight and smell are gratified in a most complete and innocent way, and there seems, indeed, to be no reason why the studies of horticulture, botany, ornamental gardening, and rural architecture should not be pursued to great advantage by your students if proper facilities are offered at the outset, and due importance is attached to that influential automatic education which depends entirely on an habitual daily contemplation of good examples.

The general plan for the buildings is a preliminary one; it embraces what has been already done, and shows how the idea can be developed in future so as to harmonize fully with our conceptions in reference to the general treatment of the design as a whole.

A road, twenty-two feet wide, is shown in addition to the two hundred feet proposed to be taken.

This, as you see, is a matter open for consideration. It will, however, if practicable, make the plan more complete, as it will furnish a private entrance to the houses on that side of the property.

Hoping that the results of our study may be in accordance with your views, we remain, dear sir, very respectfully,

OLMSTED, VAUX & CO.

E. M. Gallaudet, Esq.,
President of the Columbia Institution for the Deaf and Dumb

ADDITIONS TO CENTRAL PARK: JULY 1866

To Richard Grant White

Clifton, S.I.
23d July, 1866

My Dear White,

You will give me leave to say how much I am pleased to read your article in the Galaxy upon the C. Park gateways. The style in which Hunt's plans have been publicly discussed in most cases hitherto has been very distasteful to me, and the subject oweing to misunderstandings and misrepresentations has become exceedingly vexatious.

I am not sure that I should not be content to wait the period of this life to see more than a mile or two of the architecture of the Louvre under any associations. I don't greatly dislike it for once, where it is, but I don't hanker after it so much that I would have it everywhere in small editions. Therefore I should go a little further than, or not quite so far, as you go, on that one point, but in all else you express my views most pleasantly.

Now, I remember one other point, indeed, in which possibly, I differ with you—but it is merely a question of degree and of convenience, not of taste.

I was very glad to see your warning in regard to statues. We have headed off, or fought outright and conquered a number of projects for statues and other constructions. I always feel that this is the great rock ahead for the park. Indeed if I should criticise the park as it stands, today, I should have to say, it contains already too much incident, or too frequent incident. Our design admits and was intended to be adapted to the introduction of statuary at the Terrace and on each side of the mall— symmetrically with the avenue trees. (The Shakespeare Statue, you know has the first place assigned it here). But it is frequently proposed to erect statues, and various other monumental constructions, on the lawns and in the bays of shrubbery. The worst is perhaps before us. There is a project on foot, of which I am forbidden to speak, and which I can allude to only very vaguely and confidentially, for a construction on the park which shall rival the tower of Babel. You would say that such a project could never receive favor from the Commission, but when our friend Hunt brought forward a plan for a building of the Historical Society last winter; one of Committee on Architecture described it to me by saying: "You would not know it from the Louvre; it would cost two or three million dollars," and when I hinted that no suitable ground for so vast a building could be found in the park and that if there could, it would dwarf and ruin everything about it of a park character, he replied with great animation that he would not think of that for a moment. He would put it "right in the middle of the great green, or right across the mall." There was nothing on the park to be considered before such a magnificent building, and I am sure he would not only put all regard for the park aside but willingly throw in the Hudson river, the White Mountains and Niagara to secure a promise of the tower of Babel. What would he not have given twenty years ago if the Washington monument could have been started in the park instead of in Washington?

I am most strongly of your opinion that American architects are to make their distinctive mark in the application of study to small structures and especially those of the domestic type—I do not mean family homes alone but public buildings the general form and decoration of which is significant of the liberty of the individual, and of consideration for the comfort of men when alone or in small numbers, not merely when taking part in great pageants. I have shown my disposition in this respect in a report made recently to the Trustees of the Mass. Agricl. College. If they don't print it, I shall, by and by, and will send you a copy. You will see it also, in a less distinct way in a report which I lately made to a California corporation.

Excuse my running off into egotisms. I meant merely to thank you for putting a disagreeable discussion upon a more respectable level than it has hitherto occupied.

Very cordially Yours

Fred Law Olmsted

NOTES FOR A BOYS' SCHOOL PRINCIPAL: OCTOBER 1866

To Frederick Newman Knapp

OLMSTED, VAUX & CO., Landscape Architects,
No. 110 Broadway, New-York
Octr 8th, 1866

My Dear Knapp,

The short visit I made yesterday to Eagleswood suggested some thoughts which as I may not see you again for some time I should like to communicate in writing. I have, however, but a few minutes to spare from my engagements & must give them crudely.

Looking back at my own experience, I see plainly a great advantage in education which my son would have over me, if I sent him to your school. There are certain others which I imagine possible which, as things are, he would not enjoy to the extent I should wish, and finally I see certain advantages which I enjoyed that your boys do not. These latter came to me chiefly not by systematic arrangment or deliberate and intelligent forethought on the part of my educational superintendents but through opportunities incidentally or accidentally presented to me & which I used with good will. Yet I feel that they have been worth a great deal to me and that education of the same kind might have been systematically given me to a much greater extent with greater advantage.

Reflecting upon this I am convinced that a boy who has no opportunities and inducements to educate himself, should have systematic instruction & practice in a great variety of matters with regard to which I saw little or no provision at Eagleswood. Yet the large majority of boys who spend four years there are very unlikely to have good opportunities for the kind of education to which I refer, after they leave you, or if they have, are unlikely to have time, inclination or to be constrained to make good use of them.

To show you what I mean I will ask you to consider what would be the value to every boy on leaving Eagleswood to be able to do such things as these following, and to instruct and superintend others efficiently in matters involving them. To saddle & bridle a horse—to harness him. To make temporary repairs in harness & carriage. To ride, drive, pack, clean, feed, bleed & phisic a horse. To put on a shoe or a substitute, to take care of his hoofs, to detect & treat with some advantage in the absence of a farrier, sprains, corns, heaves &c. To make a fire, & cook under difficulties. To swim, with & without support; to aid others in swimming, to rescue drowning persons; to come ashore in surf; to resusitate drowned or smothered persons, to avoid & treat sun stroke. To make & use a raft. To stop a leak in a boat. To keep an overloaded boat from swamping in rough water. To land in breakers with a boat or raft. To make and understand common signals & signs of seamen & woodsmen. To measure distances by the eye—by pacing—by trignometry without instruments. To graduate the sights of a rifle—to keep a rifle in good order. To serve artillery with safety. To take care of ammunition. To deal with a fire. To take horses from a burning stable. To ford a river. To kill animals without cruelty; to preserve meat. To preserve life & health under difficulties when ordinary provisions are lacking—from cold, from heat, hunger & thirst—fatigue, debility, nervous prostration, excessive excitements. To make rough maps in the field and under embarrassments. To make slight repairs in & run a steam engine safely. To take care of a watch; To preserve clothing from moths. To ventilate a house, to take care of the outside of a house; To paint & glaze. To keep turf & trees in order; To graft a tree; To train & prune a grapevine. To solder and weld; to box the compass; To know the north side of a tree; To distinguish the north star; To judge the weather; To judge & describe the conditions of a soil; To drain land. To observe conditions of malaria; To avoid or overcome conditions of malaria.

There are many more such accomplishments which would be valuable and which are easily acquired. With very little assistance comparatively, a clever boy could I think acquire an amount of knowledge in all these matters which would be likely to serve him well in an emergency (even if he could not become absolutely accomplished in them), by instruction & practice in them for an hour a day, during a period of four years, and I should be glad if my boy was to be at Eagleswood four years that he should have such use of one hour a day, even if several other things commonly taught at schools had to take their chance afterwards—Moral Philosophy, Theoretical Geometry, Rhetoric, Declamation & even French, an elegant handwriting & Gymnastics under cover, for instance.

Another thing: I should regard no boy's education as tolerably good, even as preparatory to college or other advanced schools, who could not trot 12 miles in two hours or walk 16 miles in four hours or from twenty to thirty miles in a day without painful fatigue, or who could not with a few days' special practice walk from forty to sixty miles in a day without serious inconvenience. A boy not having a great deal of active physical exercise in other ways, who would not in any weather & under all ordinary circumstances, rather take a walk of ten or twelve miles some time in the course of every day than stay quietly about a house all day, must be suffering from disease or a defective education. And a school system is not a good one which so fully occupies his time and supplies him with exercise that he has no opportunity or does not enjoy to use it for acquiring the habit of daily letting himself out in this way. It is more essential to real cleanliness of skin and lungs than washing with water; and the latter, however important to be looked after, would be better dispensed with than the former. Military drill & the Gymnasium will be a snare and a delusion if they stand in the way of it. I don't think they need.

You do a good deal to train your boys in habits of neatness, good carriage & good manners. Consequently they appear to great advantage personally. But this training is not carried out in all things. The boys are educated by example not to be neat, not to be provident, not to be elegant or refined but to be satisfied with a common and moderate degree of neatness if not to a positively shabby, neglected and careless style of manners and dressing in many respects. Your lawn, your footpaths, your roads, fences, outbuildings, your roofs, the field pieces on the parade ground, the areas under the galleries, the neglect of etiquette in the matter of the ensign, all come at once to my mind as affording instances of this incompleteness, which from what you said, it appeared were as obvious to you as to me. I refer to them again, mainly because it seems to me that the cadets should be employed for educational reasons in nearly all the practical measures which you will doubtless take to improve the appearance of these things. If a boy should be taught to make his hair,

& his teeth, his clothes & his boots clean and elegant, without the assistance of servants, should he not also be taught to make such other matters as I have indicated neat and elegant? It is as much a soldier's business to keep his barracks and parade ground in order when in garrison—to sod the glacis, gravel the ramps and sweep the platforms of a fort, as it is to black his boots and air his bedding—quite. And in respect to the practical usefulness of what would be acquired; it is much easier to get servants to brush clothes & boots properly than it is to get them to take proper care of walks and lawns. For these things a man often has to depend upon his own special knowledge & skill or go shabby; when for keeping in respectable personal attire, he can look with confidence to his tailor & household servants.

Am I not one of your "advisory Board"?

I am sincerely Your friend

Fred. Law Olmsted

"OUR FARMERS' SONS AND DAUGHTERS":
DECEMBER 1866

FROM *A Few Things to Be Thought of Before Proceeding to Plan Buildings for the National Agricultural Colleges*

At the conclusion of the debate of your Building Committee, I ventured to present in a crude form the suggestion which I have now offered you more completely, and although its practicability seemed to be doubted, the Committee desired that I would study the question further, and advise you as fully as I might see occasion to do in all respects relating to the division and disposition of your land and the adaptation of the constructions to be erected upon it to the special ends to be secured by your institution.

In undertaking this duty, I find it necessary, first of all, to ask myself, what are these special ends?

Probably no rural population in the world is as highly educated as that of Massachusetts, yet the demand for an Agricultural College indicates that it is the conviction of the people of the State that its agricultural class may, with advantage, be much better educated.

This conviction is evidently but one element of a general drift of the common sense of the people, and a recognition of its proper relation to this general drift appears to me to be necessary to a comprehensive understanding of the several ends which your college should be prepared to serve.

There have been in this country two distinct and opposing tendencies of social progress. In both, the advantage of fitting men by a special class training to serve the commonwealth, the advantage, that is to say of systematic division of labor, is recognized; in one, however, there is an effort to secure not only the special training of each class in the art belonging to it, but distinctions of general condition and habits, such as do not necessarily result from this training. In the other, such artificial distinctions as exist between different members of society are considered undesirable to be perpetuated.

In addressing an assembly of the scholars of South Carolina, for instance, Chancellor Harper felt assured of the concurrence of all who heard him, when he assumed that even the elementary instruction of a common school would not only be wasted, but would be positively detrimental to the interests of society at large, if given to men who were afterwards to be employed in occupations in which manual labor was an important element. Mr. Abbott Lawrence, on the other hand, with equal confidence, in addressing a Massachusetts audience, adopted precisely the opposite assumption.

The ideal of the school of which Mr. Lawrence was an exponent is universally understood to have been much more nearly approached in practice, as well as in theory, in the New England States than in the late slave States. Already, for instance, in the former, the working farmer or mechanic, much oftener than in the latter, reads similar books, wears similar clothing, has similar amusements, and dwells in a similar house, with similar furniture, to that of the members of professions or trades whose special labor and whose peculiar wares or services are of a widely different character from his, and a law constituting an institution for the education of farmers, with a generic title relating it to a class of educational institutions in which hitherto men have been fitted almost exclusively for quite different callings, evidently proceeds from an impulse of the same general current of conviction.

In older civilized countries, where the opposing impulse has ruled longest and most simply, the dwelling of the farmer and the lodging of his cattle, the cart-shed, the dairy, and the fowl-house are often under the same roof; manure is heaped before the door, hay stacked before the windows, and his children learn the use of their limbs and their perceptive faculties are educated in the common road, or in a yard with the calves and pigs. In these countries farmers are content so to live, and in the estimate of public opinion a farmer who was not, would be above his business, purse-proud and vulgar.

If we adopt the contrary opinion and regard the more distinct division which is commonly made in Massachusetts between the things which belong to the farmer as a farmer, and the things which belong to him as a man, as evidence of a higher tendency of civilization, we cannot logically and consistently be willing to stop just where we are in this respect. We must drift further and further in the same direction.

This conviction and faith influenced the Act of Congress, as well as the Act of your General Court, providing for the institution of an Agricultural College, quite as much at least as a desire to aid in the improvement of the mere economy of agriculture. This conviction and faith must then be consulted in all your plans of education, and this conviction and faith must have its place in the designing of your ground-plan first of all, for if it does not, your ground-plan will inevitably be a source of confusion and inefficiency in all the work that will remain before you.

The conclusion to which these reflections point is simply this, that you must embrace in your ground-plan arrangements for something more than oral instruction and practical demonstration in the science of agriculture, and for the practice of various rural arts. You must include arrangements designed to favorably affect the habits and inclinations of your students, and to qualify them for a wise and beneficent exercise of the rights and duties of citizens and of householders.

If, for instance, it is desirable that the farmer and his household should be debarred as little as possible from those enjoyments of intellect and taste which are common to men engaged in any ordinary professional calling and to their households, it is obvious that while receiving the special education necessary to his business, it is desirable also that he should be accustomed to an elevated standard of requirement in regard to the management of many common and familiar things which are not peculiar to his business. There need at least be no essential difference of character between a farmer's *home* and what would be considered a desirable home for an artist, a merchant, or a lawyer, except such as would result from actual necessities of situation.

"Yonder," we should be able to say, "is the stable and the yard, and the pasture-ground for the cattle. Here is the house and the garden and the lawn and the walks for men, women and children. Each is adapted to its purpose, and in our society the man who is a farmer, his wife, daughters and sons, have no different requirements to be met in house, lawn, walk or garden, from men of different occupations, their wives, daughters and sons."

The question is not whether this ideal is at once wholly practicable; it is, what can be done in the ground-plan of your college to bring farmers nearer to it?

It is thought by many to be an unfavorable symptom of our social condition that so many of our farmers' sons and daughters are eager to leave their homes and to abandon rural occupations. To rightly understand the facts, however, it must, I think, be considered how little provision is made by most of our farmers in their household affairs, and how little fitted most of them are to make intelligent and efficient household provision for a class of requirements of human nature, the satisfaction of which is as necessary to the moral, intellectual and physical health of their families as food or clothing, although the penalty for neglecting them is not as directly or as rapidly enforced as that of neglecting the demand of hunger or cold. No intelligent man, I believe, now doubts that the reaction from the excessive gayety or playfulness of a large part of the rural population of England which occurred with the Puritans, was itself excessive, and that it led to unhealthful habits. Nor can it be doubted that to this day the rural population of Massachusetts suffers the consequence of the intemperate resistance of their forefathers to the recreative efforts of nature, and that the disposition of our young people to get to the towns where there are daily and hourly diversions from the cares and labors of the farmer or the housekeeper, is an evidence of a wholesome tendency to grow better in this respect. If it is again sometimes excessive, or if it leads those yielding to it into idle and dissipated habits, as it must in many cases, the remedy is a perfectly simple one. It is to meet the natural disposition of young men and women to diversion, (that is to say, to experience a contrast to that which is associated with care and labor,) by well considered provisions for a daily exercise of this disposition *at home* in any way that shall be altogether healthful and healthfully educative.

That much can be done, in the arrangement of your buildings and the grounds about them, towards fitting your students to make such provisions can perhaps hardly be hoped. I must repeat, however, that it is of the more importance because of the difficulties of this element of education that it should not be entirely neglected in your plans, and that the necessity for providing for this class of our natural requirements, as well as for those of the appetites, should at least be recognized and respected in your constructions so far as opportunity can be found to do so.

There is another point upon which the rural population of Massachusetts has a distinctive reputation, which is exemplified in this fact, that nearly every farmer gives considerable thought to matters which are not those of his farm, or even of his household, but of the community generally, such as the common roads, bridges, schools, meeting-houses, public grounds, grave yards, monuments, libraries, and lyceums.

In some parts of the world, farmers have nothing to do with the direction or management of such things, and wish to have nothing. If they did, and expressed their wish, they would again be generally thought to be getting above their business. They are deemed by others, and deem themselves, by the necessities of their calling, unfit to direct or even have a voice in their design or their management. Consequently in communities composed mainly of farmers, there are but few public edifices or public works of any kind except such as are required for the convenience of strangers, and these are regarded with no personal interest or pride by the rural population.

If we can imagine a community in which an ideal the reverse of this, had been realized, we shall see what the state of things is toward which the people of Massachusetts are drifting and desire to drift.

In such a community, raw banks of earth, mud-puddles, heaps of rubbish and slatternly fences would not be likely to deface a village roadside, nor would public squares, burial grounds, buildings, fountains and monuments fail of neatness, good repair, beauty and good order, for want of systematic attention, any more than house-floors would fail to be systematically swept, or body-linen to be systematically cleansed.

But although this is the ideal toward which Massachusetts is drifting ahead of the rest of the world, and toward which it desires to drift still further, it cannot be said that it is as yet closely approached even in Massachusetts villages of the best type, while in many agricultural communities the degree of progress which has been made toward it, beyond the condition of those which are fast anchored to an opposite ideal, is hardly perceptible.

It may be argued that the circumstances of a farmer's occupation make it impossible that he or his household should enjoy equal communal privileges with those whose business enables them to live in denser neighborhoods, and consequently it cannot be expected that a consideration for his education in this direction can have any practical influence on the duty immediately before us. Should it not rather be said, that it is an essential part of that duty that everything should be done, which offers the slightest ground of hope that an influence may be exercised by your institution, which shall tend to enlarge the limits of this alleged special disability of the agricultural class?

If so, it cannot be questioned that should your students, throughout the period of their college course, live under circumstances of constant familiar observation and use of excellent provisions for meeting such common requirements of all rural communities as have been referred to, their tastes, inclinations and designing abilities would have received an education from which, if they were qualified to be men of influence in other respects, the desired result to the general agricultural population of the State would inevitably follow.

FROM *Architect's Report to the Board of Trustees
of the College of Agriculture, and the Mechanic
Arts, of the State of Maine*

A class of from five to ten students, well prepared by a superior common-school education, so that no time need be lost in studies which might just as well be pursued elsewhere, might be formed next spring, some temporary accommodation, suitable for the summer, being provided for them, before any of the College buildings proper are erected. These students would have special advantages in living on the ground, while the mechanics were employed upon the buildings, and the preliminary improvements of the farm were being planned and undertaken, and these advantages, together with the more intimate personal intercourse they would have with their instructors, would offset the lack of buildings, of apparatus, and well-organized methods. A second class might be taken on the following year; and each succeeding year, as the faculty acquired experience and confidence, and the methods of instruction and discipline were perfected, the number of the freshman class could be enlarged with advantage, until the whole number of students be as large as the faculty could at any time be expected to efficiently supervise. As long as the number of the faculty shall not exceed that which can be fairly paid by so much of the income from the present endowment as you could probably afford to appropriate to this purpose, I presume that you will hardly think it advisable to allow more than forty students to a class, a number which would probably be reached within a few years. In that case it would be bad economy to form any class-room even next year, of a size barely large enough for a smaller number than forty.

Allowing for the occasional accommodation of the Trustees and other visitors in each room, and for standing-room for apparatus which it may be desired to place before the classes, the following would seem to be the minimum of accommodation which could be economically provided for class rooms and halls for general meetings of the College respectively:

Each room for class instruction, seats for fifty.

Each hall for special meetings, seats for two hundred.

An idea of the minimum of accommodation for boarding and lodging cannot be reached until a plan of government and discipline for the College has been formed, which involves a duty that can hardly be definitely undertaken with much profit except by the person upon whom the chief responsibility for success in these all important respects will eventually devolve.

If the object were merely to accommodate the students at the least possible expense, the more they were dealt with at wholesale, (that is to say, the more nearly the arrangements approached in character to those which would be economical if it was shelter and feed for so many head of live stock that was to be provided,) the better. In that case, questionably the whole would be brought under the roof of one common barn or barrack-like building. But it is absolutely essential to the success of the institution that during the four years in which students shall be subject to its direct influence, certain tastes, inclinations and habits shall be established with them. These tastes, inclinations and habits are such as they can afterwards continue to follow, exercise and gratify under the conditions which ordinarily surround citizens who are actively and usefully and satisfactorily engaged in the pursuit of the common industrial avocations of an American community. So far as the College shall fail in this respect, it must fail to accomplish the sole end had in view in its endowment. In making a plan of arrangements for the board and lodging of the students, therefore, we are most imperatively bound to consider the question of economy, not as with reference merely to the least possible cost of keeping so much live stock, but with reference to the probable result upon the character, tastes, inclinations and habits of young men.

The useful, influential and successful followers of the industrial callings lodge neither in barns, barracks nor monasteries. Ninety-nine times out of a hundred they lodge with a family which occupies a detached house with a domestic territory of its own, in which each of the inmates of the house has his own special interest and enjoyment, while he also shares with all the others in certain common means of comfort.

It is true that a close similarity in all respects to the ordinary conditions of family life cannot be expected to be secured to the students in the arrangements for their board and lodging. There are no necessities to be provided for similar to many which control the furniture and the method of housekeeping appropriate to the home of a family. In respect to internal arrangements therefore, the necessity for something different must be acknowledged, and must be met as a problem by itself. But in all other respects the arrangements for board and lodging should, it appears to me, approximate as nearly as practicable to those which would be considered models of healthy, cheerful, convenient family homes.

With regard to the internal arrangements, on the other hand, it must be considered that to a certain extent, the government and discipline of the college is required to be of a military character. Of course there must be a military organization. It will probably be found best to form companies of about forty. It will be absolutely necessary, from considerations of economy, that the officers of these companies should be students themselves. It follows that within certain limits the students must be a self-governed body. In all the military schools of which I have knowledge this is the case. In one which I have recently visited, to which students come from all parts of the country and from abroad (the greater part of whom are younger, of less orderly habits, and less advanced in education than yours will unquestionably be), I found that the direct government of the students in their lodgings, and generally in respect to all that which does not come within the care of teachers of our common schools, was entirely in the hands of officers chosen from among themselves, and that the efficiency of these officers, and the loyalty of the students in respecting their authority, was all that could be desired.

If the minimum number of persons to be accommodated in each lodging-house be fixed at twenty, this will allow one commissioned officer, and one full platoon of rank and file to be quartered in each.

The general character of the houses might in that case be similar to that of the cottages commonly built for officers' quarters in the cantonments of our western military stations. The two cottages of one company might be placed near each other, the gable ends toward the road. In the rear of the ground between them might stand a house with its gables at right angles to these, containing the company kitchen and mess-room, commissary store-room and office, a sick-room and a study-room. To show the advantages of such an arrangement I must discuss still further the question of a plan of adminstration adapted to meet the end designed to be secured by the national endowment.

It is very doubtful if real family government, parental admin-istration or domestic order is possible in any large boarding-school or College, and, if not, it is certain that any system of management which assumes to be of that character must be felt to be false, and held in contempt, concealed or avowed, by those who are expected to be subordinate to it. It must conse-quently breed bad manners and immorality. The students of the Agricultural College will be generally of that intermediate age between childhood and manhood when, in a healthy natural development of the character, there is the strongest impulse to independent self-control and self-guidance, and consequently the strongest inclination to question the right and propriety of all merely personal authority. For the same reason however that pupils at this age are strongly indisposed to yield a filial subordination to instructors who have no claim upon their filial gratitude and affection, they are most disposed to respect any degree of authority which is systematically measured by the responsibility of those exercising it, because such authority im-plies entire respect for the personal responsibilities of those subject to it. Now this is the ruling principle of military author-ity. In the largest and most powerful military system of modern times: if an officer neglects to return the salute of a private, the private can compel him to be brought before a court martial, and to suffer punishment for his want of respect to the rights of a subordinate. We have lately seen the efficiency of this system of discipline. In a three months' campaign, it has conquered an empire, and to-day it holds every power in Europe at defiance.

It is clearly the intention of the act of congress to secure as an incidental advantage of the national system of Industrial Col-leges, the preparation of a certain number of young men in each state for acting as officers and instructors of volunteer forces, and thus to save the nation from ever again being so completely unprepared for the duty of self-defence as it was found to be at the outbreak of the rebellion.*

A careful study of the subject, which I made as an official duty during the war, led me to the conclusion that the element of their theoretical responsibility in which regimental and company officers at its commencement most failed; in which they most needed instruction; in which they acquired instruction by experience with the most difficulty; and in which their ignorance caused the most misery, the greatest waste of the national resources and the most melancholy loss of life, was just this of boarding and lodging. I remember once being informed that a Maine regiment had been without food for twenty-four hours, simply because the officers were ignorant of the routine to be pursued in procuring it. I reported the fact at the head quarters of the department, where it was received with apparent satisfaction, and I was told that nothing but starvation would teach the volunteer officers their duty in this respect. That many men died in this and every other volunteer regiment on account of the imperfect provision for maintaining them in health and vigor which was at that time universal, there can be no doubt.

I would respectfully suggest, therefore, that the arrangements for providing food for your students should be as nearly as practicable similar in character to those of the army. There should be a superintending commissary of the institution, who would of course not be a student; but the students should each in turn be required to perform the duties of an acting assistant commissary

* "The great object," says Prof. Turner, in a pamphlet recently published "that we had in view in this provision was that these universities should furnish to the States, in times of peace, a strong and able corps of teachers, to diffuse the same practice and the same spirit through all the lower schools of the nation, and in times of war, a corps of officers to drill and marshal them at once for the battle-field."

"We regard," says Adjutant General Haynie in the same publication, "justly too, intelligence as the great safeguard of the people and the nation. Not intelligence upon one branch of knowledge but upon all branches. Yet it is a startling fact that anterior to 1861, whilst any other knowledge might be obtained at our institutions of learning, the knowledge how to preserve the government in times of war had been so utterly neglected that not one man in a thousand knew how to 'shoulder arms.' And it was, I believe, taught as a part of the system of education at no schools except government schools, so that when our armies were organizing in 1861 and 1862, the first eighteen months were spent in what could have been taught the boy at school much cheaper."

for their respective companies. The forms required by the army regulations for obtaining supplies for troops in barracks should be used, and no student should be graduated with honor who could not construct and use a camp oven and a camp kitchen, or who was not prepared to undertake himself and to instruct others in all the duties of a regimental commissary officer.

This plan could, it strikes me, be accommodated to the suggestions of Mr. Barnes in regard to the self-support of the students better than any other. By establishing the company fund system, an *esprit du corps* would almost certainly be developed which would supply the best possible security for honesty and economy. As, therefore, each company, upon this plan, would have its own commissary officer, I suggest that each should have its own commissary store-room and office, its own kitchen and its own mess-room.

Accepting the general scheme of administration thus outlined, the economical minimum of accommodation for lodging and boarding may be approximately estimated as follows:

Three (3) cottages (one story and a half,) each 56 × 26 feet, including verandah and storm-house, for each forty students; that is to say, twelve such cottages to be built during the first four years after the first class is organized.

As I have before stated, there is nothing in the military arrangement of the boarding and lodging-houses proposed which would be inconsistent with a perfectly domestic character in their architecture and all their exterior arrangements. It is desirable to give the latter this character as much as possible, and especially does this apply to the laying out of the grounds about them. I can do no better than repeat the advice I have already given to the Trustees of the Massachusetts Agricultural College in this regard:

"Each house should have a little lawn between it and the road, with a few additions of a domestic character, such as arbors, trellises, summer-houses, dove-cotes, martin-boxes, bowling or croquet greens, terraces, hedges, ice-houses, &c.; constructions which would supply in every case real additions to the comfort and health of the proposed inmates, and at the same time aid their *education in the art of making a home cheerful and attractive*. There should be pots of window plants, a Wardian case or two, cages of singing birds, and some not expensive musical instruments in each house; a bed of hardy ferns and delicate evergreens on the north side, and a few tender shrubs on the lawn, which would require to be laid down or strawed up for the winter. The care of these things—the mowing of the lawn—the trimming of the hedges—the rolling and sweeping of the gravel—the training of the vines on the trellises—and even the occasional painting, white-washing and glazing of the houses, should be a part of the duty and of the education of the students."

A squad from each platoon would of course be detailed at a certain hour each day for police duty. After putting their respective houses in order in all respects, those so detailed should be allowed a certain time for taking care of their lawn, their gravel walks, and all the ground and fittings in connection with their quarters and mess-room. An honorable rivalry between companies would doubtless secure great care on the part of each to give the best possible appearance to the ground before its quarters, open to constant observation, as it would be, by the public, passing along the road, and thus a most valuable system of self-education would be established.

Among all the means of education which can be obtained for this peculiar establishment—we must constantly bear in mind, and I shall therefore be excused for repeating once more that— means for establishing certain tastes and habits are of more importance than any other, because if the institution fails in this respect, it fails in the primary object for which it is founded, the Board of Trustees fail to meet their responsibility to the State, and the State fails to meet the obligations which it assumed to the nation in accepting the land grant.

The two most important classes of means with reference to this end must be, in my judgment, the library and the gardens; one with reference to indoor recreations, the other with reference to out of door recreations. The records of your Board of Agriculture show that timely consideration has been given to the first. The second, I submit, is of no less importance. We hear regrets expressed every day that our best young men are deserting the country and rushing to the cities. In many rural towns of New England it is said that there are no middle-aged people left of those farmers' families which twenty or thirty years ago were notable for their thrift, cultivation and intelligence. So far as this is true, the reason of it, in my judgment, will be found not less in the character of the men than in that of the women. If a young woman who has had good educational advantages marries a farmer, let him be ever so thrifty and so successful in his pursuit, she is apt to find but little that is gratifying to her tastes in the circumstances of her residence, or the habits of her husband. Out of doors he is given up to his interests in his crops and stock; indoors he cares more for food and rest and speculations upon the prospects of his crops and the markets, than for anything with which a woman has a womanly sympathy. Consequently his wife is often lonely; there is but little relief to the drudgery of her housekeeping duties; during the working days she seldom goes out of the house, because there is nothing to draw her out, and she finds her life monotonous and dull beyond endurance. She pines for the variety of interest, the stir and society of town life. Against this misfortune there is but one precaution that you can take. It is to establish tastes in your students with which young women of refined impulses can cordially sympathize, and to offer them facilities for training themselves in ways of gratifying these tastes, which young women can admire, encourage, contribute to and be grateful for.

For these, among other reasons, a domestic character in the exterior of the habitations of the students, and surroundings to these habitations which shall be of a model character with reference to the ground which a farmer or mechanic may, without excessive trouble, keep in order for the gratification of his family about his house, constitute desiderata in your general plan really of more importance than any other which it comes within my province to consider. To provide for them, the general village-like arrangement which I have proposed of all the buildings to be erected either within a few years or in the distant future is almost essential, and this village-like arrangement cannot be appropriately realized unless all your buildings should correspond in size and general style exteriorly with those which would appropriately meet the ordinary requirements of a rural community. If this view is adopted, all the buildings which you erect will, in important respects, themselves form models and veritable means of practical instruction to your students, as well as serve each its more obvious special purposes.

To Andrew Dickson White

OLMSTED, VAUX & CO., Landscape Architects
No. 110 Broadway, New-York
June 13th 1867

Dear Mr White,

I had a very pleasant journey, after leaving you, to Syracuse, with Mr Fiske. What a nice, excellent fellow he is! I should think he would be of great value to you, but I confess I hope that you will spare him to Hartford a little longer. He would do a world of good there if he could remain a year or two.

On the train we had the pleasure of meeting of Mr Wilcox. I found that he was not at all prejudiced against either shifting your line of buildings to the Southward, or forming them en echalon. The first plan he thought Mr Cornell would object to because it would require him to give up his wife's reserve. The second he said he had always thought would be better, as the buildings would group much better & would be much better accommodated to the ground. That is my judgment very decidedly. If you place them as you propose, you will have made the same mistake which all the large colleges of the country are now repenting. We have twice been consulted within the year as to the possibility of recasting the general ground plan of college buildings from a straight quadrangular system to a more free, liberal, picturesque & convenient one, without demolishing the old buildings. You ought to anticipate such a growth of the University as will eventually require ten times the building accommodation that is provided for in your present plan. Do you doubt that far finer buildings than any you are now proposing to construct will be erected for University purposes in the course of a century or two? I do not. And if so,—that is to say if the University is to be a great success—is to have a healthy, steady growth, is to draw out the affections, the gratitude—the patriotism & benevolence of other noble men & women besides its founders, then your proposed *line*, complete in itself, or the "quadrangle" (which is not a quadrangle) complete in itself & with but one front of dignity, will be simply another monument of shortsightedness, inconsideration & complacency with our little present, like those at Yale & Amherst. The Treasurer at Amherst told me that the founders of the College took a very fine site for their buildings and put them in a line upon it, where a magnificent view was commanded, but when by bequests new buildings were required, no suitable place could be found for them except by entirely disregarding the plan of the founders and destroying the effect which they valued. Accordingly the plan of the present edifices as something as follows: the shaded blocks being the older brick buildings, the others new & mainly of stone. Now they have a bequest of $100,000 which is the basis of a fund for a chapel, and another large sum for another buildg, both of which are intended to be much more dignified  than any of those now standing. One of the professors strongly advocated placing the largest one of them at the point X entirely ignoring the old line & the half suggested quadrangle. Being the finest building it should be put before all but what would go to the rear; certainly it should not be put on the back side of buildings so much inferior to it as those in the line would be. But X is on the slope of the hill—lower than the old line—so he asked me if a terrace could not be built out there thirty feet high as a foundation for it. You see how in placing the building A which has been lately the pride of the college, the formal effect has been given the coup de grace at one blow. The position very closely corresponds to yours, except that the declivity is steeper & the scale smaller. This is for your eye alone & I shall say nothing of it, professionally, having been informed that it was no longer open to debate, but the more I think of it the more I am impressed with the conviction that you are making a great mistake, & between ourselves, I feel it a duty to tell you so. Your Trustees it appears have decided the question contrary to the judgment, if not to the advice, of their architect. They take a grave responsibility in doing so, for if your architect is fit for his duty at all, his judgment ought to be almost controlling on such a question. If it is open to reconsideration, and your suggestion of shifting the whole line to the Southward indicates that you may consider that it is, I would advise you to call a council of architects & if you please of artists. It is a point of great importance & you had better delay another year rather than make what will hereafter possibly be always felt as a fundamental mistake. Don't, I beg of you, if you can possibly avoid it begin by tying yourself to formality & straight lacing. It is obvious already that you will not, would not if you could, carry out the theme consistently. You are deliberately proposing to arrange half a dozen initiatory buildings formally and to arrange everything else informally. The result will inevitably be unhappy. You can yet secure picturesque unity, but if you go on, a year hence neither unity nor picturesqueness, in high degree will be possible. You will have a little important formality & a great deal of helter skelter. I don't mean to say that the result will be positively bad, on that point there will probably be difference of opinion, but that a great opportunity will have been wasted, and unless the progress of taste in the U.S. gets a set back, or the university fails of a great success, I will lay you a wager payable t'other side of Styx that within two centuries some of your buildings will be demolished in order to break up the line and allow new buildings to group in with the hill top and with such old buildings & trees as will be allowed to remain in a manner which shall be just to the architecture of the age and consistent with the comfort of the public eye.

These frankly are my views on that point, and now I have done with it; I have said what I have now & so strongly, in order to get past that point, before I again see Mr Cornell, from whom I hope next week to receive definite & final instructions as to the limits within which my imagination will be free to work, and with whom I do not propose to discuss the question of site of buildings, which must be the most important of these limits.

Please not to forget to send me sevrl copies of the Plan of Organization, as I wish to send it to England.

I found Norton here on my return; he is greatly interested in your enterprise & wants much to see you. He may come to Ithaca with me later in the summer. I shall probably visit him at Cambridge in July. Is there any chance of you being there?

I trust Mrs White reached home the better for her journey.
Yours Very Truly

Fred. Law Olmsted

FROM *Report of the Landscape Architects and Superintendents*

THE OPPORTUNITY OF BROOKLYN

Here, then, there is ample room for an extension of the habitation part of the metropolis upon a plan fully adapted to the most intelligent requirements of modern town life. A large part of the elevated land which has been referred to lies not more than half as far from the commercial centre as the habitation district of New York island, the ground is better formed with reference to sanitary considerations; it is open to the sea breezes and lies in full view of the ocean; it can never be enclosed on all sides by commerce as the habitable part of New York island soon will be; and, its immediate back country being bounded by the sea, the commercial traffic through it is always likely to be light and will be easily provided for in a few special channels. Thus it seems set apart and guarded by nature as a place for the tranquil habitation of those whom the business of the world requires should reside within convenient access of the waters of New York harbor.

It does not follow, however, that it will be so occupied. In the drift of the population of towns it is generally found that natural advantages alone go for but little, and except in the part controlled by your Commission no other arrangements as yet exist with reference to the convenience, health, and pleasure of residents upon this land than such as would have been formed if it were desired to invite to it nothing but factories, ship yards, or the warehouses and offices of merchants. One or two streets were laid out through it some years ago with an avowed intention of being especially adapted to residences; they were so designed however, as to offer every advantage to commercial transportation and consequently for shops and factories but, except in mere width, without intelligent regard to the alleged purpose in view. They are nevertheless adapted to serve an important purpose in concentrating such commercial traffic as must pass through their neighborhoods and in furnishing sites for shops and public buildings which will in any case be needed to meet local requirements.

Upon the manner in which there are good grounds for confidence that the elevated district which has been indicated will be occupied in the future, depends the valuation which can justly and sagaciously be now placed upon it, and upon this valuation mainly depends the financial prosperity of the city of Brooklyn.

HOW THE OPPORTUNITY MAY BE MISUSED
AND HOW AVAILED OF

It would be a perfectly simple problem to cause this land to be given up in a few years almost exclusively to shanties, stables, breweries, distilleries, and swine-yards, and eventually to make the greater part of it a district corresponding, in the larger metropolis which is hereafter to exist on the shores of New York harbor, to that which the Five Points has been in the comparatively small town we have known.

The means by which it may be made a more suitable and attractive place of domestic residence than it is possible that any other point of the metropolis ever will be, are equally within command.

INFLUENCE OF THE PARK ON THE
VALUE OF PROPERTY

The effect of what has already been done, under the direction of your Commission, has been to more than quadruple the value of a certain portion of this land, and we have thus an expression of the most simple character, in regard to the commercial estimate which, at this period in the history of towns, is placed upon the circumstance of convenient access from a residence to a public pleasure-ground, and upon the sanitary and social advantages of a habitation thus situated. The advance in value, in this case, is quite marked at a distance of a mile, and this local advantage has certainly not been attended by any falling back in the value of other land in Brooklyn.

If we analyze the conditions of this change in value, we shall find that it is not altogether, or even in any large degree, dependent upon mere vicinity to the sylvan and rural attractions of the Park, but in very large part, in the first place, upon the degree in which these attractions can be approached with security from the common annoyances of the streets, and with pleasure in the approach itself. If, for instance, the greater part of the Park were long and narrow in form, other things being equal, the demand for building sites, fronting on this portion of it, would not, probably, be appreciably less than for those fronting on the broader part. Secondly, the advance in value will be found to be largely dependent on the advantages of having near a residence, a place where, without reference to the sylvan attractions found in a large park, driving, riding, and walking can be conveniently pursued in association with pleasant people, and without the liability of encountering the unpleasant sights and sounds which must generally accompany those who seek rest, recreation or pleasure in the common streets.

There are other things to be valued in a Park besides these, but these are the main positive advantages which would make the value of a residence, if upon the Park, much greater than if at a distance from it.

HOW THE ADVANTAGES OF VICINITY
TO A PARK MAY BE EXTENDED

So far, then, as it is practicable, without an enlargement of the Park in its full breadth and compass, to extend its attractions in these especial respects, so far is it also practicable to enlarge the district within which land will have a correspondingly increased attraction for domestic residences. The further the process can be carried, the more will Brooklyn, as a whole, become desirable as a place of residence, the higher will be the valuation of land, on an average, within the city, and the lighter will be the financial burden of the Corporation.

EXAMPLE OF A FOURTH STAGE OF
STREET ARRANGEMENTS

We come, then, to the question of the means by which such an extension can be accomplished. Although no perfect example can be referred to, there have been in Europe a few works by which a similar end, to a certain extent, has been reached. Of these, the most notable is the Avenue of the Empress, in Paris, which connects a palace and a pleasure-ground within the town, with a large park situated far out in the suburbs. This avenue, with its planted border, occupies so much ground (it is 429 feet in width) that it may be considered to constitute rather an intermediate pleasure-ground than a part of the general street system. It is lined with a series of detached villa residences, and building-lots facing upon it are much more valuable than those facing upon the Park.

The celebrated Linden Avenue, at Berlin, leads likewise from a palace and palace grounds, to a great rural park on the opposite side of the town, through the very midst of which it passes. The finest private residences and hotels of the town, as well as many public buildings, such as Art Galleries and Museums, front upon it, and it is equally convenient for all the ordinary purposes of a street with any other. It nevertheless differs essentially from an ordinary business street, in that the process which we have described, by which wagon-ways were introduced into the old streets, has been carried one step further, the wagon-way having itself been divided as the foot-way formerly was, and a space of ground having been introduced, within which there is a shaded walk or mall, and a bridle-road, with strips of turf and trees.

THE PARKWAY—A FIFTH STAGE

The "Parkway" plan which we now propose advances still another step, the mall being again divided into two parts to make room for a central road-way, prepared with express reference to pleasure-riding and driving, the ordinary paved, traffic road-ways, with their flagged sidewalks remaining still on the outside of the public mall for pedestrians, as in the Berlin example. The plan in this way provides for each of the several requirements which we have thus far examined, giving access for the purposes of ordinary traffic to all the houses that front upon it, offering a special road for driving and riding without turning commercial vehicles from the right of way, and furnishing ample public walks, with room for seats, and with borders of turf in which trees may grow of the most stately character. It would contain six rows of trees, and the space from house to house being two hundred and sixty feet, would constitute a perfect barrier to the progress of fire.

PRACTICABLE FUTURE EXTENSIONS
OF THE PARKWAY

With modifications to adapt it to variations of the topography and the connecting street arrangements, the plan should eventually be extended from the Park, in one direction, to Fort Hamilton, where ground for a small Marine Promenade should be secured, overlooking the Narrows and the Bay; and in the other to Ravenswood, where it should be connected by a bridge with one of the broad streets leading on the New York side to the Central Park. A branch should extend from it to the ocean beach at Coney Island, and other branches might lead out from it to any points at which it should appear that large dwelling quarters were likely to be formed, at such a distance from the main stem that access to it from them would otherwise be inconvenient.

There are scarcely any houses at present standing on the general line indicated and it would pass nearly parallel to, and be everywhere within from fifteen to thirty minutes walk of the wharves of the East River. The distance between its extreme points would be about ten miles and the average distance of residences upon it from Wall Street would be about half the distance to the Central Park. Spacious and healthful accommodations for a population of 500,000 could be made within ten minutes walk of this Parkway.

PLAN OF THE PARKWAY NEIGHBORHOOD

Our plan, it will be observed, covers more ground than is necessarily required to be taken for the purposes which have been indicated. The object of this is that in addition to providing for an enlargement of the Park advantages, throughout its whole extent, the Parkway may also constitute the centre of a continuous neighborhood of residences of a more than usually open, elegant, and healthy character. It is believed that such a neighborhood would not merely be more attractive, to the prosperous class generally, of the metropolis, than any which can be elsewhere formed within a much greater distance from the commercial centre, but that it will especially meet the requirements of an element in the community that is constantly growing larger and that is influenced by associations and natural tastes that unquestionably deserve to be fostered and encouraged. A typical case, for the sake of illustrating the class in view may be thus presented. A country boy receives a common school education, exhibits ability and at a comparatively early age finds himself engaged in business in a provincial town; as his experience and capacity increase, he seeks enlarged opportunities for the exercise of his powers and being of superior calibre, ultimately finds himself drawn by an irresistible magnetic force to the commercial cities; here he succeeds in becoming wealthy by close attention to his specialty and the sharp country boy becomes the keen city man. Trees and grass are, however, wrought into the very texture and fibre of his constitution and without being aware of it, he feels day by day that his life needs a suggestion of the old country flavor to make it palatable as well as profitable. This is one aspect of the natural phenomena with which we are now attempting to deal; no broad question of country life in comparison with city life is involved; it is confessedly a question of delicate adjustment, but we feel confident that whenever and wherever, in the vicinity of New York, this delicate adjustment is best attended to, and the real needs of these city-bred country boys are most judiciously considered, there they will certainly throng. We do not of course mean to argue that the tastes to which we have referred are limited solely to citizens whose early life has been passed in the country, but only that the existence of the special social element thus typified gives one of the many assurances that such a scheme as the proposed Parkway neighborhood would be successful, if judiciously carried out within the lines suggested, before the demand is more or less perfectly met in some other locality.

It is clear that the house lots facing on the proposed Parkway would be desirable, and we assume that the most profitable arrangement would be to make them, say 100 feet wide, and of the full depth between two streets, convenient sites for stables being thus provided. The usual effect of such a plan of operations would be an occupation of the rear street by houses of inferior class, and it is with a view of avoiding any such unsatisfactory result that the design is extended over four blocks of ground. If the two outermost streets are widened to 100 feet and sidewalks shaded by double rows of trees introduced in connection with them, the house lots on these streets will be but little inferior to those immediately facing the Parkway, for they also will be of unusual depth and will be supplied with stable lots that can be entered from the street already mentioned, which should be made suitable for its special purpose, and with the idea that it is only to be occupied by such buildings as may be required in connection with the large lots which are intended to be arranged throughout back to back, with the stable street between them.

Thus, so far as this arrangement should be extended, there would be a series of lots adapted to be occupied by detached villas each in the midst of a small private garden. This arrangement would offer the largest advantages possible to be secured in a town residence, and there is no good reason why they should not be of a permanent character. With the modern advantages for locomotion which would be available, the departure from the old-fashioned compactness of towns might be carried to this extent, in that part of them devoted to residences, without any serious inconvenience. The unwholesome fashion of packing dwelling-houses closely in blocks grew, as we have shown, out of the defensive requirements of old towns; it may possibly be necessary to continue it under certain circumstances, as, for the reasons already indicated, on the island of New York, but where there is no necessary boundary, either natural or artificial, to the space which is to be occupied by buildings, as is the case with Brooklyn, it is, to say the least, unwise to persist in arrangements which will permanently prevent any indulgence of this kind.

Those who availed themselves of the opportunity here proposed to be offered would not benefit themselves alone, but the whole community. The Romans seem to have been wiser than we have been in this particular. Rich people were offered every facility for surrounding their houses with open garden spaces, and the larger part of the Eternal City was composed of what we should now term detached villas, while in no part was it permitted that a new house, even though intended for the residence of slaves, should be built within five feet of walls previously erected.

How far it might be desirable for property-owners to extend the plan in the peculiar form suggested, is, of course, an open question, depending on the anticipated demand for lots of the size indicated, but it will be readily seen that as the proposed subdivisions are not of the ordinary contracted character, a comparatively small number of residents will suffice to fill up a considerable stretch of ground laid out in this way, and it is also evident that if, within a reasonable time, it should become certain that a specific number of blocks would be carried out on this plan, the lots included within the boundaries determined on would not require to be improved in regular succession, but would be selected with reference to slight, fancied advantages anywhere along the line, every purchaser feeling satisfied that the main question of good neighborhood had been settled on a satisfactory basis at the outset.

ADVANTAGES OF THE PARKWAY LIKELY TO BE SECURED TO BROOKLYN EXCLUSIVELY

Having so fully described, in its principal aspects, the question of the desirability of developing, in Brooklyn, a plan of public improvement of the general character indicated, it may be proper for us to enquire whether the broad streets which are proposed to be opened on New York island under the name of Boulevards during the next few years, are calculated to interfere with the probable success of such a scheme.

While the Central Park was in its earlier stages of progress, a Commission was appointed to prepare a plan for laying out the upper end of New York island, and some years later this responsibility was transferred to the Central Park Commission, whose plan is published in their last annual report.

The same document contains an elaborate discussion of the subject by Mr. A. H. Green, on the part of the Board, and as our professional relations with the Commissioners have not been extended over this department of their work, and we are not aware of their intention in regard to this improvement, except so far as it is set forth in the plan and public statement above mentioned, we make, for the purposes of this Report, the subjoined quotation, which sets forth clearly the limitations that are to be recognized in New York as controlling the designs of the Commissioners:

"We occasionally, in some country city, see a wide street ornamented with umbrageous trees, having spaces of green interposed in its area, the portion used for travel being very limited. This arrangement is only possible where thronging population and crowding commerce are not at liberty to overlay and smother the laws that are made to secure the legitimate use of the public streets. It would seem inexpedient, at any rate, until some better permanent administration of our streets is secured, to attempt these fanciful arrangements to any great extent in a commercial city, under our form of government."

It is clear, therefore, that the Central Park Commissioners have no intention of carrying out, in New York, any such scheme as the "Parkway," and consequently, if, as we believe, the requirements that such a plan is designed to meet are already felt to exist in this community, Brooklyn can soon be made to offer some special advantages as a place of residence to that portion of our more wealthy and influential citizens, whose temperament, taste or education leads them to seek for a certain amount of rural satisfaction in connection with their city homes.

Although the plots of ground appropriated to the Brooklyn and Central Parks are entirely different in shape, while their landscape opportunities and general possibilities of design are equally dissimilar, a generic family resemblance will yet be found between the two pleasure-grounds, simple because they are both called into existence to meet the same class of wants, in the same class of people, at the same Metropolitan centre.

The Brooklyn Parkway, on the other hand, will, if executed, be a practical development of the ideas set forth in this Report, which seem to be particularly applicable to the city of Brooklyn, and which, as we have shown, are considered by those in authority to be unsuitable for development in the city of New York; it will consequently have no such family resemblance to the New York Boulevards as exists between the two parks, and its attractions will, for a time, at any rate, be of a special and somewhat individual character.

"PARK PURPOSES": MAY 1868

Address to the Prospect Park Scientific Association

You have asked me to talk to you upon the subject of the treatment of natural woods with reference to park purposes. There is a difficulty which always stands in the way of useful debate of any of the elements by which our work here is distinguished from the great body of works in which the principles of engineering science and architectural art are more especially applied. A difficulty which arises from the insufficiency and chiefly from the looseness & vagueness of the nomenclature of the class of works in question we are prevented from comparing ideas, prevented from elaborating ideas by mutual efforts, prevented from giving & recvg instruction, by the want of words which are certain to call up in the minds of all of us or of any two of us, the same images or ideas. This arises from the fact that hitherto, there has been little occasion for exact discussion; that so far as works of this kind have been carried on at all they have been carried on without much careful thought, or at least without the benefit of exact thought in many minds. There has been but little criticism; little debate consequently little explanation or occasion for explanation of the principles of science & art upon which they are designed. In fact, public works of this class are new in the world. There have been public parks before now certainly, but till quite lately the construction of those parks has not been pursued fully & fairly as a public work, open to general, thorough & searching criticism, to anything like professional scientific criticism. Responsibility for these works has not been felt to be a responsibility to the public. Accountability has been felt only to some individual or to some few individuals and provided their intentions were realized, provided they were gratified, criticism of them has been regarded as nobody else's business. There has been no interest therefore demanding & leading to anything like precise, exact & searching debate & consequently precision of thought & clear means of expressing precise & thorough thought has not been developed.

Thus a necessity exists in the discussion of such a topic for instance as this we have in hand, to use a great deal of circumlocution or to dwell a great deal upon elementary ideas & to define elementary terms. I must do so or I shall be liable to convey impressions to you very different from those I wish you to recve. To reach good results our process must be studious, elaborate, slow, perhaps tedious.

Take this term, park purposes. What are we to understand by it. It is your business to plan and superintend constructions in which the materials of the earth's surface, clay, sand & stone, are to be largely & scientifically dealt with. You are called upon in your professional capacity to provide a certain town with a park as you might be to provide it with water-works, bridges, docks or canals. What is the idea your clients have when they demand of you a park? To begin let us say, they want a place of recreation? But that is a very insufficient definition. A theatre is a place of recreation, so is a flower garden, so is a conservatory. The vacant lots between X & XI av. & 3d & 9th St have been a place of recreation; of out of door recreation, for a long time, both the wooded parts & the open. But now we are asked to take this land & more & make a park of it. How shall we get at what it is they want? Where did they get the word? It is an English word and we must go to England if we would know to what it has been formerly applied. There are several thousand pieces of ground which for many centuries have been called parks—some of which were called parks at the period when more especially the English language was consolidated. The term park was not used to distinguish them as places set apart or fitted especially for recreation, certainly not for any kind of recreation that your modern townspeople want ground to be set apart & prepared for. What then is their common characteristic? In what did the park differ from other divisions of ground?

What was the *common quality* they possessed which made it necessary that they should have a *common designation*? They were not public properties but when the state of society was yet essentially barbarous were selected and taken possession of, prized, fought for & held solely by the rich and powerful—and when society became better organized and less rude, these same pieces of ground still remained a peculiar possession of the more fortunate and arrogant, who had residencies in the midst of them. It continued the same through all the changes of manners and customs, the increase of luxury and the progress of refinement to the present day when at length we find people who cannot have a park for a private possession uniting with others to obtain one which can be used in common. Why should the particular pieces of land to which the term park was first applied have been regarded as choice & peculiarly desireable possessions for so long a time & by men of such very different wants & habits? Pretty certainly, it appears to me, because of some topographical conditions in which they originally differed from other pieces of land, which topographical conditions have all the time been found peculiarly convenient for the indulgence of certain propensities which are a part of human nature and which the progress of civilization does not affect, as it does mere manners & customs.

To illustrate and more fully fix in your minds this hypothesis, I shall narrate to you a personal experience. When I was a young man I made a long journey through England on foot, in company with my brother, in the course of which we became very familiar with the finest & most characteristic park scenery. A few years afterwards my brother & I started to go overland by the Southern or Gila route to the Pacific. On account of the outbreak of an Indian war and the refusal of parties which we had expected to join to take the risk without military escort which could not be spared us, we were compelled to wait on the frontier during a period of several months. We undertook therefore, for our amusement and information an exploration of so much of the country beyond settlements as it was at all safe for us to cruise in, as well as some of the border land a little beyond the line of safety and of the other border a little within the line of outermost settlement.

Travelling with a pack-mule and for the most part living on the country, being in no haste, we usually broke camp about 9 o'ck, and soon after noon began to look out for a new camping ground. That is to say if at any time after noon we saw a promise anywhere to the right or left or right ahead of certain topographical conditions, we moved in that direction, and whenever we came upon a site which was particularly satisfactory to us as a place for camping, though it was but just after noon, there we would end our day's march. If we found nothing satisfactory we would keep on till dusk, and then do the best we could. If we were fortunate in this respect on Saturday we generally rested on Sunday, and sometimes at a camp that particularly pleased us laid up for several days, it being our object to keep our stock in good condition. Thus I may say that it was our chief business for some months to study the topography of the country more especially with reference to the selection of satisfactory camping places. Now with fresh recollections of the old country parks we found that the topographical conditions which we were accustomed to look for were such that we sometimes questioned whether if an Englishman had been brought blindfolded to our tent, and the scene disclosed to him he would be readily persuaded that he was not in some one of those old parks. Yet I need not say the conditions were perfectly natural, that no Engineer or gardener had had a hand in fashioning them—nay I suppose that sometimes no white man ever had before been on the ground.

What then were the governing circumstances of our selection?

First, we wanted good, clear water close at hand, both for bathing and for drinking.

2d good pasturage in which with little labor or care to us we could keep our cattle in good condition.

3d wood at convenient distance, both small wood to readily kindle up, and logs to keep the fire through the night.

4th We preferred seclusion, partly because in seclusion there was greater safety for though we did not fear the Indians or Border ruffians by day light, the chance of an attempt to steal our horses at night was just enough to make us feel a little more comfortable if our situation was a somewhat cosy one. When at the greatest distance from settlements the danger was sufficient to induce us to shift camp after cooking our supper lest the fire should have advertised us too closely. Partly for this reason we preferred seclusion, and partly because we were frequently visited after nightfall by the sudden blast of a norther, in which case an elevated or exposed position was far from comfortable either for us or our horses, which whatever the range we gave them during daylight were always staked within close pistol shot of our bed at nightfall.

5th We liked to have game near at hand, and

6th We made it a point to secure if possible as much beauty as possible in the view from our tent door.

This last brings us to the question: What is the beautiful? but it is a question which we will not here discuss. I only wish you to observe that the beauty which we enjoyed in this case depended on elements of topography of a very simple charac-ter. I assume that such beauty of scenery gives pleasure even to savages.

Now, if you think of it, you will see that all these conditions of a pleasant camp would also be the conditions of a pleasant family residence of a more permanent character, provided that the wants of the family were very simple or rude, provided, i.e. it was not greatly dependent for its comfort on the labor of others; provided it was prepared to live mainly within itself as the phrase is.

In fact we found that wherever the pioneers were settling in this country, they were selecting just such places & plainly because the less artificial wants of men were in such situations more conveniently provided for, provided for with less exertion, effort and anxiety of mind, than in any other. For example, in such a situation it would be easy to get water when wanted, easy to get wood when wanted, easy to find shelter from wind, easy to find shelter from sun, easy to make shelter from rain, easy to spy game at a distance, easy to enclose stock, easy to keep watch of stock, when turned out, easy to follow stock when strayed, easy for stock when turned out to find good grazing, water & shelter, easy, if desired, to enclose land, to cultivate it, &, to house the crops from it.

In one word the topography of such a situation is of a character which suggests to an observer an easy gratification of a great variety of the elementary human impulses and thus, leaving out of consideration entirely the impulse to associate or marry with that quality of natural objects whatever it is which we describe as the beautiful.

And this topography as I have shown is also the characteristic topography of the old parks, this is what a park was, this & nothing more when certain pieces of land were first enclosed & called parks. This gives us, therefore, the original, radical & constant definition of the topography which is wanted to be selected or constructed when a park is called for. I do not mean that this is all of a park, but that an idea of a park centres & grows upon this. If it is an insufficient definition, it is because the condition of ease is merely a negative condition. The absence of obstruction is the condition of ease of movement, and a park as a work of design should be more than this; it should be a ground which invites, encourages & facilitates movement, its topographical conditions such as make movement a pleasure; such as offer inducements in variety, on one side and the other, for easy movement, first by one promise of pleasure then by another, yet all of a simple character & such as appeal to the common & elementary impulses of all classes of mankind. But this quality of ease, must underlie the whole. You must first secure this, and if this is not all, it is at least the framework of all. But is a park, you may ask, a mere study of topography, the work merely of an engineer? I answer that that depends on what limit the engineer chooses to put upon the field of his professional study. My own opinion is that the science of the engineer is never more worthily employed than when it is made to administer to man's want of beauty. When it is carried into works not merely of art but of fine art.

Now Herbert Spencer in an Essay on Gracefulness says:

> grace as applied to motion, describes motion that is effected with an economy of muscular power, grace as applied to animal forms describes forms capable of this economy. Grace as applied to postures, describes postures which may be maintained with this economy, & grace as applied to inanimate objects, describes such as exhibit certain analogies to these attitudes & forms.
>
> That this generalization, if not the whole truth, contains at least a large part of it, will I think become obvious on considering how habitually we couple the words easy & graceful.

Whether the philosophy here is perfect & the analysis final & complete or not, we must admit that the association of ideas pointed out is inevitable; and you will see that by simply substituting the word grace for the word ease in the statement of the conclusions to which we have arrived in our study of the engineering question which we have hitherto had before us, we raise our aim at once into the region of esthetic art. Let us call grace the idealization of ease, and then let us take the final step, and add a positive quality to the negative one of ease or grace, and we shall find ourselves prepared to form what I consider to be the true conception or ideal of a park, in distinction from any other ground, or any other place of recreation.

That is to say we must study to secure a combination of elements which shall invite and stimulate the simplest, purest and most primeval action of the poetic element of human nature, and thus tend to remove those who are affected by it to the greatest possible distance from the highly elaborate, sophistical and artificial conditions of their ordinary civilized life.

Thus it must be that parks are beyond anything else recreative, recreative of that which is most apt to be lost or to become diseased and debilitated among the dwellers in towns.

With reference to construction, or the artificial formation

of topography then, we may say that park-purposes means a purpose to make gracefully beautiful in combination with a purpose to make interesting and inviting, or hospitable by the offer of a succession of simple, natural pleasures as a result of easy movements.

These, I mean, are *park*-purposes, primarily, in distinction from all other pleasure-ground purposes. So far as we are to do anything at the [...] Ground for instance, it is with these purposes we are to do it. If we cannot make it more graceful, more interesting, more inviting, more convenient, then we are to do nothing.

It does not follow that all parts of our enclosure should be of this simple easy flowing topography which I have indicated. Grace like any other quality which acts upon us through our sense of vision is enhanced by contrast, and if we can employ accessories which will have this effect & at the same time serve a direct purpose of any value they will be proper and desirable within our enclosure, but they will not be the characteristic features of the park. It is chiefly important that they do not become of so much relative importance as to lose their character as accessories.

Rocks for instance may be such accessories so may thick wood, so may shrubbery. So may buildings, monuments &c but these are not what make a park; they are not characteristic of it.

The word park as a common noun, as a descriptive word, should indicate such graceful topography, such open pastoral, inviting hospitable scenery as I have indicated.

When I speak of the treatment of wood with reference to park purposes, I mean first of all with reference to the production or improvement of such scenery, & secondly with reference to the production or improvement of such accessories.

There may be another class of park purposes, of a quite different character, & to discriminate between the two, you must recollect that the word park is used as a proper as well as a common noun.

Phoenix Park, for instance is *the* park of Dublin and includes, a vice-regal palace, with orchards & kitchen gardens; Barracks, a magazine, an arsenal; parks of artillery, & other features which are far from being graceful and equally far from presenting inducements for an indulgence in simple natural enjoyments. Yet all of which are a part of what is called the Park when the word is used as a proper noun, as much as that which, using the word again as a common noun, is the park itself, which consists of few other elements than turf and trees.

When we know that such things as barracks, arsenals and buildings intended solely for domestic or public business purposes, which are wholly incongruous with the purposes of a park, are referred to under the same general head with turf & trees, we are in no danger of confusing the common & the proper noun. But there may be accessories of a park, which contribute to its main purpose by predisposing the mind or removing impediments of the mind to the kind of recreation which it is adapted to stimulate, as by means of relief from thirst or hunger or excessive fatigue or shelter from rain and these may be included under the term park-purposes, even with reference to topographical construction and artistic design, though in themselves they are the reverse of graceful or suggestive of easy movement.

And it is possible to add these & many other auxiliaries to the means of accomplishing our primary purposes not only without lessening, but in such a manner as to positively increase the special value of the latter. For the influence of grace of topography like any other quality which influences our minds through the senses is enhanced by contrast.

Elements designed to *increase* park effects by contrast must however be used with caution, lest instead of heightening the impression sought to be primarily produced by certain elements of topography we obscure or confuse them. To this end it is chiefly important that the contrasting circumstances should be unmistakeably auxiliary, subordinate, and accessory in every respect to the general design. This principle & this caution in the application of the principle, applies to the use of woods or trees as well as to more purely constructional objects.

What then is the part; what are the duties, of trees? Christopher North asks.

But the more important qualities of trees in landscape are those of termination and obscuration of the view of an observer, though the two may be considered as one, for the termination of landscape by trees is effected by a high degree of obscuration.

You will recollect that I used the term hospitable as descriptive of the essential characteristic of park topography, and that while I hinted at a more recondite significance, in the possible appeal of a hospitable landscape to the simplest instincts of our race, I also described this quality of hospitality to consist in conditions which make the ground appear pleasant to wander over. Among such conditions, one will be the absence of anything which should cause severe exertion to the wanderer and another the presence of opportunities for agreeable rest at convenient intervals. Together these conditions imply general openness & simplicity with occasional shelter and shade, which latter will result both from trees and from graceful undulations of the surface.

Bearing in mind this deduced significance of the term hospitable as descriptive of the general character of a park topography, you will see that the more unlimited the degree of hospitality of landscape, the more unmeasured the welcome which the broad face of your park can be made to express, the better will your purpose be fulfilled, and that it follows that all absolute limits should be so screened from view by trees that the imagination will be likely to assume no limit, but only acknowledge obscurity in whatever direction the eye may rove. As, however, to comply with the conditions previously established, the range of clear vision must be constantly limited in most directions, it is desireable that there should be an occasional opportunity of looking upon a view over turf and between trees so extended that even obscurity, that is to say uncertainty of extent, to the hospitable elements of the topography, shall be impossible.

I trust you recognize the paramount importance of these purposes of trees, because ignorance of them or forgetfulness of them or the subordination of them to other purposes of trees is a besetting sin of most planters.

In subordination to them, strictly, strenuously, always & every where within a park, in subordination to them, trees are to be regarded as individuals, and as component parts of groups, which groups are again to be regarded both individually, and in relation one to another as components of landscapes as seen from special points of view.

I hope that you will see that I am not studying a mere word

all this time. I want you to see that when people ask for a park, it may be perfectly possible to please them very much with something which is not a park or which is a very poor and much adulterated kind of park and that it would nevertheless be dishonest, quackish, to do so. A park is a work of art, designed to produce certain effects upon the mind of men. There should be nothing in it absolutely nothing—not a foot of surface nor a spear of grass—which does not represent study, design, a sagacious consideration & application of known laws of cause & effect with reference to that end.

A SUBURB FOR CHICAGO: SEPTEMBER 1868

Preliminary Report upon the Proposed Suburban Village at Riverside, near Chicago

110 Broadway, New York, Sept 1, 1868

To the Riverside Improvement Company.

Gentlemen:

You have requested a report from us, upon an enterprise which you desire to bring before the public, and which appears to rest on the following grounds:

First.—Owing partly to the low, flat, miry, and forlorn character of the greater part of the country immediately about Chicago, and the bleak surface, arid soil, and exposure of the remainder to occasional harsh and frigid gusts of wind off the lake, and partly to the fact that the rapidity with which the town is being enlarged, causes all the available environs to be laid out with a view to a future demand solely for town purposes, and with no regard to the satisfaction of rural tastes, the city, as yet, has no true suburbs or quarters in which urban and rural advantages are agreeably combined with any prospect of long continuance.

Second.—If, under these circumstances, sites offering any very decided and permanent advantages for suburban residences could be put in the market, there would at once be a demand for them, which would continue and increase with the enlargement and progress in wealth and taste of the population of the city.

Third.—You have secured a large body of land, which, much beyond any other, has natural advantages for this purpose.

Fourth.—If, by a large outlay, these advantages could be developed to the utmost, and could be supplemented by abundant artificial conveniences of a high order, and the locality could thus be rendered not only very greatly superior to any other near Chicago, but could be made to compare satisfactorily, on the whole, with the most favored suburbs to be found anywhere else, a good return for such outlay might reasonably be expected.

We propose to review these grounds so far as they are not matters of fact easily put to the test of observation by those interested.

To understand the character of the probable demand for semi-rural residences near Chicago, it must be considered that the most prominent characteristic of the present period of civilization has been the strong tendency of people to flock together in great towns. This tendency unquestionably is concurrent, and probably identical, with an equally unprecedented movement of invention, energy, and skill, toward the production of certain classes of conveniencies and luxuries, which, even yet, can generally be fully enjoyed by great numbers of people only in large towns. Arrangements for the easy gratification of certain tastes, which, until recently, were possessed by but a very few, even of the most wealthy class of any country, have consequently, of late, become common to thousands in every civilized land, while numerous luxuries, that the largest fortunes in the old world could not have commanded even half a century since, are enjoyed by families of comparatively moderate means, in towns which have sprung up from the wilderness, within the memory of some still living in them.

Progress in this way was never more rapid than at the present moment, yet in respect to the corresponding movement of populations, there are symptoms of a change; a counter-tide of migration, especially affecting the more intelligent and more fortunate classes, although as yet of but moderate strength, is clearly perceptible, and almost equally so, in Paris, London, Vienna, Berlin, New York, Boston and Philadelphia. The most substantial manifestation of it perhaps, is to be found in the vast increase in value of eligible sites for dwellings near public parks, and in all localities of much natural beauty within several hours' journey of every great town. Another evidence of the same tendency, not less conclusive because it indicates an impulse as yet undecided and incomplete, is found in the constant modification which has occurred in the manner of laying out all growing towns, and which is invariably in the direction of a separation of business and dwelling streets, and toward rural spaciousness in the latter. The broader the streets are made, provided they are well prepared in respect to what are significantly designated "the modern conveniences," and especially if some slight rural element is connected with them, as by rows of trees or little enclosures of turf and foliage, the greater is the demand for dwelling-places upon them.

There is no evidence that the large class of conveniences, comforts and luxuries, which have been heretofore gained by close congregation, is beginning to have less positive attractiveness or commercial value, but it is very clear that the conviction is becoming established in the minds of great numbers of people that the advance in this respect, which has occurred in towns, has been made at too great a sacrifice of certain advantages which can at present be only enjoyed by going out of them. That this is a sound conviction, and not a mere whim, caprice, or reaction of fancy, temporarily affecting the rich, fashionable and frivolous, appears from the fact that it is universally held as the result of careful study by philanthropists, physicians and men of science. It is an established conclusion, for instance, as explained by Dr. Rumsey, in his recent annual address before the British Association for the Advancement of Social Science, that the mere proximity of dwellings which characterizes all strictly urban neighborhoods, is a prolific source of morbid conditions of the body and mind, manifesting themselves chiefly in nervous feebleness or irritability and various functional derangements, relief or exemption from which can be obtained in no way without great sacrifices of convenience and social advantages, except by removal to suburban districts.

It thus becomes evident that the present outward tendency of town populations is not so much an ebb as a higher rise of the same flood, the end of which must be, not a sacrifice of urban conveniences, but their combination with the special charms and substantial advantages of rural conditions of life. Hence a series of neighborhoods of a peculiar character is already growing up in close relation with all large towns, and though many of these are as yet little better than rude overdressed villages, or fragmentary half-made towns, it can hardly be questioned that, already, there are to be found among them the most attractive, the most refined and the most soundly wholesome forms of domestic life, and the best application of the arts of civilization to which mankind has yet attained.

It would appear then, that the demands of suburban life, with reference to civilized refinement, are not to be a retrogression from, but an advance upon, those which are characteristic of town life, and that no great town can long exist without great suburbs. It would also appear that whatever element of convenient residence is demanded in a town will soon be demanded in a suburb, so far as is possible for it to be associated with the conditions which are the peculiar advantage of the country, such as purity of air, umbrageousness, facilities for quiet out-of-door recreation and distance from the jar, noise, confusion, and bustle of commercial thoroughfares.

There need then be no fear that a happy combination of these conditions would ever fail to be exceedingly attractive to the people of Chicago, or that a demand for residences where it is found, would be liable to decline; on the contrary, it would be as sure to increase, as the city is sure to increase in population and in wealth, and for the same reason.

We proceed to consider the intrinsic value of your property for the purpose in view.

The question of access first demands attention. The centre of the proposed suburb is nine miles from the business centre of Chicago, the nearer points being about six miles apart. There is a double-track railroad from Chicago of remarkably good construction, with its first out-of-town station, at which every train is required to stop in the midst of your property. The advantages of the locality, in this respect, are already superior to those of many thriving suburbs.

A railroad, however, at the best affords a very inadequate and unsatisfactory means of communication between a rural habitation and a town, either for a family or for a man of business:

as, moreover, one of the chief advantages of a suburban home, is the opportunity which it gives of taking air and exercise in driving, riding, and walking, it is a great desideratum, especially where time is so valuable as it is generally in Chicago, that a business man should be able to enjoy such an opportunity incidentally to his necessary communication with his store or office.

We find that the surface of the country over which a drive must be taken to reach your property, examined with reference to this requirement, is like the country generally about Chicago, not merely uninteresting, but, during much of the year, positively dreary. Driving across it, at present, so far from being a diversion or matter of pleasure, is a tedious task. Being nearly a dead flat, its natural drainage is very bad, parts of it are marshy, and the whole, after storms, is miry, and remains for a long time half covered with broad mud-puddles. Since railroads were established, the intercourse between the town and country, in this direction, by ordinary-wheeled vehicles, has been so slight that the old roads, which were never tolerably well-made, are scarcely kept in sufficiently good order to be traveled safely, even by very strong and heavy wagons. In their best condition they are extremely rough, and require slow and cautious driving, while in the Spring they are sometimes quite impassible.

It is obvious that no ordinary arrangement will suffice to make a rapid drive in a light carriage, or a canter on horseback, over this region, one that can be daily taken with pleasure throughout the year, or to prevent the attempt to secure exercise and recreation in this way from becoming an intolerably tedious effort on the part of any suburban resident who wishes to attend to business in town.

It is clearly essential to your success that these objections should be removed; we, therefore, take the first serious problem of your enterprise to be—

How can the present difficulties of carriage access be overcome?

We find that drainage, not only for a road, but for the whole district through which it would pass, can be obtained by forming a series of large conduits a few miles in length, and that the neighboring land-owners are fully prepared to cooperate with you in thus removing the chief obstacle to a good road.

We find, that in such small portions of the land, through

which a direct road would pass, as have already been artificially drained, trees, several years planted, of the most valuable species for suburban purposes, are growing with great vigor and beauty.

We also find that upon the property which you have already secured at the end of the route, there are ledges of rock which will afford the means of forming a substantial foundation for frost-proof and water-proof wheel-ways, and beds of gravel for their superstructure.

On reviewing these conditions we conclude that the formation of an approach road, much better adapted to the requirements of pleasure-driving than any other leading out of Chicago, and with varied and agreeable accessories and appurtenances, is perfectly practicable.

We should advise you, in the first place, to obtain possession, if possible, of a strip of ground from two hundred to six hundred feet wide, extending from the city to the nearest border of your property, to secure its thorough drainage, to plant it with trees, and to carry through it a series of separate, but adjoining ways, especially adapted in construction—first for walking, second for riding, third for pleasure-driving, and fourth to give convenient access to houses to be built on the route and accommodate heavy freighting, without inconvenience to the through pleasure travel.

The main drive should be constructed in a very thorough and finished manner, so that, without perfect rigidity of surface, it will be storm and frost-proof.

The ride should adjoin the drive, so that equestrians can at pleasure turn from it to converse with friends in carriages; it should have a soft and slightly yielding surface, that the great jar and danger of slipping, which occurs in a paved road, may be avoided.

The grateful influences of the grove extending through the prairie, with the amelioration of climate and soil which would result from thorough drainage and wind-breaks, and the advantages which would be found in the several proposed means of communication at all seasons of the year, would be such that continuous lines of villas and gardens would undoubtedly soon be established adjoining it, and the hour's drive through it, necessary to reach your property, would be neither tedious nor fatiguing.

At certain intervals upon the route, it would be desirable to provide openings with some special decorations, and here should be sheltered seats and watering places.

We see no reason why, if this suggestion is carried out liberally, it should not provide, or, at least, begin to provide, another pressing desideratum of the city of Chicago, namely, a general promenade ground. The promenade is a social custom of great importance in all the large towns of Europe. It is an open-air gathering for the purpose of easy, friendly, unceremonious greetings, for the enjoyment of change of scene, of cheerful and exhilarating sights and sounds, and of various good cheer, to which the people of a town, of all classes, harmoniously resort on equal terms, as to a common property. There is probably no custom which so manifestly displays the advantages of a Christian, civilized and democratic community, in contra-distinction from an aggregation of families, clans, sects, or castes. There is none more favorable to a healthy civic pride, civic virtue, and civic prosperity. As yet, the promenade has hardly begun to be recognised as an institution in Chicago, but there is no doubt that it soon must be, and it is evident from the present habits and manners of the people, that when once established, the custom will nowhere else be more popular or beneficent in its influence. Even now, with no tolerable accommodations for a general out-of-door pleasure gathering, nor any drives adapted for pleasure vehicles, which are not crowded when a few hundred carriages come together, there are probably more horses, in proportion to the population, kept for pleasure use, than in any city of the old, if not of the new world. There is understood to be no ground about the city possessing natural advantages for the formation of a public pleasure-ground of the character of the great parks in which the promenades of other metropolitan cities are generally held. By making the accommodations of your approach sufficiently large and sufficiently attractive, by associating with it several turning-points and resting-places in the midst of pleasure-grounds of moderate extent, your enterprise would, therefore, not merely supply Chicago, as you propose that it shall do, with a suburb, as well adapted as any of the suburbs of other cities, both for permanent habitations and country seats, and for occasional rural fetes and holiday recreations of families living in the town, but, in all probability, would provide it also with a permanent promenade-ground, having a character peculiar to itself, and not without special advantages. This result would be greatly enhanced if, as would probably be the case, certain entirely practicable improvements of the plan of the city should be made in connection with the construction of your approach.

The benefit which would result from this to your original enterprise is evident. Having means of communication with the city through the midst of such a ground, made gay and interesting by the movement of fine horses and carriages, and of numbers of well-dressed people, mainly cheerful with the enjoyment of recreation and the common entertainment, the distance would not be too great for the interchange of friendly visits, for the exercise of hospitality to a large circle of acquaintance, or for the enjoyment of the essential, intellectual, artistic, and social privileges which specially pertain to a metropolitan condition of society; and yet it would be sufficient to justify a neglect, on the part of a suburban resident, of most of those ceremonial social duties which custom seems to require, and in which so much time is necessarily spent in all great towns.

Turning next to your present property, we find that it extends for a distance of two miles upon the banks of the Aux Plaines River. Upon the river side, the land has a somewhat higher elevation than at any point nearer Chicago; the unctuous character of the prairie soil is also somewhat modified, and for considerable spaces wholly disappears. Sandy ridges extend along the river border, but from the richer vegetation which is indigenous to them, it would appear that they are not of the same character as the barren wastes nearer the lake. We were informed that there were deep beds of clay upon the property; but wherever we happened to test the subsoil, as we did at several points, we found a porous stratum at no very great distance from the surface. We observed that the ground dried more rapidly, and that there was less chill from evaporation on the surface toward nightfall, near the river, than on any part of the prairies at a considerable distance from it. We nowhere found, even among the bushes near the water, on a warm August evening, any mosquitoes or lake flies, though both were at the time annoying the people of Chicago. We were assured by residents of the neighborhood that they were never annoyed by them, and also that no fever and ague, or other malarial disease had been known for years in the vicinity. We have since seen an old physician of the neighborhood who states, that among the earlier settlers, fever and ague was not uncommon, but gradually became so, and latterly has been very rare.

The more elevated parts of the ground, and the banks of the river everywhere, are occupied by groves of trees consisting of oaks, elms, hickories, walnuts, limes and ashes, with a scattered undergrowth of hazels, and various shrubs; most of the trees are young, but there are many specimens of large size and umbrageous form. In a private garden, planted apparently eight or ten years since, there are a number of transplanted shrubs, evergreens, and choice herbaceous plants in perfect health, and growing with such luxuriance as to indicate satisfactory conditions of soil and climate.

The water of the river is said to be ordinarily very clear, and we found it tolerably so after a heavy rain, which is remarkable in a prairie stream. It abounds with fish and wild fowl, is adapted to pleasure-boating, and can be improved in this respect. In parts, it already presents much beauty, and is everywhere susceptible of being refined and enriched by art to a degree which will render it altogether charming.

It appears to us, on the whole, as the result of our survey, that no essential natural requirement of an attractive and healthful suburb is here wanting.

We proceed to consider the artificial requirements.

The chief advantages which a suburb can possess over a town on the one hand, and over a wilderness on the other, will consist in those which favor open-air recreation beyond the limits which economy and convenience prescribe for private grounds and gardens. The main artificial requirements of a suburb then, are good roads and walks, pleasant to the eye within themselves, and having at intervals pleasant openings and outlooks, with suggestions of refined domestic life, secluded, but not far removed from the life of the community.

The misfortune of most existing suburbs is, that in such parts of them as have been built up little by little, without any general plan, the highways are usually adapted only to serve the bare irresistible requirements of agriculture, and that in such other parts as have been laid out more methodically, no intelligent

design has been pursued to secure any distinctly rural attractiveness, the only aim apparently being to have a plan, which, seen
on paper, shall suggest the possibility of an extension of the
town-streets over the suburb, and of thus giving a town value
to the lots upon them.

Exactly the opposite of this should be aimed at in your case,
and, in regard to those special features whereby the town is
distinguished from the country, there should be the greatest
possible contrast which is compatible with the convenient communication and pleasant abode of a community; economy of
room, and facilities for business, being minor considerations.

In the highways, celerity will be of less importance than comfort and convenience of movement, and as the ordinary directness of line in town-streets, with its resultant regularity of plan,
would suggest eagerness to press forward, without looking to
the right hand or the left, we should recommend the general
adoption, in the design of your roads, of gracefully-curved
lines, generous spaces, and the absence of sharp corners, the
idea being to suggest and imply leisure, contemplativeness and
happy tranquility.

Without turf, and foliage, and birds, the character of the
highways, whatever their ground plan, would differ from those
of the town chiefly in the quality of desolation and dreariness.
Turf and trees should abound then, and this implies much space
in the highways, besides that which is requisite for the passage
of vehicles and people on foot.

The first requirement of convenience in a wheel-way or foot-
way is the absence from it of whatever would serve no clearly
good purpose in it, because whatever serves no good purpose
will obviously interfere with its primary object of offering a
route of easy locomotion. In other words, the first requirement is cleanliness and smoothness of surface. The fact that this
primary requirement is found in American suburban highways,
much less frequently, even, than in towns, notwithstanding the
apparent disadvantages of towns growing out of the greater
amount of travel which their highways have to sustain, shows
how difficult it must be to secure, and makes it our business to
enquire in what the difficulty consists.

The chief essential difference between town and suburban
highway arrangements comes from the fact that in the suburb

there is much greater space on an average between the houses fronting upon the roadways than in the town. This condition involves that of a larger frontage for each lot, and this again the condition that the cost of making a given length of the highways, and keeping them in order, must be distributed among a smaller number of persons; consequently, the assessments upon each lot owner must either be much heavier, or the highways must be of less expensive character, than those of the town. Invariably, the latter alternative is taken, not merely because a complete town-street arrangement would be to each man enormously expensive, but because it seems apparent that it would be unnecessarily expensive. A suburban village road, bordered by villas and cottages and their appropriate grounds, and not a thoroughfare of general commerce, is required to sustain not a tenth part of the wear and tear from travel of an ordinary town street. This being obvious to everyone, a proposition that each house should pay more than one-tenth as much for street expenses as is paid by each house for good town streets, would be generally thought preposterous. It might be so but for the fact that the chief wear and tear to be provided against in the construction of a good wheel-way is not that of travel, either light or heavy, pleasure or commercial, but that of water and frost, the amount of which to be resisted in a suburb is not materially less than in the densest part of a town. If sufficient arrangements are not made to guard against the action of these destructive agencies, country roads and village streets become sometimes quite impassible and useless, sometimes merely very inconvenient and uncomfortable to use, and most of them are, in fact, throughout the whole of the year, untidy, shabby, uninviting, and completely contradictory to the ideal which most townspeople have in view when they seek to find a pleasant site for a suburban home.

Worse than this, they not only go far to destroy the charm of the country to the eye, but they really nullify that which is its greatest value to people seeking to escape the confinement of the town. Our country-women and girls, instead of taking more exercise in the open air, educating their perceptive faculties by a variety of observation of natural objects, and cultivating a true taste for the beautiful by familiar converse with the greatest and best of masters, are far more confined in their habits by the walls of their dwelling, than their town sisters, and mainly because they have been obliged to train and adapt themselves during a large part of the year to an avoidance of the annoyances and fatigue of going out.

These facts are perfectly familiar to every intelligent man, and yet, as we have already intimated, it is extremely rare to find an American village or suburb in which the highways can be driven through in the spring or early summer with light-pleasure vehicles, or walked through by women and children at any time, without absolute discomfort.

We find, then, that frost-proof, rain-proof wheelways and footways, let them cost what they will, should, in selecting the site of a suburban residence, be the first consideration; in planning a suburb, the first requirement to provide for. The important question then is—What is the least expensive way of providing for it?

The destructive power of storms can only be guarded against by means which will take the water away from the surface of the highways before it can form streams by which they will be worn and gullied. In most of our villages, the only means commonly employed for this purpose is that of open ditches with outlets at distant points upon natural water courses. These open ditches, at frequent intervals, become obstructed, and overflow upon the wheelway and roadsides, or they are washed into ugly gullies which must often be leaped over or waded through by people walking out, or must be bridged. They must be bridged in any case whenever it is desired to approach any nearer to a house with a carriage than the roadway itself. The covered channels thus formed are generally so small and so easily obstructed, that pools, mire-holes or gullies, across the wheelway, are usually found near them.

Pleasing exceptions to the general rule may undoubtedly be found; they usually occur in villages which are either situated on a ridge from which the water, even of heavy storms, escapes by a multitude of slight lateral depressions, so easily as not to injure the turf which has overgrown them, or upon very open sandy soils and subsoils which, except on very rare occasions, drink up the rain nearly as fast as it falls, or where both these conditions are found together.

In every such case, the water of storms is quickly and quietly removed from the surface before it has had time to form streams of strength sufficient, even when their force is increased by the concentration caused by obstructions, to form the slightest gullies.

Under ordinary circumstances, however, this can only happen upon a highway when essentially the same means are used as in well-constructed city streets, that is to say, when there are frequent outlets provided for water, connecting with underground channels, secured against the accumulation of drift-stuff by subterranean silt-basins and surface-gratings.

However expensive it is, in nearly all cases an arrangement of this kind must be considered absolutely indispensable to the maintenance of a decent and convenient country road. It must simply be a chief object, if we desire it to have a quiet rural character, to avoid anything like the ordinary high curb of the town streets, and to make the gutter as shallow and inconspicuous as, with frequent gratings, it can be, and yet be safe to accomplish the required duty.

The turf of the road-side will be cut up and destroyed if driven over when water-soaked by loaded wagons, and this it certainly will be if the proper wheelway is allowed to become miry or excessively rough. It is sure to be so when the frost comes out in the spring, if at no other time, if it is either an ordinary earth road, or a road formed by a deposit of six or eight inches in depth of gravel, or of Macadam metal, upon a substratum of earth liable to be surcharged with water. Frost, in fact, is the chief enemy of convenience and of comfort, as well as of neatness and rural prettiness in all our high roads, and the only way by which, after ceaseless experiments, it has been found possible to offer any effectual resistance to its attack, is by means of a firm, deep, solid pavement, placed upon a thoroughly-drained foundation.

A structure of this kind, as ordinarily seen, however, encounters two very strong objections. First, it is decidedly expensive; second, it is rigid, hard, jarring, noisy, hot, and fatiguing to man and horse, and discordant with the rural sentiment which should rule in a suburb. The latter class of objections can be in a great degree overcome by placing the pavement itself at a sufficient depth, and forming a surface wheelway of several layers of finely broken stone, or what amounts to the same thing, of good gravel, made so compact by heavy pressure as to be essentially waterproof. The first objection cannot be removed. A road suitable for pleasure-driving is one of the greatest common luxuries a civilized community can possess, but it is, when compared with our common, pioneer, earth teaming-ways, unavoidably an expensive luxury.

Reviewing what we have said of suburban roads, it will be evident that the two following conditions, among others, are required in their surface plan: first, they must have considerably greater breadth than is necessary merely for wheeling and walking-ways; second, wheels must be kept to the wheelways. It follows that the front line of lots, and consequently that the roadside houses, must be placed at much greater distance from the wheelways than is usual or necessary in our city streets. This, as far both as general rural effect and domestic seclusion is concerned, gives a clear advantage, against which, experience will simply place the greater inconvenience of communication between the carriage-way and the house-door.

There is but one remedy for this inconvenience which will not be destructive of neatness and good order in the road, and that is the adoption of private roads leading into the house lots.

It should here be considered that there is nothing in all the expensive constructions which have been prescribed as the necessary foundation work of a satisfactory suburban highway, that would attract as much attention as the rude and inefficient appointments ordinarily seen. There is nothing town-like about them, narrow strips of clean gravel, with other strips of undulating turf from the higher parts of which trees would spring, are all that would appear of them above ground. But all that can be said of this arrangement is that it is inoffensive; it is convenient and tidy, nothing more. Line a highway, so formed, with coal-yards, breweries, forges, warehouses, soap-works, shambles, and shanties, and there certainly would be nothing charming about it. Line it with ill-proportioned, vilely-colored, shabby-genteel dwelling-houses, pushing their gables or eaveboards impertinently over the sidewalk as if for the advertising of domestic infelicity and eagerness for public sympathy, and it would be anything but attractive to people of taste and refinement. Line it again with high dead-walls, as of a series of private mad houses, as is done in some English suburbs, and it will be more repulsive to many than the window-lighted walls of the town blocks. Nothing of this kind is wanted in a suburb or a rural village. Nothing of this kind must be permitted if we would have it wholly satisfactory. On the contrary, we must secure something very different.

We cannot judiciously attempt to control the form of the houses which men shall build, we can only, at most, take care that if they build very ugly and inappropriate houses, they shall not be allowed to force them disagreeably upon our attention when we desire to pass along the road upon which they stand. We can require that no house shall be built within a certain number of feet of the highway, and we can insist that each house-holder shall maintain one or two living trees between his house and his highway-line.

A few simple precautions of this kind, added to a tasteful and convenient disposition of shade trees, and other planting along the road-sides and public places, will, in a few years, cause the whole locality, no matter how far the plan may be extended, to possess, not only the attraction of neatness and convenience, and the charm of refined sylvan beauty and grateful umbrageousness, but an aspect of secluded peacefulness and tranquility more general and pervading than can possibly be found in suburbs which have grown up in a desultory hap-hazard way. If the general plan of such a suburb is properly designed on the principles which have been suggested, its character will inevitably also, notwithstanding its tidiness, be not only informal, but, in a moderate way, positively picturesque, and when contrasted with the constantly repeated right angles, straight lines, and flat surfaces which characterize our large modern towns, thoroughly refreshing.

We have thus far addressed ourselves mainly to questions of construction, because in them the difficulties of your undertaking will be chiefly found. If you can afford to construct wheel-ways and drainage-ways, such as we have described, there is but little more difficulty or expense in laying them out, and decorating them in such a manner as will increase the more important natural attractions which we have shown the site to possess, than in making straight streets in the ordinary way without the slightest respect for nature.

The suggestion that your property might be formed into a "park," most of the land within which might be divided by lines, mainly imaginary, into building lots, and sold as demand should require, has been publicly made with apparent confidence in its feasibility and advantage, and as it seems to have attractions, we shall endeavor to show why we cannot advise you to adopt it.

The landscape character of a park, or of any ground to which that term is applied with strict propriety, is that of an idealized, broad stretch of pasture, offering in its fair, sloping surfaces, dressed with fine, close herbage, its ready alternatives of shade with sunny spaces, and its still waters of easy approach, attractive promises in every direction, and, consequently, invitations to movement on all sides, go through it where one may. Thus the essential qualification of a park is *range*, and to the emphasizing of the idea of range in a park, buildings and all artificial constructions should be subordinated.

But the essential qualification of a suburb is domesticity, and to the emphasizing of the idea of habitation, all that favors movement should be subordinated. Thus the two ideals are not likely to be successfully followed on the same ground. One or the other should be abandoned wholly. The greater part of your Riverside property has hardly any specially good conditions for a park, while it has many for a suburb.

There are two aspects of suburban habitation that need to be considered to ensure success; first, that of the domiciliation of men by families, each family being well provided for in regard to its domestic in-door and out-door private life; second, that of the harmonious association and co-operation of men in a community, and the intimate relationship and constant intercourse, and inter-dependence between families. Each has its charm, and the charm of both should be aided and acknowledged by all means in the general plan of every suburb.

As, however, it can be no part of a general plan to provide for the interior arrangements of ground which is to be private, the domestic advantages which a suburb will possess can be little more than suggested through the arrangement of the means of division, and of passage between private and public ground.

It is especially desirable, therefore, that these means of division and of passage should be carefully studied. They should be enjoyable in themselves; they should on no account be imaginary lines, nor should they be obscured or concealed, as it would be better that they should be if such divisions or means of restraint were unfortunately required for any reason in a park.

On the public side of all such dividing lines, the fact that the families dwelling within a suburb enjoy much in common, and all the more enjoy it because it is in common, the grand fact, in short, that they are christians, loving one another, and not Pagans, fearing one another, should be everywhere manifest in the completeness, and choiceness, and beauty of the means they possess of coming together, of being together, and especially of recreating and enjoying them together on common ground, and under common shades.

We should recommend the appropriation of some of the best of your property for public grounds, and that most of these should have the character of informal village-greens, commons and play-grounds, rather than of enclosed and defended parks or gardens. We would have, indeed, at frequent intervals in every road, an opening large enough for a natural group of trees, and often provide at such points croquet or ball grounds, sheltered seats and drinking fountains, or some other objects which would be of general interest or convenience to passers-by.

It will probably be best to increase the height of the mill-dam so as to enlarge the area of the public water suitable for boating and skating, and so as to completely cover some low, flat ground now exposed in low stages of the river. At the same time, a larger outlet should be provided to prevent floods above the dam from injuring the shore. A public drive and walk should be carried near the edge of the bank in such a way as to avoid destroying the more valuable trees growing upon it, and there should be pretty boat-landings, terraces, balconies overhanging the water, and pavilions at points desirable for observing regattas, mainly of rustic character, and to be half overgrown with vines.

All desirable improvements of this character, more and better than can be found in any existing suburb in the United States, can be easily supplied at comparatively small cost. That which it is of far more consequence to secure at the outset, and which cannot be obtained at small cost, unfortunately, is a system of public ways of thoroughly good construction.

As we have already shown, in speaking upon the question of approach, your property is not without special advantages for this purpose, and, on the whole, we feel warranted in expressing the opinion that your scheme, though it will necessarily require a large outlay of capital, is a perfectly practicable one, and if carried out would give Chicago a suburb of highly attractive and substantially excellent character.

It should be well understood that this is a preliminary report, and that our observations have been necessarily of a somewhat superficial character. A complete topographical survey, and a much more deliberate study of the conditions to be dealt with, must precede the preparation of a definite plan, if it is to have any assured value.

Respectfully,

OLMSTED, VAUX & CO.,
Landscape Architects

RURALIZING THE URBAN, URBANIZING THE RUSTIC:
OCTOBER 1869

To Edward Everett Hale

110 Broadway, N. York
21st Oct. 1869

Dear Mr Hale,

I have been reading and rereading your last book with great enjoyment & sometimes with real delight. It occurs to me that you will be interested to run your eyes over some of our professional reports and I herewith send you a lot, in all of which there is matter having more or less direct bearing upon the Sybaritic problem.

It was I believe a conviction of the importance of the general duty which you are urging upon the public that influenced the first steps of the course which has become my business. As I pursue my business as a business however, the laws of supply & demand compel me to work chiefly for the rich & to study rich men's wants, fashions and prejudices. I never lose an opportunity however, & sometimes, as you will see, force opportunity and strain patience even to urge principles, plans & measures tending to the ruralizing of *all* our urban population and the urbanizing of our rustic population. For I regard it as doubtful which of two slants toward savage condition is most to be deplored and to be struggled with, that which we see in the dense, poor quarters of our great cities & manufacturing towns or that which is impending over the scattered agricultural population of—more especially the more sterile parts of the great West.

Touching the plans of the reports, all that is essential of that advised in the close of the *Street Plans* pamphlet, has been adopted in Brooklyn, Buffalo and Chicago. About twenty miles of what we call *park-way* being provided for in these three cities. You will see that this means, if successful, the suburbanizing of the residence parts of large towns, elbow room about a house without going into the country, without sacrifice of butchers, bakers & theatres. I say provided for—nothing has been actually done on construction except upon the Riverside approach road, three miles of which is graded & half of all under contract. But the rest is now I believe all provided for by ordinance and the land has been acquired for the larger part by the cities interested. I expect before winter to contract eight or ten miles more.

The Riverside operation is going on and is the most interesting of all the undertakings we have been connected with. It is a regular flyaway speculation and is managed on Gold Exchange and Erie principles. We have had to commence legal proceedings twice to hold our own position as Superintendents in a satisfactory way, but we do so and have spent perhaps 150,000 dols in construction this year and the result appears to be satisfactory. That is to say the place is ten miles out of town, the R.R. Co as yet gives no special facilities or advantages but only promises in case of success to do so. Nothing is finished but since our roads & walks and few buildings have begun to show, the Company has sold a considerable number of sites at the rate of $20 pr front foot to men intending & more or less pledged to build—some beginning to do so this fall. The land when we began being farm land. Land adjoining of similar character has sold since we began for less than $100 pr acre, and any quantity, even better with regard to sanitary conditions, can now be had at less than $100 pr ac. within two miles on the same Rail Road. Success then cannot fail to give great stimulus to enterprises in the general direction of your purpose.

I have been long trying to get a Rosedale, for city working men, started, but tho' there is much talk of it by land speculators, it comes to nothing. We have looked at several sites proposed, but condemned them all—one for malaria, one for distance &c.

You will see by the Berkeley & Riverside reports that I favor fences, as apparently you do not. They are of great value as making emphatic the division of freehold property—the independence of the freeholder relatively to the public & to his neighbors. In the present stage of civilization, people are not in a healthy way who do not want to make the line between their own families & family belongings and others, a rather sharp—at least a well defined one, & the fence helps. Doing without does not seem to me to work well—i.e. I don't find it is satisfactory for a long time except to eccentrics.

The point I stand for is that no house is a fit place for a family that has not both public & *private outside apartments.* Consequently I am bound to regard the fence as a sort of outer wall of the house. I think that the want of fences, of distinct family separation out of the house, is the real cause of the ill-success or want of great success of Mr. Haskell's undertaking at Orange, Llewellyn Park. See page 12—Berkeley Neighborhood—page 26–27 Prelimy Report, Riverside.

Very Truly Yours,

                                    Fred. Law Olmsted

Public Parks and
the Enlargement of Towns *

The last "Overland Monthly" tells us that in California "only an inferior class of people can be induced to live out of towns. There is something in the country which repels men. In the city alone can they nourish the juices of life."

This of newly built and but half-equipped cities, where the people are never quite free from dread of earthquakes, and of a country in which the productions of agriculture and horticulture are more varied, and the rewards of rural enterprise larger, than in any other under civilized government! With a hundred million acres of arable and grazing land, with thousands of outcropping gold veins, with the finest forests in the world, fully half the white people live in towns, a quarter of all in one town, and this quarter pays more than half the taxes of all. "Over the mountains the miners," says Mr. Bowles, "talk of going to San Francisco as to Paradise, and the rural members of the Legislature declare that 'San Francisco sucks the life out of the country.'"

Nearer home the newspapers again tell us that twenty-five thousand men, to say nothing of women, are asking for work in Chicago; each of the great cities of the Mississippi region is reported to be increasing in population at a wonderful rate; gold and wheat are fast falling in their markets, but rents keep up, and it is complained that builders do not supply the demand for dwellings suited to the requirements of new-comers, who are chiefly men of small capital and young families, anxious to make a lodgment in the city on almost any conditions which will leave them a chance of earning a right to remain.

To this I can add, from personal observation, that if we stand, any day before noon, at the railway stations of these cities, we may notice women and girls arriving by the score, who, it will be apparent, have just run in to do a little shopping, intending

* A paper read before the American Social Science Association at the Lowell Institute, Boston, February 25, 1870.

to return by supper time to farms perhaps a hundred miles away. We shall observe trains advertised with special reference to the attendance of country people upon the evening entertainments of the town. Leaving the cars at some remote and lonely station, we may find a poster in its waiting-room, announcing matinée performances at a city theatre. If we push across the prairie, and call on a farmer who has been settled and doing well upon his land for twenty years, an intelligent and forehanded man, we shall hardly fail to see that very little remains to him or his family of what we formerly, and not very long ago, regarded as the most essential characteristics of rural life.

Formerly it was a matter of pride with the better sort of our country people that they could raise on their own land, and manufacture in their own household, almost everything needed for domestic consumption. Now their tables are furnished with all kinds of city delicacies. The housewife complains of her servants. There is no difficulty in getting them from the intelligence offices in town, such as they are; but only the poorest, who cannot find employment in the city, will come to the country, and these, as soon as they have got a few dollars ahead, are crazy to get back to town. It is much the same with the men, the farmer will add; he has to go up in the morning and find someone to take "Wolf's" place. You will find, too, that one of his sons is in a lawyer's office, another at a commercial college, and his oldest daughter at an "institute," all in town. I know several girls who travel eighty miles a day to attend school in Chicago. If under these circumstances the occupation of the country school-master, shoe-maker, and doctor, the country store-keeper, dress-maker and lawyer, is not actually gone, it must be that the business they have to do is much less relatively to the population about them than it used to be; not less in amount only, but less in importance. An inferior class of men will meet the requirements.

And how are things going here in Massachusetts? A correspondent of the "Springfield Republican" gave the other day an account of a visit lately made to two or three old agricultural neighborhoods, such as fifty years ago were the glory of New England. When he last knew them, their society was spoken of with pride, and the influence of not a few of their citizens was felt throughout the State, and indeed far beyond it. But as he found them now, they might almost be sung by Goldsmith. The meeting-house closed, the church dilapidated; the famous old taverns, stores, shops, mills, and offices dropping to pieces and vacant, or perhaps with a mere corner occupied by day laborers; but a third as many children as formerly to be seen in the schoolhouses, and of these less than half of American-born parents.

Walking through such a district last summer, my eyes were gladdened by a single house with exceptional signs of thrift in fresh paint, roofs, and fences, and newly planted door-yard trees; but happening as I passed to speak to the owner, in the second sentence of our conversation he told me that he had been slicking his place up in hopes that some city gentleman would take a fancy to it for a country seat. He was getting old, had worked hard, and felt as if the time had fully come when he was entitled to take some enjoyment of what remained to him of life by retiring to the town. Nearly all his old neighbors were gone; his children had left years ago. His town-bred grand-daughters were playing croquet in the front yard.

You know how it is here in Boston. Let us go on to the Old World. We read in our youth that among no other people were rural tastes so strong, and rural habits so fixed, as with those of Old England, and there is surely no other country where the rural life of the more fortunate classes compares so attractively with their town life. Yet in the "Transactions of the British Social Science Association," we find one debater asserting that there are now very few more persons living in the rural districts of England and Wales than there were fifty years ago; another referring to "the still increasing growth of our overgrown towns and the stationary or rather retrograding numbers of our rural population;"* while a third remarks that the social and educational advantages of the towns are drawing to them a large proportion of "the wealthy and independent," as well as all of the working classes not required for field labor.[†]

When I was last in England, the change that had occurred even in ten years could be perceived by a rapid traveler. Not only had the country gentleman and especially the country

* *Transactions*, 1864.
[†] *Transactions*, 1861.

gentlewoman of Irving departed wholly with all their following, but the very embers had been swept away of that manner
of life upon which, so little while ago, everything in England
seemed to be dependent. In all the country I found a smack of
the suburbs—hampers and packages from metropolitan tradesmen, and purveyors arriving by every train, and a constant communication kept up with town by penny-post and telegraph.

In the early part of the century, the continued growth of
London was talked of as something marvelous and fearful; but
where ten houses were then required to accommodate new
residents, there are now a hundred. The average rate at which
population increases in the six principal towns is twice as great
as in the country at large, including the hundreds of other flourishing towns. So also Glasgow has been growing six times faster
than all Scotland; and Dublin has held its own, while Ireland as
a whole has been losing ground.

Crossing to the Continent, we find Paris absorbing half of all
the increase of France in population; Berlin growing twice as
fast as all Prussia; Hamburg, Stettin, Stuttgart, Brussels, and a
score or two of other towns, all building out into the country at
a rate never before known, while many agricultural districts are
actually losing population. In Russia special provision is made in
the laws to regulate the gradual compensation of the nobles for
their losses by the emancipation of the serfs, to prevent the de-
population of certain parts of the country, which was in danger
of occurring from the eagerness of the peasantry to move into
the large towns.*

Going still further to the eastward, we may find a people to
whom the movement has not thus far been communicated;
but it is only where obscurity affords the best hope of safety
from oppression, where men number their women with their
horses, and where labor-saving inventions are as inventions of
the enemy.

Of the fact of the general townward movement of the civilized world, and its comprehensiveness, there can be no doubt.
There is a difference of opinion apparently as to its causes and
as to the probability of its continuance, for we hear anticipations
of a reaction expressed. I see no grounds for them. It appears

* *Nation*, vol. x. p. 161.

to me to look much more as if what we had thus far witnessed was but the beginning. I do not propose to go to the root of the matter; it is sufficient for our purpose to point out that the strength of the movement at any point seems to correspond closely with the degree in which the habits of the people have been recently changed by the abolition of feudalism, slavery, and government by divine right; by the multiplication and cheapening of schools, newspapers, and books; and by the introduction of labor-saving arrangements, especially of that class which are only available at all where they can be used to the direct benefit of many, such as railroads and telegraphs.

Consider that the standard of education is still advancing. There is yet no halt in the onward march of liberty of thought; telegraph stations are multiplying, new railroads are building, and the working capacity of old ones is increasing. Consider what we have been doing in our own country. Our public lands have been divided in square plats, so as to discourage the closer agricultural settlement which long and narrow divisions favor. We have given away the pick of them under a plan well adapted to induce a scattering settlement for a time, but also calculated to encourage waste of resources. We have no longer the best to offer.

Again, we have said to the world, "Here are countless deposits of the precious metals, scattered about over many millions of acres of wild land. We will give them away as fast as they can be found. First come, first served. Disperse then, and look for them." In spite of this policy, we find that the rate of increase of our principal towns is even now greater than that of the country.

But the same cause has also had the effect of giving us, for a time, great command of ready money and easy credit, and we have thus been induced to spend an immense sum—say two thousand millions—in providing ourselves with the fixtures and machinery of our railroad system. This system, while encouraging the greater dispersion of our food-producers, has tended most of all to render them, as we have seen, independent of all the old neighborhood agencies of demand and supply, manufacture and exchange, and to educate them and their children in familiarity with and dependence on the conveniences and habits of towns-people.

We all recognize that the tastes and dispositions of women are more and more potent in shaping the course of civilized progress, and again we must acknowledge that women are even more susceptible to this townward drift than men. Ofttimes the husband and father gives up his country occupations, taking others less attractive to him in town, out of consideration for his wife and daughters. Not long since I conveyed to a very sensible and provident man what I thought to be an offer of great preferment. I was surprised that he hesitated to accept it, until the question was referred to his wife, a bright, tidy American-born woman, who promptly said: "If I were offered a deed of the best farm that I ever saw, on condition of going back to the country to live, I would not take it. I would rather face starvation in town." She had been brought up and lived the greater part of her life in one of the most convenient and agreeable farming countries in the United States. Few have lived long in the city without having experiences of a similar feeling. Is it astonishing? Compare advantages in respect simply to schools, libraries, music and the fine arts. People of the greatest wealth can hardly command as much of these in the country as the poorest work-girl is offered here in Boston at the mere cost of a walk for a short distance over a good, firm, clean pathway, lighted at night and made interesting to her by shop fronts and the variety of people passing.

It is true the poorer work-girls make little use of these special advantages, but this simply because they are not yet educated up to them. When, however, they come from the country to town, are they not moving in the way of this education? In all probability, as is indicated by the report (in the "New York Tribune") of a recent skillful examination of the condition and habits of the poor sewing women of that city, a frantic desire to escape from the dull lives which they have seen before them in the country, a craving for recreation, especially for more companionship in yielding to playful girlish impulses, innocent in themselves, drives more young women to the town than anything else. Dr. Holmes may exaggerate the clumsiness and dreariness of New England village social parties; but go further back into the country among the outlying farms, and if you have ever had part in the working up of some of the rare occasions in which what stands for festivity is attempted, you will hardly think that the ardent desire of a young woman to escape to the town is wholly unreasonable.

The civilized woman is above all things a tidy woman. She enjoys being surrounded by bright and gay things perhaps not less than the savage, but she shrinks from draggling, smirching, fouling things and "things out of keeping" more. By the keenness with which she avoids subjecting herself to annoyances of this class, indeed, we may judge the degree in which a woman has advanced in civilization. Think what a country road and roadside, and what the back yard of a farm-house, commonly is, in winter and spring-time; and what far-away farmers' gardens are in haying time, or most of them at any time. Think, again, how hard it is when you city people go into the country for a few weeks in summer, to keep your things in order, to get a thousand little things done which you regard as trifles when at home, how far you have to go, and with how much uncertainty, how much unaccustomed management you have to exercise. For the perfection and delicacy—the cleanness—with which any human want is provided for depends on the concentration of human ingenuity and skill upon that particular want. The greater the division of labor at any point, the greater the perfection with which all wants may be satisfied. Everywhere in the country the number and variety of workmen, not agricultural laborers, proportionately to the population, is lessening as the facility for reaching workmen in town is increasing. In one year we find fifty-four new divisions of trade added to the "London Directory."

Think of all these things, and you will possibly find yourself growing a little impatient of the common cant which assumes that the strong tendency of women to town life, even though it involves great privations and dangers, is a purely senseless, giddy, vain, frivolous, and degrading one.

The consideration which most influences this tendency of women in families, however, seems to be the amount of time and labor, and wear and tear of nerves and mind, which is saved to them by the organization of labor in those forms, more especially, by which the menial service of households is simplified and reduced. Consider, for instance, what is done (that in the country is not done at all or is done by each household for itself, and, if efficiently, with a wearing, constant effort of superintendence) by the butcher, baker, fishmonger, grocer, by the provision venders of all sorts, by the ice-man, dust-man, scavenger, by the postman, carrier, expressmen, and messengers, all serving you at your house when required; by the sewers, gutters, pavements, crossings, sidewalks, public conveyances, and gas and water works.

But here again there is every reason to suppose that what we see is but a foretaste of what is yet to come. Take the difference of demand upon invention in respect to cheap conveyance for example. We began experimentally with street railways twenty years ago. At present, in New York, one pair of horses serves to convey one hundred people, on an average, every day at a rate of fare about one fiftieth of the old hackney-coach rates, and the total number of fares collected annually is equal to that of the population of the United States. And yet thousands walk a number of miles every day because they cannot be seated in the cars. It is impossible to fix a limit to the amount of travel which really ample, convenient, and still cheap means of transportation for short distances would develop. Certain improvements have caused the whole number of people seeking conveyances in London to be doubled in the last five years, and yet the supply keeps nowhere near the demand.

See how rapidly we are really gaining and what we have to expect. Two recent inventions give us the means of reducing by a third, under favorable circumstances, the cost of good McAdam roads. There have been sixteen patents issued from one office for other new forms of perfectly smooth and nearly noiseless street pavement, some of which, after two or three years' trial, promise so well as to render it certain that some improvement will soon come by which more than one of the present special annoyances of town life will be abated. An improvement in our sewer system seems near at hand also, which will add considerably to the comparative advantages of a residence in towns, and especially the more open town suburbs.

Experiments indicate that it is feasible to send heated air through a town in pipes like water, and that it may be drawn upon, and the heat which is taken measured and paid for according to quantity required. Thus may come a great saving of fuel and trouble in a very difficult department of domestic economy. No one will think of applying such a system to farm-houses.

Again, it is plain that we have scarcely begun to turn to ac-count the advantages offered to towns-people in the electric telegraph; we really have not made a beginning with those of-fered in the pneumatic tube, though their substantial character has been demonstrated. By the use of these two instruments, a tradesman ten miles away on the other side of a town may be communicated with, and goods obtained from him by a house-keeper, as quickly and with as little personal inconvenience as now if he were in the next block. A single tube station for five hundred families, acoustic pipes for the transmission of orders to it from each house, with a carriers' service for local distribu-tion of packages, is all that is needed for this purpose.

As to the economy which comes by systematizing and con-centrating, by the application of a large apparatus, of processes which are otherwise conducted in a desultory way, wasteful of human strength, as by public laundries, bakeries, and kitchens, we are yet, in America, even in our larger cities, far behind many of the smaller towns of the Old World.

While in all these directions enterprise and the progress of invention are quite sure to add rapidly to the economy and convenience of town life, and thus increase its comparative at-tractions, in other directions every step tends to reduce the man-power required on the farms for the production of a given amount of the raw material of food. Such is the effect, for in-stance, of every improvement of apparatus or process in plough-ing, mowing, reaping, curing, thrashing, and marketing.

Another tendency arising from the improvement of agricul-tural apparatus, and which will be much accelerated when steam shall have been as successfully applied to tillage as it is already to harvesting and marketing operations, is that to the enlarge-ment of fields and of farms. From this will follow the reduction in number and the greater separation and greater isolation of rural homesteads; for with our long-fronted farms, it will be centuries before we can hope to have tolerable roads on which rapid steam travelling from farm to farm will be practicable, though we may be close upon it wherever hard, firm, and always smooth roads can be afforded.

It should be observed that possession of the various advantages of the town to which we have referred, and, indeed, of all the advantages which are peculiar to large towns, while it very certainly cannot be acquired by people living in houses a quarter or a half mile apart, does not, on the other hand, by any means involve an unhealthy density of population. Probably the advantages of civilization can be found illustrated and demonstrated under no other circumstances so completely as in some suburban neighborhoods where each family abode stands fifty or a hundred feet or more apart from all others, and at some distance from the public road. And it must be remembered, also, that man's enjoyment of rural beauty has clearly increased rather than diminished with his advance in civilization. There is no reason, except in the loss of time, the inconvenience, discomfort, and expense of our present arrangements for short travel, why suburban advantages should not be almost indefinitely extended. Let us have a cheap and enjoyable method of conveyance, and a building law like that of old Rome, and they surely will be.

As railroads are improved, all the important stations will become centres or sub-centres of towns, and all the minor stations suburbs. For most ordinary every-day purposes, especially house-keepers' purposes, these will need no very large population before they can obtain urban advantages. I have seen a settlement, the resident population of which was under three hundred, in which there was a public laundry, bath-house, barber's shop, billiard-room, beer-garden, and bakery. Fresh rolls and fresh milk were supplied to families before breakfast time every morning; fair fruit and succulent vegetables were delivered at house doors not half an hour after picking; and newspapers and magazines were distributed by a carrier. I have seen a town of not more than twelve hundred inhabitants, the streets and the yards, alleys, and places of which were swept every day as regularly as the house floors, and all dust removed by a public dust-man.

The construction of good roads and walks, the laying of sewer, water, and gas pipes, and the supplying of sufficiently cheap, rapid, and comfortable conveyances to town centres, is all that is necessary to give any farming land in a healthy and attractive situation the value of town lots. And whoever has observed in the French agricultural colonies how much more readily and cheaply railroads, telegraph, gas, water, sewer, and nearly all other advantages of towns may be made available to the whole population than under our present helter-skelter methods of settlement, will not believe that even the occupation of a farm laborer must necessarily and finally exclude his family from a very large share of urban conveniences.

But this opens a subject of speculation, which I am not now free to pursue. It is hardly a matter of speculation, I am disposed to think, but almost of demonstration, that the larger a town becomes because simply of its advantages for commercial purposes, the greater will be the convenience available to those who live in and near it for coöperation, as well with reference to the accumulation of wealth in the higher forms,—as in seats of learning, of science, and of art—as with reference to merely domestic economy and the emancipation of both men and women from petty, confining, and narrowing cares.

It also appears to be nearly certain that the recent rapid enlargement of towns and withdrawal of people from rural conditions of living is the result mainly of circumstances of a permanent character.

We have reason to believe, then, that towns which of late have been increasing rapidly on account of their commercial advantages, are likely to be still more attractive to population in the future; that there will in consequence soon be larger towns than any the world has yet known, and that the further progress of civilization is to depend mainly upon the influences by which men's minds and characters will be affected while living in large towns.

Now, knowing that the average length of the life of mankind in towns has been much less than in the country, and that the average amount of disease and misery and of vice and crime has been much greater in towns, this would be a very dark prospect for civilization, if it were not that modern Science has beyond all question determined many of the causes of the special evils by which men are afflicted in towns, and placed means in our hands for guarding against them. It has shown, for example, that under ordinary circumstances, in the interior parts of large and closely built towns, a given quantity of air contains considerably less of the elements which we require to receive through the lungs than the air of the country or even of the outer and more open parts of a town, and that instead of them it carries in to the lungs highly corrupt and irritating matters, the action of which tends strongly to vitiate all our sources of vigor—how strongly may perhaps be indicated in the shortest way by the statement that even metallic plates and statues corrode and wear away under the atmospheric influences which prevail in the midst of large towns, more rapidly than in the country.

The irritation and waste of the physical powers which result from the same cause, doubtless indirectly affect and very seriously affect the mind and the moral strength; but there is a general impression that a class of men are bred in towns whose peculiarities are not perhaps adequately accounted for in this way. We may understand these better if we consider that whenever we walk through the denser part of a town, to merely avoid collision with those we meet and pass upon the sidewalks, we have constantly to watch, to foresee, and to guard against their movements. This involves a consideration of their intentions, a calculation of their strength and weakness, which is not so much for their benefit as our own. Our minds are thus brought into close dealings with other minds without any friendly flowing toward them, but rather a drawing from them. Much of the intercourse between men when engaged in the pursuits of commerce has the same tendency—a tendency to regard others in a hard if not always hardening way. Each detail of observation and of the process of thought required in this kind of intercourse or contact of minds is so slight and so common in the experience of towns-people that they are seldom conscious of it. It certainly involves some expenditure nevertheless. People from the country are ever conscious of the effect on their nerves and minds of the street contact—often complaining that they feel confused by it; and if we had no relief from it at all during our waking hours, we should all be conscious of suffering from it. It is upon our opportunities of relief from it, therefore, that not only our comfort in town life, but our ability to maintain a temperate, good-natured, and healthy state of mind, depends. This is one of many ways in which it happens that men who have been brought up, as the saying is, in the streets, who have been the most directly and completely affected by town influences, so generally show, along with a remarkable quickness of apprehension, a peculiarly hard sort of selfishness. Every day of their lives they have seen thousands of their fellow-men, have met them face to face, have brushed against them, and yet have had no experience of anything in common with them.

It has happened several times within the last century, when old artificial obstructions to the spreading out of a city have been removed, and especially where there has been a demolition of and rebuilding on a new ground plan of some part which had previously been noted for the frequency of certain crimes, the prevalence of certain diseases, and the shortness of life among its inhabitants, that a marked improvement in all these respects has immediately followed, and has been maintained not alone in the dark parts, but in the city as a whole.

But although it has been demonstrated by such experiments that we have it in our power to greatly lessen and counteract the two classes of evils we have had under consideration, it must be remembered that these means are made use of only with great difficulty—how great, one or two illustrations from experience will enable us perhaps better to understand.

When the business quarter of New York was burnt over, thirty years ago, there was a rare opportunity for laying out a district expressly with a view to facilitate commerce. The old plan had been arrived at in a desultory way; and so far as it had been the result of design, it had been with reference more especially to the residence of a semi-rural population. This had long since passed away; its inconvenience for commercial purposes had been experienced for many years; no one supposed from the relation of the ground to the adjacent navigable waters that it would ever be required for other than commercial purposes. Yet the difficulties of equalizing benefits and damages among the various owners of the land prevented any considerable change of the old street lines. Every working day thousands of dollars are subtracted from the profits of business, by the disadvantages thus reëstablished. The annual loss amounts to millions.

Men of barbarous habits laid out a part of London in a way which a thousand years later was found to be a cause of immeasurable waste of life, strength, and property. There had been much talk, but no effective action, looking toward improvement, when the great fire came, and left every building a heap of ashes. Immediately upon this, while the fire was still burning, a great man, Sir Christopher Wren, prepared a plan for avoiding the old evils. This plan, a simple, excellent, and economical one, he took to the king, who at once approved it, took a strong interest in it, and used all his royal power to have it carried out. It was hailed with satisfaction by all wise and good men, and yet so difficult was it to overcome the difficulties entailed by the original rural laying out of the ground, that the attempt was finally abandoned, and the new city was built with immaterial modifications under the old barbarous plan; and so it remains with only slight improvement, and that purchased at enormous cost, to this day.

Remedy for a bad plan, once built upon, being thus impracticable, now that we understand the matter we are surely bound, wherever it is by any means in our power, to prevent mistakes in the construction of towns. Strange to say, however, here in the New World, where great towns by the hundred are springing into existence, no care at all is taken to avoid bad plans. The most brutal Pagans to whom we have sent our missionaries have never shown greater indifference to the sufferings of others than is exhibited in the plans of some of our most promising cities, for which men now living in them are responsible.

Not long since I was asked by the mayor of one of these to go before its common council and explain the advantages of certain suggested changes, including especially the widening of two roads leading out of town and as yet but partially opened and not at all built upon. After I had done so, two of the aldermen in succession came to me, and each privately said in effect: "It is quite plain that the proposition is a good one, and it ought to be adopted; the city would undoubtedly gain by it; but the people of the ward I represent have less interest in it than some others: they do not look far ahead, and they are jealous of those who would be more directly benefited than themselves; consequently I don't think that they would like it if I voted for it, and I shall not, but I hope it will be carried."

They were unwilling that even a stranger should have so poor an opinion of their own intelligence as to suppose that they did not see the advantage of the change proposed; but it was not even suggested to their minds that there might be something shameful in repudiating their obligations to serve, according to the best of their judgment, the general and permanent interests committed to them as legislators of the city.

It is evident that if we go on in this way, the progress of civilized mankind in health, virtue, and happiness will be seriously endangered.

It is practically certain that the Boston of to-day is the mere nucleus of the Boston that is to be. It is practically certain that it is to extend over many miles of country now thoroughly rural in character, in parts of which farmers are now laying out roads with a view to shortening the teaming distance between their wood lots and a railway station, being governed in their courses by old property lines, which were first run simply with reference to the equitable division of heritages, and in other parts of which, perhaps, some wild speculators are having streets staked off from plans which they have formed with a rule and pencil in a broker's office, with a view chiefly to the impressions they would make when seen by other speculators on a lithographed map. And by this manner of planning, unless views of duty or of interest prevail that are not yet common, if Boston continues to grow at its present rate even for but a few generations longer, and then simply holds its own until it shall be as old as the Boston in Lincolnshire now is, more men, women, and children are to be seriously affected in health and morals than are now living on this Continent.

Is this a small matter—a mere matter of taste; a sentimental speculation?

It must be within the observation of most of us that where, in the city, wheel-ways originally twenty feet wide were with great difficulty and cost enlarged to thirty, the present width is already less nearly adequate to the present business than the former was to the former business; obstructions are more frequent, movements are slower and oftener arrested, and the liability to collision is greater. The same is true of sidewalks. Trees thus have been cut down, porches, bow-windows, and other encroachments removed but every year the walk is less sufficient for the comfortable passing of those who wish to use it.

It is certain that as the distance from the interior to the circumference of towns shall increase with the enlargement of their population, the less sufficient relatively to the service to be performed will be any given space between buildings.

In like manner every evil to which men are specially liable when living in towns, is likely to be aggravated in the future, unless means are devised and adapted in advance to prevent it.

Let us proceed, then, to the question of means, and with a seriousness in some degree befitting a question, upon our dealing with which we know the misery or happiness of many millions of our fellow-beings will depend.

We will for the present set before our minds the two sources of wear and corruption which we have seen to be remediable and therefore preventive. We may admit that commerce requires that in some parts of a town there shall be an arrangement of buildings, and a character of streets and of traffic in them which will establish conditions of corruption and of irritation, physical and mental. But commerce does not require the same conditions to be maintained in all parts of a town.

Air is disinfected by sunlight and foliage. Foliage also acts mechanically to purify the air by screening it. Opportunity and inducement to escape at frequent intervals from the confined and vitiated air of the commercial quarter, and to supply the lungs with air screened and purified by trees, and recently acted upon by sunlight, together with the opportunity and inducement to escape from conditions requiring vigilance, wariness, and activity toward other men—if these could be supplied economically, our problem would be solved.

In the old days of walled towns all tradesmen lived under the roof of their shops, and their children and apprentices and servants sat together with them in the evening about the kitchen fire. But now that the dwelling is built by itself and there is greater room, the inmates have a parlor to spend their evenings in; they spread carpets on the floor to gain in quiet, and hang drapery in their windows and papers on their walls to gain in seclusion and beauty. Now that our towns are built without walls, and we can have all the room that we like, is there any good reason why we should not make some similar difference between parts which are likely to be dwelt in, and those which will be required exclusively for commerce?

Would trees, for seclusion and shade and beauty, be out of place, for instance, by the side of certain of our streets? It will, perhaps, appear to you that it is hardly necessary to ask such a question, as throughout the United States trees are commonly planted at the sides of streets. Unfortunately, they are seldom so planted as to have fairly settled the question of the desirableness of systematically maintaining trees under these circumstances.

In the first place, the streets are planned, wherever they are, essentially alike. Trees are planted in the space assigned for sidewalks, where at first, while they are saplings, and the vicinity is rural or suburban, they are not much in the way, but where, as they grow larger, and the vicinity becomes urban, they take up more and more space, while space is more and more required for passage. That is not all. Thousands and tens of thousands are planted every year in a manner and under conditions as nearly certain as possible either to kill them outright, or to so lessen their vitality as to prevent their natural and beautiful development, and to cause premature decrepitude. Often, too, as their lower limbs are found inconvenient, no space having been provided for trees in laying out the street, they are deformed by butcherly amputations. If by rare good fortune they are suffered to become beautiful, they still stand subject to be condemned to death at any time, as obstructions in the highway.*

What I would ask is, whether we might not with economy make special provision in some of our streets—in a twentieth or a fiftieth part, if you please, of all—for trees to remain as a permanent furniture of the city? I mean, to make a place for them in which they would have room to grow naturally and gracefully. Even if the distance between the houses should have to be made half as much again as it is required to be in our commercial streets, could not the space be afforded? Out of town space is not costly when measures to secure it are taken early. The assessments for benefit where such streets were provided for, would, in nearly all cases, defray the cost of the land required.

---

* On the border of the first street laid out in the oldest town in New England, there yet stands what has long been known as "the Town Tree," its trunk having served for generations as a publication post for official notices. "The selectmen," having last year removed the lower branches of all the younger roadside trees of the town, and thereby its chief beauty, have this year deliberately resolved that they would have this tree cut down, for no other reason, so far as appears in their official record, than that if two persons came carelessly together on the roadway side of it, one of them might chance to put his foot in the adjoining shallow street-gutter. It might cost ten dollars to deepen and bridge this gutter substantially. The call to arms for the Old French War, for the War of the Revolution, the war for the freedom of the seas, the Mexican War, and the War of the Rebellion, was first made in this town under the shade of this tree, which is an American elm, and, notwithstanding its great age, is perfectly healthy and almost as beautiful as it is venerable.

The strips of ground reserved for the trees, six, twelve, twenty feet wide, would cost nothing for paving or flagging.

The change both of scene and of air which would be obtained by people engaged for the most part in the necessarily confined interior commercial parts of the town, on passing into a street of this character after the trees had become stately and graceful, would be worth a good deal. If such streets were made still broader in some parts, with spacious malls, the advantage would be increased. If each of them were given the proper capacity, and laid out with laterals and connections in suitable directions to serve as a convenient trunk-line of communication between two large districts of the town or the business centre and the suburbs, a very great number of people might thus be placed every day under influences counteracting those with which we desire to contend.

These, however, would be merely very simple improvements upon arrangements which are in common use in every considerable town. Their advantages would be incidental to the general uses of streets as they are. But people are willing very often to seek recreation as well as take it by the way. Provisions may indeed be made expressly for recreation, with certainty that if convenient, they will be used.

The various kinds of recreation may be divided primarily under two heads. Under one will be included all of which the predominating influence is to stimulate exertion of any part or parts needing it; under the other, all which cause us to receive pleasure or benefit without conscious exertion. Games chiefly of mental skill, as chess, or athletic sports, as base-ball, are examples of means of recreation of the first division, which may be termed that of *exertive* recreation; music and the fine arts generally, of the second or *receptive* division.

Considering the first by itself, it will be found not a very simple matter to determine for what forms of exertive recreations opportunities can be provided in a large town, consistently with good order, safety, and economy of management. Mr. Anthony Trollope might recommend fox-hunting; hurdle-racing has been seriously urged by gentlemen who have given special attention to the advantages of that form of exercise. In New York, on the other hand, after several years' deliberation, and some experiments in a small way, it has been decided that the city cannot expediently undertake to provide grounds even for base-ball, cricket, and foot-ball clubs, to the great disappointment of a very large and influential element of the population.

I do not propose now to discuss the various details of this question, but to leave out of consideration all that class of pastimes which, except in the open country, cannot easily be pursued without danger to persons not taking part in them, and to adopt the conclusion that only school-boys should be provided at public expense with every-day grounds for ball-playing, and this as a part of the educational rather than the recreative system of the town. I will only remark that you will find no purposes of athletic recreation which cannot be accommodated either by such trunk roads as I have suggested we should here and there introduce, or by a sufficient number of comparatively small spaces of open ground, and that, although there are certain advantages more particularly to be gained by pursuing the forms of exertive recreation named on grounds of large rather than small area, it would be better on the whole to have a number of small grounds than to establish any very large ground with special reference to them.

Let us now proceed to the consideration of receptive recreations. As we shall consider such forms of recreation as are pursued socially or by a number of persons together, it will be convenient to again divide our subjects into sub-heads, according to the degree in which the average enjoyment of them is greatest when a large congregation of persons is assembled, or when the number coming together is small, and the circumstances favorable to the exercise of personal friendliness. Our pleasure in recreations of the first of these classes appears to me to be dependent upon the existence of an instinct in us of which I think not enough account is commonly made, and I shall therefore term it the *gregarious* class of social receptive recreations. The other will be sufficiently distinguished from it by the term *neighborly*.

Purely gregarious recreation seems to be generally looked upon in New England society as childish and savage, because, I suppose, there is so little of what we call intellectual gratification in it. We are inclined to engage in it indirectly, furtively, and with complication. Yet there are certain forms of recreation, a large share of the attraction of which must, I think, lie in the gratification of the gregarious inclination, and which, with those who can afford to indulge in them, are so popular as to establish their importance of the requirement.

If I ask myself where I have experienced the most complete gratification of this instinct in public and out of doors, among trees, I find that it has been in the promenade of the Champs Elysées. As closely following it I should name other promenades of Europe, and our own upon the New York parks. I have studiously watched the latter for several years. I have several times seen fifty thousand people participating in them; and the more I have seen of them, the more highly have I been led to estimate their value as means of counteracting the evils of town life.

Consider that the New York Park and the Brooklyn Park are the only places in those associated cities where, in this eighteen hundred and seventieth year after Christ, you will find a body of Christians coming together, and with an evident glee in the prospect of coming together, all classes largely represented, with a common purpose, not at all intellectual, competitive with none, disposing to jealousy and spiritual or intellectual pride toward none, each individual adding by his mere presence to the pleasure of all others, all helping to the greater happiness of each. You may thus often see vast numbers of persons brought closely together, poor and rich, young and old, Jew and Gentile. I have seen a hundred thousand thus congregated, and I assure you that though there have been not a few that seemed a little dazed, as if they did not quite understand it, and were, perhaps, a little ashamed of it, I have looked studiously but vainly among them for a single face completely unsympathetic with the prevailing expression of good nature and lightheartedness.

Is it doubtful that it does men good to come together in this way in pure air and under the light of heaven, or that it must have an influence directly counteractive to that of the ordinary hard, hustling working hours of town life?

You will agree with me, I am sure, that it is not, and that opportunity, convenient, attractive opportunity, for such congregation, is a very good thing to provide for, in planning the extension of a town.

I referred especially to the Champs Elysées, because the promenade there is a very old custom, not a fashion of the day, and because I must needs admit that this most striking example is one in which no large area of ground—nothing like a park—has been appropriated for the purpose. I must acknowledge, also, that the alamedas of Spain and Portugal supply another and very interesting instance of the same fact. You will observe, however, that small local grounds, such as we have said might be the best for most exertive recreations, are not at all adapted to receptive recreations of the type described.

One thing more under this head. I have but little personal familiarity with Boston customs; but I have lived or sojourned in several other towns of New England, as well as of other parts of the country. I have never been long in any one locality, south or north, east or west, without observing a *custom* of gregarious out-of-door recreation in some miserably imperfect form, usually covered by a wretched pretext of a wholly different purpose, as perhaps, for instance, visiting a grave-yard. I am sure that it would be much better, less expensive, less harmful in all ways, more health-giving to body, mind, and soul, if it were admitted to be a distinct requirement of all human beings, and appropriately provided for.

I have next to see what opportunities are wanted to induce people to engage in what I have termed neighborly receptive recreations, under conditions which shall be highly counteractive to the prevailing bias to degeneration and demoralization in large towns. To make clearer what I mean, I need an illustration which I find in a familiar domestic gathering, where the prattle of the children mingles with the easy conversation of the more sedate, the bodily requirements satisfied with good cheer, fresh air, agreeable light, moderate temperature, snug shelter, and furniture and decorations adapted to please the eye, without calling for profound admiration on the one hand, or tending to fatigue or disgust on the other. The circumstances are all favorable to a pleasurable wakefulness of the mind without stimulating exertion; and the close relation of family life, the association of children, of mothers, of lovers, or those who may be lovers, stimulate and keep alive the more tender sympathies, and give play to faculties such as may be dormant in business or on the promenade; while at the same time the cares of providing in detail for all the wants of the family, guidance, instruction, and reproof, and the dutiful reception of guidance, instruction, and reproof, are, as matters of conscious exertion, as far as possible laid aside.

There is an instinctive inclination to this social, neighborly, unexertive form of recreation among all of us. In one way or another it is sure to be constantly operating upon those millions on millions of men and women who are to pass their lives within a few miles of where we now stand. To what extent it shall operate so as to develop health and virtue, will, on many occasions, be simply a question of opportunity and inducement. And this question is one for the determination of which for a thousand years we here to-day are largely responsible.

Think what the ordinary state of things to many is at this beginning of the town. The public is reading just now a little book in which some of your streets of which you are not proud are described.* Go into one of those red cross streets any fine evening next summer, and ask how it is with their residents? Oftentimes you will see half a dozen sitting together on the doorsteps, or, all in a row, on the curb-stones, with their feet in the gutter, driven out of doors by the closeness within; mothers among them anxiously regarding their children who are dodging about at their play, among the noisy wheels on the pavement.

Again, consider how often you see young men in knots of perhaps half a dozen in lounging attitudes rudely obstructing the sidewalks, chiefly led in their little conversation by the suggestions given to their minds by what or whom they may see passing in the street, men, women, or children, whom they do not know, and for whom they have no respect or sympathy. There is nothing among them or about them which is adapted to bring into play a spark of admiration, of delicacy, manliness, or tenderness. You see them presently descend in search of physical comfort to a brilliantly lighted basement, where they find others of their sort, see, hear, smell, drink, and eat all manner of vile things.

Whether on the curb-stones or in the dram-shops, these young men are all under the influence of the same impulse which some satisfy about the tea-table with neighbors and wives and mothers and children, and all things clean and wholesome, softening and refining.

If the great city to arise here is to be laid out little by little, and chiefly to suit the views of land-owners, acting only

* *Sybaris*, by the Rev. E. E. Hale.

individually, and thinking only of how what they do is to affect the value in the next week or the next year of the few lots that each may hold at the time, the opportunities of so obeying this inclination as at the same time to give the lungs a bath of pure sunny air, to give the mind a suggestion of rest from the devouring eagerness and intellectual strife of town life, will always be few to any, to many will amount to nothing.

But is it possible to make public provision for recreation of this class, essentially domestic and secluded as it is?

It is a question which can, of course, be conclusively answered only from experience. And from experience in some slight degree I shall answer it. There is one large American town, in which it may happen that a man of any class shall say to his wife, when he is going out in the morning: "My dear, when the children come home from school, put some bread and butter and salad in a basket, and go to the spring under the chestnut-tree where we found the Johnsons last week. I will join you there as soon as I can get away from the office. We will walk to the dairy-man's cottage and get some tea, and some fresh milk for the children, and take our supper by the brook-side;" and this shall be no joke, but the most refreshing earnest.

There will be room enough in the Brooklyn Park, when it is finished, for several thousand little family and neighborly parties to bivouac at frequent intervals through the summer, without discommoding one another, or interfering with any other purpose, to say nothing of those who can be drawn out to make a day of it, as many thousand were last year. And although the arrangements for the purpose were yet very incomplete, and but little ground was at all prepared for such use, besides these small parties, consisting of one or two families, there came also, in companies of from thirty to a hundred and fifty, somewhere near twenty thousand children with their parents, Sunday-school teachers, or other guides and friends, who spent the best part of a day under the trees and on the turf, in recreations of which the predominating element was of this neighborly receptive class. Often they would bring a fiddle, flute, and harp, or other music. Tables, seats, shade, turf, swings, cool spring-water, and a pleasing rural prospect, stretching off half a mile or more each way, unbroken by a carriage road or the slightest evidence of the vicinity of the town, were supplied them without charge, and bread and milk and ice-cream at moderate fixed charges. In all my life I have never seen such joyous collections of people. I have, in fact, more than once observed tears of gratitude in the eyes of poor women, as they watched their children thus enjoying themselves.

The whole cost of such neighborly festivals, even when they include excursions by rail from the distant parts of the town, does not exceed for each person, on an average, a quarter of a dollar; and when the arrangements are complete, I see no reason why thousands should not come every day where hundreds come now to use them; and if so, who can measure the value, generation after generation, of such provisions for recreation to the overwrought, much-confined people of the great town that is to be?

For this purpose neither of the forms of ground we have heretofore considered are at all suitable. We want a ground to which people may easily go after their day's work is done, and where they may stroll for an hour, seeing, hearing, and feeling nothing of the bustle and jar of the streets, where they shall, in effect, find the city put far away from them. We want the greatest possible contrast with the streets and the shops and the rooms of the town which will be consistent with convenience and the preservation of good order and neatness. We want, especially, the greatest possible contrast with the restraining and confining conditions of the town, those conditions which compel us to walk circumspectly, watchfully, jealously, which compel us to look closely upon others without sympathy. Practically, what we most want is a simply, broad, open space of clean greensward, with sufficient play of surface and a sufficient number of trees about it to supply a variety of light and shade. This we want as a central feature. We want depth of wood enough about it not only for comfort in hot weather, but to completely shut out the city from our landscapes. These are the distinguishing elements of what is properly called a park.

There is no provision for recreation so valuable as this would be; there is none which will be so important to place judiciously in the plan of the city merely as a space, and as an interruption of direct communication between its different parts. There is nothing, therefore, for which we should be more anxious to find and early secure and hold in reserve a suitable site.

A Promenade may, with great advantage, be carried along the outer part of the surrounding groves of a park; and it will do no harm if here and there a broad opening among the trees discloses its open landscapes to those upon the promenade. But recollect that the object of the latter for the time being should be to see *congregated human life* under glorious and necessarily artificial conditions, and the natural landscape is not essential to them; though there is no more beautiful picture, and none can be more pleasing incidentally to the gregarious purpose, than that of beautiful meadows, over which clusters of level-armed sheltering trees cast broad shadows, and upon which are scattered dainty cows and flocks of black-faced sheep, while men, women, and children are seen sitting here and there forming groups in the shade, or moving in and out among the woody points and bays.

It may be inferred from what I have said, that very rugged ground, abrupt eminences, and what is technically called picturesque in distinction from merely beautiful or simply pleasing scenery, is not the most desirable for a town park. Decidedly not in my opinion. The park should, as far as possible, complement the town. Openness is the one thing you cannot get in buildings. Picturesqueness you can get. Let your buildings be as picturesque as your artists can make them. This is the beauty of a town. Consequently, the beauty of the park should be the other. It should be the beauty of the fields, the meadow, the prairie, of the green pastures, and the still waters. What we want to gain is tranquillity and rest to the mind. Mountains suggest effort. But besides this objection there are others of what I may indicate as the house-keeping class. It is impossible to give the public range over a large extent of ground of a highly picturesque character, unless under very exceptional circumstances, and sufficiently guard against the occurrence of opportunities and temptations to shabbiness, disorder, indecorum, and indecency, that will be subversive of every good purpose the park should be designed to fulfill.

Nor can I think that *in the park proper*, what is called gardenesque beauty is to be courted; still less that highly artificial and exotic form of it, which, under the name of subtropical planting, the French have lately introduced, and in suitable positions with interesting and charming results, but in following which indiscreetly, the English are sacrificing the peculiar beauty of their simple and useful parks of the old time. Both these may have places, and very important places, but they do not belong within a park, unless as side scenes and incidents. Twenty years ago Hyde Park had a most pleasing, open, free, and inviting expression, though certainly it was too rude, too much wanting in art; but now art is vexed with long harsh lines of repellant iron-work, and here and there behind it bouquets of hot house plants, between which the public pass like hospital convalescents, who have been turned into the yard to walk about while their beds are making. We should undertake nothing in a park which involves the treating of the public as prisoners or wild beasts. A great object of all that is done in a park, of *all* the art of a park, is to influence the mind of men through their imagination, and the influence of iron hurdles can never be good.

We have, perhaps, sufficiently defined the ideal of a park for a large town. It will seldom happen that this ideal can be realized fully. The next thing is to select the situation in which it can be most nearly approached without great cost; and by cost I do not mean simply cost of land or of construction, but cost of inconvenience and cost of keeping in order, which is a very much more serious matter, and should have a great deal more study.

A park fairly well managed near a large town, will surely become a new centre of that town. With the determination of location, size, and boundaries should therefore be associated the duty of arranging new trunk routes of communication between it and the distant parts of the town existing and forecasted.

These may be either narrow informal elongations of the park, varying say from two to five hundred feet in width, and radiating irregularly from it, or if, unfortunately, the town is already laid out in the unhappy way that New York and Brooklyn, San Francisco and Chicago, are, and, I am glad to say, Boston is not, on a plan made long years ago by a man who never saw a spring-carriage, and who had a conscientious dread of the Graces, then we must probably adopt formal Park-ways. They should be so planned and constructed as never to be noisy and seldom crowded, and so also that the straightforward movement of pleasure-carriages need never be obstructed, unless at absolutely necessary crossings, by slow-going heavy vehicles used for commercial purposes. If possible, also, they should be branched or reticulated with other ways of a similar class, so that no part of the town should finally be many minutes' walk from some one of them; and they should be made interesting by a process of planting and decoration, so that in necessarily passing through them, whether in going to or from the park, or to and from business, some substantial recreative advantage may be incidentally gained. It is a common error to regard a park as something to be produced complete in itself, as a picture to be painted on canvas. It should rather be planned as one to be done in fresco, with constant consideration of exterior objects, some of them quite at a distance and even existing as yet only in the imagination of the painter.

I have thus barely indicated a few of the points from which we may perceive our duty to apply the means in our hands to ends far distant, with reference to this problem of public recreations. Large operations of construction may not soon be desirable, but I hope you will agree with me that there is little room for question, that reserves of ground for the purposes I have referred to should be fixed upon as soon as possible, before the difficulty of arranging them, which arises from private building, shall be greatly more formidable than now.

To these reserves,—though not a dollar should be spent in construction during the present generation,—the plans of private construction would necessarily, from the moment they were established, be conformed.

I by no means wish to suggest that nothing should be done for the present generation; but only, that whatever happens to the present generation, it should not be allowed to go on heaping up difficulties and expenses for its successors, for want of a little comprehensive and business-like foresight and study. In all probability it will be found that much can be done even for the present generation without greatly if at all increasing taxation, as has been found in New York.

But the question now perhaps comes up: How can a community best take this work in hand?

It is a work in which private and local and special interests will be found so antagonistic one to another, in which heated prejudices are so liable to be unconsciously established, and in which those who would be disappointed in their personal greeds by whatever good scheme may be studied out, are so likely to combine and concentrate force to kill it (manufacture public opinion, as the phrase is), that the ordinary organizations for municipal business are unsuitable agencies for the purpose. It would, perhaps, be a bold thing to say that the public in its own interest, and in the interest of all of whom the present public are the trustees, should see to it that the problem is as soon as possible put clean out of its own hands, in order that it may be taken up efficiently by a small body of select men. But I will venture to say that until this in effect is done, the danger that public opinion may be led, by the application of industry, ingenuity, and business ability on the part of men whose real objects are perhaps unconsciously very close to their own pockets, to overrule the results of more comprehensive and impartial study, is much greater than in most questions of public interest.

You will not understand me as opposing or undervaluing the advantages of public discussion. What I would urge is, that park questions, and even the most elementary park questions, questions of site and outlines and approaches, are not questions to which the rule applies, that every man should look after his own interests, judge for himself what will favor his own interests, and exert his influence so as to favor them; but questions rather of that class, which in his private affairs every man of common sense is anxious, as soon as possible, to put into the hands of somebody who is able to take hold of them comprehensively as a matter of direct, grave, business responsibility.

It is upon this last point far more than upon any other that the experience of New York is instructive to other communities. I propose, therefore, to occupy your time a little while longer by a narration of those parts of this experience which bear most directly upon this point, and which will also supply certain other information which has been desired of me.

The New York legislature of 1851 passed a bill providing for a park on the east side of the island. Afterwards, the same legislature, precipitately and quite as an after-thought, passed the act under which the city took title to the site of the greater part of the present Central Park.

This final action is said to have been the result of a counter movement, started after the passage of the first bill merely to gratify a private grudge of one of the city aldermen.

When in the formation of the counter project, the question

was reached, what land shall be named in the second bill, the originator turned to a map and asked: "*Now where shall I go?*" His comrade, looking over his shoulder, without a moment's reflection, put his finger down and said, "Go there;" the point indicated appearing to be about the middle of the island, and therefore, as it occurred to him, one which would least excite local prejudices.

The primary selection of the site was thus made in an off-hand way, by a man who had no special responsibility in the premises, and whose previous studies had not at all led him to be well informed or interested in the purposes of a park.

It would have been difficult to find another body of land of six hundred acres upon the island (unless by taking a long narrow strip upon the precipitous side of a ridge), which possessed less of what we have seen to be the most desirable characteristics of a park, or upon which more time, labor, and expense would be required to establish them.

But besides the topographical objections, when the work of providing suitable facilities for the recreation of the people upon this ground came to be practically and definitely considered, defects of outline were discerned, the incomplete remedy for which has since cost the city more than a million of dollars. The amount which intelligent study would have saved in this way if applied at the outset, might have provided for an amplification of some one of the approaches to the Park, such as, if it were now possible to be gained at a cost of two or three million dollars, I am confident would, if fairly set forth, be ordered by an almost unanimous vote of the tax-payers of the city. Public discussion at the time utterly failed to set this blundering right. Nor was public opinion then clearly dissatisfied with what was done or with those who did it.

During the following six years there was much public and private discussion of park questions; but the progress of public opinion, judged simply by the standard which it has since formed for itself, seems to have been chiefly backward.

This may be, to a considerable degree, accounted for by the fact that many men of wealth and influence—who, through ignorance and lack of mature reflection on this subject, were unable to anticipate any personal advantage from the construction of a park—feared that it would only add to their taxes, and thus were led to form a habit of crying down any hopeful anticipations.

The argument that certain towns of the old country did obtain some advantage from their parks, could not be refuted, but it was easy to say, and it was said, that "our circumstances are very different: surrounded by broad waters on all sides, open to the sea breezes, we need no artificial breathing-places; even if we did, nothing like the parks of the old cities under aristocratic government would be at all practicable here."

This assertion made such an impression as to lead many to believe that little more had better be done than to give the name of park to the ground which it was now too late to avoid taking. A leading citizen suggested that nothing more was necessary than to plough up a strip just within the boundary of the ground and plant it with young trees, and chiefly with cuttings of the poplar, which afterwards, as they came to good size, could be transplanted to the interior, and thus the Park would be furnished economically and quite well enough for the purposes it would be required to serve.

Another of distinguished professional reputation seriously urged through the public press, that the ground should be rented as a sheep-walk. In going to and from their folds the flocks would be sure to form trails which would serve the public perfectly well for foot-paths; nature would in time supply whatever else was essential to form a quite picturesque and perfectly suitable strolling ground for such as would wish to resort to it.

It was frequently alleged, and with truth, that the use made of the existing public grounds was such as to develop riotous and licentious habits. A large park, it was argued, would inevitably present larger opportunities, and would be likely to exhibit an aggravated form of the same tendencies, consequently anything like refinement of treatment would be entirely wasted.

A few passages from a leading article of the "Herald" newspaper, in the seventh year of the enterprise, will indicate what estimate its astute editor had then formed of the prevailing convictions of the public on the subject:—

> "It is all folly to expect in this country to have parks like those in old aristocratic countries. When we open a public park Sam will air himself in it. He will take his friends whether from church, street, or elsewhere. He will knock down any better dressed man

who remonstrates with him. He will talk and sing, and fill his share of the bench, and flirt with the nursery-maids in his own coarse way. Now we ask what chance have William B. Astor and Edward Everett against this fellow-citizen of theirs? Can they and he enjoy the same place? Is it not obvious that he will turn them out, and that the great Central Park will be nothing but a great beer-garden for the lowest denizens of the city, of which we shall yet pray litanies to be delivered?"

In the same article it was argued that the effect of the construction of the Park would be unfavorable to the value of property in its neighborhood, except as, to a limited extent, it might be taken up by Irish and German liquor dealers as sites for dram-shops and lager-bier gardens.

There were many eminent citizens, who to my personal knowledge, in the sixth, seventh, and eighth year after the passage of the act, entertained similar views to those I have quoted.

I have been asked if I supposed that "gentlemen" would ever resort to the Park, or would allow their wives and daughters to visit it? I heard a renowned lawyer argue that it was preposterous to suppose that a police force would do anything toward preserving order and decency in any broad piece of ground open to the general public of New York. And after the work began, I often heard the conviction expressed that if what was called the reckless, extravagant, inconsiderate policy of those who had the making of the Park in charge, could not be arrested, the weight of taxation and the general disgust which would be aroused among the wealthy classes would drive them from the city, and thus prove a serious injury to its prosperity.

"Why," said one, a man whom you all know by reputation, and many personally, "I should not ask for anything finer in my private grounds for the use of my own family." To whom it was replied that possibly grounds might not unwisely be prepared even more carefully when designed for the use of two hundred thousand families and their guests, than when designed for the use of one.

The constantly growing conviction that it was a rash and ill-considered undertaking, and the apprehension that a great deal would be spent upon it for no good purpose, doubtless had something to do with the choice of men, who in the sixth year were appointed by the Governor of the State, commissioners to manage the work and the very extraordinary powers given them. At all events, it so happened that a majority of them were much better known from their places in the directory of banks, railroads, mining, and manufacturing enterprises, than from their previous services in politics; and their freedom to follow their own judgment and will, in respect to all the interior matters of the Park, was larger than had for a long time been given to any body of men charged with a public duty of similar importance.

I suppose that few of them knew or cared more about the subject of their duties at the time of their appointment, than most other active businessmen. They probably embodied very fairly the average opinion of the public, as to the way in which it was desirable that the work should be managed. If, then, it is asked, how did they come to adopt and resolutely pursue a course so very different from that which the public opinion seemed to expect of them, I think that the answer must be found in the fact that they had not wanted or asked the appointment; that it was made absolutely free from any condition or obligation to serve a party, a faction, or a person; that owing to the extraordinary powers given them, their sense of responsibility in the matter was of an uncommonly simple and direct character, and led them with the trained skill of business men to go straight to the question:—

"Here is a piece of property put into our hands. By what policy can we turn it to the best account for our stockholders?"

It has happened that instead of being turned out about the time they had got to know something about their special business, these commissioners have been allowed to remain in office to this time—a period of twelve years.

As to their method of work, it was as like as possible to that of a board of directors of a commercial corporation. They quite set at defiance the ordinary ideas of propriety applied to public servants, by holding their sessions with closed doors, their clerk being directed merely to supply the newspapers with reports of their acts. They spent the whole of the first year on questions simply of policy, organization, and plan, doing no practical work, as it was said, at all.

When the business of construction was taken hold of, they refused to occupy themselves personally with questions of the class which in New York usually take up nine tenths of the time and mind of all public servants, who have it in their power to arrange contracts and determine appointments, promotions, and discharges. All of these they turned over to the heads of the executive operations.

Now, when these deviations from usage were conjoined with the adoption of a policy of construction for which the public was entirely unprepared, and to which the largest tax-payers of the city were strongly opposed, when also those who had a variety of private axes to grind, found themselves and their influence, and their friends' influence, made nothing of by the commissioners, you may be sure that public opinion was manufactured against them at a great rate. The Mayor denounced them in his messages; the Common Council and other departments of the city government refused to coöperate with them, and were frequently induced to put obstructions in their way; they were threatened with impeachment and indictment; some of the city newspapers attacked them for a time in every issue; they were caricatured and lampooned; their session was once broken up by a mob, their business was five times examined (once or twice at great expense, lawyers, accountants, engineers, and other experts being employed for the purpose) by legislative investigating committees. Thus for a time public opinion, through nearly all the channels open to it, apparently set against them like a torrent.

No men less strong, and no men less confident in their strength than these men—by virtue in part of personal character, in part of the extraordinary powers vested in them by the legislature, and in part by the accident of certain anomalous political circumstances—happened to be, could have carried through a policy and a method which commanded so little immediate public favor. As it was, nothing but personal character, the common impression that after all they were honest, saved them. By barely a saber's length they kept ahead of their pursuers, and of this you may still see evidence here and there in the park, chiefly where something left to stop a gap for the time being has been suffered to remain as if a permanence. At one time nearly four thousand laborers were employed; and for a year at one point, work went on night and day in order to put it as quickly as possible beyond the reach of those who were bent on stopping it. Necessarily, under such circumstances, the rule obtains: "Look out for the main chance; we may save the horses, we must save the guns;" and if now you do not find everything in perfect parade order, the guns, at all events, were saved.

To fully understand the significance of the result so far, it must be considered that the Park is to this day, at some points, incomplete; that from the centre of population to the midst of the Park the distance is still four miles; that there is no steam transit; that other means of communication are indirect and excessively uncomfortable, or too expensive. For practical every-day purposes to the great mass of the people, the Park might as well be a hundred miles away. There are hundreds of thousands who have never seen it, more hundreds of thousands who have seen it only on a Sunday or holiday. The children of the city to whom it should be of the greatest use, can only get to it on holidays or in vacations, and then must pay car-fare both ways.

It must be remembered, also, that the Park is not planned for such use as is now made of it, but with regard to the future use, when it will be in the centre of a population of two millions hemmed in by water at a short distance on all sides; and that much of the work done upon it is, for this reason, as yet quite barren of results.

The question of the relative value of what is called off-hand common sense, and of special, deliberate, business-like study, must be settled in the case of the Central Park, by a comparison of benefit with cost. During the last four years over thirty million visits have been made to the Park by actual count, and many have passed uncounted. From fifty to eighty thousand persons on foot, thirty thousand in carriages, and four to five thousand on horseback, have frequently entered it in a day.

Among the frequent visitors, I have found all those who, a few years ago, believed it impossible that there should ever be a park in this republican country,—and especially in New York of all places in this country,—which would be a suitable place of resort for "gentlemen." They, their wives and daughters, frequent the Park more than they do the opera or the church.

There are many men of wealth who resort to the Park habitually and regularly, as much so as business men to their places of business. Of course, there is a reason for it, and a reason based upon their experience.

As to the effect on public health, there is no question that it is already great. The testimony of the older physicians of the city will be found unanimous on this point. Says one: "Where I formerly ordered patients of a certain class to give up their business altogether and go out of town, I now often advise simply moderation, and prescribe a ride in the Park before going to their offices, and again a drive with their families before dinner. By simply adopting this course as a habit, men who have been breaking down frequently recover tone rapidly, and are able to retain an active and controlling influence in an important business, from which they would have otherwise been forced to retire. I direct school-girls, under certain circumstances, to be taken wholly, or in part, from their studies, and sent to spend several hours a day rambling on foot in the Park."

The lives of women and children too poor to be sent to the country, can now be saved in thousands of instances, by making them go to the Park. During a hot day in July last, I counted at one time in the Park eighteen separate groups, consisting of mothers with their children, most of whom were under school-age, taking picnic dinners which they had brought from home with them. The practice is increasing under medical advice, especially when summer complaint is rife.

The much greater rapidity with which patients convalesce, and may be returned with safety to their ordinary occupations after severe illness, when they can be sent to the Park for a few hours a day, is beginning to be understood. The addition thus made to the productive labor of the city is not unimportant.

The Park, moreover, has had a very marked effect in making the city attractive to visitors, and in thus increasing its trade, and causing many who have made fortunes elsewhere to take up their residence and become tax-payers in it,—a much greater effect in this way, beyond all question, than all the colleges, schools, libraries, museums, and art-galleries which the city possesses. It has also induced many foreigners who have grown rich in the country, and who would otherwise have gone to Europe to enjoy their wealth, to settle permanently in the city.

And what has become of the great Bugaboo? This is what the "Herald" of later date answers:—

"When one is inclined to despair of the country, let him go to the Central Park on a Saturday, and spend a few hours there in looking at the people, not at those who come in gorgeous carriages, but at those who arrive on foot, or in those exceedingly

democratic conveyances, the street-cars; and if, when the sun begins to sink behind the trees, he does not arise and go homeward
with a happy swelling heart," and so on, the effusion winding
up thus: "We regret to say that the more brilliant becomes the
display of vehicles and toilettes, the more shameful is the display
of bad manners on the part of the——extremely fine-looking
people who ride in carriages and wear the fine dresses. We must
add that the pedestrians always behave well."

Here we touch a fact of more value to social science than any
other in the history of the Park; but to fully set it before you
would take an evening by itself. The difficulty of preventing ruffianism and disorder in a park to be frequented indiscriminately
by such a population as that of New York, was from the first
regarded as the greatest of all those which the commission had
to meet, and the means of overcoming it cost more study than
all other things.

It is, perhaps, too soon to judge of the value of the expedients
resorted to, but there are as yet a great many parents who are willing to trust their school-girl daughters to ramble without special
protection in the Park, as they would almost nowhere else in
New York. One is no more likely to see ruffianism or indecen-
cies in the Park than in the churches, and the arrests for offenses
of all classes, including the most venial, which arise simply from
the ignorance of country people, have amounted to but twenty
in the million of the number of visitors, and of these, an exceedingly small proportion have been of that class which was so
confidently expected to take possession of the Park and make it
a place unsafe and unfit for decent people.

There is a good deal of delicate work on the Park, some of
it placed there by private liberality—much that a girl with a
parasol, or a boy throwing a pebble, could render valueless in a
minute. Except in one or two cases where the ruling policy of
the management has been departed from,—cases which prove
the rule,—not the slightest injury from wantonness, carelessness, or ruffianism has occurred.

Jeremy Bentham, in treating of "The Means of Preventing
Crimes," remarks that any innocent amusement that the human
heart can invent is useful under a double point of view: first, for
the pleasure itself which results from it; second, from its tendency to weaken the dangerous inclinations which man derives
from his nature.

No one who has closely observed the conduct of the people who visit the Park, can doubt that it exercises a distinctly harmonizing and refining influence upon the most unfortunate and most lawless classes of the city,—an influence favorable to courtesy, self-control, and temperance.

At three or four points in the midst of the Park, beer, wine, and cider are sold with other refreshments to visitors, not at bars, but served at tables where men sit in company with women. Whatever harm may have resulted, it has apparently had the good effect of preventing the establishment of drinking-places on the borders of the Park, these not having increased in number since it was opened, as it was originally supposed they would.

I have never seen or heard of a man or woman the worse for liquor taken at the Park, except in a few instances where visitors had brought it with them, and in which it had been drank secretly and unsocially. The present arrangements for refreshments I should say are temporary and imperfect.

Every Sunday in summer from thirty to forty thousand persons, on an average, enter the Park on foot, the number on a very fine day being sometimes nearly a hundred thousand. While most of the grog-shops of the city were effectually closed by the police under the Excise Law on Sunday, the number of visitors to the Park was considerably larger than before. There was no similar increase at the churches.

Shortly after the Park first became attractive, and before any serious attempt was made to interfere with the Sunday liquor trade, the head-keeper told me that he saw among the visitors the proprietor of one of the largest saloons in the city. He accosted him and expressed some surprise; the man replied, "I came to see what the devil you'd got here that took off so many of my Sunday customers."

I believe it may be justly inferred that the Park stands in competition with grog-shops and worse places, and not with the churches and Sunday-schools.

Land immediately about the Park, the frontage on it being seven miles in length, instead of taking the course anticipated by those opposed to the policy of the Commission, has advanced in value at the rate of two hundred per cent. per annum.

The cost of forming the Park, owing to the necessity of overcoming the special difficulties of the locality by extraordinary expedients, has been very great ($5,000,000); but the interest on it would even now be fully met by a toll of three cents on visitors coming on foot, and six cents on all others; and it should be remembered that nearly every visitor in coming from a distance voluntarily pays much more than this for the privilege.

It is universally admitted, however, that the cost, including that of the original off-hand common-sense blunders, has been long since much more than compensated by the additional capital drawn to the city through the influence of the Park.

Finally, to come back to the question of worldly wisdom. As soon as the Park came fairly into use, public opinion began to turn, and in a few months faced square about. The commissioners have long since, by simple persistence in minding their own proper business, come to be by far the most popular men who have had to do with any civic affairs in the time of the present generation. They have been, indeed, almost uncomfortably popular, having had need occasionally to "lobby" off some of the responsibilities which there was an effort to put upon them.

A few facts will show you what the change in public opinion has been. When the commissioners began their work, six hundred acres of ground was thought by many of the friends of the enterprise to be too much, by none too little for all park purposes. Since the Park has come into use, the amount of land laid out and reserved for parks in the two principal cities on the bay of New York has been increased to more than three times that amount, the total reserve for parks alone now being about two thousand acres, and the public demand is now for more, not less. Twelve years ago there was almost no pleasure-driving in New York. There are now, at least, ten thousand horses kept for pleasure-driving. Twelve years ago there were no road-ways adapted to light carriages. There are now fourteen miles of rural drive within the parks complete and in use, and often crowded, and ground has been reserved in the two cities and their suburbs for fifty miles of park-ways, averaging, with their planted borders and inter-spaces, at least one hundred and fifty feet wide.

The land-owners had been trying for years to agree upon a new plan of roads for the upper part of Manhattan Island. A special commission of their own number had been appointed at their solicitation, but had utterly failed to harmonize conflicting interests. A year or two after the Park was opened, they went again to the legislature and asked that the work might be put upon the Park Commissioners, which was done, giving them absolute control of the matter, and under them it has been arranged in a manner, which appears to be generally satisfactory, and has caused an enormous advance of the property of all those interested.

At the petition of the people of the adjoining counties, the field of the commissioners' operations has been extended over their territory, and their scheme of trunk-ways for pleasure-driving, riding, and walking has thus already been carried far out into what are still perfectly rural districts.

On the west side of the harbor there are other commissioners forming plans for extending a similar system thirty or forty miles back in to the country, and the Legislature of New Jersey has a bill before it for laying out another park of seven hundred acres.

In speaking of parks I have not had in mind the private enterprises, of which there are several. One of the very men who, twelve years ago, thought that anyone who pretended that the people of New York wanted a park must be more knave than fool, has himself lately devoted one hundred and fifty acres of his private property to a park designed for public use, and simply as a commercial operation, to improve the adjoining property.

I could enforce the chief lesson of this history from other examples at home and abroad. I could show you that where parks have been laid out and managed in a temporary, off-hand, common-sense way, it has proved a penny-wise pound-foolish way, injurious to the property in their neighborhood. I could show you more particularly how the experience of New York, on the other hand, has been repeated over the river in Brooklyn.

But I have already held you too long. I hope that I have fully satisfied you that this problem of public recreation grounds is one which, from its necessary relation to the larger problem of the future growth of your honored city, should at once be made a subject of responsibility of a very definite, very exacting, and, consequently, very generous character. In no other way can it be adequately dealt with.

Report of the Landscape Architects
and Superintendents

Brooklyn, January, 1871

To the Brooklyn Park Commissioners:

GENTLEMEN:—

The primary construction of the Park is now essentially complete in all of the territory which was at first placed under your control, and in the greater part of the remainder, or in all of the Park from the Plaza gate to the Lookout Hill, the design is so thoroughly fixed upon the ground that the character of the scenery, and of the public accommodations aimed at, can hardly be questioned.

As mistaken ideas of the intention of the design have evidently gained some currency, it seems timely, before referring to what is now in course of preparation, to review what has thus far been done.

When the formation of the Park was begun, there was little pleasure-driving in Brooklyn, except of fast trotters; the gay procession now seen, every fine day, was scarcely at all foreshadowed, there were fewer private carriages relatively to the population than there had been at an earlier period, and probably fewer than in any other city of equal population in the country. In driving for pleasure,—not merely for conveyance from point to point,—it had always been an object to get as soon as possible out into the country, and, if tolerable roads could be found, into the midst of woods and scenes of a secluded and rural character. It was even more of an object to do so with those who walked or rode for recreation, and still again more so with those who made up picnic parties for a holiday. It was from the rapid destruction of all rural charm in the suburban roads, and the constantly increasing difficulty of finding any place near the city in which natural landscapes or a rural ramble could be quietly enjoyed, that the want of a public park was experimentally known.

After the works on the ground appropriated to a park were begun, it was for a year or two impossible for most observers to see any intention in them of developing natural scenes, while their obvious extent and costliness, and the amount of building material which seemed to be accumulating, gave the impression that the original features of the site were to be utterly destroyed, and a stiff, formal, garden-like ground was to be formed, dependent largely for its interest on artificial objects. Such an apprehension was not unreasonable, for, under the name of the gardenesque style, a method of treatment of public grounds has been much advocated, the result of which is very liable to be an incongruous mixture of nature, with what is called art. An impression that such would be the prevailing character of the Brooklyn Park became at this period so strongly fixed, that with many no confidence seems even yet to be felt that a different result has at any time, or in any place, been designed.

It is therefore more especially with reference to this question that an examination of the completed construction is invited.

A considerable part of the ground in question was originally wooded. None of this, with the exception of swampy spots where the trees were sickly and decaying, has been cleared further than necessary to open the way for the roads, nor has its original form been anywhere more than slightly modified, and this chiefly in the filling up of depressions, mostly artificial, of the surface. The cleared land of the site was in many places crossed by the excavations and embankments of the old country roads and the later formation of the rectangular system of streets, and there were several large clay and gravel pits upon it, as well as many acres of peat swamps, some of which had been partially excavated, and some partially filled over. The heaviest earthwork has been in draining, filling, and restoring the surface in and about these places to a natural character. No hill, not previously marred by excavations in street construction, has been leveled or its general elevation reduced. The tendency of all the changes of the surface has been to enlarge and make more distinct the original natural features. Swamps, pond-holes, and hillocks which obstructed the general flow of the surface, alone have been obliterated.

There are two small districts in which it may be questioned if this general intention of magnifying the natural features, and idealizing the natural suggestions, has been strictly adhered to. Even in these cases, however, it will be seen that depressions have been deepened, and steep hill-sides made steeper. One of the districts referred to is designed especially for the amusement and education of children; the other, with reference to objects which will be hereafter described. In neither case have the special purposes to which the locality is devoted, been pursued at the expense of the general intention. In looking over either district from the surrounding parts of the Park, nothing is observable that does not harmonize with and aid intended landscape effects.

The drives, rides and walks, the grading for which has given occasion for the largest disturbance of the ground not directed, as above stated, to the restoration and emphasizing of its original characteristics, are nowhere designed to arrest or withhold attention from the natural features, but are solely adapted, and are no more spacious or multiplied than is necessary, for the convenient passage of the number of persons who even now occasionally resort together to the Park. It is common, in public pleasure grounds, to make prominent circumstances of the ways through them, and to emphasize their course so that they cannot escape attention, even from a distance, by continuous rows of trees or distinct borders, with various decorations, architectural and otherwise.

It will be readily seen that there has been, so far, no such purpose in your park; the least possible break in the turf and natural plantations which is consistent with convenient movement, is everywhere studied in their course, grading, and method of construction. The walks are parted from the drives, in order that the necessary breaks of the turf and trees may be as narrow as possible, and except where elevation is sought to open a distant view, both are kept below the general level and are without guards or distinct curbs, so that the range of vision passes over them and catches only the green swells upon their borders.

At a short distance from the principal entrance, the course of the walks is designed to invite dispersion; for this purpose, and to aid in inducing a feeling of security and of freedom from the hurry, bustling and watchfulness necessary to safety while walking in the streets of the City, two of the four archways which have been built on the Park are used. By means of these, the drives which must otherwise need to be crossed, can, if desired, be passed without dodging among carriages, and without compelling drivers or horsemen to pull up. The lack of a provision of this kind in most of the popular parks abroad leads to many accidents and much inconvenience. The arches are as short, as narrow, and in all respects as unobtrusive as they can well be made, consistently with their objects, with sound, permanent construction, and with an honest expression of their purpose. They are always in recesses and depressions of the general surface of the ground, are always flanked and additionally secluded by thickets of foliage, and their masonry is half covered with vines and creepers. Generally, they have no parapet, but a ridge of earth and rocks, covered by a loose hedge of shrubs with a falling habit, rambling over their face. In the Enterdale and Eastwood arches (which were the first built), the planting has now been done long enough to fully exhibit this character. If the object of these constructions, instead of the simple safety and convenience of those using both drives and walks, had been, as seems to be yet quite generally supposed, the making of an architectural display, none of these precautions would have entered into their design. As it is, so far from being obtrusive objects, they are passed by those in carriages, in most cases, without being observed. They serve the purpose of shelter, upon occasion, from showers, and make a less number of special structures necessary for this purpose. They are lined with wood to avoid the drip which would occur from the condensation of moisture on stone under the circumstances.

Such other sheltered seats as have been thought to be required, are mainly low structures of sassafras logs, are, or are to be, in the shadow of trees, and draped with creeping foliage, and are as modest and secluded as is consistent with their purpose, which requires that they should be readily distinguished when the need for them arises. Besides these shelters, and some low, vine-covered trellises, only two buildings, a cottage and barn, have been placed on the ground. These are in the midst of wood, and only their rooftrees can be discerned from the more frequented parts of the Park. The cottage commands a distant view through a vista among the trees, but itself enters decidedly into no landscape. With one exception, the bridges thus far built are of wood, or rude field-stones, low, for the most part lost in foliage, and as inconspicuous as without greatly increased expense it would have been possible to make them. There is one bridge which serves four different routes of connection, besides spanning a water-course, and which commands two distinct districts seen comprehensively from no other point. A considerable and prominent construction was here a necessity, and it has received a careful architectural treatment. Its position is nevertheless retired rather than conspicuous, and it will be flanked and deeply shadowed by the associated plantations. When the colors of the now fresh cut stone shall have been subdued, the bridge will be much less obtrusive in the landscape than an ordinary farm-house or barn.

As to the apprehension, sometimes expressed, that the Park is to be everywhere disturbed, as some foreign parks are, with artificial objects, such as monuments, statues, temples, kiosks, pagodas, obelisks, fountains, vases, terraces, stiff avenues, and trim parterres, there is nothing of the kind to be found upon all this ground, and except the indication of a site for a simple block of stone, three or four feet high, as an historical landmark (and this in a position where it could not be observed from any of the drives or leading walks), no proposition or suggestion for the introduction of anything of the kind upon it has ever been presented to you, or appeared upon any of your plans. There is not a single construction or artificial object upon all this ground which is designed to attract the eye or arrest attention.

But the question will be asked if the scenery of the Park is, after all, only of a common-place, natural, rural character, why has its preparation needed so much more labor than a farmer ordinarily bestows upon his woodlands and pastures? These may often be found, in parts at least, much more beautiful than any part of the Park, and may be bought outright with everything on them, for a tithe of what has been spent in the construction of the Park. It may be answered, that the object of the larger part of the study, skill, and labor expended, has been to reconcile the purpose of a gradual and slow development of a special type of rural landscape, with the constant convenient use of the ground as a place of recreation by a very great number of people; and if it appears to have been unnecessarily large, it is in part because the difficulty of maintaining a natural and rustic character, and at the same time of keeping the ground in neat and convenient order, under these circumstances, is much greater than is generally realized. The character of the evidence which shows this difficulty may be indicated by a reference to what has passed under the eyes of many citizens of Brooklyn upon the Park.

During the first two years of the work, interest in what was promised, and curiosity as to the progress of construction, led many to visit the site of the park, and, as much of the ground was constantly crossed by trains of carts, and thus made dusty or miry, or was freshly dug or manured or otherwise rendered disagreeable by the works in progress, most of these visitors were driven to find a place of more quiet and comfort in the uninclosed woods a little on one side of the line of operations. In the parts of these to which the largest numbers came, and where there was most lounging, though constantly patrolled by the Park Keepers, and though all convenient pains were taken to preserve order and neatness and prevent injury to the trees and shrubs, all of the herbage, and of the foliage growing within six feet of the ground, except a few briery thickets, wholly disappeared; the soil was worn to dust, and blown and washed away so much that within two years, the roots of the trees everywhere protruded, and many withered in consequence. Whenever it rained, the old wood trails were gullied, the hollow places became sloughs, and the whole surface slimy and disagreeable to see or to walk upon.

Reflecting that the number of people using this ground was hardly as one to a hundred of those to be expected in the future upon the Park, no one could observe the progress of wear and tear, under these circumstances, without being convinced that to permanently secure a high degree of rural charm in the public ground of a large city, special preparations are required of a skillful, elaborate, and substantial character. The result of acting upon the contrary assumption was shown in Washington Park, before it was revised by your Commission. Nine-tenths of the trees originally planted on it had received serious injuries; and much the larger part were, upon inspection, condemned as damaged beyond recovery, and have been burned. The spaces laid with turf had been worn bare, or had become everywhere untidy and forlorn. It was not an attractive, a suitable, hardly a safe resort for women and children, and was regarded rather as a nuisance, than as an advantage, to the neighborhood. This experience has been gone through with many times, in many places, in Europe and America. The common result, after the shabbiness and uselessness becomes scandalous, is that which is illustrated in Boston Common, and which is now being applied to the Battery in New York, a style of improvement being adopted in which an evident effort is made to avoid formality, but in which, nevertheless, not the least approach to a free, natural, rural character is attempted, and the public is then invited to pass through the grounds by a complicated series of gangways guarded by chains or rails. Recreation may be obtained in such grounds, but it can hardly be called rural recreation, and it is even a question whether convenience, economy, and good taste would not all have been better served by the adoption, at the outset, of a formal and elegant architectural style.

As the park has come more and more into use, new habits and customs, and with them new tastes, have been developed. There is already many times as much pleasure-driving as there was five years ago, and not a few persons are more attracted to the Park by what is to be seen upon the road than by any conscious enjoyment of the inanimate nature to be seen from it; consequently, a new class of comments upon the design are now sometimes heard; unfavorable comparisons are made between the Park and certain foreign pleasure grounds, both with respect to the lack of opportunity for enjoying the sight of a large, gay assemblage, and its entire want of stateliness and artistic grandeur. In these comparisons, and in the demands which they suggest, there are some important considerations which are generally overlooked.

In Southern Europe, where the ground is parched, and turf and delicate low foliage withers unless carefully and laboriously watered and tended; where also, in most cases, rambling in the country, or beyond the outskirts of towns, is not only toilsome but dangerous; where ladies seldom go out of doors until after sunset, unless closely vailed; and where the people look for amusement almost exclusively to social excitements, public pleasure grounds have usually been important, chiefly, as places of rendezvous and general congregation. Their plans have been characterized by formal and stately plantations, and much architectural and floral decoration. Where anything like landscape effects have been attempted to be added to these, it has generally been, not as an invitation to exercise, but simply as a picture usually of a romantic, and often of a distinctly theatrical character.

The primary and avowed object of such grounds is to supply people with accommodation for coming together to see one another, not merely as personal acquaintances, but as an assemblage.

A style of laying out grounds adapted to this purpose has, till recently at least, prevailed, not only in Italy, Spain, and Portugal, but throughout France, and where French influence has been strong, the woods of both public and private parks and chases are nearly always traversed by straight avenues with well-defined circular carrefoures, often emphasized by architectural objects at their points of junction, as may be seen in the Bois de Boulogne. While, however, the custom of out-door assemblage, and of the promenade for recreation has been maintained, and has even become more important, a tendency to a different style in the preparation of pleasure grounds has been growing wherever the climate admits of its being adapted with success. The changes made in the plan of the Bois de Boulogne under the late Empire, those also in the Bois de Vincennes, the Parc de Monceau and other grounds in France, and the plan of the new park at Brussels, all show progress in this direction, though the liking for detached scenic effects which might be suitable for framing, or for the background of a ballet, still influences most French landscape work.

It is to be observed, too, that upon the completion of the Avenue de l'Impératrice as an approach to the Bois de Boulogne, and of the informal and narrow drive around the Lake with its various landscape effects, that part of this system of pleasure grounds which is laid out in the natural style was immediately adopted as the daylight promenade of Paris, in preference to the much wider, more accessible, more stately, and in every way more convenient and magnificent avenue of the Champs Elysees.

It will thus be seen that the grander and more splendid style of public pleasure grounds, while it is peculiarly adapted to display a great body of well-dressed people and of equipages to advantage, and is most fitting for processions, pomps, and ceremonies, while also it seems admirably to extend and soften architectural grandeur, is not preferred where there are moderate advantages for the adoption of a natural style, even for the purposes of a promenade. The reason may be that where carriages are used, in the frequent passing over the long spaces of bare surface which they make necessary, formal arrangements and confined scenes become very tiresome. In passing along a curving road, its borders planted irregularly, the play of light and shade, and the succession of objects more or less distinct which are disclosed and obscured in succession, is never wholly without interest, while an agreeable open landscape is always refreshing, in contrast to the habitual confinement of the city.

In Northern Europe, congregative recreation has, until recently, been a comparatively unimportant object in public parks, the popular idea of them being that of grounds in which people could stray away from the towns, either apart or in small detached parties. The difference of the two tastes and customs is shown by the fact that, while before the recent improvements, the roadways of the Bois de Boulogne (although then only an occasional resort for the Parisian public) were nearly a hundred feet wide, with clean-cut borders, the principal promenade drive of London, though right in the midst of the town, was, so late as twelve years ago, a mere rural road from thirty to forty feet wide, encroached upon and made still narrower at some points by trees growing naturally.

If parks laid out in the manner of those of the North were attempted on the Mediterranean, or in this country on the Gulf of Mexico or in California, they would be exceedingly dreary. Under such circumstances it is not, therefore, simply a matter of taste or convenience, but, in some degree, a necessity that devices of an obviously artificial character are used to make public grounds attractive.

In this latitude on the Atlantic slope, however, although a formal and highly ornate treatment is perfectly appropriate where the chief object of a public ground is that of a social rendezvous and promenade, it is not the only, nor always the most desirable treatment of it. If it is so situated as to command interesting views, for instance, it may be better that it should be laid out and furnished in such a way that these views will be seen through harmonious and suitable foregrounds. If there are disagreeable or incongruous objects near by, it is better that it should be supplied with boscage borders, which will be manageable screens against them.

In the nature of the case, adequate provision for simple, rural recreation requires large space of ground, it being a primary object to secure the greatest possible change of scene from the confinement and rigidity of the city, and to induce a sense of freedom and a disposition to ramble. This object has, moreover, to be reconciled, as has been shown, with that of maintaining neatness and good order, in spite of the careless and often reckless movement of many thousand people all turning out for exercise and recreation at once; and it is impossible of accomplishment, except on a site of considerable breadth, where large opportunity and invitation for dispersion can be given. It is better, on the other hand, that a drive intended to be used as a promenade, should not be so far extended that a long period will be required to pass through it and see all who are upon it, nor should it be so wide that friends cannot be easily distinguished when passing on the opposite side. The avenue beyond the Arch, and the drive about the Lake in the Bois de Boulogne, which is preferred to the wide avenues nearer Paris, is everywhere less than sixty feet wide, and in some parts less than forty.

It may then be said, that in the design of public grounds, two quite different uses of them, and two quite different artistic ideals, may properly be had in view, and that under certain conditions of situation, soil, climate, and society, one only of these uses, and one only of these ideals can properly be controlling. Individuals must be expected to place a greater value on one or the other use, and to be better pleased with one or the other style of grounds, according to their habits and the bias of their natural or acquired tastes. There can be no greater mistake, however, than to suppose that what has given great gratification in one place, or under one class of circumstances, will do so everywhere and anywhere, and that the neglect to use every opportunity of introducing it is an evidence of ignorance or bad taste. Because it is a very pleasant thing to see a great body of well-dressed people enjoying themselves in the open air, it does not follow that every pleasure ground should be designed with reference exclusively to that pleasure and all its parts, furniture, and decorations, be specially adapted to it; nor because, also, it is a very pleasant thing to find in the midst of a large town a winding road or walk, with borders on either side of dense luxuriant foliage, or with a fair landscape opening from it as completely free, as far as the eye can see, of anything artificial as if in the country, that nowhere in a public ground should there be conveniences for congregation or any obvious display of human handiwork. In a park of five hundred acres, provision of both kinds may be furnished, but it is not wise to undertake to provide both at all points, and if the ground has a varied surface, it is unwise to pursue the congregative purpose in those parts where the suggestions of natural scenery are most interesting.

When the plan of your park was first outlined, it was intended to provide a ground within which citizens could not only withdraw themselves at some few points from the sight of town houses and town traffic, but in which they could wander for hours at a time, constantly finding new scenes of natural beauty. The whole of it was laid out with this purpose in view. At the same time, the growth of the tastes and habits which are gratified by joining a gay assemblage or throng was anticipated, and, to provide more completely for the demand which was thus expected to arise, it was recommended that two series of stately avenues should be provided outside the Park. This recommendation was repeated and urged in three of your Annual Reports, and measures were at length taken to carry out the suggestion before any public demand for the purpose began to be manifested.

But experience teaches, as we have indicated, that no matter how fine and well adapted to their purpose such avenues may be made, even when their drives are exclusively used for pleasure carriages, where there is a rural park with good roads through it, also conveniently accessible, it will likewise be more or less used as a promenade, and this whether well adapted to that purpose or not.

Accommodations for large throngs of people, and advantages for observing these throngs, are then at some points desirable and necessary, and means must be carefully studied of reconciling such accommodations with the purpose of giving the public the largest practicable extent of rural scenery, and of rural exercising ground. As, for this purpose, the drives must not, as already explained, be very wide, and as the movement both ways (in order to give opportunity for the recognition of acquaintances) must be slow, it is desirable that such provision should be originally secured in such a place that people can make a considerable circuit within the Park, if they choose, without entering upon them at all.

The part of your park thus intended exclusively for rural recreation is complete within itself, and a circuit of it can be made upon both its drives and walks without entering upon the promenade district, which, indeed, lies completely hidden from it, except as the tree-tops and the water within it extend the background of the view from certain points.

According to the plans you have approved, the portion of the drive more especially intended to be used as a promenade, is to be nowhere less than fifty feet in width; in the greater part, sixty feet. Its length, not including the turning-places at the ends, is to be three-quarters of a mile. A pad for saddle-horses will adjoin it, thirty feet wide. At certain points it will be separated a short distance from the drive in order to avoid too extended a bare surface. Adjoining the pad, and again on the opposite side of the drive, are to be walks fifteen to twenty feet wide. Near the middle of the system, sheltered galleries are arranged, where those who wish can sit and look upon those moving by. The width of the whole promenade ways at this point, for a distance of two hundred and fifty feet, is to be one hundred and eighty feet; the pad and the drive being thrown together, and the walks brought to curbs upon them. One of the walks will spread laterally to beaches or bays of the Lake, and there will be an outlet from it upon a boat-landing. Throughout the whole extent of the promenade ways a succession of views will be commanded with the back to the sun over the Lake. On the side toward the sun will be a dense plantation of trees and underwood. Planted points and islands are arranged to cover the broader bare spaces of the promenade from the view of boating parties and the opposite shores, and to supply strong foregrounds to the views northward. There are to be rows of trees within and upon the edge of the drive, it being impossible to avoid long spaces, which would be unpleasantly exposed to the sun by any wholly natural arrangement of trees consistently with convenience of movement where so many are expected to be passing together, but the bordering plantations are so arranged, that the formality of these rows will not be noticed, except when close upon them. Looking beyond the exterior lines of the promenade walks, the scene will be perfectly natural and rural in character; so also the whole Lake shore, except at one point, where preparation is making for promenade concerts.

Promenade concerts are common in many European pleasure grounds, but nowhere are the arrangements for them such as would be at all satisfactory to an American audience of the number which has frequently been found already in your park. They may be divided into two classes: those universal in German towns, common in French and less so in British, where the audience is standing, walking, or sitting upon chairs, and frequently at tables at which refreshments are served, and those in which the greater part of the audience is in carriages, or walking about among carriages, as the Cascine at Florence, and on the Pincian Hill at Rome.

The music of a proper promenade band can be best heard only at a greater distance from the instruments than is desirable when listening to an ordinary indoor orchestra. It does not require close attention, and may be enjoyed while walking among the trees. It is common, however, for at least the central part of the audience to rest during the performance of each piece, and for the greater part of it to stroll or drive off and return between the pieces. Where the audience is largely in carriages, there is always more or less movement in its outer part, and this, with the room necessarily taken by each vehicle and its horses, makes the number of those who can enjoy the music at all, with any arrangement hitherto used, very small. There is no carriage promenade concert in Europe which is largely attended by people on foot. In the best and most popular promenade concerts, it is customary for all who come in carriages to leave them on arriving at the ground, and this both in small and large towns.

The plan of the concert grounds in your Park is designed to secure the advantages of both the classes which have been described, and to avoid, as far as practicable, their disadvantages.

The orchestra is to be placed upon a small island, about one hundred feet from a semicircular sweep of shore, in the direction where the audience is expected chiefly to congregate. It is believed, that with suitable instruments, at this distance over water nothing will be lost of the sound, while it will prevent the disagreeable crowding together of a large number of persons close before the stand where the music cannot be heard to advantage. Provision, however, is made for small boats to fasten along the shore below the level of the audience and of the floor of the music-stand, and a large fleet may lie about it. The circuit drive of the Park passes parallel with the shore, at a distance from it of five hundred and thirty feet; a short loop from it opens into a concourse, nearly five acres in area, sloping toward the shore, and occupying a quadrant of a circle surrounding the music stand. All parts of this are open to drivers and riders. Its southward outlets open into the promenade drive and ride.

A smaller carriage concourse (two acres) is situated upon the top of an eminence, five hundred feet to the northward, and carriages can either be driven to this and back, or a turn be taken in the promenade drive, if desired, between the pieces. It is believed that most music will be heard very well upon the higher concourse, which has the advantage for a hot summer's day of being strongly swept by the sea breeze passing over the music island.

North of the principal carriage concourse is an esplanade, with a grove for a promenade on foot. The lower part of this, for a distance of one hundred and seventy-five feet, is to be planted with plane trees, arranged at the intersection of concentric circular lines with others radiating from the music island, as may be understood from the plan accompanying this report. Back of this, at a higher elevation, is to be a grove, pierced by three alleys on the lines of vistas opening toward the music island. In the rear will be an open pavilion, with tables and seats, and back of it a low house containing cloak and dressing rooms, and from which coffee and ices may be served. A series of awnings on fixed standards will cover seats in front of the trees on the esplanade, the passage in front of which is to be closed during the performance of music. There are also to be seats in the rear of the esplanade. It is expected, however, that the larger part of the audience collecting here will be moving during the intervals of the music, and will stand among the planes or continue walking in the alleys of the upper grove during its performance. There are walks leading from the concert ground along the shore each way, and upon the face of Breeze Hill, looking toward the music stand. The music will float across the Lake, and be heard very well on the opposite shore, and more or less clearly at various more distant points.

As an agreeable, natural decoration of a space like the concert ground, designed to be mostly occupied by an audience, is impracticable, its plan is formal, and its decorations will be mainly architectural.

The ground-work of the whole of the Park south of the Lookout Hill, having to be made from material excavated from the Lake site, and every tree, shrub, and stone to be moved to it, and every variation from a plain surface to be formed, it will be some time before the design can be fully realized, but it is hoped that this statement of its intention will sufficiently show, that while the simplest form of healthful and educative rural education has been studiously provided for, the use of the park as a place to see people under pleasant circumstances, and in which to be cheered by the pervading gayety of a great company coming together simply for pleasure, has not been neglected.

No part of the Park is designed with reference to use after nightfall. There are many reasons why it should not be. The attempt to light any large ground, planted closely, or with underwood in the natural style, sufficiently to make it a safe resort, always fails. If in the midst of a large town, its use for immoral and criminal purposes more than balances any advantages it may offer. It has been shown that where the climate makes the night the most agreeable time for open-air recreation, formal promenades between rows of trees on regular, strongly defined and well-lighted walks, are customary. Not only the parkways now under construction are of this character, but the Park is designed to be surrounded on all sides with a broad avenue for carriages, and a well-lighted mall, thirty feet wide, for walking. Wherever practicable, this is made to overlook the Park, from which it is to be divided by a parapet three feet in height, the total height of the interior wall being eight feet. The Plaza is designed with a similar purpose, and the planting and lighting arrangements have been studied with special reference to night effects.

In our last Report we spoke of that intention of the plan which is to be more especially realized in the pastoral district of the Long Meadow, and among the scattered trees of the West and Mid woods which border it. The central walk leading from the Plaza to the hills and the promenade district, after passing through this open, and for the present rather too sunny ground, reaches the edge of a pool of water in the lowest part of the meadow, which is also intended to be sunny and bright; it is then carried to the left, and passes through a shady ravine, from which it issues through the Nethermead Arches upon another broad and open space of greensward, with placid water in view beyond it. The ravine is designed to provide favorable conditions for rich, dark, cool, and secluded effects in contrast with the neighboring meadow, and with the scenery of the Park generally, and connects with a small district of similar character, now under construction, which extends with a series of rambling walks and sheltered seats to the Dairy Cottage.

The usual statistics of construction, of the force employed, and of the public use of the Park (which, it will be observed, has largely increased during the year), will be found in the appended reports of the engineers.

Respectfully,

OLMSTED, VAUX & CO.,
Landscape Architects and Superintendents

Suburban Home Grounds*

Not one in a thousand, probably, of all those who, in this country, every year set about the preparation of a suburban home for their families, can readily obtain the aid of a landscape-gardener, properly so called. To those who cannot, Mr. Frank J. Scott, of Toledo, Ohio, undertakes to give elementary instruction in the art, which he defines to be that of "creating lovely examples of landscape in miniature," but which, in its application to such small spaces of ground as he has more particularly in view, might, perhaps, better be stated to be that of preparing agreeable *passages* of landscape scenery. This work is in two parts, the first relating to questions of site, extent, plan, and method; the second, to the special qualities for landscape planting of each of several hundred trees and shrubs. The two parts are of about equal bulk, and might very well have been bound apart; together, they form an inconveniently heavy volume. The advice given in the first part is copious and distinct, and may be understood and applied by most town-bred men. The principles of art are freshly, if incompletely, stated, and although a new and elaborate series of symbols is used, the numerous illustrative plans, upon which it is evident that much study has been spent, are intelligible and instructive.

In one respect, Mr. Scott abandons the usage of the established authorities, and adopts, to the fullest extent, what he regards as an improved, popular American practice. It has generally been thought desirable by the older landscape gardeners, in forming their plans, that certain objects standing outside the ground placed under their control should be given a greater apparent distance, or, perhaps, without entire concealment, should be rendered partially obscure from points of view within it. For this purpose, a plantation is generally laid out along the

---

* "The Art of Beautifying Suburban Home Grounds of small extent, etc., etc. Illustrated by upwards of two hundred plates and engravings of plans for residences and their grounds, of trees and shrubs, and garden embellishments, with descriptions of the beautiful and hardy shrubs grown in the United States. By Frank J. Scott." New York: D. Appleton & Co. 1870.

boundary which is designed eventually to establish a verdant middle distance in the landscape. Perhaps still more frequently, it has been desired to shut out completely objects which were originally in view, but which were discordant with more important landscape elements nearer the points of view, in which case plantations have been planned with the design of forming complete new backgrounds. Skilful use of boundary plantations for these purposes was originally made by Kent and his immediate associates and successors, but the practice being followed, in a mechanical way, by the famous Brown and other stupid pretenders, gave rise to "the belt," so unmercifully ridiculed by Uvedale Price in his prolonged discussion with Repton and others. Mr. Scott uses no boundary plantations, and, unless to shut out some special deformity, would merge the surface of his grounds with whatever may lie beyond them. He would do without a fence if he could, and, not being allowed to, would have it as nearly as possible transparent. It may be said for his plans that, in attempting to secure even miniature passages of landscape *of a complete character* within the usual limits of a suburban building lot, the inexperienced planter would be so likely to run into fussy confusion, that it would almost always be better for him to accept whatever objects there may be on or across the street or boundary as primary matters of interest, and that the main motive of his planting should be to gain elegance of foreground only. There is a sweet passage in the last work of Repton in which he justifies the pleasure he had taken in a design of this simple character. But Mr. Scott argues that the practice of planting closely along the boundary is a bad conventionalism, handed down from a period of "rude improvements and ruder men"; that it is a peculiarity of English gardening, which "it would be as unfortunate to follow as to imitate the surly self-assertion of English travelling manners"; and, finally, that not to lay our private grounds open to the public gaze is ill-bred, inhospitable, unneighborly, and unchristian (pp. 51 and 61).

We are confident that Mr. Scott, in the passages to which we refer, has got upon a wrong road, and as he has, in general, evidently studied his way with care, we are anxious to see what has led him astray. On reflection, it appears to us that so far as there is a distinct American practice in the respect indicated, it has grown out of the fact that the motive of what Mr. Scott calls home grounds in this country has hitherto been, in most cases, almost exclusively a motive of decoration. They have been designed to be looked upon from a window, or from the street; much less generally than in Europe to be familiarly and frequently occupied and lived in. The difference of custom in this respect has been often remarked, and generally attributed to differences of climate. We are disposed, however, to think that it should be connected with a considerable series of tolerably well-marked distinctions, now passing away, with which climate has had little to do—with habits of more constant, more desultory, and, with individuals, more varied labor; with the habit of looking with suspicion upon anything tending to withdraw attention from productive occupations, unless it were to distinctly religious exercises; with the customs which have forced young people generally to seek social enjoyment much more apart from their parents than is thought necessary, desirable, or prudent, in old countries; and, in short, with many direct results of the necessary privations and hardships of the pioneer period. It is not impossible, even in this country, with patience, ingenuity, and skill, to establish conditions under which, while engaged in many common domestic occupations, we may spend a good deal of time out of doors, but it is much more difficult than in the old countries, and while our emigrating fathers had their full stint to keep the wolf and savage from their doors, it is not surprising that they did not undertake the task. Their houses were commonly built, at most, with but two doors, of which one opened upon a working yard, always more or less blocked up with logs saved for fuel or timber, and the larger implements of the farm, the other upon the trail, which afterwards became a high road or village street. After a certain period, someone in each neighborhood would acquire an enviable distinction by "slicking up" a place, and planting some slips of lilac or poplar, obtained from the older settlements, or perhaps direct from the mother country. The most available ground for such a purpose was just within the door opposite the working yard, where, accordingly, to protect the plants from cattle, a space would be fenced in. As a better class of houses were substituted for the original cabins, with increasing security and prosperity, front-door yards increased in number, until, at length, the distinction was reversed, and it became almost disreputable in many districts to live in a house without such an appendage. The notion of furnishing them with broad, clean, smooth floors of gravel, or carpets of fine, close turf, with sewing and reading seats; of coaxing nature to decorate their convenience, or protect them from sun and wind, or to give them any degree of seclusion or coziness; or of ever using them as *al-fresco* parlors, or tea-rooms, or workrooms, or kindergartens, was not at all entertained. Regarded simply as ornaments of the house front, or as badges of respectability, like chaises and green blinds, it would have been folly to hide them behind walls, hedges, or thickets.

Between home-grounds of this class, however enlarged and improved, and the characteristic miniature pleasure-grounds of the suburban villas of any part of Europe, there can be no comparison. The private planting of public roadsides, and the contribution of a small piece of decorated ground in front of every dwelling to public use, is an excellent custom; and, in contrast with it, the habit of regarding the highway as a strictly government or parish affair, and its improvement in any respect as no man's private concern, and the somewhat stern and often rude face which suburban homes often present to the street in Europe, seems churlish and clownish. But between this extreme and that of forbidding all family privacy out of doors, there is a wide range. Croquet is doing something to unsettle the traditional idea that the only use of a home-ground is to set off the house; but few among us yet suspect how much time can be spent profitably, agreeably, and healthfully, or how large a share of our ordinary household duties, as well as our recreations, can be attended to in the open air, provided we have grounds suitably arranged and furnished.

There is reason for questioning whether women in this country are not gradually becoming disqualified for much enjoyment of nature. We have spent some months in a neighborhood so famed for its landscape beauty that it was, at the time, visited by hundreds of strangers. Notwithstanding the fact that there were the most inviting groves, ravines, and mountains on all sides, far and near, that the temperature was generally agreeably cool, and the walks in several directions not at all difficult, it was rare to meet women on foot a mile away from the houses at which they were staying; rare to meet them out of doors at all dressed otherwise than as for church or a shopping expedition in Broadway. In their driving and sailing, it was obviously the social opportunity, not the scenery, that was sought. A flower in the grass, a bunch of ash-keys, a birch trunk, the bark of which suggested the making of a house ornament, the most commonplace objects thus associated with indoor life, would at once take, and completely withhold, attention from the finest view. To have been once upon a certain road, or to a certain point, was a reason for not going there again. We have seen also, recently, seven carloads of people wait at Suspension Bridge, the greater part all the time in their seats, for half an hour of a fine autumn afternoon, but two of the whole number, and these men, taking the trouble to step the length of the train ahead, where, instead of the gloom of the station-house, there was a view that would repay a voyage across the Atlantic. To be sure, the greater number had been over the road, and had seen it before, from the car-windows, as they passed the bridge. Not one in a hundred of the women who can command a carriage in the Central Park has ever been in the Ramble; not one in a thousand has cared to walk in it twice. This lack of interest in nature is not often found in Europe except among the lowest peasantry. The vulgarest Englishwomen make at least an effort to appear superior to it, and they cannot do this without benefiting their children. At places of resort in Great Britain and Germany which may be compared with that we have referred to, go where we would, within a good half-day's walk, we have always found scores of women and girls, many of them showing by their attitude and occupation that they were not only really enjoying but studying nature with earnestness and deliberation. If there is such a defect, and it is growing upon us, how is it to be accounted for? We are inclined to think that the too exclusively indoor life, with intervals of church, lecture-room, and street, to which the better part of our women have been hitherto led, tends to disqualify them for observing truly, and consequently for enjoying, the beauty of nature on a large scale. With constant training of his faculties, no artist feels that he can appreciate or fully enjoy a landscape the first time or the first hour that he looks upon it.

Our American homes are, in some respects, the best for women in the world, but they are far from faultless, and they do not, in all respects, compare favorably, class for class, with those of the Old Country; and the weakest point of our suburban and rural homes is their lack of open-air family apartments, adapted to the climate and other conditions of our country—pieces of ground designed not so much to form pretty pictures from the windows, and thus add to our wall decorations, or from the street, and thus add to our cheap and showy house-fronts, but to be enjoyed from their own interior; to be occupied and lived in as an integral part of the home, as the grounds of Old-Country homes so much more commonly are. In suburban building-lots of the ordinary dimensions, the space between the building line, established by a good custom, if not by law, and the street is not often a suitable one to be used for this purpose, while the limited space in the rear of the house is commonly required for other necessary purposes. Mr. Scott urges that building-lots should generally be laid off twice the depth they usually are; but his plans are adapted to the customary conditions, and the question of attempting to secure family privacy out of doors by means of close plantations, under these artificial conditions, may, as we have already admitted, be considered as an open one. We simply protest against the principle involved in his argument. His work is intended and adapted to have a large influence in cultivating out-of-door habits and a love of nature, and the apparently unqualified support given in such passages as we have cited of a common prejudice against out-of-door domestic privacy is the more to be regretted.

In the second part, some seven hundred species and varieties of trees and shrubs are enumerated, and, as far as practicable, their landscape qualities indicated. The report made in regard to many of the acquisitions of the last twenty years is the best that we have seen; and it is gratifying to observe that, in numerous instances, it is based on observations of specimens found in our public grounds. In regard to many novelties, the mature character of which in this climate cannot be known for some years to come, we are glad to notice a commendable and unusual caution observed. The foliage of many of the new conifers, which is most attractive while they are in the sapling stage, changes character so greatly when they begin to bear seed, as to render them quite valueless for home plantations. With regard to shrubs, Mr. Scott truly says that if half a dozen of the commonest of the old kinds are thrown out of the long and bewildering series named in the catalogues of the great foreign nurseries, we shall find it difficult to select as many that will be their equals in beauty of form, foliage, or bloom. But it should be known also that, notwithstanding the number of high-priced and far-fetched novelties now offered, for some of the bushes that are of the highest value for landscape planting, we shall ask both our own and the foreign dealers in vain. We must look them up, as Mr. Scott shows that he has done, in our woodland pastures and along our neglected roadsides.

Of each part of Mr. Scott's work it may be said that it is the most valuable of its class that has been published in America since Mr. Downing's "Landscape Gardening."

PLANTINGS IN CENTRAL PARK: MARCH 1872

Memorandum Relating to Certain Work to Be Done, as Soon as Possible, Under General Direction of Mr. Demcker

March 1st 1872

1   The North Meadows, the Green and the Play ground, except where large rocks prevent, are to be bordered by scattered trees, singly and in small clusters or loose groups, all of kinds which will grow large and spread widely; that is to say with characteristic park trees. They are to be formed with low heads but not so low that sheep cannot graze under them. Oaks and such as have horizontal limbs should be trimmed with a trunk clean to height of about seven feet. Those which, like the American elm, branch more obtusely upward, may be allowed to branch lower. Trees on these grounds which have been trimmed to long naked trunks are to be shortened in to force new lower branching. Groves of trees on the border of the meadows, (as those near the Mineral Spring Pavilion) where either branches or roots are generally interlocking or likely soon to do so, are to be thinned to groups, clusters and single trees, with sufficient intervals to favor the desired general open park effect. In thinning those are to be spared when practicable which are likely to have long-lived, low branches; others, such as black oak and

sassafras to be generally cut out. Where shrubs have been set in the borders of these open grounds, unless to screen out some inharmonious object (as a barren rocky knoll) they are to be removed.

2 The above instructions in regard to thinning do not apply to trees intended for the shade of the walks and drive, the branches of which must be kept sufficiently high not to interfere with the passage required by the public on these ways, but trees trimmed unnecessarily and excessively high are to be headed in to force new branching.

3 Where trees have been planted at a regular distance from the edge of a drive or walk and at regular intervals, as in ordinary road-side planting, this character is to be changed, either by making some slight shift of position, or the entire removal, of the majority. Those allowed to remain will generally require heading in to force lower growth.

4 The last paragraph does not apply to trees on the outer malls, the trunks of which have been trimmed too high but the improvement of which may be postponed.

5 Hedge plants (spruces) on the transverse roads which are overgrown are to be reduced and trimmed with reference to a flat face flush with the retaining wall below them. Gaps are to be filled as far as possible by thinnings from existing plantations, trees with one side well filled to the bottom being preferred. These hedges are to be backed with a thicket chiefly of conifers and low thorny shrubs, the conifers will be mostly supplied by thinning. The transverse roads not hitherto planted are to be treated in the same way.

6 Spruces, Thujas and fastigiate conifers standing so near walks and drives that they will interfere with passage unless the lower branches are cut off, or so shortened in as to give them an ugly distorted character, are to be removed. Smaller conifers, as yews and retinosporas may sometimes be substituted for them; more frequently, especially on the winter drive, thickets of bayberry, winterberry, inkberry, hollies, kalmias, andromedas, mahonias, tree box, fiery thorn &c.

7 The last class of plants (but only such as are thoroughly hardy) is especially to be set on all the arches of the transverse roads, in loose hedges to form permanent screens thick from the ground. This is a matter of imperative importance this

season. The part of the screen which will be visable from the park is to be irregular and natural in character.

8   Clusters and groups of coniferous trees throughout the Park generally require numbers to be removed to secure the health and good development of the lower branches of those which will remain.

9   The middle parts of the Ramble in a line from the Terrace to Vista Rock are to be cleared of trees. The rocks in the upper part of the Ramble are to be made permanently visible from the terrace. Tall trees are to be retained and encouraged in the outer parts; dark evergreens on the nearer parts of the ridges, right and left, with a general gradation to light foliage upon and near Vista Rock. The recently made moss gardens are to be revised and the ground rendered natural by the removal of some of the boulders, making larger plain surfaces and by the introduction of more varied and common materials. Evergreen shrubs, ferns, moss, ivy, periwinkle, rock plants and common bulbs, (snow drop, dog tooth violet, crocusses &c.) are to be largely planted in the Ramble, and while carefully keeping to the landscape character required in the general view from the Terrace, and aiming at a much more natural wild character in the interior views than at present, much greater variety and more interest of detail is to be introduced.

10   Rock edges and clefts at various points, particularly the following; viz, in the Ramble; on both sides of the drive near the Sixth Avenue entrance; South of the Playground between the Dairy and South pond; North of the green; East of the Mall; between the Arsenal and the Mall; along the water-course of the upper park, the bridges and lakes; and on the drive north of Observatory Hill, are to be dressed with peat and wood earth and planted with ferns, mosses and Alpine plants.

11   Of the trees now standing in groves, except on the border of the larger turf surfaces, the poorer class need to be taken out, the others often to be headed down to remedy the effects of the mistaken trimming of the last two years, and generally these plantations should be given a naturally dense or obscure bottom character, by encouraging low growth and planting in underwood irregularly.

12   Wherever, in the parts of the park which have been planted, owing either to density of shade or the presence of

rock and general roughness of surface, fine close turf will either be out of character, liable to die out from drought or very difficult to mow, thickets of low mountain shrubs, broom, furze, heaths or mats of vines or herbacious plants, such as asters, gentians, lobelia, hepatica, southern wood, camomile, tansy, vervain, wild arum, wake robin, epigea, Solomons seal, golden rod, lysimachia, lycopodium, convolvulus, vinca are to be diligently introduced in patches and encouraged to completely cover the surface.

13 The patches of shrubs are now generally much too garden like. They are to be made more natural and picturesque, especially those on hillsides and broken ground by taking out some of the plants when there are many together of one kind, and introducing others; more upright growing or fastigiate species in some parts and many more low and spreading species (such as Forsythia suspensa, Rubus odorata and brambles) in others. Shrubs growing together must be made to blend more, both by the means above suggested and by special pruning for the purpose also by introducing clematis, lycium, wistaria, honeysuckles, and, for immediate effect, convolvulus, vetches &c.

14 Norway spruce and other spirey topped trees are soon likely to be too conspicuous, prominent and controlling on much of the winter drive. In thinning these plantations, pines should be more generally given the front place and in the place of some of the spruces, yews, mountain pines, Cembran pine, glaucous and weeping red cedar, retinosporas, cryptomeria &c. are to be introduced. The West drive north of 79th Street is to be made more cheerful by the introduction of a much larger number of such deciduous trees as by the character of the spray, color of bark, or their berries, will be interesting in the winter and will also associate well with the conifers; as birches, mountain ash and red twigged dogwood. Evergreen and other shrubs as mentioned in paragraphs 6 and 12 are also to be largely introduced in this district.

Where the tops of ridges have been planted with spirey topped conifers, as that west of the South pond, a portion of them are to be removed and pines substituted so as to establish a more quiet and flowing sky line.

Fred. Law Olmsted

To Gardeners

The work which has been done in getting ready that part of the park which is now out of sight, underneath the turf, trees and bushes, gravel and water, (including the purchased material such as the drain and water pipes), is equivalent to the labor of 1000 men during a period of sixteen years. The sole use of all this work is that of a foundation for something to be formed upon it and much the most important part of this something is to be produced by work to be hereafter done by and under the direction of the District Gardeners. Upon the intelligence and efficiency of the district Gardeners therefore, the value of the immense preparatory work which has been already done is dependent. So far as they work with different general motives or to obtain a different class of results from those for which the preparatory work was designed, that work will have been wasted. Even therefore, when it would be possible to aim at something better than was originally intended, it will be the part of an honest man to pursue that intention and make the best of it. Different and better purposes of gardening should be reserved to be worked out on ground where so much has not already been done for the purposes which have been in view in the Central Park.

It is, therefore, desired that the district gardeners should understand and intelligently adopt these original purposes and exert all their ability in a sincere endeavor to carry them out.

The object of this paper is to present a few leading points of these purposes with cautions against certain wrong views which many gardeners will be likely to hold.

The land and the construction of the park has not only cost the people of the city a great deal and its keeping up is not only to cost a great deal but the taking of so many building sites and the stopping of so many Avenues and Streets and causing people to go so much further around on their business than they would have otherwise needed to is a serious inconvenience. Every gardener should understand and bear in mind what all this outlay and inconvenience is for. It is not simply to give the people of the city an opportunity for getting fresh air and exercise; if it were it could have been obtained by other means than those to be provided on the park at much less cost. It is not simply to make a place of amusement or for the gratification of curiosity or for gaining knowledge. The main object and justification is simply to produce a certain influence on the minds of people and through this to make life in the city healthier and happier. The character of this influence is a poetic one and it is to be produced by means of scenes through observation of which the mind may be more or less lifted out of moods and habits into which it is, under the ordinary conditions of life in the city, likely to fall. As a general rule the more there is that is natural and simple and the less there is that is apparently artificial, or suggestive of the work of men, the better the scenery would be adapted to this purpose, and for this reason if there were but a few persons to be benefitted, it would be better that there were no roads or bridges or buildings; but the object being to offer the benefits of the park to a great many thousand people, of all classes and conditions, it is necessary to make extensive provision for their accommodation and to occupy a good deal of the ground with appliances for this purpose. So far as this consideration does not apply therefore, it may be said that the object of all the work that has been done on the park is to induce the formation, chiefly by the growth of trees and plants, of a considerable variety of natural landscape scenery. The rocks and water help to the same end, and the roads, walks, seats and other prominent structures are meant to be only such as will help the people the better to enjoy it.

It is desireable that all who are allowed to use discretion in working or directing work on or among trees, plants and turf on the Central Park, in order that they may proceed safely and intelligently without requiring constant instruction as to details of their duty, should understand what is the use of the Park and in just what way everything with which they will have to do will best help make the Park better for that use.

To foremen, gardeners and others who may have discretionary duties in the Central Park.

There are certain general considerations which every man

who is given any discretion in taking care of the Park should all the time bear in mind.

1   The people who are to visit the park this year or next are but a small fraction of those who must be expected to visit it hereafter. If the park had to be laid out, and especially if it had to be planted with reference only to the use of the next few years, a very different general plan, a very different way of planting and a very different way of managing the trees, would be proper from that which is required. No man is to use the discretion given him to secure pretty temporary effects at the expense of advantages for the future.

2   The special value of the Central Park to the city of New York will lie, and even now lies, in its comparative largeness. There are certain kinds of beauty possible to be had in it which it is not possible for the city to have anywhere else because on no other ground of the city is there scope and breadth enough for them. Such beauty as there is in a flower bed, such beauty as there is in a fir tree or a cluster of fir trees can be enjoyed on any piece of flat ground of quarter of an acre, can be had even in the back yard of a city house. The seven hundred acres of the Central Park can be better used. That which is expected to be especially valuable on the Central Park is the beauty of broad landscape scenes and of combinations of trees with trees and with rocks and turf and water.

No man is to use the discretion given him to secure pretty little local effects, at the expense of general effects and especially of broad landscape effects.

3   It must be remembered that what is good and beautiful in one place may be far from good & beautiful in another.

Gardeners and others are apt to think that work which would be regarded as excellent in a pleasure ground connected with a private house, or in a fine flower garden, must also be excellent anywhere in the Central Park. This is a great mistake; as great a mistake [...]

A great number of visitors have to be provided for in the park, for this reason the ground has to be cut up with roads and walks and encumbered with frequent buildings and other structures and appliances. Rocks have to be placed and trees and shrubs planted in some degree so as to fit these artificial features and with a view to convenience and economy in maintaining order. But, except for this reason, every bit of work done on the park should be done for the single purpose of making the visitor feel as if he had got far away from the town. Except in those things which are designed for the comfortable accommodation of visitors, the less anything that is seen appears to have been dressed up by human hands, the better.

For example it is intended in the Mall to give accommodations for a large number of visitors walking together and to let them have as open a prospect as is possible under the circumstances. To make this purpose obvious and to carry it out completely, the ground immediately adjoining the broad walk cannot be too evenly or flatly graded, the turf too fine or closely kept, nor the trees too carefully arranged to afford the largest degree of shade with the least degree of obstruction to the view. But a similar treatment of the ground and a similar disposition of trees is desireable nowhere else in the park.

To secure interest, it is necessary that some parts of the park should strongly contrast with others. As far as space will allow, therefore, smooth, simple, clean surfaces of turf on which the light falls evenly and the shadows are broad, and trees which have grown freely with plenty of room to stretch out their limbs are intended to be brought in contrast with surfaces which are very much broken and on which there is a great profusion of lines and colors and lights and shades, and with trees and bushes and plants which have grown in a somewhat crowded way, bent and mingled together as they generally are where nature plants them on rough ground, especially if the soil is rich and neither over dry nor over wet.

The perfection of such meadow and glade surfaces is found in nature only in the spring, when the turf is still short and growing evenly, but by shaving the grass closely at frequent intervals, this perfection can be nearly maintained through the summer. Consequently in preparing those parts of the ground where this effect is wanted, the surface, without being so flat as to be evidently artificial, can hardly be made too fine or too smooth and even, nor can the turf afterwards be kept too free of every plant except the grasses, nor the grass be kept too short or be too smoothly rolled. But with the same general object in view, precisely the opposite sort of treatment is required in other places. In these the surface should be more or less rough & rude, the trees & shrubs should grow more or less in bunches, there should be a great variety of character in them, some stretching up & some straggling along the ground; instead of a smooth surface of clean short grass there should be varied sorts of herbage, one crowding over another and all running together without any order, or there should be vines and creepers and mosses and ferns. There will be places where these two kinds of ground should play into one another and the surface and the plantations be of an intermediate character.

"USE OF THE CENTRAL PARK": MAY 1872

To William Robinson

Personal

110 Broadway
New York, May 17th 1872

My Dear Mr Robinson;

I have just read with interest and pleasure your introductory article on the Central Park. There is one consideration to which as an Englishman you are liable not to give due weight & to which I am sure that you will be glad to have your attention called.

You assume that the attendance at the Central Park will be much less than that at the London & Paris parks. This is natural when you see it as at present situated four miles from the centre of population of a town of less than a million inhabitants with very inconvenient means of access to it. The consideration I wish to present to you is that it was designed as a park to be situated at the precise centre of population of city of two millions, that population cut off from all rural suburbs and this its only park; Whether with good judgement or not the designers made their calculations upon a much larger attendance than they had been accustomed to see in the London & Paris parks. Up to the present time the attendance fully equals their anticipations; in ten years more there is every reason to believe that the park will be enclosed by the compact town, the borders of which were a mile away when it was laid out. As yet the streets which bound the park are incompletely graded. At present we rarely have over 100,000 at a time on the park. But as commerce drives the people northward for their homes and means of communication are improved, if this number should not often be several times multiplied, it can only be because the attractions of the park are counterweighed by the dangers, discomforts and annoyances which will arise from its crowded condition.

It may be oweing to its peculiar form, and the disposition of the people, after having travelled so far to reach it, not to walk two or three miles to enjoy its further parts, but I have never seen the parks of London or Paris appear to be as much used as the lower division of the Central Park is already every fine Saturday and Sunday. Last Sunday the count of those entering the gates on foot was over 70,000 and a large number were taken in in omnibuses—special park vehicles carrying ten or twelve each—and the most of them must have travelled at least three miles to reach the lower end of the park.

The park is so far away that of course working people cannot yet get to it after the work of the day is over and have only holiday use of it, but I think that we ordinarily in fair weather have an attendance of ten to twenty thousand a day.

I have no statistics of the London parks but of course a larger number than this would be likely to saunter through some of them on their way from one point outside them to another—a kind of use of the Central Park which has not yet begun.

We have given our view of the bearing of this consideration upon the question of the sub-ways in the second of a series of letters printed last winter by the Central Park authorities, & which I will send you. I don't hope to change your opinion by a mere statement of our theory & it is difficult to cite facts, but you may find it worth your while to read from page 28 to 32.

Sincerely Yours,

Fred. Law Olmsted

To Samuel Bowles

City of New York
Department of Public Parks
265 Broadway
May 7th 1872

My Dear Bowles;

I have not seen the Republican since the wreck but I see it named among the papers that accept Greeley. I can only imagine it true on the presumption that it is intended to influence the other conventions toward some desired course. The Republican has thus far represented my views, as usual, rather more exactly than any other paper, though expressing more faith in the Cincinnati movement than I had had for some time. But it passes my understanding how any man who has held the views it has expressed can prefer Greeley and the crowd who go with and possess Greeley to Grant and his crowd. Grant is ignorant, fails to understand his duties and blunders badly. His faults are chiefly negative. Greeley's faults are positive. He will do with set purpose what Grant does by failure. He will do systematically what Grant does occasionally and in a perfectly innocent desultory way. Greeley acts the virtues as far as he can which Grant takes naturally, and he goes naturally to the vices into which Grant stumbles.

A thousand years of Grant, say I, before one minute of Greeley.

I have taken some pains to find what others are thinking and at the Club and elsewhere have seen a good many of those who looked hopefully toward Cincinnati. I have not seen one who does not feel outraged or who will not vote for Grant rather than Greeley.

Yours Vry Truly

Fred. Law Olmsted

To Samuel Bowles

Fred. Law Olmsted. Calvert Vaux. F. C. Withers.
Olmsted, Vaux & Co.,
Landscape Archt's,
110 Broadway
May 11th 1872

My Dear Bowles;

All I can say is that I differ with your estimate of Greeley most completely. A more dangerous man for the presidency, a man more sure to humiliate us beyond endurance, to help educate our youth in the tendencies most hazardous to the nation, to foster and stimulate our worst conceits could not be found. If you help to elect him, you will curse the day through endless years of torment.

What Godkin will say or do I don't know, but if what you say, then I shall say that the damn'd infection of an excited rabble has made him crazy along with the rest and I am sorry for him, for myself & the country. An angel from heaven will not make two and two five.

Sorrowfully.

F.L.O.

To Samuel Bowles

New York, May 13th 1872

My Dear Bowles;

About Godkin again, I saw the Nation before I saw the Republican and appalled by its feeble tone I wrote to Godkin as I wrote to you, for it wholly passes my comprehension how any man of common sense & a fair knowledge of the world can speak of Greeley's nomination with any patience. It is to me the most stinging insult I ever met to be soberly asked to vote that such a man should be President—Chief Magistrate of my country. I say again I cannot understand how respectable gentlemen can have been cajoled into such an act, into complicity in such an act. Well I have seen Godkin and I am happy to say that he is—almost as crazy as I am. He is a zealous Free Trader which I am not, and he has a strong anger with Grant which I have not, but if he were to choose between Greeley & Grant today I think he would be compelled to take Grant.

But I take more comfort in the Post. Find the answer to your praises—nay, apologies—for Greeley in the leader tonight. I cannot believe the good sense of the country and I have so far parted company, that after sober consideration—examination of history—Greeley will be preferred to Grant or any other man who can be set up. I say the Post appears to me to tell the whole or more nearly the whole of your half truths. But it is, I swear! too bad to reason about. My whole reason is a woman's reason. I know he is an imposter. You knew he was an imposter before you went to Cincinnati. As an imposter his method & the success of his method was amusing but now you soberly ask me to help him impose on the country. If I do I'm damned. If all the world went for him & I stood all alone, it would be the unforgiveable sin to my moral nature to have any patience with such an outrage to it. Certainly I am not speaking coolly or deliberately—but that I speak my deliberate convictions I know.

If I seemed to refer, as your letter seems to indicate, to some special known swindle at Cincinnati, as a reason for my indignation, I was wrong. Judge you. Some months ago I dined with Dorsheimer in Buffalo and argued the case against Grant as well as I could, Dorsheimer sustaining & apologizing for Grant. By & by Dorsheimer sent for me: told me the story of his conversion—of Selden & others—argued the necessity of a demonstration Cincinnati-ward, read his pronunciamento and urged me to sign it. I was half disposed to do so, and fully disposed to go to Cincinnati, had partially agreed to do so, when he told me that Greeley was wanting to come in, had sent for him, and that Waldo Hutchins had actually signed it. I said at once "is it possible you would take Waldo Hutchins and that you think of letting Greeley get on? You are going to be swindled out of your boots, I will have nothing to do with it." Two days after came the cast of Greeley's first bait for the Free

Traders. I said to Godkin when I saw who were in it—"It is hardly possible the honest reformers are not going to be sold at Cincinnati." I have no more doubt they were sold than I have that corruption breeds pestilence. There has not been a big scheme of political swindling going on here for years that this white hatted old patriarch has not been mooning round innocently while such dirty little steamtugs as Waldo Hutchins & John Cochrane were doing his work in them.

Well! if everybody who thinks as I do, feels as I do, there'll be a sharp fight before he is elected and till the fight is over, I will not despair of the republic, but when such a man can have the countenance of such men as Sam Bowles in asking to be made President of the United States, it is the darkest day I have known. Bull Run was bright to it. I gird up my loins but can't help the sentimental howl.

F.L.O.

The longer I have to think of it the more astoundingly bad it seems to me. I cannot reconcile myself to it—on the contrary I am more & more outraged and I keep coming back to the question: am I mad, or are you? If Greeley's elected we shall soon see.

"THE WORST HABIT POSSIBLE FOR A PRESIDENT":
MAY 1872

To Samuel Bowles

Fred. Law Olmsted. Calvert Vaux. F. C. Withers
Olmsted, Vaux & Co.,
Landscape Archt's,
110 Broadway
May 16th 1872

My Dear Bowles;

Yours of 14th & 15th are recvd. Thank you & thank you.

It is simply because I feel that "he *is* the greatest imposter who ever played upon the American people"—just that, that I feel so ashamed of the whole performance. You write as if you questioned his being an imposter. You don't in your heart the least bit. You know he is an imposter. He pretends to be a plain, careless, even rude farmer like man, simple and free of self consciousness to the point of eccentricity—a just man, a generous compassionate man, temperate, unsophisticated, guileless. Now you know that he is a fop, excessively self conscious, studying effect with more elaboration & skill than any living actor or noted charlatan; that he is selfish, cruel, unjust, frantically passionate and self willed and that he has been hand and glove with the most deeply damn'd villains in this great sinful city.

I think you are right he is a greater imposter than even Fremont. Fremont could not afford to open his mouth.

I respect your weakness for a successful journalist, but while journalism may be & should be & is something much better, it remains a trade. Mr Greeley is a dealer in the market of public opinion—a measurer of public prejudices & whims & fashions. He habitually values a principle, (or the utterance of a principle or the application of a principle) very much with reference to the ad captandum, sensational presentation of it and the demand which as so presented, it will for the moment command among busy touch & go minds.

Just the worst habit possible for a President of the United States, who should be a balance wheel.

It is a bad doctrine that a successful editor, or a successful trader in anything, will be successful in dealing with questions for all time, questions of the permanent interest of a nation, questions of statesmanship.

I can't think of a worse thing to do, among possible things, than for us to make this old humbug of a patriarch President. It is carrying the joke altogether too far. I can't but hope the reaction will come before the election, sure as it is to come.—I say this knowing too that there are hundreds of thousands still bound to Fremont.

I bought a nine dollar steeple crowned black silk hat yesterday; the first time I have had one in twenty years, or since I was married. I am going to get straps on my trousers. I am also cultivating a chest voice. When you come to see me I shall not give you any milk.

More in anger than in sorrow.

F.L.O.

DECLINING A VICE PRESIDENTIAL NOMINATION:
JUNE 1872

To the New-York Evening Post

My name was used without my knowledge in the resolutions of
the gentlemen who met on Friday at the Fifth Avenue Hotel.
Their action does not call for any expression of opinion on
my part on the questions of the present political canvass; but,
while thanking them sincerely for their good opinion, I must
express my regret that they should have thought it expedient
to take up as a representative of their requirements one who is
so completely separated from the political field, and so much
absorbed in professional and official duties as I am.

"I WOULD NOT ACCEPT AN OFFICE": JUNE 1872

To James Miller McKim

DEPT PARKS, 265 Broadway
June 28th 1872

Dear Mr McKim;

Thanks for your note of 24th. Really I had not read the Tribune article and did not know how it treated the matter. When
Collins first informed me of what had occurred I was much
overcome. It appeared to me in the highest degree absurd. (It
is absurd). And I could not but think that others would see it
as I did and therefore that it was another gross blunder of the
gentlemen concerned. I am surprized & gratified that it is so
well received.

But if I were elected I would not accept an office for which I
am so particularly disqualified and I still must feel that to seem
to assent to the suggestion would be wrong.

I have the greatest possible respect for the gentlemen who so
greatly honored me and would not for the world do anything
that I could avoid to disconcert or disappoint them.

Very Truly Yours

Fred. Law Olmsted

Report of the Landscape Architects

January 1, 1874

To the Brooklyn Park Commissioners:
Gentlemen:

The object of the work which has been done on the Brooklyn Park, during the eight years in which we have had the honor to serve your Commission, has been the creation of scenes of natural character as attractive and graceful as the local conditions would allow, and their advantageous presentation.

With respect to the improvement of the scenery, the work done has, so far, been but preparatory to the greater work asked of nature; the constructions, through the use of which it was to be enjoyed, such as roads, walks, shelters, and places of refreshment, were, on the other hand, to be turned out complete at once. It was therefore inevitable that these constructions should, for a certain period, assume undue importance. In the greater part of the Park that period is already well-nigh passed; special search must be made to find a scene in which nature does not reign supreme, or in which, if artificial objects are to be recognized, they are not relatively unimportant and unobtrusive incidents of convenience.

The general character of the scenery of the Park, even in its present formative condition, is undeniably broad, simple, and quiet, yet the variations of the surface, and the disposition of open woods, thickets, glades, meadows, and of still and running waters, is such that it cannot be deemed monotonous. Its characteristic features in these respects are to be strengthened not only by growth, but also almost equally by timely reduction of whatever will tend to the weakening of distinctive qualities, or to the repression of elements intended to be aggrandized.

There were originally two main bodies of natural wood on the site of the Park, connected by a narrow belt at the point where the Long Meadow is now most contracted; the eastern body being broken by bays where the Nethermead, the head of the Lull-water, and the Deer Paddock now are.

The trees had grown thickly, their lower limbs were dead or

dying, and two-thirds of all, though yet of but moderate size, were decayed in the trunk. Many had, also, been mangled by violence.

Where a sufficient proportion of these old trees were not yet decrepid and drawn up by the effect of excessive shade beyond the possibility of restoration to moderately well-proportioned and umbrageous forms, the less promising have been taken out and an attempt made to develop open-wooded or park-like scenery. So far as proper means for this purpose have been used, the result at this time is even better than had been expected, but apprehension of the effect of wind and unwillingness to even temporarily destroy the beauty and materially lessen the shade of those parts of the Park which, until the advance of new plantations, would alone be attractive resorts, has so far caused twice as many trees to be spared as is desirable, and has prevented the adequate topping of others. In this respect much in the way of judicious removal remains to be done to enhance the beauty of the Park.

In other parts of the old woods, where trees which possessed either dignity or picturesqueness were more rare, it has been sought, by planting young trees and underwood about and among them, to develop bosky masses of foliage, in which the old trees should supply the upper parts, their poverty below being hidden by the new. Effects which are very satisfactory were thus obtained with great rapidity in those portions of the East Woods where foot visitors are confined to the walks.

These effects are, however, dependent on the maintenance of a rich, low growth, which without attention will soon fail.

Great care has been taken to secure a natural and picturesque edge to the old woods, both by breaking into them and by planting beyond them the lowest-headed large trees that could be procured. Similar trees have also been used to prevent as far as possible the occurrence of a strong contrast between the old woods and the new plantations. The shape of the ground (its natural features being almost invariably enlarged in the process of grading) has been favorable to the desired result, the outer and more conspicuous parts of the masses being on lower ground than those interior, and the few large trees under these circumstances giving character to the whole.

Most of the plantations, especially on the northern part of

the Park, are on very bleak ground, and to lessen the severity of the exposure of the young plants, as well as to provide against and secure greater immediate effects to the eye, many trees have been planted in addition to those intended to remain. That the permanent trees may have the required vigor and not be crowded into ungainly forms, a gradual thinning out of these plantations, a little every year for many years to come, is essential.

The chief defect in the scenery of the Park, at the present time, lies in the backward condition of the plantations in the southern part of the Long Meadow, west of the Lake, and south and west of Lookout Hill. This is primarily due to the fact that they were the last made, but it also should be remembered that there has been much more difficulty in procuring suitable soil for these parts in adequate quantities, and that to bring them to a satisfactory condition unusually liberal top-dressing will therefore be needed.

We have not in previous reports duly expressed our obligations to Mr. Bullard, who throughout the work has been in direct superintendence of the planting. Comprehending with a true artistic spirit the intention of the landscape design as a whole, he has spared no study or personal labor to secure the means of its realization in detail.

The surface of the water in the Lake is not yet ordinarily seen at the elevation with reference to which all the associated elements of scenery have been designed. This serious defect, which detracts much from the variety of the shore lines, and consequently from the beauty of the Lake itself (to a degree which can be hardly imagined), is due to the leakage of the water basin, and is expected to be gradually corrected by the action of natural causes.

The charm of the Park will lie chiefly in the contrast of its occasional bodies of low foliage, intricate, obscure, and mysterious, with the more open groves and woods, and of both with its fair expanses of unbroken turf. Its beauty will, therefore, depend on the care and skill with which these respective qualities, each in its appropriate place, are nursed and guarded.

The areas of the Long Meadow and the Nethermead are so large, that it has been deemed unnecessary to maintain the restrictions usually enforced in public grounds in this climate upon walking on the turf. The attractions and the public value of the Park have thus been undoubtedly very much enhanced. But the two dangers which attend this course already begin to be manifest, and it is evident that unless strenuously guarded against, serious evils will sooner or later result. One of these dangers is that of the wearing out of the turf in streaks and patches, the other is that of the destruction of underwood, shrubs, and plants, and the hazardous and inconvenient straggling of visitors across drives and rides, arising from the difficulty of restricting the privilege of walking on the turf within proper limits. The first is to be prevented by so limiting the use of the turf that it will not be trodden upon when in a poachy condition, or when it is excessively dry and inelastic, and by the use of slight guards, frequently shifted from point to point, as patches or streaks of wear become evident. The other may be particularly guarded against by concealed or inconspicuous barriers, and by cautionary signs, but can be permanently kept within tolerable bounds only by special efforts for the purpose made by an active, vigilant, faithful, and numerous body of keepers.

There are certain conveniences still wanting in the Park, which can only be adequately and appropriately supplied by architectural structures of some magnitude. The rapid growth of the young woods would now, however, in nearly every case, save these from being unduly prominent, and the erection of the Lookout Tower, with the adjoining shelters, and of the Refectory at the east foot of the Lookout Hill, with the bridge near it, would be found not only to add much to the accommodation of visitors and the comfort with which the scenery of the Park would be enjoyed, but to make more intelligible and give needed emphasis to important elements of its general design.

We desire here to acknowledge the value of the services rendered to us and to your Commission by Mr. E. C. Miller, who was principal assistant when the working drawings were made for the Plaza and for the Endale, Meadowport, Nethermead, and Eastwood arches; also, by Mr. Bassett Jones, who prepared the working drawings required for the Cleftridge Span and for the Tower to be erected on Lookout Hill; also by Mr. Thomas Wisedell, who had charge of the working drawings needed for the Concert Grove buildings and stonework and for the Martyrs Memorial at Fort Greene.

The main entrance to the Park, as yet, falls much short of

manifesting the value of the arrangements which have been in large part carried out in connection with it, and we take the occasion to explain its design more fully than we have yet done.

The principal entrance to a large metropolitan park admits in its design of more than one theory of artistic arrangement. The contrast between the urban and rural requires in some cases to be sharply drawn, the city enclosing the park as squarely and completely as a picture-frame encloses a picture. In other situations and under different circumstances a series of intermediate, partly rural and partly urban, effects may, with propriety, be introduced at the point of junction. In the Brooklyn Park, the latter arrangement seemed to be preferable for several reasons.

When the Reservoir and East Side Lands were, in accordance with our recommendation, discarded from the design, the Park at once became a unit of agreeable form. Its breadth of territory gradually increased as the visitor passed farther and farther from the main city entrance, and an opportunity evidently existed for a desirable and comparatively cheap extension of its southern boundary at some future time. The unsatisfactory feature was the shape of the entrance itself, left at the apex of a triangle which was apparently struggling to wedge its way into the street system of the city. To overcome this serious difficulty, the Plaza was introduced as a main elementary feature in the general design, and the land necessary for its construction was added to the Park territory before any improvements made by the Park Commission at the public expense had enhanced its value.

The intention controlling the arrangement of the Plaza plan will now probably be comprehended by the ordinary visitor to the Park, but the effect will be much more complete and artistic a few years hence, when the trees planted in the walks shall have attained a sufficient growth to give the definite skyline which is so much needed. As the design now stands, the apex of the triangle which forms the actual entrance has become a mere segment of an ellipse, eight hundred feet in diameter, and, therefore, on a scale large enough to contrast favorably even with such a wide street of approach as Flatbush avenue. Three large masses of plantation are introduced outside the Park boundary in connection with the Plaza design, so that the rural element may be strongly suggested before the main entrance is reached.

The Park gateway should be a handsome architectural

structure, with an arcade extending over the walk, so that many persons may with comfort wait for the cars at this point under cover when the weather is showery, and the pavement necessary to carry out this feature of the design has been designed and laid.

A platform for public meetings connects the centre of the Plaza with the city, and a large fountain basin is introduced as a central feature.

In the design for the fountain the aim has been to express clearly its special artistic purpose. An artificial flow of water on a liberal scale is prepared for, and has been calculated on from the outset. So long as the supply to the various jets is inadequate, this design will of course appear to be out of proportion to the result produced, but when the necessary additional forcing power is brought into operation, the stone base, with its bronze corona, will hardly be seen, and therefore will certainly not be considered too large an element in the general design.

It was evident that artificial light should be freely introduced in the Plaza, as it is a public promenade intended for night use; but it was also clear that the lines formed by the play of water and the general artistic effect in the Large Fountain would be much interfered with if a series of lamps elevated on the ordinary high posts should be a part of the design. The lighting has, therefore, been arranged for in connection with the railing for protection that surrounds the Fountain, the intention being, as mentioned in our last report, to have an interior circular line or ring of light below the eye and a few feet only above the water surface, so that the reflection of the globes would form a corresponding line that would be recognized as an element in the design, even by the ordinary observer.

At the north end of the platform, opposite the Lincoln statue, a public rostrum is proposed to be placed, the United States flag being displayed in connection with it. Whenever this feature is added the temporary staffs for the flags of the city and State now erected in the Plaza should be replaced by others of more elaborate and elegant design.

Respectfully,

OLMSTED & VAUX,
Landscape Architects

A REPORT ON RENOVATIONS AT THE CAPITOL:
NOVEMBER 1874

The National Capitol

Mr. Fred. Law Olmsted on the
Improvements in Progress

CHARACTERISTICS OF THE OLD CAPITOL
GROUNDS—DETAILS OF THE IMPROVEMENTS—
DUE ALLOWANCE TO BE MADE FOR ARCHITECTURAL
EFFECT—PROGRESS OF THE CHANGES

New York, Nov. 27, 1874

To the Editor of the Tribune.

SIR:

I cheerfully comply with your request for the means of laying before your readers a more complete and detailed explanation than that supplied by the report of the Secretary of the Interior, of the operations in progress on the ground east of the National Capitol. The need for it I presume to lie in the fact that, while much destruction is evident and a large force is at work, nothing is approaching completion, no improvement is found, and no intelligible plan can yet be recognized.

The place was originally a flat table, slightly inclined toward the west, where a straight street, crossing it from north to south, formed the only approach for carriages to the Capitol from any direction. East of this street there was a rectangular grass-plat bounded by straight walks; other trees appear to have been planted, at an early day, in imperfect rows alongside these walks, most of which died young. At various periods since then trees have been planted in and adjoining the first rows, some to take the place of those dying; some because of unwise haste to secure shade; some because they were of species newly arrived in the country and fashionable, and some with no intelligent purpose. A great number of rank upstarts were allowed to crowd and distort and starve the more permanent and valuable sort. The original thin soil had probably been worn out and washed away under colonial tobacco culture, and left little but a sterile and exceedingly stiff brick clay, over which street-sweepings from the old dirt roads of Washington, with some Tiber mud, have from time to time been laid. A careful forester's survey made this Summer indicated that the trees must have been generally taken from the woods, poorly lifted and poorly planted, and that their roots had rarely attempted to penetrate the clay but had sought food by running far and wide close to the surface. Three-fourths of them were in unsound condition, many far gone with decay, and the foliage of nearly all began to wilt after lacking rain but two weeks. With two exceptions the largest and best stood near the east boundary, their roots breaking out on a bank eight feet in hight formed by the recent grading down of First-st., which bank barred both approach and vision toward the Capitol. Shrubs and flower beds were dropped about here and there, many of the shrubs being of late sick or dead, and the flower beds overgrown by grass and weeds.

THE OLD GROUNDS NOT IN HARMONY WITH THE CAPITOL

Looked at by itself, without reference to the Capitol; looked at in comparison with what is now to be seen in the early building stage of a designed improvement, or with any of the desert tracts which lie at short distances in all directions about it, it might be regarded as a beautiful place, and it tolerably served the purpose of a local playground for residents of the neighborhood. Its devastation could not therefore be projected without some pathetic feeling, nor without giving occasion for honest, earnest, and rational remonstrance. The beauty of the trees and old associations connected with them have been feelingly described, and it has been urged that once removed they could not be replaced in fifty years.

On the other hand, it was to be said that the Capitol could not be replaced at a cost of less that than $20,000,000, of which sum but a small part represents the body of conveniences provided for the transaction of the business of Congress, the remainder and larger part standing for the means of a suitably dignified, beautiful, and imposing effect in the vestment of these conveniences; that the ground, as it was, contributed not in the slightest degree to the conveniences for business of the Capitol, while, because of the inclination of the surface toward

the building and the position of the trees, not half its due architectural effect could be enjoyed; that scarcely one of the larger
trees had 50 or even 20 years' life in it; and the Capitol, being
a permanent and monumental structure, the ground about it
should be managed with reference not merely to present but
to future effect.

THE OLD PARK SWEPT AWAY

This view has prevailed, and the old park has accordingly been
swept away. Congress, at the close of its last session, having
provided means for the purpose, the work began under contract
on the 17th of August, since when there has been not yet quite
time, with all the men who could be employed economically,
to accomplish the grading, the amount of earth to be removed
being about 150,000 cubic yards. Other operations seen in
progress on ground where the grading is complete are the tillage and tempering of the newly exposed subsoil to the depth
of two feet; the return to it of the old soil with additions to
the depth of a foot; the taking up of the old sewer, drainage,
water, and gas pipes, and the laying of new and much better and
more elaborate systems of each; the transplanting of some of the
more thrifty of the old trees which have been preserved, to new
places; and some laying of curb, gutters, gratings, and road and
walk foundations, with a little pavement. These operations have
seemed detached and purposeless because divided by those of
grading, but the missing links are expected to be for the most
part inserted before Winter stops work, when the plan will be
more intelligible.

MAIN PURPOSE OF THE DESIGN

The general design is very simple, and will be easily understood.
It has two purposes: First, to provide convenient approaches
to and standing room about the Capitol; second, to allow its
imposing dimensions and the beauty of its architecture to have
due effect, and so far as possible, to aid and highten that effect.
    The idea of a park, flower-garden and play-ground is dis-
carded, and the whole meager area of the little lot in which the
Capitol is placed is to be treated as a court-yard and dependency
of the building. A paved carriage-court is to extend all along its
east front, giving access to each door. Walks and carriage-ways

are to be formed between it and each of the fifteen streets leading from all sides toward the Capitol; the course of these approaches, with one exception, will be curved, but each curve is to be governed by reference to a purpose of convenience. Where two purposes of convenience come in competition, that one is to be allowed the advantage by yielding to which greater breadth for turf surface will be gained; and by humoring this secondary purpose as much as possible, without an essential sacrifice of convenience on the whole, two elliptical spaces are to be obtained, measuring each from 400 to 600 feet across, in which a field of slightly undulating surface may be formed, unbroken, except by a few groups of trees.

SUBORDINATION OF THE GROUNDS TO THE BUILDING

As the trees to be planted grow, the larger part of the road and walk space will be shaded, but the object of happy compositions of the foliage with the Capitol, and of pleasant views from important points of the Capitol is not to be sacrificed to the object of making its court-yard, in all its parts and in all seasons, a perfectly comfortable lounging place or exercise ground.

The same principle of subordination to the building will prevent the introduction in any part of the ground of local ornaments, whether in flowers, leaf-plants, or other objects simply curious or beautiful in themselves. Those matters only will be decorated which by their position and form carry out, repeat, and support the architectural design, nor will any decoration be such as to hold the eye of an observer when in a position to take a general view of the Capitol.

The carriage-court will be bounded opposite the building by a walk or esplanade, laid with colored tile, and this will be separated from the broad turf spaces beyond it by a structure combining the purposes of a parapet or barrier, and a seat, so curved in plan, that unobstructed views of the Capitol may be obtained from it at various distances from 100 to 300 feet from the nearest point of its front, and at every practicable angle of vision. The parapet is to be formed of blue and red stone, and is to be also divided by piers, supporting bronze gas-posts. This work is under contract, and, if the weather is favorable, sections of it are expected to be complete before Congress meets.

FURTHER PLANS IN PROGRESS

The roads are designed to be of concrete, but only the base of gravel will be laid this year.

Other details can hardly be explained without drawings, and what has been said will sufficiently indicate the general intention.

No work has been done on the ground west of the Capitol, except in the deposit for storage of material taken from the east side. Designs for important improvements are, however, advanced, and are soon to be submitted to the Committee of Congress. Your obedient servant,

Fred. Law Olmsted

"AN IDEAL IN VIEW": 1877

Landscape Gardening

Landscape gardening is a branch of horticulture, the highest results of which may be attained by processes of a comparatively simple character—simpler, for instance, than those of kitchen or of floral gardening. Failure of success in it being oftener due to a halting purpose than to lack of science, of means, or of skill, this article will be chiefly given to establishing the definition and limitation of the general end proper to the art; some indications being incidentally presented of the manner in which, under the requirement of different individual tastes and different local conditions, it may be judiciously pursued.

There are two other branches of horticulture, which in ordinary practice are often so much confounded with that of landscape gardening that the reader may find it convenient to have them set apart from it at the outset. One of them is the cultivation of plants with special regard to an interest in their distinctive individual qualities. The other is the cultivation of plants (trees, shrubs, perennials, and annuals) with a view to the production of effects on the principles commonly studied in the arrangement of precious stones, enamel, and gold in an elaborate piece of jewelry, or of flowers when sorted by colors and arranged for the decoration of a head-dress, a dinner-table, or a terrace. Whether, in any undertaking, one of these two leading motives or that of landscape gardening be adopted, it may be presumed that the result will satisfy that motive in proportion as it shall be followed to the end with singleness of purpose. We now turn, therefore, from the two which have been defined to consider what, in distinction from them, the leading motive of landscape gardening may be.

Derivatively, the word "landscape" is thought to apply only to such a scene as enables the observer to comprehend the shape of the earth's surface far before him, or, as we say in common idiom, "to get the lie of the land," the land's shape. Consistently with this view, it will be found, on comparing a variety of scenes, that those which would be most unhesitatingly classed as landscapes are distinguished by a certain degree of breadth and distance of view. Looking at the face of a thick wood near at hand or of a precipitous rock, we do not use the term. Pursuing the comparison farther, it will be found that in each of those scenes to which the word more aptly applies there is a more marked subordination of various details to a characteristic effect of the scene as a whole. As Lowell says, "A real landscape never presents itself to us as a disjointed succession of isolated particulars; we take it in with one sweep of the eyes—its light, its shadow, its melting gradations of distance." But there are many situations in which plant-beauty is desired where the area to be operated upon is so limited, or so shaped and circumstanced, that the depth and breadth of a landscape scene must be considered impracticable of attainment. In America gardening is required for the decoration of places of this class many thousand times for one in which such restraining conditions are not encountered; and the question may be asked whether they must all be excluded from the field of landscape gardening, and if not, what, in these cases, can be the significance of the prefix "landscape"? As a general rule, probably, so many purposes require to be served, and so many diverse conditions to be reconciled, that the only rule of art that can be consistently applied is that of architecture, which would prescribe that every plant, as well as every moulding, shall bear its part in the "adornment of a service." To this end, parterre and specimen gardening are more available than landscape gardening. But it may happen that where, with due regard to considerations of health and convenience, there would be scant space for more than two or three middle-sized trees to grow, there will yet be room for a great deal of careful study, and, with careful study, of success in producing effects the value of which has nothing in common with either of the objects of horticulture thus far defined.

As an example, suppose a common village dooryard, in which are found, as too often there may be, a dozen trees of different sorts planted twenty years before, and that, by good chance, among them there is one, standing a little way from the centre, of that royal variety of European linden called *Alba pendula*. Trampled under by its coarser and greedier fellows, and half starved, youth and a good constitution may yet have left it in such condition that, all the rest being rooted out, sunlight given it on all sides, shortened in, balanced, cleaned, watered, drained, stimulated, fed, guarded from insidious enemies, its twigs will grow long, delicate, and pliant; its branches low and trailing, its bark become like a soft, finely-grained leather, its upper leaf-surface like silk, and its lower leaf-surface of such texture and tint that, with the faintest sunlight and the softest summer breeze, a constant wavering sheen, as of a damask hanging, will be flowing over the whole body of its foliage. While it regains its birthright in this respect it will also acquire, with fullness of form and moderate play of contour, a stateliness of carriage unusual in a tree of its age and stature. If landscape gardening is for the time to take its order from this princess of the fields, and all within the little court made becoming with her state, the original level surface of the ground need be but slightly modified, yet it may perceptibly fall away from near her, dipping in a long and very gentle wave to rise again with a varying double curve on all sides. There cannot, then, be too much pains taken to spread over it a velvet carpet of perfect turf, uniform in color and quality. Looking upon this from the house, it should seem to be margined on all sides by a rich, thick bank, generally low in front and rising as it recedes, of shrubs and flowering plants; the preparation for which may have required for years a clean-lined border, curve playing into curve, all the way round. A very few plants of delicate and refined character may stand out in advance, but such interruptions of the quiet of the turf must be made very cautiously. Of furniture or artificial ornaments there must be none, or next to none, for even bodily comfort may willingly defer a little to the dainty genius of the place. They may well walk, for instance, a few steps farther who would take a lounging seat, put up their feet, and knock the ashes from their pipes. Yet a single Chinese garden-stool of a softly mottled turquoise-blue will have a good effect if set where a flickering light will fall upon it on the shady side of the tree. The rear rank of shrubs will need to stand so far back that there will be no room to cultivate a suitable hedge against the street. The fence will then best be a wall of cut stone, with decorated gate-piers; or with a base of stone it may be of deftly-wrought iron touched with gilt. By no means a casting with clumsy and overdone effort at feeble ornament—much better a wooden construction of less cost, in which there is a reflection, with variety, of the style of the house if that is of wood also, or if it is not, then something like a banister-rail of turned work, but with no obviously weak parts. The gateway being formed in a symmetrical recess of the fence nearly opposite the tree, the house-door being on the side, the approach to it will bend, with a moderate double curve, in such a way as to seem to give place to the tree, and at the same time allow the greatest expanse of unbroken lawn-surface. Near the gateway, and again near the corner farthest from it, there may be a small tree or a cluster of small trees or large shrubs, forming low, broad heads (dogwood grown in tree-form, sassafras kept low, or, to save time, the neat white mulberry), the tops of which, playing into that of the loftier linden on the right, will in time give to those sitting at the bay-window of the living-room a flowing sky-line, depressed and apparently receding along the middle. If there is a tall building over the way with signs, or which otherwise offends, and the sidewalk space outside admits, we will plant upon it two trees only, adjusting them, as to both kind and position, so that they will almost repeat the depressed line of the nearer foliage, at no greater distance than is necessary to obscure the building. Quite hidden it need not be, lest, also, there should be some of the sky lost, banishment from the lower fields of the sky being a punishment that we should strive not to need. But let us hope that at the worst we have but our neighbor's stable opposite, and that the tops of more distant trees may be seen over it; we shall then still be glad to have the chance of bringing up two trees, set somewhat farther apart than before, on the roadside, as their effect will be to make an enlarged consistency of character, to close in and gather together all that makes up the home-scene, and to aid the turf in relieving it of a tendency to pettiness and excitement which lies in and under the shrubbery.

Let a different theme be sung on the same ground. Suppose that it is an aged beech that we have found, badly used in its middle age as the linden in its youth—storm-bent, lop-limbed, and one-sided, its veteran trunk furrowed, scarred, patched, scaly, and spreading far out to its knotted roots, that heave all the ground about like taut-set cables. If we had wanted a fine-dressy place, this interesting object would have been cut away though it were the last tree within a mile. Accepting it, nothing would be more common, and nothing less like landscape gardening, than to attempt to make a smooth and even surface under it. Let it be acknowledged that fitness and propriety require that there should be some place before the house of repose for the eye, and that nowhere in the little property, to all parts of which we may wish at times to lead our friends in fine attire, can we risk danger of a dusty or a muddy surface. Starting from the corner nearest the tree, and running broader and deeper after it has passed it and before the house, there shall be a swale (a gentle water-way) of cleanly turf (best kept so by the cropping of a tethered cosset and a little play now and then of a grasshook, but if this is unhandy we will admit the hand lawn-mower). Now, to carry this fine turf right up over the exposed roots of the beech would be the height of landscape gardening indelicacy; to let it come near, but cut a clean circle out about the tree, would be a landscape gardening barbarism. What is required is a very nice management, under which the turf in rising from the lower and presumably more humid ground shall become gradually thinner and looser, and at length darned with moss, and finally patched with plants that on the linden's lawn would be a sin—tufts of clover and locks and mats of loosestrife, liverwort, and dogtooth-violets; even plantain and sorrel may timidly appear. The surface of the ground will continue rising, but with a broken swell towards the tree, and, in deference to its bent form, hold rising for a space on the other side; but nowhere will its superior roots be fully covered.

Suppose that we are to come to this house, as it is likely we may, three times out of four from the side opposite to where the beech stands; our path then shall strike in, well over on that opposite side and diagonally to the line of the road; there will be a little branch from it leading towards and lost near the tree (the children's path), while the main stem bends short away toward a broad bowery porch facing the road at the corner nearest the gate. The path must needs be smooth for ease of foot and welcomeness, but if its edges chance to be trodden out a little, we will not be in haste to fully repair them. Slanting and sagging off from a ringbolt in the porch there is to be a hammock slung, its farther lanyard caught with two half-hitches on an old stub well up on the trunk of the beech. A strong, brown, seafaring hammock. There shall be a seat, too, under the tree of stout stuff, deep, high-backed, armed, and, whether of rustic-work or plank, fitted by jointing (not held together by nails, bolts, or screws). It may even be rough-hewn, and the more checked, weatherworn, and gray it becomes, without dilapidation or discomfort to the sitter, the better; here you may draw your matches and clean out your pipe, and welcome. We will have nothing in front to prevent a hedge, but must that mean a poor pretence of a wall in leafage? Perhaps it must have that character for a few years till it has become thick and strong enough at bottom, and always it may be a moderately trim affair on the roadside, otherwise we should be trespassers on our neighbors' rights. But its bushes shall not be all of one sort, and in good time they shall be bushes in earnest, leaping up with loose and feathery tops, six, eight, and sometimes ten feet high. And they shall leap out also towards us. Yet from the house half their height shall be lost behind an under and out-growth of brake and bindweed, dog-rose and golden-rod, asters, gentians, buttercups, poppies, and irises. Here and there a spray of low brambles shall be thrown out before all, and the dead gray canes of last year shall not be every one removed. There will be coves and capes and islands of chickweed, catnip, cinquefoil, wild strawberry, hepatica, forget-me-not, and lilies-of-the-valley, and, still farther out, shoals under the turf, where crocuses and daffodils are waiting to gladden the children and welcome the bluebird in the spring. But near the gate the hedge shall be a little overrun and the gateposts overhung and lost in sweet clematis; nay, as the gate must be set-in a little, because the path enters sidewise, there shall be a strong bit of lattice over it, and from the other side a honeysuckle shall reinforce the clematis; and if it whirls off also into the thorn tree that is to grow beyond, the thorn tree will be none the worse to be held to a lowly attitude, bowing stiffly towards the beech. Inside the gate, by the pathside, and again down by the porch, there may be cockscombs, marygolds, pinks, and pansies. But nothing of plants tied to the stake, or of plants the names of which, before they can command due interest, must be set before us on enameled cards, as properly in a botanic garden or museum. Above all, no priggish little spruces and arborvitæs, whether native or from Satsuma; if the neighbors harbor them, any common woodside or fence-row bushes of the vicinity may be set near the edge of the property to put them out of sight; nannyberry, hazel, shadbush, dogwood, even elder, or if an evergreen (conifer) will befit the place, a stout, short, shock-headed mountain-pine, with two or three low savins and a prostrate juniper at their feet. Finally, let the roadside be managed as before. Then, if the gate be left open not much will be lost by it; not all the world will so much as look in, and some who do will afterwards choose to keep the other side of the way, as it is better they should. Yet from the porch, the window beyond, or the old seat under the tree there will be nothing under view that is raw or rude or vulgar; on the contrary, there will be a scene of much refinement as well as of much beauty, and those who live in the house, especially if they have a way of getting their work or their books out under the beech, will find, as the sun goes round and the clouds drift over, that taking it altogether there is a quality more lovable in it than is to be found in all the glasshouses, all the ribbon borders, all the crown jewels of the world.

The same will be equally true of the result of the very different kind of gardening design first supposed. We come thus to the question, What is the distinctive quality of this beauty? In each case there has been an ideal in view, and in each element introduced a consistent pursuit of that ideal, but it is not in this fact of consistency that we find the beauty. We term it landscape beauty, although there is none of the expanse which is the first distinguishing quality of a landscape. This brings us to the consideration that from the point of view of art or of the science of the imagination we may ask for something more in a landscape than breadth, depth, composition, and consistency. A traveller, suddenly turning his eyes upon a landscape that is new to him, and which cannot be directly associated with any former experience, may find himself touched as if by a deep sympathy, so that in an instant his eyes moisten. After long and intimate acquaintance with such a landscape it will often be found to have a persistent influence which may be called its charm—a charm possibly of such power as to appreciably affect the development of the character and shape the course of life. Landscapes of particular type associate naturally and agreeably with certain events. Their fitness in this respect is due to the fact that, through some subtle action on the imagination, they affect the same or kindred sensibilities. If in these dooryards there is something to which every element contributes, comparable in this respect to a poetic or a musical theme, as well, in the one case, of elegance and neatness, carried perhaps to the point of quaint primness, as in the other of homely comfort and good-nature, carried close to the point of careless habits, then the design and process by which it has been attained may lay some slight claim to be considered as a work of art, and the highest art-significance of the term landscape may properly be used to distinguish its character in this respect.

In the possibility, not of making a perfect copy of any charming natural landscape, or of any parts or elements of it, but of leading to the production, where it does not exist, under required conditions and restrictions, of some degree of the poetic beauty of all natural landscapes, we shall thus find not only the special function and the justification of the term landscape gardening, but also the first object of study for the landscape gardener, and the standard by which alone his work is to be fairly judged.

There are those who will question the propriety of regarding the production of the poetic beauty of natural landscape as the end of landscape gardening, on the ground that the very term "natural beauty" means beauty not of man's design, and that the best result of all man's labor will be but a poor counterfeit, in which it is vain to look for the poetry of nature. Much has been written to this effect; with what truth to the nature of man it will be well cautiously to consider.

It is to be remembered, however, with reference to landscape effect, that nature acts both happily and unhappily. A man may take measures to secure the happy action and to guard against the unhappy action in this respect with no more effrontery than with respect to the production of food or protection from lightning, storm, frost, or malaria. He need not take the chance that a certain thick growth of saplings will be so thinned by the operation of what are called natural causes that a few of them may yet have a chance to become vigorous, long-lived, umbrageous trees. Knowing how much more valuable a very few of these will be in the situation, with the adjoining turf holding green under their canopy, than the thousands that for long years may otherwise occupy it, struggling with one another and barring out the light which is the life of all beneath them he may make sure of what is best with axe and billhook. The ultimate result is not less natural or beautiful when he has done so than it would have been if at the same time the same trees had been eaten out by worms or taken away, as trees sometimes are, by an epidemic disease.

On the other hand, there are several considerations, neglect of which is apt to cause too much to be asked of landscape gardening, and sometimes perhaps too much to be professed and attempted. The common comparison of the work of a landscape gardener with that of a landscape painter, for example, easily becomes a very unjust one. The artist in landscape gardening can never have, like the landscape painter, a clean canvas to work upon. Always there will be conditions of local topography, soil, and climate by which his operations must be limited. He cannot whenever it suits him introduce the ocean or a snow-capped mountain into his background. He cannot illuminate his picture with constant sunshine nor soften it by a perpetual Indian summer. Commonly, he is allowed only to modify the elements of scenery, or perhaps to bring about unity and distinctness of expression and suggestion in a locality where elements of beautiful landscape already abound, but are partly obscured or seen in awkward, confusing, and contradicting associations. This is especially likely to be the case in undulating and partially wooded localities, such as in America are oftenest chosen for rural homes. Again, the artist in landscape gardening cannot determine precisely the form and color of the details of his work, because each species of plant will grow up with features which cannot be exactly foreknown in its seed or sapling condition. Thus, he can see his designed and imaginary landscape only as one may see an existing and tangible landscape with half-closed eyes, its finer details not being wholly lost, yet nowhere perfectly definable. Still, again, it is to be remembered that works in landscape gardening have, as a general rule, to be seen from many points of view. The trees which form the background, still oftener those which form the middle distance, of one view must be in the foreground of another. Thus, the working out of one motive must be limited by the necessities of the working out of others on the same ground, and to a greater or less degree of the same materials. Finally, the conditions of health and convenience in connection with a dwelling are incompatible with various forms of captivating landscape beauty. A house may be placed in a lovely situation, therefore, and the end of long and costly labors of improvement about it prove comparatively dull, formal, and uninteresting. What is lost is a part of the price of health and convenience of dwelling. The landscape gardener may have made the best of the case under the conditions prescribed to him.

It has been said that landscapes of a particular type associate naturally and agreeably with certain events. It is to be added that the merit of landscape gardening consists largely in the degree in which their designer has been inspired by a spirit congenial to elements of locality and occasion which are not, strictly speaking, gardening elements. The grounds for an ordinary modest home, for instance, may desirably be designed to give the house, gardens, and offices an aspect of retirement and seclusion, as if these had nestled cozily down together among the trees in escape from the outside world. The grounds of a great public building—a monument of architecture—will, on the other hand, be desirably as large in scale, as open, simple, and broad in spaces of turf and masses of foliage, as convenience of approach will allow, and every tree arranged in subordination to, and support of, the building. The grounds of a church and of an inn, of a cottage and of an arsenal, of a burying-place and of a place of amusement, will thus differ, in each case correspondingly to their primary purpose. Realizing this, it will be recognized that the choice of the site, of the elevation, aspect, entrances, and outlooks of a building for no purpose can be judiciously determined except in connection with a study of the leading features of a plan, of its approaches, and grounds. Also, that in the design of roads, walks, lakes, and bridges, of the method of dealing with various natural circumstances, as standing wood, rocks, and water; in a determination of what is possible and desirable in respect to drainage, water-supply, distant prospects to be opened or shut out, the avoidance of malaria and other evils,—all these and many other duties are necessarily intimately associated with those of gardening (or the cultivation of plants) with a view to landscape effects.

"HEALTHY SUBURBAN NEIGHBORHOODS": DECEMBER 1879

The Future of New-York

VIEWS OF FREDERICK LAW OLMSTED.
ORGANIZING THE BUSINESS OF A CONTINENT—
NEW-YORK'S COMMERCIAL ADVANTAGES—DEFECTS
IN ITS STREETS AND HOUSES—THE VICIOUS SYSTEM
OF BLOCKS—WHAT A CITY MUST HAVE TO TAKE
RANK AS A TRUE METROPOLIS

Considerable changes are occurring in the courses of trade, and some branches of business which have hitherto contributed to the prosperity of New-York are passing from it. The question what is likely to be the result on the whole is one of the deepest interest to New-Yorkers. The following observations upon this question were mainly drawn out in a recent casual conversation by a Tribune representative with Frederick Law Olmsted. The commercial advantages of New-York are touched upon. Its recent progress toward the rank of a true metropolis is referred to, and some of the evils and obstacles in the way of that progress are pointed out. The bad results of the unfortunate plan of the streets and the crowding together of houses in blocks are dwelt upon, and the tendency in large cities to concentration for business purposes and dispersion for domestic purposes is considered.

AIDS AND CHECKS TO PROGRESS

If a wise despot had undertaken to organize the business of this continent, he would have begun by selecting for his headquarters a point where advantages for direct dealing with all parts of it were combined with advantages for direct dealing with all parts of Europe. He would then have established a series of great and small trading posts, determining their positions by regard, first, to the local resources of various parts of the country, and secondly, to facilities of transportation. Each of these would be an agency of exchange for a district, but, the several districts not being strictly defined, there would, as trade developed and individual enterprise came more and more into play, be much competition between different agencies, and by greater economy of management one would often draw away trade from and prosper to the disadvantage of, another. But except in a limited and superficial way, abnormal to the system, the interests of the central and of the local agencies would be identical, and the relation between them not one of rivalry but of coöperative and reciprocal service. The business of the general agency would be proportionate to the business of the country; its local profits to the profits of trade generally. Whatever it gained would as a rule be a gain to every community on the continent.

The general agency would, unless special obstacles interposed, soon come to be the best place for comparing, testing, appraising and interchanging information and ideas on all concerns common to the New World and the Old. It would therefore take the foremost place in affairs of fashion and luxury. It would be the headquarters of dramatic and musical enterprises. It would be a centre of interest in matters of science and art. It would be the readiest point for making collections and for comparing and testing values for a great variety of affairs not usually classed as commercial. All this would cause people to resort to it, either as occasional visitors, or with a view to residence, more than to any other place on the continent. It would thus become the best market for high ability in crafts of refinement. It would be the best "shopping place." As the resources of the continent were more and more fully exploited, it would thus tend to become a metropolis. Special advantages of climate, topography or of personal leadership and particular enterprise might give a local agency a leadership in some particular field; but the tendency, as a matter of continental economy, to concentrate leadership in general, even social leadership, at the trade centre, could be permanently overcome only by local conditions which would make life in it decidedly less secure, healthy, peaceful, cleanly and economical than elsewhere. Considerable natural disadvantages in this respect, even, might be gradually overcome.

The Great Peter of Russia and his successors, in fact, proceeded much in this way which has been supposed. The position which he selected for a general centre of exchange for Eastern Europe and Western Asia was in many respects unpromising; the harbor shallow and nearly half the year closed by ice, the land marshy and malarious, natural scenery tame and sad, and the climate most inclement. Nevertheless St. Petersburg has been made not only the centre of commercial exchanges, but the chief seat of learning, science and art, and of all intellectual and social activities, for a vast population of more varied and antagonistic races, creeds, tastes and customs than that of America.

COMMERCIAL POSITION OF NEW-YORK

New-York has long been the general centre of commercial exchanges for the continent. There is not the least likelihood that any other city will supercede it. Even if any other had somewhat superior local advantages for the purpose, it is not desirable in the general interests of commerce at this stage that a change should be made. The cost of the rearrangement would be too great. Such transfer of particular branches of business to other growing towns, as now occurs, is simply a modification of commercial organization by which the mutual business of New-York and the country at large is to be done with more profit on the whole to both. St. Louis, Cincinnati and Chicago are in rivalry with one another but never except in a temporary and superficial way, with New-York. Boston, Philadelphia and Baltimore are more plainly in competition with New-York; yet in the main they likewise so far coöperate with her that New-York gains more than she loses by every advance that is made by either of them.

But New-York is yet hardly ready to assume the full duty and take the full profits of a metropolis. In some respects Boston leads New-York, Philadelphia in others; in still others Cincinnati at least aims to do so. And in many respects New-York is not as yet nearly as well equipped as many cities of Europe of less than half her population and commercial prosperity. Treasures of art and the results of popular familiarity with treasures of art must be gained slowly, and New-York can in a long time only partially overcome its inevitable disadvantages in this respect. Yet, as to the higher results of human labor, in general attractiveness to cultivated minds and as a place of luxury, New-York has probably been gaining of late, even during the hard times, more rapidly than any other city in the world. She has gained, for instance, the Natural History Museum, the Art Museum, the Lenox Library, the Cathedral, the railways to and the great plant for healthful recreation at Coney Island. She is decidedly richer and more attractive in libraries, churches, clubs and hotels. The display of her shops is very greatly finer than it was a few years ago. Shops more attractive in general effect are now hardly to be found in any older city. Great advances have been made also by half a dozen of her business concerns which are all large employers of the finer artisans and artificers: wood carvers, workers in metal, enamels, glass and precious stones, decorative painters. Better workmanship can now be had here in almost anything than was available five years ago. Take pottery, wood-engraving, upholstery, gas-fixtures, furniture, for example; in all these we could now make a better show than we did in the Centennial Exhibition. Without doubt that exhibition did much for New-York; possibly more than for Philadelphia. It is, at least, certain that New-York has since had better workmen, better designers, better tools and a more highly educated market; and all these things have distinctly advanced her metropolitan position.

UNFORTUNATE PLAN OF THE CITY

Next to the direct results of a slipshod, temporizing government of amateurs, the great disadvantage under which New-York labors is one growing out of the senseless manner in which its streets have been laid out. No city is more unfortunately planned with reference to metropolitan attractiveness. True, it may be said that large parts of many old world cities have not been planned at all, but their accidental defects are compensated by their accidental advantages. The tenement-house, which is the product of uniform 200-feet-wide blocks, is beginning to be recognized as the primary cause of whatever is peculiarly disgraceful in New-York City politics, through the demoralization which it works in the more incapable class of working-people. It is a calamity more to be deplored than the yellow fever at New-Orleans, because more impregnable; more than the fogs of London, the cold of St. Petersburg, or the malaria of Rome, because more constant in its tyranny.

On the other hand, the first-class brown-stone, high-stoop, fashionable modern dwelling house is really a confession that it is impossible to build a convenient and tasteful residence in New-York, adapted to the ordinary civilized requirements of a single family, except at a cost which even rich men find generally prohibitory.

Dr. Bellows once described the typical New-York private house as "a slice of house fifteen feet wide, slid into a block, with seven long flights of stairs between the place where the cook works and sleeps;" and really, the family is now fortunate which gets twenty feet and which has more than two rooms out of three of tolerable proportions with windows looking into the open air.

There are actually houses of less than fifteen feet wide, to which men, who anywhere else in the world would be in comfortable circumstances, are obliged to condemn their families. A gentleman of rare attainments and in every way a most valuable addition to any community, whose private professional library and collections must have cost him $10,000, has been obliged to compress his family into a five-floored stack, the party walls of which are but twelve feet apart.

In none of those older towns in which domestic convenience has been systematically sacrificed to considerations of military expediency is a man of like value condemned to such a preposterous form of habitation. Its plan is more nearly that of a light house built upon a wave-lashed rock, than of a civilized family home. New-York has need of great attractions to draw people into quarters of this kind from such houses as they could better afford in any other American city.

THE SAME DEFECTS UP-TOWN

But what is worst in the lookout for New-York is that the elevated roads and the up-town movement lead as yet to nothing better; for even at Yorkville, Harlem and Manhattanville, five or six miles away from the centre of population, there are new houses of the ridiculous jammed-up pattern, as dark and noisome in their middle parts and as inconvenient throughout as if they were parts of a besieged fortress.

Nay, there is a prospect of even worse to come, for on the slopes south of Manhattanville there are new streets, some of them paved and flagged, which, out of respect to the popular prejudice in favor of continuing the regular system, are laid out on just the worst course possible, so that in passing through them you must mount an inclination of one in six, eight or ten. What this means may be guessed by thinking of the steeper grades in the lower part of the city. That of Fifth-ave, north of Thirty-fourth-st., for instance, is one in twenty-five, and it brings every omnibus and most hackney coaches from a trot to a walk. Every ton of coal dragged up such a street, every load of garbage gathered and taken from it, is to cost three or four times as much in horsepower as it would in the lower part of the town, and yet in the lower part of the town we cannot afford to prevent great mounds of garbage from lying before our doors for weeks at a time. Its daily removal is found to be too costly.

Small families who do not wish to entertain many friends may find some relief in the better of the new apartment houses. But still, what these offer, as compared with what is offered in other cities, is of most extravagant cost. They are no places for children, and to any really good arrangement of apartments the 200-foot block still bars the way. Apartment houses in the old countries, of corresponding luxury in other respects, have much more spacious courts. The court, instead of being regarded as a backyard and every inch given to it and every dollar laid out upon it begrudged, often gives the noblest and usually the pleasantest fronts to the house. What are advertised as apartment houses for people in New-York of more moderate means, such as must be looked to by teachers, artists, artisans, writers, and nearly all the rank and file of the superior life of a metropolis, are as yet only a more decent sort of tenement-house, nearly half their rooms being without direct light and ventilation. The same classes that are compelled to live in them in New-York would regard them as intolerable in Philadelphia, or in London, Paris or Vienna.

Many attempts have been made to subdivide the block so that comfortable small houses which would come in competition with the tenement-houses might be built. The result in the best cases is that family privacy and general decency in fact and appearance are attained at an outlay which in any other large city would be thought preposterous. A better arrangement than any which has been tried is probably that proposed by Mr. Potter, which consists essentially in subdividing the block by a series of lanes running from street to street; but capitalists as yet draw back from it.

ORIGIN OF THE EVIL

How did the city come to be saddled with this misfortune? Probably by a process of degeneration. In the old city of Amsterdam, after which it was first named, many houses are still to be found which approach in proportions the fashionable New-York house. But from the beginning these had one great advantage. At their back, running lengthwise through the middle of the block, there was a canal. Into this the closet and kitchen drains had direct discharge. Dust, ashes and garbage could be shot down to the lower floor and then passed directly into boats and floated off to farms in the suburbs. At the base of the house, on the street, there was a narrow brick terrace, and outside the front door a little open-air sitting-room, and everything on that side was kept as neat as a pin. The streets of old Amsterdam were, indeed, as much celebrated in the seventeenth century for their cleanliness as those of New-Amsterdam have since ever been for their filthiness.

New-York is in short a Dutch town with its canals and cleanliness omitted and its streets straightened and magnified. Long after the present street plan was adopted it was the custom of its citizens to throw their slops and garbage out of the front door, and droves of hogs got their living in the gutters. Out of this state of things New-York streets have been slowly improved to their present condition and New-York houses have come to be more inconvenient, uncomfortable and unhealthy, for the money and labor spent upon them, than those of any other American city.

But when we speculate upon the future of New-York as a metropolis we must not think of it as confined by arbitrary political boundaries. As a metropolis, Newark, Newport and Bridgeport, as well as Brooklyn, Yonkers and Jersey City, are essential parts of it. For all scholarly and scientific purposes Yale College with its thousand students is already annexed to New-York, and is possibly today a more actively important element of its intellectual life than either or all of the four colleges which stand within its political limits.

In fact, the railway, the telegraph and the telephone make a few miles more or less of so little consequence that a large part of the ideas of a city, which have been transmitted to us from the period when cities were walled about and necessarily compact and crowded, must be put away.

CONCENTRATION AND DISPERSION

There is now a marked tendency in most large and thriving towns in two opposite directions—one to concentration for business and social purposes, the other to dispersion for domestic purposes. The first leads toward more compact and higher building in business quarters, the other toward broader, lower and more open building in residence quarters. The old-fashioned "country houses" of city people are growing more and more out of vogue, but residences in a greater or less degree combining urban and rural advantages, neither solitary on the one hand nor a mere slice of a block on the other, wherever they can be had in healthy and pleasing localities, with quick and frequent transit to business, social, artistic, literary and scholarly centres, are gaining favor. They are springing up in hundreds of charming neighborhoods about London and Paris; Boston and our Western cities are largely formed of them. They are as yet less used by New-Yorkers than by the people of any other large town. The reason is simply that hitherto there have been no thoroughly healthy suburban neighborhoods sufficiently accessible about New-York. In time such neighborhoods will be formed. Whenever they are, the metropolitan advantages of New-York and the profits of its local trade must be greatly increased by constantly increasing accessions to its population of men who have accumulated means elsewhere, and who wish to engage in other than purely money-making occupations. Such men, living under favorable circumstances and with capital and energies economically directed to matters of general interest, are the most valuable constituents of a city; and it is by their numbers, wealth and influence, more than anything else, that a city takes the rank in the world of a metropolis.

PRESERVING NIAGARA FALLS: MARCH 1880

"Notes" in the Special Report of the New York State Survey on the Preservation of the Scenery of Niagara Falls

James T. Gardner, Director
Notes by Mr. Olmsted

The few notes which I propose to append to Mr. Gardner's report will be directed to a single point.

There are those, and I fear that most of the people of Niagara are among them, to whom it appears that the waterfall has so supreme an interest to the public that what happens to the adjoining scenery is of trifling consequence. Were all the trees cut away, quarries opened in the ledges, the banks packed with hotels and factories, and every chance-open space occupied by a circus tent, the Falls would still, these think, draw the world to them. Whatever has been done to the injury of the scenery has been done, say they, with the motive of profit, and the profit realized is the public's verdict of acquittal.

It must be considered, therefore, that the public has not had the case fairly before it. The great body of visitors to Niagara come as strangers. Their movements are necessarily controlled by the arrangements made for them. They take what is offered, and pay what is required with little exercise of choice. The fact that they accept the arrangements is no evidence of their approval.

The real question is, how, in the long run, is the general experience of visitors affected by measures and courses which are determined with no regard to the influence of the scenery?

I have myself been an occasional visitor at Niagara for forty-five years. My attention was first called to the rapidly approaching ruin of its characteristic scenery by Mr. F. E. Church, about ten years ago. Shortly afterwards, several gentlemen, frequenters of the Falls, met at my request, to consider this danger, one of them being a member of the Commission now reporting on the subject. I have thus had both occasion and opportunity for observing the changed courses into which the public has been gradually led and of studying these courses and their results.

When the arrangements by which visitors were conducted were yet simple; when there were few carriages, and these little used; when a visit to the Falls was a series of expeditions, and in each expedition hours were occupied in wandering slowly among the trees, going from place to place, with many intervals of rest, there was not only a much greater degree of enjoyment, there was a different kind of enjoyment from any now generally obtained. People, then, were loth to leave the place; many lingered on from day to day after they had prepared to go, revisiting ground they had gone over before, turning and returning; and when they went away it was with grateful hearts and grateful words.

The change from this to what is described in the second section of the Commissioners' report has been gradual and, while something must be attributed to modern ease of travel, a greater influx of visitors and to habits of quicker movement and greater restlessness; much must also be referred to the fact that visitors are so much more constrained to be guided and instructed, to be led and stopped, to be "put through," and so little left to natural and healthy individual intuitions.

The aim to make money by the showman's methods; the idea that Niagara is a spectacular and sensational exhibition, of which rope-walking, diving, brass bands, fireworks and various "side-shows" are appropriate accompaniments, is so presented to the visitor that he is forced to yield to it, and see and feel little else than that prescribed to him.

But all the time there are some who, because of better information and opportunities, and as the result of previous training, get the better of this difficulty, and to these the old charm remains. Take, as an illustration, the experience of the writer of the following passage. It is that of a man who has traveled extensively for the express purpose of observing scenery and

comparing the value, as determined by the influence on the imagination, of different types of scenery. It is recorded in a little book which treats more especially of the scenery of the Alps and of what are designated "nature's gardens" among them.*
But says the author:

"The noblest of nature's gardens that I have yet seen is that of the surroundings and neighborhood of the Falls of Niagara. Grand as are the colossal falls, the rapids and the course of the river for a considerable distance above and below possess more interest and beauty.

"As the river courses far below the falls, confined between vast walls of rock—the clear water of a peculiar light-greenish hue, and white here and there with circlets of yet unsoothed foam—the effect is startlingly beautiful, quite apart from the falls. The high cliffs are crested with woods; the ruins of the great rock walls forming wide, irregular banks between them and the water, are also beautifully clothed with wood to the river's edge, often so far below that you sometimes look from the upper brink down on the top of tall pines that seem diminished in size. The wild vines scramble among the trees; many shrubs and flowers seam the high rocks; in moist spots, here and there a sharp eye may detect many flowered tufts of the beautiful fringed Gentian, strange to European eyes; and beyond all, and at the upper end of the wood-embowered deep river bed, a portion of the crowning glory of the scene—the falls—a vast cliff of illuminated foam, with a zone towards its upper edge as of green molten glass. Above the falls the scene is quite different. A wide and peaceful river carrying the surplus waters of an inland sea, till it gradually finds itself in the coils of the rapids, and is soon lashed into such a turmoil as we might expect if a dozen unpolluted Shannons or Seines were running a race together. A river no more, but a sea unreined. By walking about a mile above the falls on the Canadian shore this effect is finely seen, the breadth of the river helping to carry out the illusion. As the great waste of waters descends from its dark grey and smooth bed and falls whitening into foam, it seems as if tide after tide were gale-heaped one on another on a sea strand. The islands just above the falls enable one to stand in the midst of these rapids, where they rush by lashed into passionate haste; now boiling over some hidden swellings in the rocky bed, or dashing over greater but yet hidden obstructions with such force that the crest of the uplifted mass is dashed about as freely

* *Alpine Flowers*, by William Robinson, F.L.S. London: John Murray, 1875.

as a white charger's mane; now darkly falling into a cavity several yards below the level of the surrounding water, and, when unobstructed, surging by in countless eddies to the mist-crested falls below; and so rapidly that the driftwood dashes on swift as swallow on the wing. Undisturbed in their peaceful shadiness, garlanded with wild vine and wild flowers, the islands stand in the midst of all this fierce commotion of waters—below, the vast ever-mining falls; above, a complication of torrents that seem fitted to wear away iron shores; yet there they stand, safe as if the spirit of beauty had in mercy exempted them from decay. Several islets are so small that it is really remarkable how they support vegetation; one, looking no bigger than a washing-tub, not only holds its own in the very thick of the torrents just above the falls, but actually bears a small forest, including one stricken and half cast-down pine. Most fortunate is it that these beautifully verdant islands and islets occur just above the falls, adding immeasurably to the effect of the scene."

I have spoken of the *distinctive* charms of Niagara scenery. If it were possible to have the same conditions detached from the falls (which it is not, as I shall show), Niagara would still be a place of singular fascination; possibly to some, upon whom the falls have a terrifying effect, even more so than it is now.

Saying nothing of the infinitely varied beauties of water and spray, and of water-worn rock, I will, for a purpose, mention a few elements which contribute to this distinctive charm.

The eminent English botanist, Sir Joseph Hooker, has said that he found upon Goat Island a greater variety of vegetation within a given space than anywhere in Europe, or east of the Sierras, in America; and the first of American botanists, Dr. Asa Gray, has repeated the statement. I have followed the Apalachian chain almost from end to end, and traveled on horseback, "in search of the picturesque," over four thousand miles of the most promising parts of the continent without finding elsewhere the same quality of forest beauty which was once abundant about the falls, and which is still to be observed in those parts of Goat Island where the original growth of trees and shrubs has not been disturbed, and where, from caving banks, trees are not now exposed to excessive dryness at the root.

Nor have I found anywhere else such tender effects of foliage as were once to be seen in the drapery hanging down the wall of rock on the American shore below the fall, and rolling up the slope below it, or with that still to be seen in a favorable season and under favorable lights, on the Canadian steeps and crags between the falls and the ferry.

All these distinctive qualities,—the great variety of the indigenous perennials and annuals, the rare beauty of the old woods, and the exceeding loveliness of the rock foliage,—I believe to be a direct effect of the falls, and as much a part of its majesty as the mist-cloud and the rainbow.

They are all, as it appears to me, to be explained by the circumstance that at two periods of the year when the northern American forest elsewhere is liable to suffer actual constitutional depressions, that of Niagara is insured against like ills, and thus retains youthful luxuriance to an unusual age.

First, the masses of ice, which, every winter are piled to a great height below the falls, and the great rushing body of ice-cold water coming from the northern lakes in the spring, prevent at Niagara the hardship under which trees elsewhere often suffer through sudden checks to premature growth; and, second, when droughts elsewhere occur, as they do, every few years, of such severity that trees in full foliage droop and dwindle, and even sometimes cast their leaves, the atmosphere at Niagara is more or less moistened by the constantly evaporating spray of the falls, and in certain situations frequently bathed by drifting clouds of mist.

Something of the beauty of the hanging foliage below the falls is also probably due to the fact, that the effect of the frozen spray upon it is equivalent to the horticultural process of "shortening in;" compelling a denser and closer growth than is, under other circumstances, natural.

Reference is made at page 9, of the Commissioners' report to a marvelous effect in scenery above the Falls. It is that to which the following account by the Duke of Argyll applies:

> The river Niagara, above the falls, runs in a channel very broad, and very little depressed below the general level of the country. But there is a steep declivity in the bed of the stream for a considerable distance above the precipice, and this constitutes what are called the rapids. The consequence is that when we stand at any point near the edge of the Falls, and look up the course of the stream, the foaming waters of the rapids constitute the sky line.

No indication of land is visible—nothing to express the fact that we are looking at a river. The crests of the breakers, the leaping and the rushing of the waters, are still seen against the clouds, as they are seen in the ocean, when the ship from which we look is in the trough of the sea. It is impossible to resist the effect on the imagination. It is as if the fountains of the great deep were being broken up, and that a new deluge were coming on the world. The impression is rather increased than diminished, by the perspective of the low wooded banks on either shore, running down to a vanishing point and seeming to be lost in the advancing waters. An apparently shoreless sea tumbling toward one is a very grand and a very awful sight. Forgetting, then, what one knows, and giving oneself to what one only sees, I do not know that there is anything in nature more majestic than the *view of the rapids* above the falls of Niagara.

FREDERICK LAW OLMSTED

PATRONAGE AND CORRUPTION IN THE PARKS
DEPARTMENT: FEBRUARY 1882

FROM *The Spoils of the Park*

WITH A FEW LEAVES FROM THE
DEEP-LADEN NOTE-BOOKS OF
"A WHOLLY UNPRACTICAL MAN"

I have shown what the highest authorities in the commercial business of the city hold to be the essence of the Commissioners' business with the Park, and what is essential to their success in it. But it must be known that a strong party has always stood opposed to this view, and from the start has been incessantly laboring, and never without some measure of success, to compel a disregard for it. The counter view is commonly termed by those urging it the *practical* view; and, if this seems strange, it must be considered that a given course is called practical or otherwise, according to the object had in view at the moment by the speaker. To relieve the charity of friends of the support of a half-blind and half-witted man by employing him at the public expense as an inspector of cement may not be practical with reference to the permanent firmness of a wall, while it is perfectly so with reference to the triumph of sound doctrine at an election. It will be important, in what follows, to keep in mind this relativeness of meaning in the word.

First and last, there have been some pretty dark rams in the Park Commission; but on the whole it has been the worthiest and best intentioned body having any important responsibility under the city administration in our time, and it has, till lately, had rightly more of public respect and confidence than any other, its distinction in this respect being not always pleasing to some other constituents of the government. Yet with all the advantage their high standing might seem to give them, the Commissioners have rarely been able, when agreed among themselves, to move at all straight-forwardly upon the course, which, left to themselves, they would have marked out. Commissioner Wales has more than once, of late, referred to what he calls the "embarrassments" of the department, and has been careful to state, that, so far from these being new, he had in former years, when the public confidence in the Commissioners was much greater than at present, matched his strength with them till the breaking-point was reached, when he was compelled to resign, and go abroad to recruit his vigor in preparation for the renewed struggle in which he is now engaged.

He will excuse me for thinking that he has left the nature of these embarrassments in some obscurity, and for wishing to throw a little light upon it. I am going further on to mention circumstances connected with the dissociation of landscape-gardening from the business of the Park, which, if I had been in New York when the Commissioners' action for the purpose was taken, and had been disposed to make them public, would have added to the distrust and apprehension so generally expressed. They will even now cause surprise, even tax the credulity of many; and partly to lay a foundation for them, partly to give a clew to their significance, partly to reveal what Mr. Wales probably means by the embarrassments of the Board, I will, in this chapter, relate a few incidents of my earlier experience. My object being to throw light on methods and manners, for which we, citizens of New York, are every man responsible, and not to assail parties or persons, I shall aim to avoid names and dates.

My first narration will be of a commonplace character, and
be given only to supply a starting-point.

1. The mayor once wanted to nominate me for the office of
Street Commissioner. After some persuasion, perfectly aware
that I was taking part in a play, though the mayor solemnly assured me otherwise, I assented, with the distinct understanding,
that, if the office came to me, it should be free from political obligations; that I should be allowed to choose my own assistants,
and, keeping within the law, my own method of administration.
"Which," said the mayor, "is just what I want. It is because I felt
sure that you would insist on that, that I sent for you." I smiled.
The mayor preserved his gravity, and I took my leave. Within
half an hour I received a call from a gentleman whom I had held
in much esteem, to whom I had had reason to be grateful; who
had once been a member of Congress,—a man of wealth and
social position, but at the time holding no public office, and not
conspicuous in politics. He congratulated me warmly, hoping
that at last New York would be able to enjoy the luxury of clean
streets. Conversation turned upon the character of the Board of
Aldermen. The gentleman thought there need be no difficulty
in getting their confirmation, but suggested that it might be
better for me to let him give a few confidential assurances to
some who did not know me as well as he did, as to my more
important appointments. He soon afterwards left, regretting
plaintively to have found me so "unpractical" in my ideas. It was
his opinion that half a loaf of reform was better than no bread.
It was mine, that a man could not rightly undertake to clean the
streets of New York with his hands tied confidentially.*

Soon another, also not holding an office, but president of a
ward club, and as such having a certain familiarity with practical
politics, called to advise me that —— wanted an understanding
that I would give him fifteen per cent of my patronage. Not
having it, he feared that —— would throw his weight against
me. I need not go on. When one of the mayor's friends in the
city-hall understood that I seriously meant to be my own master, or defeated, he exclaimed, "Why, the man must be a fool!"

---

* The word "unpractical" is not found in common dictionaries, but is so useful
in our mandarin dialect, that I shall make bold for this occasion to adopt it.

2. At one time, in a temporary emergency, I had the honor to be called to the quarter-deck, having been appointed a commissioner, and elected by the board of the period to be its president. In the few months that I held the position, I had some wonderful experiences, of which, for the present purpose, I will relate, because of their bearing on what follows, but five. That unpractical men may realize the wonder of them, it must be remembered that I was riding on the very crest of the glorious reform wave.

(1) A "delegation" from a great political organization called on me by appointment. After introductions and handshakings, a circle was formed, and a gentleman stepped before me, and said, "We know how much pressed you must be, Mr. President, and we don't want to be obtrusive, sir, nor exacting; but at your convenience our association would like to have you determine what share of your patronage we can expect, and make suitable arrangements for our using it. We will take the liberty to suggest, sir, that there could be no more convenient way than that you should send us our due quota of tickets, if you please, sir, in this form, *leaving us to fill in the name.*" Here a pack of printed tickets was produced, from which I took one at random. It was a blank appointment, and bore the signature of Mr. Tweed. "That," continued the spokesman, "was the way we arranged it last year, and we don't think there can be anything better."

(2) Four gentlemen called by appointment on "important business." Three were official servants of the city: the fourth stated that he came from and was authorized to represent a statesman of national importance. Their business was to present a request, or rather a demand, so nearly naked that it would have been decenter if there had been no pretence of clothing it, for the removal of some of the minor officers of the Park, in order to make places for new men, whose names they were ready to give me. They said nothing to recommend their candidates, except that they were reformers. The fact that the men whose removal they called for had been long enough employed to understand their duties, and to have proved their faithfulness and unpracticalness, was a sufficient reason that they should go. They had had their "suck." After a little conversation, which I made as pleasant as I could, I said smiling, "But excuse me,

gentlemen, if I ask if you consider this to be reform?" There was no responsive smile (rather the contrary), and the representative of statesmanship said sharply, "What's the use of being a reformer, if it isn't?" And seriously, to these efficient public servants, this was the high-water mark of reform.

(3) Calling at this period upon another department head, and finding his lobby packed as mine was, when, after half an hour's waiting, I was admitted to a private interview,—of which the head took advantage to eat a cold lunch that had been waiting for him,—I said, "Is it possible that you are as hard beset by these gentlemen as I am?"—"Oh! more so, I think."—"Then, when do you get time for the proper business of your office?"—"Only before and after office-hours, when they think I am gone."

(4) Among those calling on me was one official of the city, who came regularly once a week, and, having been admitted, remained sometimes two hours, saying plainly that he did not mean to go until I had given him at least one appointment. At length I remonstrated with him somewhat severely. "Well, Mr. President," he replied, "you must excuse me. You know this is my business now, and I must attend to it. If I didn't, where should I be? But I'll let you off for to-day, and go round to ——'s office, and see what I can do with him."

(5) Twice it occurred to me, after passing through a large public office with many deputies and clerks, that the Chief remarked to me, "Among them all, there is but one man who is here by my own free choice, or in whose faithfulness I have confidence."

3. It has occurred five times in succession that I have been at the headquarters of the Department of Parks on the first visit of a new commissioner, and when, after a few passages of introductory courtesy, he has, as his first official movement in the business of the parks, asked to be furnished with a list showing the places at its disposal, the value of each, and the vacancies at the time existing. I believe that each of these gentlemen had been certified to the reporters to be entirely free from political obligations, and to owe his appointment solely to his eminent qualifications for the particular post of a park commissioner; but it will not be surprising, that, in view of my experience, I doubted the accuracy of the certificate.

4. A commissioner once said in my presence, "I don't get any salary for being here; it would be a pretty business if I couldn't oblige a friend now and then:" this being his reason for urging a most unfit appointment.

5. Writing of unfit appointments, nothing could be more ludicrous, if the anxiety they gave me had left room for a humorous view of them, than many most strenuously urged. A young man was pressed for my nomination as a topographical draughtsman. I asked to see some of his work, and, after explanations, was answered, "I don't know that he ever made any maps or drawings on paper."—"How could you think he was qualified as a draughtsman?" To which the reluctant reply was this: "The fact is, he was a little wild a few years ago, and ran away to sea on a whaler, and when he came back he brought a whale's tooth, on which he had made a picture of his ship as natural as life. Now I think that a boy who could do that, you could do most anything with in the drawing way." The very man who said this, and, incredible as it will be thought, said it seriously, was nominated by the mayor for a park commissioner. Can the reader say, that, if the favorite remedy for the moment, and that advocated by Mr. Wales, for all the evils of the present park mismanagement, shall be adopted, this same good business-man may not next year be chosen to exemplify the efficiency of a single-headed administration?

6. I once expressed to a gentleman surprise at the accuracy of certain information of which I found him possessed. "Oh! that's nothing," he said. "There is not a workingman living in my district, or who comes into it, or goes out of it, that I have not got him down on my books, with the name and ages of his wife and all his children, what house they are in, what rooms they occupy, what his work is, who employs him, who is to look after his vote, and so on. I have it all tabulated, and posted up. I have to make a business of it, you know. If a man means to succeed in politics, he must. It is not a business you can play with."

7. Another illustration of practical business-methods was given by a president of the Department as follows:—

"I want you to know," he said, after opening the door, looking out, closing and locking it, "of some things going on here. Yesterday a man applied for a certain position, bringing a letter dated at Albany the day before, in which the writer stated that he understood that the late holder of the position had been discharged. I told the applicant that he was mistaken; but he insisted that he was not, and I could hardly get rid of him. Here is a report coming this morning from the Park, making charges against the man in question, and advising his discharge. Information of a prospective opportunity of an appointment had gone to Albany and back, before it came to me here. You see how closely they watch us. But here is another example of it. I signed to-day an appointment which I had not determined to make five minutes before. I sent the appointee directly up to the Park, starting myself, at the same moment, for the city-hall. When I reached there, reference was made to the appointment by the first man who spoke to me, showing that not a moment had been lost in reporting it. But who made the report, and how, so quickly? I confess I hardly dare inquire. But there is something yet more inscrutable. I suspected the lock of my private drawer to have been tampered with. Last night I placed a bit of paper where it would be dislodged if the drawer was opened, and another in my memorandum-book of vacancies, applications and intended appointments. This morning I found both displaced."

8. There was an intrigue to remove a valuable officer by destroying his character, in order to make an opening for the advancement of a subordinate strongly backed with "influence." I asked and obtained a committee of the Board to try the case. The subordinate made oath to a statement which was proved to be false; and for the perjury he was dismissed. Shortly afterwards he met me on the Park, offered me his hand, and, with much flourish, thanked me for having brought about his removal, as it had compelled his friends to make proper exertions, and he now held a position much more to his taste than any on the Park could have been.

9. At a dignified public ceremony on the Park, I saw, while listening to the oration of the day, a roughly-dressed man approach the point where the Commissioners were arrayed, all in proper black, and facing a great crowd. As the man neared their position from the rear, he reached out a walking-stick, and punched one of them. The commissioner turned; and the man threw his head back, as if to say, "Come here, I want a word with you." The commissioner fell out, and there was a

whispered conversation. "Now, what does that mean?" I asked. "Don't you know? Why, that is one of our new foremen; and he and the commissioner are both members of the same district committee. He is laying in with him to make a place for some fellow whose help they need in the primaries."

10. I suspended a man because of evidence of gross disobedience of a standing rule. He told a very improbable story; and I gave him a fortnight to produce corroborative evidence of it. Instead of doing so, he set a number of his "friends" after me. His special patron was a man in office, and proprietor of a weekly newspaper. A copy of it was sent me, with a marked article containing absurd and scurrilous abuse of me, and of the Commission for employing me. As this official had shortly before called at my house, and been profuse in compliments and professions of regard, I went to see him. Referring to the article, I said, "It would have given you but the slightest trouble to ascertain that you had been imposed upon in the statements to which you have given currency." He smiled, and asked, "Would you like to see an article I intend to publish to-morrow?" handing a galley-proof to me. I read it, and said, "I have marked and numbered with my pencil seven statements in this article, which, I give you my word, can be ascertained, by anyone coming to the Park, to be quite untrue." The next day a copy of the paper was sent me containing the article without the change of a word. The suspended man at last confessed, hoping to be pardoned, but was dismissed. The paper continued to be sent me every week for perhaps a year, and I was told that every number had some attack on the Park. At another period another paper pursued a similar course. One day the editor, finding the president of the Department on a railway-train going to Albany, gayly saluted him in terms of friendship. "I am surprised, sir," said the president, "that, after what you have been saying of our Board in your paper, you can offer me your hand."—"Oh!" replied the editor, "but that was business."

11. During all my park work it was a common thing to receive newspapers, addressed by unknown hands, containing matter designed to injure me; sometimes, also, anonymous threats and filthy caricatures. The object I take to have been to impress me with the insecurity of my position, and the folly of the unpractical view of its duties.

12. A foreman of laborers, discharged from the Park against strong political influence, was, at the next election, a candidate for the Legislature.

13. At one time, shortly after the police of the Park had a second time been put under my superintendence, I undertook an improvement of it. Asking the officer in charge to account for his own failure to secure the conviction and removal of some whom he described as "regular dead-beats," who had "never performed one honest tour of duty since they were taken on," he answered, "Why, damn 'em, they are every man laying wires to go to the Legislature, and they carry too many guns for me."

14. As my first step, I wrote an order to the surgeon, directing a medical survey of the force. The surgeon called on me, and said, "I am under your orders, sir, and if you insist I shall act on them to the letter; but perhaps you do not realize, as I do, what the consequences will be to me."—"What will they be?"—"Only that I shall have to eat my bread without butter for a while."—"I understand; but I must do my duty, and you must do yours." He did, reporting a quarter part of the entire force physically incapacitated for any active duty, and indicating that it had been used as an asylum for aggravated cases of hernia, varicose veins, rheumatism, partial blindness, and other infirmities compelling sedentary occupations. The surgeon was supported by the highest authorities of his profession, and had established on the Park an excellent character, professionally and otherwise. He had gained the affection and confidence of the force, but, in obeying orders without consulting its friends, had proved himself an unpractical man, and, as he had anticipated, was soon afterwards dismissed by order of the Board.

15. I asked an officer before me on a grave charge what he had to say. With a laugh, and a wink to his comrades, he answered, "You want to know what I have to say? Well, that's what I have to say," handing me a crumpled note which read, "If there is anything against officer ——, please remember that he is my man, and charge it to account of Yours Truly, —— ——." He was dismissed.

16. I set a watch upon the night-watch; and five men, receiving three dollars a night for patrol-duty on beats of which two were a mile and a half apart, were found together in the middle of their watch in a necessary building, which they had entered

with false keys. They had made a fire, taken off their boots, and, using their rolled-up coats for pillows, were fast asleep; and this had doubtless been long their habit. With the sanction of the Board I changed the system, much reducing its cost, and employed mechanical detectors on the principle of those used for the night-watch of great mills. They were broken from their fastenings, and carried away. I devised a stronger and simpler apparatus. In several instances, within a week it was broken, as if by sledges, great force being necessary.

17. The eldest of the watchmen had been originally employed for several years in the Park as a land-surveyor. He had received a good education, and, after his discharge as a surveyor, had suffered grievous domestic afflictions, and been left very poor. He was a religious man, had been active in church charities; and it was in part upon a letter from his pastor setting forth his trustworthiness that I had obtained his appointment as watchman. He had refused to join the others in their conspiracy, and was looked upon as a spy—wrongly, for he had given me no information. He was waylaid at night, murderously struck down, and left for dead. It was several weeks before he was able to leave his bed, and when he did so he was scarred for life.

18. Several other measures were adopted, all with the knowledge and sanction of the Board, and believed at the time, by the excellent gentlemen composing it, to be perfectly business-like. But they were all very unpractical in the view taken by many of the force and their friends, who consequently united in measures designed to convince the Commissioners of their mistake, and for self-protection against my cruelty. A fund was raised, and a "literary gentleman" regularly employed to write me down. At this time I received confidential warnings indirectly from high quarters outside the Commission, that I would not be allowed to succeed in what I was attempting, and had better drop it. I did not drop it, but worked on with all my might; and presently the literary gentleman got also to his work, first in some of the Sunday papers. At length, by one of those accidents that seem liable to occur in any great newspaper establishment, he managed to get a powerful article prominently displayed in a leading daily, in which, after referring to the reputation of the force with the public, gained by its alleged uniform activity, efficiency, civility; its high state of discipline and *esprit du corps*,

it was represented, that, through some unaccountable freak of the Board, it had recently been placed under the orders of a silly, heartless, upstart, sophomorical theorist, through whose boyish experiments it was being driven into complete and rebellious demoralization. One of the Commissioners told me that he was asked a day or two afterwards, "Who is this young chap that you have put in charge of the police? How could you have been stuck with such an unpractical fellow?" Now it happened that I was one of the few men then in America who had made it a business to be well informed on the subject of police organization and management. I had made some examination of the French system; had when in London known Sir Richard Mayne, the organizer of the Metropolitan force, upon the model of which our New York Metropolitan force is formed; had been favored by him with a long personal discourse on the principles of its management, and been given the best opportunities for seeing them in operation, both in the park service and in all other departments. I had made a similar study of the Irish constabulary. I had originally organized, instructed, and disciplined, and under infinite difficulties secured the reputation of this same Central Park force. Finally, by a singular coincidence, I had nearly twenty years before, when my defamer was himself a school-boy, been an occasional editorial writer for the journal which he thus turned upon my work, and had contributed to it much of the matter, which, collected in a volume, had been later twice reprinted in London, and in translations in Paris and Leipsic.

I was asked by the president of the Department to make a public reply, and was allowed by the editor to do so in the same columns. I must gratefully add that the editor afterwards made all reparation in his power consistently with the ordinary rules of newspaper business. Nevertheless, the article served its purpose, was largely circulated among practical men, and I had reason to believe that even some of my friends thought there must be something in its ridiculous falsifications. The end was, that I was relieved of responsibility for the police of the Park. My duty was mainly assumed by a committee a majority of whom were new to the business; and the only two men who, besides the surgeon, had been conspicuously resolute in carrying out my orders, and sincere and faithful in efforts to enforce them, were dismissed—neither honorably nor dishonorably discharged, but simply notified that their services were no longer required. I am sure that the commissioners whose votes frustrated my efforts had been thoroughly convinced by the advice of friends that they were acting for the best interests of the city; that my intentions were good but impractical; and that in everything they were doing God's service. The president to the last sustained me. Because he did so, and asked it as a personal favor and act of friendship, I consented, after having resigned my office, to resume service under the Commission upon a modified arrangement, vindicating my professional standing and securing me against another similar experience.

19. Within two years the rules which the Board had been persuaded to adopt to prevent unsuitable men from being recruited, and to secure advancement by proved merit, had become a dead-letter; and the force was left to drift into the condition in which one of the Commissioners lately stated in a Board meeting that he had found it, and which led to a beautifully drawn resolution that hereafter no man who could not read and write should be taken for it. How soon to become in its turn a dead-letter, who can say? Some time after my defeat, a gentleman told me that he had walked, in a fine day, through the interior of the Park from end to end without seeing an officer. There was no lack of them on the fashionable drives; but in the most secluded and sylvan districts prostitutes were seeking their prey without hindrance, and it was no place for a decent poor woman to bring her children. I myself, since I left the Park, have seen an officer within a hundred yards of a carriage when it stopped, and when the coachman bent down an overhanging lilac-bush loaded with bloom, from which the occupants broke large branches, afterwards driving off without interruption or reproof. The officer, doubtless, thought it an unpractical thing to have lilac-bushes in the Park, as the present Commissioners think anything like sylvan seclusion unsanitary.

At another time I met seven small boys coming from the Park, all carrying baskets. They were showing one another the contents of these as I came upon them; and I found that they were each filled with beautiful rock-moss, which they were going to sell for the decoration of hanging-baskets. The Park has always been very deficient in this lovely accompaniment of rocks, and it is difficult to secure it. I asked the boys if the police allowed them to strip it off. "No," said one: "we waits till their heads is turned." "No," said another: "they don't care; they just minds the carriages, they does." Nor are these incidents by any means the most alarming that I might report.

Do the owners of houses building near the Park fancy that its vicinity will be a more agreeable place of residence because of this practical style of management? I have seen a newspaper report that already last summer great numbers of tramps and gypsies regularly lodged in the Park. When the police was under unpractical direction, I have repeatedly walked through its entire length after midnight, finding every officer in his place, and not one straggling visitor. Hyde Park is closed at nightfall, as are all other city parks in Europe; but one surface road is kept open across Hyde Park, and the superintendent of the Metropolitan Police told me that a man's chances of being garroted or robbed were, because of the facilities for concealment to be found in the Park, greater in passing at night along this road than any-where else in London.

If these incidents give little idea of the number, weight, and constancy of the embarrassments with which the Park Board has to struggle, they may have made plainer the nature of them, and the soil on which they grow.

But I must add a few more, that may, in some degree, remove misapprehensions as to the responsibility for various matters which are occasionally referred to in the interest of practical park management, as if they were the result of the ignorance or perversity of which the Commissioners intended to rid the Park in abolishing the landscape office.

For several years before that event, the management of the parks had, as before stated, not been under my direction. I had only to advise about it. But even before this, there was, for some time, a standing order in force, forbidding me to have a single tree felled without a specific order, to be obtained by a major-ity vote of the Board. Before this order was passed, men seen cutting trees under my directions have been interrupted and indignantly rebuked by individual commissioners, and even by the "friends" of commissioners, having no more right to do so than they would for like action on a man-of-war. I have had men beg me, from fear of dismissal, to excuse them from cutting trees, and, to relieve them, have taken the axe from them, and felled the trees myself. I have been denounced to commissioners by their friends as "a Vandal" and a "public robber," because nurse-trees were cut from the plantations of the Park under my directions. It may have been noticed, that, notwithstanding much talk of the necessity of thinning plantations, Mr. Wales, in a triumphant way, announced lately that not a single live tree had been cut this winter. Why not? Nothing had been cut but bushes, the removal of which, one by one, would pass with little notice from the vigilant friends of the Commissioners. Who is there, with any authority on the Park, competent to judge what trees should and what should not be cut, with a view to the purpose for which the Park has been formed?

Rocky passages of the Park, which had been furnished under my direction with a natural growth of characteristic rocky hillside perennials, have been more than once "cleaned up," and so thoroughly that the leaf-mould, with which the crevices of the ledge had been carefully filled for the sustenance of the plants, was swept out with house-brooms in the interest of that good taste which delights in a house painted white with green blinds, whitewashed cherry-trees, plaster statuettes on stumps; and patty-cakes of bedding-plants set between rocks scraped of their dirty old lichens and mosses,—and all in the heart of an Appalachian glen. Whereupon Mr. Robinson, in that invaluable addition to the literature of landscape art, Alpine Flowers, writes (I quote from a copy kindly sent me by my good friend the author, 2d London edition, p. 8),—

"In the Central Park of New York are scores of noble and picturesque breaks of rock, which have not been adorned with a single Alpine plant or rock-bush." He might have said, from which not only all such adornments, but even all the natural growth of rock-bushes, vines, perennials, and mosses, has again and again been cleaned away as exhibiting a low, depraved, and unpractical taste. The work is going on, I am assured, at this moment; and when it is finished, and August comes round again, and all the yellow turf and the dead, half-covered outcrops of smooth-faced, gray and brown ledge are fully exposed to view, God help the poor man who can find no better place of escape from the town!

20. The landscape office had been twice dispensed with for

a time before its last abolition in 1879. During one of these intervals a much boasted improvement in the plan of the Park had been put through with the energy and efficiency character-istic of a bull earning his passage through a China shop. Later, something was found defective in the drainage of the adjoining region. After a tedious and costly exploration, it was ascertained that a large main drain had been cut through at a critical point, and that the tile had been so broken and deranged as to make a complete dam, after which the excavation had been filled up, and built over. This led me to look at the drainage-maps, several sheets of which proved to have been lost. I begged to have a survey made for their renewal; and a man was employed for it who had been previously engaged in the work. While he was still occupied with the duty, what passes for economy in practi-cal park management came and dismissed him. I doubt if com-plete drainage-maps will be found in the Department to-day. I will undertake to satisfy a fair jury of respectable sanitarians, that, if there is reason to believe that a single case of malarial disease has originated in the Park in twenty years, it has been due to conditions which have been established or maintained against the advice of the landscape office. The reverse has been asserted or implied in scores of publications, for which no com-missioner, as such, has ever been responsible.

21. The more "practical" Commissioners have often given me advice received by them from friends having no official respon-sibility for the parks, and which betrayed exceptional ignorance, even for city-bred men, on matters which had been my life-study; which ran also directly counter to the practice of every respectable member of my profession; the folly of which I have often seen exposed in our agricultural journals, and the agri-cultural columns of our newspapers, but which they regarded, and expected me to regard, as of controlling weight. Some such advice I have, since I left the Park, seen carried out in practice.

22. The president once notified me that a friend of his was to come before the Board as spokesman for a "delegation" of citizens, to advocate the introduction of a running-course on the Park. He would ask me to explain some of the objections to the project, but hoped that I would do so in a way as little likely to provoke the gentleman as possible, as he had great weight in politics, and it would be in his power to much embarrass the

Department. I followed these instructions as I best could; but it was impossible for me not to refer to the landscape considerations. At the first mention of the word the gentleman exclaimed, and by no means "aside," "Oh, damn the landscape!" then, rising, he addressed the president to this effect: "We came here, sir, as practical men, to discuss with your Board a simple, practical, common-sense question. We don't know anything about your landscape, and we don't know what landscape has to do with the matter before us."

23. It will have been asked by many, as they have been reading, Why did you not appeal to public opinion? Why did not the Commissioners, who were superior to the courses through which your professional judgment was overruled, if they could not otherwise overcome these embarrassments, lay them frankly before us, and see what we could do? Might not a corresponding question be asked in regard to what everybody knows is going on at this moment, and has been for years going on, of the highest officer of the nation?

If the reference seems presumptuous in one respect, let me show that it hardly can be so in another; I mean in respect to the absorption of time and energy of public servants, through the pressure of "practical advice." As superintendent of the Park, I once received in six days more than seven thousand letters of advice as to appointments, nearly all from men in office, and the greater part in legislative offices upon which the Commissioners have been much dependent for the means of accomplishing anything they might wish to do,—either written by them directly, or by Commissioners at their request. I have heard a candidate for a magisterial office in the city addressing from my doorsteps a crowd of such advice-bearers, telling them that I was bound to give them employment, and suggesting plainly, that, if I was slow about it, a rope round my neck might serve to lessen my reluctance to take good counsel. I have had a dozen men force their way into my house before I had risen from bed on a Sunday morning, and some break into my drawing-room in their eagerness to deliver letters of advice. I have seen a president of the Park Board surrounded by a mob of similar bearers of advice, in Union Square, carried hither and thither by them, perfectly helpless; have seen policemen make their way in to him with clubs, drag him out, force him into a passing carriage, and lash the horses to a gallop, to secure his temporary relief from "embarrassments," the nature of which I trust that I have now sufficiently illustrated.

I do not remember ever to have seen the office of the Board without a poster, reading, "No laborers wanted;" and I do not believe that there has in twenty years been a time when nine-tenths of the intellectual force and nervous energy of the Board has not been given to recruiting duty.

A CIVIL WAR MEMORIAL: APRIL 1882

To Oakes Angier Ames

A triangular grass-plat is to be made in the fork of the roads opposite the Memorial Hall and a short cross road carried along the South side of it by which carriages coming from the East will be led directly to the South approach to the Hall. When this is done there will remain a bank and strip of higher ground between the new road and the old road in front of the school house. To support this bank a wall is to be built and on the terrace which will thus be formed a public walk is to be laid out with seats and shade trees.

The lowest point of this walk will be on a level with the highest point of the present side walk next the school house ground and it will be carried on to the eastward at about the same elevation. At the Eastern end there will be a circular space 30 feet in diameter, in the centre of which a flag-staff is to be planted to replace the old one which has to be taken down.

The retaining wall is to be formed of rough field-stone laid up dry, with a considerable slope that its general aspect may be consistent with the rocky elevation of the Memorial Hall Grounds—numerous crannies, niches and pockets opening to soil behind will be formed in it with a view to the growth of rock plants and the face is to be everywhere decorated with foliage and flowers, that it may appear pleasingly from the walks about the lower grass plat and in the view from the Memorial Hall Terrace.

Having ultimately in view out-of-door concerts and meetings in front of the Memorial Hall, the terrace is designed to serve the purpose of a gallery for parts of the audiences.

The retaining wall will be carried up three feet higher than the floor of the terrace walk, forming a parapet in front of it. The top of the parapet opposite the flag-staff will be twenty five feet above the base of the wall and the road on the North of it, and as the line of the wall must here be curved in adaptation to the form of the circle it will appear like the base of a round tower or an old warlike bastion half obscured by drapery of peace in the form of evergreens, vines, shrubs and flowering rock-plants.

In very old times it was customary to commemorate important events by a form of monument in the raising of which all the members of a community could have a direct part. This was done by their bringing together at a place agreed upon a great quantity of loose field stones and laying them up in a conical pile known as a cairn. The outside stones of a cairn are usually so heavy that they could only have been lifted to their place by machinery or with great labor of many men but the interior mass is more generally in part of smaller stones, some of which might have been brought by the hands of the youngest and feeblest of the community. The oldest and most enduring monuments in the world are of this class and some of them, because of the beautiful plants—that have become rooted in them and which spring out of their crevices or have grown over them from the soil at their base—are far more interesting and pleasant to see than the greater number of those since constructed of massive masonry and elaborately sculptured.

As the structure to be made at the East end of the proposed terrace-walk, above described, would otherwise have much the character of a cairn, being of the proper size, form, material and mode of construction, it is considered that it may be appropriately used to commemorate the anxious and heroic days of the great struggle through the results of which the American people are today a free and united Nation.

The better to carry out this idea, it is proposed that the names of all honorably discharged soldiers and Sailors going out from North Easton shall be deeply cut in the stones of the parapet; where they will always be conspicuous from the terrace walk and that the names of all who fell shall be inscribed upon a suitable stone at the foot of the flag staff. It is desired that the custody of the flag to be hoisted on this staff shall be with the veterans of the war living in North Easton as long as any shall survive and that it shall be set by them on Decoration day and other suitable occasions. It is further hoped that under their leadership, the school children of the village may be given conspicuous duties in all observances connected with the memorial; that in the first place for instance, they as well as all older persons, shall be asked to bring each a stone to be placed about the base of the flag staff; that their help shall be invited in the setting of plants and the sowing of flower seeds and that a custom may be inaugurated of some simple annual ceremony suitable to be carried out by them and their successors, generation after generation, carrying down the lessons of the war and keeping green the memory of its heroes.

"THE HIGHEST VALUE OF A PARK": SEPTEMBER 1882

Trees in Streets and in Parks *

I am looking upon a crooked, hill-side village street, lined with trees. I was about to say beautiful trees. But this may be questionable, for I have a book on my table which says with distinguished authority that nature is not beautiful, the word being applicable, in the opinion of the author, only to matters of design,† and it occurs to me that what is of design in these trees cannot be called beautiful. It is not symmetrical; it is not stately; it is not picturesque. A part of the trees crowd upon the gutter, a part upon the sidewalk so that two wayfarers can hardly pass between them and the fence. Soon a decision must be forced whether they shall be cut away, the street widened or the passage abandoned. The sidewalk is laid with tar-concrete on a base of stone; the gutter and wheel-way are laid a foot deep with road-metal. Were moisture, air and mould of vegetation to be carefully kept from the roots, the arrangement could be little improved. The trees are, indeed, so poorly fed that others nearby of the same species and of the same age are nearly twice as large. Everyone bears great scars from wounds

* From a letter written by request on the subject and read in abstract before the National Association for Sanitary and Rural Improvement, at Warwick Woodlands, N.J., July 10, 1882.
† *Art in Ornament,* by Charles Blanc, Member of the Institute of France, and formerly Director of Fine Arts.

and mutilations, which a little care would have avoided. Several show dead wood. Having been challenged to find a perfectly thrifty and sound tree among hundreds, I pointed to one of extraordinary beauty. Upon examination I had to acknowledge that it was of spontaneous growth, taking by chance a position in which the line and grade of the street could be accommodated to it, and that it obtained its sustenance neither from tar-concrete nor broken stone, but through roots running under the sidewalk into a deep, rich alluvial soil.

I lament all that I have described of these my neighbor trees, and looking down upon it I say it is not beautiful. But looking up at the continuous green canopy which these maltreated trunks support, swaying in the light summer breeze against the serene blue beyond—swaying not only with the utmost grace of motion, but with the utmost stately majesty—I say that cheaply, inconsiderately as the planting work was done, if the result is not to be called beautiful, it is only because it has more of sublimity than beauty. And, I ask, if man is not to live by bread alone, what is better worth doing well than the planting of trees?

Few who have not traveled with their attention specially given to the point can be aware how rarely trees are suitably selected, suitably placed, protected and cared for in our streets. There are not many towns that present a single example of a well-planted street, if even of a well-planted tree. I know of but one in which a well-considered planting system has been generally, or even extensively, carried out. I am glad to say that that one is our federal capital, in the streets of which more than fifty thousand trees now stand, with but a single defect, and that not of intention but of incompleteness, to be repaired as soon as public opinion shall have been educated—educated, be it observed, not simply to admire and demand verdant vistas and canopies, but to admit and respect the elemental conditions of life and health in the trees of which they must be framed.*

But if public opinion is uneducated to sustain what it is educated to demand in the planting of trees, how much more in the planting of parks? Yet here the trouble lies, less in ignorance

---

* There are some trees in the Washington planting of unsuitable species, and the beds of soil generally need enlargement.

and the prevalence of inadequate and shiftless ideas, than in the cross-currents and want of co-ordination of right ideas.

Parks are now as much a part of the sanitary apparatus of a large town as aqueducts and sewers. Their management should be as much a matter of sanitary economy, and as rigidly subject to sanitary tests.

As it is, in applying such tests, two great errors prevail. As the second of these grows out of the first, I would like to trace the first up from what I believe to be its roots.

It is not long since the capital cities of the world were so ill-provided with means of cleanliness, that much of the waste now carried off by sewers was deposited in the streets. Not forty years ago hogs roved in the fashionable residence quarters of New York under protection of the law, and for the same reason that excuses the turkey-buzzards of Charleston and the dogs of Constantinople:—without them the odor from filthy garbage and putrid animal wastes would have been even more intolerable than it was.

The custom of throwing offal and ordure into the streets had not gone out in large parts of Edinburgh and of Paris even thirty years ago, nor some time later in the principal cities of Italy. It had prevailed throughout London a few years earlier, and, there being no general water supply, it was a question of Heaven's pleasure how long the streets should remain uncleansed. No mere brooming over the rude pavements of that period being sufficient to fully remove the chief cause of offense, the air was nearly everywhere perceptibly foul, and this to a degree often provocative, in time of epidemics, of a panicky disposition to flee the town. Where there were parks, they gave the highest assurance of safety, as well as a grateful sense of peculiarly fresh and pure air. In London, besides the better known large parks, there were, early in this century, nearly a hundred small parks—more than three times as many as we yet have in New York. The political economy of the day valued them almost exclusively because of their cleaner air, and few travelers' stories or other general accounts of London, until lately, failed to refer to them as "airing grounds," "breathing places," as "the lungs of London," and so on. It has been recognized by men of science and leaders of public opinion that they were pleasant and useful in other ways, but, until within a few years, these other ways have been considered as of incidental and relatively insignificant value.

The current of public opinion thus established is still so strong that scientific sanitarians are often carried off their feet by it. I have a pamphlet prepared by an eminent physician, not ten years ago, in which the project of a park, now being formed at great cost, is advocated solely with reference to the value of its air.

Supposing the question to be taken up, as a problem of sanitary engineering, how to supply the people of a city with a certain amount of air, as the problem of supplying a certain amount of water or of gas-light often is, it may be considered certain that the solution would take nothing like the form which we find represented in our large parks.

An expedient is in general use, however, for reconciling the actual practice of park-making and management with an apparent adherence to the atmospheric theory of their value. It would be formalized briefly somewhat in this way: "It being desired that people should benefit by the sanitary advantage of breathing, even for one or two hours a week, the air of the parks, it is reasonable and economical to beguile them into doing so by making the parks *attractive*. Hence, besides building roads and walks and supplying shade, seats and opportunities of refreshment, large sums may be wisely expended in the planting of trees, and the introduction of other objects purely with *decorative* motives." (I say nothing of exercise, because it is an incident of taking the air, and is allowed for in any theory of value.)

But will the airing theory, as thus amended, account for the value which is generally recognized to be found in our parks?

Perhaps the shortest way to show that it will not, may be to state my own professional experience. Within four parks, there have been planted, under my supervision, more than half a million trees and shrubs, in the selection, disposition, planting and care of which I am not conscious that the first thought has been given to their comparative air-purifying value or to their decorative effect. Beyond the number referred to, wind-breaks have been planted, and in small special districts—episodes of these parks, foreign to their main themes—a few trees, with a distinctly decorative motive. But much more than ninety-nine of every hundred have been planted and managed throughout, as far as under my direction, with a very different motive. Nor do I think that any flowers, fountains, monuments, statues, or other so-called decorative objects, have ever been placed in parks of my motion, with a decorative motive, except as just explained as to the few decorative trees.

Perhaps I have been disposed to resist overmuch those who could see nothing in a park but an airing apparatus, to be made attractive by decorations; perhaps, too little. I assume nothing in either respect, but only argue that I must have taken a very different view of the requirements of the public in a park, and that if this view had little to recommend it to the public and was perplexing and displeasing to common sense, the fact would have been much more clearly established than it has been. As it is, I have been pursuing a purpose of an entirely distinct character, and in so far as I have done so successfully, it would appear that the result is not unsatisfactory to the public. On the contrary, with every renewed attempt to set it aside, or to thwart it, on the theory that a park should be but a decorated airing ground, the more decorated at all points the better, and that nothing else is of consequence, the more plainly it appears that the public finds in the park something of value not to be thus explained.

I must not neglect to point out that the pursuit of this other purpose cannot in the least interfere with or lessen the value of a park as an airing ground; I claim that it does not make it less, but in the long run much more attractive than the exclusively decorative motive, while a consistent pursuit of it, if long sustained, would not be more, but much less the costlier. On the other hand, the pursuit of the decorative motive, in planting or otherwise, is in its tendency, destructive of the objects which I claim should be paramount.

Now to the question, what is this other motive? It is plainly not enough to answer that it is to move the mind recreatively, because that is equally the motive of Punch and Judy, of a flower-garden, of a cabinet of curiosities, of jewelry.

A skilled man may appraise a show-case of jewelry, considering, as to each piece in turn, the weight and fineness of its gold, the size and color of its stone, the refinement of its chasing, and the degree in which its design and workmanship are of the ruling fashion, and thus come in the end to a close estimate of the value of the whole. One may go through a park and take account of the decorative value of the trees and all other notable objects in much the same way. But when the inventory is complete, the estimate of the recreative value of the collection will hardly have been begun.

In attempting to distinguish the action in the mind, and through the mind upon the entire organization of men, that I suppose should constitute the special recreative and sanative value of large parks, I shall be obliged to grope my way in a branch of science in which I have no claim to be adept. My apology for doing so is my desire to interest in the search those better qualified for it.

If a convalescent, leaving a bed for the first time in months, tries to walk straight from door to door across a clear, smooth, level floor, he will be conscious that several distinct mental efforts are needed to the ordering of his every step. A month later it may happen that the same man shall walk through a forest, rough, stony and with tangled undergrowth, constantly adapting his movements to numerous and complicated obstacles, both near and distant, and this with so little mental effort that he is conscious of none. All the time he may be sustaining a conversation, whistling a tune, or keeping close watch of a bird or a dog. So far from the necessary exercise of judgment interrupting or disturbing consecutive thought, the most profound courses of thought known to man have been pursued under such circumstances and with such absorption of mind, that obstacles of considerable difficulty, ordinarily calling for watchfulness and skill, have been overcome so lightly that no recollection of having passed them has remained on the mind.

We all act much and often most wisely on opinions, or mental impulses which we use as opinions, that have come to us through no process of thought that we can recall. We say, while engaged in conversation, that we think thus and so, not having been aware of such thought until it was passing our lips. Much that we call tact, sense, genius, inspiration, instinct, is of this unconscious process.

Holding this experience in view, it will seem probable that the mind not only produces thoughts and gives direction to the body without conscious effort, or process to be recalled, but that it *receives* impressions, information, suggestions, the raw material of thought; that it stores and holds them for after use; that it is fed, refreshed, revived and restocked by what it thus receives, all unconscious of the process.

I write with no effort for verbal accuracy, being sure that everyone knows from experience that of which I wish these phrases to be a reminder, and with such experience in view, I am equally sure that the distinction will be intelligible that I propose to make between what I shall call conscious, or direct recreation, and *unconscious, or indirect recreation.*

The probability may also be recognized that objects and arrangements (a choice and disposition of trees for example), best adapted to supply or augment direct recreation, is not that which should be chosen with a view to indirect recreation. It may even appear that objects before which people are called to a halt, and to utter mental exclamations of surprise or admiration, are often adapted to interrupt and prevent, or interfere with processes of indirect or unconscious recreation.

I do not intend here to discuss how the motive of unconscious recreation would lead us to lay out or to plant a park; I do not assume to have defined with precision what this so-called unconscious recreation is. But after such light upon it as may have been given, if there be any to whom the idea is not familiar, I may be allowed to submit that the highest value of a park must be expected to lie in elements and qualities of scenery to which the mind of those benefiting by them, is liable, at the time the benefit is received, to give little conscious cogitation, and which, though not at all beyond study, are of too complex, subtle and spiritual a nature to be readily checked off, item by item, like a jeweler's or a florist's wares.

There is one thought more that comes to me in connection with this of unconscious recreation, that I may yet be excused for suggesting.

It will be felt, I think, that as between the beauty of a common wild flower seen at home, nearby others of its class, peeping through dead leaves or a bank of mossy turf, and that of a hybrid of the same genus, double, of a rare color, just brought from Japan, now first blooming in America, taken from under glass, and shown us in a bunch of twenty, set in an enameled vase against an artfully-managed back-ground, there is something of this difference: The latter is beyond comparison the more decorative, superb, attractive, only, perhaps, not quite as much so as it is rare, distinguished and—costly. But the former, while we have passed it by without stopping, and while it has not interrupted our conversation or called for remark, may possibly, with other objects of the same class, have touched us more, may have come home to us more, may have had a more soothing and refreshing sanitary influence.

There is an association between scenes and objects such as we are apt to call simple and natural, and such as touch us so quietly that we are hardly conscious of them.

Many of the latter class, while they have been the solace and inspiration of the most intelligent and cultivated men the world has known, have been enjoyed by cottagers in peasant villages, living all their lives in a meagre and stinted way. It is folly, therefore, to say of the art that would provide these forms of recreation, either that it is too high for some or too low for others.

But this is to be said and said sadly: As a result of the massing of population in cities; of the centering of communication in cities; of the increasing resort to cities for recreation; of the tendency of fashions to rise in and go out from the wealthy class in cities; of the prominence given by the press to the latest matters of interest to the rich and the fashion-setting classes, and of the natural assumption that people of great wealth get that for themselves that is most enjoyable—as a result of all this—the population of our country is being rapidly educated to look for the gratification of taste, to find beauty, and to respect art, in forms not of the simple and natural class; in forms not to be used by the mass domestically, but only as a holiday and costly luxury, and with deference to men standing as a class apart from the mass.

All this tends to our impoverishment through the obscuration, supercession and dissipation of tastes which, under our older national habits, and especially under our older village habits, were productive of a great deal of happiness, and a most important source of national wealth.

And I submit that, both in the planting of village streets and in the planting of town parks, this tendency is rather to be resisted by sanitarians than to be enthusiastically pursued.

Very truly yours,

FRED'K LAW OLMSTED

PLANTINGS AT THE CAPITOL: 1882

FROM *Annual Report of the Architect
of the United States Capitol*

HISTORICAL NOTES OF THE CAPITOL GROUND

The intelligent visitor, reflecting that it is nearly ninety years since the site of the Capitol was determined, and more than eighty since Congress first held its sessions upon it, will need some explanation of its present sylvan juvenility.

Since building work first began upon it several efforts for the improvement of the ground have been made before the present, but no plan for the purpose has long been adhered to, and little of the work done has been adapted to secure lastingly satisfactory results. There is, mainly in consequence of a wavering policy and make-shift temporizing operations, but one tree on the ground that yet approaches a condition of tree majesty, and beside it probably not one of fifty years' growth from the seed—not a dozen of ten years' healthy, thrifty, and unmutilated growth. It may be added that many hundred trees are known to have been planted in the streets of the city early in the century, of which not one remains alive, nor is it probable that one was ever allowed a full development of its proper beauty. Yet, to show what easily might have been, if due judgment and pains-taking had been used, it is enough that one planted tree of even an earlier date may be pointed to, which is yet in the full vigor of its growth. (The "Washington elm" on the Capital ground, originally a street side tree.)

The following notes, chiefly upon the past misfortunes of the nation in its Capitol ground, have been largely based on conversations with the late venerable Dr. J. B. Blake, sometime Commissioner of Public Grounds.

When government, near the close of the last century, took possession of the site of the Capitol, it was a sterile place, partly overgrown with "scrub oak." The soil was described (by Oliver Wolcott) as an "*exceedingly stiff* clay, becoming dust in dry and mortar in rainy weather." For a number of years the ground about the Capitol was treated as a common, roads crossing it in all directions, and a map of the period indicates an intention to treat it permanently as an open public place. The year before his death, Washington built the brick house, still standing prominently, but injured by recent additions, a little to the north of the Capitol. A picture showing this house, with a young plantation of trees (none now living) between it and the Capitol, together with an autograph letter about it from Washington to his business agent, may be seen in the Lower division of the National Library. The first local improvement ordered by Congress, after occupying the rooms partially prepared for it in the incomplete Capitol, was a *walk* to be made between these and Georgetown (West Washington), where, there being yet no comfortable houses nearer, most of the members lodged. The Capitol and the house of Washington had both been built upon the assumption that the future city, which Washington avoided calling by his own name, continuing to use the original designation of the "Federal City," would arise on the higher ground to the eastward. Both buildings were expected to stand as far as practicable in its outskirts, backing upon the turbid creek with swampy borders which then flowed along the base of Capitol Hill. When this stream was in freshet it was not fordable, and members of Congress were often compelled to hitch their riding horses on the further side and cross it, first, on fallen trees, afterwards on a foot-bridge. There was an alder swamp where the Botanic Garden is now, which spread also far along the site of Pennsylvania avenue. Tall woods on its border shut off the views of the ground south and west of it. This wood, said to contain many noble trees, mostly oaks, was felled for fire-wood, by permission of Congress, as a measure of economy, sometime after the war of 1812.

These circumstances may give a little clue to the habit at the outset adopted, and of which Congress has since never been wholly disembarrassed, of regarding the ground immediately to the west of the Capitol as its "back yard," and all in connection with it as comparatively ignoble. With the city on the west, the transformation of the creek and swamp, and the opening of the magnificent view on that side, it is incomparably the nobler front.

It is a tradition, and is probable, that Washington, while building his brick house, planted some trees on the east side of the Capitol, of which the elm above referred to was one, and is the only one remaining. Another of equal age, but rotting prematurely, probably from unskillful or neglected pruning, was blown down a few years ago, and a third was removed in consequence of the enlargement of the Capitol. The last was a tree of graceful habit, and Mr. Smith, of the Botanic Garden, has distributed, through members of Congress, many rooted cuttings of it to different parts of the country. The surviving tree, having a girth of but ten feet at four feet from the ground, has been of slow growth, and been badly wounded within twenty years, three cavities showing the removal of considerable limbs by barbarous excision. On the east side a strip of bark, the entire length of the trunk, has been torn off. The ground, at a little distance on three sides, having been trenched and enriched, and that nearer the trunk forked over and top-dressed, the tree has, within three years, gained greatly in health and vigor; its wounds are closing over, and it may yet outlive several generations of men.

Some years after the death of Washington a space of ground nearly half as large as the present ground was inclosed in connection with the Capitol, and a street laid out around it. The Washington elm stands near where this bounding street intersected another which formed the northern approach to the Capitol, and on the opposite side, to the north, an inn of some celebrity, long known as the "Yellow Tavern," was built. This was the dining place for members still lodging at a distance.

Whatever improvement had been made upon the original ground before the burning of the Capitol in 1814 was probably then, or during the subsequent building operations, wholly laid waste, the three or four trees first planted alone escaping.

In 1825 another plan for laying out the grounds was devised, which was sustained in the main for nearly fifteen years, during most of which period John Foy had charge, and, as far as he was allowed, pursued the ends had in view in its adoption consistently. It was that of an enlarged form of the ordinary village-door yards of the time, flat, rectangular "grass plats," bordered by rows of trees, flower-beds, and gravel walks, with a belt of close planting on the outside of all. So long as the trees were saplings and the turf and flowers could be kept nicely, it was pretty and becoming. But as the trees grew they robbed and dried out the flower-beds, leaving hardly anything to flourish in them but violets and periwinkle. Weeds came in, and the grass, becoming sparse and uneven, was much tracked across, and grew forlorn and untidy; appropriations were irregular and insufficient to restore it or supply proper nourishment. Foy was superseded for political reasons, and his successor had other gardening ambitions to gratify.

At this time, though even some years later, George Combe described the city as "a straggling village, reared in a drained swamp;" it had become clear that it was not to grow up on the east front of the Capitol. John Quincy Adams, on retiring from the Presidency, had, like Washington, determined to build a town house for himself in Washington, and had chosen to do so far to the west. Much other private building had followed, including one large and excellent hotel, and government had undertaken several important public buildings in the same quarter.

It was then determined to make an addition (about seven acres), and considerable improvement of the premises in the "rear" of the Capitol, and this improvement led on, without any special act of Congress, to a gradual change of motive in the management of the old ground on the east, under the management of James Maher, who is described by his friends as a jovial and witty Irishman, owing his appointment to the personal friendship of General Jackson.*

The soil at the foot of the hill was much better than that of the east ground; but the trees planted by Maher were chiefly silver poplars and silver maples, brittle and short-lived. After doing more or less injury to the more valuable sorts, they have all now disappeared, but there remain of the planting of this period several fine occidental planes, scarlet maples, horse-chestnuts, a pecan, and a holly.

South of the "Washington elm," adjoining the east court of the Capitol, there are a dozen long-stemmed trees, relics of

---

* The following story is repeated from the best authority: The President once sent for Maher and said: "I am your friend, Jimmy, but I have often warned you, and this time I must turn you out." "Why, what's the matter now, General?" "I am told that you had a bad drunk again yesterday." "Why, now, General, if every bad story that's told against yourself was to be believed, would it be you that would be putting me in and putting me out?" He remained with another warning.

two circular plantations introduced in the midst of Foy's largest "grass plats," by Maher, for "barbecue groves," one probably intended for Democratic the other for Whig jollifications. These were also largely of quick-growing trees, closely planted, poorly fed, and never properly thinned or pruned. Forty years after their planting the larger number of those remaining alive were found feeble, top heavy, and ill grown.

Foy had planted in his outer belts some garden-like trees, very suitable to his purpose, magnolias, tree-boxes, hollies, and also some conifers, mostly thuyas, it is believed, but among them there was at least one Cedar of Lebanon. With them, however, or subsequently, more rapid growing deciduous trees unfortunately were also planted, and through neglect of thinning, the effect of drip and exhaustion of the soil the choicer sorts were nearly all smothered, starved, or sickened. A few crippled hollies (*Ilex opaca*) only remain. The violets and periwinkle (*Vinca*) now on the ground are largely of direct descent from those planted by Foy.

Most other trees within the limits of the Capitol inclosure before the enlargement of the Capitol in 1857 were removed to make way for the new building operations, or in consequence of the changes required in the grade of the ground to adapt it to the new work, or, later, to the grading done by the District government of the adjoining streets. It was found that the roots of most of the old trees, after having grown out of the small pits in which they were planted, had been unable to penetrate the clay around them, but had pushed upward and outward, spreading upon its surface and within a thin stratum of looser and darker material, consisting, it is believed, almost entirely of street sweepings which had at different times been laid on as a top-dressing. Though none were half-grown, nearly all had the characteristics of old age, many were rotten at the butt, and few were wholly sound. The more thrifty and manageable of them were retransplanted in 1875, and under more favorable conditions, presently to be stated, the larger part of them now appear rejuvenated. When moved they were generally from 8 to 15 inches in diameter of trunk.

Except under the "barbecue trees" the entire ground east of the Capitol and all that newly planted in the west, has been regraded. Near the eastern boundary the old surface was eight

feet higher than at present; the Capitol standing at the foot
of a long slope. The revised grade having been attained, the
ground was thoroughly drained with collared, cylindrical tile,
and trench-plowed and subsoiled to a depth of two feet or more
from the present surface. (In the outer parts where evergreen
thickets under scattered deciduous trees were to be attempted,
fully three feet, and here the liming was omitted.) It was then
ridged up and exposed to a winter's frost, dressed with oyster-
shell lime, and with swamp muck previously treated with salt
and lime, then plowed, harrowed, and rolled and plowed again.
The old surface soil was laid upon this improved subsoil with
a sufficient addition of the same poor soil drawn from without
the ground to make the stratum one foot (loose) in depth. With
this well pulverized, a compost of stable manure and prepared
swamp muck was mixed. It is still found to have too much of
the quality ascribed to the original by Wolcott, quickly drying
very hard. It would seem, however, to be wholesome and sufficiently friable for the growth of the trees planted; the death
of all the few that have failed being reasonably attributed to gas
leaks, severe wounds, or to extraordinary cold, or to a severe
attack of vermin before their recovery from the shock of removal. It is hoped that the more northern trees have been induced to root so deeply as to suffer less than they usually do
in Washington during periods of extreme heat and drought,
and that, in view of the thorough preparation and large outlay
for the purpose, the methods of administration will hereafter
be more continuously favorable than they had been for the
longevity of the trees and their attaining the proper full stature
of their families.

THE PRESENT DESIGN

Questions why, in the present scheme, certain trees and plants
have been taken for the Capitol ground and others neglected,
and why certain dispositions of trees have been made and others, offering obvious advantages in some respects, avoided, may
be best answered in a general way by a relation of the leading
motives of the design, some of which it is evident do not spontaneously occur to many inquirers.

The ground is in design part of the Capitol, but in all respects
subsidiary to the central structure. The primary motives of its

design are, therefore, that, first, of convenience of business of and with Congress and the Supreme Court, and, second, that of supporting and presenting to advantage a great national monument.

The problem of convenience to be met in the plan of the ground lay in the requirement to supply ready access to the different entrances to the building from the twenty-one streets by which the boundary of the ground was to be reached from the city. The number of foot and of carriage entrances is forty-six, and, as the entire space to be crossed between these and the open court and the terrace, upon which doors of the Capitol open, is but forty-six acres in extent, it had to be cut up so much as to put ordinary landscape gardening ideals of breadth and repose of surface, applicable to a park or private residence grounds, to a great degree out of the question. The difficulty was complicated by the hillside position of the building, compelling circuitous courses to be taken as a means of avoiding oversteep grades in the carriage approaches from the west.*

That the Capitol, in its several more admirable aspects, might be happily presented to view, it was necessary that the plantations should be so disposed as to leave numerous clear spaces between the central and the outer parts of the ground, and desirable that the openings or vistas should be disturbed as little as practicable by roads or other constructions. At the same time, the summer climate of Washington and the glaring whiteness of the great central mass made a general umbrageousness of character desirable in the ground, and a bare, bald, unfurnished quality to be, as much as possible, guarded against. It was then to be considered that customs are established that bring at intervals great processions and ceremonious assemblies into the ground, and that attending these, vast bodies of people, without

---

*Some may ask whether, under these circumstances, a strictly architectural design would not have had advantages. It is enough to say that, for several reasons, no such plan, if understood, would have been acceptable to Congress or the public taste of the period. It would, therefore, have soon been ruined in the treatment of details. Public taste strangely admits topiary work to be mixed up with natural forms of vegetation, and applauds a profusion of artificial features in what passes for natural gardening. Nevertheless, it condemns, even in situations where they would be most pardonable, the grander and more essential aims of ancient gardening.

order or discipline, surge through it in a manner that overrules all ordinary guardianship, and that, with increasing population and increasing means of communication, such throngs are likely to grow larger and more sweeping. This difficulty was increased by the long-established habit of regarding the Capitol ground as a common to be crossed or occupied in any part as suited individual convenience.

These considerations not only called for multiplied routes of passage, but for a degree of amplitude in pavements and flagging unfortunate with reference to the desired general effect of umbrageousness and verdancy. They also compelled a resort to many expedients for inoffensively restraining the movements of visitors in certain directions and leading them easily in others.

If these several more or less conflicting requirements are weighed, it will be seen that no attempt to reconcile them or compromise between them could be made that did not involve a disjointedness in the plantations unfavorable to the general aspect of dignity and composure desirable to be associated with so stately a building. Hence, where it remained permissible to plant trees at all, to have selected and arranged them with a view to exhibit marked individual qualities, would, as tending to increase such disjointedness, have been an unwise policy. The better motive was to select and place trees with a view to their growing together in groups in which their individual qualities would gradually merge harmoniously; to avoid a distinct definition of these groups, to aim to draw them into broader compositions, and to secure as much effect of depth and distance as possible by obscuring minor objects, especially in the outer part of the ground.

In the undergrowth, however, a degree of variety, cheerfulness, and vivacity, to be gained by moderate contrasts of form and color, might be studied. Hence not only the amount but the range of shrubbery used has been considerable, so much so that it must be admitted that at present it holds attention too much. As beyond a certain point the landscape effect of trees increases with age many times faster than that of bushes, the general effect will soon be much quieter. The chief reason for what would otherwise be an excessive proportion of shrubs and low growth is the necessity of mitigating the effect of the large extent of dead ground in the roads, walks, and adjoining streets, otherwise to be looked down upon from the Capitol and to be conspicuous in views across the ground.

Two minor motives influencing the choice and disposition of the undergrowth may be noted.

The summer climate of Washington being unfavorable to turf in situations where, owing to the number of trees growing in them, or for other reasons, the care of the turf would be difficult, the aim has been to cover the ground with foliage of creepers and of low perennials likely to retain greenness during droughts and requiring little labor to keep tidy. These low plantings also serve the purpose of connecting and merging the higher foliage with the verdure of the lawns and of increasing apparent perspective distance.

The shrubbery has been selected from regard to its fitness in foliage qualities, form, and size, when grown, to serve general purposes in the several localities in which it is placed. Its blooming qualities have been regarded as of subordinate consequence, but simple and natural bloom has been generally preferred to the more large, striking, and showy quality of flowers resulting from the art of the florist, the design being always not to make a lounging place or hold attention to details.

No spruces or other large-growing coniferous trees have been included in the recent planting, because if placed in the central parts they would obstruct views of the building; if placed on the outer parts they would disturb the general quiet and unobtrusive foliage effects desired, and lessen the apparent depth of the local sylvan scene. A few clusters of junipers, yews, and thuyas (*Chamæcyparis*), of established hardiness, will be found at points where they cannot interrupt views toward the Capitol, and where they will be obscured and overlooked in views from it.

The number of broad-leafed (laurel-like) evergreens that can be trusted to flourish in the climate of Washington is unfortunately limited. The fact that the ground is more visited in winter than in summer makes this the more regrettable. For this reason a considerable number of sorts have been introduced, the permanent success of which is not thought fully assured. All such are of low growth in this climate, and should they fail to meet expectations may be withdrawn without permanent injury to the designed summer landscape character. Should they flourish, it is hoped that others will be thinned out and the evergreens grow into moderate masses.*

The Capitol ground is declared by act of Congress to be formed "to serve the quiet and dignity of the Capitol and to prevent the occurrence near it of such disturbances as are incident to the ordinary use of public streets and places." Incidentally to this purpose, however, it is much used as a public park, especially during the hot season or when Congress is not in session. The need to provide seats in which people could rest for a moment in passing up the Capitol hill from Pennsylvania avenue, which is the point of entrance for most, and the need of a place in which children could obtain water being apparent, and as the necessary extent of accommodation in these respects would otherwise cause an unseemly obstruction of the walks or become too conspicuous a feature of the scenery, a summer-house was designed, with a view to the following advantages: It is entered by a few steps from three different lines of walk; it contains separate seats for twenty-five people, protected under all circumstances from ordinary summer showers; it allows six children to take water from the fountain at once; it is very airy, the softest breeze passing freely through it. The seats are so disposed as, though shadowed, to be well lighted, and to be each under constant inspection of the passing watchmen and the public through an opposite archway. The house is closed at nightfall and in winter. These precautions have enabled ladies to use it in large numbers, free from the annoyances which often deter them from entering sheltered resting places in parks. Standing on sloping ground, the floor is kept at the lower level and the walls and roof of brick and tile as low as practicable, so that at a short distance the eye ranges over them. That they may be more inconspicuous, the walls are banked about with natural rock, and slopes of specially-prepared soils favorable to the growth of various creepers and rock plants, by which, except

* The Evergreen Thorn (*Cratægus pyracanthas*), the Oregon Grape (*Berberis aquifolium*), the Coton-easter (*C. microphilla*), the Chinese evergreen Azalea (*A. amœna*), and an English hot-house shrub (*Abelia rupestris*), have each passed through without injury several severe summers and winters, and promise to be of the highest value for the landscape purposes for which they have been tentatively used. The three first are already to be seen in profusion and in vigorous health.

to one standing opposite to the entrance arches and turning to observe them, the entire structure will be wholly lost to view. From within the walls there opens on the up-hill side a cool dark runnel of water, supplied from the overflow of the fountain at the west entrance to the Capitol. The spray of this rapid rivulet, with that from the waste water of the drinking-fountain, maintains a moisture of the air favorable to the growth of ferns and mosses upon the inner rock-work. What is chiefly hoped for, however, is that under the conditions provided, a growth of ivy may have been secured, gradually reproducing the characteristic exquisite beauty of this evergreen in its native haunts. Many good examples of it, though not of its best estate, may be seen about Washington. The visitor interested is particularly advised to see those in the cemetery at West Washington (Georgetown).

The trees about the summer-house, though hardy and suited to the circumstances, will all have a somewhat quaint or exotic aspect. They include the Willow oak, the Cedrella, the Oleaster, two sorts of Aralias, and the Golden Catalpa.

The vistas or general lines of view to which all the planting and all the structures upon the ground have been fitted may be more fully stated.

Disregarding shrubbery, to be kept below the plane of sight toward the Capitol, openings are maintained, through which direct front views of the central portico and the dome will be had from the outer parts of the ground, upon opposite sides, and diagonal perspective views of the entire facades from four directions. In six other directions from the center of the structure only low-headed trees are planted, so that in each case the Capitol may be seen rising above banks of foliage from points several miles distant.

It is unnecessary to say that by the same disposition of the plantations, views outwardly from the Capitol are kept open, but attention may be called to the beauty and breadth, almost approaching grandeur, of the prospect up and down and across the valley of the Potomac, and to the design that when the present young plantations are full-grown this great advantage of the Capitol shall not be lost. The introduction of the proposed architectural terrace will indeed admit no trees to stand so near, or on ground so elevated, that they will ever obstruct the present distant view from the main or even the ground floor. The plantations in this direction, however, will in time obscure the nearer part of the city and form a continuous strong, consistent foreground to the further sylvan slopes.

From the terrace these plantations will in some degree limit the views to the northward and southward, but through the removal of the old central avenue and the broad gap left between the trees on the west an outlook is obtained between the northern and the southern divisions of the city in which a slope of unbroken turf, seen over a strongly-defined and darkly-shadowed architectural base, will be the foreground; a wooded plain, extending a mile beyond the foot of the slope, the middle distance, and the partly-overgrown, partly-cultivated hills beyond the depression of the Potomac, the background; the latter so far removed that in summer conditions of light and atmosphere it is often blue, misty, and etherial. Because, perhaps, of the influence of the cool waters of the river passing between the dry hills from north to south across this field of vision, sunset effects are often to be enjoyed from the west face of the Capitol of a rare loveliness.

A SUMMER RETREAT IN MAINE: MAY 1883

Report on Cushing's Island

BROOKLINE, Mass., 10th May, 1883
To the Trustees of the Cushing's Island Company:
GENTLEMEN:—I last week visited Cushing's Island with a view to giving you, as requested, my judgment of its fitness as a place of summer residence and as to measures desirable for its improvement.

The situation, dimensions, form and general character of the island as far as shown by maps, drawings and such written accounts of it as I have seen are probably known to all who may read this report, and such information as they present need not be repeated. I found that they had not impressed the more attractive qualities of its scenery upon me in several particulars. It is in parts much wilder and more rugged than I had been led to suppose, and has much more beauty of a delicate character, dependent on its minor vegetation, and the form, texture and color of its rocks. I will mention two incidents of its scenery which I found particularly enjoyable to which I had seen no reference. One is the rare picturesqueness of certain groups of vertically splintered rocks, close off the south shore against and among which the full swell of the ocean was surging at the time of my visit with a charm of motion and beauty of color quite indescribable; the other, the lovely tints, due I presume to lichens and mosses, in crannies and on the face of the beetling crags of White Head.

The Island is not a good place for a neighborhood of smart and fine suburban residences such as many prefer to pass their summers in. Streets suitable to such an occupancy of it would be difficult of construction, costly and a blemish upon its natural scenery. Villas and cottages of the class in question would appear out of place, tawdry and vulgar, upon it. Lawns and gardens appropriate to them are in large parts of the island out of the question. Notions of improving the island based on what has generally been attempted at many public favored places of summer resort should therefore be wholly abandoned. But to persons who wish to take as complete a vacation from urban conditions of life as is practicable without being obliged to dispense with good markets, shops and the occasional ready use of city conveniences; who have a taste for wildness of nature and who value favorable conditions for sea bathing, boating and fishing, the island offers attractions such as can be found, I believe, nowhere else on the Atlantic seaboard. To all such I recommend it unreservedly. The only danger of reasonable disappointment to such persons lies in the chance that others of incompatible tastes and ambitions will aim to make "improvements" of various sorts, and attempt a style of life incongruous with the natural circumstances and repugnant to tastes that the island is otherwise adapted to gratify.

If the island could in effect be owned by a club of families of congenial tastes united only for the purpose of preserving and developing its characteristic advantages and of providing convenience of habitation in a manner harmonious each with all, and all with nature, it would, under judicious management, soon acquire a value to each member such as could be obtained in a summer residence nowhere else nearly as economically.

It is with a view to a disposition of it essentially of this character that I shall suggest measures for its fittings and improvement.

From what has been said it will be obvious that the value of a summer residence upon Cushing's Island rather than in a thousand other localities along the coast, depends on scenery much of which can only be enjoyed either from points of view inaccessible to carriages and near which it will always be undesirable in the interests of those who will take the greatest pleasure in it, that carriages should be brought, or from elevated places in the interior. It is of the first importance to secure the free common use of these points of observation of both classes and to prevent their outlooks from being either obstructed or put out of countenance by structures for private convenience.

To this end certain elevated interior localities and a strip of land bordering the entire coast, should be made a constituent part of the property attached to each summer residence, these adjuncts being held in common. Certain other grounds should be disposed of for private use only in such large areas that houses to be built upon them will be scattered, leaving large spaces unencumbered by artificial objects. The deeds to be given for these large areas should provide against more than one residence within a distance of 500 feet, measured in a line parallel with the shore line, and with the condition that houses to be built upon them shall not be more than two stories in height: that at least their lower stories shall be of the local stone and that no fence or other structure shall be placed between them and the sea, except of rough local stone.

In the sketch plan herewith presented, about a hundred acres are proposed to be held as common property, this including all the outer parts of the island, its cliffs, crags, shingles and beaches, and sufficient space of the adjoining upland to allow continuous foot paths following the shore. At the more interesting points this upper space is enlarged. At each point of the island giving upon the ocean and the harbor's mouths considerable spaces are reserved and these are connected by a narrow common along the central heights which will command views both ways. Roads are projected with a view to a subdivision of the property and to a convenient connection between the interior building sites and the different parts of the shore. One main road, leading through the middle of the island from the present

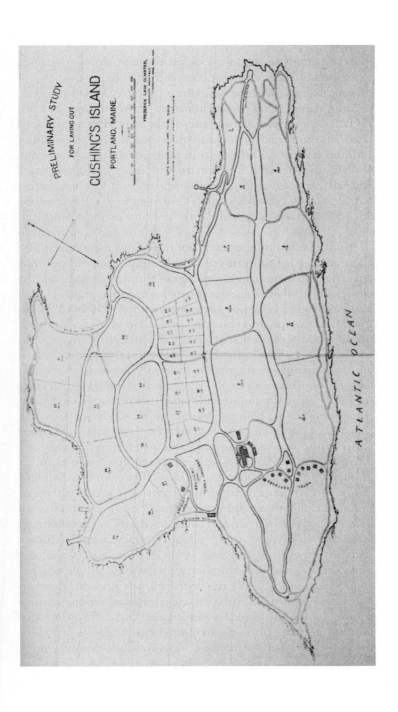

PRELIMINARY STUDY

FOR LAYING OUT

CUSHING'S ISLAND

PORTLAND, MAINE.

FREDERICK LAW OLMSTED,
LANDSCAPE ARCHITECT.

ATLANTIC OCEAN

landing of the Portland ferry boat, is proposed to be seventy feet wide so as to admit of its being planted with trees. Other roads are generally forty feet wide and a few by-paths for short cuts between different points of interest are proposed.

Residence sites in that part of the island where houses will be overlooked from the heights, and where neither rocks nor declivities will make difficulties in building, are generally from half an acre to an acre in area, elsewhere they vary according to circumstances, from two to seven acres.

With a view to unity, harmony and congruity of general effect, it is advised that no house shall be allowed to stand within 30 feet of the road line on the smaller lots, nor within 60 feet on lots of over an acre in extent; that no house shall be more than two stories in height, or 30 feet to the top of the roof, or furnished in its upper or more exposed and conspicuous parts with jig-saw or other extrinsic and puerile ornaments.

All the northern part of the island is at present comparatively bare and bleak of aspect, but there is evidence enough in the existing foliage that trees, shrubs and perennial plants may be easily and satisfactorily grown. It is very desirable for the value of the property as a whole that trees should be planted and that the narrow roads should be lined with low hedges and thickets. For this reason, and with a view to suitably planting the roads, walks and common grounds, the Trustees are recommended to establish at once a small nursery from which a variety of plants, especially shrubs and low-headed trees, adapted to the local soil, topography and climate, shall be provided for private planting on the island, without charge or at cost. Also to encourage the building of stone houses and fences, the free use of the present farm walls and all loose stone is advised to be allowed and quarries are recommended to be opened from which building stone for use on the island may be taken without charge. The stone of the island may apparently be very cheaply quarried, and if the outside of all its buildings shall present to view only the local stone or shingles without paint or gingerbread work, or shall be draped with the foliage of vines natural to the locality, the general result will be most effective.

The abundance of stone is such that where railings, parapets or small structures for seats and outlooks are required in the common grounds, ordinary slight painted work should not be admitted, nor should any structure be made more conspicuous than its leading purpose requires, it being kept constantly in view that the value of the property in the long run and on the whole will be dependent on the art which conceals rather than displays itself, and which favors the large and most unsophisticated enjoyment of nature that can be reconciled with a fair measure of convenience.

To the same general end provision should at once be made for a gradual replacement of the present spruce and fir woods of the higher parts of the island. Such a removal and improvement of the old natural growth, if not delayed, can be secured at slight expense. A few years hence it is likely to be practicable only by an outlay many times as large. The present natural beauty of the island may, simply by the sowing of seeds at trifling cost, be greatly increased.

The topography of the island is favorable to drainage, and, as far as can be judged in a cursory survey, there will be ready and moderately direct descent from all the lots shown on the accompanying plan, to the sea. Possibly in a few cases, to avoid rock cuts it may be desirable to carry outlets for short distances through adjoining properties, and the Trustees should retain the right to direct this when necessary.

Respectfully,

FRED'K LAW OLMSTED

To Bronson Case Rumsey

Brookline Mass Nov 1884

B. C. Rumsey Esq

Dear Sir

Last week I made a cursory examination of the property shown on the map herewith returned and the country near it.

The long steep slopes of a large part of the property are likely to be saleable only with reference to the larger class of suburban villas and the advantages offered for this disposition of it are considerably lessened by the circumstance that it is divided into five belts by a stream, an aqueduct a railroad and a carriage road, all slicing it from North to South and barring what would otherwise be the best system of roads for giving access to the hillside building sites. Some land may in consequence have to be sold either in undesirably small plots, or attached to larger plots without adding much to their value, or made public property. Still a division fairly satisfactory for villa sites a considerable part of which would be from four to six acres in extent is practicable.

Unfortunately there is little demand for villa property of this class near New York, less than almost any other city the environs of which are not specially inviting, and villas and villa grounds of the better sort rarely sell to advantage. Many can be bought at half their original cost. Thrifty men are consequently cautious of having much capital in them. The reason generally given is that so many of such properties have proved to be malarious or otherwise unhealthy. I have examined many with the result of a conviction that they could be in most cases made healthful at a cost that would not be inordinate but that the disposition of owners to sell and the indisposition of others to buy is only partially due to this cause. Remove it entirely and the fact would remain that villa life in the near vicinity of New York does not prove generally satisfactory and consequently that villa places and villa sites are comparatively poor property. Poor I mean comparatively with a similar class of property near other cities looking so far away even as London, Liverpool and Paris. The comparison that I am best able to make however is with Boston near which city I have been advised with as to several villa neighborhoods. In each of these before land has been put in the market, good roads have been built, their borders made graceful and neat, drainage secured and the healthfulness of the locality secured. It follows that lots have been rapidly sold at prices fully meeting the calculations of the owners and that numerous villa houses have been built and grounds prepared of a much more attractive sort than any often seen near New York.

Among the people who have done this some are of abundant wealth and of the highest social standing and there is no doubt that they are following a strong bent of taste and a conviction that the health and well being of their families are better served by a suburban villa manner of life than by any other. Some of these suburban residents that I know have moved from New York. While there they did not think of taking out of town places. Here they do so at once and are glad of the opportunity.

The difference does not lie wholly or mainly in the more careful judicious and substantial way in which lands naturally well adapted to villas are prepared and put in the market near Boston. It is due in large measure to the greater assurance felt by purchasers that such lands will not only not be taken up for other and widely incongruous purposes but that in a large neighborhood there will be a constant advance and improvement in the direction of an unbroken community of people of not excessively uncongenial tastes purposes and modes of life; a community likely therefore to be measurably united and constant in its demands and its influence upon the management of local public affairs and in which there will be an active public opinion repressing roadside exhibitions of excessively bad taste shabbiness or slatternliness.

In 1875 when engaged in devising the street plan for that part of the City of New York adjoining your property on the South I saw how little confidence a purchaser could have in a similar growth of a villa neighborhood within it. It contained not a few places in themselves attractive but always at no great distance from these were circumstances putting them out of countenance. Rough clearings in old wood land with blocks of gaunt trees left standing; patches of waste land and ill kept fields; raw banks by the side of the road, puddles and swamps; road side taverns and beer gardens; shanties; dilapidated stables or small groups of buildings such as are to be looked for in the most repulsive outskirts of cities with cinders and garbage strewn before them New York fashion. These things scattered at intervals neutralize the attractiveness of a suburban neighborhood no matter how nice its better parts may be. And being closely associated with most villa properties about New York they have come to be regarded as natural and necessary elements of suburban scenery, just as crowded cars and shabby and incommodious railroad stations are. There are a dozen stations about Boston finer and better kept than the best in the suburbs of New York. So there are about Philadelphia.

After examining your property the other day I looked again through parts of this adjoining New Ward district and it seemed to me that in the progress from its original rural condition the recent drift had been rather more toward a squalid outskirt of the town than toward a permanently inviting suburb. I do not see how confidence can be had that any part of it will acquire a continuous fixed character such as seems easy to establish for neighborhoods about Boston.

There are many times more people in New York than in Boston of the tastes habits and inclinations that are represented in the more attractive Boston suburbs. If the same advantages could be secured in your property with the same confidence of a lasting attractive consistent character that are secured in many Boston suburbs I think that a corresponding demand might be reckoned upon.

There are two special difficulties in the way of giving these advantages and this public confidence for your property. The first is the topographical difficulty to which I have referred which can only be got the better of by devising arrangements of an unusual if not an entirely original character in respect to roads and drainage.

The second is the difficulty of overcoming the inert imagination of possible purchasers and of setting them to think out the problems of providing such a class of homes for themselves as they might obtain upon these hillsides. New Yorkers are not accustomed to build except on shelves or plateaux of land and know nothing that is good of hillside gardening.

They need some tangible illustrations of what can be well done in such a locality to put them in train to a market demand.

I do not think that experience gives reason to suppose that any easy and moderate improvement such as has been characteristic of New York suburban real estate speculations will make your property saleable except at prices at which it can be again held for speculation by small investors or occupied scatteringly by people of small means such as those who are building on the outskirts of Brooklyn with a view to getting houses at less rent than they can be had for in the city. The ground is much less adapted to a method of subdivision suitable to such an occupation of it than it is to that which I have aimed to suggest.

A JEWEL IN BOSTON'S EMERALD NECKLACE:
APRIL 1886

Paper on the Back Bay Problem and Its Solution
Read Before the Boston Society of Architects

I have been asked to give you some account of the public work at the outlet of Back Bay.

The central purpose of this work is simply that of a basin for holding water, as an adjunct of the general drainage system of the city. With this basin a variety of arrangments have been planned to lessen the unseemliness and inconvenience of an affair for such a purpose in the midst of a residential quarter, the more important of these being expedients for controlling the movements of water in the basin and to it and from it.

How it happens that it is universally called a park, criticised as a park and the beauty and usefulness of a park anticipated for it I will explain presently. It might as well be called a dry dock or rural cemetery or a cathedral close, and discussed from a corresponding point of view, and the persistance with which it is thus held to be what it is not, never was and never can be, is an interesting illustration of the absurd difficulty that a professional man must be prepared to find sometimes standing in his way of getting a fair hearing from the public.

It occurs to me that the most instructive aspect in which this work can be presented to you as architects, is that in which it will appear as an illustration of the advantages that may be had from professional combination.

The professional fields respectively of the Architect, the Engineer, the Sanitary Engineer and the Landscape Gardener or Landscape Architect are in the main well-defined. Yet, at certain points, one merges into the other in such a manner that they may be regarded as so many convenient subdivisions of one field and each profession as a branch of one trunk profession. You see engineering journals giving plans of buildings, and architectural journals discussing plans of drainage of bridges and of parks. But as yet there is much less disposition to ready and cordial cooperation between these branch professions than is desirable for the public interests.

At a very late stage in the construction of the Brooklyn Bridge, the trustees of that work concluded to employ a board of architects in consultation with their engineer. The result is to be seen by walking through some of the narrow streets that pass under the inclined approaches to the bridge proper, and it is a very interesting result. By and by, when the granite gains the tints of age, the painters and etchers will find it out and instruct the public about it. As yet it is almost unknown. Suppose that the great engineer who planned the main structure had been led to seek the cooperation of the same architects in planning the towers of that edifice and all other parts of the structure, how much the public would have gained.

There is a bridge over the Schuylkill planned by another eminent engineer, in which, as it is really a part of the great park of Philadelphia, much effort for magnificent effect is evident. There is not a member of this Association who if he had been consulted by the engineer before the plan was fully conceived would not have shown him in a moment how much a greater degree, of the effect he desired, could be obtained, with no addition to the cost of the bridge.

As an illustration of the reverse practice, the employment of Mr Hunt at the suggestion of General Stone, the engineer of the base work of the Bartholdi statue may be referred to.

This work of Back Bay is instructive of the advantage of interprofessional cooperation in another way. That a landscape artist should have been associated with a sewer engineer in the planning and superintendence of a public work, and of the two should rather have been given the first place is certainly remarkable. Supposing it to be a wise arrangment you may be curious to know how it could have been brought about through the working of our present methods of city government. The best way to explain it will be by a narrative which would be unduly personal, egotistical and confidential if you had not done me the honor to make me an honorary comrad, and I were talking to you at any other time than after dinner.

In 1876, three gentlemen of notable position and character, of great commercial ability, liberal & public spirited were appointed Park Commissioners of the city of Boston with the duty of considering a variety of projects for the advancement of which there had been more or less public demand. As is apt to be the case in the early days of any such undertaking there was a disposition with these gentlemen to enter as soon as possible upon some scheme, the practical results of which would not be very remote. The scheme that first engaged their attention, and with reference to which there seemed to them to be the most immediately pressing demand, was the project of a pleasure ground within or adjoining that quarter of the city toward which fashion was setting, and in which there was the most activity of trade or speculation in real estate. Anything else the Commission could have in contemplation seemed by comparison, distant and obscure.

They therefore soon advised the City Council to authorize the purchase of 100 acres of land for a park on Back Bay. The City Council was not disposed to comply but under various influences, an order was at length adopted which permitted the Park Commissioners to buy, if they could, not less than 100 acres of land within certain defined limits, provided the whole could be obtained at a sum not exceeding $450.000, or at a rate of 10 cts a foot. This success was not brought about without some log-rolling and compromising among the members of the Council, and the order would not have been passed, it is said, and I have no doubt truly, had not some of those who voted for it felt quite sure that it would be impossible to buy the required amount of land at the price fixed.

After a great deal of skillful bargaining, however, the result was accomplished, a little being picked up here and a little there, until finally an area was obtained of 106 acres of the singular shape that you see.

If you ask how it came to take such a shape, the answer is

to be found in the circumstance that the principal part of the ground the Commissioners were able to purchase at the fixed price, was a gulf of mud and water of such depth that the cost of filling it up and preparing it to be built upon would be so great that it offered no prospect of a return for the needed investment. The substance of the locality was not like that found in those parts of the Back Bay that have been built upon, but was a flowing mud. Its surface was in considerable parts 20 feet below the grade of Commonwealth Ave and at one point soundings could be taken in it twenty feet deeper so that the solid ground was 40 feet below street grade.

Another circumstance was that the owners of the property wanted as large a frontage of lots as possible, consequently the more extended the outline of the park in proportion to its area, the better for any sellers who could retain a portion of their land.

By the way, you will here please reflect that the disadvantages which these circumstances established with reference to building purposes, applied almost equally to what are ordinarily and rightly understood to be the purposes of a park. In my opinion the whole scheme of a park at this point was an ill considered one. As Mr Davis the City Engineer afterwards told the Commissioners: If the state of Massachusetts had been hunted over, a space combining more disadvantages for a park could not have been found.

Having obtained the land, or rather the space of marsh, mud and water, they had sought, the Commissioners went through the usual form of conciliating an ignorant public opinion, which is called a Competition for plans. They did so I have no doubt in perfect good faith, more or less sharing the delusion of the public with respect to this expedient.

Now I come to my personal narrative. I was in Europe at the time this competition was entered upon. I returned about the time it ended, and immediately received an invitation to assist the Commissioners in selecting the prize plan. I declined to do so and when pressed, told the Commissioners that I considered that the terms of the competition were thoroughly unfair and the result could not but be most unsatisfactory and prejudicial to their undertaking. I predicted certain misfortunes which, do the best they could, must result from it. Misfortunes for which I was unwilling to bear any responsibility.

Several months afterwards the Commissioners sought me again, and said:—"It is turning out just as you said that it would. We realize that the Competition was unfortunate. Not one of the twenty odd plans comes near to suiting our views. We have only raised a swarm of hornets to plague us. Now we want to see what you can do. Will you make us a plan?"

"I will not," I first answered. "The only possible justification that can be made for your inducing a score of educated men to direct their ambition and spend their brains for some months in preparing plans for you for which they would receive no compensation, is that by such a course you might be helped to pick out from among them the man best fitted to advise you in the matter. If you don't like your prize plan, nevertheless you have found the man who comes most nearly among twenty to meeting your ideas. Take him into council, and you will soon obtain what you want. That is due to him."

They answered, "That we shall never do. The man would not suit us. We have paid him $500, and he is perfectly satisfied. He wanted nothing more."

After turning the matter over for a week I saw the Commissioners again and said, "I will not make you a plan to be accepted or rejected as you may be disposed, but for certain considerations I offer to become your professional counsel in this matter for a period of not less than three years. I will discuss the subject of a plan with you and will aid you to advance such discussion to profitable conclusions by means of drawings, until a plan is attained that shall be satisfactory to you."

An engagment was made on those terms, my office being entitled that of Advisory Landscape Architect.

Three successive studies were made and finally a plan was reached acceptable to the Commissioners. I had before, more than once, suggested that it would be a good plan to call the City Engineer in consultation with regard to the project, and I now advised that the plan should not be formally adopted without a conference with that officer, and this was assented to and a meeting arranged for the purpose.

At this meeting the City Engineer said, "I never have seen how it was practicable to have a park in the locality that you have chosen, and if you had given me an opportunity I should long ago have pointed out what I think to be insuperable difficulties in the way of it. But the question is one in which the

Superintendant of Sewers is better prepared in some respects to advise you than I am. You had better send for him."

This was done and there followed a discussion of four hours at the end of which the Engineers retired, leaving the Commissioners fully convinced that all their movements in the matter had been precipitate and that all the labor given to a park on Back Bay had been wasted.

The fact to be faced was this:—

Within the territory of which they had obtained possession, there was an estuary formed by the coming together of two streams, one being the Muddy River which flows through Brookline; the other Stony Brook flowing through Roxbury, and of which you have some knowledge from the full accounts of it given in the Press during the Freshet of last February. At the ebb of the tide the water of both these streams moved steadily into Charles River under a bridge upon the mill dam road. But as the tide rose there was a back set, the banks of the estuary were overflowed, forming mud flats. Beyond these there were plateaus of sedge and salt grass, over which the tide occasionally flowed, and in time of freshet, especially if at the same time there was a spring tide and an Easterly wind, a district about 300 acres in extent was flooded. There was thus a natural tidal basin of this extent.

For some time before and after full flood of the tide, the body of water set back in this natural basin was at rest and under these conditions it became a settling basin. Both the streams flowing into it had long served the purpose of main sewers for the people of a large territory, and the matter brought down by them, being constantly precipitated, had been incorporated with the mud of the estuary. The water moving over it became exceedingly filthy so that even eels could not live in it. Then, as the water went out with the tide the mud was exposed to the sun, and a stench arose that became an insufferable nuisance to people living half a mile away.

These conditions you will consider existed at a point toward which population was moving more rapidly than any other and close about which there was soon to be an irresistable demand for building ground as soon as the nuisance could be abated.

What could be done? The tide could be shut out by a dam. But the dam that would bar the tide at high water would also

bar the outflow of the streams at low water; and at such junc-
tures as have been referred to, of which the freshet of last winter
affords an example, a great accumulation would occur before
the tide would fall so low that it could be let out through a
gate in the dam.

A basin to hold it, then, was a necessity, and if there was to be
a reasonable development of the neighborhood as a residence
quarter, it was necessary that it should be one of much less
extent than the natural basin and one of much less disagreeable aspect.

The regular thing to do under these circumstances would, I
suppose, be to form a basin like that at Providence—a basin in
which the water would be allowed to rise to a height of perhaps
15 ft above low water, and its extent made sufficient to hold all
the water likely to accumulate while the tide was too high for
an outflow. It would be formed by a retaining wall of stone
and the city could be built up closely about it. Such an arrangment would be very costly and would be far from an attractive
circumstance in the Back Bay quarter of the city. Its character
being realized, the prospect of it would not advance the value
of neighboring real estate or enlarge the basis of taxation.

But being the simplest thing to be done and, so to say, the
normal engineering idea of a basin, it was the natural starting
point for the discussion that now ensued between the City Engineer and the Landscape Architect, and which proceeded from
step to step, somewhat in this way.

"Can sewage matter be kept out of the basin?"

Answer, "yes, by intercepting sewers."

"But the ordinary flow of the streams will yet be often foul;
can this flow, except in the emergencies for which the basin is
needed, be kept out of it?"

Answer, "Yes, by conduits of moderate dimensions laid outside the basin."

"That being the case, can the basin when not required for its
main purpose be kept clean and sweet?"

Answer, "yes, by flooding it as far as necessary for the purpose
with salt water, letting this move in and out enough to avoid
stagnation."

"But suppose we go to the very expensive expedient of high
retaining walls, will not the deposit that will occasionally be

made above these, when the water subsides after a flood, leave a slime upon them offensive both to the eye and the nose, and would not their aspect be in all respects unpleasant?"

Answer, "It could not be otherwise."

"Sloping earthen banks instead of masonry would answer the purpose of holding the water, what would be the objection to them."

Ans. "The slope would need to be as nearly level as that of a sea beach, or, to be pitched with stone in all that part liable to be flooded and for some feet above it. Otherwise it would be undermined and washed out by waves beating against it. Such a slope for the necessary depth would require a great space of ground and it would not have a pleasing appearance. Moreover such a lining of stone would be open to the same objections as a vertical wall of stone."

"Suppose the wash of waves could be avoided, the lining of stone dispensed with, the margin of the water be made inoffensive, could a basin of sufficient extent be formed within the area now under control of the Park Department?"

By calculation it was found that it could.

"By taking care that there shall nowhere be any great breadth of water for the wind to act upon, we may avoid the liability to waves of destructive force. By taking care that the slope of the bank between high and low water level, shall be at an inclination of about 1 to 6; by making the breadth of ground to be flooded during freshets so great that the difference between high and low water need not exceed four feet and by providing for a growth of foliage on the banks, not liable to be flooded with salt water, that will obscure the margin, should we not have a result that would serve all the engineering requirements as well as they would be served in a basin of masonry and be much less objectionable on the score of taste?"

Ans. "We should."

"And would not a basin of this character cost much less than a basin of masonry?"

Ans. "It would."

Thus we came to the problem of which the plan now being carried out was finally accepted as a tolerably satisfactory solution.

I will give you a description of the apparatus for controlling the movements of the water, reading most of it from a paper prepared for the Boston Society of Civil Engineers by Mr Howe, the Assistant Engineer in Superintendence of the work, and printed by the Society. This was written five years ago, and as you will see under the influence of the habit and the popular understanding which still with the public generally leads the locality to be called a park and any water in it a lake. He is describing the intentions which have since been carried out.

> Muddy River is to be taken to Charles River by an independent conduit. A conduit is to be made for carrying the ordinary flow of Stony Brook also to Charles River, but as the water in Charles River would be liable to rise at times so as to back up the water in this conduit about the street level in parts of Roxbury, a lower outlet for such occasions must be provided.
>
> The ordinary area of water within the basin will be 30 acres with its surface at 8 feet above city datum. In times of freshet the water of Stony Brook will be turned by an automatic arrangment into this basin, and the water as it rises will spread over an area of fifty acres—p. 130

So much for the appliances for regulating the flow of the water.

Now as to the design of the basin; this is the drawing of the plan originally presented to the Commissioners. You will see that a public street is carried all around the territory and at several points across it. This was required by the City Council and the space needed for the streets was to be taken, as you see that it has been, out of the 100 acres to be purchased. These streets are broader than ordinary city streets; they have very broad side walks and between the walks and the wheelway, planting spaces. On one side of the basin provision is made for a riding pad in addition to the wheelway, and half a mile of this is guarded from being crossed either by carriages or by people on foot so that a gallop can be safely taken upon it.

The basin lies within these circumferential highways. The water within the basin at its ordinary height is ten feet below the level of the highways, and the distance between the edge of the highways and the high-water line is about seventy feet on an average but constantly varying in most parts from forty to a hundred feet. Where it is ordinarily liable to be flooded, the surface of the bank has an inclination of about one vertical in

1879
PARK DEPARTMENT. CITY OF BOSTON.

PROPOSED IMPROVEMENT
or
BACK BAY.

—Figures show intended elevation of surface above low water of Charles River.
— Water is represented as intended to be maintained under ordinary conditions, at an
elevation of eight feet above the same datum.   During freshets and extraordinary
tides, it would rise and spread over all the sedgy grounds.

SCALE OF FEET

SCALE OF METERS

J.P.DAVIS,
CITY ENGINEER.

F.L.OLMSTED,
LANDSCAPE ARCHITECT.

CHARLES.H.DALTON ,

WILLIAM GRAY Jʳ ,

HENRY LEE ,
COMMISSIONERS.

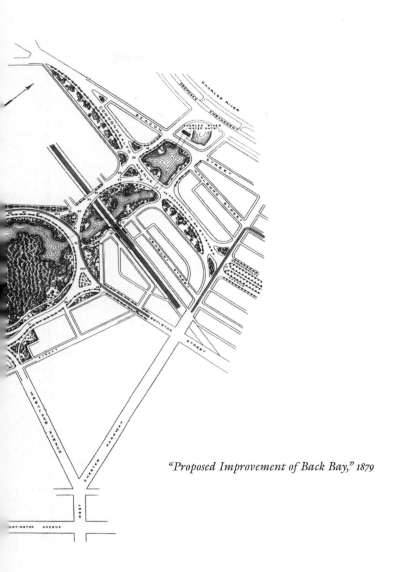

"Proposed Improvement of Back Bay," 1879

six horizontal. Above that it has an ogee section until a swell is formed generally a foot or two above the surface of the highways to the border of which it is brought with another ogee.

Such a section constantly varying in its curvature, corresponds with that naturally formed on the banks of streams, where the soil is moderately friable but somewhat variable in density.

The visible bottom of the basin is to have the character of a salt marsh, through, and on the border of which, a tidal creek flows in rapidly winding courses, there being nowhere any straight reach. The object of this crookedness is to prevent the surface of the water from being raked by the wind for any considerable distance and consequently to prevent a swell from forming. The ordinary level of the water will be from three inches to a foot below the level of the salt marsh but, it can be readily raised when necessary to keep the sedge and salt grass in flourishing condition.

When floods come and the tide is up so that there can be no outflow from the basin, the water will rise rapidly until it reaches the salt marsh level, then, having double the area to spread over, more slowly. Very rarely, according to the calculations of the engineers, will it rise more than a foot above the surface of the roots. The sedge tops will generally be more than that height above the roots, and with the obstacle they will provide, it will remain impossible for the wind to raise a destructive swell over the enlarged water surface. If the water ever rises still higher, which it may do once only in several years, the space of time before the tide outside will have fallen so that an outflow can again be had will be short, the swell raised above the sedge cannot be heavy and the damage to the banks is likely to be slight and readily repaired. With these conditions in view the engineer yielded the point of a formal zone of stone for the protection of the bank, which would have destroyed all possibility of giving the basin a picturesque or natural aspect.

The further treatment of the banks became then an ordinary question of landscape gardening under certain motives that need not be here particularly explained.

The best result that can be hoped for is that after trees have grown and nature has in various ways not to be minutely anticipated come to our aid, and in effect adopted and given a truly natural character to the details of the salt creek and salt marsh elements, it will appear that there is nothing artificial about the affair except the roads and bridges required for convenience, but that the city has grown up about the locality leaving all within its boundaries in an undisturbed natural state.

For convenience, I have confined my account thus far exclusively to the Basin proper. What will have been more conspicuous to any of you passing near the locality is the outlet or passage between the basin and Charles River. There are special local features in this part of the work of which the more important, being that of the causeway and arch, will not need description. The outline of these having been established, I requested the Commissioners to employ an architect for designing them and they engaged Mr H. H. Richardson for the duty. My intention had been that the causeway if built at all of stone, should be of field stone so laid with pockets and with a heavy batter in the manner of the wall built in Franklin Park that it would be much overgrown with foliage and its artificial character except at the parapet be unobservable. Mr Richardson fell in with this idea, and his first plans for the Boylston Street arch were for a very picturesque structure of field stone, harmonizing in character with the proposed plan of the causeway. The cost of the work on the whole would have been much less if this had been adopted but the Commissioners were afraid to undertake anything so out of common, and so we had to come to what you now see. It is very agreeable as a matter of general outlines and of color, but I think it would have suited the circumstances better if it had not been quite so nice.

As to the treatment of this outlet district in other respects I will read from my published report for 1884. (page 14)

The work is now so far advanced and in respect to its hydraulic apparatus so far in operation as to have already been fairly tested with respect to its main purposes. The flood of last winter was an extraordinary one and all the conditions were as unfavorable as they are ever likely to be. The great destruction of property which it caused in the valley of Stoney Brook is evidence of this. But within the field of our operations not the slightest disturbance occurred. The whole self-acting apparatus did its work smoothly and continuously. The water in the basin rose at no time while the tide was too high for an outflow as much as four feet above its ordinary level. There was no wash of consequence.

There has been some question whether we could succeed in making an artificial salt grass or sedge meadow marsh. If you look over the Western parapet of Mr Richardson's bridge, you will see that we have done so on a space of several acres, quite sufficient to show that our plans for the purpose are practical. We have tried two methods, one by sodding and one by sowing; both are successful.

Where we are not successful as yet is in establishing any satisfactory vegetation between salt sedge and a line about three feet above it, within which salt appears to be deposited probably by evaporation of salt water, carried up by capillary attraction, but until last year we had no proper organization for planting, being dependent on a contractor, and I am confident that we shall yet succeed. Even if we fail, it is but a question of time when this zone will be obscured by overhanging foliage from the trees and bushes growing above it.

It has been thought that the place would be a breeding ground for muskitoes. No evidence that it was so appeared last summer.

It was thought that our plan would not overcome the filthiness of the locality, that the stench would not be relieved and that the water in the basin would be always disgustingly foul. The air was perfectly sweet all of last summer, and notwithstanding the fact that steam dredgers were at work in the upper part of the basin and a steamboat with scows loaded with mud was often moving in the lower part, the water was generally fairly clean. I have no doubt that it will be perfectly so when the work ends.

The plans for the Basin having been adopted, I asked the City Engineer, "what are your plans for dealing with the Muddy River above the Basin?"

"We have none."

"What are you likely to have there eventually—a big conduit of masonry to carry the flood, several miles in length, and intercepting pipes for the sewerage from both sides?"

"That is not unlikely."

"Such arrangment will be very costly and will be delayed many years because of its cost. Meantime and before many years the Muddy River valley will be very dirty, unhealthy, squalid. No one will want to live in the neighborhood of it. Property will have little value and there will grow up near the best residence district of the city an unhealthy and pestilential neighborhood."

"All that is not improbable."

"Why not make an open channel there and treat the banks of it as we are going to treat the banks of the Basin. Would not that be an economical move?"

"I don't see but it would."

"Then the roads leading up that valley to Jamaica Pond would be the beginning of a Park-way leading from the Back Bay to the Arboretum and West Roxbury Park."

"They might be."

"Suppose then that we put our two professional heads together again and see if we can't make a practicable plan for that purpose and get the city to adopt it."

"Agreed."

And from that conference came this plan which you will see is essentially an extension of the Back Bay Plan, and has been fully adopted by [...] Brookline and Boston.

"LOCAL RESOURCES": OCTOBER 1886

"A Healthy Change in the Tone of the Human Heart"

(SUGGESTIONS TO CITIES)

This is the term used by a great writer to describe what indolent people would be apt to call a difference of taste, the difference between the "taste" that led to the building of the Parthenon and that evinced in the building of cathedrals, and, again, between the public taste of the period of cathedral-building and the time of the building of—what shall be said?—our soldiers' monuments? our patent iron bridges?

In the fifteenth century, Mr. Ruskin tells us, the most cultivated of men found delight in scenes of which the chief characteristics were trimness, orderliness, framedness, surface fineness,— sources of gratification that could be so only through a conspicuous manifestation of human painstaking. The water in which they took pleasure was water flowing in a channel paved at the bottom, walled at the sides, rimmed at the surface, and bordered by parallel floral fringes, specimen trees, or hedges. The rocks they enjoyed were any but crannied, craggy, mossy, and weather-stained rocks. They liked best to look on forest trees when they had been trimmed, shorn, and disposed in rows by the side of a road. They disliked all that we mean by depth, intricacy, mystery, in scenery. They liked clear outlines, fences, walls, defining circumstances, scenes fretted with bits of bright color, turf patched with flower-beds, nature dressed on the principles of our drawing-room and garden decorative art. They fairly hated the sight of the disorderly, unconfinable sea, with its fluctuating lights and shadows and fugitive hues. The civilization of our times, Mr. Ruskin thinks, finds a greater pleasure in rivers than in canals; it enjoys the sea, it enjoys the distinctive qualities of mountains, crags, rocks; it is pleasantly affected by all that in natural scenery which is indefinite, blending, evasive. It is less agreeably moved by trees when standing out with marked singularity of form or color than when the distinctive qualities of one are partly merged with those of others, in groups and masses, as in natural woodsides. It takes pleasure in breadth, sedateness, serenity of landscape. If modern art has any advantage over that of the middle ages, it is through its awakening to the value of these aspects of nature and its less respect for the more material wealth of man's manifest creation.

This doctrine is not Mr. Ruskin's alone. Scholars in general have substantially taken the same view from the time of Addison and Horace Walpole down. Mr. Ruskin has but presented it more fully and accurately than others. But if we accept it, what are we to think of the neglect that is apparent at many of our centers of civilization to preserve, develop, and make richly available their chief local resources of this form of wealth? Let me refer to a few examples.

At our national capital, while we are every year adding to its outfit new decorations in marble and bronze, formal plantations, specimen trees, and floral and bushy millinery, we leave the charmingly wooded glen of Rock Creek in private hands, subject any day to be laid waste. Once gone, the wealth of the nation could not buy for Washington half the value of landscape beauty that would thus have been lost.

Again, one of our Northern cities has always had lying at its feet a passage of scenery in which, with some protection and aid to nature, and a little provision of convenience, there might be more of grandeur, picturesqueness, and poetic charm than it is possible that this city shall ever otherwise be able to possess, though it should increase a hundred-fold in population and wealth, and command the talents of greater artists than any now living. No effort is made to hold the opportunity. No thought is given to it. The real estate in which it lies, as yet mainly if not wholly unproductive, is from year to year bought and sold as private property with regard alone to its possible future value for some industrial purpose to which thousands of acres nearby can easily be as well adapted. There is a river running through it, but its chief interest to "the human heart" does not lie in the water. The water is of no small value, yet it might be wholly drawn off to turn wheels and all that I have said remain true.

We have another fine city, a city of some repute for its poets, its architecture, sculpture, music, gardening, its galleries and its schools of art. Liberal, provident, thrifty, clean, it sits at the head of a harbor giving directly on the sea. The harbor has made the city. Various islands and headlands make the harbor. The islands and headlands are thus the life of the city. Following Mr. Ruskin, one would suppose that whatever of beauty lies in them would long since have engaged all the art-sense of its people. But, in fact, hitherto, a stranger wishing to look down the harbor toward the sea could not find a foot of ground along the shore prepared for the purpose. Once the islands were bodies of foliage. Seen one against another and grouping with woody headlands, they formed scenery of grace and amenity, cheerful, genial, hospitable. But long ago they were despoiled for petty private gains, and the harbor made artificially bald, raw, bleak, prosaic, inhospitable. Each island now stands by itself, as sharply defined in all its outlines as the most mediæval mind could desire. Several of them are the property of the city and are in use for excellent purposes. It would not lessen but enhance their value for these purposes to dress them again with the graces of naturally disposed foliage; and under a well-prepared system, patiently followed, it would cost little more every year to do this than is spent for an hour's exhibition of fireworks. The harbor is often more crowded than any other on the coast with pleasure-seeking yachts and yachtlets; all that has been stated is perfectly plain; but the opportunity remains not only unused, but, so far as publicly appears, unconsidered,—a matter of no account.

One of the most impressive (and by its impressiveness the most recreative, and by its recreativeness most valuable) city grounds that I have known, I strayed into by accident, never having heard of it before. This was thirty years ago, and I have not heard of it since; but the impression it made was so strong that being asked for a note on this topic, it is instantly and vividly recalled. The entire value of this city property lay in its situation. Otherwise it was barbarous—barbarous in its squirming gravel-walks, its dilapidated essays of puerile decoration, its shabby gentility; its hogs and its hoodlums. But far below flowed a great river, and one looked beyond the river downward upon the unbroken surface of an unlimited forest; looked upon it as one looks from a height upon the sea.

No matter what is beyond, an expanse of water, as you say, can never fail to have a refreshing counter interest to the inner parts of a city; it supplies a tonic change at times even from the finest churches, libraries, picture galleries, conservatories, gardens, soldiers' monuments, parks, and landward outskirts. What is easier than to provide a grateful convenience for such refreshment? Yet if one wants it at Troy, Albany, Newburgh, Springfield, Hartford, Middletown, New London, Trenton, Norfolk, Louisville, St. Louis, Memphis, Vicksburg, what is offered? What was lost for Brooklyn when the brow of its heights was wholly given up to paved streets and private occupation! What resources is Burlington wasting!

The wayfarer in Lynchburg may come to know by a chance glimpse at a street-corner that that city holds one of the greatest treasures of scenery at its command; but if he would see more of it, he must ask leave to climb a church-steeple, or, what is better, plod off by a dusty road to a point beyond the city's squalid outskirts, where the James river will give him undisturbed space for western contemplation. Many such illustrations of the general fact might be given.

But one who believes that Ruskin is describing tendencies of civilized movement rather than stages attained, as he looks over our land, is not left cheerless. Years ago a traveler arriving in Buffalo asked in vain where he could go to look out on the lake. "The lake?" he would be answered in the spirit of the middle ages; "nobody here wants to look at the lake; we hate the lake." And he might find that two large public squares had been laid out, furnished and planted, leaving a block between them and the edge of a bluff to be so built over as to shut off all view from the squares toward the lake and toward sunset. But lately land has been bought and prepared, and is much resorted to, expressly for the enjoyment of this view. This new public property also commands a river effect such as can be seen, I believe, nowhere else,—a certain quivering of the surface and a rare tone of color, the result of the crowding upward of the lake waters as they enter the deep portal of the Niagara. Is the regard paid to these elements of natural scenery by the city less an evidence of growing civilization than is given in the granite statues on its court-house or in its soldiers' monument? San Francisco holds a grand outlook upon the Pacific; New Haven has acquired a noble eminence overlooking the Sound. Be it remembered, also, that at Chicago and at Detroit, at Halifax and at Bridgeport, sites have been secured at which the public interest in great, simple, undecorated waters may be worthily cared for.

Between the two neighboring cities of St. Paul and Minneapolis the Mississippi flows majestically. Its banks are bold and nobly wooded, a virgin American forest. Mr. Horace Cleveland, a veteran artist, a kinsman of the President's, is urging upon the people of these two cities that they secure the opportunity thus offered for a public ground common to both with which no other city recreation-ground could be brought in comparison. If Mr. Ruskin be right, it speaks well for the health of these two wonderfully growing communities that the suggestion has been gravely received and is earnestly debated.

A small space, it should not be forgotten, may serve to present a choice refreshment to a city, provided the circumstances are favorable for an extended outlook upon natural elements of scenery. This is seen in Durham Terrace at Montreal, the inward as well as the riverward characteristic scenes of which Mr.

Howells has described in "Their Wedding Journey." Another illustration of the fact may be found in a queer little half-public place, half-domestic back-yard, from which the river may be overlooked if anyone cares for it, at Hudson, New York. Yet another may be come upon at Providence, a public balcony, not more than a hundred feet square, thrown out from a hill-side street. A trifling affair, but a trifle that expresses much of public civilization.

For low-lying towns upon the sea or lake coasts, promenade piers will generally offer the best means to the purpose. A simple promenade pier built with tree-trunks from neighboring woods, nicely hewn, nicely adzed, nicely notched, nicely pinned, without a bolt or strap of iron, with no paint or applied "gingerbread," built by a village bee, would be a work worthy to be celebrated in a woodcut poem of THE CENTURY.

A DISPUTE WITH A COLLABORATOR: JULY 1887

To Calvert Vaux

9th July, 1887

My Dear Vaux,

I had hoped to find a note at Cameron's giving me some understanding to work upon of what you would like me to aim at & was disappointed. I had been asked to come to the park office at 11 o'ck; had at the moment made a memorandum of it and verified it. Nevertheless, I was told when I arrived there that the Commission had met at ten and adjourned. It was said however, that if I would wait Commissioners would be sent for and a special meeting held. They were supposed to be about the City Hall. I waited and they came and went and came for some hours but no formal meeting was held.

I had before written Crimmins that to avoid further waste of time in discussion of impracticable propositions, such as presented to me the week before, he and they would do well to consider that no arrangement could be made with me which did not recognize you—essentially as in my discussion with them of last year. Verbally with the Commissioners I held the same ground. But at last, when it was nearly time for me to go to catch a train for Boston, seeing no prospect of a move on that line, as they were plying me with questions about Riverside plan, having it in mind that the arrangement of last year was no longer satisfactory to you and that I had been unable to draw from you any indication of what you would like me to aim for, except that you had two or three times recalled to me that Riverside & Morningside plans were not the same to you that they were to me, I admitted that an arrangement might be practicable for revising the Riverside and Morningside plans which did not involve a partnership interest. Crimmins asked me to repeat this, and began taking a memorandum of it. I asked him not to as it had been said carelessly but then said "if you want a memorandum suggesting such an arrangement I will write one" and thereupon I did so. The President took the note and having read it said something to the effect that something like that might be feasible and he would like to talk it over with the then absent Commissioners and if I wanted to get the next train to Boston he would not detain me longer. We were not likely to come nearer to a point this time.

Since I began writing I have recvd your note of yesterday. I must say that I do not see how you can put the construction you seem to upon my course or why it should please you to wish to. You write as you might if I had been coming to New York of my own notion with the purpose to obtain some employment of the Park Commissioners and that had moved for this purpose in such a manner as to crowd you—at least to take the "lead" out of your hands. You say that I have undertaken to lead but finding that I could not have been trying to ease myself of responsibility of leadership by teazing you for advice, or for information of your plans. I think that this is what anyone else reading your letter would suppose. I cannot suppose it because I know that you know that there is not the slightest word of truth in it. Yet even I cannot make anything else out of your letter and am obliged to think that you do not fully realize how far any such notion would be from the facts. If you don't, you ought.

For ten years past I have been sick of New York. Its infernal politics had wrought the most intense and ruinous disappointment with me. And occurrences made this, day after day, more and more mortifying and aggravating. After a time it did not appear that I had any duty to myself, my profession or to the public that should anchor me there. I came here for no business purpose. I had not a particle of business or prospect of business here when I came and I was further from such business as I had elsewhere when in Boston than when in New York and I left New York only because I was sick of it—its park commission and its infernal underground politics and after coming here I diligently cut myself away from New York and its associations. You must know that I have done so. I have not been to New York except for a business purpose, I have stayed no longer than was necessary and have rarely seen a New York friend in New York. I have done nothing that would help me to hold or extend influence there. I have meddled not at all with park affairs except in such organic public matters as the Menagerie and Parade and when writing on these or other matters at special request have done so in a way to avoid connecting my name with the agitation. When Mr Crimmins wrote inviting me to come to him with a view to an arrangement for my employment, I had not seen him. I knew none of the Commissioners and wanted nothing to do with them; I declined the invitation. When it came again in an official form and as a business proceeding, I concluded after advising with several of our friends that it would not be right to refuse to give the Commissioners this counsel asked in their behalf by their President. The first word I said to them was that you were the proper man for them to consult and that I wished to make no engagement with them. Since then in all that has passed nine parts out of ten of all that I have said to them has been with a plain purpose to strengthen you and Parsons and to further your views as far as I could understand them. The first word I had with them and the last— addressed to the President as I was taking leave of him Thursday last was an earnest appeal to him to first of all put you on a proper professional footing. My last letter to Mr Crimmins was an effort to convince and persuade him that it was bad policy to keep you at arm's length and that it would be better to deal directly with you. I probably have never placed myself under bonds to have nothing to do with them until they had given you a proper position because I have never fully intended, if the obstacles to your appointment as resident Landscape Architect could not at last be overcome, to give them no alternative but to employ some one, as the Commissioners more than once had done before, not at all in sympathy with us, (as Mould or Jones or Johnson who was with them last year with letters from Ruskin) but I have come as near to it as I could with truth and have gone far to create that impression.

Further, I have taken no step; have presented no suggestion to them which I did not believe to be in accordance with your wishes, or the least discordant with them that the circumstances allowed. It has never occurred to me that I was leading—much less that I was leading against your lead and I have no idea what you mean when you imply that. Certainly I have never desired to lead or to move in the matter at all except side by side with you. I have not thought of leading the Commissioners except in the view that I wanted nothing that, rightly informed, they would not want. I have had no concealed thoughts from them, have been plain and blunt. And so with you. If I have ever concealed anything from you that you ought to know or would wish to know, I am not aware of it. If I have in the least taken a lead that you did not wish me it has been your fault, not mine. It has been in some technical sense, not in spirit purpose or principle. I am not playing a game and am not ground by technical rules.

—Here as I write comes in your second letter of yesterday, again, I have to say that I do not feel that I am on the ground of it. It would seem to bear the implication that I have been willing that, through the Tribune or otherwise, a wrongful impression, harmful, as it chances, to your interests and to Radford's, should be spread, such an impression as you say Mr Duncan had received. I think that you would hardly be willing that I should understand just that from your letter. But what else can I understand? I see nothing else but an argument to that effect in all of these two pages. But I know that you have not the slightest ground for a suspicion that I have been willing that such a report should be propagated. But considering it a wrong report and one injurious to you, what could have been your reason for telling him that "*The Tribune was, of course right.*" It was, *of course wrong*—(according to your statement, I have never seen the report). And you knew it to be wrong. I have not the remotest idea for what purpose you went out of your way to propagate the wrong.

I am apt to talk loosely when led on to do so in apparently friendly conversation and to overcome feebleness of expression by exaggerated rattle and I might easily have given some body with access to newspapers some wrong notion when asked what had occurred between me & the Commissioners. But in this I am sure that I have not. I have been twice interviewed with a view to a newspaper report but have at once said that nothing had occurred worth mentioning. I have referred to you as better able to talk about coming improvements, these in New York being matters of your business rather than mine, and have pleaded haste to get away. My aim has been to prevent newspaper reporting not lead it. And I suppose that I have succeeded.

My name has not been mentioned at any time since I left New York in connection with New York parks with my knowledge and consent. I have several times prevented it from being mentioned when it otherwise might have been.

I suppose that there is something lying back of what you say which you expect me to see and I cannot. Something "technical." If I were a prisoner before a criminal court and you the prosecuting attorney I should expect to be hanged by a technical rope. All the same I should know that I really was not guilty. I have been assuming that your letter meant what I say and have been contradicting it; but I don't quite think so—only if not that it is incomprehensible to me. That after all these years we should be no better able to understand one another is one of the strangest of life's experiences. I seem as near to you sometimes as to any old friend—I have not many left. Yet sometimes we have as little insight of each other's meaning and motives as if we were beings of two different planets.

I still hope that what is best on the cards for you and Parsons will come out of all this otherwise wasted time. Not that your interests are my primary object, of course. But I suppose that they lie right along with my primary object. I don't want to have to come back to New York but I am not sure that I shouldn't even do that rather than lose all chance of bringing the parks back to original principles so far as that is now possible. To that end, with you or without you, I shall always do what seems to me best. There is nothing else I care so much for.

Affectionately Yours

F. L. O.

PLANS FOR A NEWPORT ESTATE: AUGUST 1888

To Frederick William Vanderbilt

2d August, 1888

Dear Mr Vanderbilt;

I think I ought to say to you that the more I reflect upon the matter the less I am near to reconciling myself to the conclusions reached in our last discussion. As I said then, the place must be prepared with a view to your taste and your comfort and not at all to mine. But the question is for me to consider what plan when carried out, and, years hence, after mature results have been reached, you are likely to be permanently satisfied with. Taking fully into account your present predilections, I do not believe that the arrangements to which you provisionally assented the other day would prove permanently satisfactory. In my opinion if you proceed upon them it will not be five years before you will abandon them and seek to make changes & variations. The result will be little less satisfactory, there being two classes of motives in conflict, producing a weak and imperfect compromise.

Therefore before anything is done in that direction, I must give you my advice distinctly against what I may have seemed the other day to have assented to.

The one thing that I hold to is that there should be no attempt at "lawn" treatment of the ground immediately in connection with the outcrop of ledge on the Rough side of the house. There should be an abrupt and clean separation between all dressy ground and these bold storm-beaten features of the place. Any attempt to have the dressed ground fade off into the wild ground will be a failure. As I said a thicket of shore growing shrubs, such as Myrica (candle-berry), lambskill, sweet fern and sweet briar, could possibly be interposed between the lawn and the rocks, but it would be years before it could be brought to satisfactory condition; it would be a failure with any ordinary gardening and the probability is that you would get tired of it and let your gardener seek to improve it by the introduction of elements that would destroy its character.

And the fact is that it would not accomplish your purpose. It would, if it succeeded, just as effectually separate visually your lawn from your wild ground as the terrace or a wall.

I am confident that you are mistaken in supposing that the effect of what I have advised would have the effect of belittling the place. I am sure it would have the contrary effect.

I am the freer to urge my opinion upon you (as to the division of the dressed ground from the "cliffs") because when first asked to take the matter up I gave my opinion in writing upon the point and if I did not clearly intimate in that note, I did distinctly state to Mr Peabody, that if you should not be disposed to accept my opinion in this particular I should wish to decline the commission. So far as I advised you as to the form and position of the house it was with the object of making the house and its outworks constitute, as far as possible the desired separation, and while I have since urged the terrace on other grounds it is only as a means of completing this division that I think it, or some substitute in the same locality, essential to a good general design of the place. I do not believe that you are as able as I am to forecast what will be permanently satisfactory to you in this respect.

I am bound to say, now that I am giving you a professional opinion on this point that I feel the design not to be quite satisfactory in one other. I have never liked the plat of turf that you have wanted between the two platforms on the rough side of the house and which you agreed the other day that you would discard. My reason for not liking it was that it was petty and insignificant and would make the two platforms which it separated petty also. It is much better to make one affair of the three things. But I think that the feeling which was at the bottom of your inclination to have a plat of turf (or of something) intermediate between the platforms, (and the house), and the undulating, broken and rocky ground before it was a sound one. A defined flat space of turf or of turf and gravel would be more convenient and would look more convenient and be in better taste at the foot of the steps than an abrupt passage from tiled floors and cut stone walk to rough ledges and undressed turf in slopes and declivities of various inclinations.

Yours Truly

Fred^k Law Olmsted

A DEFENSE OF FOREIGN PLANTS: OCTOBER 1888

Foreign Plants and American Scenery

October 24, 1888

To the Editor of GARDEN AND FOREST:

Sir.—In GARDEN AND FOREST of August 1st, page 266, the law seems to me to have been laid down that the introduction of foreign plants in our scenery is destructive of landscape repose and harmony. No exception was suggested, and the word harmony was used, if I am not mistaken, as it commonly is in criticism of landscape painting, not of matters of scientific interest; not as if the question were one of what, in matters of literary criticism, is called "the unities."

That a fashion of planting far-fetched trees with little discrimination has led to deplorable results, no good observer can doubt. That these results are of such a character that we should, from horror of them, be led, as a rule, in our landscape planting, to taboo all trees coming from over sea, many of your readers will not, I am sure, be ready to admit, and if no one else has yet offered to say why, I will ask you to let me assume that duty.

Suppose anywhere in our Northern Atlantic States an abandoned clearing, such as in Virginia is called an "old-field;"—suppose it to be bordered by the aboriginal forest, with such brushwood as is natural to its glades and skirts straggling out upon the open;—suppose that mixing with this there is a more recent, yet well advanced, growth of trees and bushes sprung from seed, of which a part has drifted from the forest, a part from a neighboring abandoned homestead, while a part has been brought by birds from distant gardens, so that along with the natives, there is a remarkable variety of trees and bushes of foreign ancestry;—suppose a road through more open parts of the old-field, and that on this road a man is passing who, having lately come from New Zealand (or the moon), knows nothing of the vegetation of Europe, Asia or North America, yet has a good eye and susceptibility to the influences of scenery.

Now suppose, lastly, that this man is asked to point out, one after another, so that a list can be made, trees and bushes in an order that will represent the degree in which they appear to him to have an aspect of distinctiveness; No. 1 being that which stands out from among the others as the most of all incongruous, unblending, unassimilating, inharmonious and apparently exotic; No. 2 the next so, and so on.

The question, as we understand it, is essentially this: Would all of the trees and bushes that had come of a foreign ancestry be noted before any of the old native stock?

Some of them surely would stand high on the list, and some of much popularity, such as Horse Chestnut and Ginkgo and numerous sorts of trees in themselves, at least, less objectionable on this score, as, for example, Weeping Beech and most of the more pronounced weepers; most of the Japanese Maples, also, and the dwarf, motley-hued and monstrous sorts of Conifers.

But, all? or, as a rule, with unimportant exceptions? So far from it, to our eyes, that we doubt whether, even of different species of the same genus, the visitor would not point out some of the native before some of the foreign—some of the American Magnolias, for example, before any of the Asiatic. We doubt if the European Red Bud, the Oriental Plane or the Chinese Wistaria (out of bloom) would be selected before their American cousins. It appears to us that *Rubus odoratus* would be noticed before *Rubus fruticosus.* Passing from the nearer relatives, it seems to us likely, also, that many of the European and Asiatic Maples, Elms, Ashes, Limes and Beeches would be named *after* such common American forest trees as the Catalpas, Sassafras, Liquidambar, Tulip, Tupelo and Honey Locust; that the American Chionanthus, Angelica, Cercis, Ptelea, Sumachs, Flowering Dogwood, Pipevine and Rhododendrons would be placed before some of the foreign Barberries, Privets, Spireas, Loniceras, Forsythias, Diervillas or even Lilacs. We doubt if the stranger, seeing some of these latter bushes forming groups spontaneously with the natives, would suspect them to be of foreign origin, or that they would appear to him any more strange and discordant notes in the landscape than such common and generally distributed natives as have been named. We doubt if Barberry, Privet, Sweetbriar and Cherokee Rose, which, in parts of our country, are among the commonest wild shrubs, or the Fall Dandelion, Buttercups, Mints, Hemp Nettle and a dozen others, which, in parts, are among the commonest wild herbaceous plants, though it is believed all of foreign descent, would ever be thought, by such an observer, out of place in our scenery because of their disreposeful and inharmonious influence. Two hundred years hence are not Japanese Honeysuckle, "Japanese Ivy" and "Japanese Box" (*Euonymus radicans*) likely to be equally bone of our bone in scenery?

The forest scenery of northern Europe is distinguished from most of ours by greater landscape sedateness. It is to be doubted if many of the trees that come thence to us, judiciously introduced among our own, provided they are suited with our climate, will not often have more of a quieting than of a disturbing influence on our scenery.

We have much ground which it is difficult and costly, with any plants natural to it, to redeem from a dull, dreary, forlorn and tamely rude condition. There are parts of the world where, in ground otherwise of similar aspect, plants spread naturally, of such a character and in such a manner, that the scenery is made by them interesting, pleasing and stimulating to the imagination—picturesque, in short. Heather, Broom and Furze are such plants in the British Islands. It happens that neither of these has yet flourished long with us, though it is said that Broom appears to have got a foothold in some of our exhausted tobacco lands. But if we cannot have these, it does not follow that nowhere in the world are there plants that would serve the same purpose with us. If any such offer, should not every American give them welcome? The Woad-waxen is a plant inferior to those above named as an element of landscape, but superior in cosmopolitan toughness. As a matter simply of scenery is such heroic settlement as it has effected (it is often winter-killed to the ground, but not to the root), upon the bleak, barren fells back of Salem, as lately described in GARDEN AND FOREST, a misfortune? We believe that to most persons it adds (and otherwise than through its floral beauty) much to the landscape charm of these hills, while detracting nothing from their wildly natural character.

Again, may we not (as artists) think that there are places with us in which a landscape composition might be given a touch of grace, delicacy and fineness by the blending into a body of low, native tree foliage that of the Tamarisk or the Oleaster, that would not be supplied in a given situation by any of our native trees?

Is there a plant that more provokes poetic sentiment than the Ivy? Is there any country in which Ivy grows with happier effect or more thriftily than it does in company with the native Madrona, Yew and Douglas Spruce on our north-west coast? Yet it must have been introduced there not long since from the opposite side of the world. Would not the man be a public benefactor who would bring us from anywhere an evergreen vine of at all corresponding influence in landscape that would equally adapt itself to the climatic conditions of our north-eastern coast?

Imagining possibilities in this direction, let us suppose that, from remote wilds of Central Asia or Africa, we should be offered an herb, or a close-growing, dwarf, woody plant like the Leiophyllum, as it occurs in the Carolina Mountains, that would form a sod with a leafage never rising more than three inches from the roots and never failing in greenness or elasticity during our August droughts. Would not the matting of many a large, quiet, open space among our trees, with such a plant, favor harmony of scenery much more than it is ever favored by the result of the best gardening skill, aided by special fertilizers, lawn mowers, rollers and automatic sprinklers, in dealing with any of our native grasses? Such an acquisition we may think too improbable to be considered. But is it really much more improbable than, 200 years ago, would have been a prediction of the present distribution in some parts of our country of Timothy Grass, Red Clover and Canada Thistle, or in other parts of Bermuda Grass, Alfalfa and Japan Clover?

Before agreeing that no addition can be made to our native forest, except to its injury, we should consider that trees for landscape improvement are not solely those that please simply from their fitness to merely fall quietly into harmony with such as are already established. Trees would be of no less value to us that, being adapted to our climate, would supply elements of vivacity, emphasis, accent, to points of our scenery, such as we see happily produced by the Upright Cypress and the horizontally branching Stone Pine when growing out of Ilex groves on the Mediterranean. And this is a reminder that some scholar has said that we can form little idea of what the scenery of Italy was in the time of Virgil from what we see there now. This because so many trees and plants, which were then common, have since become rare, and because so many, then unknown, have since become common. Is there reason for believing that the primitive scenery of Italy was, on this account, more pleasing than the present?

The large majority of foreign trees that have been introduced with us during the last fifty years, and which have promised well for a time, have been found unable to permanently endure the alternate extremes of our climate, but that there are many perfectly suited with it we have abundant evidence. Does the White Willow flourish better or grow older or larger in any of the meadows of its native land than in ours? Was it not under this tree that the most American of our poets sung of the family of trees, "Surely there are times when they consent to own me of their kin, and condescend to me and call me cousin," forgetting that, if so, it was the case of "a certain condescension of foreigners"? How is it with the English Elm, the Norway Maple, the Horse Chestnut? The Ailanthus, the Paulownia, the Pride of China, all introduced from Asia within the memory of living men, are spreading as wild trees and elbowing places for themselves in the midst of our native forests. The Eucalypti, from Australia, have come, in thirty years, to be a marked (not generally an agreeable) feature in the scenery of California, and while the climate of our Atlantic coast does not quite agree with the Hawthorns, in Oregon, notwithstanding its greatly drier summer, they seem to be as much at home as in Kent or Surrey.

But on this point of the adaptability of many foreign trees to flourish in American climates, only think of Peaches, Pears and Apples.

Frederick Law Olmsted

Brookline, September, 1888.

A SUMMER RESORT IN COLORADO: JANUARY 1889

To General Bela M. Hughes

January 15, 1889

Gen'l B.M. Hughes,
President of the Redstone Company.
Dear Sir:

I enclose a quotable professional opinion of the character of your property of Perry Park as a site for a summer resort.

In the present communication I propose to offer suggestions for the carrying out of your purpose to establish a small summer colony in the park at any early day.

The ultimate value of the whole property will depend much on the impression which this proposed early settlement will make upon possible future purchasers of land, even at considerable distance from it. The success of the early settlement, therefore, is to be measured but very partially by its immediate profit to you or by the satisfaction that shall be taken by those having part in it. The settlers you count upon will be, for some time, chiefly Denver people of a class disposed to make but very moderate outlays for buildings; not ambitious of display, yet unready to dispense with neatness and taste even while passing a vacation in a region mainly attractive to them because of its wildness and seclusion from the fashionable world. Among the people that you want to be prepared to impress favorably in the future there will be many of more luxurious tastes and who are readier to make liberal outlays to gratify them.

The point of policy to be considered is: How the pioneer settlement can be made, without excessive cost, to acquire and hold a character and reputation by which the value of the whole property will be favorably affected? Answering this question, there are, in my opinion, two reasons why you should stringently insist that the settlement shall not be made in a straggling, fragmentary or scattered way. They are:—

First, that spaces of bare ground which may have a not unpleasing aspect if in the midst of a region generally in a state of nature, when seen as waste places between neat houses and planted door-yards, are, in the climate of Colorado apt to appear forlorn, untidy and the reverse of attractive. If the houses are at all fine they will, by contrast with the vacancies, make the village as a whole appear a jumble of incongruities. If they are rude their association with the waste ground will give the village a raw and hopelessly mean character. A collection of even extremely rude cabins on the other hand, is apt to be pleasingly picturesque if they are seen to form parts of a group or composition the other parts of which are in good proportion pleasingly natural.

More or less this objection to scattered settlements is of general application but it often happens that in our eastern villages, what would otherwise be dreary waste places between houses are quite as agreeable elements of the local landscape as if they were under the highest garden cultivation because in the spontaneous course of nature they are clothed with rich turf and decorated with pretty bushes and perennials. The course of nature is very different on Colorado.

Second, the cost of providing common conveniences such as walks and roads and those of water supply and for the removal of waste, and of keeping them always efficient and neat, will be much less in a closely built than in a scattering settlement. And cost in this case does not mean money cost alone but housekeeping trouble. It is also to be considered that in a compact village a man would be ashamed to neglect the simplest requirements of good taste in the care of his place who, living in an isolated house, would allow its surroundings to fall into a condition likely to impress a passing stranger unpleasantly and injure the prestige of the property.

Assuming that the Company will not sell or lease land to people who are unwilling to live in a moderately compact village and to take obligations which will insure between each house and its neighbors a constant state of tidy verdure, what character in other particulars is it desirable that the village should acquire with respect to the lasting advantage of the park property as a whole?

It appears to me that the aim should be to give it some general excellence of its own, distinguishing it at least so far that no visitor will be liable to remember it only as one of numerous villages that he has seen. Even though to give it such a distinction there should be some elements to which many people would object it is better that it should provoke discussion on these points rather than fail to be distinguished. The great point is to make it complete in its own way and prevent the introduction of features confusing and out of character with that which is its notable excellence.

How could such a distinction be obtained without excessive expense?

Suppose that one who had been travelling for a few weeks in Colorado should come into a village in which there were no raw, dry, dusty and dirty places either in the streets or adjoining them: in which there were no houses so big and "stuck up" as to dwarf the greater numbers of all others; in which no house called for *particular notice* solely because of its evident newness or the freshness of its paint, none in which less seem to have been done for immediate display than for a kind of beauty that, nourished by nature would be increasing from year to year and would express unobtrusive domestic taste rather than fashion or smartness. Suppose that owing in part to local circumstances, in part to customs universally followed by its people, the houses of the village did not hold the eye of one passing among them more than the verdure growing before between and about them and that, notwithstanding the unassuming style of its constructions and the informal and apparently unarranged character of its natural elements, the village, *as a whole*, appeared strikingly pretty. Suppose a village so different as this must be from what is commonly brought about by the ambitions of those through whose efforts, moved more by a competitive than a cooperative spirit, villages are generally formed. Suppose this and you will see that situated in the midst of a naturally attractive region it could not fail to acquire celebrity in a degree greatly disproportionate to the necessary cost of securing it, a celebrity due, first, to its modesty and the apparent absence of effort with its people to make a display; second, to the evidence it presented of genuine refinement, good sense and good taste.

It is not to be supposed that such a distinction could be gained without cost both in the way of outlay for common improvements and by restrictions upon private enterprise that would prevent as rapid and early growth of the place as might otherwise be secured.

But it is my opinion that the cost would be well repaid in a few years and that much more would be gained by aiming steadily at such a distinction and keeping under control whatever would interfere with the pursuit of it than by taking a course more nearly parallel with that commonly followed in the building of summer resorts.

On one of the above points I will dwell a little more.

As a rule people will go to Perry Park rather than to some other place, under the lead of men who, in the first instance, will have taken land because its natural landscape was particularly pleasing to them. Now upon such a natural landscape a village—a settlement of summer visitors—never failed to jar unless its houses were not only subdued in color as houses only can be brought to be slowly, without paint, but unless they were comparatively unimportant features in the midst of a wealth of foliage growing on and about them.

But wealth of such foliage as would be desirable does not come of itself to a village, and when it is made to come in Colorado, it does not appear to belong to the natural landscape. Two precepts follow: First, you should choose a locality and devise a plan for your village favorable to a rapid growth of foliage in the midst of it. Second, you should seek to have the village so situated that it will not be a prominent feature in the general landscape but rather an episode.

The required conditions will be fully provided on the shores of the pond which you propose to form, surrounded as they will be at a short distance by hills that will frame in and give landscape seclusion to the locality.

Suppose that you have a road made along the natural margin of this pond, far enough from it to allow a nearly continuous belt of trees and bushes to grow with their roots in its moist edges, the road as narrow as convenience will permit in order to avoid all unnecessary exposure of dead earth and all unnecessary expense of keeping it smooth and tidy. Suppose that a little back from this road you let a series of "bungalows" be built, all low walled and roofed with only the face toward the pond presented distinctly to view and this face mostly shaded by verandas, galleries or awnings. Suppose that there is a little garden in front of each with a hydrant for watering it supplied by pipes from higher points of the brook which is to feed the pond, and you will see that you have the leading elements of a very charming sort of village.

As a centre to such a village nothing could be so pleasing as a pond such as you expect to have embowered with such foliage as could be soon established on its banks. Given such an oasis with a road about it, and it would be natural and reasonable that a circle of cultivated people should cluster closely about it, and, having only summer quarters in view and an intention to live much out of doors, that they should build inexpensively just the class of rustic and unassuming but neat and cozy habitations that would be more desirable from the point of view of an artist. It would be equally natural and agreeable that, these houses being on a hill side, those living in them should terrace off little gardens before them from the road with rustic walls made of the loose stone abounding on the hill-side in their rear; that there should be seen a profusion of vines falling over these walls and climbing over the gate ways, trellises, porches and verandas of the cottages, and that they should be flanked and backed by such trees and bushes as with little effort could be grown for the purpose.

It is unnecessary at this point to carry the general suggestion thus presented into fuller particulars. If it strikes you favorably and you are disposed to have it elaborated in the form of a plan, the topographical map of the ground, for which we have already furnished instructions will be a necessary preliminary to our aiding you to obtain it.

It seems to me premature to undertake to plan the improvement of the park much further at present than has thus been proposed.

But to guard against others gaining to your disadvantage from such work as you may do, I advise that the Company get into its own direct possession enough additional land at a point that I indicated to you when on the ground to hold the control of all from which a good general view could be of the rock district and the two prairies, one stretching northwardly, the other southwardly, from near the old saw mill site.

Respectfully Yours

Frederick Law Olmsted
F. L. & J. C. Olmsted
Landscape Architects

Brookline, Mass.
15th January, 1889

Having been asked to report on the availability of Perry Park as a summer resort, on the 26th and 27th of December, 1888, I made such examination of it as was at the time practicable.

The ground being frozen and lightly powdered with snow and an unusual drought prevailing, my observations were not such as would be needed for an assured judgment on questions of water-supply and cultural capabilities but I saw three streams flowing from as many ravines in the adjoining mountains, and evidences elsewhere of water beneath the surface. The form of the ravines seemed favorable for the storage of water at high elevations.

It was, however, as a place for the enjoyment of local scenery and for rural rides and rambles that I more particularly considered the park. In this respect its more important features are to be found in several bodies of prairie land each bordered and separated from others by low and gently sloping, rounded hills. The comparatively small extent of the glade-like openings and the more continuous slight undulations of the surface, both of the openings and the wooded ground, make the term park a perfectly descriptive designation of the topography— much more so than it is as usually applied in Colorado to much broader and less varied surfaces, unbroken it may be for miles, by trees.

Although in Perry Park all trees of certain age had been taken out for timber some years since, enough remain of good size and so disposed, singly and in loose groups, as to give the landscape not only a well-furnished but in its distances an intricate and mysterious character. One can move in no direction that new and attractive passages do not open before him adapted to act subtly upon the imagination.

With the territory to which the above observations more particularly apply there is closely associated, first, the grandeur of an immense mountain range with bold acclivities divided by darkly shadowed glens, and second, the interest of a remarkable body of rocks projecting in great variety of towering forms from the surface of the ground. Few of these are smaller than an ordinary dwelling, many are larger than the grandest of cathedrals. Most are so scattered and disposed, and associated with the other landscape elements as to form interesting and agreeable incidents of scenery. Looked at one by one, some are entertaining because of their extremely fantastic forms which bring to mind the quaint rocks often represented in Japanese pictures. Others might be taken from a distance for stately monuments. There are several extended ranges which present splintered, craggy and curiously crannied cliff-like faces. Often these are topped with lofty pinnacles and serrated crestings. Some have much beauty from the fretted texture of the stone of which they are composed and its varied soft tints.

Kept clear of such puerile and cockneyfied structures as are too generally allowed to put nature out of countenance in places of summer resort, as well as of such as would be offensive from their rudeness and shabbyness, I should think that Perry Park would soon be found very attractive, first, to tourists, led chiefly by curiosity, second, to persons seeking rest and refreshment under the influence of invigorating mountain air, of a landscape that will grow more pleasing as it becomes more familiar and of incitements to out of door contemplative occupations such as are to be found abundantly in the conditions that have been described.

I shall elsewhere offer a few suggestions as to the manner in which provisions for sojourners in the park may be made with the least injury to its natural attractions.

F. L. & J. C. Olmsted,
Landscape Architects

BILTMORE: JULY 1889

To George Washington Vanderbilt

Brookline, Mass., July 12th 1889

Mr. Geo. W. Vanderbilt:

My Dear Sir; I am advised by Mr. McNamee, that you are expected to arrive in New York next week and will probably be going a few days afterwards to Mt. Desert. If you can offer me a chance to see you as you go through Boston I shall be glad to discuss the matter of your North Carolina Estate with you in a more satisfactory way than I can on paper. Even if this should be practicable, however, you may like to have a report of the movement of my judgment as it has been affected by my recent reconnaissance of the Estate, to be read at your leisure. I will try to give it to you under successive heads.

I

THE RESIDENCE

The principal points of the residence and its dependencies, as the plan stood when you went away, have been marked on the ground by stout stakes, and two scaffolds have been erected from one of which the view from the Music Room window can be had, from the other the view from the south end of the Terrace. I think that you will be pleased to find how much is to be gained by setting out the building well over the hillside as advised by Mr. Hunt, and also what a considerable variation of view will be had by walking to the end of the Terrace. You will observe that the scope of the scenery to be enjoyed from the house will be much enlarged by cutting down the crest of the hill-top on the East and by breaking into the woods on the North. The woods are poorer near at hand on all sides than they are at a little distance and it will be desirable to thin them boldly.

We shall send you a key-map before you go to the ground, showing the position of the stakes. Letters on the map will correspond with letters on the stakes, and a number on a stake will show, in feet, the cut or fill required to reach the intended level at the point where the stake stands. The building being set so far down the slope, the grading will be a heavy piece of work but the advantage to be gained, is very great.

I have found a better place than that proposed on the preliminary sketch of last spring as a suitable one for the green-house and service garden and have asked Mr. Thompson to extend the survey so as to include this place. When he has done so I shall be prepared to suggest some improvements of the plan south and east from the court.

I doubt whether the court might not with advantage be made a little more spacious. Please consider the question when on the ground and with regard to what I shall later say under the head of The Approach.

II
WATER SUPPLY FOR THE RESIDENCE

I had thought last year that it was highly important to find, if practicable, means of water supply that, under the most trying conditions of drought, would be abundant without resort to pumping, and had asked Mr. Aston to make certain explorations for this purpose. He apparently was not successful in doing so and proposed instead a source of supply which in my judgment would be inadequate and require engines and pumps. At my request Mr. McNamee had put Mr. Thompson, who succeeds Mr. Aston, upon the line of examination which I originally had in view, and this he had pursued before my visit with results so promising that I instructed him to follow it up thoroughly and prepare a complete project. I expect a report from him and thereupon before long, to advise you fully on the subject.

III
THE FOREST

Knowing that at no great distance from the Estate and under conditions of climate as far as I could judge, less favorable at least to southern forms of vegetation, there was the finest natural forest and the most varied in its constituents, to be found in the United States, or possibly in the temperate regions of the world, I was last year greatly disappointed to find your property so deficient in respect both to variety of trees and to local beauty of trees in mass. Exploring the narrow valleys I have found this impression a little relieved. In the main, however, it remains and it holds with regard to your new as well as to your earlier purchases.

From such study as I could give the circumstances, aided by Mr. Douglas, I was led to think that the defects to which I have referred had been of comparatively recent occurrence and that there had been once and might be again, for any natural obstacles, a much greater variety of trees and shrubs than are found at present on the Estate, and a large majority of them grown to the highest perfection.

As to the way in which the present conditions have been brought about it appears probable that although there have been no permanent residents on the greater part of the Estate it has been occupied for generations past by a succession of campers, squatters and transient settlers in such numbers that the final effect of their operations has been not unlike what would be expected from those of a much denser population. I saw the remains of four saw mills on the Estate, three of which must have been at work a good many years; there have been others, probably, on the Estate, for all that I saw were within much less than half its entire space, and yet others near it, drawing from it. Almost certainly, also, shingles and boards have been worked on it in large quantity without mill saws. For these purposes and those of the mills, every tree desirable for any sort of salable lumber has been felled. What is now seen is the refuse. As is always the case, to get out the best trees, many a little less choice have been felled or broken down and ruined. Of what remained the settlers have taken great numbers for their cabins, fences and fuel. Big fires are the one luxury of the pioneer cabins. Then more have been taken to feed Asheville hearths than you can readily imagine. With many, when anything was wanted from a store, the readiest way to get it was to take a load of fire-wood to town. You may often see distant settlers, even now, drawing jags of hickory cordwood with a runty bull before a creaking cart into Asheville for the same purpose, and, undoubtedly, similar expeditions have been made from the region of the Estate constantly for many years past.

All the large Cherries, Tulips and Black-Walnuts have been taken by speculators to be sold after going through the mills, to cabinets makers; the large Black-Birches if there were any, to bedstead makers; the large locusts have been taken for posts, the large Dogwoods sold for spools and woodcutters blocks. Nearly all of the large trees of any of the species that I have named now standing on the Estate you will find to have long been rotten at the core. These have not been thought worth cutting. But the largest of the standing trees are Chestnuts. These I suppose to have been preserved by the owners of the land as a resource for rails when others should fail. You will observe that there are hardly any medium sized Chestnuts but many stumps, showing where such have formerly stood. The reserved Chestnuts are often hollow-hearted or partly burned or both, so that fewer rails would be obtained from them for the same labor than from those of medium size. Of the trees that remain standing,

Oaks greatly preponderate. The reason I suppose to be that Oaks are hard to fell and hard to work, especially with cheap, frontier implements and machinery, while there has been no near demand for oak timber as there has been at all points near the Atlantic coast. For a thousand Oaks with trunks of from two to four feet thick now standing, you may not see more than one Ash, Linden, Sugar-Maple, Liquid-Ambar, Tulip or Locust, of corresponding size. You may pass ten thousand such Oaks without having come upon one Magnolia or Virgilia or White-Fringe or Catalpa, or Honey-Locust, or Persimmon, or Tupelo, or Holly, or White-Pine or Hemlock. Yet of all these species I saw a few small examples on or near the Estate and have no doubt that they were once common. I hoped to find the Silvery Linden which I have seen growing finely on the Blue Ridge but I did not. I hoped to find specimens of a species of Hemlock lately discovered at a point not twenty miles distant from the Estate, but though there are localities exactly suited to it, I found none. Nor did I notice a single native Elm, Coffee-tree, Nettle-tree, Papaw or Silver Bell, all of which are believed to be indigenous to the region. In the narrower glens and swampy places I did find a few splendid Rhododendrons and Kalmias—taller specimens than I remember to have seen in any of the great English collections, but I found none of the Cypresses, Evergreen Magnolias or Andromedas that might naturally have grown in such situations and that undoubtedly would flourish in them if planted. I found no "Jasmines" such as grow elsewhere in the State.

The characteristic and greatly predominating trees of the Estate are Oaks, as I have said. Now Oaks of all the sorts seen, (I found none of the delicate Willow Oak or of the Laurel-leaved Oaks) to exhibit their best character and beauty require, more, perhaps, than any other tree, to be allowed to stretch out their branches horizontally and take spreading and umbrageous forms. I did not see a single large Oak on the Estate that had had this advantage. All the older had evidently been extremely crowded by other trees until they had grown to be too firm in structure to expand when their neighbors were cut out.

I must speak of one other unfortunate circumstance in the present sylvan condition of the Estate. Except near the water courses or in a few rocky or swampy places, there is a remarkable paucity of underwood and of herbaceous plants, so that a great deal of nearly bare ground is seen. Moreover this bare ground has a notably sterile appearance. Often, even in the depths of the woods, not the slightest leaf-mould is to be seen.

With this circumstance another is to be associated:

There are a great many sapling Oaks growing up thickly together and there are as I have said, more scattered Oaks of from two to three feet thickness of trunk than of all other trees. Between Oaks which may have not been growing more than twenty years and these larger ones, that may be a century old, there are few or none. This fact indicates that where other old trees have been cut out and the old Oaks left standing, young Oaks have taken possession of the ground to the exclusion of other young trees. There are two ways of accounting for the circumstance. First, the woods have been a range for stock and the stock has been often hard pressed, forcing the hogs to root searchingly for seeds of trees in the soil and the horned cattle to close browsing. Oak sprouts are comparatively tough and astringent and sprouts of other trees have been selected by the cattle in preference to them.

(I do not mean that Oaks of different upland species have not always predominated in this forest. I am accounting for what I believe to be an extraordinary predominance of young Oaks at this time.)

Second, in addition to the destruction by stock there has been the destruction by fire. I suppose young Oaks to be better able to resist fire than young trees of other of the indigenous species.

Fires have been of two classes; first, comparatively light fires, generally started intentionally in the spring, to clear the surface of dead leaves and stubs so that a better growth of annual grasses and other herbage might spring up for the pasturage of cattle and hogs. This is said to have been a custom of the Indians inhabiting the region and to have been taken up by the earliest white settlers and perpetuated to this time.

Second, fires starting accidentally in the late summer and autumn, which, in times of drought and when forced by strong winds, seizing upon the dead trees and lopped limbs and brushwood of the timber that has been removed, have sometimes been fierce. These fires have, I imagine, destroyed the seed previously in the surface soil, and the younger crop of Oaks has grown from seed subsequently falling from the older Oaks left standing.

To the effect of such fires, I suppose is due, also the absence of undergrowth and of superficial leaf-mould and the sterile aspect of the surface of the ground in many places, where stumps and standing old trees show that it really is not sterile.

I should say that the condition of things that I have described is not at all peculiar to the locality. It is frequently found in all parts of the Cotton States. It is not often found in the better wooded, higher mountain regions of North Carolina because these have had fewer inhabitants; it has been harder to get lumber to market from them and, the summers being shorter and, (because of higher elevation and more frequent showers), less drying, they have been less affected by fires.

Where forests have been systematically cleared for crops, as they have been in many small patches on the Estate, aggregating, I judge near two thousand acres, the ground has been cultivated in a very shallow way, the plow often being a mere prong drawn by one small bullock and its operation a scratch but three or four inches deep. With such tillage, corn and grain and tobacco have been grown year after year until the land was "worn out," which means until the thin upper stratum of cultivated soil had parted with nearly all it had originally possessed of the constituents of these crops. I saw several crops of this year ripening, the value of which would not probably repay the labor, merely of harvesting, at a dollar a day.

When thoroughly exhausted, the land has been "turned out," and then, as a rule, after a few years, a growth of one or two or three species of Pines peculiar to barren lands has sprung up, that most common being known as the Scrub Pine. All the Pine woods of the Estate, several hundred acres in extent, are of this character. The trees never became large; their timber is practically valueless; they sometimes have an agreeable effect in landscape if looked down upon from a distance, but from ground near them or under them they are not pleasing and they are generally recognized as a badge of poverty.

It is a question of great importance relatively to a general plan for dealing with the Estate how far the superficial appearance of the soil that I have described is to be accepted as authentic.

I turned this part of my examination largely over to Mr. Douglas who for three days went from end to end of the Estate, sampling soil and subsoil. I shall refer to certain particulars of his report later. The general result of our study is a conviction that, with moderately deep tillage, soil would nearly everywhere be found of a very choice quality for trees, and that if dressed with lime and manure and well tilled, it would probably be productive agriculturally. My belief is that, a clear, fine and lasting grass sod, such as I have never seen in the South, can be formed upon it.

Speaking more particularly of its capabilities for forestry, I should say that I have never examined ground upon which as large variety of trees and shrubs was likely to grow as rapidly.

I will mention one or two circumstances that seem to sustain the view I have taken of the causes of the present apparent barrenness of the soil and of the comparative scarcity of other trees than Oaks.

At a few points on the Estate there are patches of ground that have been parts of clearings and have been fenced in and trees better protected than they otherwise would have been from fires and from the browsing of stock, yet, perhaps because they could not be as conveniently plowed as the rest of the ground enclosed with them, have not been as severely cropped. In some such places I noticed a remarkably thrifty growth of young trees other than Oaks. If, when you are on the ground again, you will follow down the glen that has its head a few hundred yards east from the residence site, until you reach the edge of the old fields that spread south-westerly from Shiloh meeting house, you will find such a place. The present predominating growth is of the Tulip tree. Tulips are outgrowing everything else. They are as fine trees of the species, of their age, as I ever saw and growing with remarkable rapidity. The probability is that Tulip-trees were originally very common; that they grew to majestic size, and that the forest having been cleared of them, had it not been for burning and browsing, seedlings from them would have been now growing everywhere as thriftily as in this accidentally protected locality.

Again, in one valley I found a few Rhododendrons thriving but near by others, larger, that had plainly been ruined by fire not more than two years ago. If sweeping fires, largely due to litter left to become dry by tree cutters, had been avoided, Rhododendrons would probably have been growing abundantly in every valley.

Considering that you were likely to use the Estate as a winter resort I suggested last year that there would be a considerable advantage in having considerable portions of it planted with White Pines, having in view, first a contrast to prevailing Oaks; second, winter verdure; third, the pleasant footing that is always found under a White Pine wood; fourth the agreeable balsamic odor of the tree, and, lastly, its probable future economic value. As to the feasibility of growing it thriftily on the Estate I more particularly sought Mr. Douglas's opinion. This was entirely favorable, and I have asked a proposition from him, looking to the immediate planting on the old fields of several hundred acres of White Pines, by contract. Other suggestions as to general planting and the management of the forest I reserve for the present. I will simply say, at this point, that I am inclined to advise you to have in view the establishment and maintenance of an unbroken forest from the north to the south end of the Estate, to extend from the east border, as a general rule, to the edge of the river bottom on the west, but with a "Park" to be taken out near the residence as to be hereafter proposed. Perhaps with certain fields to be also taken out for agricultural purposes. Your property on the left bank of the river to be also maintained in forest condition and improved.

From these forests you would gradually eliminate the overgrown ill-formed Oaks, replacing them with more valuable and pleasing trees; you would thin out and make thrifty the younger Oaks and other trees, and in desirable localities establish underwood.

The chief peril of forest property is that of fires. And the chief source of forest fires in the future is likely to be railroads. The topography of the Estate is not inviting to new railroads. Your river and tributaries give you advantages for contending against fires spreading from railroads on the West, North and South. It would be desirable to have your forest bounded on the East by a broad road such as is already in considerable part, I believe, provided.

Further, good management will require that the forest be traversed at intervals by common roads and that these be so laid out as to serve as a means of checking the advance of possible fires from one division of it to another. Certain topographical advantages for this purpose, I shall refer to later. Fires are rarely destructive under good forest management.

Looking over what is above written I see that it may not quite clearly indicate the line of policy that I have meant to suggest as applicable to the main body of the ridge land of the Estate. Allow me to make a partial re-statement.

The ridgeland is now occupied chiefly by Oaks of two classes; first, old trees the remnants of a thickly grown forest out of which great numbers of other trees than Oaks have, years ago, been taken. These Oaks have acquired ungainly forms because of the crowding to which they were subject when young. Second, Oaks which have sprung up since the forest was thinned of other trees. These younger Oaks are not now growing very well, partly because many of them are shaded by the older Oaks and partly because the roots of the older Oaks are still taking the lion's share of the moisture and a certain part of the remaining constituents of the soil needed for their nourishment. These younger Oaks are not yet stunted, however, nor are they yet so cramped by crowding that, judiciously thinned, they would not soon acquire fine, characteristic, stalwart and umbrageous forms, such as you have seen Oaks taking in Windsor Forest, for example.

Remove all of the old Oaks that are not of exceptional and admirable character; let the thickets of the younger Oaks be judiciously thinned; give the other trees, (Hickories, Chestnuts, Limes, (Basswood) Tupelos, Beeches, Maples, Tulips, Birches,) that are sparsely growing with them, a fair chance; plant occasional vacant spaces with yet other trees, natural to the circumstances, such as I have named; encourage a growth of underwood, and a forest would result that would easily come in time to be the finest in the country. Finer than any natural forest of the same trees because always in the natural forest, under favorable conditions of soil and climate, the struggle for existence of trees, one with another, prevents the attainment of a high development with any. Finer than any other planted forest because no other yet planted will have equal advantages of soil and climate.

You may ask, if forest undertakings are desirable in this country why are there no notable examples of them other than those recently entered upon by Railway Corporations in the treeless regions of the far West? Simply because no considerable "investment" in forests can be made with the large *early* profits that necessity, and custom growing out of general necessity, lead our people beyond all others to be passionately eager to secure. For the harvest of a forest crop one must look more years ahead than he does months for the harvest of other crops. But, so looking ahead, a well managed forest is likely to be as good a property, all things considered as any other. Mean time, the management of it; the oversight of its development and improvement from year to year, would be a most interesting rural occupation; far more interesting, I am sure, to a man of poetic temperament than any of those commonly considered appropriate to a country-seat life. Certainly there can be no prospect of success, of profit or pleasure from year to year, in any other use to be made of your ridge lands to compare with it. You cannot find an upland farm in all the mountain region that has a thoroughly pleasant aspect; hardly one that does not make a doleful impression. But where the native forest has not been wholly ruined in the manner I have described it to be; wherever it has been but moderately injured, its beauty, its mystery, its solemnity, are really fascinating. Years ago I rode alone for a full month through the North Carolina forests, and it was with great regret that at last I emerged from them. There is no experience of my life to which I could return with more satisfaction.

I have written in a too desultory way but you will see that in what I have said there is the substance of a proposition which is much the most important of all that I have to submit to your consideration. That the subject may be more completely and intelligently brought before you, I advise you to read the pamphlet by my friend Mr. Cleveland that I send herewith. Reading it you will see what I meant when I said last year, that adopting the suggestion, as then less fully presented, you would not only make the best use of the property for the direct satisfaction of yourself and friends but would be doing the country an inestimable service and thus from the start give the Estate a rank like that which Blair Atholl has among the great British estates.

IV
THE QUESTION OF A NAME

"Blair Atholl" suggests the question of a name. Mr. McNamee has been looking thus far vainly for an Indian name. An Indian name, to be advisable, should have a suitable significance; at least a significance not provocative of punning, sarcasm or ridicule; should be sonorous; should fall trippingly from the tongue, and should not have been appropriated. It is not probable that an Indian name will offer having all these advantages. For a concocted English name there are the following suggestive circumstances: First, the river; second, the forest; third, the ridge or line of hills; fourth the central of both sides of the river. I don't suppose the Indian name of the river is available. If it had been Mr. McNamee would have proposed it. Probably it has been appropriated. French Broad will not do. But possibly something might be done with "Broad," Broadwood, for example, while short, simple, unaffected and appropriate as suggested by the river and the broad wooded hills between which it flows, has to me a quiet respectable air, (perhaps from association with Lord Palmerston's seat, Broadlands.)

V
AGRICULTURE

You know that what passes with us as "gentleman farming," is generally a very costly, and that after a time, it usually comes to be a very unsatisfactory, amusement. Why should you undertake farming on any large scale? The only reason that I can see is that to a rapid improvement of the Estate as a forestral country seat you need to have at command a great deal more manure than you can economically obtain except by a certain kind of farming. Adopting this as the real motive of what you shall do, incidentally you will have the pleasure of raising and keeping as much fine stock of all kinds as you choose. Considering fine stock as an incidental feature of your operations, to which you can give as much attention as you please, (making the Estate famous as a head-quarters for particular herds and strains, if your inclination ultimately runs that way), the main agricultural question is how to maintain a large stock most economically.

From the little study that I was able to give this question my impression is that it will be best to confine tillage mainly to the river bottoms and a few fields near them and, as a rule, sell no farm product except live stock and this mostly fat and fine, such as, for example, there will be a growing demand for at special prices, as population and luxury increase in Asheville, Atlanta and other cities not as far away as those on the Atlantic. This policy would lead you to raise as much forage as possible on the ground given to farming. As far as I can judge the bottom lands are all good for forage crops. The poorest are those upon which sand has lodged and the grain crops on them are this year very poor. Mr. Alexander was away during my visit and I could get no information of value from anyone I saw but I am much mistaken if these sandy bottoms would not with fertilizers, bear heavy crops of the coarse forage pea (cowpea, I think it is called) that is elsewhere largely grown at the South, and I have heard that a mixture of this pea with corn-fodder, in silos, makes the best ensilage that is known. Probably you can raise, at first with commercial fertilizers, great crops of fodder corn, alfalfa and clover on the bottoms, while improving their fertility. They have been exhausted by grain growing. Avoid taking grain (including corn) from them until they have recovered fertility. If necessary to fatten off stock for market for the time being, buy corn.

You have unusual advantages (in a number of brooks coming to the bottoms from higher ground and in a more or less sandy soil and good outlets) for an inexpensive trial of water meadows (irrigatable grass lands) hardly ever used in the Eastern States but found highly profitable for forage crops in the south of England.

I think that you will find it best to have two centres of operations, one for the upper, one for the lower bottoms, with silos and feeding stations at each. (The meadows before the residence, I do not think that you will want to cultivate after once putting them in order. They may be made a part of the park, or kept permanently for hay and pasturage.)

As your stock-keeping capacity increases you may bring all the agricultural land of the Estate under a regular system of rotation; manuring for corn, grain, cut fodder and roots, and leaving a due proportion of land, after being thus prepared, to be successively laid down in fields to be kept for a course of years for hay and pasturage; selling off, as a rule, nothing but live stock, and husbanding manure in every reasonable way.

VI
THE PARK

There is no *park-like* land on the Estate. None in which park-like scenery of a notably pleasing character, could be gained in a life time. Plenty of land in which agreeable, wild, woodland scenery can be had in a few years.

The best place in which to keep deer or other animals where they may be seen to advantage, and which will, as far as practicable, have what is otherwise to be desired in a private park, will be on the westside of the residence where it can be looked into from its windows and terrace. So situated, the inconvenience of having gates wherever transit is to be made in any direction toward or from the residence on the entrance front will be avoided.

The park would differ from the forest in having a much larger proportion of un-wooded ground; in having a larger proportion of its trees standing singly and in groups; in being more free from underwood; and in having a turf surface, forming a fine pasture and giving a pleasant footing for riding or walking freely in all directions. It might be grazed and the turf kept moderately close by herds of the native fallow deer, of the Antelope of the Rocky Mountains and of South Downs or some other herd of small, choice mutton sheep. The latter would probably have to be folded at night on account of dogs.

A park that would answer every desirable purpose would not, I think, exceed two hundred and fifty acres. If much larger it would be a worrisome business to take care of it and the needed fences, gates and other requirements of keeping would be inconvenient. The central parts of it would be nearly midway between the residence and the river. It would include the valley next north of the residence; extend southwardly to the neighborhood of the Alexander place and would take in the lower hill, at present nearly covered with scrub-pine, which is very prominent in the view westward from the scaffolds. Also, probably, the hill on the north of this, beyond the conspicuous road. This road will desirably be abolished and in place of it a road carried on the edge of the bottom land at least as far as the next opening of the hills, where there is now a tolerable farm road. You will observe, when looking from the scaffolds, that by the removal of a few trees a considerably larger space of the river will be brought under view from the windows of the Residence.

VII

THE ARBORETUM

As to the suggested Arboretum, I have conceived the outline of a plan for it the general nature of which I will try to indicate, but before offering any final recommendation, even as to its general scope, I should want to give the matter more study.

This plan would be to lay out a road starting from the residence in such a manner that, bending to the valley southward, it would follow up Four Mile Creek to the meadow above the second dam, across from the meadow near, (if I recollect aright) the Hart place, and so to the valley of the next creek south; down this valley to the French Broad bottom-land, then back to the point of departure by the Four Mile valley. A dam could be built on the site of the present lower dam of Four Mile Creek and ten feet higher, which would form a lake, extending up the north valley of the creek to a point a little above where the steam saw mill stood. This lake would probably be visible from the residence garden and perhaps from the terrace. In a branch of the Four Mile valley, where there is now a vacant house a little north east of what would be the head of the lake, is probably the best place for your service gardens, propagating houses, etc.

Such a road as I have thus indicated would make convenient subdivisions of the forest and in connection with the streams which it would follow would be a guard against the spread of fires. It would be a very picturesque road, and on its borders there would be situations of great variety in respect to soil and exposure and generally of the highest fertility to be found on the Estate. Some would be rocky; some marshy; some meadowy; the most, fair upland. My idea, in a word, is to form the Arboretum by cutting back and thinning out the present standing wood on the borders of this road, leaving the best trees and bushes but making place for the planting of the collection, choosing for each representative tree a position adapted to develop its highest character and exhibit it, in several specimens, to the best advantage. Water-side trees by the lake; Ash, on the fertile well-drained meadow; Magnolias in the dingles opening southward; Oaks on the higher upland, and so on.

Without doubt an arboretum could be formed in this way by far finer and more instructive than other in the world, an arboretum to which naturalists would resort from all parts of the world.

It would, of course, be backed at all points by the main forest of the Estate and the trees would group with those of the forest.

VIII
THE APPROACH

The present roads of the Estate have been laid out as far as practicable on the ridge lands, where they could be made and kept passable at the least cost. Near them the timber has been naturally poorer and has been worse used than elsewhere and the local scenery is monotonous and forlorn. It is in the valleys or gulches between the ridges that the most interesting foliage is to be seen; where there is the greatest moisture and all conditions are the more picturesque.

I suggest that the most striking and pleasing impression of the Estate will be obtained if an approach can be made that shall have throughout a natural and comparatively wild and secluded character; its borders rich with varied forms of vegetation, with incidents growing out of the vicinity of springs and streams and pools, steep banks and rocks, all consistent with the sensation of passing through the remote depths of a natural forest. Such scenery to be maintained with no distant outlook and no open spaces spreading from the road; with nothing showing obvious art, until the visitor passes with an abrupt transition into the enclosure of the trim, level, open, airy *spacious*, thoroughly artificial Court, and the Residence, with its orderly dependencies, breaks suddenly and fully upon him. Then, after passing through the building, the grandeur of the mountains, the beauty of the valley, the openness and tranquility of the park would be most effectively and even surprisingly presented, from the windows, balconies and terrace.

A sketch map showing a route by which such a result could be obtained will soon be sent you, and when you go to the

Estate you will find this route approximately indicated by stakes on the ground.

This plan assumes a crossing of Swananoah creek by a bridge a little below the Haunted House ford, from which point a road would be carried so as to skirt the bottom land to a point where a large beech tree stands on the road you now ordinarily take in visiting the Estate, and where that road is crossed by a brook. Thence it follows near the easternmost and largest branch of this brook, to its source; thence at a slight depression of the ridge, it crosses into a branch of the valley next north of the Residence; runs down this to the brook of the valley; follows up a branch of the brook to its head, where it swings out on the upper part of a hillside, along which it winds to the gate of the Court.

I believe that fairly easy grades, with occasional levels, can be had on all of this line, without heavy construction and without curves that would be inconvenient for four-in-hand driving, but I shall be able to advise you on this point and others much better after Mr. Thompson has made the survey that I have requested of him. As to details, some suggestions will come under the next head.

IX
NURSERY

Many of the trees, shrubs and vines that you will find it desirable to plant in considerable quantity cannot be obtained at the Commercial nurseries; certainly cannot except in small numbers and at the price of rarities. To obtain them in quantity, of a desirable planting size, will take several years. Some can best be propagated on the ground; some obtained as small seedlings in Europe, or from Japan, and advanced in a nursery on the Estate. There are numerous plants that may well be used that are not quite rare but for which there is no demand at the North because of their tenderness and no sufficient demand at the South to have led to their being grown for sale except at the price of rarities and in very small numbers.

I have mentioned several smooth-leaved evergreens of which a few can be found on the Estate, or in the Asheville gardens, showing that they are hardy, such as the evergreen Magnolia, the American Holly and Rhododendron Maximum. There are others which I know from trials at Washington will endure the Asheville climate, and of which for winter enjoyment you should have, near your residence and in sheltered places along your roads, in much larger quantities than they can be obtained at this time from all the nurseries in the country or, as to some of them, in all the nurseries of Europe. Propagating and rearing them on a scale large enough to warrant the employment of a good gardener with a suitable plant for the purpose they would cost you not quarter as much as the commercial price. There are others for which contracts could be made for delivery after two years at half the present market price.

Taking such measures there are shrubs which are yet luxuries, seen only as "specimens," and many of these in New York only under glass, which you could easily have as profusely on the borders of your roads as you see rock ferns and "huckleberries" growing along the roads of Mt. Desert. You can have a stretch of bamboos, at little less cost than one of blackberries, have it quarter of a mile long if you like, provided you make preparations for it three or four years in advance. The nursery price of *Rhododendron Maximum* in New York, three feet high, has been $2.00 a plant. You can have plants gathered for you within twenty miles of your residence, by the thousand, probably at ten cents a plant, and after two years in nursery they will be better plants than I have been able to get from any nurseryman in Europe or America.

Plant 10,000 of them along your road, as a back ground and in front of them 5000 of the most splendid hybrid Rhododendrons (such as they exhibit under tents at the Horticultural Gardens in London) and of the Himalayan and Alpine Rhododendrons; scatter among them clusters of Kalmias, the native and Japanese Andromedas, the Japanese Euonymus of which there are a dozen sorts that will surely be hardy with you, though they cannot live out in Philadelphia; the Japanese Aucubas, the refined little *Abelia rupestris* with a cloud of most delicate bloom (I have had a hundred of them growing fully exposed for several years in Washington though I have never seen a specimen elsewhere except in a hot house); *Mahonia aquifolia* which must be guarded here and is often scorched and sometimes killed, but would be at home with you; the Japanese Mahonia, still less hardy but safe with you; All these are smooth-leaved, (laurel-like) evergreen shrubs, which can be had, under a well organized system, in a few years, by the thousand, costing no more than people generally pay for the commonest deciduous bushes of our northern woods. I suppose that you could naturalize in your woods more than five times as many sorts of fine, smooth-leaved evergreens as can be grown in the open air near New York. Some that I have named rarely grow more than three feet high. Some ten, some twenty feet. *Magnolia Grandiflora*, of which I saw one specimen in Asheville, grows to be a towering, stately tree, sometimes one hundred feet high.

These are hints of the capabilities of the Estate. Making good use of them where would there be anything to compare with it? You would have people crossing the Atlantic to see it.

With these possibilities in view, so unusual with tree buyers that commerce is not in the least adapted to them, the early starting of a propagating house, nursery and trial garden, will recommend itself to your consideration.

Yours Very Truly,

Fred^k Law Olmsted
F.L. & J.C. Olmsted;
Landscape Architects

"NOTHING OF AN ARTIFICIAL CHARACTER":
MARCH 1890

Governmental Preservation of Natural Scenery

Brookline, Mass.,
8th March, 1890

In a communication that has been given to the public from the Governor of California to the Senators and Representatives in Congress of that State, I am surprised to find my name introduced in a manner that compels me to make the following statement.

In the year 1864, being then a citizen of California, I had the honor to be made chairman of the first Yosemite Commission, and in that capacity to take possession of the Valley for the State, to organize and direct the survey of it and to be the executive of various measures taken to guard the elements of its scenery from fires, trespassers and abuse. In the performance of these duties, I visited the Valley frequently, established a permanent camp in it and virtually acted as its superintendent. It was then to be reached from the nearest village only by a sixty mile journey in the saddle, and there were many more Indians in it than white men. The office had come to me unexpectedly and in a manner that earned my devotion. So far from a salary coming with it, it was an affair of considerable cost to me, which I have not asked to be reimbursed. Moving out of the State in the autumn of 1867, I presented my resignation of the office, which was accepted by the Governor with expressions of regret and gratitude.

I have not been in the Valley since; but because of some knowledge of this pioneer duty of mine, travelers returning from it have often told me of what they thought missteps in its administration. I have never expressed an opinion on the subject. These travelers have also now and then urged that some proceeding should be taken to expostulate with the State against the manner in which it was believed by them to be abusing its trust. I have always declined to move, or take any part in any movement, for the purpose.

Several years ago, one of the editorial staff of the Century Magazine, Mr. R. U. Johnson, called on me with a letter of introduction. In the conversation that ensued, the subject came up of the danger to treasures of natural scenery that is more and more growing out of modern developments of commerce and modern habits of travel. The thought came to the surface that with reference to this danger, a sentiment needs to be cultivated such as would appear in any crisis threatening a national treasure of art. I do not remember that the Yosemite was referred to, but it followed from the conversation that I wrote a short paper, afterwards published in the Century, upon the duty of towns to guard for their future people eminently valuable passages of scenery near them, and in this paper the Yosemite was mentioned; but not reproachfully to the Commissioners.

Last summer I received a second call from Mr. Johnson. He had just returned from the Yosemite, and his object was to invite me to prepare an article upon it. I declined, giving as one reason for doing so that I could not properly write on the subject without making a prolonged personal examination of the present condition of the Valley and investigating the grounds of the complaints made by travelers as to the management of it. I was then asked if I would undertake to make such an examination and investigation at a suitable professional compensation from the Magazine, taking with me an accomplished artist to prepare illustrations for the desired article. I was loth to decline so liberal a proposition, but concluded that I must in justice to my existing professional engagements.

Mr. Johnson then said that he would be obliged to write it himself, and thereupon mentioned several points upon which he desired my opinion. One was in regard to a proposition which I understood to involve the systematic cutting out of all young trees in the Valley. He asked what I thought of it. A proper system of management for woods valued because of their effect in scenery, must be directed as much to the renewal and perpetuation of the constituent trees as to anything else; a common rule being that for every hundred or thousand trees going off, there shall be a hundred or a thousand more, advancing, to take their place. To provide against accidents, and in order that the replacing trees shall be of choice quality, a much larger number of young trees are kept growing, those not selected to remain because of their choiceness being gradually thinned out. A systematic removal of all the young trees of the Valley would be equivalent to the destruction, in course of time, of just what the State of California stands voluntarily pledged to "*hold, inalienably, for all time.*" That is to say, the distinctive charm of the scenery of the Yosemite does not depend, as it is a vulgar blunder to suppose, on the greatness of its walls and the length of its little early summer cascades; the height of certain of its trees, the reflections in its pools, and such other matters as can be entered in statistical tables, pointed out by guides and represented within picture frames. So far, perhaps, as can be told in a few words, it lies in the rare association with the grandeur of its rocky elements, of brooks flowing quietly through the ferny and bosky glades of very beautifully disposed great bodies, groups and clusters of trees. In this respect, its charm is greater than that of any other scenery that, with much search-ing, I have found. There is nothing in the least like it in the canyon of the Colorado, sometimes foolishly compared with the Yosemite. I felt the charm of the Yosemite much more at the end of a week than at the end of a day, much more after six weeks when the cascades were nearly dry, than after one week, and when, after having been in it, off and on, several months, I was going out, I said, "I have not yet half taken it in." To the perpetuation of this charm nothing is more essential than the constant renewal of its wood. There will always be danger that fire will too much interfere with what is necessary to provide in this respect.

These views having been for years fixed in my mind, to Mr. Johnson's inquiry I replied, that to carry out such a rule as he said had been advocated, would be "a calamity to the civilized world." I remember that I said this because he introduced the phrase in what he afterwards wrote, and this has been my sole contribution, hitherto, to the agitation of the subject. It did not occur to me at the time, nor do I think now, that Mr. Johnson was trying to "make a case" against the State. His questions were such as would be asked by any intelligent man of one known to have given many years of serious and business-like study to a subject about which the inquirer was preparing to address the public. To me he only seemed patient and pains-taking, just and loyal in the performance of a not at all pleas-ing duty. He was apparently seeking to avoid injustice to the Commissioners whom I judged that he regarded as honest and well meaning men. He distinctly agreed with me in discrediting much that had been charged against them. He spoke disrespect-fully of no one of them, but showed, I think, that he had an im-pression that, as a body, they had taken a narrow, short-sighted and market-place view of the duty of the State in the premises.

I have thus shown all that I have had to do with the mat-ter, and all that I know concerning Mr. Johnson's motives and methods. I believe that the latter were simple, honorable, public spirited and perfectly in character with the distinguished high tone of the Magazine he represents. The Governor has been led to state in an official paper, given to the world, that Mr. Johnson is my nephew, and that all he wanted in this business was to bulldoze the Commissioners into giving me employment, as to the latter of which delusions I may say that I have never been so unfortunate as to need to solicit public employment, or to have any one solicit it for me.

After the above narration, may I not suggest that if the attitude of the State of California toward the trust it accepted in 1864, from the Nation, were what it ought to be, its Governor would hardly have missed the point of the remonstrance of the Century, so completely as his letter indicates that he has.

That remonstrance points to nothing in the methods of the Commissioners that would be objectionable if the concern of the Nation in the matter were of the same kind that it is with the State's dealings with mineral deposits, irrigation, militia, schools, railroads, or even forests. If the Governor and the Commissioners are in error, their error probably lies not in any intentional disregard of the State's obligation, but in overlooking the fact that in natural scenery that which is of essential value lies in conditions of a character not to be exactly described and made the subject of specific injunctions in an Act of Congress, and not to be perfectly discriminated without other wisdom than that which is gained in schools and colleges, counting-rooms and banks. Such qualities as are attributed by the Governor to his Commissioners—integrity, general education, business experience and what is comprehensively called good taste—do not, in themselves, qualify men to guard against the waste of such essential value, much less do they fit them to devise with artistic refinement means for reconciling with its preservation, its development and its exhibition, such requirements of convenience for multitudes of travelers as must be provided in the Yosemite. Whether it is the case with these Commissioners or not, there are thousands of such estimable men who have no more sense in this respect than children, and it must be said that those most wanting in it are those least conscious of the want. Men of the qualifications attributed to the Commissioners are the best sort of men for the proper duties of an auditing and controlling board. There could be no better men for the usual business of a board of hospital trustees, for example. But the best board of hospital trustees would commit what the law regards as a crime, if they assumed the duties of physicians and nurses. Ability in a landscape *designer* is, in some small degree, a native endowment, but much more it is a matter of penetrative study, discipline, training, and the development through practice of a special knack. Even men of unusually happy endowment and education, who have not, also, the results of considerable working experience, can rarely have much forecasting realization of the manner in which charm of scenery is to be affected by such operations as commonly pass under the name of "improvements."

I should say no more had I not observed in a California publication on the subject an assumption that a professional field-student of that which constitutes the charm of natural scenery would be more inclined than other men to crowd the Yosemite with "artificialities." Its error may be shown by quoting the advice, given several years ago, by the Landscape Architects employed by the State of New York to outline a plan for the restoration, preservation, development and exhibition, of the scenery of Niagara Falls. The paragraph which follows was the only italicised passage in their report, this distinction meaning that they regarded the principle stated as the corner stone of their work.

"Having regard to the enjoyment of natural scenery, and considering that the means of making this enjoyment available to large numbers will unavoidably lessen the extent and value of the primary elements of natural scenery, nothing of an artificial character should be allowed a place on the property, no matter how valuable it might be under other circumstances, and no matter at how little cost it may be had, the presence of which can be avoided consistently with the provision of necessary conditions for making the enjoyment of the natural scenery available."

FREDERICK LAW OLMSTED

"OPEN AIR GYMNASIUMS": APRIL 1890

To Robert Treat Paine

5th April, 1890

My dear Mr. Paine:—

I have just received your note of the 4th instant.

As I may not be able to attend the meeting to which you invite me, I wish to express the interest that I have long had in the subject to be considered.

You are aware that five years ago, I had a map and table prepared, showing the location, area and other particulars, of nearly two hundred parcels of public land in Boston and its immediate suburbs, many of these being, it is understood, lands which have come into the possession of the City under some legal process, wholly unimproved, and, in their present condition, useless. With regard to them, I urged at the time that "many are well situated for play grounds for school children, and could be adapted to that use at moderate expense; while others, smaller, even single house lots, would be available for open air gymnasiums." This statement was laid by the Park Commissioners before the City Council and widely published, and I have, on various occasions since, drawn the attention of the Mayor, Park Commissioners, School Committee and others to the matter.

I hope that special consideration may be given to the question of the desirability of open air gymnasiums expressly for the physical training of *school children*. The Charlesbank Gymnasium is designed for the benefit more particularly of working men of sedentary occupations, and ordinarily, under the rules of the Park Commission, school children are not admitted to use the apparatus with which it is furnished. But, by special arrangement, the School Committee last year had squads of boys sent to it from certain schools, at regular intervals, for several weeks, and an experiment was made in training these boys under a competent instructor. I do not know that a report of the result has been published, but I was personally informed, both by the instructor and by the president of the School Committee, that it was most promising. If so, should not the question be well

considered whether suitable provision for such training, both
for boys and girls, might not be made at several points in the
City, at convenient distance from the school houses, as a part
of its regular educational system? I am under the impression
that the space required at each point would be small, that suitable ground could be selected from public properties that are
now useless, and that the apparatus needed would not be very
costly. If nothing more is done immediately, might it not be
well, before any of these pieces of land are otherwise disposed
of, to have certain of the more suitable of them selected and an
assignment of these secured for the purpose?

The Park Commissioners are intending this Summer to prepare a small, open-air gymnasium for women and girls under a
plan that has been approved by Dr. Sargent, and if this should
be found to work well, it is probable that it will be the forerun-
ner of others.

I am, dear Mr Paine,
Yours Very Truly

Fred^k Law Olmsted

"THE NATURAL ADVANTAGES OF THE SITE": APRIL 1890

To Archie Campbell Fisk

Brookline, Mass.,
21st April, 1890

Mr. A. E. Fisk, President,
Denver & Lookout Mountain Resort Company.
Dear Sir:—

In previous letters we advised you that there were two conditions to be satisfied before we could engage to furnish what
your Company sought from us.

The first was that, after a personal examination of the property, our estimate of its advantages should agree with that of the
Company. Upon this point, one of us having since made such
an examination, we are glad that we can report that the results
are satisfactory. The views from various points of the property,
both towards the Mountains and towards the Plains, are found
to be finer and, in our judgment, are likely to be more attractive

to the public, than your representations had led us to suppose, while no unexpected draw-backs to the advantage of the situation have been found.

The second condition was that the Company should not expect from us a plan that would be suitable to a pleasure resort in the Eastern States. We wish now to set forth our views on this point more fully. They are the result of much observation in the dry countries bordering on the Mediterranean visited with a special view to a study of the subject, and of a residence of some years, as well as of several thousand miles of travel in the dryer part of our own country.

Briefly stated, they are that eastern-bred people coming to live in the dryer regions of the far West should give up, to a greater degree than they anywhere yet have, the ideas in which they have been trained, as to what is desirable to be seen in the immediate surroundings of a villa, or a farm-house, or in a village street, or a rural or suburban neighborhood.

The great advantages that are, in many respects, so conspicuous in these dryer regions depend on climatic conditions that are disadvantageous for the production of many kinds of luxury that the poorest may possess in the East. How greatly disadvantageous may be seen in the fact that the cleanliness, the beauty and the comfort which is found in the turf that forms spontaneously, and which maintains itself naturally on road-sides and in pastures and waste places, in regions of more humid climate, is not to be had at any cost in the dry regions. It is true that, with a sufficient expenditure of labor in watering and otherwise, turf may be formed and kept verdant, but it is a very different thing from the turf of regions in which turf is a natural production, and in no single respect does it serve the same purpose. In the far West of our country a lawn is a perfectly exotic affair. It does not follow that a small lawn may not be made an agreeable decoration of a dwelling place. There are situations about houses in New England, in which a small palm tree growing in a tub may be introduced for a few months in the Summer with good effect, but if an over-rich man should form a grove of palms in the neighborhood, it would completely destroy the charm of the natural scenery and be an offensive piece of bad taste. It is in equally bad taste to aim at effects of a landscape character in dry regions, such as the best taste demands on the borders of the Atlantic.

Another illustration of the principle for which we contend may be offered in this way. The charm that has given great celebrity and added ten fold to the value of land in Stockbridge, Lenox, Litchfield, and numerous other New England villages, is due greatly to their broad streets. Let anything occur by which the turf in these streets would be deadened, or take the character of irrigated turf, or cease to become a pleasing cushion for the feet of wayfarers choosing to cross it, and this charm would disappear. In some cases where population has flocked into such villages until they have become so densely peopled that their street turf is worn out, the old charm is departed, and people are moving to the outskirts of the town, abandoning to shops and hotels what were once the most attractive residence streets.

Lacking the protection that a fabric of living, knitted vegetation supplies, the surface of the ground in dry regions, becoming parched, is pulverized by a slight blow or pressure. Two things follow; first, that in all unpaved places frequented by men or animals, the ground wears away rapidly; is excessively subject to gullying when rain comes, and much labor is required to keep it nice; second, that in hot weather, there is a great deal of dust in the air (largely in an impalpable and invisible form) near such places, and that it is constantly settling on all neighboring objects. Wherever this dust becomes visible on leaves, the natural effect of a prolonged drought appears to be aggravated and all trees and bushes, unless often washed, assume hues, which, though not disagreeable at a little distance, give all foliage near the eye a more or less dull, pallid and lifeless aspect. Another effect of this fine dust is that no roadside objects, unless lately washed, appear clean or inviting for a clean person to come in contact with.

For reasons thus sufficiently suggested, it is a mistake, even where expense is no consideration, to attempt anything like the landscape gardening of the East and of the North of Europe, in these dryer regions. We have visited places, upon the care of which quite ten times the outlay had been made annually, for a series of years, than would be required to keep similar places in the finest condition at Newport, or on the North River, with results that were pitiably unsatisfactory. Our advice has been asked as to how the expense of one of these places could be reduced, and we have had to answer that no material reduction of it was probably possible, which did not involve an abandonment of the particular forms of landscape beauty with regard to which the place has been laid out. In one of these places, as many as ten men were kept at work all night long watering the turf, for several successive months.

In all the dryer regions of the world in which men have been living in a condition approaching that of civilization, it has, from time immemorial, been customary to plan buildings and grounds with a view to pleasure, in a manner looking to four classes of results. These are; first, to leave little naked ground, such as would be covered with turf in regions of humid climate, fully exposed to view near the eye; second, to have objects in the foreground of dwellings and of frequented places and ways, arranged in such a manner that it is comparatively easy to so apply water to them that they may be kept clean, fresh and in nice order; third, to have these foreground objects so arranged that other objects coming in view beyond them will be at such a distance that effects of drought and dust upon them will not be disagreeably evident; fourth, that a picturesquely intimate association of natural and artificial objects may be secured, as, for example, by the mantling of walls, fences, gateways, verandas, balconies and pavilions with a foliage of vines, and by growing upon them plants that need little moisture, such as Agaves, Yuccas, Cacti, Sedums and Houseleeks. These, sometimes growing with obvious art, as decorations, in vases and pots; sometimes naturally, in crannies and cavities of rocks and stone work.

We have thus sufficiently indicated the general direction in which, if we undertake to make plans for you, we should wish to be free to depart, in a moderate and reasonable degree, from the beaten ways of the Eastern States. It is unnecessary to our present purpose that we should try to show in particulars to what such a departure would probably lead. We may say however, that we should aim to discourage future residents from holding more land near a public street than they were likely to take good care of, and should aim to keep down the common expense of the community for the care of roads and for the water needed for private premises. These motives would lead to compacter arrangements and to smaller building lots than would generally be thought desirable in an Eastern resort.

Further to realize our views in these respects, we should probably recommend the Company:—

First, to sell no building sites except with the obligation on the part of the purchaser to soon occupy them and deal with them in a manner that would be pleasing to those passing on the street before them.

Second, that, on ground to be improved by the Company, little use should be made of turf, this little only where special facilities are to be had for keeping it fresh and nice, and that, in lieu of turf, free use should be made of vines and creepers, spreading from roots in pockets, as a covering for ground that would otherwise be bare, parched and dusty in the late Summer, the native trailing plants of the locality being largely used for this purpose.

Third, that certain of the hill-tops and other prominent points of view should be reserved from sale and held for the benefit of the community at large; that, in these places, suitable shelters and concourses should be constructed for the better enjoyment of the natural scenery opening from them, and that roads should be made on easy grades, by which these points would be comfortably approached.

With regard to early preliminary operations, we offer the following advice:

First, that an immediate beginning be made of a nursery for the growing of trees, shrubs and vines suitable to be used freely in the locality. These cannot be obtained in desirable quantities from commercial nurseries, and the cost of such as can be, if bought ready grown, would be greater than if they were raised by the Company on its own ground. We also recommend that preparations be soon made for forest planting, on a liberal scale, in some of the less attractive places, which, by these means, can be made, in a few years, much more agreeable and interesting than they now are.

Second, we advise the Company to see that its property is guarded against the danger of forest fires, and that as soon as practicable, it be fenced to keep out cattle which are now rapidly destroying the natural under-growth, which, if protected and allowed to develop, will become an element of much value in the beauty of the property.

Third, that measures be taken to secure as copious a supply of water upon the ground as circumstances admit, the success of the scheme unquestionably depending upon the ability of the Company to supply water freely, both for public and private use.

Fourth, we advise that the proposed hotel be placed on the site designated by our Mr. Codman, when on the ground; that it be constructed with a rustic exterior of the native stone which lies scattered near by in great abundance; that it be not more than two stories in height, solid, substantial and plain in outward aspect, not putting the mountain scenery out of countenance, yet with more luxury of outworks, attracting its guests out of doors, and more care for pleasing combinations of its masonry with foliage than it has been hitherto common to use in the design of large rural hotels; that it be designed by an architect of experience in the tasteful adaptation of rough stone to building purposes, and that it be so planned and fitted to the ground that convenient enlargements of it may be made when required.

We believe that a good hotel of some marked originality of character, this originality having been suggested in a great degree by the materials used and the natural advantages of the site, would attract many visitors from a much greater distance than Denver, and would aid much more than a hotel of the ordinary fashionable type, such as would stand as fittingly on the plains as on the mountains, to bring the advantages of the locality as a summer resort, to the knowledge of the public.

If, with such an understanding as we have aimed to give you of the views with which we should enter upon the duty, you wish to employ us professionally in the improvement of the Company's property, we shall be glad to be,

Respectfully,

At your service,

F. L. Olmsted & C°
Landscape Architects

"PREPARATIONS FOR THE WORLD'S FAIR": AUGUST 1890

To Lyman J. Gage

N. Y. C. R. R. en route,
Aug. 21st, 1890

Dear Mr. Gage:—

Looking back at this distance from Chicago, I am inclined to offer you a few scattered observations, unofficially and unprofessionally, as one after another they come to me in review of what we learned while with you of the progress of preparations for the World's Fair.

You know that just before we left we were offered the position of Landscape Architects to your Board. Thinking it over, we see that to undertake the duties of that office, we should be obliged to decline a good deal of business that will be offered us, and should find it difficult to do justice to all our existing important engagements. Our situation is such, that we could not think of doing this without feeling assured that we were to have opportunities, means and facilities for securing a result that, compared with those secured at previous World's Fairs by our English, French and German professional brethren, would be creditable to the country and would sustain the reputation we have earned.

The best of the sites you have in view is a wretchedly poor one compared with any site heretofore taken for a great Exposition. To secure a fairly respectable result under the conditions of topography soil and climate of any one of them, within the period of time to which we shall be limited will require much ingenuity in design, most sagacious and industrious management, liberal outlay, and after all perhaps some favor of luck. With reference to a desirable result to be economically obtained, the North Lake Site would be a far better site than either of the others; the West Side much the worst. A good thing could be done at Jackson Park if but a part, and not too large a part were to be accommodated there.

Looking over your by-laws (which we had not seen until today), we notice (Article 15), that you appear to contemplate having all your work done by contract. A good deal of what we should design could not be done well by contract. It would be impossible to make sufficiently stringent specifications for it, or to enforce them. You can't get good plants of such sorts as would be necessary, by contract. What some Members of your Board have seemed to us to understand to be Landscape Architecture, would not in our judgment be at all suitable for the premises of a World's Fair; no more than window gardening would be suitable, spread over a door-yard, or door-yard gardening over a park. In a study of the proportion of the parts to the whole, it is not so much the extent of ground that is to be considered, as the size and number of buildings.

The Directory is disposed to think it necessary that it should proceed at once upon estimates of the cost of the Landscape Improvements to be made. We are surprised that they do not realize the utter worthlessness of any estimates that could possibly be made, without any understanding of the number and size of the buildings and other construction to be considered. It would not necessarily cost half as much to lay out approaches, and shape and finish grounds and plant them suitably for ten large buildings of one character, arranged systematically and snugly about a spacious Court, as for twenty similar buildings scattered about the same centre much less symmetrically, with entrances and outlets differently disposed, and with requirements of a picturesque rather than of a formal, architectural character. Any estimates that could be made within a month, with no better data in respect to building plans than you can have for sometime to come, would be but a delusion and a snare. Any man who would give them to you would be a quack.

An Architect can give you a rough approximate idea of how much it would cost to build a fire proof building, of a certain number of stories, of a given floor space, upon a given foundation; but could any one tell you how much you will need to pay for the furnishing and decoration of such a house when it is still undetermined whether there are two, three or six stories under the roof; whether there are to be ten or twenty rooms on a floor, and whether the building is to be lighted on four sides, on three sides or only at the two ends?

In a loose way it may be assumed that an equally satisfactory result could be obtained at half the cost on the North Lake Site that it could on the Jackson Park Site, and at half the cost on the Jackson Park as on the Garfield Park, and yet this is a most imperfect statement. For with four times the outlay you could not make the Fair nearly as good in outward effect on the Garfield Park Site as on the North Lake Site, while to make use of Jackson Park a wholly different principle of arrangement would be used by any Artist. You might as well judge the value of a horse by comparing his points with those of a cow of a certain value.

You must settle the question of Site with reference to the probable result in admittance fees, and this is most likely as we judge, to bring you back at last to your original intention of having a part of the Fair on the Lake Front, and a part at Jackson Park. There are many great, very great, objections to the "Dual Site," but if you have two parts the objection to three is not much greater than to two. Possibly then it would be better to have one part on the Lake Front, one at Jackson Park, and the Agricultural division on the West Site.

We would not like to recommend it without a formal consultation with the Architect, but it strikes us as a question to be well considered before you think of taking all of the Exposition, or all but the Agricultural part to Jackson Park, whether a much more compact arrangement than you have hitherto had in view for the Lake Front might not be made satisfactory.

Suppose; for example, that we have on Michigan Avenue, a building as long as you can make it, that is to say, if I recollect aright, giving you nearly a mile frontage, unbroken in the upper part and with a colonnade below like that of the Rue de Rivoli. Give it a high basement so that the main floor extended would be say eighteen feet above the track of the Illinois Central Railroad; suppose that outside of the Railroad you had another similar building half a mile long to be approached from the first by bridging over the Railroad, and on the Lake Site of the last building a good broad promenade upon a terrace over the water of the Lake. You would then have floor space enough, and roof enough to accommodate all those parts of the Exposition desirable to be visited at night. Then from seventy-five to one hundred acres more of floor space at Jackson Park for large buildings and ten or twenty more for small scattered buildings, would provide amply for all the rest of the Exposition, except the Agricultural Department. For this, provisions could be made either by filling on the Pierce property, or if preferred upon a body of land near Garfield Park, if you do not object to a triplicate ticket of admission.

Yours very truly,

Lyman J. Gage Esq,
Chicago, Ill.

To Charles A. Roberts

9th December, 1890

Dear Mr. Roberts:—

On returning from a long journey in the South and West, I have read your note to us of December 1st. Mr. Codman is attending to the matter of the plan, and I only wish now to make one observation. You write as follows:—

"Your ideas are very sound as to the width of lots, but occasionally we are liable to sell to a party who is perfectly able to pay for the things you mention, and he is the one who wants the room."

It is evident from your saying this that you still do not quite understand our ideas. Our entire plan is based on the conviction that, under the circumstances of the case, the settlement will, in the end, be a great deal more attractive if it produces very distinctly the impression of a *community* in which the private dwellings are brought as closely together as practicable, without appearing crowded, and without an absolute denial of any private grounds about the house, while each family is allowed equal enjoyment of more extensive pleasure grounds held in common. We consider that, with this object, you cannot, at any price, afford to allow any single family to monopolize a large extent of ground as private property. The expense of providing so large an extent of public ground, including the ornamental waters, as you propose to provide, can only appear justified when you shall have this ground surrounded by as large a number of family residences as is practicable. Any single large place will be an injury in this respect to the general effect desired, and, considering the question to be in a great degree one of the effect of what is seen upon the imagination, we do not think that you can afford to have wide lots, even if you can sell them at many times the rate per front foot at which you would sell narrower lots. Those who wish larger places than are provided for on our plan should get them elsewhere.

Yours Very Truly.

Fred^k Law Olmsted

Mr. C.A. Roberts,
Denver, Colorado

A "MOST DIFFICULT UNDERTAKING": JANUARY 1891

To Clarence Pullen

7th January, 1891

Dear Mr. Pullen;

We are going to New York tonight and from there, in company with the New York Architects of the Exposition, tomorrow to Chicago. We are exceedingly pressed to get our drawings done and other preparations made in time for this conference and it has been quite impossible for us to give the time we would like to before we go to your article. What you send us is but a desultory collection of dislocated memoranda, many of them repetitions, and it would appear to me a great feat to work out a coherent and orderly article from them in the time you will have.

I will try to go over the paper and make suggestions on its margins while on the train and send it to your house early tomorrow morning.

Among points to be made I did think are these:—

It's a vast complicated and most difficult undertaking. No one *could* be expected to take it all in and see at once the grand fundamental conditions of success and place the different elements of success in due relation & subordination one to another. It was a necessary result of the manner in which the Commission & the Directory were composed that at first the most conflicting notions of what should be aimed at and of the proper methods of proceeding should *exist*. To the public & especially that portion of the public predisposed to fault-finding; it was inevitable that such preliminary discussion as was absolutely essential to a good start, should have the appearance of a prolonged, useless and wasteful wrangle. (There must be a good deal more of it). Considering what diametrically opposite opinions were held by different men of weight; how warmly they were represented, it is quite wonderful how *frank* debate has been effective in *overcoming* difficulties and securing cooperation in a broad policy. A great deal remains to be *discussed*; wide differences *still appear*, but there has been great progress and out of all the row the fact appears unquestionable that the enterprise is one of great popular interest, especially in all the West; that this interest of the West will give it some very distinctive qualities; that the pride of the people of Chicago is strongly interested to make the affair creditable to the city, and that their action for the purpose will be liberal and hospitable. *Wise*, able and energetic men are *already secured* and at work in various departments and that *progress is being* made cautiously and *thoughtfully*.

I shd say that your memoranda gave *me* too much prominence generally, considering how it has been compiled. The one thing that [...] instruction to the public in [...] is that we have not come here for advantages for gardening or for native display, which many wld suppose to be our only care as Landscape Architects; have urged a site as far as possible of such advantages—a desert place of drifting sand and water—simply out of respect for the one feature of natural—*purely natural*—beauty, in which there can be no display of our professional skill, the Lake.

I would suggest that you be cautious in speaking of plans as if anything had been decided beyond a few general ideas. We are still engaged only on "studies" rather than plans, these being presented tentatively to aid in advancing discussions. There will yet be much discussion before even outlines can be considered as finally determined.

It is doubtful whether any use will be made of the Plaisance for the Exhibition. Economy requires as snug and compact an arrangement as will answer the purpose.

To many foreigners if not to many Americans Chicago itself

will be the most interesting exhibition of the Fair. The manner in which it has been built up and of the novel and great local difficulties overcome in securing for it a decent equipment. The manner in which the site of the Exhibition will be built up out of a swamp will add to this characteristic interest of the city. It is as in keeping with the entire history of the city that, in order to provide the esthetic value of a view over the Lake, the difficulties in these and horticultural disadvantages of building up a site out of a swamp divided by barren sand dunes should have been disregarded. The boldness of the proposition is quite in line with that so successfully carried out of screwing up thousands of houses in order to get their front doors above a satisfactory level for streets. (See article on Chicago in Johnsons Cyclopedia).

I am obliged to close now but I think that I have written all I had intended.

Yours Truly

Fred^k Law Olmsted

"A POETIC AND TRANQUILIZING INFLUENCE":
JANUARY 1891

To Henry Van Brunt

22nd January, 1891

My dear Mr. Van Brunt:—

I have just received, gratefully, your letter of the 17th instant. I feel with you warmly that the meeting at Chicago was a most happy, useful and promising occasion and I look forward with much pleasure to others to follow.

I am a most unfluent and clumsy writer and can publish nothing without an appalling amount of revision and trimming. I have always applications in this way beyond my ability to meet. I cannot now possibly undertake what you suggest that I should for the Atlantic.

The latest information I have of the class you need is in the form of a Report from the Earl of Meath to the New Town Government for London, called the County Council. Lord Meath was at my house while here and his Report is largely based on information compiled from various sources in our office, or which were collected for him by direct correspondence with the different cities. It is neither full nor accurate, and there are omissions in it of matter we gave him, for which I cannot account. Perhaps he thought it too vague or incomplete. For example, Denver possesses a public park site not yet much improved. I presume that you have correspondents there. If not, you could address the Mayor, or our friends Andrews and Jacques, who have an office there now, would get accurate information for you. A public park, parkway and small grounds are being laid out at Omaha by our friend, H.W.S. Cleveland, a most worthy old gentleman, formerly a partner of Copeland and of Follen in Boston, whom you could address, mentioning that I advised you, care of the Park Commission of Omaha. He would gladly aid you, I know.

There is an article of mine on "Parks" in the American Encyclopedia, and one on "Landscape Gardening" in Johnson's Encyclopedia, that you might like to run over.

You will find some information in Waring's contribution to the Census of 1880; "Social Statistics of Cities." See columns "Parks" in the index of each of the two volumes (XVIII and XIX); but it will hardly pay for the gathering.

Hyatt's interest in the subject has grown entirely out of efforts of mine to get the Boston Society of Natural History to move with reference to out-of-door scientific and educational museums. I will try to send you copies of correspondence on the subject. I mention the fact only that you may recognize that my prevailing purpose has been to guard against the injection of such museums into park designs.

This brings me to what would be chiefly interesting to me in anything that you may write on the subject of parks.

The grand difficulty with which, from the outset, Vaux and I had to contend, and with which all who have a serious interest in the subject are incessantly struggling, is the almost universal want of discrimination between the special purposes, motives and reasons for being, of different species of public grounds. From the beginning of work on Central Park, as you must in some degree recollect, the disposition of the public, of the liberally educated, cultivated men, of the majority of newly appointed Park Commissioners, of all snobs and Philistines like Judge Hilton, and of nearly all members of City Councils and other city officers, has been to consider land appropriated for a public park as a vacant space in which anything of public interest could be dumped that would not be better placed on land in the form of city lots to be specially purchased for the purpose. Half the strength of my life has been spent in various forms of contention with this difficulty. I send you a copy of the last private letter I have written on the subject. This was in reply to an inquiry addressed to me a few weeks ago by Paul Dana almost immediately after his appointment as a Park Commissioner. During the last thirty years I have written many such letters, and also a great deal for the public on the subject, mostly through newspapers with reference to special occasions. I will send you one of these writings, of a less fugitive character than most, addressed to the Social Science Association in 1880. You will not need to read it all, but I wish you would glance at the first half dozen and the last three pages at least, in order to see for what I am always contending.

You may observe that Lord Meath quotes from this pamphlet a passage, the object of which was really the opposite of that he apparently assumes: i.e. the passage was intended as an introduction to an argument for large parks (preserves) of rural scenery, such as cannot be had in public grounds of small area. Doubtless, he accidentally missed the point, but the fact that he did so shows you how hard it is to get the less intelligent public, and less liberal Park Commissioners to apprehend the point.

(Lord Meath has officially to do with no large public park, but only with small public grounds. He is Chairman of an Association, the chief object of which is to get the disused burial grounds of London turned into gardens—not parks—and opened to the public,—a most useful institution.)

My notion is that whatever grounds a great city may need for other public purposes, for parades, for athletic sports, for fireworks, for museums of art or science, such as botanic gardens, it also needs a large ground scientifically and artistically prepared to provide such a poetic and tranquilizing influence on its people as comes through a pleased contemplation of natural *scenery*, especially sequestered and limitless natural scenery.

What should be aimed at in this respect is always a special problem to be solved by special study of the landscape capabilities of each city.

Please preserve and return to me the Meath Report and the pamphlet by Eckman. You need not return the others.

Suppose that you had been commissioned to build a really grand, opera house; that after the construction work had been nearly completed and your scheme of decoration fully designed, you should be instructed that the building was to be used on Sundays as a Baptist Tabernacle, and that a suitable place must be made for a huge organ, a pulpit and a dipping pool. Then at intervals afterwards, you should be advised that it must be so re-fitted and furnished that parts of it could be used for a court room, a jail, a concert hall, hotel, skating rink, for surgical cliniques, for a circus, dog show, drill room, ball room, railway station and shot tower? What chance would you see for making a fine affair, in any respect, of your building?

Again, suppose that once in three or four years an ordinary house painter and paper hanger, or even a theatrical scene painter, should be called in to revamp and improve your decoration of the auditorium? Could you think of such a history without indignation and disgust?

But that, more or less, is what is nearly always going on with public parks. Pardon me if I overwhelm you; it is a matter of chronic anger with me.

Cordially Yours,

Fred^k Law Olmsted

"COMPLEX DISPOSITIONS OF LIGHT AND SHADE":
MARCH 1891

Memorandum As to What Is to Be Aimed At in the Planting of the Lagoon District of the Chicago Exposition, As Proposed March, 1891

As far as it is possible, between the present time and May, 1893, the Lagoon must be made to look like a natural bayou, secluded, shallow and placid, but not suggestive of stagnancy or any form of foulness or unhealthfulness. Its low, sterile, sandy shores must be given a rich, affluent, picturesque aspect, in striking contrast alike with that of the present ground, the shores of the great lake, the margins of the Basin in the great Court and the canals yet to be formed, and with the bare and prosaic shores of the ponds heretofore made in Jackson and Washington Parks.

The desired result in this respect is to be accomplished largely by thick, luxuriant growths of herbaceous, aquatic vegetation along the shore, rooted partly above and partly below the surface of the water.

The best of the few poor trees now growing on the island are to be retained and, if possible, forced by an enrichment of the soil into finer foliage. Between them and the water plants, bushes and young trees are to be introduced so as to make the island from the east appear a broad, continuous, close bank of verdure.

Nearly everywhere else, except where formal terraces are to be formed near the shore, three main objects are to be had in view in the shore planting:

First, to make an agreeable low foreground over which the great buildings of the Exposition will rise, gaining in grandeur of effect upon the imagination because appearing at a greater distance, and more lofty than they would but for such a foreground;

Second, to establish a considerable extent of broad and apparently natural scenery, in contemplation of which a degree of quieting influence will be had, counteractive to the effect of the artificial grandeur and the crowds, pomp, splendor and bustle of the rest of the Exposition;

Third, without losing a general unity and continuity of character in the shores, to secure whatever time, with all possible exercise of skill for the purpose, will allow, of mysterious poetic effect, through the mingling intricately together of many forms of foliage, the alternation and complicated crossing of salient leaves and stalks of varying green tints in high lights with other leaves and stalks, behind and under them, and therefore less defined and more shaded, yet partly illumined by light reflected from the water. So far as consistent with this last purpose of obscure and subdued poetic beauty through the intricate conjunction of various forms of vegetation and complex dispositions of light and shade, it is intended that the shores should have a somewhat gay and festive aspect through a profusion of flowers. But it is not desired that there should anywhere appear to be a display of flowers demanding attention as such. Rather the flowers to be used for the purpose should have the effect of flecks and glimmers of bright color imperfectly breaking through the general greenery. Anything approaching a gorgeous, garish or gaudy display of flowers is to be avoided. It will be easier to accomplish what is thus to be aimed at, even if flowers are used profusely, because, to the great body of visitors, the Lagoon plantations will only be seen from a distance, and from a nearly horizontal point of view, on the shore opposite that on which they stand. Boats will be prevented from closely approaching the plantations.

While the greater number of plants to be used will be such as are indigenous to the river banks and swamps of Northern Illinois, and therefore hardy, in order to increase intricacy and richness of general effect, many are to be scattered among them that a botanist, looking closely, would know could not have grown in the locality naturally. The work is thus to be in some degree of the character of a theatrical scene, to occupy the Exposition stage for a single Summer. But it is not intended that the slightly exotic forms of verdure to be thus used shall call, any more than the flowers, for individual notice. Rather, seen as they will generally be, at some distance, they will merge indistinguishably with other forms of verdure, and not suggest a question as to what they are, or how they have come to be where they are.

The line at which the water meets the shore is intended hardly ever to be seen, being obscured by aquatic plants growing above and below it.

There are several serious difficulties to be overcome in realizing this design thus set forth, and they must be met by original expedients. The chief of these difficulties is that of the uncertainty of the normal elevation which the water will have during the period of the Exposition, and the certainty that whatever this normal elevation shall be, it will fluctuate irregularly from day to day, so that what is dry ground at one time will be flooded at another. The only means of dealing with this difficulty thus far proposed to be used is that of providing plants very liberally which will stand a good chance to flourish, although their roots are sometimes high above water, and sometimes submerged. Trials of numerous plants must be made in the Summer of 1891 with reference to this purpose, and large reserves of a class of plants of small cost, sure to succeed, must be prepared for replanting any ground where better sorts shall either be drowned or dried out, so that in no case will the shores at any points appear sparsely furnished, much less unfurnished or barren.

Another difficulty is that of guarding against the danger that plants that will have been established on the shore in the Summer of 1892, will be lifted or bruised destructively by the ice of the following Winter. This can be provided against, in some degree, by cutting the plants closely and by laying loose litter over and about them late in the Fall; by cutting the shore ice free from the central body of ice in the Lagoon, and by stakes or otherwise preventing it from floating off until it gradually melts in place.

Another difficulty is that as there will be several miles in length of the shore planting to be done, and as the planting season will be short, and the men employed working at disadvantage in the ice cold water, a satisfactory direction and oversight of the large number of unskilled laborers required can only be had through an extensive and elaborate system of management, carefully organized in advance, with a view to this difficulty. At best, the work of planting must be expected to be done in a comparatively rude way which it will be difficult to get gardening foremen to efficiently direct. Plants, therefore, that require delicate treatment, or that do not take root readily in wet, sandy ground, can be little depended on. The plants must be set thickly and there will be little or no opportunity to cultivate them after they are set.

Another restriction on the class of plants to be extensively used is that, owing to the packing of ice along the shore in the southern part of Lake Michigan, the water often remains at a wintry temperature until after the time set in the Spring for the opening of the Exposition, nor does it become as warm during the entire Summer as the water in many streams, ponds and swamps in the same latitude. Hence, many water plants natural to such localities are likely to grow but slowly, if at all, in the Lagoon. It is hoped that this difficulty may be, in some degree provided against by making many shallow bays and pools along the shores, especially of the west side of the island. But the main planting must everywhere be done with thoroughly hardy and tough aquatic plants, common further north than Chicago.

Letters on the Preliminary Planting Map of the Lagoon are intended to indicate a little more fully and definitely the character of planting desired in different localities, by reference to corresponding letters in the schedule below. But while the plants named are to predominate, it is not intended to closely restrict the planting to them at any point. Certain plants, such as bulrushes, sedges and ferns, are intended to be placed wherever they are likely to flourish among others, in order to give increased density, intricacy and naturalness of effect, and to slightly screen, without hiding, flowers otherwise likely to be too obtrusive.

The various so-called pond-lilies are also to be scattered somewhat freely along the edges of all waterside plantations, and on the lower parts of slopes.

Except against the terraces, as to be later explained, and at a few other points where they would rise too high for the effects desired, cat-tails, (Typha) are to predominate in the planting, large patches of them being formed; these are to be broken and diversified chiefly with flags, (Acorus) and bulrushes, (Juncus) and Irises, and among them there should be numerous little patches and recesses, if necessary, on slightly raised ground, where blooming plants can be seen, such as the smaller Irises, Lobelia cardinalis, Ranunculus repens and Viola cucullata. Patches, also, of ferns suitable to the situation. Farther from the water, and to be seen through openings of the Typhas and Acorus, taller flowering plants may be seen, such as Bacharis halimifolia and Nicotiana affinis.

For young trees to be planted with a view to fill out vacancies in the edge of the woods on the island, it is important to use such as are most sure to be in rapid growth, with abundant and vigorous leafage, in ground well above water, in 1893. It has been ascertained that for this purpose, trees of the following sorts can be obtained in Western nurseries, in fair condition, from 10 to 15 feet high: White Maple, Catalpa speciosa, Box Elder (Negundo), Russian Mulberry, American Linden. To these, certain Poplars and Willows of natural growth can probably be added. For crowding under and facing the stems of these, good plants are to be had of the European Alder, Larch, American Mountain Ash. For the lower parts of the mass, Cornels and most of the common nursery shrubs can be had, 3 to 4 feet high, and various Willows can be grown. Aralia spinosa may be used freely; also, Pawlonia, cut short to force

Wooded Island and Footprint of Surrounding Buildings, World's Columbian Exposition

large leaves near the ground and water. Cat-tails, Flags, etc. can be scattered at intervals in the water outside of these, and *occasionally* still further out, Water-lilies, etc.

Looking at the map, it will be seen that, for long distances the shore of the Lagoon is intended to be near, and with a general trend parallel to, the straight walls sustaining terraces at the base of several of the Exposition Buildings.

The strip of ground between these retaining walls and the water is to be commonly from 25 to 50 feet broad, and to have a sloping face towards the water. (These strips are marked E on the map).

Nearly all of the Lagoon margin of this character is expected to be submerged for a few hours at uncertain intervals, but ordinarily the upper part will be dry and the lower part, or waterside, water-soaked. Plants upon the upper part will be nearer to the greater body of visitors, and will be more closely observed than any others on the Lagoon shores. They will be looked down upon from the terrace, the roots of the nearest being 7 to 9 feet; of the furthest 9 to 13 feet, below the eye. Seen from boats, or from the opposite shore, the plants should appear a low thicket, or bank, of verdure, more or less broken, irregular and tufty in its profile, the upper part of the wall and the parapet or balustrade of the terrace, being generally seen rising a little above it. To this end, few plants can be grown on this strip that, during the Summer of 1893, will come to have a height of more than 3 to 4 feet.

More flowers can be shown with advantage on the upper part of the strip than anywhere else on the Lagoon shore, precaution being taken, where they would otherwise be too showy, to slightly veil them from the opposite shore by a few bulrushes, Eulalia, or other thin plants, to grow on the waterside of them. With a little care in this respect, Irises, especially versicolor, prismatica and Germanica, set from 2 to 15 feet from the wall, will be exactly suitable to the situation. Care must be taken to avoid anything like a continuous bed of such flowering plants, or any monotony of arrangement, by constantly grouping them with Funkias, Ferns and other plants. Large bodies of low and spreading plants of Clethra alnifolia and cephalanthus occidentalis will be desirable all along the strip, these being valued because of the fragrance of their bloom. Besides these, there are to be set profusely, adjoining the wall, on what will be the driest part of the strip, other plants from which pleasing scents will rise to visitors on the terrace. Viola cucullata, Hemerocallis flava, Lonicera brachiopoda, Rosa rubiginosa, lucida, Carolina and multiflora will, for example, serve the purpose.

To make sure that a dense growth of foliage will be everywhere interposed at some point between the wall and the water, straggling thickets may be formed of young plants of various Willows, so shortened in, or pinned down, that they will seldom rise more than 2 to 3 feet from the ground. Among and around these should be Flags, Acorus, calamus and Bulrushes (Juncus), various Sedges (Carex) and other waterside grass and reed-like plants. Small channels may be made to let the water flow into these wherever desirable, such channels being easily made inconspicuous.

The same class of plants, together with Sagittarias and a variety of broad-leaved water plants, such as Saxifraga, Callas, Symphoricarpos, Nuphas and Nympheas should be planted above and below the water's side.

SCHEDULE SUGGESTING WHAT SORTS OF PLANTS MAY BE USED CONSISTENTLY WITH THE LEADING PURPOSES OF THE GENERAL DESIGN IN THE VARIOUS LOCALITIES INDICATED ON THIS MAP BY LETTERS CORRESPONDING WITH THE LETTERS ON THE MARGIN BELOW

T. Sufficiently described in the memorandum above.

W. Typha (nearly everywhere predominating); Acorus calamus; Juncus, Iris Sibirica, Kaempferia, Virginica; Struthiopteris Germanica, Eryngius Yuccafolium; Yucca filamentosa; Osmunda regalis and cinnamonia.

M. Native grasses and sedges (on the ground) with scattering patches of native Golden-rod and Asters; Rose mallow (Hibiscus); Swamp Loosestrife (Lychium); Swamp Milkweed (Asclepias); Cassia Marilandica; Lilium superbum and canadense; Veronica; Rudbeckia laciniata; Nicotiana affinis; (This district will be secluded by surrounding plantations and the above plants seen at a distance in tufts through small openings.)

E. Iris versicolor, prismatica, Germanica; Sisyrinchium, (Blue

Eyed Grass); Xyris flexuosa and Carolina; Liatris spicata;
Eulalia Japonica (mainly of the green varieties, few of the
striped and those not set prominently out); Viola cucullata
(Marsh Violet); Hemerocallis fulva and flava, and other
fragrant sorts; Lonicera brachiopoda; Rosa rubiginiosa, lucida, Carolina and multiflora; Funkia (Day lilies); Veratrum
viride; Sagittaria; Acorus calamus; Caltha palustris; Oron-
tium aquatica; Calla palustris; Meyanthes trifoliata; Alisma
plantago; Nasturtium officinale (seed); Saxifraga crassifolia;
Juncus; Corex, various species; Cyperus, various species;
Lobelia cardinalis and syphilitica; Spiraeas lobata; Ranunculus repens; Geum rivale (Water avens); Hydrophyllum
canadense; Virginicum and appendiculatum; Saururus
cernuus; Solidago lanceolata, tenuifolia; Aster linariifolius
and laevis; Rudbeckia Newmani; Erigeron Philadelphicum;
Physostegia Virginica.

L. Nymphaea odorata and Nymphaea odorata minor; Nymphaea tuberosa and lutea; Nupha advena; Limnanthemum
lacunosum; Brasonia peltata; Potamogetons; Marsilea
quadrifolia;

B. Juncus, Cyperus, Carex, Onoclea sensibilis, Aspidium The-
lypteris, Spiranthes and low ferns.

C. Lawn-like turf.

"LIKE THE BANKS OF SOME TROPICAL RIVERS":
MARCH 1891

To Rudolph Ulrich

24th March, 1891
Dear Mr. Ulrich:

Please think well over the Memorandum about the Lagoon
which Mr Codman will give you. It is most important that you
should get the right ideal in your mind and work for it heartily.

The thing is to make it appear that we *found* this body of
water and its shores and have done nothing to them except
at the landings and bridges. They were rich, rank, luxurious,
crowded with vegetation, like the banks of some tropical rivers
that I have seen or Louisiana bayous. The vegetation must

18. Olmsted and friends, New Haven, 1846. Back row (*l. to r.*):
Charles Trask, Frederick Kingsbury, John Hull Olmsted.
Front row: Charles Loring Brace, Frederick Law Olmsted.

19. The Colfax party in Yosemite Valley, August 1865. Olmsted and his wife are second and third from left, front row.

20. Mary Perkins Olmsted, 1863.

21. Pruning ladder used in Prospect Park, Brooklyn, c. 1870.

22. Tree-moving machine, Prospect Park, Brooklyn, c. 1870.

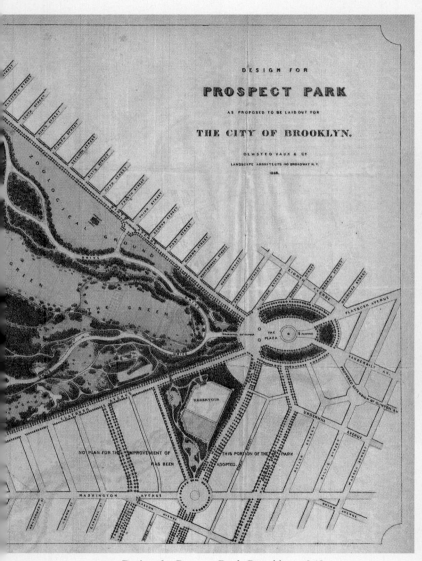

23. *Design for Prospect Park*, Brooklyn, 1868.

24. View of Long Meadow, Prospect Park, Brooklyn, 1902.

25. General Plan of Riverside, Illinois, 1869.

26. *General Plan for the Improvement of the U.S. Capitol Grounds*, 1875.
Drawn by Thomas Wisedell.

27. The Riverway section of the Muddy River, Boston.
Top: Under construction in 1892. *Bottom:* Twenty-eight years later.

28. The lagoon at the World's Columbian Exposition, Chicago, 1892.

29. Tennis in Boston's Franklin Park, c. 1894.

30. Ellicottdale in Franklin Park, part of Olmsted's "Emerald Necklace" around Boston, 1892.

31. Olmsted with daughter Marion on the grounds of the Biltmore estate, North Carolina, early 1890s.

32. Olmsted, c. 1890.

33. "Fairsted," Olmsted's home and office in Brookline, Massachusetts, 1904.

appear spontaneous and thoroughly wild (to all unlearned visitors). The stronger the contrast thus to be obtained with the highly gardened, finished and kept ground, the better the latter will be—the more effective. We cannot get trees that will be large and fine and effective as trees. The highest things that we can grow that will appear flourishing, indigenous and natural to the locality as we shall be supposed to have found it, will be Typhas. I hope that in two years we can have these in perfection in great bodies and grouping with them flags (acorus) and lots of other things of less height that will group with them and fringe the shores. A sort of fringe of luxurient vegetation is all that we can hope in perfection. We must be very careful not to attempt anything small, local and petty and nothing in which we *cannot make sure of perfect success.* We cannot in the poor sandy sour soil be sure of high success, on the necessary large scale, with anything radically different from what the Memorandum proposes, I think. The neat sloping lawns of a common pleasure ground could not be made in time so that they would not compare unfavorably with what many of our visitors will have been accustomed to. The natural condition of the locality is a swamp. Chicago has grown out of a swamp, and as far as I know a swamp without beauty. Let us try to show the possible beauty of a swamp, even without trees.

A very difficult thing to do, I fully recognize, but not, I believe, impossible. Nor do I see that there is anything else that can be done on the grand scale required and within the limits of time and expense imposed upon us, that has not greater difficulties.

We must depend on you to anticipate and contrive means in advance for conquering the difficulties. If you succeed it will be a great surprise and delight to the people of Chicago and they will have learned something of our art of which they have no conception.

The whole lagoon district must, through its wildness, luxurience, unrestrained and informal aspect of natural scenery of a type rarely seen in close connection with grand affairs, be a foil for the highly enriched, refined and delicate gardening decoration of other parts of the Fair Ground.

Yours Truly

Fred^k Law Olmsted

To William James

8th July, 1891

Dear Professor James:—

I have received your note in which you say that you would be glad to have a fuller narrative of my experiences in what I believe to have been a condition of sleeping with open eyes.

The first was when I was twenty years old, one of the crew of an American ship, in the South Atlantic, homeward bound from China. I was at the time but imperfectly recovering from typhoid fever, on such unsuitable diet that it resulted in scurvy before we reached home. The ship was short-handed and the time usually allowed for sleep had been curtailed; "all hands" being kept on deck during the morning and the afternoon watches.

At two o'clock in the morning, it was my turn to keep the lookout on the forecastle. I realized that I was in a state of cruel drowsiness and struggled resolutely to get the better of it. Soon, while standing erect and looking vigilantly ahead, I fell sound asleep and was awakened by falling upon the deck. I then determined not to allow myself to stand still for a moment. The ship was being painted and some spars had been temporarily lashed upon the forecastle so that I could find no place for walking which would allow me to move more than five steps each way, back and forth. In walking this distance, if I staggered sidewise towards the stern, I should fall over the break of the forecastle down upon the main deck, and if I moved more than five steps, there was nothing at one end of my beat but a small life-line at the height of my knee, to prevent me from stepping overboard. Walking to and fro in the situation, I repeatedly struck my forehead and temples with my fists, trying to overcome the inclination to sleep. Nevertheless, I three times went sound asleep between one end of my beat and the other and the third time was saved from being pitched into the sea only by catching the life-line with my hand. I reflected that to continue this walk would be suicide and looked about for some more effective means of keeping myself awake. The expedient I adopted was to sit on a spar at a point where the heavy bolt-rope forming the bottom of the foresail would, as the ship rolled, first strike me from behind; then rake my head, compelling me to bend downward and let it pass, and then strike me in front and force me again to move as it swung backward. Thus I should be sharply struck and compelled to crouch uncomfortably two or three times a minute. So situated, I looked forward upon the sea; imagined that for an instant I had caught sight of a dipping light on the horizon; roused myself to the utmost vigilance in searching for its reappearance, and, while so vigilantly searching, lost consciousness, as I have no doubt, with my eyes wide open. How long I remained in this condition I do not know, but it must have been a number of minutes; possibly half an hour. When consciousness began to return to me, I felt the stroke of the sail upon my head as it swung forward, and, at the same time, knew that I had been seeing, before my mind took hold of the fact, a pair of eyes looking into mine. Then I heard a voice, asking: "What is the matter with you?" It came to me as if part of a dream, but waked me completely and on the instant I knew that the Captain was standing on the windlass and so bending over and turning his body as to look me in the face. I was able to answer promptly and in a quick, natural, decisive way: "There is nothing the matter with me, sir." "Why don't you answer when you are hailed?" "I have heard no hail, sir." "What do you mean? I hailed you from the quarter deck; I hailed you from the waist, and when you did not answer I came to the windlass and hailed you within three feet of your ear. I thought you must be asleep until I saw that your eyes were open." "I don't understand it, sir; I certainly did not hear you." The Captain believed me and turned away, saying: "Keep a sharp lookout," and I did not fall asleep again until after I had been regularly relieved.

The next experience to which I have referred occurred more than forty years afterwards, when, sitting at a table with several other persons, I was suddenly attacked with sleepiness and could with difficulty keep my attention upon the topic of conversation. I resisted the tendency all I could. I lifted a spoon, turned my eyes towards it with a determination that they would not close, gave my head a shake, and, the next moment was asleep and dreaming. I do not think I remained so more than a few seconds. When I awoke, my eyes were still fixed on the spoon which I was turning in my fingers; I could not define my dream, but had an imperfect recollection of it. I was sure that I had been dreaming and that my dream had carried me through much more time than had actually passed. I said to myself:— "My eyes cannot have been closed." No one at the table had observed me and I entered again into the conversation that was advancing, having no more trouble to keep awake.

My third experience occurred last year. I was in a common car upon a railroad, occupying the right hand place upon a double seat; this bringing me next to the aisle. A gentleman traveling with me, who had both our passage tickets, was seated on my left. Here again I fell asleep, as I am convinced, with my eyes open, and with no consciousness at any time that I was "going off." I saw a conductor coming through the car. When he came near me, he turned to collect the tickets from the occupants of the opposite seats and then swung half around and touched me on the right shoulder. I lifted my right hand and moved it as a gesture toward my companion who had the tickets. With the movement, I recovered full waking consciousness. The instant before I did so, and the instant after I did so, my hand, passing to the left, was seen by me in a continuous motion. Also, when awake, I saw the people on the seats before me just as I had been seeing them in my dream. But now the conductor was no longer at my side or in the car, and I realized instantly that he had existed only in my dream. I asked myself at once if I could entertain a doubt that my eyes had been open through this dream, and I could not. It seemed to me that while I was asleep, my eyes had not ceased to see, but that there had been a disconnection, or a partial disconnection, between them and my mind. I say partial, because I had once, when under the influence of morphine, administered by a surgeon, experienced what is called "double consciousness" very vividly and curiously and I thought that I was aware that there had been a slight degree of double consciousness in this case, and that I had it in memory that my eyes had not been obscured; that there had been no interruption of actual vision. I had not looked squarely and attentively at the conductor, but as he moved slowly toward me in the aisle, turning from one passenger to another, I had obtained a clear impression of his personal appearance. He was under-sized, his face dull and hard, his hair and beard untidy, his coat was unbuttoned and shabby, and I had been led to the thought while I was asleep, that on the Pennsylvania Company's roads, no conductor would ever be seen so slouchy and ill-favored. Had I been a little less conscious of the change from a partially dreaming to a fully awake condition, I should probably have explained the experience as a hallucination in which the ghost of a railroad conductor appeared, touched me and vanished, while all other things within my vision remained as they were, fixed and tangible.

Having written what is above, another circumstance has been brought to my mind, which, as it may be instructive as to the possible origin, growth and ripening of what might be taken for household words, and being regardful of your wish for accounts of personal experience of this nature, I will also narrate:

Forty-three years ago, I became possessed of a farm on the seacoast near New York. Shortly afterwards, I heard an old man, native of the neighborhood, refer to the farm as the "Tosomock Place." Upon inquiry, he said that had been the name of the locality when he was a boy. I said that it sounded like an Indian name and he observed that there were shell heaps on the shore and that he supposed the name came from the Indians. Thereafter I called the farm Tosomock Farm and was accustomed to say, when asked, that it was the Indian name of the locality. Years afterwards I ascertained that, in the previous century, the farm had once been the home of a family, of which no descendant was now living in the county. The name of the family was Teschemaker.

Upon this farm there had been, until within a few years of my time, a house described to me as "a real old Dutch farmhouse"; long and low, of one story fully above ground covered with a peaked and curved roof. Its main floor was on the level of the ground at one end and, as the surface sloped away, seven feet above it at the other, where a level entrance was given to the cellar. My predecessor had removed the roof, added a story; given it a commonplace roof, and built a veranda on three sides of the house. The old walls, having been formed principally of large boulders collected on the farm, were very thick and the openings for windows in them, short and narrow.

Soon after I came to live in this house, a guest remarking the quaintness of the room in which we were dining and the fortress-like windows, said: "A house like this ought to have a ghost." Recalling a statement of the old man's, that he had heard that a gang of tories had occupied the house during the Revolution, I answered my friend: "Yes, it has a ghost; I bought it with the live stock." "What's the story?" he asked. "The story is," I replied, "that during the Revolution the house was occupied by a company of Tory Cow Boys. Once, at night, during a fearful easterly storm, an alarm was given, throwing them into a panic and they fled to get under cover of the British frigates at the Narrows. There is a place below divided from the rest of the cellar by bars or narrow plank slat work, in which cider used to be kept under lock. This had been taken by the Tory garrison for a dungeon and in it, the day before the storm set in, the drummer of the corps had been confined for drunkenness. In the flight he was forgotten and left to starve to death. Ever since, when an easterly gale is rising, and the sea begins to roar on the beach, he is to be heard groaning and sighing; trying to wrench or force apart the bars of his cage, or playing the Devil's tattoo on an empty cider barrel."

This yarn, invented on the moment, and recited with suitable gravity, was heard by the maid waiting upon us and so passed out. Some years afterwards, when we had other domestic service, it came back to us as a veritable legend of the house. Then it became a custom with us, when an easterly storm arose, to imagine that we heard the drummer, and there were noises made by the wind swaying the timber framework of the new parts of the house and passing through the trees near it and the trelliswork under the veranda, which it was easy to think resembled those of subdued drumming, with sighs and groans, and convulsive wrenching, straining and creaking of wooden bars. There were those in the kitchen part of the house who were sure that these resemblances were more than imaginary. They were confirmed in this conviction when, at length, in making repairs of the premises, there was found an oval brass plate having an inscription showing that it had been a British military belt-plate.

I was about to write, in all honesty, that this plate was found imbedded in the earthen floor of the cider cellar and that the inscription upon it read: "THE QUEEN'S LOYAL RANGERS," but a doubt came to me as to the word Rangers. I reflected that I had not seen the plate since, some thirty years ago, our furniture had been lost in a fire, and that, when in Texas, I had become familiar with the word as applied to irregular troops. So, questioning if memory were not playing tricks with me as to this word, I consulted my wife, who said: "The plate was not found in the cider cellar; it was found in removing the floor of the cock-loft over the old carriage-house, and the inscription on it was, "The King's Loyal Dragoons." I give up the Rangers, but think that I am right as to the Queen, else, why, King being the more probable word, should I have thought of Queen?

But so, even in one lifetime, a piece of the simplest, innocent, playful imagination has acquired something of domestic, traditional and legendary character; its authenticity confirmed by an accidental discovery, and particulars of that discovery become misty, and evidence respecting it hopelessly conflicting.

Upon this matter of conflicting testimony, I may add this experience:

Ten years after the War of the Rebellion, I was dining with a Virginia farmer and his family. There were at the table, also, his brother and another man, both of whom lived near by. The farmer had mentioned that, during the War, he had lost all his fences. I observed that he must have suffered from both sides, as the region had been occupied several times alternately, one army driving out the other. "No," he said, "the Confederates were never here." I thought that I knew the contrary, but his brother repeated the statement. I stated my grounds for having supposed that the Confederates had been much on the ground and the farmer replied that I had been misinformed, no Confederates had been near the place in all the War. He looked around the table and, apparently, all present but myself confirmed the statement. Courtesy forbade me to say anything further. Here, then, was positive evidence, taken on the spot, ten years after a highly important historical occurrence, by a number of persons, all of whom must have been eye witnesses, much interested and personally affected by the circumstance in question. In conversation, afterwards, with the third man of the region, something he said led me to ask, "Surely you remember then, do you not, that the Confederate army was in this region?" "Certainly, Sir," he replied, "again and again; they were all through here. Reckon they were camped on that man's farm." "What did he and all of them mean, then, when they said they were never here?" "Reckon they were forgetful, Sir." "But why did you not say so, when we were at the dinner table?" "Why, they were all so positive I did not think it would do any good, and I did not care to have a difference with them."

Yours Very Truly

Fred^k Law Olmsted

Professor William James,
Chocorua, New Hampshire

"IN SYMPATHY WITH NATURE": SEPTEMBER 1892

To William Robinson

The villages in the Cotswold region to which I referred as well built were Camden, Broadway, and Middle Hill. I do not remember if I wrote you about our little tour in the Sherwood Forest, the Dukeries, Chatsworth, and Haddon Hall. Briefly, I enjoyed the remains of the forest and the villages on its borders very much; was much pleased with Thoresby; enjoyed Haddon Hall; enjoyed the more unsophisticated scenery of Derbyshire greatly, including the bleak heathery moorland; enjoyed the park at Chatsworth, did not like the terrace but found, notwithstanding some bad anomalies, the results of Paxton's work in the pleasure grounds more agreeably interesting than I had in some way been led to suppose or than I remembered them. I suppose this is the result of growth. Justice can often not be done a landscape gardener's design in less than fifty years after the work has been initiated. Nor then or ever, unless it has been in the hands of one in sympathy with Nature.

Reviewing all that I have seen in England, it appears to me that the selection and disposition of trees and plants, the modeling of surfaces and the arrangement of roads and walks and architectural conveniences, with a view to pleasing general effects of scenery, have been of late much confused and often lost sight of in efforts to provide brilliant local spectacles, to display rarities, curiosities and luxuries of vegetation, and to exhibit masterpieces of horticultural craft and costly garden *bric-a-brac*. Vast numbers of trees have been planted without knowledge or soundly formed anticipations of what they will become. Many of them are failing, and many that are not failing are conspicuously offensive, because of their unfitness to combine with the native elements of English scenery. Since my earlier visits the country has lost something of picturesque interest, mainly, I think, through agricultural and economical improvements, but a little, I am inclined to think, because of some slight and probably temporary turn of public sentiment toward prosaic neatness and formality.

Since my last visit there has been a decided abatement of the bedding-out nuisance and of all the garish and childish fashions that came in with it. The gardeners and others with whom I have talked have been generally conceding—some with evident regret—that it was going out of fashion. Any who think that with it their occupation will be gone had better come quickly to America, where all the beauty that I have been aiming to provide on various grounds is wholly put out of countenance by it. There has never been a square yard of bedding out on any ground under my direction.

"A NEW IDEAL OF LOCAL SCENERY": MAY 1893

To Mariana Griswold Van Rensselaer

22nd May, 1893

Dear Mrs. Van Rensselaer:—

I came home late last night and have only just now known of "Art Out of Doors." I have but glimpsed through it, keeping it to read when I shall be less subject to interruptions.

I am proud of the elevation in which it places me, but must say that it makes me feel a little giddy and unsafe to stand in such a position and that I am carried further in the direction that my note written the other day at your house indicated that I was then tending. I have all confidence in your judgment and I shall gladly help you as best I can in all that about which you will let me help you, (I am writing on the text of Mr. Johnson's note to me), but it seems to me that a magazine article on my works can be little more than a catalogue raisonné, and that something more comprehensive, or something more limited in scope, would have greater public value. To show what I mean by this alternative, I will mention that I have had some professional responsibility for close upon a hundred public grounds, but I am not accustomed to class more than twenty of these as "parks," reserving that term for places distinguished not for trees or for groups and masses of trees, or for flowers or statues, or roads or bridges, or for collections of these and other fine things, nor for landscapes as painters use the term, nor for anything related to what the word garden formerly meant, and in common popular use means now. I reserve the word park for places with breadth and space enough, and with all other needed qualities to justify the application to what you find in them of the word scenery, or of the word landscape in its older and more radical sense, which is much the same as that of scenery. (By the way, do you know that Sir Walter Scott protested against the introduction of the word landscape-gardening as likely to confuse two distinct arts: that is to say, the art of gardening and the art of landscape or scenery-making? And, by the way again, did not Milton use the word architecture for the working out of the divine design for the heavens? Architecture is not rightly to be limited to works of buildings. Gardening is rightly to be limited to garden work, which work does not conveniently include that, for instance, of exposing great ledges, damming streams, making lakes, tunnels, bridges, terraces and canals).

The question I wish you to consider is whether it would not be better to have a more comprehensive handle to a more distinctly limited topic; whether you might not write, for example, on scenery-making and scenery-mending, with illustrations, or the citing of examples, if you please, from American public works that would come under that category? It would now be possible to refer to several public works in which considerable progress had been made towards a new ideal of local scenery. Vaux and I agreed, when we began to design the Central Park, that we would have in view effects to be attained in not less than forty years. Thirty-seven years of that time will have passed next Winter.

There is a special reason why I shrink from what Mr. Johnson proposes, which I can perhaps explain in this way: I should have had nothing to do with the design of the Central Park, or of

Prospect Park, had not Vaux invited me to join him in those works. But for his invitation I should not have been a landscape architect. I should have been a farmer. He was then already established as a landscape architect, having been a partner of Mr. Downing. I do not like to be given credit for the design of these works when he is not given quite equal credit. It is distinctly unjust that I should.

Then, to quite half my works my son John has contributed in an important degree. It is impossible to apportion credit, so much to one, so much to another, for the general result that may come from the striking together of two or more minds in prolonged, practical discussions. Consider this point with reference to Harry. You and others try to be just to him, but you cannot rightly give me the smallest credit for one part of a common work, to him for another part, and to John for a third part. Not one of us has done anything that the others have not helped him to do. In every one of our works there has been a merging of thought into thought, so that to differentiate individual originations is quite out of the question.

Nothing can be written on the subject with profit in my opinion in which extreme care is not taken to discriminate between what is meant in common use of the words garden, gardening, gardener, and the art which I try to pursue. I am tired almost to death in struggling with the confusion of mind which is manifest in this confusion of terms, and I know that the fight is not yet fairly begun and that I shall die before it does begin.

Sincerely & gratefully Yours

Fred^k Law Olmsted

To Mariana Griswold Van Rensselaer

June 18, 1893

Dear Mrs Van Rensselaer;

I write in this way because I am in bed. Excuse me. I always have to spend at least a day or two in bed when I come here. It seems to be a matter of acclimation to the rarified air of the mountain region. The trouble this time is mild but enforces caution if I am to reach Cambridge on the 28th. It is a notable circumstance that at the same time that Burnham and I go to Harvard to receive honors for our professions, Hunt goes to England to receive his medal.

The most interesting general fact of my life seems to me to be that it was not as a gardener, a florist, a botanist or as one in any way specially interested in plants and flowers as such or specially susceptible to the beauty of flowers and plants that I was drawn to the work which is to give me the Harvard distinction. (I am ignorant and unwise and inept in that field and largely dependent on others) The root of all my good work is an early *respect* for, regard and enjoyment of scenery (the word tells much better of the fact than landscape) and extraordinary opportunities of cultivating susceptibility to the power of scenery. Not so much grand or sensational scenery as scenery of a more domestic order. Scenery to be looked upon contemplatively and which is provocative of musing moods. I think that I was largely educated for my profession by the enjoyment which my father and mother (step-mother) took in loitering journeys; in afternoon drives on the Connecticut meadows. This at first, helping to give me a bent, which, when book study was restricted by the trouble of my eyes, and when I had chanced to get some reading of Price and Gilpin, led me, in long and leisurely tramps and visits to friends on farms, to take a more intelligent, discriminating, analytical and cultivated interest in such scenery. So the habit thus begun to be formed led me, when I came to visit parks & promenades abroad to view them, for a time, less from the point of view of a member of society, than as an amateur of scenery and so to look upon trees and plants and weeds less from regard to their beauty as such, than from regard to their value as elements of compositions of scenery. To look upon roads and walks in parks, correspondingly, as [...] according to their [...] through the use of which scenery was to be enjoyed. I believe that I have before said something about this. I am inclined to urge it because so rarely do people discriminate between a love of nature, such as be shown in admiration of flowers in a vase, or even in admiration for a *hortus siccus* or a botanic garden, and a love of nature such as used to lead my father and mother to take quiet drives upon meadow and wood land roads, for the most part regarding the scenery silently and never in a way to lead to exclamations—My mother, by the way, used to have a very unusual number of wild plants in her garden, both bushes and herbs, gathered with her own hands, sometimes with my help, when I was a very small boy. She regularly carried a basket and a trowel for gathering plants, in our journeyings.

I have often thought there was less regard for scenery and consequently for landscape architecture now than then, and been inclined to trace the loss to modern methods of travel. A man in a hurry; a man moving fast, cannot enjoy scenery contemplatively. Scenery is enjoyed not because it is in itself beautiful but because contemplating it quietly the mind is led into a musing mood—a poetic mood, perhaps. Modern means of travel are most unfavorable to the enjoyment of scenery. The longer one lives in a place, the more he becomes accustomed to its scenery & to enjoy it without thinking or talking about it, the more influence it has upon him.

I am not disposed to under-value the scientific or the "practical" side of the profession. But in seeking for a reason why Harvard and why the Century should do what is proposed, it seems to me that it must be found in the fact of a cultivated sensitiveness to the sentiment of scenery, and that the value of any biography of F.L.O. must turn on the manner and degree in which it draws attention to the class of circumstances by which in early life he was led to look for his pleasure largely to leisurely quiet, unsystematic familiar intercourse with natural scenery. I do not express my idea quite correctly. I cannot. That is where I fail. That, if you get the idea by review of the facts in which it lies, is what you can do so much better. But I may suggest it again in this way. I have not been a man of leisure, have not been a contemplative man (in the way of Isaac Walton) with regard to matters of art and literature, but I was so placed and circumstanced that with reference to scenery I was a man of leisure and was indolently contemplative at a period of life when most men are held very closely to the study of books or scientific observation.

I don't like to be talking so much of myself. I do so only that you may better see how in the guise of a biographical statement, you can educate the public to a better understanding of what the art in its essence is, that I profess; a love for and intelligent cultivated regard for scenery—commonly called with danger of a confusion of ideas—landscape. I purposely do not say "natural scenery," because the association of farm houses and barns, of smoke and roads, and the planted elms of village streets and door yards with natural elements of scenery was an essential element of that of which my early life was an unconscious study. Herein lies the lesson that I would have you teach, that study and industry are not all that are wanted for education.

But of course the more important end is to increase the respect of the Am^n public for the art—to show that it is an Art, and that appreciation of and power to work in it is not an accident of birth; that evy man does not possess it, and that those qualities & habits by means of which success in the accumulation of wealth & social & political strength—those of the practical man, whether banker or alderman, are not the qualities that shd give them the confidence so many are disposed to use, in overruling & superceding those of an artist.

The main question is: Should L. Architecture be regarded as an art and a profession, or as a matter of common sense in wh. one man's ideas are of equal weight with another's? The less you make of me, except as a text, the more of the essence of the art, and the need of the profession in American Society & civilization the better—

Sincerely Yours

Fred^k Law Olmsted—

"MEN OF PARISIAN TRAINING AND ASSOCIATIONS":
MARCH 1895

To William A. Stiles

March 10, 1895

Dear Stiles:—

I have considered that you probably determined your course after consultation with Vaux, and have therefore felt freer than I otherwise should to follow you in declining to serve on the Committee, but I came to the conclusion to do so with some reluctance and hesitation, because of the fear that the result would be a Committee essentially packed against natural landscape and against Vaux, and having the doubt whether a minority of such a Committee sustaining Vaux might not have weight in forming public opinion.

It makes me grind my teeth to see how Vaux is treated. But, the harder it is, the more expedient it is, to keep one's temper in anything that is to come before the public.

White and those who follow him are sincere and unquestioningly strong in their convictions. They are even *fanatical*. Vaux and I have had to contend with men of like convictions before. In the original Park Board Commissioner Dillon represented them. It might be worthwhile to rake up his demonstration against our plan, and his demand for a broad avenue entering the park at the middle of the south end and going straight to the reservoir regardless of topographical obstacles. His plan for the purpose was sent to the newspapers, and the Tribune editorially favored it. Thereupon I invited Raymond of the Times and Dana to breakfast with me. I seated them at table in a tent set on a grand rock in the Ramble, right on the line of the proposed avenue. When they were smoking I asked them to look southward and consider what destruction even of existing natural beauty; what excessive belittling of the already too petty scenery, the proposition meant. They at once both confessed that they had not realized its import, and if they did not both come out against it publicly, they at least ceased to favor it. It was a case of natural eloquence versus grandiloquence. About 1868, after the lower park had been fully blocked out and planted, Dillon again moved in the Board of the Park Commission for the construction of a broad Central Avenue between 59th Street and the Reservoir. His resolution was referred to me and I wrote a report on the subject. His proposition had in it the making of all the rest of the park a decorative attachment to a grand central place of assembly; a Champs Elysées. That would have made it an affair of the south of Europe where there can be no turf, and where natural landscape is rightly made subordinate to the stateliness of an effect essentially architectural; an intensification and aggrandizement of urban art rather than a means of recreation from the town; any broad rural effect being considered out of place and anacronistic.

The proposition was referred to me and again I reported against it and it was rejected, Dillon himself acknowledging that after the progress that had been made in working out a radically different motive, it would, directly and indirectly, cost too much, but not abandoning his view, which was, essentially, that an Alameda or a Champs Elysées was a more desirable means of recreation for the people of a city than a place of rural character.

Mind you, I am not in hot contention with this view. What I am fighting is a *weak, fragmentary and vaccilating* compromise between two leading general motives. Such artificial elements as are necessary to the convenience of public use in a park I believe in making, and sometimes I think it best to display and aggrandize the display of them. But I would make them distinctly as means for the better enjoyment of natural scenery where I well could.

Now I want you to take my assurance that there is a strenuous fight coming on between those of our side and those who are disposed to revise every body of public land that has been laid out regardfully of natural beauty with the object of transforming it as far as possible into a field of architectural beauty. There is to be a strong and able, organized, systematic and methodic renaissantic movement in this direction. It is already afoot; not perhaps consciously to all those engaged in it, but to certain of the leaders, I believe, it is consciously so, and that it is to be advanced with deliberate campaigning, plotting, strategy and tactics. We are and have been this past year, just as distinctly engaged with it in Brooklyn Park, for example, as if war had been formally declared; nay, as if we were engaged in an actual assault upon an entrenched position which Stanford White had been, has been, and is now, month after month, building in the single Brooklyn Commissioner's mind. That is to say Stanford White has been and is trying to establish the rule of motives that are at war with those that ruled in the original laying out of Brooklyn Park. He distinctly hates these older motives. He would at least, now that so much has been established in the spirit of the original design, get the Commissioner to make the Park an incongruous hybrid between that which was aimed at in this design and that which would be aimed at in such a design as a French architect would have made early in the century, introducing sentimental passages of "Nature," like that attempted at Petit Trianon, but making them secondary, and as interludes of efforts approaching the ruling Versailles character. Of course this is theory and conjecture. It is not an assertion. It is the only way that I have been able to imagine by which his course can be explained. And in certain lines he is gifted. The talent, even the literary talent, which he and those with him, can apply to their purpose, is not to wisely be underrated.

I want to write a great deal more; feeling that in what I have written no justice has been done the subject or to my feelings, but I am pressed with other duties. You can show this to Prof. Sargent if you think best. It is time that we, who are essentially of one faith in this matter, however we may differ among ourselves, should be closing our ranks and be moving more warily than we have been. We have an organized enemy before us, strong in its convictions, able, proud even to superciliousness, confident and enthusiastic. They have struck down Vaux and are doing their best to kill him in the name of the Lord and of France. They are strong; they are sincere; they are confident; they are mostly cultivated gentlemen to be dealt with courteously, but they are doctrinaires and fanatics and essentially cockneys, with no more knowledge of nor interest in real rurality than most men of Parisian training and associations.

Reading over what Rick has type-written for me, I am dissatisfied with it, but if you will translate the metaphoric into plain language you will have what I have wanted to say *in the main*. You know that these men of the enemy are my friends; that here and at other points (at Chicago, for example) I have managed to work in hearty, active, friendly cooperation with them. A sufficient explanation of the apparent anomaly is that there is a place for everything. At Chicago we sought for a site, first, that would be favorable to formality and architectural gardening. There was none available. Taking the site that in all other respects was most suitable we tried to reconcile a picturesque motive of natural scenery with the formal stateliness that our architectural associates were determined to have in the buildings, and we succeeded to their satisfaction. The site was not ill-adapted to the purpose. Here, again, at Biltmore we have managed to reconcile the requirements of Hunt in his renaissance buildings with a generally picturesque natural character in the approaches, and in the main landscape features; introducing more or less formal spurs and outworks of architectural motive for that purpose. And Hunt has accepted our way of doing it, and even, at my request, has aided in marrying the two motives, extending, modifying and altering architectural outworks at my suggestion. Getting well away from the transcendent architectural features there is not in the whole 9000 acres a suggestion of any other than natural landscape motives. There has not been the slightest break of harmony between us. He has accepted every single suggestion that I have made and I have accepted every single suggestion that he has made and I do not think that in the end there will be a note of discord in the combined work. (I am not quite certain. There are one or two points about which I am nervous and this is because I am not quite at home when required to merge stately architectural work into natural or naturalistic landscape work. I am taking heavier risks in this respect here than I did at Chicago. But as yet nobody seems aware of it but myself.) I write as if I were doing it but not a step has been taken here, nor was there one at Chicago which was settled without thorough discussion and cordial agreement with my partners before engaging with Hunt.

As soon as you can you must be prepared to come here and go over it with me and give us the benefit of your criticism. When do you look for a vacation next? There are points—the flower garden, for instance—where we distrust ourselves. And there is one point, at least, where I hardly dare undertake what I am nevertheless contemplating. I shall probably come here next in May or June.

Very Truly Yours,

Fred[k] Law Olmsted

A Homestead;
Its Constituent Parts and Essentials

The word homestead is derived from two roots, both fertile of words. Thus hatch, hedge, hold (of a ship), hat, hide and holy (set apart), all growing from the same root with home, alike carry as an essential sense the idea of shelter or defence by a method which involves seclusion. Home is that which does this for a family. Stead is from a root which is the parent of stow (to fit a thing snugly to a place), stop, stay, stand, stable, stall, settle, and stake, all conveying the idea of attachment to a place. As an active verb, it means to support, to assist. Thus Shakespeare says, "It nothing steads us."

A homestead then is a house together with so much of the ground about as, with the house, forms a constituent part of the seclusion and abode of a family.

A homestead then is a place prepared and furnished suitably for the seclusion, shelter and staying of a family. Not the mere shelter from the elements alone of a family, but all that which being of a fixed rather than a moveable character pertains to the locality of which such a shelter is the centre and supplements what it provides for the comfort of the family staying thereat.

It is not necessary that the means of maintaining the family with food and clothing, whether in a farm or shop, should be a part of the homestead. A seafaring man may have a homestead for his family. That which produces, increases or maintains the means of supporting a home is not an essential part of a homestead. The farm or garden or shop which in some cases is attached to a homestead may be laid waste and entirely removed or disconnected with it and the homestead remains unimpaired, or even be the better for it. All conveniences for mere commercial gain should therefore be considered apart from the homestead. But as supplies of various kinds—more especially of food—are essential to the maintenance of a homestead, it follows that a homestead cannot be conceived of apart from its outlets and inlets, including those belonging to others in common with it, and generally in law what is called the public

road is not possessed wholly by the public; every householder
or homestead holder has a special right of property in that part
of it which adjoins his private land. It cannot be closed against
him. It is therefore a part of his homestead.

The first question is, what is essential to be associated (in
contiguity) with the shelter of a house. Vegetables and fruit can
be brought in from a distance; so can flowers. These therefore
may be put away till other things are secured. What is wanted
that can't be in a house? Flowers can be brought in; trees and
turf cannot; open air cannot. We must have facilities for enjoying open air outside.

Most of us or of our fathers, on emigration were advanced
in but a comparatively small degree, if at all, above the savage
condition in this respect. See how the laboring, servile and
vagabond classes of the Old World (and not one in ten thousand of us came from any other classes) live at the present day,
and it will be obvious that this could be no otherwise. In the last
centuries when most of our parents were brought out, the life
of the great body of the people of the old countries was greatly
less civilized than at present, and pioneer life is by no means
favorable to direct advance in refinement, only sometimes to the
formation of a strong common sense base for refinement. The
true and last and only safe measure therefore of real prosperity
in the United States is a measure of the willingness of the people
to expend study and labor with reference to delicate distinctions
in matters of form and color. The test of prosperity is advance
in civilization; the test of civilization is delicacy. The test of delicacy in civilized progress, I may add, is whatever shows ability
to finely see truth and to follow it in an exact way.

Therefore, it is not enough that a house affords a shelter for
a family from rain and wind and sun, which bunting off of a
certain class of animal discomforts is all that a savage requires of
a house; nor is it enough that it should be adapted to protect its
inmates from many other discomforts which those who live in
wigwams accept meekly, such as dirt, darkness and vermin, for
instance. Nor is it enough that means for regulating the degree
of temperature and of light in its different parts, advantages
of neatness, conveniences for association and for retirement
and other provisions against discomfort should exist in it. The
slightest apprehension of discomfort from the neglect of such

provisions should not be possible. The existence of such provisions, therefore, should be made obvious with scrupulous truthfulness, not with ostentation or extravagance,—that is to say,
but with delicacy and refinement, which is to say, in the way of
truth followed with painstaking delicacy. But then, though this
is much and any appearance of design or effort of decoration
without it is childish folly—in no better taste than the gewgaws
hung from the nose of a filthy savage—it is not all; it is not even
civilization; it is merely release from barbarism. Active, positive
civilization comes with the addition of the positive pleasures
which are given by a nice adaptation of the forms and lines and
colors of all the parts and which are secured at no sacrifice of the
finest truth, of none of the requirements of negative comfort
before named, and at no extravagant cost, or sacrifice of other
desirable things of any kind whatever, but which add *positive*
beauty to these. That is to say, beauty which is good in itself and
not beauty the good of which is dependent on its fitness for or
expression of something else that is good, as light, air, warmth,
and so on. However rich a man may be by comparison with a
savage, a peasant or a slave, who is not able to desire, to pay for,
and to enjoy this in his homestead, he is an utterly poor man
measured by a truly civilized standard of wealth.

In all Fifth Avenue there are not a score of homes the out-
sides of which do not fail not merely of beauty but which do
not fail even in that without which the effort at beauty is nasty,
honesty of expression. Hundreds of farm houses, which have
cost not so many thousands as these tens of thousands, show
at least this degree of wealth, and to this degree of wealth positive beauty might be added, did their owners but care enough
for it, at a cost of a tenth part of what has been wasted in barbarous decorations laid upon the brown stone skins of these
metropolitan wigwams. And no patriot should flatter himself
that they are better within. No, the true wealth of our country
is in its homesteads. The rest is mainly rubbish, the more barbarous for the deceitful glaze which much of it has. And the
field of investment in which the real wealth of the country can
be most rapidly multiplied is this field of the improvement of
homesteads. The way in which investment can alone be made
in it is by the expenditure of sincere, patient, painstaking study,
in the consideration of what is desirable, and of the means of

procuring that which is desirable. There can be no question in the mind of a competent student that every dollar that is earned in the United States would be worth many times as much as it is, if our people were able to exercise their common sense in a fine way with as much ability as they do exercise it in a coarse way. Delicacy is not in great demand, nor is it much cultivated in the management of corn, tobacco, wheat or cotton crops, in fatting swine, beef or mutton, in mining, in lumbering or in many other undertakings wherein we are consequently successful and make money. Thus while the average money wages of a man in such employments are much greater than in Europe, and capital is accumulated several times more rapidly, a given amount of money is commonly exchanged in Europe for, a vastly greater amount of comfort, because positive comfort, in distinction from mere brute satisfaction, is dependent mainly on the satisfaction of delicate requirements, and our means of education, extraordinary as they are up to a certain point, are so poor beyond that point that we generally blunder in a most distressing way in trying to buy a small degree of positive comfort. This is particularly the case in respect to all homestead comfort.

Chronology

1822–25   Born Frederick Law Olmsted on April 26, 1822, in Hartford, Connecticut, the first child of John Olmsted, a prosperous dry-goods merchant, and Charlotte Hull, the daughter of a farmer. Brother John Hull Olmsted is born three-and-a-half years later, on September 2, 1825.

1826–27   Mother dies on February 28, 1826, of an overdose of laudanum; father marries Mary Ann Bull in April of the next year, and sends Frederick to Hartford "dame's schools." Father and stepmother will have six children: Charlotte (1828–1832), Mary (1832–1875), Bertha (1834–1926), Owen (1836–1838), Ada Theodosia (1839–1846), and Albert Henry (1842–1929).

1828–30   Spends four months with uncle Owen Pitkin Olmsted in Geneseo, New York; they visit Niagara Falls. In November, 1828, is sent to study with the Reverend Zolva Whitmore in North Guilford, Connecticut, where he boards for just under a year. Subsequently enrolls in Hartford Grammar School.

1831–36   Beginning in May 1831, attends Ellington High School in Ellington, Connecticut, living with a local minister; father withdraws him after a teacher punishes him severely. In October becomes one of four pupils of the Reverend Joab Brace of Newington, Connecticut, remaining for four-and-a-half years. Suffers from a severe case of sumac poisoning and persistent eye troubles; is advised to avoid close work. Returns to Hartford Grammar School in September 1836.

1837–40   Travels to Andover, Massachusetts, in November 1837, to learn the surveyor's trade with Frederick A. Barton. Vacations with family in the White Mountains of New Hampshire. Visits Washington, D.C., with father. Continues as Barton's student until April 1840, following him to Collinsville, Connecticut. Four months later, takes job as a clerk for a New York dry-goods importer.

1841–42   Lives in Brooklyn. Learns French, commonly spoken where he works. Leaves New York in March 1842, returning to

Hartford. Takes music and dancing lessons. With brother John, sails a small boat down the Connecticut River to the sea. Visits brother at Yale.

1843   On April 23 departs for China aboard the bark *Ronaldson* as an apprentice seaman. Arrives at Whampoa Beach, near Canton (Guangzhou), on September 8, remaining until the end of the year.

1844   The *Ronaldson* returns to New York on April 15. Recuperates from the voyage over the summer, in Hartford. Decides on a career as a gentleman farmer and takes an interest in agricultural science; lives and works for four months on a farm in Cheshire, Connecticut, owned by his uncle David Brooks.

1845   During the summer, studies farming with Joseph Welton in Waterbury, Connecticut. In the fall, spends time at Yale with brother John. Joins brother's circle of friends, including Charles Loring Brace, Frederick Kingsbury, and Charles Trask; they claim him as an "honorary member of the class of '47." Audits Benjamin Silliman's scientific lectures. Encouraged by pious stepmother, attends revival meetings in New Haven.

1846   Spends six months as an apprentice at Fairmount, George Geddes's prize-winning farm near Camillus, New York, to learn new agricultural methods. Visits the offices of *The Cultivator*, where he meets Andrew Jackson Downing, a prominent young writer on landscape gardening and domestic architecture. During the summer, sees Niagara Falls, Montreal, Quebec, and Lake Champlain with father and brother; reads Thomas Carlyle's *Sartor Resartus*. In November, with $4,000 from his father, purchases a small, rocky farm on Sachem's Head, a peninsula in Long Island Sound near the town of Guilford, Connecticut.

1847   Moves to Sachem's Head in February, living in a small farmhouse with two hired hands and their families and his two dogs, Neptune and Pepper. Family vacations at Sachem's Head House, a nearby resort hotel. In August, writes to *The Horticulturist*, edited by Downing, with questions about the care of fruit trees in coastal areas. Buys apple and quince trees; harvests onions, potatoes, and turnips.

1848   In March, moves to a larger farm on Staten Island, overlooking Raritan Bay; he later names it Tosomock. His aunt Maria, with maids and a young manservant, keeps house; six fieldhands and other occasional laborers help work the land. Family begins regular summer visits; brother and friends arrive on weekends. Socializes with prominent neighbors including William Cullen Bryant and publisher George Palmer Putnam. Grows fruit trees, especially French pears, for the nursery trade—a more lucrative business than food crops.

1849   Becomes corresponding secretary of the Richmond County Agricultural Society; in December, publishes an "Appeal to the Citizens of Staten Island," encouraging participation.

1850   Sails for Liverpool with his brother and Charles Loring Brace, arriving in late May. Walks through rural England, and travels in France, Belgium, Holland, Germany, Ireland, and Scotland; meets farmers and nurserymen. Returns to New York at the end of October.

1851   In May, article on "The People's Park at Birkenhead, Near Liverpool" appears in *The Horticulturist* (under the pseudonym "Wayfarer"). Neighbor George Putnam encourages him to turn his English letters and diaries into a book. In August is formally engaged to Emily Baldwin Peters, daughter of a Hartford politician, but she soon breaks the engagement off; father notes his son "seems like a man who has thrown off a tremendous weight." Publishes "A Voice from the Sea"—about the hard lives of working seamen and the need for reform—in the *American Whig Review*.

1852   Wins "First Prize for Pears" at a Staten Island agricultural fair, and writes on pears for *The Horticulturist*. Publishes *Walks and Talks of an American Farmer in England*, the first volume in February and the second in October. (The latter he dedicates to Andrew Jackson Downing, who had died in a steamboat accident a few months before.) Visits Fourierist utopian community at Red Bank, New Jersey, in July, contributing an account of his visit (by "An American Farmer") to the *New-York Daily Tribune*. Is recommended by Charles Loring Brace to the editor of the *New-York Daily Times*, then searching for a correspondent to report from the South. Sets off in December, traveling through Virginia, the Carolinas, Georgia, Alabama, Louisiana, and

Mississippi. Hopes to "make a valuable book of observations on Southern Agriculture & general economy as affected by Slavery."

1853 First of fifty letters on "The South" appears in the *Times* on February 16 (under the pseudonym "Yeoman"). Returns from his first southern trip in April. Embarks on a second, with brother, in November. In Nashville meets Samuel Perkins Allison, a "good specimen of the first class gentleman of the South" and classmate of his brother, who challenges his understanding of the differences between northern and southern society.

1854 Series on "The South" concludes on February 13; "A Tour in the Southwest" begins on March 6 and continues through June 7. Spends time in "very agreeable" German-immigrant settlements around San Antonio, based on free labor; hopes for the creation of a free state or states in western Texas. Returns from second trip in August after an absence of almost nine months. In October, helps to raise funds to aid the *San Antonio Zeitung*, an antislavery paper whose editor C. D. Adolph Douai he and his brother had met in Texas.

1855 Moves to New York City, becoming a partner in publishing firm Dix, Edwards, & Company. Joins *Putnam's Monthly Magazine* as managing editor. Tours New England visiting potential contributors including Emerson, Irving, Longfellow, and Stowe; solicits work from Melville and Thoreau; meets Thackeray, then lecturing in the United States. ("If we can get the writers," he tells his father, "there is little fear that we shall get the readers.") Corresponds with Edward Everett Hale, a leader of the Emigrant Aid Society, in support of antislavery settlement in Kansas. Raises money to help purchase munitions for free-soil settlers in Lawrence, Kansas; negotiates with arms dealers and consults an expert in guerrilla warfare to select appropriate weapons.

1856 *A Journey in the Seaboard Slave States* is published in January to laudatory reviews but disappointing sales. (Harriet Beecher Stowe praises the book, "written in a style so lively and with so much dramatic incident as to hold the attention like a work of fiction." English critics review a London edition widely and warmly.) In February, with half-sister Mary, sails to London, where he seeks relationships for his firm with British publishers. With half-sister Bertha and friend Sophia Hitchcock, tours the French Riviera, Italy, and central Europe. In August, accompanies father, stepmother, and half-brother Albert in travel to Germany. Returns to New York in October. Worried about the conduct of his partners in the publishing business, considers resigning from Dix, Edwards, & Co.; is persuaded not to when new partners invest in the firm, but reduces the extent of his managerial involvement.

1857   *A Journey through Texas* appears in January; based on his travel journals, it is finished and edited by his brother John. Strongly opposes "any further extension or annexation of slavery" in its introduction. Warns in another introduction (to Thomas Gladstone's *The Englishman in Kansas*, which he persuades Dix, Edwards & Co. to publish) that "this Union is bound straight to disastrous shipwreck" over the issue of slavery. In April, Dix, Edwards' creditors force his partners out of the business; he too resigns three months later. Publishes a series of letters in the *New-York Daily Tribune*, "The Southerners at Home." In August meets Charles Wyllys Elliott, recently appointed to the Board of Commissioners of New York's Central Park, who encourages him to apply for the position of superintendent. Seeks the support of prominent friends and acquaintances including William Cullen Bryant, credited with first proposing the idea of a New York park in 1844. The Board solicits park designs in a public competition. Named superintendent on September 11, prepares reports on park drainage and tree planting that impress the commissioners, who increase his authority and salary. Approached by Calvert Vaux—an English architect who had been working in America since 1850, with Andrew Jackson Downing—decides to collaborate on a design for the park. On November 24, brother John Hull Olmsted dies of tuberculosis in Nice.

1858   Meets with Vaux in the evenings to finish their competition entry, the "Greensward Plan," which they submit at the beginning of April. A month later, after many rounds of voting, their plan wins. In mid-May, is promoted to superintendent and architect-in-chief, and hires Vaux as his associate; the park's chief engineer, Col. Egbert Viele, is dismissed. Enlists literary friends in a successful campaign to resist changes to the Greensward Plan proposed by

Commissioners Robert Dillon and August Belmont. More than 2,300 artisans, gardeners, engineers, and laborers are at work in the park by the end of the year. Hires William H. Grant as superintending engineer, Jacob Wrey Mould as Vaux's assistant, Ignaz Pilat as foreman of gardeners, and George Edwin Waring Jr. as agricultural engineer.

1859   Organizes a park police force and writes park regulations. On June 13, marries Mary Perkins Olmsted, his brother's widow, adopting her three children, John (b. 1852), Charlotte (b. 1855), and Owen (b. 1857). They move into an apartment in a former convent in the park; Vaux and his family occupy another convent building. On September 28, sails alone to Europe; visits parks, country estates, arboretums, and zoological gardens in England, France, and Belgium, returning in mid-December. Shortly before his departure, friend Andrew Haswell Green is appointed Central Park comptroller.

1860   Son John Theodore Olmsted is born on June 14, but lives only two months. In July, with Vaux, is hired by the Central Park Commission to propose a plan for the development of northern Manhattan. *A Journey in the Back Country* appears in August to substantial praise in the northern states and England. Breaks his leg in a riding accident, acquiring a permanent limp. On point of honor, assumes $8,000 in debt in the wake of the bankruptcy of Dix, Edwards' successor firm Miller & Curtis; signs over his royalties to *A Journey in the Back Country* in partial payment.

1861   Collaborates with Vaux and others on designs for the grounds of Hartford Retreat for the Insane. On January 22, frustrated by Andrew Green's micromanagement, offers resignation to the Board of Commissioners; they offer compromises and persuade him to remain. In February, hires Daniel R. Goodloe to help prepare an abridged edition of his three travel volumes; titled *The Cotton Kingdom*, it is published in London in November. Soon after the attack on Fort Sumter, begins drilling a home guard of Central Park volunteers; imagines a wartime role for himself as superintendent of contrabands, or freed slaves. ("I have, I suppose, given more thought to the special question of the proper management of negroes in a state of limbo between slavery & freedom than any one else in the country," he writes Henry W. Bellows.) In early June, the Board of Commissioners sides with Green on questions of fiscal authority. At the end of the month, accepts an offer from Bellows to become executive secretary of the newly formed United States Sanitary Commission, an officially sanctioned volunteer relief organization. Obtaining a leave of absence at half-pay from his park responsibilities, heads to Washington, D.C. Inspects troops encamped around the city; appalled at their disorganized state, official obstruction, and the high cost of living in Washington, wishes privately he had not taken the position. After the Union defeat at Bull Run, writes a sharply critical "Report on the Demoralization of the Volunteers." (Fearing its effects on morale, the commission chooses not to publish it, but they redouble their philanthropic efforts and begin to prepare for a long war.) Oversees the growth of Sanitary Commission staff, coordinating volunteer organizations and donations and establishing field depots. In October, with other members of the commission, fails in an attempt to convince President Lincoln to replace the surgeon general, Clement A. Finley; successfully deflects public criticism of the organization with a "Report to the Secretary of War" about its activities. Daughter Marion Olmsted is born on October 28. Returns occasionally to New York to attend to Central Park business. In December, works on legislation designed to reform the Medical Bureau, passed the next April.

1862   In April, learns that two positions he had hoped for—one as New York's street commissioner, another overseeing former slaves on plantations taken from the Confederacy—have both been given to others. Works on Sanitary Commission plans for a fleet of more than a dozen ships, the Hospital Transport Service, taking the *Wilson Small* as his headquarters. In early June, after the Battle of Fair Oaks (Seven Pines), the flotilla takes on thousands of wounded men. ("The horror of war can never be known but on the field," he writes his wife. "It is beyond, far beyond all imagination.") In poor health, spends time with family on Staten Island; with his friend Frederick Knapp in Walpole, New Hampshire; and with Sanitary Commission member Cornelius Agnew in Saratoga Springs, New York. In October, family moves to Washington.

1863   Differs with Sanitary Commission board members on question of independence of its branches in the west. Some members worry about his habits and health. ("He works like a dog all day and sits up nearly all night," George Templeton Strong reports in his diary; "doesn't go home to his family . . . for five days and nights altogether, works with a steady, feverish intensity till four in the morning, sleeps on a sofa in his clothes, and breakfasts on *strong coffee and pickles!!!*"). Tours commission operations in Pittsburgh, Cincinnati, and St. Louis and visits Army of the Cumberland at Murfreesboro, Tennessee. With Edwin L. Godkin, makes plans to publish "a first class weekly paper," later named *The Nation*. Resigning from the Sanitary Commission, sails alone from New York in September to take a more lucrative position as superintendent of the Mariposa Estate, a large gold-mining property in the foothills of the Sierra Nevada. On the way, delights in Panama's tropical foliage ("the reality far beyond my imagination," he writes Ignaz Pilat, Central Park's chief gardener). Arrives at estate in mid-October via San Francisco; warns wife she "must be prepared for a very hard life" there. Visits Mariposa Big Tree Grove.

1864   Finds the estate's financial situation much worse than previously represented. Reduces miners' wages, and when they go on strike as a result, orders the strike suppressed by force. Family arrives in San Francisco in March. Visits site of Mountain View Cemetery, which he is invited to design, in Oakland. Spends summer riding, camping, and exploring with family; they tour Yosemite. In late September is appointed de facto chairman of a new Yosemite Valley commission, charged with its preservation. Hires geologist Clarence King to complete a boundary survey.

1865   Seeks new employment prospects as the Mariposa company proves unable to pay its creditors. Visits and purchases stock in nearby oil properties. Proposes a joint-stock company offering shares in a Sonoma Valley vineyard. Writes to the *San Francisco Daily Evening Bulletin* to advocate a "Great Park" for the city. Camps at Yosemite with his family and several commissioners in a party led by Speaker of the House Schuyler Colfax; submits plans for the preservation and maintenance of Yosemite to California legislature. Works on designs for the grounds of the College of California at Berkeley. Begins writing a book, never published, on "Society in the United States—the influence of pioneer-life—& of Democracy." Resigning Mariposa position, departs for New York on October 2. Resumes partnership with Calvert Vaux: they do business as Olmsted, Vaux & Company, Landscape Architects, serving once again as landscape architects to the Central Park Commission, and beginning work on plans for Prospect Park, in Brooklyn.

1866 Becomes associate editor of *The Nation*, probably contributing several unsigned articles, but resigns as work on Prospect Park plans intensifies. Settles with family at Clifton, Staten Island, commuting to Vaux's Manhattan office by ferry. In May, with Vaux, is formally appointed landscape architect for Prospect Park; superintends its construction beginning in July, overseeing a workforce ultimately numbering almost 2,000. Completes plans for the Massachusetts Agricultural College at Amherst and the Columbia Institution for the Deaf and Dumb (now Gallaudet University) in Washington, D.C. A son, unnamed, dies in infancy.

1867 In February joins the executive committee of the Southern Famine Relief Commission, helping to coordinate aid to the South. Visits Ithaca, New York, advising founders of Cornell University on plans for their new institution. Submits a design proposal for the renovation of Washington Park (now Fort Greene Park), in Brooklyn, and meets with the Newark Park Commission.

1868 Visits Buffalo, New York, in August, touring park sites and presenting proposals for an extensive park system, the firm's largest project to date. From Buffalo travels to Chicago, where he meets with the president of the Riverside Improvement Company to discuss plans and contract terms for the development of a new garden suburb.

1869 Describes Riverside as "the most interesting of all the undertakings we have been connected with." (It is also a "great speculation," which will ultimately involve the firm in legal disputes and for which they will receive far less compensation than they expect.) Recommends the construction of a parkway between the new development and the city. In August, meets with Vaux and others at Calvert House, near Niagara Falls, with the aim of preserving Niagara scenery.

1870 Submits plans for parks in New Britain, Connecticut, and Fall River, Massachusetts, and for the expansion of Amherst

College. Addresses Social Science Association at Lowell Institute on "Public Parks and the Enlargement of Towns." Son Henry Perkins Olmsted is born on July 24 (he is later renamed Frederick Law Olmsted Jr.). After the passage of a new city charter in New York, his authority over Central Park affairs is diminished and official position finally eliminated; publicly opposes the construction of a zoological garden in the park. Works on a regional plan for the Staten Island Improvement Commission.

1871   Reports that "preliminary construction" of Prospect Park is complete. Publishes designs for South Park in Chicago (now referred to separately as Jackson Park, Washington Park, and the Midway Plaisance). Plans park system for Hartford, Connecticut, and the grounds for the Buffalo State Asylum for the Insane, in the latter case collaborating with architect Henry Hobson Richardson. With the indictment of New York mayor William "Boss" Tweed, allies regain control of Central Park; Olmsted and Vaux become "Landscape Architects and General Superintendents." Describes aftermath of Chicago fire for readers of *The Nation*, in "Chicago in Distress."

1872   Publishes a "Prospectus of the New Suburban District of Tarrytown Heights," envisioning a new 900-acre subdivision in New York state. In May becomes acting president of the New York Department of Public Parks; works to repair the "great injury" done to Central Park during previous administrations. Over the summer, without his involvement, is nominated by a faction of the Republican Party as a vice-presidential candidate; immediately declines the nomination, but is "surprised & gratified that it is so well received." Partnership with Vaux is dissolved, on mutually agreeable terms, on October 18. Moves with family into a Manhattan brownstone, at 209 West Forty-Sixth Street.

1873   Father dies on January 25. In February, proposes a set of "Instructions to the Keepers of Central Park," reforming park policing; his reforms are attacked in the press, and in the wake of the controversy his authority over park police and other matters is curtailed. Offers to resign from park duties but board asks him to remain. Developer of Tarrytown Heights project declares bankruptcy. Suffers severe depression, unable to work for four months. Takes a long vacation trip through Canada.

1874   Named landscape architect to the United States Capitol; visits Washington and prepares plans for Capitol grounds. In November, submits designs for a new park at Mount Royal, Montreal.

1875   Recommendations for Riverside Park in upper Manhattan formally adopted in March. Offers a new street plan for Riverdale, north of New York City and newly annexed to it; replaces the grid system with a scheme designed to follow the "highly picturesque" local topography. Authority over Central Park gardeners is restored. Stepson John joins firm as draftsman.

1876   Reports on projects for Buffalo City Hall, a resort community on Lake Chautauqua, New York, a new capitol in Albany, and park sites in Boston (in the latter case making the first in a series of recommendations that will ultimately produce the city's "Emerald Necklace").

1877   Gives two lectures in Montreal on his vision and hopes for Mount Royal. At the end of the year, New York's park commissioners abolish his position. Though friends and prominent supporters protest, chooses not to fight the dismissal.

1878   Sails to England early in January; travels through England, the Netherlands, Belgium, Germany, Italy, and France, visiting zoos, gardens, and parks. In his absence, wife quarrels with Calvert Vaux over statements in the press that fail to credit Vaux as codesigner of Central Park. Returning to the United States, spends summer with his family in Cambridge, Massachusetts, at the home of E. L. Godkin. Submits preliminary scheme for a park in Boston's Back Bay fens, and is hired by the Boston park commission to proceed with detailed drawings. With Charles Sprague Sargent, Harvard professor of botany, lays out and helps to develop the collections of the Arnold Arboretum, in Boston; plans capitol grounds for Hartford and Albany. Stepdaughter Charlotte marries.

1879   Visits Niagara Falls in May with James T. Gardiner, director of the State Survey; they envision a reservation to protect the surrounding landscapes. Orchestrates a campaign to obtain international support for the falls.

1880   Enlists H. H. Richardson to design bridges for the Back Bay. Suggests the addition of the Muddy River and its wetlands to the Boston park system.

1881   New York governor Alonzo Cornell opposes efforts to purchase land around Niagara Falls. Moves with family to suburban Brookline, Massachusetts, renting out his New York house. Publishes *Mount Royal, Montreal,* a report on the mixed progress of his Montreal park plans and a defense of his original vision for the park. Stepson Owen sends telegram from Montana, where he runs a cattle ranch; in poor health, he dies before his brother John can bring him safely home. Makes recommendations for a new campus for the Lawrenceville School in New Jersey.

1882   Designs The Rockery, a war-memorial cairn, to be built alongside a new town hall in North Easton, Massachusetts. Publishes "Trees in Streets and Parks" in the *Sanitarian.* Spends two weeks in Detroit, where he discusses ideas for a park on Belle Isle, in the Detroit River, with the city park commissioner. Appears before a joint committee of Congress to describe his proposals for an extensive renovation of the Capitol grounds. Publishes pamphlet *The Spoils of the Park,* an account of corruption and political patronage in the management of Central Park. "I fear that its ruin is inevitable," he writes of the park to Charles Loring Brace.

1883   In the spring, begins renovations on a house in Brookline, "Fairsted"; it will serve as home and office. Is elected to the Saturday Club, which holds monthly dinners at the Palmer House in Boston. New York governor Grover Cleveland passes law authorizing the New York State Reservation at Niagara Falls. Theodore Roosevelt, a young New York state legislator, writes to praise *The Spoils of the Park,* and solicits advice on the reform of Central Park's governance and management. Stepdaughter Charlotte, suffering from mental illness, is institutionalized after the birth of her third child.

1884   Stepson John C. Olmsted is named a partner in the Olmsted firm; visits Detroit with him to work on park at Belle Isle. Henry Sargent Codman joins firm as apprentice.

1885   Works on designs for Franklin Park, in Boston. A site at the northern end of Riverside Park in Manhattan is chosen for the tomb of General Grant; though Olmsted worries the tomb "should not be an incident to a festive promenade," yields to the proposal and suggests Vaux be consulted.

1886　Is entreated by Henry Beekman, new president of New York's board of park commissioners, to return as manager of Central Park and other city parks. Considers the offer seriously but ultimately declines; relationship with Vaux, who suspects Olmsted of attempting to displace him, deteriorates in the wake of negotiations. Invited by Leland Stanford to design the grounds for a new university in Palo Alto, travels to California in August, accompanied by Henry Codman and son Frederick Jr. After a visit to the Mariposa sequoia grove, they tour Stanford's estate, dissuading him from the "New England scenery, New England turf and trees" he envisions for the arid site.

1887　Olmsted & Vaux's "General Plan for the Improvement of the Niagara Reservation" is published; they collaborate on a revised design for Morningside Park in upper Manhattan. Works with architect Richard Morris Hunt on a mausoleum for the Vanderbilt family at New Dorp, Staten Island. Travels again to Palo Alto; Stanford demands major changes to proposals for the university submitted by Olmsted and architect Charles Coolidge. ("The matter is not going well," Olmsted remarks in a private letter, "but not ruinously.")

1888　Offers financial support to the founders of *Garden and Forest: A Journal of Horticulture, Landscape Art, and Forestry*, William A. Stiles and Charles Sprague Sargent. In August, visits Lone Pine Mountain near Asheville, North Carolina, with George Washington Vanderbilt, a "delicate, refined, and bookish" multimillionaire who hopes to build a country estate on land he has acquired there. Encourages Vanderbilt to commit most of the property to forestry instead of farming or a park.

1889　Plans for an arboretum on Stanford campus rejected. Begins drawings for grounds at Vanderbilt's Biltmore, which he will call "a private work of very rare public interest." Selects site for main house, designed by Richard Morris Hunt, and designs formal gardens to complement it; devotes great attention to three-mile approach road to the house. Establishes a nursery on the grounds.

1890   Stanford's project manager dismisses Olmsted's field engineer over the summer and ceases reporting to Olmsted; failing in an appeal to have him reinstated, Olmsted withdraws from active participation in the building of the campus. Friend Charles Loring Brace dies on August 11. Travels to Chicago with Henry Codman, recently named a partner to the firm; they select a site beside Lake Michigan for the World's Columbian Exposition, scheduled to open three years later. Named consulting landscape architects, they open a Chicago office, and collaborating with fair director Daniel Burnham and his partner John Root produce a plan imagining a network of waterways and lagoons traversed by small boats. Continues frequent trips to Biltmore, Vanderbilt offering him the use of his private rail car, the *Swannanoa*.

1891   Develops a planting scheme for the exposition grounds; resists efforts to build on the naturalistic Wooded Island he has designed for the lagoons. Hires Gifford Pinchot to manage forestry at Biltmore.

1892   Travels to Biltmore, Knoxville, Louisville, and Rochester. In April, sails to Europe for a five-month stay with son and daughter. Inspects the site of the 1889 Exposition Universelle in Paris and chateaux in the Loire Valley; spends time in Paris with landscape architect Edouard André. In London, consults a specialist in nervous disorders, who recommends a rest cure.

1893   In March, former apprentice Charles Eliot joins firm, which becomes Olmsted, Olmsted, and Eliot. Attends opening of exposition on May 1, along with half a million others. Spends summer on Deer Isle, Maine, with wife and daughter Marion.

1894   Agrees to serve as consulting landscape architect for Prospect Park, hoping to restore features "wholly ruined" by neglect. Supports Vaux in debates over a plan to build a speedway along Harlem River Drive, in New York. ("It makes me grind my teeth to see how Vaux is treated," he writes privately.) Counsels son Frederick, hoping he will take over as head of firm.

1895   In May, at Biltmore, sits for a portrait by John Singer Sargent. Begins to notice clear signs of senile dementia; seeks son's help in making his "confusion" appear less conspicuous to others. ("I have rarely felt so little master of myself," he writes Frederick.) Condition worsens over the summer, on Deer Island, Maine; worries that partners are plotting an office "coup" against his interests. In October, doctors recommend treatment in England; sails with wife, daughter, and son the next month. Calvert Vaux drowns in Gravesend Bay, Brooklyn, but family withholds the news for several months, fearful of his reaction.

1896   Treatment in England fails to improve condition.

1897   Early in the year, moves into a house on Deer Island with wife Mary, who has planned its construction for his sake.

1898–   In September 1898, Mary unable to continue as his care-
1903   taker, is committed to McLean Asylum in Waverly, Massachusetts, for which he had selected the site a few years before. Firm becomes Olmsted Brothers. Dislikes his situation intensely, complains often about infirmities, and has few moments of lucidity. Dies on August 28, 1903, son Frederick at his bedside, Mary and stepson John having just departed. After a small private funeral service at Fairsted, is cremated, his ashes interred at Old North Cemetery in Hartford, Connecticut. Olmsted Brothers persists and prospers, completing unfinished projects, maintaining existing ones, and embarking on new ones; it ceased operation in 1980.

Note on the Texts

This volume contains 107 items written by Frederick Law Olmsted between 1843 and 1895, including public and private letters, newspaper and magazine articles, professional reports and memoranda, speeches, parts of an unfinished book, and other works. The texts of all of these items have been taken from the first ten volumes of *The Papers of Frederick Law Olmsted*, published by the Johns Hopkins University Press between 1977 and 2015. They are arranged in approximate chronological order of composition, with a few exceptions: some autobiographical pieces appear at the approximate date of the events they describe.

A wide variety of source material is gathered in *The Papers of Frederick Law Olmsted*, ranging from published works that Olmsted saw through the press to unfinished or fragmentary drafts in the hands of clerks or copyists. The editors of *The Papers* provide texts of these documents that are, as they put it, "as close to the original as possible without causing undue difficulty for the reader," emending only typographical errors in published works, inadvertently repeated words, certain habitual misspellings, missing apostrophes or awkward or unclear contractions, and punctuation where Olmsted's meaning would otherwise be unclear. In cases where words are missing or unintelligible in Olmsted's original manuscripts (or those written for him by a clerk), they supply the missing or unintelligible words in roman type in square brackets; the present volume accepts these conjectural readings and prints them without brackets. In cases where Olmsted cancelled a word or passage in his manuscripts, the editors print the cancelled material in bracketed italics; the present volume omits the cancelled material entirely.

The Notes to the present volume provide information about the publication history of those items that appeared in print during Olmsted's lifetime. They also describe two instances in which the texts given in *The Papers of Frederick Law Olmsted* have been taken from more than one source: his "Preliminary Report upon the Yosemite and Big Tree Grove," reconstructed from a fragmentary manuscript and a published newspaper article in the absence of a complete copy of Olmsted's original oral presentation; and his memorandum "To Gardeners," reconstructed from fragments of what are probably separate drafts of a presentation no longer known to exist in its finished form.

The list below gives the source of each item in the present volume within the individual volumes of *The Papers of Frederick Law Olmsted*, published in Baltimore by the Johns Hopkins University Press (Vol. I: *The Formative Years, 1822–1852*, Charles Capen McLaughlin, ed.; Charles E. Beveridge, assoc. ed. [1977]; Vol. II: *Slavery and the South, 1852–1857,* Charles E. Beveridge and Charles Capen McLaughlin, eds.; David Schuyler, asst. ed. [1981]; Vol. III: *Creating Central Park, 1857–1861,* Charles E. Beveridge and David Schuyler, eds. [1983]; Vol. IV: *Defending the Union. The Civil War and the U.S. Sanitary Commission, 1861–1863,* Jane Turner Censer, ed. [1986]; Vol. V: *The California Frontier, 1863–1865,* Victoria Post Ranney, ed.; Gerard J. Rauluk, assoc. ed.; Carolyn F. Hoffman, asst. ed. [1990]; Vol. VI: *The Years of Olmsted, Vaux & Company, 1865–1874,* David Schuyler and Jane Turner Censer, eds.; Carolyn F. Hoffman, assoc. ed.; Kenneth Hawkins, asst. ed. [1992]; Vol. VII: *Parks, Politics, and Patronage, 1874–1882,* Charles E. Beveridge, Carolyn F. Hoffman, and Kenneth Hawkins, eds.; Tina Hummel, asst. ed. [2007]; Vol. VIII: *The Early Boston Years, 1882–1890,* Ethan Carr, Amanda Gagel, and Michael Shapiro, eds. [2013]; Vol. IX: *The Last Great Projects, 1890–1895,* David Schuyler and Gregory Kaliss, eds.; Jeffrey Schlossberg, asst. ed. [2015]; Supplementary Series I: *Writings on Public Parks, Parkways, and Park Systems,* Charles E. Beveridge and Carolyn F. Hoffman, eds. [1997]):

Autobiographical Fragment B. I, 113–19.
To John Olmsted & Mary Ann Bull. I, 148–52.
To Maria Olmsted. I, 173–79.
The Real China. I, 187–90.
To John Hull Olmsted. I, 212–13.
To Charles Loring Brace. I, 221–23.
To Frederick Kingsbury. I, 275–77.
To Charles Loring Brace. I, 313–17.
The People's Park at Birkenhead, near Liverpool. Supplementary
    Series I, 69–75.
To Charles Loring Brace. I, 375–84.
The South. Number Seven. II, 103–10.
The South. Number Eight. II, 115–20.
The South. Number Nine. II, 121–25.
The South. Number Twenty-Eight. II, 182–87.
To Charles Loring Brace. II, 232–36.
The South. Number Forty-Seven. II, 247–54.
A Tour in the Southwest. Number Eight. II, 275–80.
Passages in the Life of an Unpractical Man. III, 84–90.
Description of a Plan for the Improvement of the Central Park,
    "Greensward." III, 119–51.
To Henry H. Elliott. III, 259–68.
Park. III, 346–59.
To Mary Perkins Olmsted. IV, 130–31.
from Report on the Demoralization of the Volunteers. IV, 162–67.

To Gen. Bela M. Hughes. VIII, 556–60.
To George Washington Vanderbilt. VIII, 680–96.
Governmental Preservation of Natural Scenery. VIII, 778–81.
To Robert Treat Paine. IX, 88–89.
To Archie Campbell Fisk. IX, 95–99.
To Lyman J. Gage. IX, 194–97.
To Charles A. Roberts. IX, 237–38.
To Clarence Pullen. IX, 287–89.
To Henry Van Brunt. IX, 294–97.
Memorandum As to What Is to Be Aimed At in the Planting of the District of the Chicago Exposition, as Proposed March, 1891. IX, 322–28.
To Randolph Ulrich. IX, 330–31.
To William James. IX, 359–63.
To William Robinson. IX, 564–65.
To Mariana Griswold Van Rensselaer. IX, 623–25.
To Mariana Griswold Van Rensselaer. IX, 653–55.
To William A. Stiles. IX, 905–8.
A Homestead; Its Constituent Parts and Essentials. IX, 982–85.

This volume presents the texts of the *Papers* chosen for inclusion here (with the two kinds of alterations mentioned above), but it does not attempt to reproduce features of that edition's typographic design, such as the display capitalization of chapter openings. The texts are reprinted without change, except for the correction of typographical errors. Spelling, punctuation, and capitalization are often expressive features, and they are not altered, even when inconsistent or irregular. The following is a list of typographical errors corrected, cited by page and line number: 4.33, moments; 11.33, miles); 27.6, 'spose; 80.5, legistation; 84.17, Grey.; 93.37, slighest; 116.32, overunning; 136.32 (and *passim*), Abbott; 163.21, McIntee; 164.28, (Elsey's); 167.24, their's.; 179.20, transportion,; 184.13 (and *passim*), Forster,; 185.25, Spaulding.; 190.37, altogether:; 219.19, exclusivly; 234.6, parvenu's;; 238.6, give; 245.37, writes."; 246.10, map."; 246.14, right."; 248.3, Garasche,; 253.33, Hurlbert; 274.37, Clancey; 275.31 (and *passim*), Fisher; 352.9, mineing; 353.6 (and *passim*), specemin; 353.39–375.23, indians; 359.4, priveledged; 360.37, itself;; 366.20, seperate; 380.2, (Presidential election),; 418.8, Fisk.; 420.18, tother; 436.31, production of; 441.28, Rumsay,; 483.20–21, compliment; 489.7, bear-garden; 520.17, *Dempker*; 530.9 (and *passim*), Greely; 533.8, Cochran; 564.14, Gardener's; 568.32, Argyle; 612.13, acqueduct; 613.28, A; 619.16, him.; 628.1, self-acting; 637.36–37, *right"* It; 647.33, than; 651.16, it's; 654.26, relived.; 654.30 (and *passim*), Douglass,; 654.35, grow.

Note on the Illustrations

estate, North Carolina, early 1890s. Courtesy of the National Park Service, Frederick Law Olmsted National Historic Site.

32. Olmsted, c. 1890. Courtesy Historic New England.

33. "Fairsted," Olmsted's home and office in Brookline, Massachusetts, photographed in 1904. Courtesy of the National Park Service, Frederick Law Olmsted National Historic Site.

Notes

In the notes below, the reference numbers denote page and line of this volume (the line count includes chapter headings but not blank lines). No note is made for material included in standard desk-reference works. Quotations from Shakespeare are keyed to *The Riverside Shakespeare*, ed. G. Blakemore Evans (Boston: Houghton Mifflin, 1974). For further information about Olmsted's life and works, and references to other studies, see *The Papers of Frederick Law Olmsted* (Baltimore: Johns Hopkins University Press, 1977–), the individual volumes of which are further described in the "Note on the Texts." See also Charles E. Beveridge and Paul Rocheleau, *Frederick Law Olmsted: Designing the American Landscape* (New York: Rizzoli, 1995); Morrison H. Heckscher, *Creating Central Park* (New York: Metropolitan Museum of Art, 2008); Melvin Kalfus, *Frederick Law Olmsted: The Passion of a Public Artist* (New York: New York University Press, 1990); Lucy Lawliss, Caroline Loughlin, and Lauren Meier, eds., *The Master List of Design Projects of the Olmsted Firm, 1857–1979* (Washington, D.C.: National Association for Olmsted Parks, 2008); Justin Martin, *Genius of Place: The Life of Frederick Law Olmsted* (Cambridge, MA: Da Capo, 2011); Witold Rybczynski, *A Clearing in the Distance: Frederick Law Olmsted and America in the 19th Century* (New York: Simon & Schuster, 1999); Elizabeth Stevenson, *Park Maker: A Life of Frederick Law Olmsted* (New York: Macmillan, 1977); and Cynthia Zaitzevsky, *Frederick Law Olmsted and the Boston Park System* (Cambridge: Harvard University Press, 1982).

The Library of America and the editor wish to thank Ethan Carr, Jane Turner Censer, Victoria Post Ranney, and David Schuyler for their advice and suggestions about the contents of this volume.

3.3 *Autobiographical Fragment B*] Olmsted probably wrote these posthumously titled reminiscences in the mid-1870s, as part of a book he envisioned but never completed on landscape design in the United States.

3.4 My father's father and two of my father's great uncles] Olmsted's grandfather was Benjamin Olmsted (1751–1832) and his great-uncles Epaphras Olmsted (c. 1742–1836) and Gideon Olmsted (c. 1749–1845).

3.11–12 their brother . . . Wallabout] Along with more than 10,000 others, Ezekiel Olmsted (1755–1782) died on one of the British prison ships in Wallabout Bay, near the present-day Brooklyn Navy Yard.

5.10–19 a poor scholar . . . education.] Jonathan Law (1784–1859), a lawyer who had served as Hartford's postmaster.

5.20–21 The other . . . calling.] Charles Hyde Olmsted (1798–1878), a cousin active in the Hartford Natural History Society.

6.23   a topographical engineer] Frederick Augustus Barton (1811–1881), a surveyor and divinity student with whom Olmsted lived and studied for a year beginning in November 1837.

6.33–34   Price, Gilpin, Shenstone and Marshall] Prominent English writers on landscape gardening Uvedale Price (1747–1829), William Gilpin (1724–1804), William Shenstone (1714–1763), and William Marshall (c. 1745–1818).

8.21   "Anjer"] A town in western Java on the Sunda Strait, frequented by vessels in the China trade; now more commonly spelled *Anyer.*

8.37   Cochin China] A region in the southernmost part of what is now Vietnam.

21.2   *The Real China*] Olmsted completed this short memoir in February 1856, intending it to appear in *Putnam's Monthly,* but his manuscript was misplaced and it went unpublished.

25.29   *John Hull Olmsted*] Olmsted's younger brother (1825–1857).

25.30   Chateau L'eau roche] From May 12 to August 13, 1845, Olmsted lived on a farm in Waterbury, Connecticut.

27.3   the boat] Olmsted and his brother often took their small sailboat out onto the Connecticut River and Long Island Sound.

27.25   *Charles Loring Brace*] Olmsted became friendly with Brace (1826–1890), his brother John's freshman-year roommate at Yale, during his visits to New Haven in 1842 and 1845. They remained lifelong correspondents.

27.31–32   Emma . . . and John] Charles Loring's younger sister Emma Brace (1828–1850) and Olmsted's brother John.

30.36   "liph,"] Eliphalet Terry (1826–1896), one of Brace's school friends.

31.7   *Frederick Kingsbury*] Olmsted met and became friendly with Kingsbury (1823–1910) at Yale, through his brother John.

31.8   Fairmount] A prize-winning farm near Camillus, New York, where Olmsted served as an apprentice in mid-1846, working for George Geddes (1809–1883).

31.24–25   Norton's farm . . . East Haven] John Treadwell Norton (1795–1869), of Farmington, and William Kneeland Townsend (1796–1849), of East Haven, had both advised Olmsted as he contemplated a career as a farmer.

31.36   Mrs. Baldwin] Emily Perkins Baldwin (1796–1874).

33.7–9   Sartor Resartus . . . "Everlasting No!"] In Book II, Chapter 7 of *Sartor Resartus* (1833–34) by Thomas Carlyle (1795–1881), the philosopher Diogenes Teufelsdröckh falls into a mood of skepticism and despair, animated by what he comes to refer to as "the EVERLASTING NO."

34.3–6 South side . . . Sachem's Head"] On March 5, 1845, Olmsted had moved from his farm on Sachem's Head, near Guilford, Connecticut, to another on Staten Island.

35.8 Drs. Taylor, Edwards] American theologians Nathaniel William Taylor (1786–1858) and Jonathan Edwards (1703–1758).

36.25–31 A Bishop . . . Christianity itself."] On January 10, 1847, at Norwich Cathedral, Edward Stanley (1779–1849), Bishop of Norwich, delivered a funeral sermon for an evangelical minister of the Society of Friends, Joseph John Gurney (1788–1847). Though Gurney was "not of our community" and did not subscribe to the Church of England's doctrinal thirty-nine articles, Stanley had no doubt of his salvation.

37.1–2 in Horace Greeley's shoes . . . Dr. Taylor's.] Olmsted contrasts Greeley (1811–1872), a Universalist and editor of the *New-York Daily Tribune* who supported several social reform movements, with Leonard Bacon (1802–1881) and Nathaniel W. Taylor (1786–1858), both Congregationalists of New Haven, the former a minister and the latter recently a professor of theology at the Yale Divinity School.

38.6–7 the *French Revolution* . . . steamer arrives.] Several days before Olmsted's letter, New York newspapers had reported the abdication of Louis Philippe (1773–1850) and the formation of a provisional government headed by Alphonse de Lamartine (1790–1869), but the political outcome remained uncertain.

38.10–11 *It is too late.*] Louis Philippe abdicated in favor of his grandson Philippe d'Orléans (1838–1894), with the Duchess of Orléans (1814–1858) to serve as regent; when she presented her son before the Chamber of Deputies, a voice from the gallery is reported to have shouted this remark.

39.2 *The People's Park at Birkenhead, near Liverpool*] Olmsted published this article in the *Horticulturist* in May 1851, and later included it, in revised form, as a chapter in his book *Walks and Talks of an American Farmer* in England (1852).

42.6 Mr. Paxton] Sir Joseph Paxton (1803–1865), an English architect, gardener, and member of Parliament; he designed the Crystal Palace for the Great Exhibition of 1851.

43.31–36 "When the important . . . toil-worn."] See *The Stranger's Guide to Birkenhead* (1847).

43.37–41 "Few towns, . . . *Robertson.*] From *The Present Sanatory Condition of Birkenhead* (1847), by James Hunter Robinson, as quoted in *The Stranger's Guide to Birkenhead*.

45.19 *To Charles Loring Brace*] Olmsted probably wrote this undated letter on July 26, 1852.

45.21 Mr. & Mrs. Field, Rosa, Dr. Neidhard] Alfred T. Field (1814–1884), a Staten Island neighbor and friend of Olmsted's, active in the Richmond

County Agricultural Society; Charlotte Errington Field (c. 1817–1880), his wife; their daughter Rosa (d. 1931); and Philadelphia homeopath Charles Neidhard (1809–1895).

45.26   your letters . . . book.] Brace's letters from Hungary, originally published in the *Philadelphia Bulletin*, had been collected as *Hungary in 1851* (1852).

46.28   Spring] Marcus Spring (1810–1874), a Quaker cotton merchant who was one of the Phalanx's main nonresident stockholders.

46.30   Mrs. Arnold] Lydia Spring Arnold (1801–1854), wife of the Phalanx president George B. Arnold and sister of Marcus Spring.

49.24–25   the Shuss cogsslocken del Espelntatzellin] A nonsense phrase, suggestive of philosophical German.

51.25   Mr. Arnold's history.] George B. Arnold (1804–1899), a former minister and nurseryman, served as Phalanx president.

52.7   * Fuller] Sarah Margaret Fuller (1810–1850), author of *Summer on the Lakes*, in 1843 (1844), *Woman in the Nineteenth Century* (1845), and *Papers on Literature and Art* (1846), signed many of her contributions to the *New-York Daily Tribune* with an asterisk. She traveled to Europe with the Springs in 1846.

53.23–24   Foxes & Fishes] Spiritualists Margaret Fox (c. 1833–1893), Catherine Fox (c. 1839–1892), and Ann Leah Fox Fish (c. 1818–1890).

53.27–29   reading Tribune . . . Judge Edmonds.] *The New-York Daily Tribune* of July 24, 1852—in a notice of the publication of the first volume of *The Shekinah*, a journal "devoted to the elucidation of spiritual phenomena"—reprinted a selection from that journal's July issue about the experiences of John Worth Edmonds (1799–1874), a justice of the New York Supreme Court who had come to believe that his deceased wife was attempting to communicate with him.

54.17   Charles Elliott] Charles Wyllys Elliott (1817–1883), who had studied landscape gardening and horticulture and published *Cottages and Cottage Life* (1848), would later, as a member of the Board of Commissioners of the Central Park, suggest that Olmsted apply for the position of park superintendent.

55.10   I have condensed . . . Tribune.] See "The Phalanstery and the Phalansterians. By an Outsider," *New-York Daily Tribune*, June 29, 1852, published under the pseudonym "An American Farmer."

55.14–17   *The South* . . . SEVEN] Olmsted left New York in December 1852 at the invitation of Henry J. Raymond (1820–1869), editor of the *New-York Daily Times*, to work as a traveling correspondent in the South. From February 16, 1853, to February 13, 1854—under the pseudonym "Yeoman"—he published fifty "Letters on the Productions, Industry and Resources of the Southern States." He later extensively revised and expanded these letters in *A Journey in the Seaboard Slave States; with Remarks on their Economy* (1856), a book subsequently further revised and abridged as *Journeys and Explorations in the Cotton Kingdom* (1861). The seventh letter in his original series was first published in the *New-York Daily Times* on March 17, 1853.

58.35–36   as I have before shown, . . . disease.] In the fourth of his letters from the South, published in the *New-York Daily Times* on March 4, 1853, Olmsted quotes from the writings of New Orleans physician Samuel A. Cartwright (1793–1863), who argued that slave "rascality" was the result of a disease he named "Dysæsthesia Æthiopica."

64.17–20   *The South* . . . EIGHT] First published in the *New-York Daily Times* on March 30, 1853.

71.8–11   *The South* . . . NINE] First published in the *New-York Daily Times* on April 5, 1853.

72.11–12   Mr. Randolph's slaves] John Randolph of Roanoke (1773–1833), a planter and politician who served in both the House and Senate, made provision in his will for his slaves' manumission; in 1846, nearly 400 were resettled in Ohio with funds from his estate.

77.2–5   *The South* . . . TWENTY-EIGHT] First published in the *New-York Daily Times* on July 8, 1853.

77.9–19   the plantation . . . Mr. A.] White Hall, a large rice and cotton plantation in Bryan County, Georgia, owned by Richard James Arnold (1796–1873), a Rhode Island businessman whose wife had inherited the property.

79.12–22   a writer in the *Times* . . . "Walpole"] See "Southern Slavery. A Glance at Uncle Tom's Cabin. By a Southerner. Second Paper," published in the *New-York Daily Times* on June 26, 1853, under the pseudonym "Walpole"— probably Andrew Adgate Lipscomb (1816–1890), an Alabama clergyman and educator.

84.10–12   we called on Prentice . . . C. M. Clay . . . Greeley and to Raymond] George Dennison Prentice (1802–1870), editor of the *Louisville Daily Journal*; Cassius M. Clay (1810–1903), editor of the antislavery *True American*; Horace Greeley (1811–1872), editor of the *New-York Daily Tribune*; Henry J. Raymond (1820–1869), editor of the *New-York Daily Times*.

84.16–17   Dr. Short . . . Dr. Gray.] Charles Wilkins Short (1794–1863), a retired physician interested in botany; Asa Gray (1810–1888), Harvard botany professor.

84.22   a classmate . . . *Allison*.] Samuel Perkins Allison (1827–1858), of the Yale class of 1847.

85.35   Seward] William H. Seward (1801–1872), U.S. senator from New York and a prominent opponent of slavery.

85.39   D. S. Dickinson] Daniel Stevens Dickinson (1800–1866), a lawyer and former U.S. senator from New York.

86.32–33   Strauss' life . . . Parker's books.] In his controversial *Life of Jesus, Critically Examined*—first published as *Das Leben Jesu* in 1835–36 and translated in 1846—German theologian David Friedrich Strauss (1808–1874) attempted to distinguish between historical and mythical elements in the gospels. Theodore Parker (1810–1860), a Boston Unitarian who had reviewed Strauss's book sympathetically in 1840 and who opposed slavery.

88.19   Peter Cooper . . . Reds.] Cooper (1791–1883), the wealthy son of a working-class family, conceived and funded the construction of the Cooper Union for the Advancement of Science and Art, begun in September 1853; it promised an education that would be "free and open to all." The phrase "red republican" was used to describe supporters of the European revolutions of 1848 and those espousing extreme anti-aristocratic views.

88.34   Field, Elliott] Alfred T. Field (see note 45.21) and Charles Wyllys Elliott (see note 54.17).

90.8–11   *The South* . . . FORTY-SEVEN] First published in the *New-York Daily Times* on January 26, 1854.

94.40   *consols*] A type of government bond issued in Great Britain.

96.6–11   Jefferson . . . Expediency.] See Query XVIII ("Manners") in *Notes on the State of Virginia* (1785), by Thomas Jefferson (1743–1826).

100.1   Mrs. Tyler] See "To the Duchess of Sutherland and Ladies of England" (*Southern Literary Messenger*, February 1853), a defense of slavery by Julia Gardiner Tyler (1820–1889), written in response to an English antislavery petition of November 1852.

100.22–23   *A Tour* . . . EIGHT] First published in the *New-York Daily Times* on April 24, 1854, under the pseudonym "Yeoman," one of fifteen in a series begun on March 6 and ended on June 7, 1854. Olmsted later revised these letters with the assistance of his brother and collected them as *A Journey through Texas; or, a Saddle-Trip on the Southwestern Frontier* (1857).

104.11   "their mind to them a kingdom is,"] See "My Mind to Me a Kingdom Is" (1588), a poem attributed to Edward Dyer (1543–1607).

106.2   *Passages in the Life of an Unpractical Man*] A title supplied by the editors of *The Papers of Frederick Law Olmsted* for a section of a longer manuscript memoir, probably begun in the late 1870s but left incomplete and unpublished at the time of Olmsted's death.

106.3–4   an article published by Mr. Downing in 1848] See "A Talk about Public Parks and Gardens" (*Horticulturist*, October 1848), by the landscape designer and horticulturalist Andrew Jackson Downing (1815–1852).

106.29   a chief Engineer] Egbert L. Viele (1825–1902), a former infantry officer who had served as New Jersey's state engineer.

107.40   Black Republicans] A phrase coined derisively by opponents of the Republican Party, which opposed the extension of slavery into the territories.

108.10   one of the Commissioners] Charles Wyllys Elliott (see note 54.17).

108.12–13   Journey in the Back Country.] The final volume in Olmsted's series "Our Slave States," published in 1860, following *A Journey in the Seaboard Slave States* (1856) and *A Journey through Texas* (1857).

115.2–4   *Description of a Plan . . . "Greensward"*] Olmsted and his collaborator on the Greensward Plan—the British-American architect Calvert Vaux (1824–1895)—printed this text in pamphlet form and submitted it as part of their 1858 competition entry. They also presented a large map (ink on paper, 43" high x 132" wide) of the design they proposed, and eleven smaller presentation boards featuring before and after views and other details. The images on these presentation boards have been reproduced following page 124 in the present volume.

116.35   Our present chief magistrate] Daniel F. Tiemann (1805–1899) served as New York's mayor from 1858 to 1860; for his inaugural address, see the *New-York Daily Times*, January 6, 1858.

125.30   study number 2] See Greensward Study No. 2, following page 124 in the present volume.

126.9   study number 1] See Greensward Study No. 1, following page 124 in the present volume.

127.19–20   the sketch submitted] See Greensward Study No. 11, following page 124 in the present volume.

128.2   study number 11] See Greensward Study No. 11, following page 124 in the present volume.

128.19–20   study number 3] See Greensward Study No. 3, following page 124 in the present volume.

132.19–20   study number 9] See Greensward Study No. 9, following page 124 in the present volume.

132.21–22   study number 10] See Greensward Study No. 10, following page 124 in the present volume.

132.26   study number 7] See Greensward Study No. 7, following page 124 in the present volume.

133.37   the explanatory guide to the arboretum] Olmsted and Vaux included a "Descriptive Guide to the Arboretum" at the conclusion of their "Description of a Plan for the Improvement of the Central Park, 'Greensward'," followed by an extensive "Index to Arboretum," in which tree and shrub species are keyed to numbers on their large-format design map. The "Descriptive Guide" is printed below; for the "Index," see Charles E. Beveridge and David Schuyler, eds., *The Papers of Frederick Law Olmsted*. Vol. III: *Creating Central Park, 1857–1861*, pages 164–77.

DESCRIPTIVE GUIDE TO THE ARBORETUM

The general arrangement of the arboretum is exhibited on the plan. The principal walk is intended to be so laid out, that while the trees and shrubs bordering it succeed one another in the natural order of families, each will be brought, as far as possible, into a position corresponding to its natural habits, and in which its distinguishing characteristics will be favorably exhibited. At the entrance, marked "W" on the plan, we place the Magnoliaceae, associating with them the shrubs belonging to the orders Ranunculaceae, Anonoceae, Berberidaceae, and Cistaceae. The great beauty of these families entitles them, if no other reasons prevailed, to a very prominent place on our grounds. In pursuing the path which enters here, we find on our right hand the order Tiliaceae, with the shrubs belonging to the orders Rutaceae, Anacardiaceae, and Rhamnaceae. On each side of the walk groups succeed, composed wholly of the order Sapindaceae. Next to the right, planted on high ground, among large rocks, we come to the natural order Leguminosae, distinguished for the beauty of its forms and the lightness of its foliage, and not less in some species for the exquisite fragrance and delicacy of its blossoms.

At the next turn of the path, we come upon the Rosaceae. The shrubs of this order being very beautiful, we have placed many of them singly, as well as in thickets between, and over, the large masses of rock, which occur here on both sides.

Next, we reach the order Hamamelaceae, represented by the only tree of the order, Liquid Ambar Styracifula, and with shrubbery consisting of Cyclanthaceae, Grossulaceae, Saxafragaceae, Hamamelaceae, and Arialiaceae.

On the right of the path and nearly in front of the chapel comes the family Cornaceae, which contains but two large trees, Nyssa Multiflora and Nyssa Uniflora. But to compensate for its meagerness in this respect, this and the following orders, Caprifoliaceae and Rubiaceae, contain some of our finest shrubs, which are well placed upon smooth slopes.

Next in order and occupying a large space upon the dark, fertile soil of the Harlem flats, which here extend into the park, we find the natural family Ericaceae, possessing but one large tree, Oxydendrum Arboreum. This order is remarkable for the beauty of its shrubs, which are so peculiar to this country that, when planted by themselves abroad, they form what is called an American garden, one of the choicest ornaments of the higher class of English country seats.

At the next turn are arranged three natural orders, represented by one tree each: Aquifoliaceae by Ilex Opaca, Styraceae by Halesia Tetraptera, and Ebenaceae by Diospyros virginiana. With these are the shrubs of Styraceae, Sapotaceae and Verbenaceae. At the left hand of the walk stand singly two specimens of our finest flowering tree, the Catalpa Bignoniodes (Bignoniaceae), which has no shrubs immediately associated with it. Next, the Oleaceae, with shrubs belonging to Thymeleceae; some of them scattered on a large open lawn, and some gathered in copses upon a rocky hill side. On another part of the same ledge will be seen the only species of the Laurel tribe which belong to our climate—the Sassafras officinalis, and Benzoin odoriferum (Lauraceae). The specimens will be numerous, standing both singly and in clusters.

The arboretum walk here approaches and soon crosses the One hundred and Second street entrance to the park, which will thus in the regular sequence of the natural orders be furnished with a canopy of the American elm, bordered by the other fine trees of the order, and shrubs of Elaegnaceae, Santalaceae, and Empetraceae.

South of the entrance road stands, singly and in an isolated group, the Platanus occidentalis (Platanaceae). Scattered on a grassy declivity follow the Juglandaceae. Growing as they grow in our pastures, no tree is more beautiful in groups or singly than the hickory, and shrubbery of any kind among them would be out of place.

The oak may be almost called an American tree, as in no other country are the species half so numerous. On this account, as well as for their great beauty, it has been thought proper to give them much open space. A few shrubs of Cupuliferae and Myricaceae form the underwood of the mass which will shut out the view towards Fifth avenue, which here passes at an elevated grade.

To these succeed the order Betulaceae (the graceful birches) and Salicaceae, which includes the poplars. Finally are brought in our various American Coniferae. Only single trees are provided for in this section, as masses of each are elsewhere arranged in the park.

134.12   study number 5] See *Greensward Study No. 5*, following page 124 in the present volume.

135.2   *Henry H. Elliott*] Elliott (1805–1868) was a member of a commission formed in April 1860 to oversee the extension of the street plan for Manhattan to the north of 155th Street.

135.5–11   The Herald . . . Commissioners.] See "Grand Suburban Park at Washington Heights," *New York Herald*, August 27, 1860.

135.6   slang-whang] Bullying or abusive speech or rhetoric.

136.32   Mr. Abbot] Gorham D. Abbot (1807–1874), a school principal, hoped to build a women's college in Manhattan.

145.21   *Park*] First published in 1861 in volume 12 of *The New American Cyclopædia* (1858–63), edited by George Ripley and Charles Dana.

156.31   Sidney and Adams] James Clark Sidney (c. 1819–1881) and Andrew Adams (fl. 1858–60).

156.39   Mr. Daniels] Howard Daniels (1815–1863) designed Baltimore's Druid Hill Park, which opened in 1860.

158.39–159.1   Lord Bacon to remark . . . perfection."] See the essay "Of Gardens" (1625), by Francis Bacon (1561–1626).

160.6–10 the opinion of Sir William . . . Holborn"] See Walpole's *The History of the Modern Taste in Gardening* (also titled *On Modern Gardening*), collected in the fourth volume of his *Anecdotes of Painting in England* (1780).

160.34 Kent] William Kent (c. 1685–1748).

161.22–25 "Most of our large . . . all."] See *Village Memoirs, in a Series of Letters between a Clergyman and His Family in the Country, and His Son in Town* (1774), by Joseph Craddock (1742–1820).

161.31–33 The various "Picturesque Tours" . . . Price] William Gilpin (1724–1804), a curate and schoolmaster, published many books on the picturesque qualities of places he visited, including *Observations on the River Wye, and Several Parts of South Wales, Etc., Relative Chiefly to Picturesque Beauty; Made in the Summer of the Year 1770* (1782), and *Observations, Relative Chiefly to Picturesque Beauty, Made in the Year 1776, on Several Parts of Great Britain; Particularly the High-Lands of Scotland* (1789). Price (c. 1747–1829), the owner of an extensive Herefordshire estate, first published his *Essay on the Picturesque* in 1794; an expanded edition, in three volumes, followed in 1810.

161.35 Shenstone, Mason, and Knight, by their poems] See *The Works in Verse and Prose* (3 vols., 1764–69) of William Shenstone (1714–1763), whose Shropshire, England, estate The Leasowes was celebrated for its landscape gardening; *The English Garden: A Poem* (1772–81), by William Mason (1724–1797); and *The Landscape: A Didactic Poem, in Three Books, Addressed to Uvedale Price, Esq.* (1794), by Richard Payne Knight (1750–1824).

161.37–38 Repton, Loudon, Paxton, Kemp, . . . Downing] Humphry Repton (1752–1818), author of *Sketches and Hints on Landscape Gardening* (1795), *Observations on the Theory and Practice of Landscape Gardening* (1803), and *Fragments on the Theory and Practice of Landscape Gardening* (1816), and a practitioner of the art in England beginning in 1788; John Claudius Loudon (1783–1843), Scottish landscape architect and author of many works, including *A Treatise on Forming, Improving, and Managing Country Residences* (1806), *Arboretum et Fruticetum Britannicum* (1835–38), and *The Suburban Gardener, and Villa Companion* (1838); Joseph Paxton (see note 42.6); Edward Kemp (1817–1891), designer and first superintendent of Birkenhead Park, near Liverpool, and the author of *How to Lay Out a Small Garden* (1850), among other books; and Andrew Jackson Downing (see note 106.3–4).

162.19 Beauregard] Pierre Gustave Toutant-Beauregard (1818–1893), Confederate brigadier general who led the attack on Fort Sumter and was hailed as a hero of Bull Run.

163.21 McEntee . . . Bull's Run.] Jervis McEntee (1828–1891), an artist and the brother-in-law of Olmsted's partner Calvert Vaux, served in the 20th New York State Militia, which was not present at the battle.

163.25–26 FROM *Report . . . Volunteers*] Olmsted's Bull Run report of September 1861 was printed as a pamphlet bearing the full title "Report of the

Secretary with Regard to the Probable Origin of the Recent Demoralization of the Volunteer Army at Washington, and the Duty of the Sanitary Commission with Reference to Certain Deficiencies in Existing Army Arrangements, as Suggested Thereby." The pamphlet was marked "Confidential" and "Printed for Members Only" on its title page; a much-abridged version was circulated publicly in December.

163.28   these investigations] Olmsted's report was based on empirical research: seven Sanitary Commission inspectors, visiting the regiments that had been engaged at Bull Run, posed a lengthy series of questions about the condition of the troops before, during, and after the battle. The results, amounting to "about two thousand items of evidence," were tabulated by Ezekiel Brown Elliott (1823–1888), a statistician and actuary formerly employed by the Boston Life Insurance Companies and now head of the Sanitary Commission's statistical bureau.

164.26–27   see McDowell's . . . Mercury] Olmsted cites accounts of the battle reprinted in the *New-York Daily Tribune*: Gen. Irvin McDowell's (which appeared on August 9), Dr. Josiah Clark Nott's (August 10), and those of the *Charleston Mercury* (late August–early September).

164.27–32   a single brigade . . . Cash] Gen. Arnold Elzey Jr. (1818–1871) led the Confederate 4th Brigade into battle at Bull Run, joining Col. Joseph B. Kershaw (1822–1894) of the 2nd South Carolina and Col. E.B.C. Cash (1823–1888) of the 8th South Carolina regiments.

165.22–23   Mr. Elliott] See note 163.28.

169.19   *To the Editor . . . Times*] Olmsted's letter of November 29 was published on December 4.

171.37–38   Hatteras . . . Tybee] Union naval forces had captured Confederate forts at Cape Hatteras Inlet (North Carolina) in August and at Port Royal (South Carolina) in early November, prompting the evacuation of Confederate troops from Tybee Island (Georgia), later that month, to a stronger position at Fort Pulaski.

174.11   St. Domingo massacres] Slaves in the French colony of Saint-Domingue—now Haiti—rose up against their owners beginning in August 1791.

176.3   *George Frederic Magoun*] Magoun (1821–1896), pastor of the Congregational Church in Lyons, Iowa, was appointed secretary of the Iowa Army Sanitary Commission on October 13, 1861.

176.33   "the dark and bloody ground,"] A phrase used proverbially to describe Kentucky, attributed to Cherokee chief Dragging Canoe (Tsiyu Gansini, c. 1738–1792).

178.26–27   a Commission organized by General Fremont] The Western Sanitary Commission, headquartered in St. Louis.

183.14–17 one of its Secretaries . . . his command.] John Hancock Douglas (1824–1892), a physician, arrived in St. Louis on December 16.

184.3–12 *James Reed Spalding . . .* the World of today] Olmsted wrote Spalding (1821–1872), a former editor at the *New York World*, believing him to be the author of its February 15, 1862, editorial that called for a commission to address the future of Port Royal's slave plantations. In fact, the paper's managing editor Manton Marble (1835–1917) was responsible for the editorial, and Olmsted sent him another letter the next day.

184.12–13 the Senate Bill of Mr Foster] On February 3, 1862, Olmsted sent Lafayette S. Foster (1806–1880), a Connecticut Republican, a "draft of a bill to provide for the cultivation of a portion of the land held by the United States forces in South Carolina & Georgia & for the care & management of the negroes thereon—which I have prepared at your request."

186.8–9 Dr Howe, Prof^r Bache, Dr Bellows and G W Curtis] Samuel Gridley Howe (1801–1876), A. D. Bache (1806–1867), and Henry W. Bellows (1814–1862), of the Sanitary Commission—the latter its president—and George William Curtis (1824–1892), Olmsted's friend and former business partner, in 1862 a columnist for *Harper's Monthly*.

188.2–5 *Argument Addressed . . . Sea Islands*] Olmsted presented oral arguments about the management of the Sea Islands plantations first to Secretary of the Treasury Salmon P. Chase (1808–1873), probably between March 10 and March 13, 1862, and then to Secretary of War Edwin M. Stanton (1814–1869), probably on April 13, 1862. The text presented here reflects the latter presentation, for which he made extensive revisions to the manuscript version of his argument. He left this manuscript unpublished during his lifetime.

192.15 Old Man of the Sea of Slavery] In the *Arabian Nights* tales, the Old Man of the Sea convinces travelers to carry him on their backs to cross a stream and then refuses to let go, effectively enslaving them.

195.38 your predecessor] Simon Cameron (1799–1889), who served as secretary of war from March 1861 to January 1862.

196.15–16 I called upon the Secy . . . gentleman] Olmsted met with Salmon P. Chase on January 27, 1862, along with Henry W. Bellows and A. D. Bache.

196.19–21 he had employed . . . action.] Chase appointed Edward L. Pierce (1829–1897) as his agent in the Sea Islands on March 9, 1862. Pierce had been asked in July 1861, as a private in the 3rd Massachusetts, to supervise a large group of contrabands in the construction of fortifications at Hampton, Virginia, later publishing an account of his experiences (see "The Contrabands at Fortress Monroe," *Atlantic Monthly*, November 1861).

199.7–8 *Labors of the Sanitary Commission*] Olmsted's letter to Henry W. Bellows appeared in the *New York Times* on May 24, 1862.

200.28 Dr. Grymes] James M. Grymes (c. 1828–1863) of Washington, D.C.

202.8–9 Knapp, Ware, Wheelock] Frederick Newman Knapp (1821–1889), the Sanitary Commission's superintendent of special relief; Robert Ware (1836–1863), Sanitary Commission medical inspector; George Gill Wheelock (1838–1907), a Sanitary Commission wound dresser.

202.36 Dr. Tripler] Charles Stuart Tripler (1806–1866), medical director of the Army of the Potomac.

207.2 *John Foster Jenkins*] Jenkins (1826–1882), a Massachusetts-born physician who had practiced in New York City and Yonkers, New York, joined the Sanitary Commission in 1861. He served as acting general secretary in Olmsted's absence, and later succeeded him as general secretary.

207.7–9 the enclosed sheet . . . Meals.] Olmsted had sent Jenkins a draft of a document to be posted in hospital ships and titled "Instructions for floating hospital service on the Atlantic coast."

210.9–14 As Dr. Bellows . . . the matter.] Iowa senator James Harlan (1820–1899) had accused two Sanitary Commission workers—Henry Augustus Warriner (1824–1871) and John H. Douglas (1824–1892)—of preventing his wife Ann Eliza Peck Harlan (1824–1884) from delivering supplies for the wounded after the Battle of Shiloh, and of speaking to her in "gross and threatening" terms. On investigation, Sanitary Commission president Henry W. Bellows (1814–1892) chose not to reprimand the two.

210.16 Dʳ Fisher] George Jackson Fisher (1825–1893), of Sing Sing, New York.

219.1 Sibley tents] Conical or bell tents designed by West Point graduate Henry Hopkins Sibley (1816–1886) and patented in 1856.

221.30 Leveridge farm] A farm near Olmsted's on Staten Island.

222.19–20 the Monitor] The Union Navy's first ironclad, launched in January 1862.

222.32 The Hero] A troop transport steamboat.

223.13 Letterman] Jonathan A. Letterman (1824–1872), medical director of the Army of the Potomac from 1862 to 1864 and subsequently the author of *Medical Recollections of the Army of the Potomac* (1866).

228.13 Douglas . . . Pittsburg landing.] John Hancock Douglas (1824–1892), a physician and Sanitary Commission medical inspector, helped to care for the wounded after the Battle of Shiloh (Pittsburg Landing) in April 1862.

230.30 the Governor] Henry W. Bellows (see note 186.8–9).

231.30 Agnew] Cornelius R. Agnew (1830–1888), a New York physician on the Sanitary Commission's executive committee.

231.35 Jenkins] See note 207.2.

232.2–3 the Tribune correspondent's . . . Antietam?] See "The Great Battle of Wednesday" by George W. Smalley (1833–1916), published in the *New-York Daily Tribune* on September 19, 1862.

232.10–11 Dr Brown's] Probably David Tilden Brown (1822–1889), a psychiatrist with whom Olmsted and Vaux both collaborated.

232.30 Masons?] Mason Brothers, the New York firm that had published Olmsted's *A Journey in the Backcountry* (1860), was on the verge of bankruptcy.

233.2 *Oliver Wolcott Gibbs*] Gibbs (1822–1908), who served on the Sanitary Commission's executive committee, was professor of chemistry at the Free Academy (later City College of New York) until 1863, and subsequently at Harvard.

233.5 this direful day] On November 4, 1862, Democrat Horatio Seymour (1810–1886) was elected governor of New York, and his party also won many lesser offices.

233.9 "Loyalists' Club."] Subsequently organized as the Union League Club of New York, in February 1863.

233.18 Belmont and Stebbins] August Belmont (1813–1890) and Henry G. Stebbins (1811–1881), both wealthy Democrats who served on the Central Park Commission.

234.20 Agnew, Van Buren] Cornelius R. Agnew (1830–1888) and William H. Van Buren (1819–1883), both physicians on the executive committee of the Sanitary Commission.

234.40 Minturn & Brown] Probably Robert Bowne Minturn (1805–1866), a prominent shipping merchant, and James Brown (1791–1877), of the investment bank Brown Brothers.

235.2 Strong and Jay.] George Templeton Strong (1820–1875) and John Jay (1817–1894).

235.4–5 old Col. Hamilton.] James Alexander Hamilton (1788–1878), son of the founding father.

235.15 boss devil] See note 237.38.

235.25–27 Kapp . . . Curtis, Col. Waring, Captn Worden; Col. Elliott] Friedrich Kapp (1824–1884), a lawyer who had emigrated from Germany in 1850 and the author of *Die Sklavenfrage in den Vereinigten Staaten* (1858), among other works on American history; Joseph B. Curtis (1836–1862), assistant architect for New York's Central Park; George E. Waring Jr. (1833–1898), Central Park's drainage engineer; probably John Lorimer Worden (1818–1897), commander of the U.S.S. *Monitor*; and probably Henry Hill Elliott Jr. (1833–1912), a lieutenant colonel in the 1st Louisiana Infantry (Union).

235.37 the Maison Doree] A luxurious French restaurant on Union Square, opened in 1861.

237.5 the Council] Delegates representing Sanitary Commission auxiliary groups held a conference in Washington, D.C., referred to as the "Women's Council," on November 21, 1862.

237.15   Dr Newberry] John Strong Newberry (1822–1892), physician and secretary of the Western Department of the Sanitary Commission beginning in September 1861.

237.16–17   Judge Skinner] Mark T. Skinner (1813–1887), judge of the Cook County Court of Common Pleas, led the Northwestern Sanitary Commission, headquartered in Chicago.

237.22   the Cincinnati men.] Samuel J. Broadwell (1832–1893) and Joshua Hall Bates (1817–1908), of the Sanitary Commission's Cincinnati branch.

237.38   the O.B.D.] Olmsted felt that the Sanitary Commission ought to be a national organization devoted to the common good, and derided the impulse to serve narrower groups or interests at the expense of this higher purpose as "the old boss devil."

239.16–17   The ladies . . . President of the U.S.] The delegates attending the conference met with President Lincoln on November 24, 1862.

240.2–6   *Charles Janeway Stillé* . . . Independence"] Stillé (1819–1899), active in the Philadelphia branch of the Sanitary Commission, had given Olmsted a copy of his recently published pamphlet on February 24.

240.19–20   my brother . . . a negro regiment] Albert Henry Olmsted (1842–1929), Frederick's half-brother, was camped near the 3rd Louisiana Volunteers.

240.24–25   its results seem . . . Seymour of Connecticut] Opposing the Proclamation and calling for peace negotiations with the Confederacy, Democrat Thomas Hart Seymour (1807–1868), a former governor of Connecticut, seemed poised to unseat the current Republican governor of that state, William Alfred Buckingham (1804–1875), in the election of April 1863, but lost narrowly.

243.13   K.] Frederick N. Knapp (see note 202.8–9).

248.3   Garesche] Julius Peter Garesché (1821–1862), Rosencrans's chief of staff who had been killed at the Battle of Stones River.

249.23–24   McClellan frame] A riding saddle named after George B. McClellan (1826–1885), in standard Army use beginning in 1859.

250.19   just as Mr. Trollope was at Centralia.] In *North America* (1862), Anthony Trollope (1815–1882) describes the passengers he sees waiting for a train at Crossline, Ohio. Olmsted may have remembered a stop in Centralia described by William Howard Russell (1820–1907) in his *My Diary North and South* (1863).

252.5   Mr Russell's book] See note 250.19.

253.33   Gen'l Hurlbut] Major General Stephen A. Hurlbut (1815–1852) commanded the Sixteenth Corps in the Army of the Tennessee.

253.34   Columbus] Columbus, Kentucky.

253.35   Jackson] Jackson, Tennessee.

254.1 Gen'l McPherson] Major General James B. McPherson (1828–1864) commanded the Seventeenth Corps in the Army of the Tennessee.

254.10 Col. Bissell's Western Engineer Regiment] Josiah Wolcott Bissell (1818–1891) commanded the "Engineer Regiment of the West," organized in the fall of 1861.

254.19 Admiral Porter] Acting Rear Admiral David D. Porter (1813–1891), commander of the Mississippi Squadron.

254.22–23 Sunflower and Blackwater expeditions] Unsuccessful Union attempts to reach the Yazoo River to the northeast of Vicksburg via Steele's Bayou and the Sunflower River, and by way of Yazoo Pass and the Coldwater River.

254.33 Parrotts] Muzzle-loaded, rifled artillery pieces used during the Civil War, named after manufacturer Robert Parker Parrott (1804–1877).

256.7 Cranch] Christopher Pearse Cranch (1813–1892), an American writer and artist who lived in Paris from 1853 to 1863.

256.16–17 Farragut's . . . Hartford] Rear Admiral David G. Farragut (1801–1870), commander of the West Gulf Blockading Squadron, had run past the batteries at Port Hudson, Louisiana, on the night of March 14 in his flagship the *Hartford*.

256.17–18 my quondam . . . Dick Taylor's] Major General Richard Taylor (1826–1879) commanded the Confederate District of West Louisiana. Olmsted had visited his sugarcane plantation near New Orleans in 1853.

256.22–24 grossly abused . . . Chickasaw bluffs] See "The Battle of Chickasaw Bayou," *New York Herald*, January 18, 1863.

256.31 Gen'l Steele] Major General Frederick Steele (1819–1868) commanded the First Division in Sherman's Fifteenth Corps.

256.35 Gen'l Blair's] Brigadier General Frank Blair (1821–1875) commanded a brigade in Sherman's corps.

260.23–24 his adjutant General] Lieutenant Colonel John A. Rawlins (1831–1869).

260.35 Breese his flag-captain] Lieutenant Commander Kidder Randolph Breese (1831–1881) was the captain of Porter's flagship *Black Hawk*, a converted river steamboat.

261.14–21 *Charles Eliot Norton* . . . invitation.] Norton (1827–1908) had invited Olmsted to participate in the work of the newly founded New England Loyal Publication Society, which distributed patriotic articles and editorials ("slips") to newspapers throughout the Union; "anything you may write or may select for the purpose would be welcomed," he wrote. John Murray Forbes (1813–1898), a railroad magnate and philanthropist, had helped to found and support the enterprise.

261.29–30 As Mr Seward . . . end.] In a letter to his wife Eliza dated April 23, 1863, Henry W. Bellows reported Secretary of State William H. Seward (1801–1872) to have made similar remarks at a dinner party; Bellows was probably Olmsted's source for them.

263.20 Genl Banks' arrangement] General Nathaniel Prentice Banks (1816–1894), commander of the Department of the Gulf, issued General Order 12 on January 29, 1863, governing the labor of former slaves in Union-occupied southern Louisiana.

264.2 *Prospectus for a Weekly Journal*] Olmsted completed this prospectus on or around June 25, 1863, in collaboration with Edwin Lawrence Godkin (1831–1902), who in July 1865 became the first editor of *The Nation*.

269.2 the authors of the *Federalist*] Alexander Hamilton (1755–1804), John Jay (1745–1829), and James Madison (1751–1836).

269.13–17 One of our most powerful demagogues . . . Union.] In January 1861, Mayor Fernando Wood (1812–1881) proposed that New York City declare itself a "Free City," independent of Albany and Washington, D.C.

274.1–4 The statement . . . old regiments] Probably Henry Wilson (1812–1875), Republican senator from Massachusetts, though the source of this statement is obscure. Olmsted's letter was written in the midst of the New York City draft riots, which began on July 13.

274.7–9 "The hermaphrodite . . . describes her).] Mary Edwards Walker (1832–1919), a pioneering female physician, was appointed assistant surgeon in the Army of the Cumberland in September 1863 after extensive voluntary service. Her preference for what the *Tribune*'s Potomac correspondent called "male habiliments" attracted considerable attention.

274.36–38 Let Barlow & Bennett & Brooks and Belmont & Barnard & the Woods & Andrews and Clancy . . . omit Seymour.] Olmsted lists prominent "foes of the Republic": Samuel Latham Mitchel Barlow (1826–1889), a wealthy New York lawyer and conservative Democrat; James Gordon Bennett Sr. (1795–1872), founding editor of the *New York Herald*; James Brooks (1810–1873), a New York Democratic congressman; August Belmont Sr. (1813–1890), financier and former chairman of the Democratic National Committee; George Gardner Barnard (1829–1879), judge of the New York Supreme Court; Fernando Wood (1812–1881), New York's former Democratic mayor; Benjamin Wood (1830–1900), Fernando's brother, a New York Democratic congressman; John U. Andrews (1825–1883), a Virginia-born lawyer later imprisoned for his anti-draft oratory; John Clancy (1830–1864), editor of the *New York Leader*, a Democratic newspaper; and Horatio Seymour (1810–1886), New York's sitting governor, who opposed the draft in 1863.

275.23 *Ignaz Anton Pilat*] Pilat (1820–1870), formerly director of the Imperial Botanical Gardens in Schönbrunn, Vienna, served as head gardener for New York's Central Park from 1857 until his death.

275.31 Mr. Fischer] William L. Fischer (1819–1899), a German-born landscape gardener employed as a foreman gardener at Central Park beginning in 1856; in 1884, Olmsted asked him to supervise plantings in Boston's Franklin Park and Back Bay.

284.5 Mr. Green] Andrew Haswell Green (1820–1903), treasurer of the Central Park Commission.

284.15 Pieper] John Henry Pieper (1824–1888), former head of the Central Park corps of engineers and chief engineer of the Mariposa Estate.

285.24 Mrs Fremont] Jessie Benton Frémont (1824–1902), writer of *The Story of the Guard: A Chronicle of the War* (1863) and *Far-West Sketches* (1890) and wife of the Mariposa Estate's former owner, explorer and politician John C. Frémont.

288.27 Rossville] A town on Staten Island, near the Olmsteds' farm.

289.38–39 Knapp's cottage at Walpole] Frederick Knapp (1821–1899), Olmsted's coworker at the Sanitary Commission and a friend, owned an "Anglo-Swiss" house in Walpole, New Hampshire.

291.1–2 I enclose a memorandum.] This enclosure is not known to have survived.

292.9 Martin] Howard A. Martin, Olmsted's longtime clerk.

300.7–8 *Preliminary Report . . . Grove*] As published in *The Papers of Frederick Law Olmsted*, the text of this preliminary report is taken from two sources: a fragmentary manuscript, unpublished until 1952, in the hand of Olmsted's secretary Henry Perkins, and a letter Olmsted published in the *New York Evening Post* on June 18, 1868, describing Yosemite scenery; the last lines of the letter to the *Post* correspond to lines in the fragmentary manuscript, and supply the material missing from the manuscript. Thus reconstructed, the preliminary report represents the best available text of the otherwise unpublished oral presentation Olmsted made before the Yosemite commissioners at Yosemite in August 1865.

300.27 our own Capitol] The capitol building at Sacramento, begun in 1861.

304.18 sketches of Calame] Alexandre Calame (1810–1864), a Swiss artist noted for his mountain landscapes.

312.10–22 Downing . . . in England.] See the final sentence of "The New-York Park" by Andrew Jackson Downing, published in volume 6 of the *Horticulturist* in August 1851.

319.2–4 FROM *Preliminary . . . San Francisco*] Olmsted's report to the Committee of the Board of Supervisors of the City of San Francisco is dated March 31, 1866; it was published under this title in 1866. In June 1866, Mayor Henry P. Coon (1822–1884) informed him that the committee had failed to advance the legislation "necessary . . . for carrying your report into practical operation."

336.21–24 FROM *Report* . . . your request] Olmsted's report, submitted to Samuel Hopkins Willey (1821–1914), vice president of the College of California, is dated June 29, 1866; it was published under this title by Wm. C. Bryant & Company in New York.

341.8–15 Lord Bacon . . . *perfection.*"] See note 158.39–159.1.

349.23–24 FROM *The Pioneer* . . . *America*] Olmsted never completed *The Pioneer Condition and The Drift of Civilization in America*—a title supplied by the editors of *The Papers of Frederick Law Olmsted* for a collection of fragmentary drafts produced from 1865 to 1868 or early 1869 and now at the Library of Congress. In a letter of November 29, 1864, to E. L. Godkin, he had envisioned "a heavy sort of book on Society in the United States—the influence of pioneer-life—& of Democracy"; the sections of this book-in-progress included in the present volume appear to have been written in part in 1866, during Olmsted's residence in California, and in part in 1868, looking back on his frontier experiences.

349.28 The Indians who before lived here] The Sierra Miwok.

350.19 tribal gatherings.] Olmsted included a description of one such gathering in his manuscript but wrote in the margin "This leads astray? Better omitted." It is reprinted below.

One such gathering I lately, quite by accident, took part in. I was camped with my family on the bank of a mountain trout stream, the country near which was visited only in the summer on account of the depth of snow which lay in the winter upon the trail leading to it, when Indians began to show themselves about us, their number increasing by new arrivals every few hours during two days. About sixty of them were at length camped over against us, the greater number of them being women and children. With these my own children were soon acquainted quite as intimately as could be considered desireable with reference to their education, in spite of the fact that the Indians spoke nothing of any European language except a few words which bore an obscure relation to the Spanish and two profane English exclamations. About day break one morning, I was awakened from a dream so gradually that it was some time before I was clear in my mind that I was not in Georgia and listening to a howling cry of warning to escape from the wrath to come. When I fairly gained self command, I roused myself with a start and looked about me. I had been sleeping on the ground with the boys by my side and found them both there still fast asleep and everything as it should be. Our servant was lighting a fire near by, apparently with no consciousness of hearing anything unusual. Nevertheless in my ears (I could not be mistaken) the exhortation of the camp meeting still continued. I did not ask if I was awake, I knew that I was but I turned and said very quietly as became a man who was not sure of his senses:

"This is not a camp meeting, Bell."

"Bless yer, no Boss, it's one o' them Indian medicine men that's a doin that preachin."

But the resemblance was astonishingly close, and I wondered if it were possible that John Shasta* had joined the camp in the night.

"B," I asked, "can you understand anything of what he says?" for B had lived with the Indians and could communicate with them in a crippled way.

"O I've heerd all that he's sayin now, heaps o times afore."

"Listen to him," said I, "and when he gets through tell me as much of it as you can."

Accordingly B. hung up the kettle and took a seat somewhat unwillingly facing the Indian camp while I went to my bath. At breakfast the following—a Special Report—was given me.

> Dese yer Injuns, yr see has allers bin in the habit of coming to dis yer branch ebery summer; so did all der faders afore 'em and when de moon's ware twas last night den dey begins to pizen de trouts in de branch; dey pizens 'em wid soap weed, and when dey comes belly up den dey picks em out and de women dey makes a mush of 'em. Dats wat dem holes in de rocks is for. Dars war dey cooks 'em. Well yer see deys allers bin used fore dey begin, to hab a ceremony, a kind of preachin, yer see. Dey don't hab dat dey tink it bad luck. Dat ole feller as was preachin this mornin, he tell 'em—well amount oft was, dey must be good Injuns and stick by dere tribe and be mighty kerful dey don't do nothin that'll be any good to anybody dat don't blong to dar tribe, and den dey get plenty fish, allers; and when dey die a great wite bird wid his wings as long as from dat yer mounting to dat un, 'll come and take um up up to a big meadow war de clover heads don't never dry up and dar's lots o' grasshoppers all de year roun. Dats about d'amount ov't, Sir.

Olmsted included a footnote about John Shasta:

> *John Shasta is an Indian preacher of whom the following account has been published in some California newspaper: John Shasta is the first "Indian convert who is known to have been brought to Jesus and immersed on this coast. He belongs to the Digger race of Indians, is a young man of good personal appearance, and so full of the spirit of the Master, that he longs to devote his life as a missionary among his people. It is certainly more christianlike to convert a Digger Indian than to shoot one, as has often been done, wantonly and in cold blood by the reckless miners.

354.22–23 ancient times (of Buchanan)] During James Buchanan's presidential term, from 1857 to 1861.

354.23–24 Bear Camp . . . proper name.] Bear Camp had been renamed Bear Valley.

356.32–357.2 a gentleman . . . County hospital.] J. Antoine Grandvoinet (d. 1871), a graduate of the University of Montpellier, later served as county coroner.

362.27 little Peterkin] See the second and third stanzas of "The Battle of Blenheim" (1800), a poem by Robert Southey (1774–1843).

374.39 "Lo! the poor Indian."] See *An Essay on Man* (1733) by Alexander Pope (1688–1744): "Lo! the poor Indian, whose untutor'd mind / Sees God in clouds, or hears him in the wind." Pope's apostrophe was quoted so often that "Lo" came to be used as a generic term for the Indian.

375.6–20 the correspondent . . . protect themselves.] See "Indians Disappearing," *Sacramento Daily Union*, January 26, 1865.

375.21–34 the same paper . . . *Sacramento Union*.] See "A Subject for Reflection," *Sacramento Daily Union*, September 12, 1865.

376.10 Los] See note 374.39.

377.1 [4th of July murders outlaws]] Olmsted drew a box around this phrase in his manuscript and left space for a newspaper clipping to be pasted in, as clippings are pasted in throughout, but no clipping was inserted.

377.36–378.9 Mr H. P. Arnold . . . heard.] Howard Payson Arnold (1831–1910) later collected his newspaper recollections of English author and politician Thomas Noon Talfourd (1795–1854) in a sketch titled "Gentle Dullness at Dinner," published in *The Great Exhibition; with Continental Sketches, Practical and Humorous* (1868).

381.29–30 voted for McClellan . . . election] General George B. McClellan (1826–1885) ran as a Democrat against Abraham Lincoln in 1864.

382.9–10 The official representative . . . order.] Louis A. Auger (b. 1819) was appointed pastor of Mariposa County in 1860. Born in Paris, he returned there in 1872.

394.19–24 Of the thousand . . . tribes.] See the first sentences of "The Street-Folk," the opening chapter of the first volume of *London Labour and the London Poor* (1851), by Henry Mayhew (1812–1887).

396.7 *Edward Miner Gallaudet*] Gallaudet (1837–1917), president of the Columbia Institution for the Deaf and Dumb, asked Olmsted, Vaux & Company, in early 1866, to work on a master plan for the college. Olmsted's letter was published in the *Ninth Annual Report of the Columbia Institution for the Deaf and Dumb* (1866).

399.2–8 *Richard Grant White* . . . Hunt's plans] White (1822–1885), a literary and music critic, had published "Gateways of the Central Park" in the *Galaxy* of August 1866; while praising the "nobility and elegance" of plans prepared by Richard Morris Hunt (1827–1895) for formal entrances to Central Park, he argued that such structures would be inappropriate in context, marring Olmsted & Vaux's original design.

400.26–27 a report . . . College.] See pages 404–9 in the present volume.

400.29–30 a report . . . corporation.] See pages 336–49 in the present volume.

401.2–7 *Frederick Newman Knapp* . . . Eagleswood] A Unitarian minister with whom Olmsted had become friendly when both worked for the Sanitary Commission, Knapp (1821–1889) now served as principal of Eagleswood Military Academy near Perth Amboy, New Jersey.

404.19–22 FROM *A Few Things* . . . your Building Committee] Olmsted's report, prepared for the Board of Trustees of the Massachusetts Agricultural College, was largely completed before a meeting of their building committee in June 1866. Olmsted later revised it, publishing it under the present title in late November or early December.

405.18–19 an assembly . . . Chancellor Harper] See *Memoir on Slavery, Read Before the Society for the Advancement of Learning, of South Carolina* (1838), by William Harper (1790–1847).

405.25–27 Mr. Abbott Lawrence . . . assumption.] Lawrence (1792–1855) expressed his opinions on education in a letter to Harvard College treasurer Samuel A. Eliot on June 7, 1847, offering $50,000 toward what became the Lawrence Scientific School (see *Twenty-second Annual Report of the President of the University at Cambridge, to the Overseers, Exhibiting the State of the Institution for the Academic Year 1846–47*, 1848).

406.20–21 the Act of Congress . . . General Court] The Morrill Act of 1862 (also referred to as the Land Grant College Act) and a similar Massachusetts law signed on April 28, 1863.

410.3–5 FROM *Architect's Report . . . Maine*] Published in 1867 in the "Annual Report of the State College of Agriculture and the Mechanic Arts" (Maine, House of Representatives, 46th Legislature, Document Number 57), Olmsted's report is dated January 22, 1867.

413.32–34 We have lately seen . . . defiance.] The Prussian army had defeated Austria in the Seven Weeks' War, June–August 1866.

414.27–42 "The great object . . . cheaper."] See the first volume of the *Report of the Adjutant General of the State of Illinois* (1867), which quotes both Jonathan Baldwin Turner (1805–1899), professor and education reformer, and Isham N. Haynie (1824–1868), adjutant general of the Illinois State Militia.

415.7–8 the suggestions of Mr. Barnes] See *The Colleges for the Industrial Classes Contemplated by the Act of Congress of 1862* (1866), by Phineas Barnes (1811–1871).

415.39–40 a Wardian case] A glass housing for plants; a terrarium.

418.2 *Andrew Dickson White*] White (1832–1918) served as president of Cornell University beginning in November 1866.

418.8–10 Mr. Fiske . . . Hartford] Daniel Willard Fiske (1831–1904) left the staff of the *Hartford Courant* in 1868 to become university librarian at Cornell.

418.12 Mr Wilcox.] Harlow M. Wilcox (1831–1885) of Buffalo, architect of Cornell's first building, South University Hall (now Morrill Hall).

418.15 Mr Cornell] Ezra Cornell (1807–1874), cofounder of Cornell University with Andrew Dickson White.

420.34 Norton] Charles Eliot Norton (1827–1908), editor of the *North American Review* from 1864 to 1868 and subsequently professor of art history at Harvard.

421.2–3 FROM *Report . . . Superintendents*] Published in the *Eighth Annual Report* (1868) of the Board of Commissioners of Prospect Park, Brooklyn, and dated January 1, 1868.

428.21–22 a Commission . . . New York island.] Olmsted and Vaux served as landscape architects and designers for this commission, formed in 1860, but it submitted no official report, and the task of laying out the streets of upper Manhattan fell to the Board of Commissioners of Central Park, which proceeded without Olmsted and Vaux's input.

428.23–24 the Central Park Commission . . . last annual report.] See the *Ninth Annual Report* (1866) of the Board of Commissioners of Central Park.

435.9–18 Herbert Spencer . . . graceful.] See "Gracefulness" by Herbert Spencer (1820–1903), collected in *Essays: Moral, Political, and Æsthetic* (1878).

437.34–35 What then . . . North asks.] See "Soliloquy on the Seasons" by John Wilson (1785–1854), published under the pseudonym Christopher North and collected in *The Recreations of Christopher North* (1854).

441.28–29 Dr. Rumsey . . . Social Science] Probably "Homes for the Labouring Classes" by Henry Wyldbore Rumsey (1809–1876), published in the *Journal of Social Science* in May 1866.

456.21–25 *Edward Everett Hale . . . last book*] Hale (1822–1909), a writer and Unitarian minister, had just published *Sybaris and Other Homes* (1869), which included five sections, some "cast in the form of fiction," some "statistical narratives of fact."

457.12 the *Street Plans* pamphlet] See Olmsted's *Observations on the Progress of Improvements in Street Plans, with Special Reference to the Park-Way Proposed to be Laid Out in Brooklyn* (1868).

458.4 a Rosedale] In the (fictional) section of *Sybaris and Other Homes* titled "How They Lived at Naguadavick," Rosedale is a suburban town that offers its working-class inhabitants better living conditions than they would otherwise be able to find in urban areas.

458.24–25 Mr. Haskell's . . . Llewellyn Park.] A suburban community in West Orange, New Jersey, established by Llewellyn Solomon Haskell (1815–1872) in the 1850s.

459.4–7 The last "Overland Monthly . . . life."] See "A Flock of Wool" (*Overland Monthly*, February 1870) by Stephen Powers (1840–1904), published under the pseudonym Socrates Hyacinth.

459.17–20 "Over the mountains . . . country.'"] The source of this quotation from Olmsted's friend Samuel Bowles (1826–1878), editor of the *Springfield Republican*, is obscure, but similar language appears in Bowles's book *Across the Continent: A Summer's Journey to the Rocky Mountains, the Mormons, and the Pacific States, with Speaker Colfax* (1865).

460.34–35 A correspondent . . . other day] See the *Springfield Republican*, February 5, 1870.

461.1 sung by Goldsmith.] Anglo-Irish novelist, playwright, and poet Oliver Goldsmith (1728–1774), author of *The Deserted Village* (1770).

461.37–462.1 the country gentleman . . . Irving] See *Bracebridge Hall* (1822), by Washington Irving (1783–1859).

464.29–31 the report . . . sewing women] See Shirley Dare, "One End of the Thread," *New-York Daily Tribune*, February 26, 1870.

464.36–37 Dr. Holmes . . . social parties] See *Elsie Venner: A Romance of Destiny* (1861), a novel by Oliver Wendell Holmes (1809–1894).

466.25–26 McAdam roads.] Roads paved with layers of small stones, following the method of Scottish engineer John Loudon McAdam (1756–1836).

488.33–489.13 a leading article of the "Herald" . . . lager-bier gardens.] See "The Central Park and Other City Improvements," *New York Herald*, September 6, 1857. The *Herald*'s "astute editor," until 1866, was the elder James Gordon Bennett (1795–1872).

493.36–494.8 the "Herald" . . . well."] The source of this quotation is obscure.

497.19–25 One of the very men . . . adjoining property.] Possibly Harold Potter (1826–1877), a New York banker who consulted Olmsted about plans for a 150-acre property he co-owned, in Long Branch, New Jersey.

515.8 Kent] William Kent (c. 1685–1748), English painter and landscape architect.

515.10–13 the famous Brown . . . Uvedale Price . . . Repton and others.] Lancelot "Capability" Brown (1715–1783) often called for belts of trees to be planted around the parks he designed. Uvedale Price (1747–1815), in his *Essay on the Picturesque, As Compared with the Sublime and the Beautiful* (1794), described this practice as "very unfortunate," but Humphry Repton (1752–1818) defended it in his "Letter to Uvedale Price" (1794) and elsewhere.

515.25–27 sweet passage . . . simple character.] In "Hare Street"—Fragment XXXVI of his *Fragments on the Theory and Practice of Landscape Gardening* (1816)—Repton reflects on the pleasure he finds in the landscape around his own "humble Cottage" near Romford, in Essex.

518.10–11 Suspension Bridge] The International Suspension Bridge, downstream from Niagara Falls; it was completed in 1855 and replaced in 1897.

520.15–17 *Memorandum . . . Mr. Demcker*] The original memorandum—misspelling the recipient's name as *Dempker*—was written in a clerk's hand and signed by Olmsted. Demcker (1821–1925), a Prussian immigrant, joined the Bureau of Landscape Gardening as a draftsman in 1871 and later became head gardener.

524.3 *To Gardeners*] Dated by the editors of *The Papers of Frederick Law Olmsted* to April–May 1872, the original document from which the text that follows was taken is a fragmentary manuscript draft. Written on more than one type of paper, it may combine more than one draft of an intended presentation to newly hired Central Park district gardeners, or even separate works written for different purposes, and material is certainly missing.

528.11–17 William Robinson . . . Central Park.] Robinson (1838–1934), an English landscape gardener, editor of *The Garden*, and author of *The Wild Garden* (1870) and other books, had recently published the first of a series of articles on Central Park (see "Public Gardens. The Central Park of New York," *The Garden*, May 4, May 11, June 8, July 20, 1872).

529.26–27 the second of a series of letters] See *Two Letters to the President of the Department of Public Parks on Recent Changes and Projected Changes in the Central Park. By the Landscape Architects*, published by Olmsted, Vaux & Company in 1872.

530.2 *Samuel Bowles*] Olmsted had met Bowles (1826–1878), editor of the *Springfield Republican*, in California in 1864, and the two became friendly. Bowles later supported him in his plans for the preservation of Yosemite and for several design projects.

530.8–14 the wreck . . . the Cincinnati movement] The Liberal Republican convention, held in Cincinnati at the beginning of May 1872, had nominated Greeley for president.

530.28 the Club] Probably the Union League Club of New York.

531.17 Godkin] E. L. Godkin (1831–1902), editor of *The Nation*, did not ultimately support Greeley.

532.9 I take more comfort in the Post.] An editorial in the *New York Evening Post* on May 13, 1872, criticized Greeley's candidacy.

532.28–36 Dorsheimer . . . Seldon . . . Waldo Hutchins . . . signed it.] William Edward Dorsheimer (1832–1888), U.S. attorney for the northern district of New York; Henry Rodgers Selden (1805–1885), a Rochester lawyer; and Waldo M. Hutchins (1822–1891), a New York lawyer and politician, were among the twenty signatories to a public letter ("New-York for the Cincinnati Convention") published in the *New-York Daily Tribune* on March 30, 1872, expressing dissent within the Republican Party.

533.8　John Cochrane] Cochrane (1813–1898), a former congressman, was a leading Greeley supporter.

534.10–11　a greater imposter than even Fremont.] John Charles Frémont (1813–1890), western explorer and 1856 Republican presidential candidate. Olmsted's low opinion of him was confirmed by his experience as manager of the Mariposa Estate, a property that had formerly belonged to Frémont.

534.18　ad captandum] Designed to please the crowd.

535.3–5　*To the* New-York Evening Post . . . Hotel.] Published on June 22, 1872. On the previous day, at the New York Hotel, a faction of the newly formed Liberal Republican Party opposed to the nomination of Horace Greeley for president proposed William S. Groesbeck (1815–1897) as an alternative candidate, and Olmsted as his running mate. Olmsted immediately turned down the honor, of which he was informed after the fact by Isaac Clinton Collins (1824–1879), a Cincinnati lawyer active among those opposed to Greeley.

535.14–21　*James Miller McKim* . . . overcome.] McKim (1810–1874) wrote Olmsted on June 24 to correct a report claiming it was he who had nominated Olmsted for the vice presidency (see "The Little End of Nothing," *New-York Daily Tribune*, June 22, 1872); he had mentioned Olmsted favorably, but had not felt at liberty to formally nominate him. A noted abolitionist, McKim had previously offered Olmsted a position as general secretary of the American Freedman's Aid Commission, formed to better the condition of freed slaves.

536.2　*Report of the Landscape Architects*] Published in the Brooklyn Park Commission's *Fourteenth Annual Report* (1874).

538.19　Mr. Bullard] Oliver Crosby Bullard (1822–1890), a former associate at the Sanitary Commission, assisted Olmsted in the construction and planting of Prospect Park, and later worked with him on the Capitol grounds in Washington, D.C.

542.3　*The National Capitol*] Olmsted's report appeared in the *New-York Daily Tribune*, December 5, 1874.

546.14　*Landscape Gardening*] Written for publication in *Johnson's New Universal Cyclopaedia: A Scientific and Popular Treasury of Useful Knowledge* (1878).

547.20–23　As Lowell says . . . distance."] See the essay "Spenser" (*North American Review*, April 1875) by James Russell Lowell (1819–1891).

556.13　The Future of New-York] Published in the *New-York Daily Tribune*, December 28, 1879.

560.17–20　Dr. Bellows . . . sleeps;"] See "The Townward Tendency" (*The City: An Illustrated Magazine*, January 1872), by Henry W. Bellows.

562.11–12　that proposed by Mr. Potter] See "Urban Housing in New York," a series by architect Edward T. Potter (1831–1904) published in *American Architect and Building News* from March 16, 1878, to September 27, 1879.

565.3 characteristic scenery by Mr. F. E. Church] Frederic Edwin Church (1826–1900), a landscape painter whose *Niagara Falls* (1857) is now at the Corcoran Gallery of Art.

565.4–7 Shortly afterwards . . . subject.] Olmsted met with Henry Hobson Richardson (1838–1886), William Dorsheimer (1832–1888), and others at the Cataract House, a Niagara Falls hotel, on August 7, 1869.

567.26–30 The eminent English botanist . . . statement.] Joseph Hooker (1817–1911) and Asa Gray (1810–1888) made a joint visit to Goat Island in September 1877, the former subsequently describing its flora in "The Distribution of North American Flora," *Notices of the Proceedings at the Meeting of the Members of the Royal Institute of Great Britain* (1879).

568.32 the following account . . . Argyll] See "First Impressions of the New World" (*Fraser's Magazine*, December 1879), by George Douglas Campbell (1823–1900), 8th Duke of Argyll.

569.19 FROM *The Spoils of the Park*] Olmsted published this account in pamphlet form in February 1882.

570.15–17 Commissioner Wales . . . department] Salem Howe Wales (1825–1902), who served as park commissioner from January 1873 to May 1874, complained in a letter to the *New York World* on December 18, 1871, that "intrigues" in the department had made his official life "miserable," prompting him to resign his office.

572.10–23 a great political organization . . . Mr. Tweed.] William M. "Boss" Tweed (1823–1878) led Tammany Hall beginning in 1858.

578.37–38 a powerful article . . . leading daily] See "Central Park in Danger. Alarming Results of Police Demoralization" and "The Central Park Investigation," published in the *New-York Daily Tribune* on May 28 and May 29, 1873, by an unknown author under the pseudonym Jan Vier.

579.28–30 a public reply . . . same columns.] Olmsted's reply to "Jan Vier" appeared in the *New-York Daily Tribune* on June 3, 1873, under the title "Central Park Changes."

585.9–11 *To Oakes Angier Ames* . . . Memorial Hall] Ames (1829–1899), the son of an industrialist and financier, commissioned Olmsted to design the landscape for the new Oakes Ames Memorial Town Hall in North Easton, Massachusetts, built in honor of his father. The only text of Olmsted's letter known to exist—a draft in his hand—is probably a fragment.

587.13 *Trees in Streets and Parks*] Published in the *Sanitarian*, September 1882.

590.5 a pamphlet prepared by an eminent physician] See *Public Parks: Their Effects upon the Moral, Physical and Sanitary Condition of the Inhabitants of Large Cities; with Special Reference to the City of Chicago* (1869), by John Henry Rauch (1828–1894).

595.33–35   described (by Oliver . . . .. weather."] See Oliver Wolcott (1726–1797) to his wife Lorraine (Laura) Collins Wolcott (c. 1730–1794), in a letter of July 4, 1800, printed in the second volume of *Memoirs of the Administrations of Washington and John Adams, Edited from the Papers of Oliver Wolcott, Secretary of the Treasury* (1846).

598.8–10   George Combe . . . drained swamp;"] See *Notes on the United States of North America during a Phrenological Visit in 1838–39–40* (1841) by George Combe (1788–1858), Scottish phrenologist.

606.21   *Report on Cushing's Island*] Published in *Summer Homes, Cushing's Island*, an 1883 real estate prospectus, under the title "Report of Fred'k Law Olmsted, Landscape Architect," and retitled for the present volume. Francis Cushing (1847–1911) formed the Cushing's Island Company in 1883, and hired Olmsted to lay out a summer community on his property, an island of about 250 acres in Casco Bay, Maine, now part of the city of Portland.

612.3–7   *Bronson Case Rumsey . . .* property] Rumsey (1823–1902), a businessman from Buffalo, sought to develop property in Yonkers, New York, to the south of what is now the intersection of Midland and Yonkers Avenues.

615.15–16   *Paper on the Back Bay . . . Architects*] Olmsted read his paper on April 2, 1886.

616.34–36   the employment of Mr Hunt . . . Bartholdi statue] Architect Richard Morris Hunt (1827–1895) was asked to design a base for the Statue of Liberty, by Frédéric Auguste Bartholdi (1834–1904), in 1881; he collaborated with Charles Pomeroy Stone (1824–1887), who served as chief engineer.

627.32–33   I will read . . . (page 14)] See Olmsted's "Report on Back Bay" (*Tenth Annual Report of the Board of Commissioners of the Department of Parks for the City of Boston, for the Year 1884* [Boston: Rockwell and Churchill, 1885]), the final section of which reads as follows:

> In that part of the work now more nearly completed, being the outlet part, north of Boylston Bridge, there are special local features, some reasons for which may be stated.
>
> The circumstances allow a contrast of character to be sought between the banks of this short narrow passage and the miles of banks to be found about the broad basins on the south side of the bridge and the parkway beyond them; and, to make the most of the opportunity, it is desirable here to aim at a degree of variety of form and slope that would otherwise be excessive.
>
> *The outflow channel is required by the plans of the Street Department to be carried between two straight lines of bridge abutments at five different points within a distance of less than 600 yards.* The intermediate reaches of the channel are too short for expanded pools or a quiet character in the shores and what would otherwise be an excessively wriggling disposition of the banks has the advantage of avoiding a sewer or canal-like

directness of channel. Much would have been gained if all the bridges had been of masonry; but the conditions would have made them excessively costly.

It is necessary to use a certain amount of stone at points in the facing of the banks to guard against drifting ice. This gives reason for a buttress-like abruptness of bank at these points. Such abruptness being accepted, it is better to make a decided feature of it, and let it control the character of the scenery of the outlet in contrast with that of the basins above where there can be no headlands. Large field-stones, have, therefore, been procured from the waste of the city's gravel banks and piled together to obtain boldness of projection. At present the stones, somewhat unhappy in color, are offensively conspicuous, and the several points have too much repetition of character. They will not only, in time, lose their present rawness of color, but will all, in a great measure, soon disappear under leafage, while, through the difference in the forms of vegetation growing out from between the stones and upon their flanks, their similarity of aspect will be lost.

The ground has been planted with a density which would be excessive were the conditions not extraordinarily bleak. It has been planted also with an excessive variety, and in parts not harmoniously, with the expectation of thinning out a part of the plants when they shall have served their purpose of nurses, and in the meantime of determining experimentally whether certain of them can be depended upon to grow satisfactorily under the extreme exposure of the situation.

Lombardy poplars have been planted on the side of the road by which Boylston Bridge is to be approached from Commonwealth Avenue. The situation is an exceedingly trying one, and, until buildings shall break the force of the wind from the north-west, hardly any trees can be expected to grow in it without acquiring stunted and distorted habits. It is hoped that the poplar, if frequently cut in, will by its vigorous, compact growth, for a time, serve a good purpose.

This row of poplars terminates on the north at a point where, if continued, it would interrupt the prospect from the Boylston Bridge over Charles River. The entire scheme of planting is determined with regard to this view; to the reverse view from Commonwealth Avenue through the arch of Boylston Bridge, and to the subordination, as far as practicable, of the railroad and other rigid and uncongenial features of topography.

629.25–28 "*A Healthy Change* . . . great writer] Published in the *Century Illustrated Monthly Magazine* in October 1886. The title phrase appears in "Of Mediæval Landscape:—First, the Fields," Part IV, Chapter XIV of the third volume (1856) of *Modern Painters*, by John Ruskin (1819–1900).

631.21–632.7 another fine city . . . no account.] Olmsted hoped to encourage the reforestation of city-owned islands in Boston Harbor.

633.28 Horace Cleveland] Cleveland (1814–1900) had recently published *Suggestions for a System of Parks and Parkways for the City of Minneapolis* (1883) and

Public Parks, Radial Avenues, and Boulevards: Outline Plan for a Park System, for the City of St. Paul (1885).

633.39–634.1   Durham Terrace . . . "Their Wedding Journey."] Descriptions of Durham Terrace, in Quebec City, appear in "Quebec" and "Homeward Bound," chapters in the novel *Their Wedding Journey* (1871), by William Dean Howells (1837–1920).

634.20   at Cameron's] At the office of a client, Roderick William Cameron (1825–1900), where Olmsted had informed Vaux he would be stopping on his next trip to New York.

634.30   Crimmins] John Daniel Crimmins (1844–1917), a construction contractor and philanthropist who served as a board member of the Department of Public Parks from 1883 to 1888.

636.29   Parsons] Samuel B. Parsons Jr. (1844–1923), Vaux's apprentice and business partner, who had been appointed superintendent of plantings at Central Park in January 1883, at Vaux's suggestion.

637.2–3   Mould or Jones or Johnson] Jacob Wrey Mould (1825–1886), head architect for the Department of Public Parks from 1870 to 1875; Aneurin Jones (1824–1904), superintendent of parks from 1881 to 1885; Joseph Forsyth Johnson (1840?–1906), in charge of horticulture and arboriculture for Brooklyn's parks for six months beginning in late 1886.

637.27   Radford's] George Kent Radford (1826–1908), an English civil engineer with whom both Olmsted and Vaux had collaborated.

639.2–7   *Frederick William Vanderbilt . . . the place*] Vanderbilt (1856–1938), a director of the New York Central Railroad, had engaged Olmsted to make plans for Rough Point, his estate in Newport, Rhode Island, in 1887.

640.10   Mr Peabody] Robert Swain Peabody (1845–1917), cofounder of the Boston firm Peabody & Stearns and the architect of Vanderbilt's Rough Point mansion.

641.2   *Foreign Plants and American Scenery*] Published in *Garden and Forest* on October 24, 1888.

641.4–8   To the Editor . . . harmony.] An unsigned article in *Garden and Forest* had criticized the introduction of non-native plants in Brooklyn's Prospect Park.

645.15–19   the most American of poets . . . foreigners"?] Quoted from two works by James Russell Lowell (1819–1891), both published in 1869: the poem "Under the Willows," and the essay "On a Certain Condescension in Foreigners."

646.2–8   *General Bela M. Hughes . . . resort.*] Hughes (1817–1902) was president and cofounder of the Red Stone Town, Land, and Mining Company, which had hired Olmsted as a consultant in June 1888. Olmsted's report on Perry Park—between Denver and Colorado Springs—was published in the company's promotional literature as "Feasibility of Perry Park as a Resort."

652.28–35 *George Washington Vanderbilt . . .* North Carolina Estate] Olmsted first worked with Vanderbilt (1862–1914), heir to one of the largest fortunes in the country, in 1885, when he designed the landscape around the Vanderbilt family mausoleum on Staten Island. In 1888, Vanderbilt began purchasing land in western North Carolina. Olmsted and architect Richard Morris Hunt worked together to design the grounds and the house on the estate, later named Biltmore. Charles McNamee (1865–1923), a New York lawyer, served as Vanderbilt's agent and estate manager at Biltmore from 1888 to 1904.

653.31 Mr. Thompson] William A. Thompson (1845–1933), responsible for engineering and surveying at Biltmore.

654.30 Mr. Douglas] Robert Douglas (1813–1896), a nurseryman and writer for *Garden and Forest.*

664.11 Mr. Alexander] Either B. J. or W. J. Alexander, who owned farms next to Vanderbilt's property.

671.34–35 I wrote a short paper] See "A Healthy Change in the Tone of the Human Heart" (pages 629–34 in the present volume).

673.17 what he afterwards wrote] See "The Care of the Yosemite Valley," *Century Illustrated Monthly Magazine,* January 1890.

675.21–29 *"Having regard . . . available."*] See Olmsted and Vaux, "General Plan for the Improvement of the Niagara Reservation" (1887), reprinted in *The Papers of Frederick Law Olmsted,* Supplementary Series vol. 1.

676.2 *Robert Treat Paine*] Paine (1835–1910), a Boston lawyer, had given $200,000 to a charity intended to foster the "spiritual, moral and physical welfare of the working classes."

676.26–27 The Charlesbank Gymnasium] An innovative outdoor exercise yard in Boston's West End neighborhood, open to the public at no charge, designed by Olmsted and Dudley Sargent (1849–1924), professor of physical culture at Harvard.

677.21 *Archie Campbell Fisk*] Fisk (1836–1923) was a Denver businessman and real estate developer.

682.9 our Mr. Codman] Henry Sargent Codman (1863–1893), a partner in Olmsted's firm.

683.2 *Lyman J. Gage*] Gage (1836–1927) was president of the Board of Directors of the World's Columbian Exposition.

686.9 *Charles A. Roberts*] Roberts, an investor in the Red Stone Town, Land, and Mining Company, was planning the Lake Wauconda resort community in Perry Park. (See also note 646.2–8.)

687.13 *Clarence Pullen*] Pullen (c. 1850–1902), a former engineer, was at work on an article for *Harper's Weekly* subsequently published on January 17, 1891 (with Olmsted's suggestions incorporated) as "The Site of the Columbian Exposition."

689.20   *Henry Van Brunt*] Van Brunt (1832–1903) designed the Electricity Building at the World's Columbian Exposition. His letters to Olmsted are not known to have survived.

689.33–34   a Report . . . County Council.] See *Report to the Parks and Open Spaces Committee of the London County Council on the Public Parks of America* (1890), by Reginald Brabazon, 12th Earl of Meath (1841–1929).

690.22–28   Hyatt's interest . . . park designs.] Olmsted had quarreled with Alpheus Hyatt (1838–1902) over plans to construct a large zoological garden in Franklin Park.

690.40   Judge Hilton] Henry Hilton (1824–1899), a commissioner in the New York Parks Department in 1870–71.

691.11–13   I will send you . . . in 1880.] See "The Justifying Value of a Public Park," *Journal of Social Science*, December 1880.

691.41   pamphlet by Eckman.] Probably *Public Parks. A Compilation of Facts and Statistics Relative to the Benefits and Profits Derived Therefrom* (1888) by William H. Eckman (1841–1901), a former Cleveland parks commissioner.

692.28   May, 1893] The World's Columbian Exposition was scheduled to open on May 1, 1893.

700.26   *Rudolph Ulrich*] Olmsted had hired Ulrich (1840–1906) as landscape superintendent for the World's Columbian Exposition in late 1890 or early 1891.

702.2   *William James*] James (1842–1910), professor of psychology and philosophy at Harvard, would later publish *The Varieties of Religious Experience* (1902).

708.11   *To William Robinson*] Robinson (see note 528.11–17) published this excerpt from a letter not otherwise known to have survived in his magazine *The Garden*, on September 17, 1892.

708.21   Paxton's work] See note 42.6.

709.21–25   *Mariana Griswold* . . . "Art Out of Doors."] Mariana Alley Griswold Van Rensselaer (1851–1934) discusses Olmsted in her book *Art Out-of-Doors: Hints on Good Taste in Gardening* (1893).

709.33–34   Mr. Johnson's note] On May 6, Robert Underwood Johnson (1853–1937), editor of the *Century Illustrated Monthly Magazine*, had sought Olmsted's cooperation with an article he had asked Van Rensselaer to write, subsequently published as "Frederick Law Olmsted" in October 1893.

710.15–18   Sir Walter Scott . . . scenery-making?] See "On Ornamental Plantations and Landscape Gardening," published in the *Quarterly Review* in March 1828.

711.13   Harry] Henry Sargent Codman (see note 682.9).

712.10–12   Burnham . . . Hunt goes to England to receive his medal.] Olmsted and Daniel H. Burnham (1846–1912), architect and director of the World's Columbian Exposition, were awarded honorary degrees on June 28, 1893; Richard Morris Hunt (see notes 399.2–8, 616.34–36, and 652.28–35) received the Queen's Gold Medal of the Royal Institute of Architects.

712.31   Price and Gilpin] See note 6.33–34.

713.31   the Century] See note 709.33–34.

715.3–15   *William A. Stiles . . .* treated.] William Augustus Stiles (1837–1897), a managing editor of *Garden and Forest*, had written to Olmsted recommending that they decline to serve on a committee appointed to revise Vaux's proposals for the Harlem River speedway. He would be appointed as a New York park commissioner in November 1895.

715.18   White] Stanford White (1853–1906), a prominent architect and partner in the firm McKim, Mead & White.

715.21–27   Dillon . . . favored it.] Robert J. Dillon (1811–1872) had recommended numerous alterations to Olmsted and Vaux's Greensward plan during his tenure on the original Central Park Commission; the *Tribune* praised some of his proposals in an editorial of June 8, 1858.

715.27–28   Raymond . . . Dana] Henry Jarvis Raymond (1820–1869), editor of the *New York Times*, and Charles A. Dana (1819–1897), managing editor of the *New-York Daily Tribune*.

716.41–717.2   an entrenched position . . . the single Brooklyn Commissioner's mind.] Frank Squier (1840–1908), a paper manufacturer who served as commissioner of parks for the city of Brooklyn in 1894–95, had appointed White to design several gateways and other structures for Prospect Park.

717.21–22   Prof. Sargent] Charles Sprague Sargent (1841–1927), director of the Arnold Arboretum at Harvard and editor of *Garden and Forest*.

717.34   Rick] Frederick Law Olmsted Jr. (1870–1957).

719.2–3   *A Homestead; Its Constituent Parts and Essentials*] It is unclear when Olmsted wrote this short piece, the ultimate source of which is an unsigned, undated typescript in the Olmsted papers at the Library of Congress.

719.12–13   Shakespeare . . . steads us."] See *All's Well That Ends Well*, III.7.41.

Index

THE LIBRARY OF AMERICA SERIES

The Library of America fosters appreciation and pride in America's literary heritage by publishing, and keeping permanently in print, authoritative editions of America's best and most significant writing. An independent nonprofit organization, it was founded in 1979 with seed funding from the National Endowment for the Humanities and the Ford Foundation.

To subscribe to the series or to order individual copies, please visit www.loa.org or call (800) 964–5778.

This book is set in 10 point ITC Galliard, a face
designed for digital composition by Matthew Carter and based
on the sixteenth-century face Granjon. The paper is acid-free
lightweight opaque that will not turn yellow or brittle with age.
The binding is sewn, which allows the book to open easily and lie flat.
The case board is covered in Brillianta, a woven rayon cloth
made by Van Heek–Scholco Textielfabrieken, Holland.
Composition by David Bullen Design. Printing and
binding by Edwards Brothers Malloy, Ann Arbor.
Designed by Bruce Campbell.